NORTH CAMPUS

"Salvatore provides a fresh and robust perspective on his life . . . his essential portrait of Debs is credible and exciting."
  —*Newsday* (Long Island, N.Y.)

"A major contribution to biographical literature . . . likely to stand for some time as the definitive biography of Debs."
  —*Choice*

"Nick Salvatore, then, has written more than a good book, he has written good history . . . he has brought a man and his time back to speak to the present."
  —*Worcester (Mass.) Sunday Telegram*

"The Bancroft Prize–winning biography by Cornell historian Nick Salvatore differs from all of its predecessors in . . . its persuasive analysis of aspects of nineteenth-century American culture which Debs drew upon for his own ideas."
  —*New York Times Book Review*

"Salvatore's book is thorough, sensitive, and provocative—all a fine biography should be."
  —*St. Petersburg (Fla.) Times*

W9-CUQ-711

EUGENE V. DEBS

The Working Class in American History

Editorial Advisors
James R. Barrett
Alice Kessler-Harris
Nelson Lichtenstein
David Montgomery

A list of books in the series appears at the end of this book.

921
Debs
S

NORTH CAMPUS

EUGENE V. DEBS

Citizen and Socialist

SECOND EDITION

Nick Salvatore

LYONS T.H.S. LIBRARY
LA GRANGE, ILLINOIS

University of Illinois Press
Urbana and Chicago

© 1982, 2007 by the Board of Trustees
of the University of Illinois
All rights reserved
Manufactured in the United States of America
P 5 4 3 2 1

∞ This book is printed on acid-free paper.

Library of Congress Cataloging-in-Publication Data

Salvatore, Nick, 1943–
Eugene V. Debs : citizen and socialist / Nick Salvatore. — 2nd ed.
  p.   cm. — (The working class in American history)
Includes bibliographical references and index.
ISBN-13: 978-0-252-07452-3 (pbk. : alk. paper)
ISBN-10: 0-252-07452-1 (pbk. : alk. paper)
1. Debs, Eugene V. (Eugene Victor), 1855–1926.
2. Working class—United States—Biography.
3. Socialists—United States—Biography.
I. Title.
HX84.D3S23   2007
335'.3092—dc22 [B]   2006029422

For Gabriella, Nora,
and Their Generation

Contents

Preface to the Second Edition

TWENTY-FIVE YEARS HAVE PASSED since the original publication of *Eugene V. Debs: Citizen and Socialist* in 1982. During this time much has changed that would seem to make the legacy of America's most important Socialist less relevant to Americans today. A quarter of a century ago, America remained entangled in the Cold War political culture that had dominated political life since the late 1940s. From within that vision, the Soviet Union's proclamations of ultimate Communist victory over liberal, democratic capitalism constituted the major threat to national prosperity and security. Then, in 1989, the Wall—the actual wall that divided the city of Berlin, as well as the metaphorical Iron Curtain that demarcated the extent of the Soviet Union's post-1945 consolidation of power in Eastern Europe and large segments of Asia—collapsed. More than thirty years of courageous dissenters in the Soviet Union, joined in the 1980s by striking Polish workers and their supporters, a charismatic pope, an American president, and a British prime minister, all played a role in this transformation. The fundamental cause of the collapse of the empire, however, lay in the profound distortions and contradictions created in Soviet society by seventy-five years of Communist rule. In the process of this dramatic change, the Soviet Union reverted to its historic appellation, Russia; formal commitments to political democracy and the free market economy evolved; and the People's Republic of China, formerly a bastion of revolutionary Communism, embraced capitalist economics. The prophetic vision of Karl Marx lost credibility worldwide. There was, after all, no master plan for societal change.

The years since the first publication of *Eugene V. Debs* have witnessed enormous changes in American politics that might have further marginalized Debs. The book appeared as President Ronald Reagan approached the end of his second year in office, and even his staunchest supporters would not have then predicted his massive reelection victory two years later. The Federalist Society, an organization of conservative legal scholars that would, in time, spearhead the transformation of the American judiciary, had just been founded. The evangelical Right, although a potent force in politics, had yet to evolve into the multifaith, interdenominational, broad-based conservative political force it has since become. Liberal critics talked of Reagan as an "acting" president, an imposter whose conduct as president was indistinguishable from the B-movie roles he perfected as a Hollywood actor. They anxiously awaited his political collapse, and with it the collapse of the upstart conservative movement that helped him to power. More than two decades later, as those critics still wait, the percentage of organized workers in the labor movement barely matches 1910 levels, and much of the liberal social agenda has unraveled before sustained political opposition.

Considered against these changes in American political life and culture at home and abroad, the commemoration with this anniversary edition of the life and career of America's most prominent Socialist figure may seem counterintuitive, an exercise in nostalgia. Nothing could be further from reality. Eugene Debs, with his all-too-human faults and contradictions, remains a vital component of our common national experience some eighty years after his death. Indeed, in a manner he never could have envisioned, these more recent developments in American political culture have actually restored Debs and those who joined him in a variety of social and political movements to a renewed place of relevance in our current political debates. It is not that his specific proposals for social change are relevant today; such strategic thinking was never his forte while alive. Rather, his value, then and now, lies in the vision he articulated of the promise of American life, of the meaning of American democracy, of the power yet vital when individual citizens act together. Debs's vision always owed more to his understanding of the American Revolution than to Karl Marx, and he treasured the long American tradition of dissent against remaining injustices as a cornerstone of the deepest patriotic convictions.

As a young man in the 1870s, Debs served as a local officer in the labor movement in Terre Haute, Indiana, his home town, where he lived until his death in 1926. During this long public career, Debs's thinking evolved as he considered the new challenges that confronted American democracy during the country's transition to industrial capitalism. At first he uncritically embraced the emerging corporation, with its enormous power over individual citizens, as the very fulfillment of America's promise of opportunity for all. But his experience in the labor movement, and in local and state politics in his native Indiana, led him sharply to reconsider.

The concentrated power of the corporation, he came to argue, actually curtailed opportunity for many individuals. The corporation's unilateral command of the workplace and its singular ability to implement decisions beneficial to its investors regardless of the economic impact on communities across the nation marked major threats to American democratic values. Debs was not against the

idea of progress, economic or technological; in fact, as an American Socialist he welcomed the corporation and its potential for greater productivity and
efficiency. But he insisted that, in a democratic society true to its beliefs, the
decision-making process that determined the beneficiaries of these gains must be
far more inclusive than corporate directors allowed. Even more pointedly, Debs
argued that during this era—famously labeled "the Great Barbecue" by Mark
Twain—the corporation and its lobbyists controlled many state legislatures, and
a large swath of the nation's congressmen as well. This concentration of power
constituted a fundamental violation of American democratic traditions, Debs
charged; he held that he and other dissenters in a variety of protest movements
were, in fact, the true American patriots in their opposition to the revolutionary
transformation wrought by corporate leaders. Long before some political com-
mentators would make the case for industrial democracy as an essential prereq-
uisite for the survival of political democracy in a corporate era, Debs articulated
this as the core of the class question in American life: If individual American
citizens could be so denuded of power in a workplace that commandeered up
to fourteen hours of their daily lives, how could those same individuals find
the time, energy, or the confidence to join with fellow citizens, without fear of
retribution, in the affairs of their community and their nation?

Given the corporate scandals and abuses of democratic process (now global in
their impact) that already mark the first decade of the twenty-first century, Debs's
commitment to democratic principles and his explanation of the fundamental
American values that structure them remain more instructive than ever before.
Were he present today he might well recognize, with a wry, knowledgeable smile,
the irony that—once again—those most committed to preserving democracy's
vitality are themselves considered dissenters lacking in some key ingredient of
what the powerful consider "patriotism."

In emphasizing the necessity for democratic values to guide economic as well
as political life, Debs discussed the question of class in a distinctly American
way. In his incessant travels across the country, including those during his five
campaigns for the presidency on the Socialist Party ticket, Debs stressed the common interests that so many non-elite Americans shared. He urged his audiences
to transcend their ethnic, sectional, and religious differences, to treat politics not
as something inherited from parents and grandparents, but rather as a response
to one's contemporary circumstances. But he did not treat his audiences as an
undifferentiated bloc. A constant refrain in his speeches was a direct address to
the individual in the audience to consider the message and rethink his position.
"I do not want you to follow me or anyone else," Debs expounded in a classic
statement he frequently repeated. "I would not lead you into the promised land
if I could, because if I could lead you in, someone else would lead you out.
You must use your heads as well as your hands, and get yourselves out of your
present condition."

Neither Debs's audiences then nor readers today would be wrong to sense in such expressions a direct appeal to America's valued tradition of individualism. Debs believed that each individual citizen bore a personal responsibility to consider solutions to current difficulties in concert with fellow citizens. Nor would it be misplaced to hear in Debs's language the tones of an American revival experience. His appeals were marked by an evangelical tenor, thick with biblical allusions, which focused, not unlike a revival preacher, on the individual's decision to transform his or her life. Debs, to be sure, did not advocate otherworldly salvation, and did not himself attend church; but as a native son of Indiana reared in its mid-nineteenth century culture, he came by his evangelically influenced democratic vision honestly. It was Debs, the preeminent American socialist, who, while serving a jail term in a federal penitentiary for expressing his opposition to America's entry into World War I, had but one framed picture on his cell wall—that of Christ crowned with thorns. His ability to weave these multiple strands of American culture into a political appeal that resonated with many is also relevant in our own time, when liberals and conservatives alike persist in treating their favorite strand as exclusive, if not downright hostile, to all others.

If some of Debs's more orthodox coworkers in the American Socialist movement recoiled in near-horror at these words and images, Debs never altered his approach. His Socialism was fundamentally an extension of American democracy, he affirmed across a lifetime, intended to preserve and strengthen the core values of a nation in the midst of a major economic transformation. Dissent, then, was not unpatriotic but a critical component of American democratic culture. The generation of the American Revolution understood this in the struggle against the legitimate colonial ruler, Britain, as had the abolitionists, black and white, in their effort to extend America's first principles in their campaign against slavery. In Debs's own experience, labor organizers and other contemporaries also risked much in their efforts to organize working people against the power of unprincipled employers. It was from inside this complex American tradition, one that balanced individual rights and responsibilities with concerted group action, an evangelical sensibility with social justice, and the expansion of democratic principles into ever-broader areas of common public life, that Debs sought to address his generation's problems. That he failed to convince many and was never elected to the presidency is, of course, true. But his defense of democratic values remains a guidepost to understanding the central issues of his time and, despite the changes that have occurred in recent decades, is yet vital and relevant to our contemporary political life as well.

Nick Salvatore
Ithaca, New York

Introduction

THIS IS A SOCIAL BIOGRAPHY of Eugene Victor Debs. It is a traditional biography in that it emphasizes this one individual's personal and public life as far as the evidence allows. But the book is also a piece of social history that assumes individuals do not stand outside the culture and society they grew in and from. I have stressed each aspect of Debs's story in order to present both the importance of the man and a more complete picture of the political and cultural struggles his society engaged in during his lifetime.

Debs's public career spanned the years after the Civil War to World War I, an era that witnessed the full development of American industrial capitalism. As a result of his activities both as a labor organizer and Socialist agitator, Debs occupied a prominent place in the nation's consciousness for many years. Alternately applauded and attacked, his words and deeds were discussed by Americans of all classes and political allegiances. Yet many today know little about him. When most school texts mention Debs, he is more often than not in a footnote, an historical curiosity who ran for the presidency five times on the Socialist party ticket. Until recently, much scholarly treatment followed a similar pattern. Debs remained an oddity, out of the mainstream of American political discourse, a Don Quixote tilting at windmills. Even those who viewed Debs with sympathy have frequently, if inadvertently, contributed to this perception. Too often Debs became a larger-than-life hero, a born radical eternally at odds with the culture that nurtured him. This approach does violence to his complex history and threatens to make him incomprehensible to Americans who do not already share the faith.

This dichotomy between Debs's place in the consciousness of his contemporaries and his role in our current historical imagination led me to write a new biography. However interesting Debs's personality might be, his primary claim on our historical consciousness remains rooted in the significance of his public words and actions. A symbol of the national protest against the social revolution wrought by industrial capitalism, Debs galvanized Americans in defense of their rights as citizens and working people. Debs was no Luddite, opposed to technological innovation. Rather, as he insisted throughout a long public career, if technological progress was achieved at the price of American democratic traditions, then that "victory" signalled the destruction of American republicanism. His power as a speaker before American-born and immigrant audiences resulted in large part from his profound appreciation of this indigenous democratic tradition. As a Socialist, Debs presented the reality of class struggle in America in sharp, incisive terms, but never at the expense of his commitment to democratic thought. Many in America responded to this message, as they did to Debs himself, and it remains today his most potent legacy. Debs was anything but a tilter at windmills; the core of Debs's thought and the actions that flowed from it were firmly rooted in the American experience.

But far more is at stake than just the historical record of one individual. Debs was a prominent figure in his time for two important reasons. First, the questions he raised concerning industrial capitalism and the political and cultural revolution it encouraged were serious issues for Americans of every class in his generation. These issues were not, as we are often encouraged to think today, welcomed uncritically by all Americans; nor was the outcome of the debate assured. Debs was part of a national discussion that ultimately questioned precisely how America's traditions would be reinterpreted within this changed and charged context. Second, his fellow citizens did not support Debs primarily due to his eloquent oratory. He was a powerful public speaker, but he was no manipulative "outside agitator." His appeal stemmed from the fact that his words addressed the very real experience of countless Americans as they encountered industrial capitalism. Debs symbolized their protest, but these American men and women themselves protested the forced changes in their work lives, family structure, and individual sense of self. To ignore Debs and the movements he led distorts the past in a fundamental fashion and seriously limits our vision in the present.

Neither in his time nor in ours would Debs stand as an architect of a specific program for the future. His talents were unsuited to such an approach and to that extent limited him. But his life and those of his comrades in the labor and Socialist movements have a far broader significance. The issues first raised in the transition to an industrial capitalist society are not yet resolved. The value of the individual in a corporate-dominated society; the meaning of work in a technological environment geared primarily for profits; and the importance of citizenship amid widespread malaise brought on in large part by the manipulative practices of political leaders—all these are questions of vital concern today. Eugene Victor Debs cannot speak directly to our present; the contexts are not identical. But a study of his life does suggest that the moral and political values this preeminent native son embodied shed light on the past and are still instructive today.

During the long years of researching and writing this book, first as a doctoral dissertation and now in greatly expanded form, I have benefited immensely from the help and support of many individuals and institutions. As a graduate student, I was fortunate to receive a two-year appointment as a Max Farrand Fellow at the University of California, Berkeley, and a third year of support from the Mabel McLeod Lewis Foundation. Since then, former colleagues at Holy Cross College provided me with a semester's support, and the bulk of the final draft was written while on a year's fellowship provided by the National Endowment for the Humanities. Librarians across the country have been most helpful. Although too numerous to name individually, the staffs of the institutions listed in the notes were unfailingly supportive. I would, however, especially like to thank Dr. Paul Koda, formerly of the Cunningham Library, Indiana State University; Mr. and Mrs. Ned Bush, formerly curators of the Debs Foundation; and Mr. and Mrs. Schubert Sebree of Terre Haute, Indiana. They gave me every possible assistance during a prolonged stay in Terre Haute, shared with me their personal and professional knowledge of Debs, and opened their homes to me. Without them this might be a very different book. I am sorry that neither Ned nor Schubert has lived to see its publication. James Hogan and Selina Martin of the Dinand Library at Holy Cross treated my requests with patience and imagination during my years there.

I have profited greatly from the criticism and suggestions of many friends and colleagues. Larry Gerber, William A. Green, James R. Green, David Kessler, Bruce Laurie, Staughton Lynd, Peter Mailloux, David J. O'Brien, and Michael True read all or part of the manuscript and consistently encouraged even as they sharply criticized. Roy Rosenzweig read the complete manuscript numerous times in various forms, and I deeply appreciate his intelligence and friendship. I was fortunate in having as my editor David Brody. A perceptive historian in his own right, he helped me transform an unwieldy manuscript into a more coherent book. Scott Molloy shared with me labor material from his private collection and throughout prodded me to address a diverse audience. Christine McHugh, Neil Basen, and Lois McLean shared their research on related topics. Leslie Birmingham, Timothy Dwyer, R. Ken Gilroy, and Mark Pettitt were valuable research assistants. Pearl M. Jolicoeur and Pamela O'Keefe typed various drafts of the manuscript and brought to my attention numerous errors, large and small. I thank them for their care. Hilda Rogin was of great help in preparing the final copy. Richard L. Wentworth and Susan L. Patterson of the University of Illinois Press were consistently helpful and understanding.

My friend and teacher, Leon F. Litwack, greatly influenced this work. His careful reading of various drafts and his critical encouragement were important, but even more so were the standards he set of professional craftsmanship and personal integrity. Robert N. Bellah and Robert Salzman were also important friends and critics. In their willingness to speak sensitively of the interconnection between the biographer and the subject, they helped me to discover dimensions of my work and life that had been previously shrouded. Both it and I are richer for this.

My wife, Ann H. Sullivan, lived with me with patience and love as I learned something of the art of historical writing. Amid the demands of her own career, she also became my closest critic. Many of the ideas and interpretations that follow were first suggested by her. Her spirit and involvement pervade throughout.

Ithaca, New York

NATIVE SON: 1855–1889

America is preeminently the land of great
possibilities, of great opportunities, and of no
less great probabilities. Look around us, no
matter what our position may be, we all stand on
the great field of renown, with a free and equal
chance to go to the supreme height of all that can
be desired of earthly grandeur. We all have a fair
chance and an open field. Long may it so
remain. The time, the occasion is auspicious.
Nothing like it was ever known before.

Eugene V. Debs, 1883

"Terre Haute was a straggling village" at the time of Eugene Victor Debs's birth in 1855, James Oneal observed seventy years later. A native of Terre Haute and Socialist comrade, Oneal explained Debs's political development in terms of the social changes that altered Terre Haute in the late nineteenth century. "Something of the frontier democracy still survived" in 1855, Oneal suggested; thirty years later "this democratic society of comparative social equals" remained vital. "Debs did not change," Oneal argued. Rather, the development of industrial capitalism revolutionized that democratic society, and Debs rose to national prominence because of his opposition to this revolution: "The old order was dead, but Debs did not die with it as so many others did."[1]

Debs agreed with at least part of Oneal's analysis. In a 1924 letter to his friend and biographer, David Karsner, Debs confided that he often yearned for his "beloved little community of Terre Haute, where all were neighbors and all friends." Sadly he told Karsner that in the "enchanting little village" where he was born, concrete had replaced the grass, and modern buildings—those "hideous steel prison walls"—the maple trees.[2] There was some solace, however inadequate. As Debs had earlier written his brother, Theodore: "We can at least thank God that the profit pirates can't reach into our consciousness and despoil us of our sweet and priceless memories."[3]

But what of these memories and their motivating power? Debs and Oneal imply a certain Bunyanesque quality to early Terre Haute. Industrial capitalism destroyed the pristine purity of democratic innocence, Oneal argued, and Debs, with single-minded determination, defended the values of old Terre Haute. This interpretation might appear a fitting eulogy to an aging hero's career, but it avoids a harder, more meaningful examination of both Debs and his society. Industrial capitalism did alter the heart of Terre Haute, as it did American society in general. Yet the values Debs absorbed in his youth were not as simple or self-evident as he and Oneal later indicated. The development of Terre Haute, and of the Debs family within it, encompassed a far greater complexity. The Eugene Debs who achieved national fame as a strike leader and Socialist spokesman remained most profoundly a native son, born and raised in a small Indiana city. Without understanding the continuity and the importance of that small town culture in shaping him, Debs of necessity must appear a wistful, would-be hero, an aberration separated from his time and culture.

1

An Earthly Paradise

FOUNDED IN 1818 on the banks of the Wabash River, Terre Haute drew an early sense of its civic identity from its proximity to Fort Harrison. Mrs. George Locke, wife of the Methodist circuit rider headquartered in Terre Haute in the late 1820s, remembered that the educated officers from the fort provided early settlers with "a certain sort of cultured society from the beginning."[1] Although Mrs. Locke and other religious enthusiasts regarded this as antagonistic to the Lord's work, the desire to create the appearance of refinement intensified as the prairie outpost progressed from hamlet to village to town.

In 1851 Elizabeth Peddle, wife of the master mechanic of the recently completed Terre Haute and Indianapolis Railroad, wrote to her sister-in-law of her impressions of her new community. "The generality of the people" were wealthy, she thought, and explained that she and her husband, Charles, would leave their rooms at the Prairie House the following day "as it is rather expensive for *poor folk* like us. You know it is one of those kinds of houses that the ladies dress differently three times a day."[2] In judging her family's status at the Prairie House in terms of her ability to dress the part, Mrs. Peddle was not far wrong. In Terre Haute, as throughout nineteenth-century America, women were considered curators of culture and the repository of moral virtue for society. An English visitor to Terre Haute that same year explored this aspect more thoroughly, although in the end he remained confused. J. Richard Beste, with his wife and eleven children, spent a month at the Prairie House in the summer of 1851. "The American woman," he complained, "whether rich or poor, had her rocking-chair and her fan; her simper and her sigh; her whine and her finery." After some weeks in Terre Haute, Beste knew "much of this idleness to be affected," for Terre Haute women worked, in fact, "are obliged to work in private." What ultimately confused him was not the women but the men: "The marvel to me is that American men, who are so active-minded themselves, can admire such listless apathy in the other sex. That they do admire it is proven by the fact that the women practice it."[3]

Although still mystified, Beste had indeed stumbled onto a crucial aspect of Terre Haute's self-identity. At all costs, women of the upper echelon, such as those who frequented the Prairie House, were expected to appear as living "in the grace of literature and the arts of social life." For men, such cultural activities, while desirable, were not necessary. Their duty was business, conducted honestly in the main, and they took a "democratic" pride in the belief that among the cultured at least "the possession of a fortune added nothing to respectability."[4]

The reality of life in Terre Haute was, of course, different. Most poignantly, as Beste noted, women of all classes worked. In the 1850s the town lacked the economic foundation to support a leisured class, although that was a goal some desired. Neither did the "democratic" pride of the society's leaders extend into the wards of the working people.[5] Yet, these cultural pretensions were not merely transparent lies. A sense of culture was important for the town, even if acquired in much the same fashion as other commodities in the marketplace. It developed and reinforced a belief in the town's destiny that, in turn, structured the individual expectations of the elite as well as, in theory, the less prominent. As one town father suggested in his maturing years, with perhaps less ardor than in his youth, Terre Haute was "an Earthly paradise . . . *a sort of half station to the skies.*"[6]

In its religious observance as well, the community sought to overcome its fear of commercial and social backwardness. A little more than a generation removed from the Second Great Awakening that centered in neighboring Kentucky, Terre Haute, and Indiana in general, remained affected by the spirit of that religious enthusiasm. Explicit religious values motivated many in their daily lives, and intense emotional conversions were a widely shared experience. These early religious enthusiasts attempted to create what the Reverend Allen Wiley termed "the good state of society." An itinerant Methodist minister for over forty years in Indiana, Wiley felt that this state rested on the relative equality of wealth among the first settlers and on their dependence upon each other for much of their daily sustenance. "When we met at any of our business meetings, our social meetings, or religious meetings," he wrote, " . . . we felt as a band of brothers and sisters."[7] As one descendant of another early Methodist minister, who grew to maturity in post–Civil War Indiana, commented of the society of his youth: "Rank and file alike looked upon themselves as soldiers of the Lamb. . . . Their modes of thought and forms of speech were full of militant images, while their hymns and songs throbbed with the spirit of battle and of victory, and the banner of the cross was the watchword of old and young, men and women."[8]

Yet religious enthusiasm did vary throughout the state. South of the National Road, whose western terminus bisected Terre Haute, southern origins and influences combined with rural poverty to nurture a traditional revival atmosphere—and also helped create a Democratic party stronghold that endured for much of the nineteenth century. In contrast, the central plains to the north of Terre Haute, more heavily populated by immigrants from New England, became less effusive in its religious practice, more successful in its agriculture, and eventually Republican in its politics.[9] Differences also existed between the rural and urban experience. The center of religious activity lay among Indiana's dominant rural population, who suspiciously observed the apparent lack of fervor in the growing urban centers.[10]

The fourth largest town in Indiana in 1860, with a population of 8,500, Terre Haute received its share of such criticism. One Presbyterian minister described the town in 1834 as "an interesting place, large and growing, delightfully situated on the Wabash . . . but in a moral point of view everything is the reverse. A little feeble church, and they divided, and without much moral courage."[11] A decade later, Colonel Thomas Dowling, a lay Methodist leader in Terre Haute, complained of a distinct lack of religious feeling in the town and characterized Terre Haute as still a "frontier town" in terms of religious development. While Dowling tended to see this as a result of the strict Methodist discipline, other sects fared as poorly. Curry's Prairie Baptist Association, formed in 1834 to organize the counties of Clay, Sullivan, and Vigo, had but seven ministers and 1,400 members in 1860, the great majority outside Vigo County's seat, Terre Haute.[12] This belief in "urban sinfulness" has led one historian of Indiana religion to suggest that "in many of the towns, the property holders and office seekers were opposed to all forms of religion."[13]

Despite Terre Haute's worldly tone, this vision of urban disdain toward religion is misleading. As in other new communities, Terre Hauteans recognized quite early that the observance of certain religious forms was the *sine qua non* of civilized life.[14] In 1834 a Presbyterian minister journeying to St. Louis held a religious service in a Terre Haute saloon because no permanent church buildings existed. After services, the community's leading citizens induced the Reverend Merrick Jewett to settle in Terre Haute with a pledge of funds for a church and his salary. For many years the church lacked a formal profession of faith or denominational affiliation, but it gradually evolved into the First Congregational Church.

In 1860 the Reverend Lyman Abbott replaced Jewett as minister. In the course of his four-year tenure in Terre Haute, Abbott discovered that the chairman of the citizens' committee that founded his church in 1834 was a famous local gambler, who desired a church "as he might have interested himself in getting a railway, a school, or a library, and no more thought it necessary to be a member of the church than he would have thought it necessary to be a stockholder in a railway, a pupil in the school, or a reader of books." But Abbott thought it commendable that an "entire community should recognize the need of a church, as it might recognize the need of a fire department."[15] When the church was rebuilt in 1871, a concern for the town's civic reputation was again evident. Three of Terre Haute's leading Methodist laymen—Dowling, Richard W. Thompson, and William Riley McKeen—all purchased family pews in the Congregational Church and were prominent in the fund-raising drive.[16]

Terre Haute, then, was not "opposed to all forms of religion." On the contrary, religion remained a cornerstone of civic identity. Terre Hauteans were "full of militant images" and "throbbed with the spirit of battle and of victory," but in an adaptation of traditional theology they held that the millennium was already at hand. In political speeches and newspaper editorials, civic dedications and Sunday sermons, they asserted that the Kingdom of God had already arrived and that their town was destined to be the center of the Kingdom's Midwest development. Most significant was the townspeople's belief that the struggle against evil was over. Hard work, shrewd manipulation, and time itself would develop the millennium to its fullness. Abraham's God, Jehovah who spoke in flames, needed only the emergence of a fire department to be removed from daily consciousness.

In their secular use of millennial imagery for their own "half station to the skies," the people of Terre Haute were part of a nationalist movement that swept America and that interpreted the complex belief that Americans were God's chosen people as a simple affirmation of that God's uncritical approval of their greatest aspirations.[17] Although traditional religion retained a place in the culture of even this worldly small town, in part because the very alteration in its meaning found expression in familiar religious symbols, the rural suspicions were well founded. In Terre Haute the Reverend Wiley's community of believers searching for the "good state" had become but another buttress in the construction of an entrepreneur's delight.

A belief that businessmen were destiny's instrument to lift the town closer to the heavens was not unique to Terre Haute. As one foreign traveler noted of America at mid-century, "Every man is in business, and the business is never over.''[18] In this pre-industrial yet capitalist society, however, business did not imply the more formal and rigid class distinctions of the early twentieth century. Many men aspired to better their positions and felt that they could be successful if they so chose. Yet in Terre Haute, as in other small towns throughout America, a business elite did develop, and the deference paid this elite followed from three realities of pre-industrial life. First, the local elite had actual political and economic power and with it the ability to affect the daily lives of their neighbors. The remnants of a democratic ideology, combined with the close personal ties between these elites and their employees, tended in most cases to mute the direct use of this power, at least for a time. Nonetheless, it remained a demarcation line demanding respect from those on its far side.

Second, deference paradoxically derived from the belief held by most in society that a widespread potential for social mobility did exist. The relative fluidity of the social structure in the antebellum years allowed for a realistic hope of individual advancement and even prompted the identification of others' mobility as a sign of eventual personal success. Finally, deference rested upon the very foundation of the town's social ideology—the concept of community. Originally rooted in the conditions of the frontier, with its imperative to make "the solitary place glad" and carry "genius, learning and refinement throughout a land lately occupied by savages and wild beasts,"[19] the idea of community at first had an egalitarian ethos—for white males at least—reminiscent of Wiley's efforts to create the good society. But as more than one historian has suggested of this tradition of frontier democracy, the pioneers themselves were most ambitious men, eager to transform themselves into the "image of the bankers and merchants and landlords back home."[20] Yet in this economically underdeveloped society, individual success seemed to demand the progress of the community as a whole. One could not aspire to financial greatness in a small Midwest backwater. The individual was firmly wedded to his community both by the bonds of daily life and by the expectations of future success, and the development of an elite was welcomed even by many who remained outside it. In the process, the ideas of individualism, self-interest, and community appeared to meld.

But this sense of community proved more fragile than appeared to most at mid-century. It would last only as long as the hope for individual mobility remained feasible, and as long as the community itself could entertain expectations of dramatic future progress. Never quite as egalitarian as Oneal and Debs remembered, Terre Haute nonetheless appeared inviting to families such as the Debses as they established residence there in the 1850s. The bustling activity on its streets and the resounding affirmation heard in its pulpits and papers indicated that Terre Haute might be a good community in which to raise a family.

Eugene Victor Debs was born into this community on 5 November 1855. The third of six surviving children, Eugene was the first son born to Jean Daniel and Marguerite (Bettrich) Debs. Natives of Colmar, Alsace, the Debses migrated first to New York in 1849. Unlike other immigrants at the time, notably the Irish, neither parent was motivated by poverty. Daniel's father, Jean Daniel, Sr., owned a textile firm in Colmar and his father, Eugene's great-grandfather, achieved a certain prominence as a delegate to the National Assembly and as assistant attorney general for Alsace during the French Revolution. Marguerite Bettrich, while not wealthy, came from a respectable working-class family and had worked as a hand in her future father-in-law's factory. As a young man, Daniel studied literature in school and refused repeated requests by his father that he join the family business. Family tension increased when Daniel announced his intention to marry Marguerite, who was not only a family employee but a Catholic—the Debses were Protestant. So intense were these arguments that Daniel's father consistently refused his son permission to migrate to the United States. Finally, in January 1849, a year after his father's death, the twenty-nine-year-old Daniel arrived in New York. Marguerite joined him in September of that year, and two days later they married.[21]

Disinherited after their marriage, neither Daniel nor Marguerite ever lost their bitterness toward their European relatives. Some seventy-five years later, their son Theodore would describe those relatives, most of whom he had never met, as "a gang of cold-blooded thieves" who had robbed his father "of the last frank they could get their hands on, even to looting the linen closet." His mother also, he added, had good reason for "not forgetting, or forgiving them, and she didn't to her dying day—nor shall I while there is a breath in my body."[22] In contrast with their European kin, the Debs family in America would be extremely tight-knit and loyal.

The Debses remained in New York for a year after their marriage. In September 1850 they moved to Cincinnati and in the spring of 1851 to Terre Haute. With the exception of a six-month return to Brooklyn in 1854, the family remained there for the rest of their lives. Despite the town's bustle, life was difficult at first for Daniel and Marguerite. That Daniel possessed no obvious skill demanded by this brash, raw community complicated the task of supporting his wife and two daughters, Marie and Louise. He first held a series of ill-paid jobs, two of which, as a laborer at a pork packing firm and on the Terre Haute and Indianapolis Railroad, he quit due to his health. In desperate financial condition in 1855, a depressed Daniel watched as his pregnant wife took their last cash reserves to open a grocery store in their front room. Shortly thereafter a son, Eugene Victor, was born.[23]

In the decade following Eugene's birth, the family's financial condition improved markedly. The store proved a success, and in 1857 a more bouyant Daniel purchased two lots on Wabash Avenue, Terre Haute's main business street. Three years later he began construction of a building into which he permanently moved the family business. The continued expansion of Terre Haute coupled with a war-induced economic boom between 1861 and 1865 assured the business's continued success.[24] During this same decade, the Debs family also grew in numbers. Following the births of Eugene and Emma, the second Debs son and last child, Theodore, arrived in 1864. Established and prospering after a difficult start, Daniel and Marguerite could indeed look with pleasure on their community.

Eugene Debs's early years reflected this growing prosperity. The oldest son, he assumed a position of leadership among his siblings. As a young boy he might accompany his father to the store, meet some of Daniel's increasingly comfortable customers, and bask in the sense of himself as the little heir-apparent. He shunned the rough competitive games of his playmates but took great pleasure in the long walks through the woods with his father (and later with Theodore), tagging along at first but when older joining his father in hunting game. Eugene's fondest memory of these preteen years were the Sunday evening sessions he and the other children had with Daniel. Along with the talk and banter, Daniel read to his children each week from the classics of French literature, Voltaire, Rousseau, Dumas, Eugene Sue, and Victor Hugo—all were familiar during childhood. Named as he was for Sue and Hugo, his father's particular favorites, these evening sessions reinforced in Eugene a sense of his prominence within the family as they awakened him to a world beyond Terre Haute.[25]

As with many nineteenth-century children, Debs's first sustained experience outside the home came through the schools. Established by 1860 in Terre Haute, the public school quickly assumed the role of the main promulgator of the community's democratic ideology. As the school superintendent of Terre Haute argued in 1875: "If we shall limit the education of the masses, and trust to the extended education of the few for directive power and skill, we must expect to be ruled by monopolies, demagogues and partisans."[26] But such democratic sentiments were not meant to include Terre Haute's black population. The city excluded them by ordinance from the outset, and not until 1869 did it provide separate school facilities for black children.[27]

The schools in Terre Haute followed a familiar pattern of deferential democracy. On the original board of trustees sat many of Terre Haute's business leaders. Using the McGuffey speller, Harper's reader, and Goodrich's history, the school curriculum stressed training and skills as a means of social mobility. But the most pervasive lesson concerned the development of a proper Christian morality. The books used in reading and history oozed with moral exhortations to do good and avoid evil, and the board specifically commanded Terre Haute's teachers to "give careful and constant attention to the instruction, discipline, manners and habits of their pupils."[28]

Eugene attended both private and public schools. At first he attended the Old Seminary School, at a cost of some sixteen dollars per semester, because Daniel doubted the financial stability of the public system. After the Civil War, when the state guaranteed aid to the public schools, Eugene transferred to Terre Haute's first district school. Each school, however, was similar in its course of instruction and in the values it sought to inculcate in students. Eugene did well at school and seemed to thrive in its rigid atmosphere. In 1868 his eighth grade teacher, Abbie Flag, ranked him within the top 20 percent of his class in deportment—a catchall category that included appearance, punctuality, manners, and attitude as well as scholarly preparation. That same semester, he won a Bible for a perfect score in spelling. On the flyleaf of the Bible Flag wrote, "Read and Obey." Years later Debs commented that he had done neither, but there is no contemporary evidence to support that claim. Indeed, Eugene prospered in school, respected his teachers, and won their approval. He learned quite young that Terre Haute's democratic vision did not reward rebellion or deviance.[29]

The young Debs was not alone in absorbing the message of deference and obedience imbedded in a more formal democratic language. As Clarence Darrow, a product of a small-town Ohio education, reflected, the surface meaning of his school lessons offered a democratic vision that stressed individual potential and community progress within the context of the political traditions of the American Revolutionary heritage. Yet, Darrow recalled, the constant moral preaching also emphasized respect for and submission to parents, teachers, and, by implication, all authority. Hard work, industry, and individual success appeared as absolutes, without any indication "that any possible evil ever grew from thrift, or diligence." Ultimately these stories held as the reward for virtue not a strengthened community but a personal success which "was in no way uncertain or etheral, but was always paid in cash, or something just as material or good." Such a combination of morality and materialism conflicted sharply with a more independent democratic ideology. After rereading his grade school texts many years later, Darrow reflected on their power: "I try to recall the feelings of one child who read those stories in the little white schoolhouse by the country road. What did they mean to me? Did I laugh at them, as I do today? Or did I really think that they were true, and try and try, and then fail in all I tried, as I do now? I presume the latter was the case."[30]

As a thirteen-year-old, Debs, like Darrow, tried to follow his teacher's advice. Yet in a way perhaps unique to him among the town's children, he was aware, however dimly, of another tradition. Through his father he could claim kinship with the French republican tradition and from his earliest days he knew of the great Enlightenment and Romantic writers. In Hugo's *Les Misérables*, which even during these years Debs frequently reread in the original French, he first encountered an alternative moral order to the strictures of a deferential democracy.[31] As a young man, however, Eugene evidenced little recognition of this potential.

After completing grade school, Eugene attended the high school for one year, where his classmates were children from some of Terre Haute's leading families, among them the McKeens, the Peddles, and the Thompsons. He appeared neither awed by this proximity to the local elite nor oppressed by it. Rather, he felt that there was little difference between him and them that time and hard work would not overcome. Although he left high school after one year, Eugene remained impressed with the potential for advancement available to an educated man and attended a business college at night during the next three years. His heroes at this point in his life were men like Barney Barnato, an Englishman who had risen in three years from poverty to millions.[32] With local success stories more immediately before his eyes, Eugene entered Terre Haute's promising world of work in 1870.

In 1870 Terre Haute felt itself on the edge of dramatic development. Its population had increased almost 300 percent since 1850, and five different railroads already serviced the town, with five more either under construction or contemplated. The third ranking coal-producing county in Indiana, Vigo County was also fifth of ninety-two counties in manufacturing. The excitement that swept the town was not based solely on past accomplishments. Although the value of the county's manufactured products increased almost 200 percent during the 1860s, the recent discovery of bituminous coal deposits in adjoining Clay County indicated that the economic boom might have just begun. Within a few years, many suggested, Terre Haute would surpass both Chicago and Cincinnati as the Midwest's center of commerce and manufacturing.[33]

Achieving such distinction had long been a dream of Terre Haute. Even before it was incorporated as a city in 1854, an anonymous writer in the Cincinnati *Gazette* argued that Terre Haute, with its developing transportation facilities, was but one of several Indiana cities about to surpass Cincinnati.[34] "A pleasantly-situated town of rising importance," as one visitor described it prior to the Civil War, Terre Haute perceived itself as a distinguished if still growing community, whose early years had already provided it with a firm economic structure.[35]

This economic development began modestly enough. When Chauncey Rose, a native of Wethersfield, Connecticut, arrived in 1818, Terre Haute was little more than an agricultural village. Quickly establishing a successful grist mill, Rose used a sizable inheritance during the next decade to buy large tracts of land as he positioned himself at the center of the local economy. In 1834, in partnership with other local businessmen, he organized and served as a director of the local branch of the State Bank of Indiana. A few years later he established the first expensive hotel, the Prairie House, and exerted his by now considerable influence to assure that the National Road passed directly in front of his hotel.[36] But Rose was neither a restaurateur nor even a financier at heart. His financial empire crested at the headwaters of the mid-nineteenth-century's economic development, where land speculation and new modes of transportation flowed together. In the 1840s Rose invested in the Wabash and Erie Canal, which was to provide transportation from the central Midwest to the Great Lakes region. A canal director, Rose encouraged civic expectations of imminent commercial success and made certain that the route passed entirely through land which he owned.[37]

But the canal was not to be the instrument to lift Terre Haute into national prominence, for at the very moment of its inception it was already an outmoded form of transportation. The railroad had begun to cobweb America and, as might be expected, in Terre Haute Rose was at the center. In 1847 he obtained a charter from the state to build the Terre Haute and Indianapolis Railroad, which was completed in 1852. Local businessmen Josephus Collett, Demas Deming, Sr., and Alexander McGregor were among the first directors, while Richard W. Thompson, a former Terre Haute Whig Congressman, served as counsel. The road was an immediate success as eight trains left daily for Indianapolis, carrying grain, packed pork, and passengers.[38]

In many ways Rose was typical of small-town entrepreneurs at mid-century. He strongly believed his personal success essential for the community's progress and in that most optimistic age had little doubt about either.[39] The importance of his inherited wealth never prevented him from espousing an ideology of individual effort and private enterprise and, by implication, urging all to follow in his steps.[40] But as befitted a businessman formally committed to civic as well as individual success, Rose was also devoted to philanthropy and gave freely of his fortune to develop his and Terre Haute's reputation.[41] Rose brought Terre Haute to one level of development, but it remained for William Riley McKeen and his associates to lead the community into the industrial era.

McKeen was born on a farm just outside Terre Haute in 1829. At age seventeen, with his father's assistance, he obtained appointment as assistant clerk for Vigo County. Two years later he accepted a position as bookkeeper at the State Bank of Indiana.[42] As a result of his own abilities and a healthy dose of good fortune, McKeen rose swiftly at the bank. In 1852 he received a promotion to cashier at the same time his father formed a business partnership with McGregor, a director of the bank and one of Riley's employers. During this same year, he contracted a well-appointed marriage with Eliza Johnson, the daughter of a prominent Terre Haute merchant. In 1855 McKeen, only twenty-four but already considered a man of "considerable means," left the state bank to establish his own private bank. Over the next decade, he came to dominate local banking circles and also became active politically. A four-time Republican city councilman between 1854 and 1867, he took his first step in state politics when he lent the nearly bankrupt state $10,000 to enable it to raise regiments for the Union army. Shortly thereafter, he was appointed treasurer and director of the State Normal School in Terre Haute.[43] In addition, McKeen held major interests in numerous local enterprises and was quite active in religious and cultural associations. He also raised thoroughbreds at his farm just outside the city and became a central figure in one of Terre Haute's major forms of popular culture, horse racing.[44]

The dominant figure in the community following the Civil War, McKeen sought even greater investment opportunities. In 1869 he purchased the controlling interest in his friend Rose's railroad. A sound economic investment, it also came at a critical period in American railroad history. Prior to 1870 the major railroad corporations pursued a policy of cooperation and alliance with the smaller roads. Concerned with the ability to manage a complex national system profitably and fearful of the political repercussions a giant railroad monopoly might invoke, railroad executives instead sought to influence the policies of these feeder lines through investment that stopped short of majority control. The year 1870 marked a turning point, however. Speculators such as Jay Gould systematically raided the smaller roads and, although not generally successful, underlined the weak link in the major railroads' corporate structure. Then the depression of 1873 quickly followed. As the economy slowed and railroad traffic plummeted, the pattern of cooperation governing rates and territorial jurisdiction simply collapsed in the mad scramble to remain solvent. In the aftermath, first the Pennsylvania and then the other major roads rejected the alliance system in favor of obtaining direct control of all subsidiary roads.[45]

McKeen's purchase of the Terre Haute and Indianapolis road was timely. He and his local co-investors owned and managed an important link between the eastern markets and St. Louis, a major rail terminus. At the same time, McKeen entered into a financial alliance with the Pennsylvania corporation to extend the road west across Illinois to St. Louis and thus control direct freight access through the heart of the Midwest. Although the Pennsylvania owned the new track, McKeen obtained a ninety-nine-year lease on quite favorable terms and renamed the whole system the Vandalia Railroad. Many in Terre Haute took great pride that the system remained in local hands. With the community expanding, they argued, it was important that one of its critical resources remain intact, free from the ironclad directives of distant directors. The accuracy of that sentiment would be tested in the years to come.[46]

These protestations of local pride notwithstanding, the business community was by no means averse to outside investment. Indeed, its leaders understood its importance if they were to fulfill their hope of surpassing Pittsburgh as the nation's leading iron center. Thus it was with pleasure that such local leaders as McKeen, McGregor, and D. W. Minshall joined with nonresident investors to establish three blast furnaces between 1870 and 1872. Although modest by national standards (only one was capitalized at more than $100,000), they generated widespread local enthusiasm. That outsiders retained majority control of two of the companies caused little negative comment. If anything, such investment rekindled excitement over Terre Haute's coming prominence. In an 1870 prospectus the town's business leaders boasted that a Pittsburgh concern founded the Vigo Iron Company and exclaimed that "heavy capitalists from the iron regions of Pennsylvania and elsewhere are almost daily visiting Terre Haute with a view to an examination of its advantages . . . with reference to the manufacture of iron." Two years later in another prospectus, written by an imported publicist, the business community went further. The railroad and the blast furnaces, they urged, combined with the community's central location and natural resources, made inevitable Terre Haute's emergence as the future center of Midwest commerce and industry. With little hesitation they crowned Terre Haute as the true "beacon star set *upon* the hills."[47]

While McKeen, like Rose before him, donated both time and money to his community's cultural and charitable institutions, his emergence as the dominant figure in the business community after 1870 signalled a new consciousness among Terre Haute's businessmen. Although he and his associates might still publicly interpret their activities as beneficial for the whole community, and even appeal to a shared common citizenship to cloud their growing ascendancy, it nonetheless became clear in the years after the Civil War that new concerns motivated these men. They no longer conceived their activities as merely of local concern. As the tone of their various prospectuses suggests, they nearly trembled with expectation at the thought of their expanding relations with the "heavy capitalists" of America. Slowly these desires helped to foster the growth of a different consciousness, one that pared away the meaning of community and citizenship to reveal more clearly than in the preceding generation the essential self-interest that lay at its core.

Collectively these leading businessmen, the "best people" as Lyman Abbott called them, were a homogeneous group. Eighty-four percent were American-born, and almost half had resided in the community since before the construction of the National Road in the 1830s. Economically well-entrenched by the Civil War, these men and their families shared cultural and civic bonds that helped separate them from others in the community. They founded schools and charitable organizations and served as directors for each other. In 1870 all joined in promoting the construction of the 1,400-seat Opera House, which they saw as tangible proof of Terre Haute's emerging status. Important for the development of this group consciousness was their tendency to intermarry. Two years after his first wife died in 1855, McKeen married Anna Crawford, whose father was then president of the Terre Haute and Indianapolis Railroad. Another second-generation businessman and banker, John Sovercool Beach, married Harriet Gilbert, the daughter of one of Terre Haute's earliest bankers and land speculators. The children of this generation also married well. In 1880 McKeen's oldest son, Frank, married Mary McGregor, the daughter of Alexander, an early employer and later associate of his father. Beach's daughter in turn married Spencer Ball, editor of the Terre Haute *Gazette*, whose family had lived in Terre Haute since the 1830s. Similarly, the grandson of S. S. Early, a prominent first-generation banker and entrepreneur, married the daughter of Preston Hussey, an important banker and investor of the Civil War era.[48]

These intermarriages suggest a pattern that encompasses three generations of Terre Haute's business families. If the first and even some of the second generation's marital alliances reflect a shrewd business sense as well as personal affection, the third generation's pattern indicates another emphasis. These marriages were less concerned with solidifying an economic empire, for executive positions in well-established family concerns awaited the sons of all three families. Rather, the choice of partners and the hearty concurrence of the families in each case point to a cultural tradition already entrenched by the 1870s. They might sit side by side with the sons and daughters of small retail merchants and railroad workers in the community's public schools, but their fathers knew, even if the young boys did not always realize it themselves, that they were being groomed for a far different future than their classmates.

By the 1870s an important new emphasis permeated Terre Haute's business community. More clearly than in Rose's day, the convergence of personal success with community-wide progress proved suspect, as the "best people" now presented themselves as a separate group of singular importance. "As a city," they proclaimed in 1873, "we are altogether dependent upon the business tact and energy, or in other words, *life* and *vigor* of our business community."[49] Increasingly these men divided their world into those who owned and managed the local economy and those who hired on as hands in the bustling world of work.

Smitten as he was by the idea of success, the fourteen-year-old Debs gave little thought to these developments. Intent on achieving his own local prominence, this handsome, slim lad excitedly left school in 1870 to join the work force. As his father before him, however, Eugene possessed no special skills. But with the aid of a family friend, Pierre Solomon, a fellow Alsatian and skilled worker for the Vandalia Railroad, he was hired as a locomotive paint-scraper at fifty cents a day by Charles Peddle, the Vandalia's master mechanic. Working at first with borrowed tools, Debs quickly bought his own paint-scraper, which he kept until the day he died. On this simple note began Eugene Debs's passionate involvement with railroad work and railroad workers.[50]

The decision to leave school caused family tension. Both parents urged their son to continue his studies and argued with him. But Eugene remained adamant. Years later he would claim that he left school because his parents were quite poor and had "in fact suffered martyrdom" that their children "might fare better."[51] But this was misleading. Neither Daniel nor Marguerite supported his choice and, as his brother Theodore noted, the family was not poor: "There was always a sufficiency of food, though life at times was hard and suffering great, but this was from other causes."[52] Similarly, Debs's memory that he wept when his high-school class graduated and he "longed to be counted with them" again misrepresented what railroad work meant to him in 1870. In part, the railroad was simply exciting and attractive to the young boy. The work appeared glamorous and offered uncommon opportunities for travel. But it promised other opportunities as well. Skilled railroad workers—the engineers, firemen, and conductors who went over the road and the carpenters, mechanics, and painters who remained in the repair shops—were among the most respected and highest paid workers in America during the 1870s and 1880s. Tradition held, and it was borne out by the experience of many, that the opportunities for advancement were impressive, even for a young lad beginning in an unskilled trade.[53]

If Debs's parents envisioned a petit-bourgeois position for their son in the family business, Eugene's choice of occupation was not without its own prestige or avenues of mobility. As his attendance at the evening business school during his first three years of employment indicated, he thought such training could prepare him for a future managerial position in business. According to one teenage companion, Debs was but one of Terre Haute's youth intent on making a name:

All we young fellows then held close together and at times expressed pretty forceably to one another, what we were going to do toward making the world go round. In those early days our admiration was likely to be more particularly extended toward Robert Flynn, the always exquisitely fashioned man about Hulman's; toward John Logan over at Paris [Illinois] who essayed to become a famous detective; toward whoever was so fortunate as to be appointed Chief of Police. . . . Our anticipations were of the time when Gene would reach an eminence in trade equal to Herman Hulman, or step into a Master Mechanics job in charge of all the engine men.[54]

Eugene Debs worked for McKeen's Vandalia Railroad for a little over four years. Debs became a fireman within the first year, the promotion occurring quickly when the regular fireman appeared too drunk for work. But in September 1874 the depression claimed his job, and Debs traveled to East St. Louis, Illinois, where he found temporary work as a substitute night fireman in the train yard. He hoped that Tom McCabe, a friend and former Terre Haute machinist, could find him a permanent position. Almost nineteen and "on the tramp" in a distant city for the first time in his life, Debs was a lonely and somewhat frightened young man. "I have a little company," he wrote his parents shortly after arriving, "but sometimes I am all alone and I am so homesick, I hardly know what to do." While he desired a job, in part perhaps to end his isolation, he did not feel optimistic at the prospects, for "times are indeed dull." East St. Louis itself seemed to Debs a strange, even alien city as he encountered there for the first time the devastating urban poverty that his family's position largely shielded him from in Terre Haute. "It makes a person's heart ache to go along some of the main sts. in the city and see men, women and children begging for something to eat," he told his parents, and then drew a lesson from that for his own family: "Sisters Lou, Jennie and Emma and brother Theodore don't know how happy they ought to be to have a comfortable home, and parents kind, to help them. I did not know it either till I came over here."[55]

Lonely and isolated, Debs was delighted when he managed to strike up a friendship with a French family who lived near his boardinghouse. As he discovered on visiting them, they had an attractive seventeen-year-old daughter with whom Eugene immediately proceeded to fall in love. So taken was he with Lena Duches, he sheepishly confessed to his sister Louise, that he "stole off their table this morning" a picture of her. Feeling charged yet hesitant, barely able to visit with Lena without acute embarrassment, Eugene began to explore new dimensions in himself. In other ways as well he asserted, at times stridently, the dawning of a new self-identity. Covering his self-doubt with youthful braggadocio, he confidently reassured his family that the railroad he hoped to work for was, despite its aged and well-worn equipment, "as safe as a bed, never having had any ill luck in any manner." Besides, as he told Louise, the inherent danger of railroad work was not the main issue: "I don't expect to stay away from home forever, nor even for an unreasonable length of time; I only want to stay long enough and to prove that I can act manly when must be."[56]

That conjunction of personal identity and public position, the definition of one's worth in terms of the performance of duties and responsibilities in society, was not unique to Debs or simply the result of a passing adolescent crisis. Rather, it represented the very core of Terre Haute's expressed values. As Debs and other male children learned from their earliest days in school, manhood was in large part defined in public fashion, through one's actions as a citizen, a member of a specific community, and as a producer of value for one's family and the community and in one's personal relations with others. This was the lesson that Daniel taught his son by example, as did other fathers their sons. Manhood found its clearest expression within a very small personal circle: the family, first as son and later father; and the business world, among the customers and business acquaintances a small retail grocer such as Daniel might acquire. In brief, the very concept of manhood hinged on the ability of any given individual to assume in his localized social group personal responsibility for his deeds. In theory there was no place for the emerging corporation.

But in 1874 the potential richness of this idea remained shrouded for the young Debs. Beyond a certain sympathy for the poor and a deep concern to become self-supporting (and one senses that the first concern fueled the second), Eugene defined himself in very personal terms that emphasized his role within the family. As he sought to harness the confusion and self-doubt within himself, he on occasion played the role of the worldly young man to his older sisters who were, given the patriarchal limits of the notion of manhood, by definition subordinate to him despite their age. But it was with his ten-year-old brother, Theodore, that Eugene sought an alternative to the confusion he himself was then experiencing. In an early note to his sister (in a letter to his parents) from East St. Louis, he told her to instruct Theodore to care for the family's chickens "and to be a good boy and obey pa and ma."[57] A week later, he wrote his brother directly. Pleased that the chickens were healthy, Eugene again urged Theodore "to do all you can to help pa and ma" and promised that "maybe, if you are right-good and work hard, I will fetch you something from St. Louis."[58] Not fully confident that he could "act manly," Eugene found a certain solace in affirming his position as the central sibling in the family. Given the family's intense loyalty and its unspoken but clear acceptance of his role, Eugene received what he needed.

But the world treated him more harshly. Unable to find a job, Debs returned to Terre Haute in October 1874 without the gifts he promised. Once home, his mother strongly urged him not to await a business up-turn to regain employment as a fireman. Marguerite was terribly concerned with the high rate of railroad accidents, and in response to her plea Eugene sought other work. At this juncture, Daniel again interceded, as he had in 1870, and spoke to his friend and business associate, Herman Hulman, the owner of one of the largest wholesale groceries west of New York. By the end of the month Eugene, to the great relief and pleasure of both his parents, joined the Hulman business as an accounting clerk. For Daniel especially his son's recent "tramp" might have appeared a rite of passage into adulthood, a necessary but potentially dangerous diversion. But now both parents seemed to feel that that problem no longer concerned them as their son appeared ready to settle down.[59]

Settle down Debs did. He remained at Hulman's through the 1870s and saw in that position a viable avenue for advancement. As befitted the son of a small yet prosperous retail merchant (who in 1877 added a full line of imported wines and liquors to his stock), Eugene took a more active role in civic affairs.[60] In frequent attendance at the Opera House for orations, theater, and concerts, Eugene also joined the Occidental Literary Society, which sponsored occasional debates and educational addresses.[61] Interested in politics, he sporadically attended Democratic party ward meetings. In general, he appeared to his neighbors as a personable young man with great potential for future success. Hulman spoke of his employee with great enthusiasm. Debs himself shared these expectations, and the potential of the community as his own still appeared vibrant to him. In this mood, in February 1875, Eugene Debs attended an organizational meeting in Terre Haute of the Brotherhood of Locomotive Firemen.

Perhaps the excitement and comradery of the distinctive culture of railroad men still attracted Debs, and he may have thought that organizational work would provide an outlet without violating his mother's request. If so, it was also true that association with the Brotherhood of Locomotive Firemen caused no tension for Debs in his other roles as son, Hulman employee, or rising young citizen in Terre Haute. Founded by Joshua Leach in 1873, the Brotherhood was primarily a benevolent association, concerned with insurance and death benefits for members. During its first two years of existence, it rarely if ever expressed any hostility toward railroad owners and managers. Its motto, "Benevolence, Sobriety and Industry," indicated neither disappointment nor discontent but rather an organization of relatively skilled workers intent on maintaining and improving their position through careful attention to their duties and responsibilities. Leach himself explained these Brotherhood goals to Debs and nine others on 26 February 1875. Urging them to return the following night with additional railroad men, they then formally organized Vigo Lodge, No. 16. A charter member, Eugene Debs was elected recording secretary, while a young fireman, Mark Miller, became the financial secretary.[62]

Debs was well suited for his new office. Personally popular with the railroaders, his education and work experience prepared him for a position that required both keeping the lodge's minutes and maintaining its correspondence with other lodges and the national office. In contrast to the working firemen who were frequently absent from Terre Haute, Debs's white-collar position gave him the time to attend to such duties. Finally, Debs seemed to have a knack for organizational responsibilities. He enjoyed the contact the position offered with similar officials across the state and country and relished the preparation of the formal reports his office demanded. Although not a bureaucrat in any modern sense, neither was Debs uncomfortable with such work. His election marked for him a new possible route to success through association with a skilled craft organization—a route, moreover, that, although different, was consonant with his position at Hulman's.

By 1875 Debs had fully entered Terre Haute's world of work. His formal education over, he was one of a coterie of young men who looked optimistically toward the future and who believed explicitly that opportunity permeated their culture. Each might define it somewhat differently—but whether Debs became the chief accountant at Hulman's or eventually replaced Peddle as master mechanic on the Vandalia mattered little in their eyes. Further, neither Debs nor his friends even thought to question the dominant place their collective employers held within Terre Haute's economic and political structure. Indeed, the promise of dramatic development offered by such men as McKeen, Hulman, D. W. Minshall, and others, coupled with the praise they bestowed on their promising employees, effectively focused Debs and his friends' attention in another direction. The opportunity they expected for themselves would wither, their attitude suggested, without the continued economic success of their employers. In 1875 Debs and his circle believed in the community of Terre Haute—"that sacred little spot" as he called it[63]—and like so many other ambitious young men he saw his future inevitably tied to the progress of the whole community.

But Terre Haute had changed. No longer "the straggling village," its democratic traditions appeared more and more muted, as if encased in bunting. Slowly, a distinct consciousness surfaced within the business elite and the term "the best people" took on added meaning. Controlling the avenues of economic development, this elite at least privately began to redefine the meaning of the word community. Despite the public appeals to a Jeffersonian rhetoric, the self-interest at the heart of their activities found increasing use within this group as the only necessary justification. Their willingness to jettison larger communal interests in order to entice "heavy capitalists" and advance their own interests resulted in a series of dramatic consequences that permanently altered the community. As events on the Vandalia only two years later would indicate, critical decisions concerning wages and work conditions—the very ability of working people to affect the basic structure of their daily lives—were made by employers more sensitive to the mandates of distant corporate executives than to the men they faced daily. Although the business community's attitude was still in formation, in 1875 the "beloved little community. . . . where all were neighbors and all friends" described less a reality than it did a wistful desire.

Ironically, this transformation occurred despite the absence of dramatic economic development. The coal boom, that expected engine of progress, simply petered out. The deposits proved neither as extensive nor as rich as hoped for, and Terre Haute's distance from the Mesabi Range, the center of America's ore resources, proved too expensive to overcome. Further, the iron industry never generated enough capital to finance the transition to modern industrial methods. Despite the hopes and dreams, there were no new iron furnaces erected in all of Indiana between 1872 and 1900.[64] Terre Haute's business leaders miscalculated in other ways as well. Myopic with excitement over the recent economic spurt, they failed to see how limited that development was. Proud to be ranked twelfth among Indiana's ninety-two counties in 1876 in the value of its railroad property, few considered that the leading Indiana county, Lake, had less than 5 percent of the state total. Thus, in such a decentralized, nonindustrial state, Vigo County's 2 percent was meaningless, particularly in light of its dreams of national power and prominence.[65]

Ultimately Terre Haute had little to contribute to industrializing America. As one local historian noted, the city could "offer no services that cannot be obtained elsewhere just as easily."[66] Isolated, without significant amounts of natural resources, Terre Haute had only its dreams and expectations. Yet these dreams had a real power for the "best people" that, when combined with their extensive control of the local economy, gradually transformed life in Terre Haute over the next decades. It was at this juncture, a critical yet dimly understood clash of expectations and basic values, that Eugene Debs began devoting his nights to the business of organizing the Terre Haute lodge of the Brotherhood of Locomotive Firemen.

2

The Blue-Eyed Boy of Destiny

THE CONCEPT OF MANHOOD that so concerned Eugene Debs in 1874 was not peculiar to him. For many workers in the decades following the Civil War, and especially for skilled men, that concern spoke to some of their deepest aspirations and fears. In part, it addressed the father and husband's role within the family that positioned him at the apex of family concerns. The breadwinner and active participant in the world, a man's duty and responsibility demanded he provide for his wife and children in a material way and, just as important, serve as a model of industry and honesty. Manhood also required an active political participation and the fulfillment of one's duty as a citizen. But at root this skilled worker's vision of manhood rested on his specific work function. It demanded that he secure a living wage; establish through industry and proper habits his own self-respect; and in this manner secure the respect of other men—goals derived primarily from the work experience. Theoretically, this concept promised that the "manly virtues" counted for more than financial differences between men and applauded the common bond held to exist between employer and worker in the grand project of ordering and advancing society.

Not unexpectedly, such understandings could lead skilled workers on the railroad and in other industries to advocate a communality of purpose with their employers. Bayless W. Hanna, a former Indiana attorney general and a member of Terre Haute's business elite, skillfully drew on this perception in an address before the Brotherhood of Locomotive Firemen in 1882. While Debs and other delegates provided nearly continuous applause, Hanna described the railroad industry as the "animating spirit of the entire physical universe. You, gentlemen," he told the cheering delegates, "are its representatives. . . . What higher distinction could you want?" Answering his own question, this investor and legal counsel for the railroad industry touched a keen aspect of this audience's self-image: "There can be no higher distinction, nor any more honorable. And the locomotive fireman is the coming engineer. Then, he will, indeed, hold the nervous helm of commerce." Urging his audience to "get ready," to develop "a sober, steady, strong hand," Hanna concluded with a final reminder that linked these men's self-esteem directly to the continued prosperity of the railroad industry: "You are a part, and a necessary part, of our entire railroad system. How important, how vast, how essential that system has become, I need not tell you."[1]

These invocations to duty and responsibility were familiar to Hanna's audience. Many workers believed that this recognition of their manhood depended upon the experience of a fundamental cohesion within their society and culture. In pursuit of this unity they, too, could deny the existence of conflicting class interests and, under the banner of harmony, stress a common purpose. As one worker, upset with attacks on that ideal, told a Congressional committee in 1879: "Now my view of capital and labor is that a community should exist between the capitalist and the laborer, instead of antagonistic feelings."[2]

This emphasis on harmonious social relations especially pervaded small-town American culture during the transition to industrial society. Employers utilized it, both manipulatively and honestly to achieve conservative goals, as did many workers and union leaders. F. W. Arnold, the grand master of the Locomotive Firemen, suggested in 1882 that the "high moral position of manliness" rested upon the three virtues that formed the Brotherhood's motto: a practical benevolence, "that enables us to regard the whole human species as one family"; sobriety, "the most important and necessary qualification"; and industry, the virtue "as one" with morality. Arnold stressed that employers were quick to comprehend "this marked advance in morality" due to the Brotherhood's influence and showed it by frequent advancement and promotion to members.[3] The quest for harmony could thus lead some to link even union activity to employer approval.

Yet even the most extremely conservative use of such a concept did not completely eliminate the potential critique at its core. The very notion of harmony—with its tradition in humankind's religious imagination as old as original sin—had a specific American anchor, and the development of religious thought during the eighteenth and nineteenth centuries gave renewed political expression to certain of those principles.[4] For many in this early labor movement, the goal of harmony demanded a rededication to the fundamental promise of the American revolution: a classless society of citizens, acting in concert with God's grace and intent on creating the new Jerusalem. All who produce value within and for the community could regard themselves as citizen-producers—respected in each other's eyes, concerned with the economic and political welfare of the community, and opposed to those monopolists and financiers who desire only to extract their wealth. In this view the term harmony was co-equal with a concept of justice that demanded active community control of the more avaricious aspects of one's personality. With the emergence of an industrialized society, one that threatened the republican and religious foundations of the older culture, many workers saw in this concept of justice a stringent critique of the new order. Insisting that even industrial capitalism was subject to these older moral and political traditions, Edward King, a type-founder and delegate to New York's Central Labor Union, told Senate investigators that workers' remedies to current industrial problems "imply something more than 'business principles'; they imply the subordination of what are regarded as 'business principles' to morality."[5]

Manhood, too, had a Janus-faced quality to its meaning. Many skilled workers believed that the ability to support their families—to allow the wife to remain at home and to obtain at least a grade school education for the children—marked a new level of success. But such goals had serious if unforeseen consequences. The "cult of domesticity," as advocated by both men and women in the latter half of the nineteenth century, tended to limit the image of women to a specific and narrow function within the family, ironically even when economic reality forced her outside the home. Her husband was equally limited, although at first glance the opposite seemed the case. His own self-worth became disproportionately tied to a marketplace economy. As industrialization destroyed the craftsman's pride of work, the very meaning of work narrowed and its value in creating self-respect diminished.

During the last half of the nineteenth century, however, these issues were still vital and largely unresolved. The concepts of manhood, dignity, and self-respect did galvanize workers to oppose the new industrial culture in defense of a deeper and broader value. Questioned by a Senate committee, John S. McClelland, a New Jersey worker and Knights of Labor official, traced his own labor activism in part to the fact that "in many of those larger institutions . . . the men are looked upon as nothing more than parts of the machinery that they work."[6] Another witness was even more direct: "When the men entered [the factory] in the morning they were numbered by checks. A man lost his identity as a man and took a number like a prisoner in a penitentiary."[7]

Manhood and harmony, then, could either fuel opposition to industrial capitalism or ease such a transition to the new social order. Much would depend upon the specific local context: the nature and pace of industrial development; the composition and traditions of the work force; and the history of a specific community. In a small town such as Terre Haute, where industrialization was slow and incomplete, a harmonious community based on mutual self-respect seemed to exist longer than in New York or Chicago. But between 1875 and 1885, as Debs became ever more immersed in his trade union work, the definition of these central concepts appeared less certain even in Terre Haute.

Almost thirty years after he joined the Brotherhood of Locomotive Firemen, Debs told a national audience what that experience had meant for him. Coloring his memory of those early days with the hues of his later life, Debs wrote that joining the Brotherhood had marked the fundamental turning point in his life. "In the very hour of my initiation I became an agitator," he proclaimed. "A new purpose entered my life, a fresh force impelled me as I repeated the obligation to serve the 'brotherhood,' and I left that meeting with a totally different and far loftier ambition than I had ever known before."[8] Disregarding the concerns that motivated him and the other charter members, Debs invented an heroic and otherworldly conversion saga more consonant with his image as a Socialist spokesman than with his thoughts at age twenty. Many of his biographers have accepted this later view and added to that mythic shroud around his life.[9] But Debs's reality was far more complex than even he at times would admit, and in the unfolding of that complexity lies the meaning of the man and an important part of the experience of his generation.

Although organized in February 1875, Vigo Lodge transacted little business at first, as most of the meetings between May and October of that year were cancelled for lack of a quorum.[10] The visit from Grand Secretary-Treasurer William N. Sayer was the best attended meeting during this period. As Debs recorded it, Sayer's address was largely ceremonious, concerned with lodge regalia, and he stressed the need for the members to "form a line of march in the anteroom, and he placed [each] in rank, according to position and station occupied."[11]

The ceremony and ritual suggested by Sayer's remarks were not merely an empty form, betraying the lack of real power the fledgling union possessed. The men of Vigo Lodge, as other workers throughout the country, were new to the labor movement. In many ways the heritage of democratic individualism ill prepared them for economic cooperation. The ceremony Sayer suggested could strengthen a feeling of solidarity, and it held within itself the seeds of a potent opposition to the highly competitive ethos of American society. As one New Jersey fireman expressed it: "The first step a fireman takes in the Lodge he is reminded of the living God, and of the undertaking. He is made to know that he is about to enter the consecrated walls of our Lodge. Then the important lessons are taught him. He is immediately surrounded by a band that has thrown off the shackles of jealousy and deceit, and he is made to know that brotherly love exists where the boys of the ironhorse meet."[12]

The ritual of the lodge was not merely empty ceremony, but neither did it demarcate a distinctive working-class attitude. The potential use of lodge ceremony as a prophetic religious ritual in opposition to industrial capitalism remained latent. The hierarchy of the Brotherhood generally opposed such an interpretation, as did most members. They declared that the Brotherhood existed for "the protection and elevation—mentally, morally and socially" of all firemen "for the purpose of working their way up to a higher position." Although concerned with wages, they placed the major emphasis on securing proper moral conduct from members in order to obtain wider community support. Vigo Lodge understood itself less as a labor organization agitating for justice than as a sifter of personnel for the railroad corporation. "It is a part of our business to secure all good members work," the *Locomotive Firemen's Magazine* stated in its first editorial, "and the many assurances from railroad officers that they will give us the preference is, in itself, a work of honor to us as locomotive firemen. . . . To place such men upon the locomotive engine as have received their education through our Order, is merely to give the public a class of men whom trust can be reposed in."[13]

Debs was an influential force within this lodge throughout the first fifteen years of its existence. Continually and usually unanimously re-elected to office as recording secretary or, from July 1883, as master of the lodge, Debs was also sent as Vigo's delegate to the national convention in three of his first four years as a member. In part, his importance was an expression of trust from members for his hard work in keeping the young lodge alive; in part, it resulted from his growing prominence within the national hierarchy. As recording secretary to No. 16, Debs had frequent contact with the national officers and early attracted their attention. Chosen to deliver the Grand Lodge address at the 1877 convention, Debs was subsequently appointed to a series of minor offices over the next two years. His career took a decided advance in 1880, when Arnold appointed him to replace Sayer as secretary-treasurer and editor of the journal after Sayer was accused of drunkenness and possible embezzlement.[14]

During these years Debs fully embraced the official ideology of the Brotherhood as explained in the magazine's first editorial. Some among the rank and file interpreted the Brotherhood's motto of "Benevolence" as an imperative to "strive to live good Christian lives, strive to elevate ourselves to a higher standing, morally and socially. Why not show our manhood by taking a firm stand against every evil, which is so prevalent through our country?'' But, Debs argued in the summer of the great railroad strike of 1877, having established an insurance program, the Brotherhood ''could with one voice exclaim, 'We have done our duty.' ''[15] Debs believed that the principle of harmony, conservatively understood, best expressed the correct relations between worker and employer. In a speech before the 1878 convention he denounced as ''sheerest folly'' the notion that the Brotherhood would conspire against the railroad corporations, since its ''interests are so closely aligned with those of their employers.'' The only ''advantage'' the Brotherhood intended to have over the corporations, Debs continued, was to ''give them a class of honest and intelligent laborers, men upon whom they can depend, men who are equal in every way to the responsibilities under which they are placed.'' Then and only then, the twenty-three-year-old Debs thundered, are we ''justified in asking recompense in accordance with the kind of labor performed.''[16]

In the pages of the *Locomotive Firemen's Magazine* as well, Debs was a leader in blunting the more radical critique that some of the members gave the term benevolence. Those who sought to widen the scope of the Brotherhood beyond its skilled craft concerns encountered a conservative, ahistorical, and individualistic moral argument that placed the onus of maintaining harmony directly on the workers. As Debs wrote in 1878:

> Our prospects in the future would be as bright as the glittering rays of sunshine, were each member to resolve within himself upon being an example of morality and a promulgator of the prospects which our Order embraces. . . . The Brotherhood of Locomotive Firemen endeavors to induce its members to exercise an unblemished influence, and thereby stimulate the victims of immorality to enter upon a more righteous course of conduct and emulate its example. This, however, cannot be effected until we have banished from our midst all threatening vices, and can point upon our own members, without exception, as being a class of men worthy of confidence and respect.[17]

Debs's influence within Vigo Lodge rested on other factors besides his rise within the national hierarchy. While his work situation at Hulman's allowed him the leisure to assume these additional responsibilities, the qualities of his own personality won him the respect of the railroad men. This angular, sharp-featured young man brought to his duties an intense dedication. At the same time Debs was anything but a dour individual. He enjoyed the comradery that came to mark the lodge meetings and enthusiastically participated in the informal discussions on social issues with other members. Debs felt comfortable with these men, and they with him.

Yet Debs's presence within the lodge held additional meaning for both him and the rank and file. An active member within the larger Terre Haute community, Debs delivered his initial public, speech—on Patrick Henry—before the Occidental Literary Society in 1875. In 1878, more at ease on the platform, Debs entered local politics, giving his first speech for the Democratic party while organizing his ward.[18] By this time Debs was a rising young figure in Terre Haute. He was friendly with William Riley McKeen and Herman Hulman, and both men encouraged Debs in his various activities and provided him with access to the town's leading citizens. A budding Democratic politician and labor leader, Debs expressed in his own life that principle of harmony he theorized about in the *Locomotive Firemen's Magazine*. His close personal contact with men such as McKeen brought the lodge a respectability and acceptance from the larger community, which was appreciated by the members. In turn, his own personal success in the Brotherhood as in Terre Haute clearly rested upon his reputation as a conservative and "sensible" leader of Vigo Lodge. In classic American fashion Debs sought to rise from the ranks, believing as he did that he fulfilled not only his own destiny but also furthered the very ranks themselves.

Debs and the lodge members shared a similar outlook. A narrow interpretation of the motto, "Benevolence, Sobriety and Industry," was the motif within the lodge as within the pages of the magazine. When, for example, Andrew Kelly, a charter member, died from work-related injuries, the brothers of No. 16 voted funeral benefits and appointed a committee to inquire of the railroad whether it would pay the doctor's bills. No outcry was raised, nor did any discussion ensue, as to the nature of the railroad's responsibility; rather the brothers resolved that "we humbly bow in submission to the will of our Lord and Master, who has deprived us of our worthy brother and associate; and as life is so uncertain we deeply feel how necessary it is, to be prepared at all times to meet the summons."[19] When another member requested full sick benefits in 1881, Debs argued, and the members concurred, that he should receive them "provided that his disability was not brought about by his own immoral conduct."[20]

While such benefits were not large—in 1879 death benefits brought but $8.25—a member had to prove himself almost a temperance man to receive them.[21] Early in its history Vigo Lodge interpreted the stricture to sobriety to mean that if a member was found drunk three times, even if off duty, he would be expelled.[22] Concern over this issue was so high that one unemployed brother felt it necessary to ask permission from the lodge to accept a job tending bar in Terre Haute. This was allowed "only until he could acquire another situation."[23] In 1882 Debs himself brought charges against Alonzo Hunt for being "drunk and disorderly in the City of Terre Haute." Adjudged guilty by a lodge committee, Hunt was merely suspended as it was his first offense.[24] But it was even possible to face expulsion from the lodge for using "abusive language" against a brother, as one member discovered in 1879.[25]

The tremendous emphasis placed on temperance and upright moral conduct within the lodge suggests the particular image these men held of themselves. Skilled workers with high aspirations, they viewed the Brotherhood as a means of their collective transformation and as a vehicle to achieve a more complete acceptance from the larger community. They wished to be understood as responsible, moral members of the community and went to great lengths to prove that they were. Hard work, sobriety, the acceptance of their responsibilities, and devotion to duty—this complex of values was their link to the wider community of businessmen, ministers, bankers, and employers; proof, as it were, that having met the duties of their station, they were now entitled to partake of the joys of harmonious social intercourse. The extent to which these firemen went to prove such worth was indicated in a *Locomotive Firemen's Magazine* editorial in January 1879, Debs's first issue as associate editor:

> We feel ourselves in duty bound . . . to give to railway corporations a class of sober and industrious men. A class of men who are not only satisfied with having performed the ordinary functions of their situations, but men who will be in the direct interest of their employers. Men who will save fuel and oil, and protect the machinery and other property entrusted to their care; in other words to give our superior officers trained and intelligent labor, shall be our highest aim. We believe that then they in return will recognize our merits and say: "Well done, my good and faithful servants." May the time soon come when these prospects will have been fully realized, and then the struggling masses of our association will not have labored in vain.[26]

If the subservience that lay at the root of the idea of harmony in this emerging industrial culture needed further clarification, it was provided by Hanna some years later. In his address at the 1882 convention he reminded the men, to their continued applause, that they should be grateful, for the corporation "has invited you to a field of such useful and profitable labor . . . has taught you self-reliance and obedience to authority; made you ready, active and faithful in service; [and] honest, just, fearless and humane in the exercise of power."[27] The officials and many of the members might have only complained that they, and not exclusively the corporation, should inculcate these virtues.

Such ideas were of major importance for Debs and the men of Vigo Lodge, and they needed expression at a more serious level than just the pages of their journal. The ultimate test came in the manner the Brotherhood acted in specific work situations. If harmony was a prized value, then the lodge itself would have to take steps to control the "base" natures of the members. It clearly attempted this with reference to liquor, a potential work-related issue, as well as with the nonwork issues of language and general manners. Significantly, as Gorm Smith discovered in 1885, this moral stewardship did extend to work issues. Taken sick in April, the lodge paid his medical expenses. The doctor reported an enlarged heart and declared him permanently incapable of continuing with the strenuous physical duties of a fireman. The lodge maintained Smith's dues for him and extended other benefits. There the matter might have rested, an example of "true benevolence." But a year later, Smith applied for and obtained a job as an engineer on the Vandalia line—a position that required less physical exertion than a fireman. On learning this, the lodge appointed a committee of three, chaired by Debs, then master of the lodge, to inform the Vandalia supervisors of Smith's earlier condition. As a result Smith was not hired, and the railroad officials profusely thanked the committee for its concern. The committee did not question Smith or ask the doctor for an updated opinion. For Debs and other members of Vigo Lodge the mere possibility of irresponsible action by a member toward his employer demanded an immediate, swift response.[28]

The major challenge to the ideal of harmony hardly came from incidents such as that involving Smith, a minor event compared to the tumultuous nationwide railroad strike of 1877. A spontaneous response to yet another wage reduction in the fourth year of a serious depression, the strike started on the Baltimore and Ohio line at Martinsburg, West Virginia, on 16 July. Within a week, the strike and accompanying riots spread as far as San Francisco. In many cities, especially Pittsburgh, Chicago, and Baltimore, widespread violence occurred. With the local militias generally siding with the strikers, among whom were friends and relatives, federal troops—for the first time in peace since Andrew Jackson's administration—were called in to suppress the strike. The New York *Tribune* called the strikers an "ignorant rabble with hungry mouths," while its competitor, the *Times*, raised the fear of communist insurrection. The Scranton *Republican* claimed the strike was an attempt to institute an American commune patterned after the great French uprising of 1871.[29] Even the Harmonists in the utopian capitalist community at Economy, some sixteen miles south of Pittsburgh, wondered "whether this reign of terror marked the beginning of the harvest-time spoken of in Scripture."[30]

Within the Brotherhood of Locomotive Firemen, the strike was a divisive issue. A faction within the national office, led by J. J. Bennett, editor of the journal, supported the strike. Bennett argued that "the great

fault lies with the railway managers, who have defied all established max-
ims and rules of correct business procedure.'' He warned that serious trouble lay in the near future, for, as long as the managers ''turn the screw
upon wages, but make no effort to reform themselves . . . labor becomes
first suspicious and then mutinous.''[31] Sayer was reputedly the leader of
the strikers at Indianapolis, although he denied this at his trial a month
later.[32] The other officers of the Brotherhood, W. R. Worth and John
Broderick, opposed the strike but had no effective control over Bennett's
editorial policy. Thus the Brotherhood was officially on record as a strike
organization.[33]

Debs and other firemen and engineers in Terre Haute felt the strike was
fraught with peril. It threatened to disrupt their organization and raised
substantive, tension-filled questions concerning the nature of their dual
identity as citizens and workingmen. For many, the strikes and riots of
1877 marked the inception of a distinct labor consciousness and raised in a
forceful way the fear of widespread class conflict.[34] But such consciousness
also threatened a belief in harmony and the meaning of manhood rooted
in that concept. Many years later, in a brief account of the strike, Debs attempted to deny this tension, suggesting that he at least ''had an active
part'' in the strike and that a full account of the event ''would make an interesting chapter of proletarian history.''[35] As with so many of Debs's
later reminiscences, however, his attempt to project himself as an active
striker is simply not true. Yet the activities of Debs and other Terre Haute
workers during and after 1877 are interesting and do indeed deepen our
understanding of ''proletarian history'' in a small, partially industrialized
city.

The industrial structure of the city in 1877 encouraged this belief in
social harmony. With few exceptions, no industry in Terre Haute averaged more than thirty employees per shop, and most employed less than
twenty. Yet even the largest employer, the Vandalia Railroad, maintained
a personalized work atmosphere despite its 1,300 employees. As far as
possible, McKeen and Charles Peddle hired the friends and family of their
work force to fill vacancies, and through the 1870s Peddle continued to interview applicants for positions. The ethnic composition of the city also
reinforced these attitudes. A community of almost 26,000 in 1877, fully 85
percent of Terre Haute's citizens were American-born, and the largest
percentage of immigrants came from Germany, Ireland, and England.
With a diverse and decentralized industrial setting, marked by a culturally
homogeneous population and personalized work relations, the belief in
harmony was pervasive. Yet the members of Vigo Lodge were clearly
angry as well, as they watched their wages plummet 23 percent between
1873 and 1876 and then another 10 percent in May 1877. When Thomas
Scott of the Pennsylvania Railroad announced another 10 percent reduc-

tion effective in June 1877, their anger reached a boiling point. They knew that the smaller lines, including the Vandalia, would imitate Scott's action.[36]

On Sunday, 22 July, just a week after the strike began in the East, the firemen and brakemen of Terre Haute called a meeting in the Engineers' hall over Oscar Baur's drugstore to discuss the national and local situation. Robert Ebbage, master of Vigo Lodge, presided while Debs, if present, left no record of his views. After some discussion the men voted to present three resolutions to McKeen. Angered by their wage cuts and motivated by the past week's nationwide activity, they "respectfully requested" a 15 percent wage increase and promised to strike the following morning if this were denied. Second, they vowed to prohibit the movement of freight cars until wages were sufficient "to keep our families from actual want." Finally, the men informed McKeen that they would not use "in any shape or form intoxicating liquor in case we quit work." Only eleven of Terre Haute's railway workers signed the petition.[37]

McKeen failed to respond the following morning and at noon, 23 July, the strike began in Terre Haute. Despite the small meeting the night before, most of the engineers, firemen, and brakemen quit work, and they were joined by the six hundred men in the Vandalia repair shops. The following day, with his employees in control of the depot, McKeen informed the strike committee that he was still undecided as to his course of action. Since events in the East were still unclear, McKeen announced that he wished to wait upon an eastern settlement before committing himself to any set figure. However, on his own in order to defuse the strike, McKeen cancelled all trains originating in Terre Haute with the exception of the mail cars.[38]

The strikers' response to McKeen explains something of the complex attitudes that motivated these men to strike and occupy the depot. In an official letter, the result of a mass discussion in the occupied depot, the strikers expressed "full faith" in their employer's "honor and integrity" and in the belief that "he will do all he can to comply with our wishes." They vowed to protect all railroad property and to prohibit "irresponsible parties, such as tramps and roughs," from strike activity. In return for this responsible behavior, the men confidently called on "fellow citizens of all classes" for aid in "our resistance to the encroachments of capital upon unprotected labor." In their analysis of the strike, they argued that the basic problem was the rate kickback that selected corporate shippers received and noted that, due to his need to stay competitive, McKeen was as much at the mercy of the larger railroads as were they. Finally, the strikers' resolution assured the people of Terre Haute that they did not intend to establish any permanent labor organization, for "as soon as our object is obtained, then this organized movement is to be abandoned."[39]

This self-understanding of the strike, which revolved around an expressed commitment to defend their vision of the Terre Haute community from outside corporate influence, remained dominant as the strike entered its fourth day. As Mark Miller, chairman of the Strike Executive Committee, explained to the Terre Haute *Express*, the committee would not issue a call for a general strike and refused the proffered aid of Clay County miners because the fight concerned only the major railroad corporations and not local businessmen.[40] Robert Nesbit, another strike leader, argued at a meeting on 26 July that the men should allow passenger trains already in transit to pass, for "we . . . are not making war upon women and children. We are warring to break down that gigantic eastern monopoly, the Pennsylvania road, in two words, we can put it—Tom Scott. It is not particularly upon Riley McKeen or Mr. Peddle, that we are warring. We are under the thumb of that road, and when they take up their thumb, they say jump."[41]

This perception, combative in a national context but stressing local harmony, also influenced the selection of speakers strikers chose or allowed to address their meetings. Daniel W. Voorhees, Indiana's Democratic U.S. Senator, and Henry Fairbanks, the mayor of Terre Haute, both expressed support of the strikers' demands, urged them to remain non-violent, and received loud applause. A Protestant minister assured them they had the support of the entire community. Most suggestive, however, was the experience of a local retail grocer. Hauled before the strikers on charges of opposing the strike, and facing a boycott of his store, he told the men that the charges were ridiculous as his very business depended upon sales to workers and thus he shared their interest in higher wages. While the grocer's very presence before the workers indicated the new collective power they held at that moment, his defense and their response echoed again the theme that this was a community-wide struggle. With great enthusiasm, the strikers rescinded the proposed boycott.[42]

But as the events of the last days of that exciting week dramatically showed, McKeen and his business associates interpreted that commitment to the community quite differently. On Saturday 28 July, a detachment of the Third U.S. Infantry, under the command of General Benjamin Spooner, left Indianapolis with orders to open the depot at Terre Haute to allow the trains of the Logansport, Crawfordsville and Southwestern Railway to pass. Spooner acted under the authority of federal Judge Walter Q. Gresham, who assumed responsibility for that railroad since it was in federal receivership. Aware of this development prior to its public announcement, McKeen declared that morning before the troops arrived that he would open his yards for work in the afternoon. As the troops approached Terre Haute, the strikers relinquished the depot and, after a short stop, the infantry continued onto Vincennes for similar duties.

Reorganizing into a mass meeting chaired by Mark Miller, the strikers reacted angrily to McKeen's opening of the yards. They reaffirmed their demand for a wage increase and informed McKeen that his letter of that morning was an insult. After the meeting, many of the men reassembled back at the depot.[43]

McKeen did not respond to this latest message from the workers. Rather, with the private support of many of Terre Haute's "best people," he wired Judge Gresham the following request: "Engineers refuse to run our trains. Strikers are turbulent and men who desire to work intimidated. I trust you will let the United States soldiers remain here for a few days. Please answer." Greshman immediately contacted Spooner at Vincennes, ordering him to return to Terre Haute. He suggested that the troops at Terre Haute would "have a good moral effect" and absolved Spooner in advance of any responsibility for potential violence: "If the Vandalia strikers think the troops are to operate against them, you will not be responsible for their mistake."[44]

But the strikers did not react with violence. When the troops arrived, they relinquished the depot again without incident. Spooner seized a mail train, staffed with master mechanics rather than the regular engineers and firemen, and accompanied it to Indianapolis. McKeen promised he would not discriminate against any striker and thus without obtaining their demands, the men voted to return to work. The nationwide movement lay in tatters, and their vision of harmony was no match for either McKeen's manipulations or federal troops. On Monday, 30 July, Nesbit spoke with Peddle to obtain further assurances. Peddle stated, in a curiously cryptic display of cooperation, that both he and McKeen would work "as silently as possible" for a wage increase and once again promised that when freight rates rose, so would wages. This central demand of the strikers continued to elicit a response that emphasized the interconnections between McKeen and the eastern railroad corporations. Ominously for Nesbit and others active in the strike, Peddle reinterpreted McKeen's pledge of no recriminations, stating that some men would be suspended pending investigation.[45] On this note "The Great Upheaval" ended in Terre Haute.

McKeen had sharply demonstrated the limits of harmony and community as applied to working people. And the strike of 1877 further solidified the business community's distinct consciousness, for McKeen did not act alone. Richard W. Thompson, his longtime associate and by then secretary of the Navy in the Rutherford B. Hayes administration, spoke for many of the "best people" when he termed the strike "nothing more or less than French Communism [and] so entirely at war with the spirit of our institutions—that it must be overcome." Thompson had nothing but praise for McKeen's handling of the Terre Haute strike. He "stood up firmly and manfully, and I regretted I was not at home to help him—or that I could not send him at least one company of my marines."[46]

Such stark sentiments, however, were not immediately apparent to the Vandalia workers. In Terre Haute, the strike of 1877 did not signal the birth of a worker consciousness. Neither class consciousness nor even a class feeling, the *Klassengefülh* that Samuel Gompers described as the basis of worker solidarity—"that primitive force that had its origins in experience only"—resulted from the strike.[47] There were a few hesitant movements in succeeding weeks to organize a labor party for future elections, but to little avail.[48] Most workers remained unaware of the extent of McKeen's manipulations and their commitment to community channeled their real if sporadic anger in other directions.

For the young Debs, even a strike called to affirm unity between workers and employers in the face of industrial capitalism proved too stringent an action. In Terre Haute during the strike Debs took no known part. Beyond signing a petition, along with all the members of the lodge, supporting Miller and Sayer in their court cases, he gave no public statement during that last week of July.[49] Two months later, at the Brotherhood's convention at Indianapolis, Debs did finally speak at length on the strike and its causes. He restated for himself and the membership the validity and vitality of the ideal of harmony as a goal for labor. Pointing to the railroad corporation as "the architect of progress," through whose "magic power the uncultivated inhabitant is lifted from the shades of ignorance and idleness," Debs argued that the railroad was essential to the nation's development. Implying that a fireman's self-respect derived from participation in this task, Debs warmed to his major theme:

> The correct guidance and management of a railway train requires conservative judgement and involves considerable responsibility on the part of the men acting in the capacity of engineer, firemen, conductor, brakemen, etc. It is strictly necessary, therefore, that these men should be thoroughly competent to fulfill their duties in a faithful manner. Admitting this, is it not equally necessary, on the other hand, that they should in turn receive an equivalent amount of compensation? To this question every fairminded man will readily answer in the affirmative. Contrary to this, however, the wages of employees have been reduced from time to time, until today these men can scarcely provide themselves and families with the necessities of life. This continual reduction of the price of labor was the direct cause of the recent strikes, which terrified the entire nation. A strike at the present time signifies anarchy and revolution, and the one of but a few days ago will never be blotted from the records of memory.

The question has often been asked, Does the Brotherhood encourage strikers?

To this question we most emphatically answer, No, Brothers. To disregard the laws which govern our land? To destroy the last vestige of order? To stain our hands with the crimson blood of our fellow beings? We again say, No, a thousand times No.

Strikes are the last means which are resorted to by men driven to desperation after all peaceful efforts to obtain justice have failed. The Brotherhood endeavors to qualify its members to become honest and upright citizens, bearing as its motto, Benevolence, Sobriety, and Industry. Benevolence being the principal object, it is obvious that we are organized to protect and not to injure.[50]

Aware that honest work should bring a fair wage, Debs ultimately disregarded this central concept of justice and fervently embraced a deferential attitude. Through its "magic power" the corporation imbued its employees with moral virtue, a path the Brotherhood wished to emulate. Recognizing a McKeen as the citizen-superior, the *primus inter pares*, Debs laid responsibility for discord on the shoulders of working people. Little wonder that McKeen, among others in Terre Haute's business community, vigorously applauded the young man who delivered that speech.[51]

In the aftermath of the strike, the Brotherhood of Locomotive Firemen nearly disintegrated. Those who actively supported the strike appeared discredited, and most members were confused and disheartened. But the strike solidified Debs's position both within Vigo Lodge and the battered national office. Where previously he had shared influence within the lodge with Miller and Ebbage, who had been lodge master throughout 1876 and early 1877, Debs alone survived the strike. Neither Miller nor Ebbage ever again held office in Vigo Lodge, and Debs replaced Ebbage as delegate to the national convention by a decisive majority. Debs's firm anti-strike position now seemed correct to a majority of lodge members.[52]

At the September convention, following his trenchant speech, this forceful young man was unanimously elected by the national delegates to the office of grand marshall for the coming year.[53] In rising within the Brotherhood, Debs was consistent in thought and action. His vision of harmony and manliness offered no barriers to his own personal success, in large part because the fulfillment of those ideals and his own ambition remained keyed to the expectations of superiors, in the union as in the broader community.

The loss of the strike in 1877 was more than simply an isolated labor defeat. In the months following the uprising, employers throughout the country used the blacklist to great effect to weed out of their labor force strikers and union members. The unions, already suffering from the effects of the depression, had few resources with which to fight organized capital. Most simply disintegrated before the employer onslaught. In late 1877 the *Labor Standard* listed only nine national unions still operating, and most of those, including the Locomotive Firemen, existed more in name than deed.[54] Yet the forces unleashed by the strike—the anger, the critique of monopoly, the incipient if sporadic class awareness—did not simply wait for the resurgence of new unions in the next decade. They found an outlet almost immediately in political action.

Even before the Depression of 1873 had begun, the Independent party formed; it demanded lower railroad rates, civil service reform, and new banking laws and opposed federal land grants to corporations.[55] Motivated by a producer ideology, it soon merged with another third party, the Greenback party, and together they continued to advance at the polls. The 1877 strike gave this movement great impetus, clarifying issues that had existed throughout the depression. The party's candidates attracted nearly one million votes in the state elections of 1878, with the core of support centered in the Midwest.[56]

Dissident political movements attempted to organize in Indiana during the 1870s. The Farmers Mutual Benefit Association, similar in objective to the Independent party, was especially strong among the poorer farmers of southern Indiana.[57] The Greenback party was also active in both state and local politics. Loosely affiliated with the Indiana Democratic party, it constituted that party's left-wing, and Greenback electoral strength varied in direct proportion to Democratic strength.[58] This close alliance with a third party actually allowed the Democrats, even in times of great unrest, to present themselves as the party opposed to "the Hosts of Mammon and Monopoly."[59] As Voorhees expressed it, the "Democratic party is in war against the unjust taxation of American labor for the benefit of enriched idlers and pampered monopolists."[60]

In this context it is not surprising that Debs was attracted to politics. The usually hard fought battles of small-town elections were even more appealing in this atmosphere of reform and unrest. Although Debs had personally sponsored a talk by the famous suffragist, Susan B. Anthony, in 1880 when the Occidental Literary Society (of which he was then president) refused, he did not join any of the reform movements.[61] As one early biographer expressed it, Debs entered politics from the first "advocating the principles of the Democratic party."[62] As he demonstrated in 1877, a program based on even a nascent class awareness threatened his and, he presumed, the whole community's understanding of citizenship. Debs rejected the Greenback-Labor party, for in its very formation that party undermined that sense of harmony and community. At a time when employers recognized their commonality of interest, Debs resisted a similar process for workers. His own deference to the "best people" obscured questions of power and rendered impotent for the moment his own intense commitment to a democratic community.

In 1879 Debs perceived few of these problems. In fact, alliance with the Democrats seemed to offer a way to avoid them. He could still affirm his belief in harmony and remain within a sphere of perceived equality with men like McKeen and Hulman—a task fraught with great difficulty had he joined a labor party. Further, given the growing Democratic identification with labor, Debs created for himself a role within that party as a labor spokesman. From the Democrats' point of view, Debs's prominence within labor circles made him that much more desirable. And there was yet another reason for this attachment. As the town's Democratic newspaper noted approvingly of Debs in 1879: "Not only had he steadily given satisfaction to his employers, serving faithfully their interests; he has also been ambitious to improve himself."[63]

In March 1879 Debs announced his candidacy for city clerk on the Democratic ticket. He was one of five candidates for the nomination; his rivals included Frank Heany, the incumbent deputy city clerk. Debs teamed with Thomas Harper, a candidate for city attorney, to create a reform slate aimed at overthrowing the entrenched Democratic regulars. At the nominating convention on 27 March, two of the regular Democratic nominees withdrew in an attempt to offset the growing influence of Debs, who had obtained bipartisan public support from Republicans like McKeen. Despite this Debs won the nomination handily, with sixteen of a possible thirty votes. Interviewed in the local Democratic paper after the nomination, a composed Debs accounted for his success and underscored his priorities: "I entered with clean hands, and if the people endorse me I will do everything I can to advance the welfare of the City and the Democracy."[64]

Endorse him the people did. McKeen and Hulman gave Debs access to Terre Haute's business community. His own appeal as a Democrat and quite respectable labor leader also assured him of traditional Democratic support, despite his vaguely defined reform platform. Running against Clifford Ross, a Republican, and Grover Crafts, the Greenback candidate, Debs swept the May election, winning decisively in all but the first of Terre Haute's six wards.[65] His total of 2,222 votes surpassed that of Benjamin Havens, the successful Democratic candidate for mayor.[66] While the *Locomotive Firemen's Magazine* saw in Debs's sweep "the triumph of a *laboring* man over politicians and money kings," the Democratic *Evening Gazette* more accurately reflected Debs's attitude when it noted that the young politician had even "better things in store for him. He is one of the rising young men of Terre Haute."[67] Even the Republican *Express* declared Debs "the blue-eyed boy of destiny."[68]

Although not due to assume office until September, Debs announced early his intention of appointing his friend, Alexander Mullen, a member of Vigo Lodge and a former Hulman employee, as his deputy.⁶⁹ The City Council rejected Debs's request and intended to retain Heany as deputy to check this young upstart. For good measure, the council also cut Debs's salary just prior to taking office. Involved in his first political dispute, Debs responded shrewdly and passionately. In a letter to the City Council, which he publicly read to that council as his first duty as clerk, he stated that he would usually never question any legal action, but "I believe it a duty I owe myself, as well as the people of this city, to question your authority. Quiet submission in this case would be the sacrifice of my honor and my manhood." Turning to the main issue, he continued:

> Since the last meeting of your body, I have consulted many of our most substantial citizens in reference to this question, and they all, irrespective of politics assure me that it is a simple matter of right against wrong, and that I must not yield from the attitude I have assumed. . . . [if] our positions in relation to each other could be reversed for a few brief moments, and you as individuals were made to feel the moral pain and discomfort to which I have been subjected, you would, when released, gladly recognize my grievance.

Having established a position of moral superiority and publicly identified himself with the town's leading citizens, Debs then proceeded to skewer the City Council with its own democratic rhetoric: "If the question as it now stands were submitted to the people for a decision, you know as well as I do in whose favor the verdict would be; then why should you, as their representatives, fail to carry out their will?"⁷⁰

When Debs concluded his reading, the spectators in the council chambers broke into prolonged applause. After gaveling for quiet, Mayor Havens and other members, realizing they had been outflanked, reversed their action and appointed Mullen as deputy. Debs's position stressed both the affront to his manhood and the ultimate good of the whole community. Significantly, he made no distinction between the "people" of his concluding question and those "substantial citizens" from whom he had sought advice.

Debs's position reflected more than just personal traits. When examined in the context of his electoral support, it also sheds light on the attitudes of railroad workers only two years following the 1877 strike. Of Terre Haute's six wards, railroad workers resided primarily in three—the fifth, the sixth, and the first—which either surrounded or immediately adjoined the Vandalia freight and passenger depots and the repair shops. The fifth and sixth wards, containing the residences of the majority of semi- and unskilled railroad workers, Debs carried by 55 and 56 percent, respectively, in this three-way race. In the first ward, a mixed area including homes of skilled railroad workers and unskilled common laborers and the residences of a few men such as McKeen, Debs lost badly, garnering only 23 percent to the Republican candidate's 52 percent.[71] He more than made up for this poor showing in two other wards. Ward three, traditionally Republican and containing the largest concentration of black voters, Debs won handily with 51 percent of the vote.

But the key to Debs's electoral success as to his political vision during these years lay in the results from the second ward. Also traditionally Republican, it housed John S. Beach, Hulman, and the majority of Terre Haute's "best people." Although he failed of an outright majority, Debs attracted over 45 percent of the vote—more than enough to insure his Republican opponent's defeat. With firm support in both working-class and upper-class wards, Debs forged an alliance across classes that assured his election. A politician with a potent appeal to working people, Debs swamped the more radical candidate by more than two to one citywide and by almost three to one in the railroad workers' wards. Simultaneously, he did well in traditional Republican strongholds.[72] For many of his supporters, as for Debs himself, his election underscored the power of that term community.[73]

Except for a more lenient attitude toward collecting the fines of the town's many prostitutes, there was little of a reform nature in Debs's actions,[74] and he was not seriously estranged from the Democratic party. He campaigned for its candidates in the 1880 election and won re-election as city clerk as a Democrat in 1881.[75] He remained on close personal terms with major figures of both parties in Terre Haute.[76] His appeal was such that when the Brotherhood held its 1882 convention in his home city, state and local politicians of both parties turned out to give, in the words of one biographer, "a long and loud laudation to one man—Eugene Victor Debs."[77] Explaining this appeal, the *American Railroader*, a trade journal of the industry's officials, commented on his re-election in 1881: "He was simply invulnerable. Wealthy men, property holders, etc., voted for him because they felt sure their interests would be safe in his keeping; and the laboring classes and the poor supported him because they knew he was their friend and practically one of them."[78] With such backing, Debs did not remain even a tame maverick for long, as the Democratic party courted him for higher office.

The idea of a career in politics had long intrigued Debs. Rumor had it that he had been approached by the Democratic organization as early as 1878 with an offer to run for Congress but had refused, claiming a desire to remain close to home and fulfill his commitment to rebuild the Brotherhood.[79] While the story is probably fanciful, as Debs legally could not have served in Congress until after his twenty-fifth birthday in

November 1880, it nonetheless does underscore important aspects of Debs's early thinking. Until the mid-1880s, politics and his Brotherhood work remained separate realities that touched only tangentially. Politics concerned the whole community, the Brotherhood but a part. In 1884, however, when offered the Democratic nomination for the state assembly, Debs accepted. By then he had come to a fuller acceptance of his role as a labor spokesman within the political arena. At the nominating convention Debs received over two-thirds of the votes and had the active support of such local leaders as Havens, Beach, William R. Hunter, and others. Newspapers as far away as Minneapolis touted Debs as the next Congressman from Indiana's Eighth District—and this time it seemed he might accept.[80]

A leader in the Vigo County Democratic organization, Debs campaigned as part of a balanced ticket that included farmer Reuben Butz and businessman Phillip Schloss.[81] The party presented a strong labor platform that included a reduction of hours for state employees, the establishment of a Bureau of Labor, an end to child labor, and opposition to corporate ownership of large tracts of farm land.[82] In the November election all three Democrats were victorious. Debs captured four of Terre Haute's six wards and did well in the surrounding townships and farming villages of Vigo County. Garnering 5,603 votes, Debs ran ahead of Grover Cleveland, the Democratic presidential candidate, in all but one Terre Haute ward, and led John Lamb, the incumbent Democratic Congressman, in all but two. While Vigo County voted Republican for both president and governor by small margins, Debs received more votes than either of those successful candidates. He was, as the *American Railroader* had noted earlier, "simply invulnerable," attracting a multiclass, bipartisan support that made plausible his belief in harmony.[83]

Debs approached his legislative duties with vigor and enthusiasm. Prior to the opening of the session in January 1885, he had already drafted a bill to require railroad corporations to assume responsibility for employees injured by faulty equipment. Under the current law the corporation avoided such claims by charging worker negligence, and Debs intended to have the railway employee "placed on the same footing as the traveling public."[84] Arriving at Indianapolis, Debs submitted his bill and was placed on three committees: on Railroads, on Corporations, and on Engrossed Bills.[85]

Debs's role in the assembly fell short of his expectations. He found legislative work boring and, as a freshman member, had little power. During the two-month session, he introduced a series of minor bills, which generated little excitement, and voted for bills that would have granted suffrage to women and abolished racial and color distinctions in all state laws. The defeat of both these bills did little to improve his opinion of the legislature.[86] The core of his interests, however, lay elsewhere, and had

Debs achieved some success with these primary interests, he might have continued as a traditional electoral candidate beyond this term. As he stated those concerns on the assembly floor, when placing Voorhees's name in nomination for re-election to the U.S. Senate, Debs came to the legislature "as a working man, with whatever duties attached to my position, as a representative of working men."[87]

A workers' representative, Debs was by no means anti-capitalist. But he did oppose the ever growing power of the corporation. A roughly developed producer ideology forced him to acknowledge with some confusion the separation of society into distinct groups. Debs attempted to develop a political position so as to use the state as a buffer between labor and capital. Theoretically, the state could remain the neutral meeting ground for all citizens, the repository of the common good somehow transcending the intense factionalism he now experienced around him. Thus he supported a bill to provide state licensing for all engineers and firemen, as "it will not only better the service but will throw around the boiler a safeguard." The bill might wreak hardship on Brotherhood members who failed the exam, but in Debs's mind this was offset by the official approval and increased professional status it would provide. Further, the worker owed such responsible actions to the larger community.[88]

While that bill failed by four votes, his own bill on railroad responsibility seemed to fare better. Fighting to get it through the Committee on Railroads, which shocked him with its lack of concern, Debs successfully amended it on the floor to prohibit any corporation from compelling workers as a condition of employment to sign a release for corporation responsibility. When the bill passed the lower house by a resounding 76-0 vote, Debs experienced "unconcealed exaltation." His joy was short-lived however. The railroad lobby "reached" sufficient numbers of state senators, and there is even some indication that the assembly vote was fixed, as a reward for the young legislator while at the same time teaching him the ropes. In any event, the Senate emasculated the bill, and Debs refused even to vote for the watered-down version.[89]

It is this experience that most of Debs's biographers point to as the significant lesson of his legislative experience. Bored by the legislative process and horrified at the callousness of political compromise, they argue that Debs returned to Terre Haute with little faith in traditional political activity and, by implication at least, suggest he had already started on the road toward the Pullman strike and eventually toward Socialism.[90] From hindsight, there appears a certain hazy truth to this view. However, Debs did not have that hindsight, and his own path to Pullman and beyond was to be long, twisted, and never smooth. His vote in 1885 on the state militia bill was at least as accurate a measure of Debs's consciousness as his more well-known reaction to legislative politics.

Since the strike of 1877, when fraternization between local police and striking workers, coupled with the weakness of the state militias, led railroad officials to demand federal troops, a movement to create and strengthen state militias had spread through the nation.[91] For the railroad corporation, the state system was more manageable, as its manipulation required less drastic political power and was less shocking to the public than demands for federal troops. Indiana was no exception to this rule. Early in 1885, when a pending strike against the Gould railroad generated fears of a repetition of 1877, the Indiana legislature debated a bill to establish a state militia system.[92] Defenders of the measure argued that their opponents had, by resisting a militia, expressed "sympathy . . . with the violators of the law."[93] Acknowledging this indirect reference to labor troubles, the bill's opponents presented a twofold argument. When the parliamentary motion failed, James B. Patten, member from Sullivan County (which adjoined Vigo County), rose to present the major attack. Noting that his G.A.R. post voted unanimously against the bill, Patten argued that the bill was simply an anti-labor measure—"a direct blow at wage laborers, and if they dare to raise their voices to oppression this militia is to declare a riot and charge upon the laborers." The bill eventually lost, but not before Debs voted with a majority of Republicans for its passage.[94]

Startling as Debs's vote appears, both from the point of his own later autobiographical sketches as well as from his current perception of himself as a workingman's representative, it is not inexplicable. Several weeks prior to the vote, Debs had announced his support of the municipal police bill passed by the Terre Haute City Council, even though one reason for its creation was to control the large group of unemployed workers in town.[95] One must see his vote on the militia bill in the context of his own railroad compensation bill, and vice-versa, for together they formed a whole pattern in his mind. Both capital and labor had responsibilities, to each other as to the community in general, and corporate irresponsibility provided no excuse for worker violence. Still searching for community amidst intense factionalism, Debs showed no concern that some in his "beloved little community" now desired a police force to protect themselves from that community's unemployed citizens.

This legislative experience did discourage Debs from future involvement as a traditional political candidate. In 1888, for example, he declined the proffered Democratic nomination for the City Council, to the regret of the organization.[96] Yet it did not keep him from all political activity. He still campaigned for Democratic candidates throughout the state and continued his role as that party's leading labor representative. In trying to maintain both roles Debs became a peculiar labor spokesman who remained silent on many important but divisive labor issues. This silence was necessary as Debs tried to maintain his prior commitments while avoiding their increasingly obvious inherent contradictions. The experience in the legislature might have raised some initial questions, but at best they remained private. In 1885 Debs appeared still secure in his belief in the viability of the harmonious community.

Debs's identification as a worker's representative was no idle boast, nor was it simply a ruse to catapult himself into an easy job. From the very organization of Vigo Lodge, he was deeply engaged in labor activities and eventually hired his brother and two of his sisters at greatly reduced salaries to keep the Brotherhood alive. Debs himself refused an offer from Major O. J. Smith, founder of the American Press Association, to become that firm's general manager.[97] In addition to his Brotherhood work, Debs organized other workers. With P. J. McGuire he helped start a carpenters' local in Terre Haute and was instrumental in the development of unions for the town's coopers and printers and of the Central Labor Union itself.[98] Away from home as frequently as his duties as city clerk allowed, Debs made many organizing trips to the East and his first visit to Texas and Oklahoma in 1882. On these journeys he organized firemen, railway conductors, brakemen, telegraphers, trainmen, and switchmen. Often paying expenses from his own pocket, Debs won the support and admiration of many railroad workers.[99]

Yet Debs remained wedded to the belief in harmony even in his labor work. Louis Kopelin, a Socialist comrade, was wrong when he suggested that as early as 1880 Debs viewed craft unionism as too conservative a method for organizing workers.[100] If anything, Debs then felt that it was too radical. When Mark Moore, a Terre Haute printer, wrote Adolph Strasser, president of the Cigar Makers Union, in 1881 urging "the need for an amalgamation of all trade unions" and proposing a conference to achieve that end, Debs remained silent. When the conference was held in August of that year, in Terre Haute, with twelve representatives of various Terre Haute unions present, Debs did not attend.[101] In similar fashion Debs never endorsed nor apparently even publicly mentioned the Knights of Labor before 1886, although twenty-three of Indiana's twenty-seven labor organizations in 1880—some of which Debs himself helped organize—affiliated with that federation.[102] Even in 1885, when thirty-one delegates, nearly evenly divided between trade unionists and Knights, met in Indianapolis to form a State Federation of Trade and Labor Unions, Debs, by this time prominent among labor men, was conspicuously absent and silent.[103]

Clearly then, although dedicated in his organizing efforts, Debs conceived of labor unions in these years as more conservative than either the Knights or the emerging American Federation of Labor (AFL). Out of this dichotomy grew yet another level of tension. Personally popular with railroad men, Debs enjoyed his incessant travels. He relished the discussions of social issues, loved to swap jokes and stories with the other men, and, although there is no direct evidence from these years, in all probability shared many a drink with his railroad brothers across the nation. But the formal message this intense young man brought with him reflected a different aspiration. For at the foundation of his view of the labor union lay a profoundly negative assessment of working people.

The source of this tension originated in Debs's understanding of manhood.[104] For him, personal honor, industry, and responsibility to one's duties were the essential attributes in the early 1880s. In an editorial entitled "The Square Man" Debs argued that "duty does not call him in vain [and] all who know him feel safe, for a square man is at the post of duty."[105] In part this reflected Debs's appreciation of Bayless Hanna's ideas, but he also perceived a deeper meaning, which held that "the most sacred and binding seal we know to civilized men is the pledge of honor. . . . No man, with any moral scruples, would be able to contemplate without a keen feeling of shame, the record of a broken pledge." This understanding of moral honor might have helped Debs to interpret the comradery of the lodge meetings as an essential bulkhead against the culture of a developing industrial capitalism. Instead, it brought Debs's attention back to a man's work-related duties and elevated the Brotherhood to a position of moral stewardship over men. Debs concluded this editorial with the admonition that the "pledge of honor" commits the members of the Brotherhood to follow its rules and adhere to its strictures. "Anyone who violates that obligation," Debs warned, "strikes down his manhood with his own hand."[106]

Although Debs argued in 1883 that "each creature has a duty to perform and to perform it well is a solemn matter,"[107] he did not feel that fate ordained people to any set role. As his own belief in mobility demanded, he felt that through hard work one could forge his own destiny.[108] In the tradition of Enlightenment rationalism, Debs held that people, through their intellectual facilities and freedom of choice, controlled their fate: "God takes the wheat of the field and places it in the human stomach; there it is changed by a wonderous chemistry into blood. . . . Most wonderous of all, a part of the wheat passes into that mysterious alembic, the brain, and a thought is born." At this point God's role ended, for as "the watch is the mechanism of man [so] man is the mechanism of God."[109] Establishing mankind on an equal footing, God retires, and for their success or failure people can only look to themselves and the quality of their own manhood. Yet Debs's understanding of the social power of the concept of manhood undercut his affirmation of the individualistic, even atomistic, responsibility of each person to his duty. His experience in

Terre Haute and the Brotherhood led him to a belief in what he termed "Masterful Men." Unchecked individualism could lead to anarchy, and therefore the individual needed a model. "Men confide in leaders," he explained in 1882: "Few men in moments of personal danger, or in days of national turmoil, act intelligently if left to their own resources. Some leader always springs to the front and assumes a command questioned by none. Such men are self-poised, heroic, calm."[110]

The memory of the 1877 strike continued to strengthen Debs's demand for proper leadership. In his report to the 1880 convention Debs argued that the violence in that strike across the nation arose from three causes: the mistreatment of workers by management; the ignorance of workers to "the true way of having their grievances adjusted"; and finally, their being "urged on, as they were, by their so-called leaders, who had nothing to lose, and with a spirit of revenge, they sought to burn and kill to their satisfaction."[111] A more positive example of leadership and manliness lay closer to home for Debs, however, in the person of William Riley McKeen.

By the time Debs was thirty, he had developed a close working relationship with McKeen. While there is no evidence that they socialized together—such conduct would have violated the boundaries of their deferential society—Debs did adopt McKeen as his model of manhood and accepted without question the railroad president's assumptions concerning the relations between labor and capital. For his part, McKeen extended concrete aid as well as praise to Debs. He encouraged Debs in his union activities, loaned him $1,000 to rebuild the Brotherhood after the 1877 strike, and in 1880 guaranteed Debs's bond when he became secretary-treasurer of the Brotherhood.[112] And, of course, he actively supported Debs in his early political career. The feeling between Debs and McKeen also encompassed the members of Vigo Lodge. Aware of McKeen's support, the brothers of the lodge at Christmas 1880 presented their employer with a gold-handled cane "for his kind and generous treatment of the most humble of [his employees] and as a tribute to his splendid manhood."[113] Five months later they presented McKeen with a scroll, and when the Brotherhood held its convention in Terre Haute in September 1882 McKeen was praised in speech and given a place of honor at the banquet.[114] For Debs, McKeen's actions were more than just the deeds of a benevolent employer. They constituted proof that proper leadership, informed by the moral qualities of manhood, could keep vital an ideal of harmony. "Mr. McKeen," Debs wrote in 1883, "is absolutely adored by his men. No General ever rode in front of his columns with a more enthusiastic and loyal following. The reason is clear—he is a just man and his employees all know it. He listens with patience and attention to all their grievances. . . . In his presence all men stand truly equal—whether they be rich or poor, high or low, in rank or position, they are sure to receive justice at his hands . . . . Such a policy as that," Debs concluded without reference to 1877, "will forever prevent discontent."[115]

If McKeen was "the model railroad president" who believed in "*honest pay for an honest day's work*,"[116] that was but one part of the equation. Workers themselves, Debs held, must actively accept such men as models, for left to themselves they tended to degenerate. In part, Debs saw himself, guided by McKeen's example and advice, fulfilling such a role. But ultimately this need passed beyond the force of personal example, and Debs saw in the Brotherhood, as an institution, the moral principles, hierarchical structure, and rigid discipline necessary to control workingmen's "baser" natures. As a national leader, Debs argued that "all honorable members" had a duty "to assist [the national officers] in ridding the Order of all worthless material." Such a course was imperative, he continued, for "just in proportion as they are tolerated, to that extent will the Order suffer from public condemnation."[117] Employers' confidence could only be won with such an organization. Without it, even the workers themselves would "have no standard by which to govern their actions" and could not give "their sacred honor that they would be honest, moral and upright."[118]

For Debs, then, the goal of harmony required a complicated balancing act. Supposedly geared to the needs of working people as part of the larger community, it yet followed at every juncture the demands of employers. Debs formally based his thinking on the long tradition of democratic individualism, yet he distrusted that individual and pioneered in the creation of a union organization to control him. Employer and employee were to be social equals, yet an employer, one of Terre Haute's "best people," consistently surfaced as a model. The onus of maintaining harmony, moreover, clearly and repeatedly fell upon the worker, and for years the strike of 1877 remained for Debs continuing proof of the workingman's need for moral uplift. In a major editorial, "United Again," Debs demonstrated to what extent social harmony depended on the deferential attitude of working people. Starting once again with the strike of 1877, Debs explained the Brotherhood's involvement as the result of the "power usurped" by one of the national officers, since removed, and reiterated the Firemen's official resolution to ignore strikes.[119] Turning to the Brotherhood, its purpose and goals, he wrote:

> The object of our institution is to make men out of crude material, and when we have succeeded in that, there will be no occasion for strikes, for when we are fully qualified to receive our rights, they will always be accorded us.
> It is no small matter to plant benevolence in the heart of stone, in-

still the love of sobriety into the putrid mind of debauchery, and create industry out of idleness. These are our aims, and if the world concedes them to be plausible, we ask that they find an anchoring place in its heart, and that in our humble efforts to carry them out, we will be beckoned onward and upward by those who have the power to assist us.[120]

In such a fashion did Debs define his role in the early 1880s.

Although but one of a number of national officers, as editor-in-chief of the official journal and secretary-treasurer of the Brotherhood, Debs was the single most influential national officer. In this role he led the opposition to any rank-and-file deviance from national policy. One of the earlier struggles occurred in May 1884, when Debs published a five-page editorial, "The Mission of the Brotherhood." In the main an attack upon the notion of strikes, Debs remarked that as the topic was controversial, he welcomed comments and criticism from readers. "The mission of the Brotherhood of Locomotive Firemen," he wrote, "is not to antagonize capital. Strikes do that; hence we oppose strikes as a remedy for the ills of which labor complains." One fireman, S. William Pettibone, objected to Debs's use of the phrase "oppose strikes," as the official Brotherhood position was only to ignore them. A small point perhaps, but Pettibone perceived in it an important change of emphasis, and he wrote a letter explaining his thinking. Debs refused to print it. Pettibone then wrote a longer article, outlining in detail the differences between these two concepts, and charged that Debs's original editorial was no different than one that "the most avaricious, grasping, tyrannical representative of monied monopoly [would] have written." This article Pettibone circulated among a group of members, and he challenged Debs to publish it.

Debs did not publish it but rather brought charges against Pettibone at the national convention the following September. Avoiding the substantive issue, Debs asserted that Pettibone had insulted him and attacked his competence. He defended the original editorial on irrelevant grounds and boasted that he never published an article in the journal that he did not think to be in "the best and highest interests of such members, the calling they represent, and the Brotherhood at large." He concluded by requesting an investigation that could have resulted in Pettibone's expulsion. The convention appointed a committee, however, which persuaded Debs to withdraw his charges in exchange for Pettibone's admission that he never intended to insult Debs. Some months later, Debs even admitted his error. And so the battle ended, the issues never fully discussed, but not before Debs's willingness to use his position against the less prominent in the rank and file had been made apparent. As with his model, McKeen, beneath Debs's paternalistic concern for the direction of the Brotherhood lay a rather keen perception of the use of power.[121]

It is unfortunate that Pettibone's article has not survived, as it would be invaluable in discovering the extent of the critique he and his supporters made of Debs's ideas. It is clear that a majority of the delegates supported Debs, although no vote was taken on the Pettibone controversy. When the delegates passed by voice vote a resolution prohibiting any national officer from holding political office, Debs, a candidate for the assembly in the November election, rose and stated that he would have to resign his offices as he would not at this late date renege on his commitment to the Vigo County Democrats. The delegates promptly reversed themselves, 149–57.[122] In the absence of other evidence, that margin might be taken as a rough estimate of Debs's support among the delegates. Most were conservative in their politics and, like Debs, believed deeply in the value of harmony. Skilled workers, intent on rising to the position of engineer, only a minority welcomed the Knights of Labor with its concern for all workers regardless of position. The majority still swelled with pride when Debs told them that the Pullman Company of Chicago had provided, without cost, "elegant sleeping cars" for the delegates to the 1883 Denver convention.[123]

Like Debs, many firemen believed in the promise of American life and held that as workers they were the very foundation of civilization, properly understood. "Civilization," Debs wrote, "has placed her hand trustingly in the hand of her mother Labor, and together they walk with majestic step along the highway of Progress, drawing after them all the honored laborers of the earth and trampling to death the drones and the worthless."[124] When the labor force is thus winnowed and is represented only by "*chevalier sans peur et sans reproche*," then all strife shall cease.[125] For as Debs understood the problem during these years, the promise of America was a given; the question was the worker's preparedness:

> America is preeminently the land of great possibilities, of great opportunities, and of no less great probabilities. Look around us, no matter what our position may be, we all stand on the great field of renown, with a free and equal chance to go to the supreme height of all that can be desired of earthly grandeur. We all have a fair chance and an open field. Long may it so remain. The time, the occasion is auspicious. Nothing like it was ever known before. The time is an exception. Let the members of our Brotherhood prove themselves exceptions in the avidity with which they take advantage of the opportunities offered. Our Order is come to lead those who will practice its precepts and preachings, to certain victory in the fairest fields of success.[126]

Concerns with status and position permeated Debs's private life as well. As he approached thirty, a national labor leader who had already expressed a desire to become president,[127] his thoughts, interwined with his ambition, turned toward securing a proper marriage.

Little is known of Debs's relations with Terre Haute's young women during the decade of his twenties. While he might have indulged in certain temporary infatuations when traveling during these years, he appears to have remained aloof from serious courtships at home. Extremely busy, he and Theodore had in addition vowed not to marry until all their sisters had arranged suitable matches for themselves.[128] But if there is little evidence of specific courtships, there are nonetheless some indications of his attitude toward women. Although Debs had early supported the suffrage movement, he still shared the major assumptions of his culture concerning women. Women were placed on a pedestal, an idealized image of sensitivity and spirituality somehow beyond the reach of men. As he declared at the Brotherhood's 1885 convention, women "have rejoiced in our prosperity, have aided us in our toil, have spurred us on to renewed effort, and no stain so deep can be put upon our organization but their tears will wash it away."[129]

Privately, Debs expressed more complicated attitudes. In 1881 he wrote his sister Eugenie of the female sensitivity as he had experienced it in a certain Helen Jeffers. A resident of Terre Haute, Jeffers had presented a series of gifts, mainly bookmarks and banners, to the firemen of Vigo Lodge.[130] Debs felt that she was a talented artist, as her handmade gifts indicated, and "one of the grandest women I ever knew . . . the embodiment of womanhood." He was amazed that Jeffers felt comfortable in the company of railroad workers and had little patience for those "who occupy a higher round on the social ladder." This concerned him, however, for a woman of her talent needed friends, as she had her "ambition to gratify." Her situation, caught as she apparently was between her feelings and her proper status, was difficult for her, as Debs felt it would be for any woman. "Man can stifle ambition—woman cannot," Debs wrote with ingenuous sincerity, and sympathized: "I can just imagine how she feels to have every aspiration of her soul trampled upon and crushed out of existence." He felt it his privilege to help her and looked forward to the day she would be famous, as "I always love to see real merit rewarded."[131]

While Jeffers never achieved the fame Debs hoped for her, his letter is quite revealing, nonetheless. The more sensitive and spiritual female nature stands in stark contrast with the baser male force, and especially evident is Debs's low regard for workingmen. In contrast, Debs's own high sensitivity to status differences within Terre Haute is obvious in his appreciation of the need for friends "a higher round on the social ladder." This feeling, so evident in his relationship with McKeen, pervaded Debs's thoughts concerning marriage as well. It was not surprising then that in

1884 when he met Katherine Metzel at the home of his sister, they began to court that very night.

Katherine, or Kate as she was known, was born in Pittsburgh on 18 April 1857, of middle-class German immigrant parents. Raised in Louisville, Kentucky, she was two when her father died. Her stepfather, John Baur, was also of German ancestry. The father of five children, Baur had worked a farm in southern Indiana just prior to the Civil War, where he owned and operated a large flour mill. In 1865 he invested his savings in Terre Haute real estate. His first wife died that same year, and Baur returned to Louisville where he had once lived and married Kate's mother within the year.[132]

The Baur family (Kate kept her father's last name) moved to Terre Haute in 1867. While not among the wealthiest of families at first, the Baurs quickly established themselves at a second level of prominence within the town. Baur opened a drugstore that soon became the largest and most successful in Terre Haute; two of his sons, Jacob and Charles, ran it after 1880. By 1890 the sons were millionaires, deriving their fortune from a formula for liquid carbonic gas originally discovered by an employee. Charles Baur also invested in real estate and in 1890 bought from McKeen the controlling interest in the Prairie House, the town's symbol of respectability now called the Terre Haute House. Others in the Baur family were in close if subordinate proximity to Terre Haute's social elite. Kate's stepsister, Amelia Baur, married Silas C. Beach, brother of the banker, John. A member of the City Council while Debs was city clerk, Silas Beach headed a construction company that did all the building for McKeen's various enterprises.[133] Thus the courting of Kate Metzel had many levels for Eugene Debs. Undoubtedly he fell in love with her, but it was also, as was said at the time, a well-appointed marriage—a young man of talent and ambition marrying considerably above his station.

The Baurs themselves were aware of this social contrast. A number of young men, most from far better families then Debs, courted Kate, and there was strong opposition within Kate's family to Eugene.[134] Eventually this was overcome and on 9 June 1885, at 6:30 A.M., Eugene and Kate married in a formal service at St. Stephen's Episcopal Church. With expensive gifts accumulating back in Terre Haute from Brotherhood lodges all over the country, the newlyweds left that morning on a two-week, thousand-dollar honeymoon to the East. It was, wrote Ida A. Harper, the women's editor of the *Locomotive Firemen's Magazine*, "a true love match, the engagement is of long standing, and they have every prospect of a happy future. Young, gifted, surrounded by friends, married to the woman he loves, the B. of L.F. may indeed congratulate their friend and leader, who deserves all the good gifts a kind fortune has bestowed upon him."[135]

Unfortunately for both Eugene and Kate, this rosy picture faded soon after their honeymoon. Returning to Terre Haute, they established house in what Kate considered a somewhat dingy set of rented rooms. Although Eugene made an excellent salary for the time—over $3,000 per year—it proved insufficient to maintain the style Kate desired.[136] This problem, inherent in their relationship from the start, was augmented by two others. When Eugene married Kate, his frenetic work schedule did not ease. Frequently away organizing railroad men of every description during these first years of marriage, he spent even his nights at home immersed in work. Moreover, these years were a time of great tension for Debs, as events in the world of labor forced him to reconsider his earlier understandings. His salary remained steady, but he consistently rejected substantial offers to enter business. For Kate, this sharply contrasted with the dramatic economic and social progress of her own family at this time. Perhaps most fundamental, the couple discovered early their inability to have children. Difficult as it is to understand the full impact of this on their marriage, it clearly had at least one effect. It turned both away from each other and toward the world in fairly predictable ways. Eugene was completely involved in his work, more often on the road than at home. Kate, for her part, tried first to share his work as his secretary. This was short-lived, and her own primary concern with the symbols of status and position resurfaced even more strongly. With money from her inheritance in 1890, she ordered an ostentatious residential showcase built in a fashionable Terre Haute neighborhood some few blocks from the Chauncey Rose mansion.[137]

This disparity was not missed by Debs's friends and family. In 1885 many described him as a friendly, open person, while his wife appeared stiff and aloof. One explanation of this relationship suggests that Debs was influenced by his parents' marriage, where Daniel was the businessman and Marguerite the "retiring housewife." Being away so frequently, Debs did not need a companion but rather a wife who was self-reliant. Thus, in a kind of marriage of convenience from the start, Debs sought a "typical wife but an unusual marriage."[138] This analysis of the marriage is misleading at a number of critical points. Most striking is that Daniel Debs, in contrast to his oldest son, gave up a promising bourgeois career in order to marry a hand in his father's factory. Moreover, Marguerite Debs was anything but a "retiring housewife." During Daniel's bleakest days in the 1850s, it was his wife, known as Daisy, and not the discouraged and demoralized Daniel, who took the family's last dollars and opened the grocery store. But more to the point, Eugene Debs did not see his mother in such a retiring role. She administered the family finances and was the parent to whom Eugene gave his salary when he worked on the Vandalia. She was also instrumental in directing Eugene's early career and was the only reason he left the Vandalia in 1874. For Eugene as for his brother, the love, spontaneity, and warmth of his mother were, by repeated admission, the major formative forces in his life. It is this felt emotional identity with his mother that perhaps best clarified the meaning of his marriage.

The year 1885 was a critical juncture in Debs's life, although he came to understand that only later. It began, optimistically enough, with the ambitious labor politician riding to Indianapolis in January for his first session in the legislature. But before too many months had passed, the contradictions inherent in Debs's social vision grew more noticeable. As industrial strife increased, the comradery of the lodge meeting assumed a more aggressive stance toward employers. In the process the social foundations of those ideals of manhood and harmony appeared to many deeply cracked. This perception forced Debs and other railroad workers to reconsider their actions and their ideology.

In his personal life a parallel development occurred. Prior to 1885, Debs rarely spoke or wrote of either parent. Rather the person he recognized as most influencial in his life was McKeen. But as Debs experienced that growing tension between the ideal and the real, McKeen lost his power of example. Hesitantly at first, and then with repeated public reference, Debs replaced McKeen with the example of his mother. From her, he stated time and again, he drew his inspiration, his impulse toward the good. In her warmth, love, and sincerity, and in her concern for all regardless of status, Debs found a model for his own life. A working-class woman, she stood in sharp contrast to McKeen.

In Debs's mind, Kate also seemed in contrast to his mother. He never attributed to his wife a central role in his life, and her concern for status and position proved increasingly nettlesome to him. Although little is known about Daniel Debs's personality, what is known suggests that he and Kate shared some traits in common. Daniel enjoyed and to an extent identified with German culture. He offered no resistance when his oldest daughter married a German of Austrian birth in 1870, and he was the only French member of a German hunting club during and after the Franco-Prussian War—which resulted in the annexation by Germany of Daniel's native province, Alsace.[139] Further, in spite of the saintly tones many biographers have adopted towards Daniel, it appears quite possible that he was as aloof and coldly reserved in his relations as was Kate. As Ray Ginger has commented, Daniel "often seemed disagreeable to the outside world." Eugene Debs understood this. At his parents' fiftieth wedding anniversary, he reserved all praise for developing humanistic and personal qualities for his mother, while thanking his father for teaching him the ways of a world he had by that time largely rejected.[140]

This is not to suggest that Debs did not care for his father or did not owe much to Daniel's influence. Nor is it to argue that he held no affection for Kate. Rather, these patterns of emotional connection highlight the complex change Debs experienced as the force and quickness of industrial capitalism deluged his culture. The example of McKeen; the self-assuredness concerning the affairs of the world, so long the linchpin of male identity; that naive yet potent belief in harmony—all were swept away as men and women throughout the country found their wages decreasing, an industrial work discipline as impersonal as it was oppressive, and federal troops prepared to shoot them in the streets at the behest of their employers. In 1885 Debs was on the verge of discovering this. His marriage was of the fabric of his earlier life, when he felt assured of the promise of America. As an old Socialist commented years later, some twenty years after Eugene's death: "The truth was that Debs married Kate at the time when he was all in the unions. She was very proud of his gifts; she was devoted. When he embraced the Socialist Movement she was, at first, a little bit hesitant, afraid that he was burning his bridges, afraid of the danger of losing a home, to which she had contributed so much *more* than he, by the way."[141]

But the world of being harmoniously "all in the unions" exploded, blown apart by its own inner contradictions. The meaning of manhood no longer seemed a given birthright, and this still earnest native son began his search for another beacon light upon the hill.

3

A Citizen, A Workingman

WHEN THE DELEGATES to the Firemen's twelfth annual convention gathered in Philadelphia in September 1885, many sensed a charged new atmosphere. The stable world of their earlier conventions now gyrated. The men they represented were angrier than they had been even a year before, quicker to take issue with their employers concerning wages and working conditions. The very concept of harmony appeared anachronistic to some for, as Joseph R. Buchanan would later explain it, "the old spirit of fraternity . . . was dead," and the new rule in American life was "every fellow for himself, the devil take the hindmost."[1]

In an important way, however, Buchanan's analysis was misleading. The central idea that marked the midyears of the 1880s was not individualism, however acquisitive or grasping it might be described, but rather cooperation. Among railroad corporations as in the banking and new oil industries, corporations based on cooperation rather than competition began to dominate, and a kind of fraternity, greatly different from that celebrated in Buchanan's lament, undermined the formal laissez-faire ideology. Albert Fink, a former vice-president of the Louisville and Nashville Railroad, expressed this bluntly before a Congressional committee in 1883: "Competition doesn't work well in the transportation business."[2]

The worker in basic industry in 1885 felt threatened by this increasing corporate cooperation. Cyclical business depressions periodically slashed the worker's living standard, and workingmen saw in the corporation's reliance on new immigrant workers a plan to reduce permanently the status of the skilled American-born men. What allowed employers to use these new unskilled workers, however, had less to do with ethnicity than with a basic alteration of work conditions then underway. The managerial reorganization of basic industry sought to concentrate all decision-making in the front office, far from the traditions and prerogatives of workers on the shop floor. To achieve this, the directors of the iron and steel, transportation, and oil industries introduced sophisticated new machinery that replaced skilled workers, increased profits and productivity, and further centralized their control of production.[3]

Railroad workers were not passive observers of these events. They, too, were taken with the idea of combination, and the successful conclusion of two recent strikes against Jay Gould's railroad empire gave many hope. When Gould reduced the wages of the shopmen on his Wabash line by 10 percent in February 1885, the men, led by the Knights of Labor, struck immediately. Within a week, the shopmen of the Missouri, Kansas and Texas and the Missouri Pacific, two other Gould roads, joined. In a critical display of labor solidarity based on a shared sense of grievance, the Engineers and Firemen supported these 4,500 strikers, and together they completely shut down the Gould system. Forced to rescind the reduction in early March, Gould also reinstated the strikers as a condition of settlement.[4] During the strike many men of both brotherhoods took out joint membership in the Knights. Indeed, the Knights' popularity grew astronomically following this strike. As John Swinton commented, although the Knights' leadership remained wary of strikes, "the first news we are likely to hear after [the strike's] close is of the union of the men with the K. of L."[5]

Gould retaliated quickly. During that spring he individually fired the Knights active in the strike. On 16 June the executive board of the Knights' District Assembly No. 93 declared another strike to protest the firings—which neither the Engineers nor Firemen supported. In early September Terence Powderly, grand master of the Knights, negotiated an agreement with A. A. Talmadge, the general manager of the Wabash, that called for the reinstatement of all employees "as fast as possible." They also agreed that the railroad officials would not "discriminate against the K. of L. or question the right of the employee to belong to the Order." In return, Powderly promised to call no further strikes until a conference with railroad officials might be held.[6]

Although the Knights did not achieve union recognition or a clear understanding of what would constitute discrimination, this settlement electrified the country. As the St. Louis *Chronicle* suggested, it was a victory of such magnitude that it had no parallel "in this or any other country."[7] Workingmen throughout the country were exhilarated and felt that in the Knights they had at last found an organization both strong and committed enough to combat the power of organized capital in defense of their rights as citizens and workers. Increasingly among the unorganized, as in the older brotherhoods, workingmen and women rushed to join. As one member wrote Powderly from LaCrosse, Wisconsin, in December 1885: "I have been here for the last week. I have three assemblies ready to organize but there is no organizer here. I wish you would inform me of the nearest organizer to this place. I have in one place here 150 members and another 93 and another 56."[8]

A few weeks following the September agreement, as he walked down the aisle of the convention hall welcoming new delegates and greeting old friends, Eugene Debs sensed this new mood among the men and tried to gauge its strength. The delegates did not direct their anger only toward Gould and other corporate leaders. For over a year dissension had brewed within the Brotherhood, directed primarily toward the conservative stance of the national officers regarding strikes and solidarity with other laboring men. There was talk now of a clean sweep, of replacing these officers with more militant men. As secretary-treasurer since 1880, Debs, and not the nominal grand master, had directed the business of the Brotherhood. When coupled with his duties as editor, it was clear that Debs had almost sole responsibility for the implementation and formation of past policy.[9] Debs might well have pondered this situation and how it might affect his own future ambitions, as he approached the podium to deliver his annual report, possibly his last as secretary-treasurer of the Firemen.

He began, as he had so many times in the past, with a short review of the purpose of the Brotherhood. It stood for "honesty, manhood and hard work" and sought to inculcate in members "probity and virtue." He then congratulated the assembled brothers for their collective efforts in eliminating drunkenness and reminded them that "to insure the respect of mankind they must respect themselves." But at this juncture the comparison with past reports ceased. Where his earlier speeches would have required an affirmation of harmony and a ringing no-strike pledge, Debs now ventured into a new area and introduced the theme of harmony in strident and unfamiliar fashion. Harmony remained the guiding principle of the Brotherhood, he asserted, and members would never use their power to gain an unfair advantage. However, this was no longer the major issue. For the first time at a national convention Debs upheld the concept of justice that had always rested, if somewhat dormant, at the core of harmony. Referring to the growing labor consciousness, Debs claimed that working people "do not ask our employers to treat us any better than we do them. All we ask is an honest day's work, and we are willing to be considerate and just. Our fundamental principle is justice . . . . It is but right that the men of brain and brawn who produce shall be recognized in the distribution. We simply ask a just proportion of the proceeds."[10]

After the completion of Debs's report, the expected repudiation of past Brotherhood policies began. C. S. McAuliffe rose to introduce a resolution rescinding the 1879 pledge to ignore strikes and to declare themselves as a labor organization that would allow strikes in order that "the lodges shall be allowed to protect themselves and their interests as their best judgement may dictate." Referred to committee for study, the resolution eventually passed overwhelmingly.[11] Turning next to the election of national officers, the delegates indicated just how sweeping was the realignment they intended. F. W. Arnold, four years the grand master, lost to Frank P. Sargent, 92–120; while Arnold's grand organizer, S. M. Stevens, lost to John J. Hannahan, 86–121. At this point, Debs rose to address the convention. Acknowledging the "prevailing disposition to abolish the old administration, with all its mistakes," Debs briefly reviewed his intimate association with those policies and then submitted his resignation as both secretary-treasurer and editor of the journal. In a dramatic vote following this speech, the delegates rejected Debs's resignation on both counts and returned him to office by a large margin.[12]

If at first glance the vote appears contradictory, it is accurate to say that the situation itself was contradictory. Debs's support within the Brotherhood rested upon diverse factors. In part, members of all political persuasions appreciated his untiring work on their behalf. He alone had revived the organization during the difficult days in 1880–81, and his frequent organizing trips throughout the country reconfirmed their respect. Further, the various factions within the Brotherhood could each in their own manner claim Debs, for they, like him, were in transition. The more conservative delegates, angered by the machinations of a Gould but wary of too close an association with the Knights, understood Debs's reference to justice and producers' rights within the context of his prior adherence to the ideal of harmony. In addition, these men had the example of Debs's handling of the William Pettibone affair in the last convention to ease any apprehensions. For those more militant in their opposition to corporate capitalism, Debs's emphasis on that same producer ideology, long a major theme in the agitation of the Knights of Labor, seemed an endorsement, if not of the Knights themselves, then at least of the principles that underlined their struggles. Thus the very ambivalence that lay at the core of Debs's thinking accurately reflected the feelings of many throughout the Brotherhood in 1885. Influenced by multiple and often contradictory impulses and perceptions, Debs attempted, nonetheless, to create from the growing social chaos some consistent responses.

Debs began this effort a year earlier when he published an editorial which, for the first time since the late 1870s, addressed the problem of labor. As the laboring people of America "create all the wealth" and "make all the money" for society, "then simple justice demands that the laws of the land, if they are not enacted with special reference to their welfare, shall not operate to their detriment." He averred that labor's demands were modest—"to live comfortably in a house"—and attacked those who opposed workers' attempts to combine "as monopolists have done." Despite such opposition, however, Debs foresaw a new era emerging, for laboring men "are beginning to realize the vastness of their members. They are taking council together, and are asking themselves why, in the halls of State and National legislation, they may not have their representatives. They have the ballots and they have the brains. . . . In this age of combination they too will combine to place men in power who will represent their interests and therefore, the best interests of the Republic."[13]

Defending the promise of equal opportunity for all, Debs also emphasized the intimate connection between producerism and political action. Social fragmentation occurred because, while labor "is alone the source of revenue among men, since all value is born of labor," yet "nowhere on God's green earth have the men, whose work creates the revenues of nations, been permitted to enjoy more than a pittance of the values they have created." Unjust legislation caused this, and he urged laborers to elect men who would repeal those laws which "permit money capital and water[ed] capital to extract dividends from labor capital and leave it to starve in sight of the wealth it creates." When workingmen so unite around the ballot, Debs prophesied, the "results will give a power and a dignity which, while it will secure for labor simple justice, will confer lasting blessings upon society at large."[14]

Debs's emphasis on the benefits that would accrue to all in society through united political effort by labor was no idle thought, a camouflage for a new, more strident tone. The belief in general social improvement went to the heart of his advocacy of producers' rights and afforded him continuity, within a changing context, with the traditional goal of harmony. Against the unbridled self-interest of the corporations, which he now saw as the agents of revolution in nineteenth-century America, Debs pitted his understanding of that same culture's eighteenth-century Revolutionary heritage. In advocating the eight-hour day, Debs contrasted the monopolist—who desired "the greatest number of hours for the least possible pay"—with the national good to be achieved from an intellectually active laboring class, for then "the government will rest upon the intelligence and virtue of the people."[15]

Throughout 1885 and 1886, as he discovered and developed the ramifications of the producer theory, Debs continually explored its roots in traditional American thought. Unlike other countries, where such struggles demanded new concepts and where to revert to the original social contract was to regress, America was different. "In the United States,"

Debs wrote, "it is true, that the government in the onset was framed upon principles which belonged to its best condition, and, therefore, it is the part of wisdom for the people to often go back to first principles, if they would escape 'unnatural and dangerous' departures."[16]

Similarly, Debs criticized the American publication of John Ruskin's essay "Work." He felt that its purpose was to reconcile British workers to a class system and assumed a like purpose in its publication here. "But such logic will not flourish on this side of the Atlantic," Debs countered. "Work—honest work—is not degrading. The man who by honest toil earns an honest living is a peer of the realm. He is not a mendicant. Equal to the richest and proudest before the law. Equal to any man in all rights and prerogatives of citizenshp, with every avenue of advancement open to him, he spurns the idea of 'upper' and 'lower' class, and says, 'we, the people.' "[17]

Debs's new stress on the "people" and the immutable tradition of the American Revolution quickly led him to reject the employer paternalism embraced in his earlier editorials on William Riley McKeen. Not to do so would denigrate the worker who "owns himself, is a man, a citizen, independent."[18] These values allowed Debs to attack employers in specific ways. In early 1886, when the Pennsylvania Railroad instituted its own relief agency for workers, Debs's first reaction was to focus on the anti-labor animus that prompted this development: workers were forced to join and contribute to a company department in direct competition with their own brotherhoods.[19] At its deepest level, however, Debs's argument was less over unionization than it was over the meaning of American citizenship. In a second editorial Debs agreed that to obtain life's necessities demanded a mutual dependency within society. But this dependency should only be temporary, he insisted, and criticized the Pennsylvania corporation from the vantage point of atomistic individualism. "It is only in 'the direction of one's own affairs without interference' that absolute independence can be secured, and it is this independence and this *absolute right* that the employes of the Pennsylvania railroad company demanded, nothing more; and by demonstrating this right, they demonstrated that they were manly men, not 'squaw men,' and the fact should elevate them in the estimation of their employers."[20]

In a very critical manner, then, Debs's evocation of the "people" was not a call to communal action. While men might band together on both economic and political planes to oppose certain corporate actions, they did so primarily in defense of their rights as individuals. It was not surprising for Debs's readers, therefore, to find, in the month following his critique of the Pennsylvania plan, an editorial opposing boycotts but supporting the right of workers to refuse to join a union. "Strike down that idea," he stated, "and the idea of *personal* liberty disappears." Of the

Cigar Makers' Union, which had used the boycott to establish a closed shop, Debs was highly critical: "The American motto is 'fair play.' Boycotting is not *fair play*—it is *not* in consonance with American ideas of justice, it is fruitful of injustice, it does not recognize *personal* liberty and *personal* rights."[21] Debs's insistence on the unique American nature of liberty revealed neither knowledge nor awareness either of the Irish immigrant worker, from whose tradition the boycott originated, or of Samuel Gompers and the many other immigrant cigar makers.

Debs's call for united political action and, to a limited degree, unified economic organization, therefore, in no way reflected a growing class awareness on his part. Rather, his increasing anger drew strength and justification from a specific American tradition that stressed economic mobility, political action, and industrious work habits as the foundation of individual dignity and manliness of character. Yet, it must be understood, Debs had traveled some distance in his thought since 1877. Significantly, as Debs developed his deeply American critique of monopoly, religious themes and symbols appeared more frequently in his writings.

The tradition of evangelical Protestant reform that had so structured the pre–Civil War abolitionist movement did not disappear in the postwar years. Both the temperance and women's suffrage movements retained part of that tradition, and labor organizers and working people often appealed to it in their struggles with industrial capitalism. The Bible provided a complex of values that justified workers' struggles against autocratic authority, values that were seen as the "fixed and eternal laws of God for the ordering of society."[22] As with the American Revolutionary heritage, itself perceived as based on these eternal truths, the folk religion of American Protestantism offered both justification for labor's opposition to aspects of industrial capitalism and assurance of ultimate success.

Although never religious in any orthodox fashion himself (he never joined a church), Debs revealed during these years how influenced he was by the religious current in American culture. Increasingly he quoted from the works of religiously influenced political thinkers, the most important of whom were Victor Hugo and Henry George;[23] when he argued in favor of the bimetallic standard, Debs returned to the Old Testament to find his argument. Recalling that Abraham paid silver for Sarah's burial plot, Debs argued that the bimetallists, as "the progressive, enterprising working class," could evoke the blessings and approval associated with Abraham, in direct contrast with the gold advocates who were "speculators upon the misfortunes of mankind."[24] Some months later, Debs went so far as to justify momentarily the use of dynamite with an appeal to this religious tradition. "Dynamite is forever saying to despots," Debs wrote in October 1885, "let my people have freedom. . . . It is the old demand made by Moses to Pharaoh 'Let my people go,' and Pharaoh's stubbornness should teach despots of the present age a lesson in prudence.''[25]

Like most Americans of every formal religious profession, Debs understood his culture's history as the progress of God's chosen people. Destined to create the "New Jerusalem," and under a powerful imperative to spread the "good news" to others, Debs and many Americans found it inconceivable that the will of God could be thwarted except by the malicious design of a few powerful individuals. This conviction grew from the belief that the resources of American society were plentiful enough for all its members to live in dignity and even comfort. Debs attacked the Malthusian theory that population and food sources were in conflict, branding it an aristocratic idea "built upon the most stupendous crime that an inscrutable God ever permitted to curse the earth"; he looked to working people to reverse these conditions caused by a few. The producing classes, he argued, are "organizing everywhere," fighting in defense of the basic principle "that there is work and food for a man born into this world, and that at the 'great banquet of Nature' a plate is laid for him, and, if not, they will see to it that he does have a plate at the banquet in the future, at least in the United States."[26]

Reflecting this traditional American emphasis on the promise of nature, Debs presented his case for the eight-hour day. Poverty existed, not due to some Malthusian theory or Darwinian selection, but because work itself was not fairly distributed. Further, wages were often below subsistence levels, and there were some "who are so demonized that they seek for their own gain to advance the price of food." An eight-hour day, at a fair wage, would create more jobs, allow leisure for intellectual development, and raise the standard of living to one "more in consonance with the dignity of American citizens."[27] Similarly Debs condemned the growing scarcity of free land. Relying on John Stuart Mill, he argued that land derived its productive power from nature and thus ought not be controlled by a few. Yet, he noted, almost 60 percent of the western land for sale between 1862 and 1871 was given to the railroad corporations to promote new lines. With these large grants came the development of large-scale corporate farming and a corresponding rise in tenancy among white agricultural workers. Tenancy, in turn, touched "the very marrow of liberty and independence, and he who does not see in the growth of landlordism in the United States dangers to the permanency of American institutions, is as blind as a bat."[28]

The conflict between his newfound grasp of America's millennial promise and what he perceived as the pseudoscience and crass manipulation of a few monopolists forced Debs to reformulate his understanding of manhood. With his new emphasis on justice and the common equality of all, the image of the forceful, shrewd, self-made businessman that so dominated his own and his era's imagination was no longer sufficient. In an article entitled "Art Thou a Man?" Debs contrasted for the first time the themes of manhood and monopoly. Rejecting physical prowess as a definition of manhood (as "it is equally well-known that mules are hard-hitters"), Debs also rejected social prominence. A banker, he pointed out, might appear to be the pillar of the church, but when his speculative enterprises collapsed he was soon revealed to be "a moral mons-ter. . . . religious that he might the more successfully play the role of rascal." Of this so-called progressive element in society, who would cor-ner the market on needed goods, Debs complained that "to call such per-sons men is to outrage the properties of speech and obliterate from the face of the earth those standards by which Christ measured men." Instead, drawing on the tradition of the Christ who chased the money changers from the temple, Debs offered his revised definition of manhood: "A MAN will not rob directly or indirectly. A MAN despises a lie, prevarica-tion and subterfuge. A man is true to wife and home, to obligation and trust. A man will recognize probity without reference to position or ar-tificial surroundings. He will estimate other men by character rather than cash or coat, by head rather than hat."[29]

In these years immediately surrounding his marriage in 1885, a more confident Debs began to emerge. His constant travels caused tension with Kate, but they provided this thirty-year-old labor organizer with the seeds of a new self-knowledge. His discussions with workers across America led him to question his earlier understandings of manhood and harmony. What Debs learned from these working people about the changing nature of work, coupled with his own observations in Terre Haute, forced him to explore the critical side of the American tradition. The deference he had so long granted McKeen he now viewed as a negation of his own manhood. Even physically Debs seemed to change. A tall and gangly young adult, Debs came to use his thin frame with effect. From the podium, his intense eyes and expressive face demanded attention while his long arms and torso eased or coiled in pace with his cadence. More than just experience pro-duced this confidence, however. As he first explored new interpretations of familiar themes, Debs discovered that his culture's Protestant religious imagery was particularly suited to both his emerging new message and to his public personality. In the patriarchs of the Old Testament and in the angry Christ of the New, Debs found a prophetic model that legitimized his critique and demanded no apologies for frank, even harsh, pro-nouncements. In the process he touched for the first time his powerful charismatic appeal with audiences.

Yet this was no instant conversion. Even as he appealed to the model of Christ, Debs also defended the French war effort in Indo-China in terms dripping with the missionary passion of American jingoism. "All

Christendom hopes for the triumph of French arms," he explained, "because the exclusiveness of the Chinese is not in consonance with the civilization of the age, and will not be tolerated."[30] Closer to home, Debs identified overproduction as the cause of declining wages and urged working people to elect representatives to Congress committed to support American corporate interests in wresting from various European powers the rich South American market. Unconcerned with the social consequences of this policy for the people of these countries, Debs argued that American working people might thus solve their own problems and to no small extent bring the blessings of the democratic millennium to these backward nations.[31]

Even as he used prophetic Christian imagery to resist corporate excesses, Debs remained culture-bound in many narrow ways. He paid scant attention to immigrant workers and people of color abroad seemed but stepping-stones for the American producer's progress. Weaving together the leveling power of the Protestant Reformation with a deep affirmation of the rational secularism of the Enlightenment, Debs seemed almost Comtean in his faith in science and in his society's foreordained progress. In this "utilitarian age," he thought, "science stands pledged to overwhelm mere idealists," and he stressed education as the means by which "the masses [can] grasp ideas possessed of lifting power."[32]

This faith, in turn, reflected the profound emphasis on people's free agency in producer thought. During these years Debs fervently believed that "people had the will to determine the course their lives would take."[33] Due to these contradictory strands in his thought, Debs's new understanding of manhood, the Christian tradition, and the centrality of the producing classes had little immediate effect upon his daily life. He remained tied to a view of the trade union that placed primary emphasis on a small coterie of national officers and was still hesitant about strikes. Although his new insights were important in liberating him from the static belief in harmony that had dominated his early public career, it proved to be a hesitant liberation. Many of the seeds only sprouted in later years as Debs struggled to keep alive the ultimate search for harmony in an increasingly hostile world.

During these same years, another idea of labor organizing with revolutionary implications for American working people began to find supporters throughout the country. Perhaps best symbolized in the person of Samuel Gompers and the organization he presided over for almost forty years—the American Federation of Labor (AFL)—this new concept also stressed the need for labor to combine to combat capital. However, it based its organizational efforts on a belief that working people were, in fact, workers in a profound class sense and should relinquish all expectations of transcending that status. Fully accepting industrial society and its hierarchical structure, Gompers and his associates insisted that the working class should concentrate their energies on improving their position within that society.[34]

Ultimately Gompers and Debs became bitter antagonists. Debs felt Gompers became in later years a Judas to the labor movement, a "grand national joke . . . the greatest political Mr. Facingbothways this country has ever had."[35] Gompers, for his part, characterized Debs in his 1925 autobiography as an "emotional intellectual" who, in the aftermath of the 1894 Pullman strike, "had lost all faith in the power of constructive work and became the advocate of revolt."[36] Their differences, great as they were, were less rooted in specific strikes, however, than in their respective conceptions of the purpose of the trade union movement. In the decade prior to the Pullman strike, they developed parallel if contradictory approaches to trade union questions. While the general darkness clouded these differences for the moment, it was, ironically, Gompers and not Debs who offered a dramatic new defense of working people in 1886.

The AFL, formed in December 1886, had its origins in the meeting held in Terre Haute, Indiana, in August 1881. When political disagreements disrupted this meeting, the trade union delegates, led by Patrick J. McGuire, called another conference for Pittsburgh the following November.[37] Neither Debs nor Gompers attended the Terre Haute meeting, but Gompers did play an important role in the Pittsburgh conference. As at the first meeting, the delegates divided over the purpose and proposed composition of the new organization. Mark Moore, elected secretary at the earlier meeting, urged the Pittsburgh conference to "let your action be cool, deliberate, and not too overreformatory. Grasp one idea, viz., less hours and better pay," and he suggested legislation to achieve these ends.[38] Ultimately the convention did adopt thirteen resolutions to improve labor's condition, all of which looked to legislative action for their fulfillment.[39]

Gompers supported these legislative demands but strongly opposed the inclusion of larger political issues. In contrast with many midwestern delegates, especially those affiliated with the Knights of Labor, Gompers was more the orthodox Marxist who stressed the primacy of economic demands over divisive political issues. He told the convention that he had come to Pittsburgh "not to air his opinions, but to work, not to build a bubble, but to lay the foundations for that superstructure that would be solid, and that would be a true federation of trade unions."[40] A member of the convention's legislative committee, Gompers proposed a resolution opposing public advocacy of any political party, while allowing support for an individual candidate "who is pledged purely and directly to labor measures." As he noted in his autobiography, "labor organizations had been the victims of so much political trickery that we felt the only way to keep this new organization free from taint was to exclude all political partisan action."[41]

The major struggle at the convention developed between advocates of the Knights of Labor and those favoring a stronger trade union and an economically oriented federation. The Knights, quite well organized in the Pittsburgh area even in 1881, comprised almost half the delegates.[42] Early in the meeting, Gompers delineated the issues dividing the two groups when he proposed that the convention adopt as its official title, the Federation of Organized Trade Unions. Richard Powers, of the Chicago Lake Seamen's Union, rose to support the resolution—which excluded the phrase "and Labor Unions"—arguing that he believed "it will keep out of the Federation political labor bodies which might try to force themselves into our future deliberations."[43]

The Gompers proposal encountered strong opposition. In a prophetic analysis, Jeremiah Grandison, a black delegate representing the Pittsburgh Knights of Labor, argued that the resolution would include only skilled craftsmen and bar from the organization those "who have no particular trade." The purpose of the convention, he insisted, was to "federate the whole laboring element of America," and he warned the delegates of the dangers of creating such an exclusionary organization: "I speak more particularly with a knowledge of my own people, and declare to you that it would be dangerous to skilled mechanics to exclude from this organization the common laborers, who might, in an emergency, be employed in positions they could easily qualify to fill themselves."[44]

The Gompers resolution ultimately lost and the name of the new organization read the Federation of Organized Trades and Labor Unions. However, it was something of a pyrrhic victory for Grandison and his supporters. The three top officers of the new federation—John Jarrett of the Amalgamated Iron and Steel Workers, Powers, and Gompers—had all supported the original resolution. By the time of the second convention in Cleveland a year later, moreover, the Knights had officially withdrawn from the federation, and the remaining trade union delegates altered the basis of representation to preclude any reentry by the assemblies of the Knights.[45] Most important, the delegates to that second convention clearly identified themselves as the representatives of an industrial working *class* and rejected any sympathy for, or identification with, the concept of the producing classes. In a manifesto that marked a revolutionary turning point in the American labor movement, the Cleveland convention proclaimed:

We favor this Federation because it is the most natural and assimilative form of bringing the trades and labor unions together. It preserves the industrial autonomy and distinctive character of each trade and labor union, and, without doing violence to their faith or traditions, blends them all into one harmonious whole. . . . Such a body looks to the organization of the working classes as workers, and not as "soldiers" (in the present deprecatory sense) or politicians. It makes the qualities of a man as a worker the only test of fitness, and sets up no political or religious test of membership.[46]

Although the bitter personal antagonism between Debs and Gompers would not surface for another decade, it was rooted in their understanding of the position of working people as they expressed it during the 1880s. Gompers was an immigrant who had early been exposed to Marxist thought. While his ideas were certainly not foreign to America, the struggles between Marxists and Lasselleans in both Europe and America had heavily influenced him. As a young cigar maker in the early 1870s, Gompers had been affected by a fellow worker, Karl Laurrell, a Swedish immigrant and a member of the executive board of the International Workingmen's Association in New York. A committed Marxist, Laurrell opposed the emphasis on political activity that the American Lasselleans in the Socialist movement advocated, and he repeatedly instructed the young Gompers to evaluate all ideas in light of trade union principles: "Study your union card, Sam," Gompers recalled him saying, "and if the idea doesn't square with that, it ain't true."[47]

Debs, however, was moving toward what he saw as a more radical critique of industrial capitalism and embraced the very principles that Gompers rejected in shaping the AFL. Inherent in the idea of the producer was the concept of a free labor economic system, stressing individual mobility and political activity and drawing heavily on the free agency theology of evangelical Protestantism.[48] To use the term industrial capitalism to describe what Debs opposed in 1886 would be misleading. Less than an understanding of an economic system, he stressed resistance to the obstacles placed in the individual's path by the machinations of a few powerful men. In using this concept, with its tradition in American culture older than the American Revolution, Debs indicated just how much he was a native son of Terre Haute and marked something of the gulf that separated him from Gompers.

The year 1886 was a fateful year for the labor movement in the United States. The formation of the AFL in December seemed less decisive than the generally weak posture of the labor movement as a whole. Buoyed by its apparently easy victory the year before, in March the Knights of Labor struck the Gould system in the Southwest. Two months later, on 4 May, in Haymarket Square, Chicago, a bomb exploded during a labor rally called to support a demand for the eight-hour day. With over seventy police injured — seven fatally — the police opened fire and killed or injured an indeterminate number of demonstrators. Responsibility for the bombing was immediately laid at the feet of the anarchists who had addressed the meeting and, despite absence of proof, a severe anti-labor sentiment swept the nation. On the night of the bombing the general executive board of the Knights, meeting in St. Louis, called off their strike without achieving a single demand. Coupled with the general failure of the eight-hour day agitation that had begun on 1 May, the labor movement was thrown on the defensive.[49]

Throughout this turmoil Debs himself was confused. On the one hand, while touring with F. P. Sargent throughout the Southwest during the Knights' strike, Debs generally spoke well of the strikers and claimed that they were misunderstood.[50] Yet he was very critical of the Knights as an organization. He thought it too pro-strike (evident, he felt, in its motto: "Injury to one is the concern of all") and held its lack of centralized organization as a major cause of the current strike.[51] Further, along with Sargent, Debs played an important role in breaking strike unity. He cautioned Brotherhood members who were also sympathetic to the Knights to "faithfully serve" their employers, and he frequently reminded members of the Brotherhood's decision to support the railroad corporations and not the Knights in this strike.[52] Debs persisted in this stand, despite the strong feeling for the Knights among many of the Brotherhood's rank and file.[53]

Characteristically Debs did attempt to formulate a synthesis, however vague, from the clash of these two contrasting positions. At a meeting in Sedalia, Missouri, on 19 April, he argued that, while the Knights had been "hasty and rash in some instances," the current strike might ultimately benefit both labor and capital. The strike "would learn each to respect the other," Debs hoped, and would establish "an honorable alliance of capital and labor, to the end that justice might be done to both." While the nature of this "honorable alliance" was not developed, Debs did assert once again his belief that "the world will not be civilized until men of labor are appreciated."[54] If this synthesis left many strikers angry, and with little practical support, it caused the opposite reaction among railway officials and their supporters. Debs himself noted at the conclusion of the trip that he and Sargent had been "treated kindly" by the railroad officials they encountered, and he reported with pleasure that "the purposes of our Brotherhood seemed to be well understood."[55] The Des Moines *Leader*, an anti-strike paper, confirmed Debs's optimism after his speech there in early July: "He is certainly the right man in the right place," the editors commented, "and so long as he holds to the splendid sentiments enunciated, and the Order follows them so long will the Brotherhood retain the friendship and best wishes of the public and railway managers."[56]

If Debs expressed little support for the Knights' strike, he evinced even less sympathy toward the anarchists accused of planting the bomb in Haymarket Square. He did not refer to the case during the trial, but when he did comment on it he viewed the eight convicted anarchists with the eyes of a conservative citizen-producer. In January 1887 Debs condemned the anarchists for their violence and narrowness of vision. "These anarchists," Debs wrote,

> saw nothing, or little, in American institutions worthy of favorable consideration. Saturated with ideas born of European methods of government, they assumed that every wrong perpetrated by individuals or corporations against the rights and interests of working men was fundamental, rather than superficial; that is to say that such wrongs are inherent in the principles upon which the government was founded, rather than innovations, at war with its spirit, and hence they sought to inculcate by speech and press, opposition to institutions which, by their liberality, permitted them to openly and defiantly antagonize them.

But these men, he concluded, should not be sentenced to death for misguided ideas. They had not been convicted for any deed—for throwing the bomb—but rather because their teachings and ideas "prepared the way and led to the throwing of the bomb." To fail to distinguish between language and action violated both freedom of speech and press, Debs argued, and was as harmful to American liberty as the anarchist *Attentat* itself.[57]

In the same issue of the *Locomotive Firemen's Magazine* Debs restated his social beliefs and, indirectly at least, commented on the disturbances and upheavals of the past year. Talk of a general war between labor and capital he termed "the creation of diseased brains," for "such a war . . . in the nature of things can not and never did have an existence." But there was an impending social crisis, Debs believed, one fought for control of public sentiment by "grasping monopolists seeking by statutes, and precedents, established usages, to maintain a crushing ascendancy over the wealth-producing millions of men." Such a war, he predicted, which pitted the few against the many, would ultimately be won by the masses at the ballot box.[58]

Opposition to strikes and insistence on a political solution to the problems caused by the aggressive economic expansion of industrial capitalism marked the enormous distance, even in these early years, between the positions of Debs and Gompers. In his defense of strikes to wrest economic improvements from capital and in his abhorrence of union involvement in politics, Gompers manifested both the strong influence of Karl Marx and the practical lessons he and his father learned from their work in London. His early years in New York only reinforced his inherent distrust of the notion of a producing class. In that complicated and expanding urban complex, Gompers found little evidence of a community of citizens committed to harmonious resolution of conflict. For Debs, though, the pull of Terre Haute, with its promise of equality and harmony, remained a strong, even dominant force in his thought.

As if to underscore these differences, Debs remained active during these years in the civic and social life of Terre Haute. Even as he questioned earlier concepts, the community of Terre Haute continued to serve him as a symbol of the proper relations within a republic. For their part, the townspeople still welcomed his participation. When Benjamin C. Cox, an important merchant and early partner of Herman Hulman, donated land for a city park in 1888, Debs was invited to give one of the dedication speeches, and he attended the gala ball later that night along with Terre Haute's "best people." Similarly, when the refurbished Terre Haute House—the old Prairie House—reopened in 1889, Debs was one of the speakers, along with Richard Thompson and Daniel Voorhees, scheduled to address the celebratory dinner-dance.[59] Debs, his brother Theodore, and Sargent all offered prizes for the best pies and breads at the Vigo County Fair; and he remained interested in the Occidental Literary Society (in which Theodore had become an active member and committeeman) and was its banquet speaker in 1888.[60] As befitted the sons of an increasingly successful local merchant, who was soon to be listed in H. C. Bradsby's *History of Vigo County* with an appropriate biographical sketch, Eugene and Theodore Debs perceived no conflict between their work as labor organizers and their active role in the town's civic life.[61]

It was during these years that Debs's relations with his siblings assumed their adult complexion. The assertive yet curiously dependent tone he had adopted toward them during the 1870s grew in intensity as Debs's public career involved him in political and personal controversy. With the transfer of the national offices of the Firemen from Indianapolis to Terre Haute, Debs fully involved his brother and sisters in his career. Both younger sisters worked in the office prior to their marriages, and relinquished far better paying jobs to do so. While he drew support from the family in general (his activities increasingly dominated his parents' dinner table conversation), he developed a quite special relationship with his younger brother Theodore. "Kude," as Debs nicknamed him, became his older brother's alter ego. As the demands on Eugene's time escalated, so did Theodore's duties. When his older brother was on the road, it was Theodore who answered the mail, kept the books, and edited the journal for the printer. Even Theodore's own marriage became interwoven within this special fraternal relationship. When he married Gertrude Toy, the daughter of a wealthy Denver realtor, Theodore continued his work with his brother at far less salary than he might otherwise command. In fact, he refused an attractive position at the Indiana State Bank of Terre Haute in the late 1880s to continue with Eugene.[62] For her part, Gertrude fully accepted this relationship in all its particulars, despite the decline in her standard of living. Eugene was most grateful. As he wrote Theodore a few years after he and Gertrude married, in an obvious if implied contrast with his own marital arrangements: "I know how loyal Gertrude is and no words in the language can express my appreciation."[63]

With family and civic relations seemingly intact, Debs continued in his role as the Democratic party's labor spokesman both in Terre Haute and throughout Indiana. Despite the appearance of a United Labor party in Terre Haute, Debs reaffirmed his allegiance to the Democrats. He spoke at ward meetings and helped establish the Businessmen's Tariff Reform Club in 1888—an anti-high tariff Democratic organization led by Hulman, John S. Beach, B. F. Havens, and Philip Schloss.[64] He even publicly admonished McKeen for his anti-labor policy, although he carefully restated his ties of personal friendship at the same time.[65] However, Debs's major contribution to the Democratic campaign during 1888 was a full-scale attack upon the labor record of the Republican presidential candidate, Benjamin Harrison—an attack that centered upon Harrison's role during the 1877 strike.

In late October, before a packed crowd that filled beyond capacity the Wigwam, the local Democratic party hall, Debs proclaimed that he would speak in a nonpartisan fashion, not "as a Democrat, but as a citizen, a working man." Pointing to Harrison's lifelong anti-labor record, Debs noted that he would still oppose him even were Harrison a Democrat, and then Debs presented the national context of the 1877 strike. The strikers had been wronged, he claimed; they had struck "for just simply enough wages to keep soul and body together." In contrast to his views in 1877, he now defended the strike on the grounds that "a man's first duty is to his family." When despite honest toil he still cannot earn enough to support them, "he owes it to his family and to himself to protest because somebody is drawing at least a portion of his wages." Emphasizing the themes of manhood and personal duty in the tradition of American citizenship, Debs explained that he had now come to realize that under certain conditions strikes were "absolutely justifiable. There is not a star, there is not a stripe in the American flag that does not tell of a strike for liberty and for independence."

Debs then examined the specific events in Indianapolis during the summer of 1877. The strikers needed a friend, he stated, for not only had their wages been cut but also their attempts at arbitration had been rejected by the railroad corporation. The mayor, John Cavin, perceiving that the strikers "were not lawbreakers," had appointed three hundred of them as special police officers. Harrison, however, had taken a quite different approach. At that time a lawyer for the railroads, Harrison defended the corporation and declared that a dollar a day was sufficient for working people. He even organized a private militia company, Debs charged, to oppose the strikers in the streets. As if this were not enough, Debs continued, Harrison led the prosecution of those arrested and was guilty of falsifying evidence to obtain convictions. In a revealing statement before his neighbors, many of whom were familiar with his actions during 1877, Debs accused Harrison of distorting the evidence against one John Reeves, who "had no more to do with the strike at that time than I had." Concluding his attack with a brief review of Harrison's record as a U.S. Senator, Debs argued that the Republican nominee had consistently voted to "place the working men of this country upon a level with the five cent Chinaman, with the man who comes from abroad and carries a five cent god in his pocket." Yet Debs felt that many, even among workers, would support Harrison. He consoled himself, however, and his highly partisan audience, with the thought that more working people than ever were becoming active in politics. The future, if not the present, thus held great promise.[66]

Harrison, of course, won the election despite Debs's efforts. In his appeal to the community, however, Debs indicated just how consistent his thought had been over the past decade. Circumstances had changed, and he could now, in the middle of a major strike against another railroad corporation, defend the 1877 strike. But he did so from within that same structure of values that had earlier led him to oppose it. Although more critical of corporate power and its local representatives, Debs had not relinquished his belief in the power of community—and that alone separated him from Gompers. James Whitcomb Riley understood this quite clearly when, in his poem, "Terry Hut," he apotheosized both McKeen and Debs in the same stanza. They were, for him as for many in Terre Haute, still the symbol of the town's ultimate harmony and community of interest.[67]

What fueled Debs's attack upon Harrison was a serious and prolonged strike against the Chicago, Burlington and Quincy Railroad that began some months earlier. It was Debs's first experience as a strike leader, one of the very few strikes in which the Brotherhood itself participated,[68] and, more than any other single event in his early career, it forced Debs to reevaluate prior opinions and strategies.

The strike of the Firemen and Engineers against the Burlington lasted from February 1888 until January 1889. It originated in a dispute that began in 1886, when a committee of engineers presented a long list of grievances to the line's general manager, T. J. Potter. Chief among these were demands to halt the classification system (by which engineers and firemen received apprentice pay for the first three years, although they performed the full job) and to establish a uniform pay scale based on mileage traveled for every line and subdivision within the Burlington system. When Potter agreed to meet all but the two major demands, P. M. Arthur, chief of the Engineers, maneuvered the men into accepting the agreement.[69] Although these issues were the immediate catalysts for the 1888 strike, a fundamental change had occurred within the Brotherhood of Locomotive Engineers as well. Long a bastion of conservative craftsmen, with a cautious and explicitly anti-militant leadership, many members were affected by the activities of the Knights of Labor during 1885–86.[70] As with the Locomotive Firemen, many engineers held dual membership in both their Brotherhood and the Knights, and some of these men developed a caucus that checked Arthur's unilateral power and gained dominance of the grievance committee on the Burlington between 1886 and 1888.[71]

Burlington officials were not unaware of these developments. As early as May 1886, Charles E. Perkins, president of the Burlington, attempted to fire all known members of the Knights "inasmuch as the Knights of Labor owe allegiance to somebody else, and not to the railroad company that employs them."[72] Many of the men were forced to choose between their jobs and their union membership. Yet, despite their common opposition to the Burlington officials, relations between the Knights and the two railway brotherhoods were cool at best. Each distrusted the other and could point to specific strikes where the scab policy of one broke the strike of another. Engineers and Firemen remembered the spring of 1877 when a number of Knights replaced them and contributed to their defeat at the hands of the Philadelphia and Reading Railroad. The Knights recalled how neither brotherhood supported them in their strike against the Gould system in 1886, and that, following the strike, Arthur ordered all engineers holding dual membership to quit either the Knights or the Brotherhood.[73]

Even more recently, however, the Knights of Labor strike against the Reading road in late 1887 generated bitter feelings. Called in sympathy with the 80,000 coal miners employed by the railroad, the engineers and firemen belonging to the Knights struck the road. Not only had the two brotherhoods refused to support the strike, but also their leaders publicly encouraged members to replace the strikers. When a majority of the Philadelphia lodge of the Firemen joined the strike, to protest the firing of a member for his strike support, Sargent took stringent action. He strongly supported the master of the lodge, Jeremiah J. Leaky, who opposed both the strike and the Knights and echoed Arthur's attitude toward the Knights. He warned that "no bulldozing on the part of the members belonging to the Knights of Labor will be permitted'' and threatened to revoke the charter if his instructions were not followed.

In a public interview following this telegram, Sargent all but interdicted the Knights from participation in the Brotherhood. ''No member of the Brotherhood who is a Knight of Labor will be allowed to bring up the subject at any of the lodge meetings,'' he announced, and again he threatened to revoke the charter if this was disregarded. In this same interview Debs lent his considerable prestige to Leaky and defended him against rank-and-file criticism. Leaky, Debs asserted, ''stands high in the order and is a first class man in every respect.''[74]

In this atmosphere of hostility and tension within the brotherhoods and between them and the Knights, the Engineers and Firemen, themselves not the best of allies, struck the Burlington road. Demanding an end to classification and a uniform pay scale, the strike appeared on the first day—27 February 1888—to be a success. Where railroad officials had estimated that fully 40 percent of the men would ignore the strike call, over 97 percent walked out, although only 66 percent belonged to either brotherhood. To avoid possible injunctions, the strikers declared that they would carry the mail trains provided no freight cars were attached.[75]

Debs was optimistic and buoyant at the start of the strike. In an interview with a Chicago reporter Debs blamed the strike on the intransigence of the Burlington officials. Noting that the Brotherhood never encouraged strikes, he pointed with pride to its record of one strike in the past fifteen years. ''In a nutshell,'' he argued, the issue was ''equal pay for equal service,'' and he expressed confidence that ''harmony will supplant discord and the largest measure of good results for all concerned will be secured.''[76] At first this optimism seemed warranted. The strikers remained united, and few if any broke ranks to return to work. Further, when it became clear that the connecting railroads still handled Burlington cars, Arthur and Sargent called a meeting of the grievance chairmen on all roads where the brotherhoods had lodges for 5 March in Chicago. A majority present agreed to boycott all Burlington freight cars on whatever road they appeared and specifically approved in advance a strike called to protest the firing of a man for participating in a boycott. The conservative Arthur, when asked whether he suppored the measure, replied: ''In times of war I believe in war measures; yes, I will sanction the strike.''[77]

Despite this show of unity, however, the main strike itself was all but lost by the time the grievance chairmen reported back to their locals the decisions of the Chicago conference. In both brotherhoods strong factions opposed not only the projected boycott but also the very strike against the Burlington itself. Many in the Knights, moreover, were anxious to take the strikers' positions. Finally, the firm and uncompromising position of the railroad officials assured the ultimate failure of the strike. With the ac-

tive support of many of their largest competitors in the transportation industry, as well as the sympathy and understanding of the federal judiciary
in Chicago, the Burlington could even look on the strike with a certain
pleasure, as the ensuing internal dissension and defeat would undoubtedly
weaken labor for years to come.

The first indication of trouble within the brotherhoods appeared when
the men of the Chicago, Milwaukee and St. Paul met to vote on the resolution to boycott. After heated discussion, they refused to support the
boycott and thus gave the Burlington crucial access to the western
markets. At the same time, the chairmen of the grievance committees to
the east of Chicago refused to even report the boycott resolution to their
local members.[78] Where the boycott was effective, it most often succeeded
because general managers on the smaller lines voluntarily supported it in
an attempt to preserve their position against the sprawling Burlington
operation. Sargent eulogized one such manager for defying "that tyrannical management" of the Burlington in his insistence upon "good wages
and just treatment for his employes."[79] But even where the boycott
originated with Brotherhood men, it compounded rather than eased tension. On 15 March, the firemen and engineers of the Atchinson, Topeka
and Santa Fe struck to prevent the Burlington from receiving continued
support from their employer. In addition to direct strike aid, they told one
reporter, they had examined the stockholders of both lines and found
"that a considerable number of the Santa Fe stockholders are also largely
interested in the 'Q.'" They then concluded to "dip into both pockets at
once, and let these men feel the full effects of the strike by crippling their
resources."[80]

Between the Chicago meeting on 5 March and the start of the Santa Fe
strike ten days later, however, the official position of Arthur, Sargent, and
Debs changed dramatically. On 8 March the Burlington sought an injunction under the provisions of the Interstate Commerce Act against the
Wabash Railroad for refusing to handle its freight. The case was argued
before the same federal judge, Walter Gresham, who had provided
McKeen with federal troops in 1877. On 9 March the Burlington requested
a similar injunction against the Union Pacific. On the 13th Gresham
issued a preliminary opinion that left no doubt but that he would side with
the Burlington.[81] The leaders of the striking brotherhoods understood
only too well the implications of Judge Gresham's preliminary decision.
Arthur, Sargent, and even Debs, according to one account, faced with jail
on the one hand and an internal conservative opposition on the other,
dropped the boycott and chose to abandon the more militant members.[82]
Referring to the Santa Fe strike as "treason" and "open rebellion," the
leaders of both brotherhoods disowned the men and demanded they
follow the new national policy. By 20 March the Santa Fe strike had col-

lapsed, and Sargent, Arthur, and Debs received widespread criticism from members of both brotherhoods.[83]

The antagonism between the brotherhoods and the Knights further complicated an already impossible strike situation. On the very eve of the strike, the leader of the St. Louis Knights, Richard Griffiths, announced that his members would immediately apply for the vacated positions, while George L. Eastman, a national organizer of the Knights, wired the Burlington general manager that he had available three hundred experienced engineers. Although Terence Powderly urged his members not to scab, his influence was seriously limited. Most of the strikebreakers were affiliated with the anti-administration "provisional committee," which opposed Powderly in part for his weak handling of recent strikes.[84]

With the Reading Knights pouring into Chicago, Debs called upon Joseph R. Buchanan, chairman of the "provisional committee," in an effort to shut off the influx. When Buchanan reminded him of past scabbing by both brotherhoods and the consistently hostile attitude of Arthur, Debs appealed to Buchanan as a dedicated labor organizer. "No matter how 'leaders' may err," Buchanan later quoted Debs as saying, "it is your duty and mine to exert what influence we may possess to prevent organized workingmen from cutting each other's throats." Impressed both by the man and his argument, Buchanan agreed to use his influence to have the Reading men return to Pennsylvania. Despite these negotiations, the Knights, and especially the Reading Knights, continued to replace the strikers. Not only was the leadership of the various factions unable to resolve this issue, but it was indicative of the deep unrest among railway workers in general that neither Powderly nor Buchanan, neither Arthur, Sargent, nor Debs could control a major portion of their own memberships.[85]

Although the strike continued into 1889, it was lost as early as March 1888. Internal disagreements limited the effectiveness of the boycott, and the threatened injunctions ended it where it had occurred. By 8 March, slightly more than a week after the strike's optimistic beginning, the Burlington corporation already hired permanent replacements for the strikers—easily available given the breakdown of negotiations with the Knights. Thus the railroad was in an excellent position to reject any agreement short of total capitulation by the striking men. Although Debs was instrumental in bringing out the brakemen and switchmen on 23 March, their sympathy strike was ineffective in closing down the line. By 29 March the Burlington replaced a majority of even these new strikers.[86] So complete was the defeat that Debs later could comment: "I do not expect ever to see another strike of engineers and firemen."[87]

Debs's role in the leadership of the strike was, in public at least, limited.

The constitutional changes inaugurated at the 1885 convention centered organizational power in the office of the grand master and, as Sargent repeatedly stated, even he played a subordinate role to Arthur of the Engineers.[88] As a supporting figure, however, Debs consistently lent his considerable prestige to the policies outlined by Sargent and Arthur. He supported Sargent's opposition to the Knights as he did Sargent's and Arthur's suppression of the Santa Fe strikers. Indeed, he cosigned with Sargent every important strike circular issued by the Brotherhood that year. In his report on the strike Sargent thanked Debs and another official for their assistance and publicly associated them with his position in the intra-union factional fighting: "They were always with me, and without them I would have lacked the courage to have withstood the darts of my adversaries."[89]

Many years later Debs claimed that he was powerless during 1888 and suffered from the unified opposition of both Sargent and Arthur in his desire for a more militant stance.[90] In part, Debs's recollections on this point seem accurate. In the early days of the strike, prior to Judge Gresham's ruling, Debs expressed private criticism of the strike leadership. After a dinner with his son on 10 March, Daniel Debs wrote to his daughter Emma that Eugene "thinks the strike is lost for the strikers and as he says for lack of right management. He is confident that he would have carried it through successfully if he had been at the head of it in place of Arthur and Sargent."[91]

Although limited, Debs had not been exactly powerless during 1888. As he himself indicated, even Arthur and Sargent wanted him to conduct the daily affairs of the strike, as much to free them to control the negotiations as in recognition of Debs's unparalleled popularity with railroad workers of every political coloration.[92] Both recognized, moreover, that the only man who could receive a hearing from the Knights of Labor or convince the switchmen to join the strike was Debs. Yet Debs did not use this acknowledged influence to press his disagreements with the course of the strike.

In part, the choices opened to Debs appeared to him too stark. While he had serious disagreements with Arthur and Sargent, he refused to embrace what he saw as the explosive and even anarchistic attitude of many in the rank-and-file opposition. He shared their anger and to an extent had changed his thinking, as they had, in response to capitalism's hardening edge. But Debs still retained a basic belief in the value of structure and hierarchy and in the concept of leaders of labor meeting in arbitration with the leaders of capital. Debs avoided an open break with the brotherhoods for another reason. He hoped that if nothing else a federation of all railway workers would emerge from the strike that would assure future labor cooperation. Federation, he hoped, would provide the necessary new leadership without destroying the old and, thus paradoxically, create a new group without risking the permanent dismemberment of the older ones.

These conflicting attitudes permeated the one vehicle Debs did control for expressing his opinions on the strike—the editorials in the *Locomotive Firemen's Magazine*. Early in the strike, at the time he had dinner with his father, Debs's public position was quite tempered and expressed none of the misgivings Daniel mentioned. Debs placed the origins of the strike in the unsatisfactory negotiations with Potter in 1886 and stressed that the strike was a last resort, the result of a two-year wait for justice. Debs specified that the problem was caused by the "managers of the system" who spent those two years denying their employees "honest pay for honest work. . . belittling them . . . denying them consideration . . . [of] grievances." The men struck, then, as an ultimate defense of their basic integrity as men and as citizens. As Debs expressed it, "Their rights and their manhood were at stake, and they would yield nothing that could, by any possible construction, be regarded as conceding what was justly their due—and whatever may be the final result, the men will have maintained their integrity and will have demonstrated that their courage was equal to their convictions."[93]

In placing responsibility with the managers of the railroad—and not the owners—Debs revealed another aspect of his thought. For in that same April issue, he strongly attacked those legislators who, angered by the greedy manipulations of the railroad corporations, sought legislation to limit their operations. Scorning the idea that railroad owners were public enemies, Debs argued that the roads were built by "philanthropists for the sole purpose of advancing the welfare of others, regardless of the interests of its investors." He also pointed out that any reduction in railroad profits would tax the workingman as much, if not more, than the railroad itself.[94] Once again, Debs attempted to fuse contradictory themes. In tones reminiscent of his earlier veneration of McKeen, Debs reaffirmed his belief in the railroad corporation as a major agent of civilization and chose not to explore the analysis offered by others within the Brotherhood such as the Santa Fe strikers. Although recognizing that the major issues concerned wages and work conditions, he stressed the indignity of the affront to the men by the managers. Ultimately, Debs remained convinced that the large issues in the strike would only be resolved by the whole community, working people as well as others, when they banded together in their common identity as citizen-producers at the ballot box.[95]

But the Burlington experience did mark a critical turning point for Debs in at least one important area. It forced him to reconsider the nature of worker solidarity and that in turn would lead over the next years to a more complete reinterpretation of the meaning of manhood and community.

Debs emerged from the strike convinced that a federation of all workers was essential, and he demanded a higher degree of group loyalty than ever before. Scabs in general he now characterized as having "no more conscience than a tarantala [*sic*],"[96] but he reserved his bitterest venom for the Order of Railway Conductors who, under the leadership of Calvin S. Wheaton and William P. Daniels, had publicly supported the Burlington officials during the strike. In a widely distributed circular Wheaton proudly announced that his members "ran engines, fired engines, acted as pilots, and performed police duty" for the railroad. The conductors, Wheaton noted with pleasure, "seemed to vie with each other in showing their loyalty in this time of trouble, and tendered their services when needed."[97]

The conduct of these workers infuriated Debs. He accused them of cringing before the corporation and, in an unprecedented statement, urged a small group within the Order who supported the strike to organize in opposition. The actions of Wheaton and Daniels placed them outside the bonds of fraternity, Debs asserted, for "when a conductor takes the place of another man who is seeking to obtain fair pay he is wanting in those essentials of manhood universally recognized among honorable men."[98] Dissenters among the Firemen received equally harsh treatment. When some during that summer expressed resentment at the continual appeals for funds to support the Burlington strikers and suggested that they take whatever settlement possible, Debs lashed out at them. They were "the camp followers of the armies of progress and independence; the Esaus, selling their birthrights for pottage." Such men had "no higher ideal of life than is embodied in rations."[99]

This new emphasis on labor solidarity provides the key to understanding Debs's development during the Burlington strike. In a fashion that had always been implicit in the idea of the citizen-producer, but that Debs had earlier shied away from, he now could unequivocally announce that in the struggles of all working people lay the preservation of traditional American values. Without labor unity, the basis of the culture's dignity and integrity would disintegrate. In January 1889 he endorsed for the first time without reservation the Knights of Labor; the order, he now asserted, "is modern—and it is American. It sounded a key-note. It recognized certain great fundamental facts—the independence and sovereignty of the American citizen." At the same time he announced his support of strikes as a necessary weapon and endorsed the boycott as a tactic that could develop labor's cohesion.[100]

The reaction of the Burlington officials, and their close association with the ubiquitous Gresham, gave Debs a glimmer of the true nature of corporate capitalism. Prophetically he warned working people that in the future they could expect to see federal troops called in to break strikes under the guise of protecting the mails. Debs found it inconceivable that this "shot-gun" policy should be seriously discussed in a country "where every working man is a sovereign citizen, the equal before the law of every other citizen." Workers must therefore judge carefully candidates for election if only, Debs hoped, to assure the fact that it was "too early to Russianize America—too early to displace the ballot box by the cartridge box."[101]

Not surprisingly, then, for those who had followed Debs's editorials, he rested his newfound defense of the strike and the importance of labor solidarity on an appeal to the traditional rights of the American citizen. "The strike," he preached in a moving editorial in June 1888, "is the weapon of the oppressed, of men capable of appreciating justice and having the courage to resist wrong and contend for principle. The Nation had for its cornerstone a strike." Raising the revolutionary banner of the citizen-producer, Debs argued that the new corporate power threatened the values of all in nineteenth-century America. When a newspaper at the behest of the corporation urged a worker to accept the company's offer rather than suffer deprivation for principle, more than that individual's manhood was at stake. All of society would suffer, as the corporations "trample upon the divine declaration 'that all men are created equal,' as pagans trample upon the cross." Attacking that narrow definition of manhood, Debs insisted that if "the dollar is to be everything," forcing society to bow to its power, then by definition "the corporation," as it has the greatest resources, "is to rule, and workingmen, with their faces in the dust, are to serve. The corporation idea" expects employees to "worship with pagan submissiveness the golden image they set up" and eventually hopes to restructure all of society in that image. In this battle the workingman obviously fought for much more than just his immediate interests.

Unfortunately, Debs acknowledged, "all too often this Nebuchadnezzaran idea is correct." Some men are weak, even "effeminate," and yield to the offerings of the new cultural masters. But there are others, Debs stressed, who would not, who were "the salt of the earth," and who would lead the struggle against encroachments of their traditional rights. For these men understood that "the right never did succeed without a strike, and while arrogant injustice throws down the gauntlet and challenges the right to conflict, strikes will come, come by virtue of irrevocable laws, destined to have a wider sweep and greater power as men advance in intelligence and independence."[102]

The Burlington strike was lost, but Debs had learned much from it. The solidarity of labor dominated his thought, and he had come some distance in freeing himself from a one-dimensional view of America's tradition. In discovering this sharp edge as regards manhood, harmony, and community, Debs illuminated for himself and others a path to a fuller understanding of the corporation—and to a far stronger critique of industrial capitalism than conceivable even shortly before the strike. With fervor and renewed hope, then, Eugene Debs turned toward the federation of all railway men as a new defense of traditional rights against the omnipresent tentacles of corporate power.

THE MEANING OF CITIZENSHIP: 1890–1900

If we could but destroy the money monopoly,
land monopoly, and the rest of them, all would
be different. You say labor organizations do not
discuss politics. I would have labor unify at the
polls and vote for an independent people's party.
Some say politics mean destruction to labor
organizations, but the reverse is the fact. There
are questions I would like to see labor interest
themselves in. Their conditions are like a cancer,
you can cover it with a poultice but the cancer
continues to spread. You must apply the knife
and root it out if you expect relief.

Eugene V. Debs, 1894

As Eugene Debs emerged from the Burlington strike in 1889, both his public image and self-understanding were substantially different than they had appeared even four years earlier. Increasingly hailed as "Gene" by workers across the country, Debs's ceaseless organizing activities (especially after he left Hulman's in 1880) and his editing of the *Locomotive Firemen's Magazine* elevated him into a position of growing national importance. The Burlington strike confirmed that prominence and, even as many railroad men disagreed with his specific policies, marked a critical turning point in his own conscious motivation as well. The meaning of citizenship, he now began to understand, had two edges. If one served to confirm the *status quo* in a gush of celebratory (and deferential) patriotism, the other called on Americans to assert their traditional rights to oppose the destructive social and economic effects of a maturing capitalist society.

As this major transition engaged his energies and engendered a reorientation of his labor work, Debs's relations with his Terre Haute neighbors, nonetheless, remained static. He was absent more, of course, and this led him to refuse renomination as master of Vigo Lodge in 1887. But he still occupied a dominant place among local railroad workers. Yet the Debs of national reputation treated Terre Haute as a special preserve, a respite from the contentious problems of the outer world. He continued to serve as the Democratic party's labor spokesman and made frequent appearances at local social and cultural events. Still close with William Riley McKeen and Herman Hulman, Debs did not publicly aid or support the city's workers during their twenty strikes between 1877 and 1894—despite the fact that he helped organize a majority of the city's labor unions.[1]

If Debs desired Terre Haute to remain his "beloved little community," others offered a sharply different conception. In the aftermath of the 1877 strike the business community continued to coalesce, recognized its own particular self-interest, and grew less hesitant to use its considerable local power in dealing with workers. As the city's population increased by some 40 percent between 1880 and 1900 and expanded further east from the Wabash River, local investors discovered important new business opportunities in that urban growth. Corporations formed to provide the city with water service, electricity, and both intra- and interurban transportation.[2] During the 1880s the telephone came to Terre Haute, with service as far as Indianapolis, and Chauncey Rose's old hotel was purchased by local investors, including two of Debs's brothers-in-law, with the intention of making it a showplace of the business community's progress and power.[3] In all these ventures local businessmen, in alliance with nonresident investors, capitalized these companies and in the process strengthened their own distinct community of interest.

The city's greatest economic excitement came with the discovery of oil underneath the streets of the downtown business district in 1889. As they had once expected of coal, Terre Haute's "best people" now saw oil as the vehicle to lift the city out of its economic stagnation. In a perfectly madcap fashion the business community tore up its very foundation in its search for the elusive fluid. The Guarantee Oil and Gas Company owned the first well—termed a "perfect gusher" by a local paper[4]—and its directors were a who's who of the local elite. McKeen, Hulman, Josephus Collett, and D. W. Minshall were the most powerful of the fifteen co-investors. During the two-year "oil fever," twenty additional companies formed, some with outside funding, and also included men in the lower ranks of the local business community such as John Heinl, a flower and greenhouse merchant and Debs's brother-in-law. Despite the warnings of an itinerant Knights of Labor organizer concerning the perils of leasing or selling plots of land to such giants as the Standard Oil Company, Terre Hauteans rushed to do just that with the result that the price of land doubled by 1891.[5]

As with coal, however, the boom was short-lived. The original gusher was the only well to produce and even that evaporated quickly. With the exception of the regionally successful Highland Steel Company, organized in 1901, Terre Haute remained during these years the quiet city in the rural sea it had always been.[6]

But the oil excitement and continued urban growth did produce two discernible results. These shared investment opportunities forged stronger links of identity within the business community and provided the context in which that identity expanded from a merely local to a national allegiance. If in 1877 McKeen was one of the few local businessmen with significant ties to major American corporations, by 1900 such contacts were far more numerous among the elite. The original local investors in the community's water, electric, and transportation companies had, by the turn of the century, sold majority control of these concerns at considerable personal profit to Chicago and Boston corporations. These local entrepreneurs, however, still retained important investments whose continued success depended less upon local conditions than on the decisions of imported managers responsive to the directives issued in distant board rooms.[7]

This change was already evident by the late 1880s. Even as Daniel Debs lauded the elite's renovation of the Terre Haute House as "great progress for the City,"[8] a local criminal trial underscored the new tone. Michael Tonhey, an active participant in the bitter strike against the Terre Haute Car Works in 1887, was charged with felonious assault for fighting with a scab. Assisting the prosecution was John T. Scott, a major stockholder in the Car Works who, but a decade earlier, had proudly defended the railroad men in their strike. Now, however, Scott scornfully dismissed defense witness Henry Bligh's definition of a scab "as a man who would turn against his mother." When Bligh attempted to explain Tonhey's motivation, stating that the scab "came here to take bread out of other people's mouths," Scott sarcastically inquired whether that was what all strikers called honest work. Finally, in some consternation, Bligh asserted his and Tonhey's basic moral defense: the scab in question "is a stranger and he came here and took a citizen's job." In a world increasingly dominated by the desire to maximize profit, Bligh's appeal to both biblical and democratic traditions merited only Scott's sneering silence.[9]

As Scott's actions indicated, much had changed in the decade following 1877. If Terre Haute's workers remained more quiescent than workers in other communities,[10] the business community honed its self-interest and was more willing to intervene directly to defend and expand it. Appeals to communal harmony faded, and the business leaders, united in the Terre Haute Businessmen's Association, now avidly discussed the local and national aspects of "the labor question."[11]

Publicly, Debs paid little attention to these developments. Engrossed in other matters, the ties of personal friendship and family network to the business community caused him to hesitate. Perhaps he could sense the basic conflict then evolving in his mind, for in a short time the economic and political reality of his native city, as of the larger society, would clash with the implications of his new and more aggressive understandings of manhood and citizenship.

4

Transcending the Brotherhoods

"THE SPIRIT OF FRATERNITY [is] abroad in the land," Eugene Debs pro-claimed in the journal, *United Labor*, in August 1890. Despite "the mad chase for the 'almighty dollar'" and the "debasing greed for gain which pre-eminently distinguishes the age, there are men, thousands of them, whose hearts throb with divine aspirations for the welfare of their fellowmen; whose sympathies never congeal; whose tongues are never still when grand, noble words are to be spoken for the poor, the friendless and the oppressed." Fraternity, Debs insisted, encompassed fellowship, "a stronger word than friendship," for it demands "brotherly love," an acknowledgment of "the ties and bonds and obligations [that] large souled and large hearted men recognize as essentials to human hap-piness." This spirit underscored the old truth that "'man shall not live by bread alone,' that is to say the mind, the soul, the spirit, one or three, as men may choose, is to be fed—bread will not suffice"; and it asserts a powerful "faith in the triumph of human nature over 'the world, the flesh and the devil,' the setting up of the Kingdom of God on earth; faith in the fatherhood of God and the brotherhood of man; a profound and active in-terest in the welfare of men." While this faith promised to "eventually restore men to their lost estate," its believers "cherish no hallucinations," for "it is not utopian." However, "it is iconoclastic," for its spirit "has touched the body politic" and serves as a "quiet but ceaseless protest against isolation, endorsing the fact that man is his brother's keeper; the fact of the interdependence of men."[1]

With these words Debs announced to one and all the meaning for him of the Burlington experience. The acrimonious and fratricidal conduct of labor during that strike, his complicity in it as well as the collaboration between business and the federal judiciary illumined his earlier assumptions with a startling clarity. No longer would he define working people as "crude material," inherently limited by "the putrid mind of debauchery." Fraternity, he had come to understand, stressed instead the "human possibilities" and "scouts the idea of total depravity." The lessons of that strike taught him something else as well. He no longer pitted manhood against brotherhood, and no longer might the ultimate value of that evocative phrase manhood find its definition in "that absolute independence" in "the direction of one's own affairs without interference." Mutual dependence, he now understood, did not weaken men or make them "effeminate" or "squaw-like." Rather, reliance of one upon the other allowed the development of each individual's potential, as it did that of the community as well.

When understood in contrast to the privileged cooperation among industrial corporations and between them and the federal government, this interpretation gave renewed hope for the revival of harmony and community as viable social goals. For in grasping ever more firmly the millennial basis of American citizenship, Debs embraced a vision of his society even more fundamental than its Revolutionary heritage. In 1890 he might have said, following John Winthrop almost three centuries earlier: "We must be knit together in this work as one man. We must entertain each other in brotherly affection; we must be willing to abridge ourselves of our superfluities, for the supply of others' necessities." In that bond, in that common fraternal purpose, lay not only his society's ultimate prosperity but also increasingly for Debs, as it was for Winthrop, a most profound choice between spiritual life and death as a people.[2]

Debs was accurate in stressing that this social vision was not utopian, knowing as he did that he drew on a deeply American tradition. But in specific interpretations of that tradition, its iconoclastic nature would prove troublesome. Manufacturing and railroad executives had long shown that they were more interested in "hands" to staff their enterprises than in the qualities of citizenship. The recent strike had also shown how difficult it would be to translate the power of fraternity into concrete organizational tactics within the labor movement. Even Debs himself would not find this process easy. His personality did not always encourage such feeling and, as with so many other working people, he too was in transition. The power of his earlier commitments could still on occasion cloud his new vision.

Yet the period immediately following 1888 remained an optimistic time for Debs. Despite years of strife with the Brotherhood of Engineers —years in which P. M. Arthur prohibited engineers from holding dual membership in the Firemen and refused Debs permission to address his convention in 1885 on this issue[3]—prospects for better relations were promising. The Burlington strike revealed strong opposition within the Engineers that would serve as a basis of future organizing. Responding to this pressure, and prodded further by both Samuel Gompers and Debs, Arthur even expressed interest in a federation of all railroad workers.

There were other signs as well. The Union Pacific men in Denver, Colorado, had long expressed interest in federation, and Debs had unofficially supported their efforts in 1886 to explore the basis for such a system.[4] The firemen and engineers among them, in turn, organized sentiment within their brotherhoods. Despite the tension with the Engineer officials, Debs had long granted that brotherhood primacy. In his editorials Debs had taught his readers well, stressing as late as 1892 that, through education and self-improvement, firemen could rise to become engineers and perhaps even master mechanics.[5] If the Engineers endorsed federation, Debs might be able to turn those long-taught lessons toward checking the growing conservative sentiment among firemen that his editorials had originally encouraged. And such developments would go far in liberating Debs himself from a subservient attitude that now felt awkward.

But the key to Debs's optimism lay in the nature of the federation he proposed. Despite his newfound enthusiasm for the Knights of Labor, Debs did not advocate the form of industrial unionism practiced by that order. Rather than organizing railroad workers of all levels of skill into one union, Debs deplored any "blending" of current organizations into a single group and proposed a federation based on existing craft divisions, which preserved the prerogatives of the various national officers. There was, however, an iconoclastic note here as well. Debs grounded this proposal for federation in the proposition that, as working people produced the wealth of the nation, they shared a common interest in securing a fair and just return. Extending his analysis beyond the railroad industry, Debs suggested that all workers should federate, as it would lead to "better citizenship" and assure "the sympathy, and at least the moral support of all" for any union in time of crisis. Coupled with his repeated attacks on the notion of a "labor aristocracy,"[6] Debs indicated that he diverged sharply—if at times contradictorily—with the prevailing opinions of other brotherhood officials as well as important segments of the rank and file.

Yet Debs hoped these differences that he sensed would not prove critical. The lessons of the Burlington strike were so clear and the appeal of producer thought so powerful that Debs hoped that his efforts at federation might transcend potential contradictions and unify the labor movement.

During June and July 1888 railway workers held meetings in New York and St. Louis to discuss proposals for future federation. In three of the five railroad brotherhoods (Engineers, Firemen, and Switchmen), strong sentiment favored federation, and even Arthur stated that he would follow the democratic decision of his next convention. On the surface, at least, it appeared that most railway workers had learned that federation was the great lesson of the recent strike.[7]

The Firemen met first at Atlanta in the fall of 1888. In his opening report, Frank P. Sargent endorsed the idea of federation and Arthur, invited to address the meeting, expressed no criticism. On the seventh day of the convention the Ways and Means Committee, chaired by W. F. Hynes of Denver, submitted its report on federation. In its preamble the report urged federation as the one means to abridge a conspiracy "that is eating into the very vitals of our liberties, and threatens the destruction of the Republic." Drawing on an analogy with the federal government, the report argued that the individual brotherhoods, like the states, would be independent but in time of crisis could call on the support of their fellows, as the states can the central government. Specifically, the report recommended a federation that decentralized the power to call strikes as much as feasible.[8]

On each railroad line or system, a Board of Federation would be established, consisting of three representatives of each federated brotherhood who would also be members of their individual brotherhood's Board of Grievance. When a dispute occurred, the brotherhood affected would first attempt settlement through its own procedures. If that failed, the grievance would be submitted to the Board of Federation. If still unsuccessful, the board would refer it back to the brotherhood for action with the assurance of financial support in case of a strike call. In order to call a sympathy strike of all other federated organizations on the line, the board must approve the specific proposal by a two-thirds vote. Thus, while the plan provided for a concentration of labor's power and kept the decision-making close to the men who intimately knew the conditions, it also provided for an intricate system of checks to prevent precipitous strike action by a few.

Although the report itself carried with little opposition, disagreement arose over the makeup of the special committee that would present this plan to the other brotherhoods. The composition of this committee assumed critical importance, as it was empowered to "make such concessions and modifications . . . as may be required to secure the approval of the other organizations." The delegates defeated a motion to elect the committee from their body and instead appointed the existing grand officers.[9] The Switchmen and Brakemen met in early October and voted to support the Firemen's plan,[10] and all attention then turned toward the Engineers, meeting in convention at Richmond, Virginia.

Arthur faced pressure from numerous sides to end the policy of isolation. Gompers twice wrote him that October, urging him to join the AFL. Hoping ultimately to attract all the railway brotherhoods to his organization, Gompers emphasized that the labor movement now jealously protected individual trade union autonomy.[11] Pressure of another sort came from the Firemen, whose grand officers were all present at the convention. Sargent and Debs hoped that the Engineers would approve federation, thus immeasurably strengthening its power. Debs, however, remained skeptical of Arthur's intentions. He unwittingly told a Pinkerton informant—apparently a friend of long-standing—that his current support of Arthur was not sincere, and he threatened to help impeach Arthur if he vetoed federation or continued aid to the Burlington strikers.[12] Finally, a faction within the Brotherhood itself pressed for federation, especially the Burlington strikers and other western members.

But the Richmond convention rejected federation. Aided by the opposition of the more conservative eastern engineers, Arthur adroitly manipulated parliamentary procedures to ensure its defeat. Knowingly or not, he was also aided by the same Pinkerton operative who had befriended Debs in removing a radical grand officer and in protecting his own position. Under Arthur's direction, moreover, the convention agreed to end the Burlington strike without consultation with the Firemen, and the delegates refused to rescind the laws passed in 1884 and 1885 that barred Firemen from membership.[13]

His suspicions borne out, Debs stepped up his criticisms of Arthur while simultaneously he prepared for a federation without the Engineers.[14] In June 1889 the grand officers of the Firemen, Switchmen, and Brakemen met in Chicago to inaugurate the new organization. Like Debs, the other brotherhood leaders felt that federation would eliminate most strikes and improve relations between labor and capital. The conference resulted in the formation of the Supreme Council of the United Order of Railway Employees, with Sargent as president; Frank Sweeny, of the Switchmen, vice-president; and Ed O'Shea, of the Brakemen, secretary-treasurer.[15] As Debs explained, the "extreme demands" of the now unified workers were in fact quite simple. All they desired were "fair pay for honest work, and fair treatment at the hands of their employers. With fair pay they can rear their families in respectability, to lives of usefulness and honor. With fair treatment they can maintain their independence and maintain the dignity of American citizenship."[16]

The Chicago meeting established a federation that contrasted sharply with the plan endorsed by the delegates to the Firemen's convention. Rejecting the system plan, it created a national or associated scheme of federation. Power was concentrated at the top, among the grand officers. Other than filing a grievance, the rank and file had little control over the procedure. Only the Supreme Council could call or cancel strikes, and it would consider a strike request only if it already had the approval of the grand officers of the affected brotherhood. This program, which Debs supported, bypassed the rank and file and threatened to destroy Debs's hopes for unity in yet another bitter factional fight among the firemen.[17]

The first hint of trouble came in October 1889. Meeting at Denver, delegates to the Firemen's Board of Adjustment on the Union Pacific line condemned *"wholly and without reserve"* the actions of their grand officers at the Chicago conference. Led by Jackson Hoover and Frank Walton, the Union Pacific firemen argued that the Atlanta convention had provided for *home rule* on each system of railways, thereby assuring those most directly interested at least a semblance of a controlling voice in their own affairs; at the same time, the Grand, or General, Federal Board could check any rash tendencies, as its decisions, in all cases, would be final. The centralization of power, they further argued, abridged "the first prerogative of American citizenship," while the provision allowing any two grand officers from the same brotherhood to veto a strike call provided a *"broad opening for bribery and treachery."* As to the Knights of Labor, Jackson and Walton wrote, the present constitution all but barred them from joining. In short, they concluded, the current Supreme Council tended "to widen the breach between organized labor rather than draw them closer" and removed the final court of appeals so far from the rank and file "as to appear in its obscurity like a powerful throne, conceived in the minds of men for the glorification of the minority, rather than for the emancipation of the majority."[18]

Debs's response to this critique, couched as it was in terms of traditional American liberties, generally avoided the specific issues raised. Ultimately he rested his defense on his loyalty "to the authority of the Brotherhood of Locomotive Firemen" and claimed his opponents were factionalists intent on destroying both the Brotherhood and the Supreme Council. Referring to one of his antagonists as "this wonderful literary freak," Debs accused the Denver delegates of unbridled radicalism and of desiring strikes despite the "untold ills which strikes inflict"—an argument in sharp conflict with an earlier editorial he wrote rejecting these same sentiments when they were suggested by the corporation. He defended the Chicago conference, stressing that the Atlanta convention gave the grand officers full powers *"in all things* necessary to effect federation" and pointed to the recent vote of the Firemen along the Santa Fe system that supported his actions. Finally, in a classic piece of practiced illogic and *ad hominem* attack, Debs argued that the very existence of the Denver meeting proved the reality of home rule; and then, in a subsequent editorial, he called the Union Pacific men a "miserable faction" similar to those within the Knights who, by attacking the regime of Terence Powderly, attempted to destroy that organization. With bitter invective Debs brought his full power and prestige to bear against a rank-and-file critique that championed the role of the individual within a large bureaucratic organization.[19]

Although both the Switchmen and Brakemen officially supported Debs,[20] the battle continued to rage throughout the spring of 1890. In March Walton responded to Debs's assertion that the Brotherhood would not allow factionalism. "Who," Walton asked, "composes the Brotherhood? . . . Does the Brotherhood consist of the rank and file, or simply of a few Grand Officers?" He charged that Debs's reply had consisted of "unmerited sarcastic abuse from first to last." Persisting in his position, Debs responded by arguing that the rank and file, through elected delegates who then elect the officers, compose the Brotherhood.[21]

Meanwhile, a new correspondent, who raised a highly sensitive issue, entered the battle. T. P. O'Rourke, an occasional contributor to the *Locomotive Firemen's Magazine* for almost a decade, wrote to criticize "a certain system of hero worship" fostered by "some" of the grand officers. Saying that he first noticed it at the 1884 convention, he suggested clear evidence of it existed again at Atlanta. By giving the officers power to amend the by-laws, the delegates, at the urging of those same officers, relinquished their legislative duties and became "passive neuters"; at the same time, this encouraged the grand officers to become "egotistic, jealous of interference and furious at criticism." Turning to federation, O'Rourke argued that since the Chicago plan differed so greatly from the Atlanta resolution, the grand officers must obtain approval from the next convention: "You have made a *Treaty*," O'Rourke asserted, "which does not become Law on your mere *ipse dixit*."[22]

Once again, Debs's response was less than complete. He totally identified his position with that of the national officers and accused O'Rourke of mounting a full-scale attack on the very existence of the Brotherhood. He defended the power granted the grand officers at the Atlanta convention and grew livid and irrational over O'Rourke's charge of "hero-worship."[23] Sensing the potency of the charge, O'Rourke returned to the theme three months later. Reviewing the issues between them, O'Rourke charged that Debs rarely answered criticism either with reason or with fact, but rather employed "a slop bucket filled with filth." He then delivered a major indictment of Debs's leadership as editor and spokesman for the Brotherhood:

> It is scarcely necessary to go outside the pages of the *Magazine* to prove that "hero-worship" is encouraged and fostered. Here we see the "faithful" lauded to the skies, patted on the back and praised for being good boys. . . . Does any sane man imagine for a moment that there is any other purpose behind all this than a desire to pose as a Sir Anthony Absolute, to be recognized as the great "I Am," and

reverenced accordingly. Is not one class entitled to just as much consideration as the other, and should they not be allowed to express their opinions in the *Magazine* without being smeared with filth by the editorial *yahoo* that presides over it?[24]

Debs's response once again raised more questions than it answered. While he claimed that the publication of O'Rourke's letters indicated his commitment to free speech, he based his argument on the belief that, as editor of the *Locomotive Firemen's Magazine*, it was his to use as he thought best. As he told O'Rourke, in a tone that confirmed O'Rourke's major critique: "To correct errors, to crush falsehood, to overthrow subterfuges and coverts, to counteract malign influences, to explore conspiracies and defeat them, becomes a duty which, however unpleasant, cannot be ignored."[25] Despite important new understandings, Debs remained impressed with his prominence and self-righteously unaware of his own motives. Vain and egocentric when attacked, Debs needed public approval, and this attribute ultimately led him to support uncritically policies he had already begun to question.

This bitter fight reverberated throughout the Brotherhood. While Debs received some support, many of the letters to the journal from members of the order not immediately identifiable with the Union Pacific men were critical of Debs. Even more correspondents thought both groups lacking in fraternal feeling and urged the next convention to take up the issue of federation again.[26] Prior to that convention, however, two important meetings occurred that eliminated the need for a showdown on this issue at the 1890 San Francisco convention.

At the second annual convention of the Supreme Council, held in Chicago on 16–17 June 1890, the twelve representatives attempted to smooth over the bitter factional fighting of the past six months. They announced with pleasure the admission of the Brotherhood of Railway Conductors, led by Grand Chief George W. Howard, and were hopeful that the rival Order of Railway Conductors, which had recently announced as a labor organization under the new leadership of E. E. Clark, would soon join as well.[27] Appealing to the "brethren . . . in the interests of harmony and good will," the Supreme Council stressed the necessity of unity and pointed to the successful settlement, without strikes, of a number of grievances during the past year. But the appeals to harmony appeared disingenuous in the face of a resolution that required every member of the council to "oppose the so-called local or system federation" and to recognize the council "as now organized as the only legitimate federation of railway employees."[28] As expected, this resolution produced another wave of protest from the Union Pacific men.

Rather than conduct the battle through the journal as in the past, Debs went to Denver in the last week of June to meet with the Union Pacific men. At a meeting of all railway workers on the 25th and the Firemen's own meeting on the 26th, Debs defended national over system federation despite the critiques of Hoover, Walton, and Hynes. He stressed the need for unity, especially to defeat an aristocratic feeling within labor's own ranks, and insisted that the Supreme Council took the best possible action based on its more complete knowledge of the circumstances. Whatever else either side said remains unreported, but this Denver meeting resulted in a cessation of hostilities between Debs and the Union Pacific men.[29] He did not win them to his position, as they continued to criticize the national plan of federation,[30] but the bitter animosity ended. Perhaps Debs convinced them that national federation was the most for which they could hope, given the political composition of the grand officers on the Supreme Council. Whatever he said, it was effective. The Union Pacific leaders were shortly singing Debs's praise in the pages of their magazine. Within two months of that June meeting, major articles by Debs appeared in the pages of *United Labor*, a journal controlled by the leaders of the Union Pacific Board of Federation.[31]

The role of Debs in this factional dispute with the more militant members of the Brotherhood is important for what it suggests about him as he approached what he thought was the apex of his career. A man of considerable ego, he was at times unscrupulous in his attacks upon opponents. His most consistent defense was to wrap himself in the authority of the Brotherhood whose best interests, he claimed, only he could interpret; and he maintained this attitude even in the face of serious contradictions between his current and past positions.

When Walton, for example, criticized the Supreme Council for dismissing the Knights of Labor because they were not yet fully organized, he in part blamed the leadership of the Firemen for this, as the Knights had been practically destroyed on the Reading and the Gould systems due to "the antagonistic or neutral attitude" of the other brotherhoods. In response, Debs did not acknowledge his support of that earlier policy or recount his own more recently altered ideas. Rather, he insisted that the Knights could join the federation if they desired—this despite his understanding that the Supreme Council had effectively precluded their participation, as it had the Brotherhood of Telegraphers, another national union with members in other industries than just the railroad.[32] For Debs, then, the demands of his own ego—especially the desire to appear consistent and to wield unquestioned authority—were partially responsible for his attitude toward the Union Pacific men.

But personal, emotional needs were not the only explanation of this conduct. Debs remained unsympathetic with any movement aimed at increasing rank-and-file control. He felt the grand officers possessed more knowledge and sensitivity than members-at-large and, despite new ideas concerning the labor movement, he still acted within the framework of an older model. As he told Walton, the rank and file's task was to elect the Brotherhood's officers, upon whom fell the duty of guiding the order. Their role complete, the members were then expected to retire until the next election of convention delegates.

This role allotted the rank and file points to yet another contradictory theme in Debs's thinking. As he increased his attacks upon the corporations for their destruction of traditional American liberties, and reinterpreted such concepts as individualism and manhood, Debs paradoxically continued to accept a major aspect of the corporate model as a guide for his own conduct within the Brotherhood. As American industrialists now insisted on their right to control the work process through the widespread use of management specialists, so, too, did Debs support the presence of labor "specialists" such as himself within the Brotherhood. At root, this contradiction stemmed from Debs's belief that only a strict defense of each brotherhood's autonomy could provide the basis of federation. This, in turn, meant complete support for the internal prerogatives and hierarchical structures of each set of grand officers.

Yet, ultimately, Debs was not as theoretically tied to trade union autonomy as were the other grand officers. His support of such a structure, while certainly not in conflict with his earlier positions, nonetheless rested more on his hopes for federation than it did in theory. To a considerable extent, Debs's critique of the corporation had altered his views more than he had publicly allowed. If federation worked, and the Supreme Council proved to be a useful organization, then perhaps the duality that marked his thought might never demand exploration.

Oddly, however, Debs remained popular even with many in the militant minority of the rank and file. He could criticize "the Spread Eagle enthusiasm" of the Burlington strikers that had led the rank and file to reject a proffered settlement that the grand officers "would gladly have taken up and felt it a victory."[33] Yet Debs must have been able to articulate forcefully, if piecemeal, the implications of his critique of the corporation. The Denver meeting with the Union Pacific men suggests his ability to convince his bitterest opponents that they ultimately shared a common goal, even if they disagreed with his tactics. Perhaps these men understood from Debs's talk something of his own restiveness at continuing his work within the imposed limitations of his earlier public career.

Following the Burlington strike, then, Debs was a confused and confusing labor leader. Perhaps more at ease and more respected by the militants than any other grand officer, he nonetheless strictly adhered to a plan of federation that left the rank and file almost powerless. He encouraged open revolt among both the Conductors and Engineers, yet fiercely defended the Sargent administration within the pages of the *Locomotive*

Firemen's Magazine. He had invested much in the success of the Supreme Council, but, even before that issue was resolved, his developing political analysis of the effects of corporate capitalism would force a serious break between this view and that of the majority in his brotherhood.

If Debs had difficulties with a vaguely defined "left wing" among the Firemen—those who favored a decentralized program of federation and a more assertive articulation of labor's position vis-à-vis capital — his relations with the more conservative members of the union proved even more explosive. This group of men had learned well the lessons presented in Debs's editorials before the Burlington strike, had deeply embraced his emphasis on harmony, and had found little in their recent experience to lead them to alter these beliefs. The delicate balance between these two tendencies, neatly straddled by Debs ever since the 1885 convention, met its most severe test in the years immediately following the collapse of the Burlington strike. Debs and only a few of his confidants knew that his future association with the Brotherhood depended in large part upon the resolution of this growing schism.

Tension over the proper attitude toward the Engineers heightened this struggle. The bitter relations between Debs and Arthur had exploded anew when, after refusing to join the federation, Arthur attacked Debs while praising the other two grand officers of the Firemen. Unleashing a tirade of abuse and counterattack upon Arthur's career and politics, Debs urged his own brotherhood to change its name to include the locomotive engineers as well.[34] Although Debs was accurate in claiming that many firemen retained their membership in that Brotherhood even when they rose to become engineers, his proposal was tantamount to creating a dual union to compete with the Engineers. This instigated an explosive debate within the Firemen. Walton, just a few months prior to leading the Union Pacific men against Debs, supported him in this dispute and wondered at the "magic" that drew some to the Engineers. He exhorted the firemen to protect their "dignity and manhood" by refusing to capitulate to the aristocratic Arthur. A large percentage of those who wrote to the magazine, however, vehemently disagreed with Debs's proposal and argued that neither Arthur nor his Brotherhood had taken actions that warranted such steps. In response Debs insisted, sometimes in vitriolic tones, that the manhood and very principles of the Firemen were at stake, and he often implied that the writer was a coward, even unmanly, for disagreeing.[35]

The most serious attack on Debs's proposal came from W. S. Carter of Taylor, Texas. In early 1890 he agreed with those who argued that the Engineers had done nothing to deserve such action. Significantly, Carter expanded his critique and focused on Debs's conduct as a labor leader and political advocate. The Engineers would have joined a federation, Carter asserted, but for their "intense ill-feeling" toward Debs himself. In this they were justified, he continued, as for some years Debs had responded less with reason than with personal animosity and "injured feelings" toward Arthur. Some years ago, Carter remembered, at the suggestion of H. M. Hoxie, the general manager of the Gould system, Sargent warned Debs to lessen his criticism of the Engineers. This Debs had done until after the Burlington strike, Carter noted, and implied that his current course contradicted the official position of the Firemen. He then connected the renewed attacks upon the Engineers with Debs's recent political emphasis. The editor has become a dictator, Carter wrote, and "the Magazine is rapidly assuming the style of some political administrative organ." Rather than explaining to his brothers the roots of his political evolution inherent in his critique of conservative, craft-orientated labor leaders, Debs responded in his usual acerbic manner. He insulted Carter and asserted—without evidence—that a majority of the membership supported his position. Surprisingly, he made no mention at all of Carter's account of Hoxie's conversation with Sargent.[36]

Carter fired off another letter, calling Debs "'The Jack the Ripper' of American literature" and accused him of radical political tendencies that were at war with the spirit of the Brotherhood. Pointedly, he referred to an editorial of March 1886 in which Debs had extolled the interdependency between engineers and firemen and had urged all to avoid ill-feelings and prejudice. Carter noted somewhat sharply that Debs failed in that attitude at the moment. Debs, for his part, refused even to answer Carter this time.[37]

Although the Brotherhood of Locomotive Firemen eventually changed its name, that did not occur until the twentieth century, well after Debs had left the Brotherhood. In 1889 and 1890, despite his assertion to the contrary, Debs did not have the support of the membership. Many, as had Carter, understood that in his attack on Arthur, Debs raised political issues at odds with prevailing sentiment. Debs's insistent demand for labor unity and a more aggressive stance by working people could not be separated from his condemnation of "aristocratic" labor officials. This, in turn, forced Debs into a war with the words and implications of his earlier editorials. Much to his chagrin, he found that the majority in the Brotherhood still adhered to his earlier, less fractious vision. Most refused to follow him, and two lodges in Connecticut actually revolted, announcing that they would "not solicit subscriptions for the *Magazine*" until its political attitude changed.[38]

Debs persisted in his critical analysis of the labor movement and proceeded to alienate even more members. In the spring of 1889 he could still blame workers' ignorance for the refusal of many to join unions.[39] Ten months later, however, he insisted that this problem had more to do with the labor organizations themselves than with working people's deficiencies. Debs pointed out that common laborers, a growing segment of the work force, were not permitted to join any existing union (save the Knights of Labor), as they had neither the skill nor craft necessary for membership. While cautiously defending the trade union ("this is no reflection upon the organization of trades"), Debs vigorously praised the Knights for their efforts to organize all workers. To the dismay of many of the craft-oriented firemen, he also proclaimed this new organizing drive essential to the success of any plan of federation. Embracing the attitude that Jeremiah Grandison advanced at the Pittsburgh meeting almost a decade earlier, Debs offered a revised goal for labor: "All that labor has demanded [is] an honest distribution of the wealth that labor creates. Fair wages, a lesser number of hours for toil. The evaluation of the American idea of citizenship, home and family. Then the wielding of the ballot. Just laws, honest officials, a pure judiciary, the annihilation of trusts and monopolies—in a word, the reign of justice."[40]

Debs's linkage of traditional political rights with a more democratic economic system became the source of much controversy among his readers. Most would agree with the assertion that the central defense against the erosion of labor's dignity was the question of higher wages. Dispute arose over the manner in which Debs explored that idea, for, finally, Debs refused to reduce all questions concerning labor to one of wages; he sought to broaden the social impact of his culture's democratic political rhetoric. Workers were neither a commodity, one of many in the capitalist market place, that could be "bought" at the right price; nor were they simply political beings, unconcerned with the controlling economic structure of their society. In arguing that a dignified wage was the *sine qua non* of a participatory citizenship, Debs presented for the first time the outlines of the creative synthesis that would dominate his future concerns.

Despite growing opposition, this synthesis provided Debs with a powerful wedge in addressing a series of related questions in the five years following the Burlington strike. Debs intensified his criticism of such corporate leaders as Austin Corbin of the Pennsylvania Railroad for their attempts to "Russianize" American workers; and, to the shock of many readers, he simultaneously defended Alexander Berkman as a man of greater moral sensitivity than Henry C. Frick, the steel executive whom Berkman attempted to assassinate during the Homestead strike of 1892. He continued to attack corporation-sponsored insurance programs and the establishment of government boards of arbitration. Such boards would encourage the collaboration already evident between business and government, give further standing to national labor leaders, and undermine the self-reliance of the rank and file. Moreover, he now proclaimed, it was precisely the leaders of this rank and file, the "valiant *labor agitator*[s]," and not the grand officers, who were responsible for labor's advances. Debs still clung to a concept of "masterful men," but the model he now advanced, based on his own new political course, seemed to many readers both dangerous doctrine and additional evidence of Debs's egotism.[41]

In stressing this working-class self-reliance, a major aspect of earlier nineteenth-century labor ideology, Debs edged paradoxically close to a rejection of all reform schemes that relied on nonworkers. He characterized the question then popular in newspaper editorials and social commentaries—"What can we do for working people?"—as the height of condescension. Rather, he asserted, workers themselves, "if they are independent, self-respecting, self-reliant men," can "teach capitalists that they do not want and will not accept their guardianship. . . . Fidelity to obligation," he warned, "is not a one-sided affair."[42]

Debs was also critical of the middle-class Nationalist movement, what he called "the Yankee Doodleisms of the Boston savants," although he did enjoy Edward Bellamy's book, *Looking Backward*. Yet he detected in the movement, as in the book, a paternalistic attitude "which dwarfs out of sight the individual, while it indefinitely expands government control to absolutism."[43] He was also cool toward the Populist party through 1893. Debs disputed the Populist claim that its cause was one with the working class. He did not understand the distinction between an "agriculturist," a farmer who employed help, and one who worked for himself; and he dramatically pointed to anti-labor bills that Populist representatives supported to justify his position.[44] Socialism as well came under attack because its millennial promise conflicted with what Debs felt was the millennial reality of America—"a country of boundless resources capable of supporting a thousand millions of people, and this country is the new earth and the new heaven of workingmen, if they can be made to understand the fact."[45]

A sharp insistence on the individual responsibility and capability of a workingman in unison with his fellows to assert, define, and defend his own rights and needs formed the core of Debs's rejection of these programs. While this emphasis certainly stemmed from earlier nineteenth-century thought, Debs's new use of this older American ideal, his critics were quick to point out, all but demanded that workers adopt a staunch, principled opposition to their corporate employers. In asserting the power of fraternal unity based on an acceptance of individual responsibility, Debs sought to revitalize a more holistic view of man—a view, he felt, that was the ultimate cultural defense against the revolutionary values of corporate industrial society.

At times, however, Debs appeared confused about how exactly to present these new ideas. If in one mood, he might echo Grandison in promoting the organization of unskilled workers, Debs could also evoke the spirit of Gompers at the same 1881 convention. Holding to a view of politics that proscribed all but traditional political activity, Debs urged workers not to "go roaming in the realms of [political] discussion . . . but rather [to] find the one thing needful and to go for it with all your might, and when found, grasp and hang on to it. Why waste time and breath," Debs asked, "over minor questions? Why clamor for a single tax? Why run mad over nationalism, another term for parentalism? Why resolve to go pell mell into some new fangled political party? Why get hoarse over the initiative and referendum? Why not, on the contrary, unify, solidify, and federate to secure honest, fair and just wages?"[46]

In emphasizing such an analysis, which often ignored and at times seemed to reject political activity, Debs appeared close to the position of Gompers. Since the Burlington strike, in fact, the two men had been in frequent contact. In 1890 Gompers addressed a long letter to both Debs and Sargent, supporting and encouraging their efforts at federation. The following year, he defended Debs and other Indiana labor leaders from criticism and praised their honesty and sincerity. In 1892, as Debs contemplated leaving the Brotherhood, Gompers expressed great anticipation over Debs's future work and suggested, since "there could scarcely be a more fitting opportunity presented to embark in that wide field," that Debs address the forthcoming convention of the AFL. When ill-health prevented Debs from accepting, Gompers expressed regret.[47]

On his part, Debs praised Gompers at almost every opportunity between 1889 and 1894. They agreed on the importance of the eight-hour movement and joined to support Illinois Governor John Altgeld's pardon of the remaining Haymarket anarchists. When Gompers criticized Arthur at the 1889 AFL convention, Debs called Gompers "one of the most brainy men now connected with the great labor movement." Similarly, after Gompers addressed a large meeting in Terre Haute, Debs praised him as "a valiant defender of the rights of labor" and wished him success in all he undertook. Debs's support was not limited to generalized fraternal well-wishes. In 1893 he supported Gompers for re-election as president of the AFL over John McBride, the Socialist candidate, and publicly rejoiced when Gompers won in a close election.[48] Debs and Gompers grew closer during these years, and it was understandable if Gompers perhaps thought that this charismatic leader of the railway men was feeling his way toward a more concrete class understanding and away from the "vagaries" of the citizen-producer idea.

But Debs was a more complicated figure than at times even he himself was aware. While Gompers and the conservative majority of the Firemen could unequivocally endorse a narrow emphasis on wages and working conditions, Debs continually insisted on transcending those limits. As his Brotherhood critics understood, even when he did not directly address political issues in his editorials, such implications were always close to the surface. Debs never retracted the basic analysis of the wage question he first developed in 1889. Wages were important, he noted, but in this "God favored land," blessed with liberty, American workers "are not to be silenced by any per diem. [Their] high resolve is to change unjust laws, and to place men in the legislative, executive and judiciary departments who will see that just laws are righteously administered."[49]

This fervent commitment to a "reign of justice" most clearly marked the gulf between Gompers and the majority of the Firemen and Debs. As he pondered the lessons of the Burlington strike, Debs was deeply affected by the writings of Henry George, Lawrence Gronlund, and Bellamy. Their critique of American reality echoed the anger railroad men, especially those on lines to the west of Chicago, expressed in talks with Debs. Together, Debs and his supporters among railway men rejected the divided, compartmentalized view of man and nature promulgated by the corporation and accepted by many in the labor movement. Yet Debs continued to reaffirm his belief in mobility and his praise of self-made men, of firemen who rose to become postmasters.[50] For Debs remained at this point less concerned with class formation than with the fulfillment of America's promise. But there remained fundamental tension between Debs and many firemen as to the ultimate meaning and interpretation of these seemingly traditional pronouncements.

As Debs focused attention on broader cultural issues within American society, he again angered many of his readers. In 1890, for example, the Women's Department of the *Magazine* came under sustained attack from male readers. Edited by Ida Husted Harper (whom Debs had appointed in 1884), this monthly commentary advocated women's equality in politics as in marriage. Debs not only supported Harper's right to such advocacy but also clearly indicated he agreed with her position. Four years later, Debs accused St. Paul of having "innoculated Christianity and the church with the virus of inferiority" and condemned the church for its institutional support of this policy which had resulted in "centuries of enslavement" for women.[51]

Revealing still another major area of disagreement with many in the rank and file, Debs offered a broader criticism of organized religion. He accused American churches of a widespread anti-labor bias, and he condemned them for failing to encourage "into a sympathetic alliance" the Dives and Lazaruses of American society. In another editorial he dismissed organized religion and asserted that the true spirit of Christianity could be found in the labor movement as "every blow organized labor strikes for the emancipation of labor has the endorsement of Christ. It is, reverently speaking, in alliance with Christ to oppose pomp and splendor.''[52] Apt sentiments for one seeking the Kingdom of God on earth, but many firemen found them offensive and even sacrilegious.

Both personally and with the membership, the most difficult political problem Debs encountered centered on the issue of race and nationality. The traditional premise of Debs's ideology rested upon an identification of the labor movement with Anglo-Saxon male Protestants intimately familiar both with the prophetic strain in Christianity and with the traditions of American democracy. Immigrants, especially those of non-English or non-German stock, and black and female workers did not fit into this conception. Yet to reject them out of hand clearly vitiated the spirit of those traditions. While Debs never completely resolved this problem, his partial solution created further tension with the membership. For two years after the Burlington strike Debs expressed a sustained hostility toward the ever-increasing waves of immigrants entering the eastern cities. He attacked the immigration agents in Europe as representatives of capital, the "enemies of American workingmen" who desired to "Chinaize the country," and he welcomed laws enabling authorities to return "to their despot cursed home" the "victims" of these agents' efforts.[53]

At times Debs also revealed a deep animus against the immigrants themselves. Responding to a newspaper report that favorably compared the new Italian immigrants' work habits with those of the earlier Teutonic and Anglo-Saxon immigrants, Debs scoffed and found the Italians even less desirable than the Chinese. "The Dago," he claimed, "works for small pay, and lives far more like a savage or a wild beast, than the Chinese." This Italian, Debs continued, "fattens on garbage" and cares little for civilization, and therefore "is able to underbid an American workingman." Only in this way can the Italian appear industrious, and Debs warned that "Italy has millions of them to spare and they are coming."[54]

Jews fared little better. When it was announced that the London Board of Guardians had instituted a program to transfer Russian-Jewish immigrants to the United States, Debs claimed that this would increase the already intense hostility toward immigrants. Identifying these immigrants as "criminals and paupers," Debs bemoaned the fact that most were able to "take up a permanent residence" and strongly asserted that "it is possible to end the infamous business."[55]

Debs made few public references concerning black Americans. Although he welcomed the end of slavery and increasingly used the symbolism of that earlier struggle to support labor's current battle against capital's wage slavery, at no time did Debs run counter to the membership's dominant anti-black feelings. He supported without any record of dissent the Brotherhood's efforts to rid southern railroads of black firemen and the anti-black clause in the Firemen's constitution. In a rare comment on the larger social condition of the black population, Debs indicated the limits of his concern during these years. Reporting that a new Texas law required separate coaches for black and white passengers on intrastate railroads, Debs stated that, though "there might come a time when in the South whites and blacks will be on terms of social equality," nonetheless, "till then, it were better to separate than to fight."[56] While the implication of this brief comment might have indicated some disagreement with the wave of Jim Crow laws sweeping the South, it also clearly suggested Debs's basic support of the segregationist policies both in the Brotherhood and in society in general. Debs obviously found it difficult during these years to break with the dominant racial attitudes of the culture that had formed him.

In these attitudes toward blacks and immigrants, Debs reflected the prevailing feelings of the majority of firemen. Given their common cultural background—which among other aspects gave prominence to the "dialect" jokes with which Debs loved to regale his friends—this is not surprising. However, while Debs did not alter his public position concerning blacks, at this time certain implications in his critique of industrial society forced him to re-think his attitude toward immigration. This, in turn, brought him into sharp and bitter antagonism with his brothers in the Firemen.

The nativist response to the new wave of immigrants from eastern and southern Europe after 1880 evolved from an aggressive dislike of foreigners *per se* into a complex, and at times rabid, theory of racial and religious superiority of the Anglo-Saxon tradition. Not surprisingly, these years also saw the growth of an expansive, imperialistic ideology in large part based on these racial theories.[57] While sharing some of these larger assumptions, Debs nonetheless came to oppose immigrant restriction. In part his deep belief in free speech and the free expression of religious sentiments separated him from the nativist appeal.[58] More important, by 1891 Debs's critique of the new corporate order had altered his thinking. The hue and cry against the "foreign pauper immigrants" he now saw as the work of the same capitalists who enticed them to America in the first place. "Trust barons and great corporations," he argued, "may be pleased with such terms, because they have the significance of slaves, or serfs, and do not suggest citizenship." If allowed to succeed, these barons would completely identify working people with the term "pauper labor"—to the degradation of all labor. While avoiding an endorsement of open immigration, Debs did suggest that, from its very origins with Columbus, America had meant "land for the world; not for those who first robbed the Indians, but for men through all time who might seek homes in the New World."[59]

Within two years Debs's analysis became more pointed and direct. In early 1893 he reviewed the history of anti-immigration policies in America and associated its advocates with the anti-democratic tradition, citing King George III, the supporters of the Alien and Sedition Acts, and the Know-Nothing movement as earlier defenders of an exclusionary policy. Noting the pressure on the labor movement to join with these forerunners, Debs claimed that "if labor is true to itself, it should be the first to denounce all laws in anywise abridging the rights of those who wear its badge."[60] What led to this strong defense of immigration was the growing power and influence of the American Protective Association. Founded in Iowa in 1887, it identified Catholicism as the country's most dangerous threat and, secondarily, emphasized opposition to alien immigration. Although branches were formed throughout the nation, its greatest source of strength was in the Midwest. Members took an oath vowing never to vote for Catholic candidates, patronize Catholic merchants, or strike with Catholic workingmen.

Debs recognized that religious and racial disputes within labor's ranks defeated many strikes and organizing drives, and he attacked the association as un-American and in violation of "every quality of manhood worthy of recognition." He claimed that railroad executives led the organization and that its major purpose was, in fact, to split the ranks of labor. To a certain extent, Debs noted, it had succeeded, while "the ruling classes" were in no way so affected.[61] Although he never unequivocally endorsed open immigration (always resisting the importation of Europe's "vagabond class"), Debs's editorial on the association marked an important change. Both in Europe and America, he now understood, the representatives of "the ruling classes" fomented unrest among workers on religious, racial, and national grounds, and he was appalled at the extent of their success even within his own union. Predictably, this editorial provoked a strong and virulent opposition from many of his readers. Debs was threatened with assassination, accused of pro-Catholic (and thus anti-American) sympathies, and condemned for criticizing a group many held to be a friend of working people.[62]

What made this struggle even more complicated for Debs was that in important ways he remained rooted in the very culture that he now attacked and that, through his readers, attacked him. In an editorial examining the Sino-Japanese war over "Corea," Debs indicated the pervasiveness of this influence. He argued that the war was essentially foolish, as Russia would never allow either Asiatic country to gain a foothold in Korea. In words reminiscent of his earlier editorial on Indo-China, however, Debs welcomed the prospect of a different kind of war. "If by some fortunate turn of affairs, both China and Japan could be involved in a war with Christian nations, much real good might be achieved.'' The ports of the "two pagan empires'' might thus be opened to western commerce, and the "barbaric exclusiveness'' of their cultures eradicated. Fully embracing the imperialistic and racist assumptions that fueled the American Protective Association, Debs stated in his conclusion that peaceful measures were simply ineffectual to achieve the goals that all Americans, within and without the labor movement, desired: "It is all folly to expect any valuable results from missionary work—these heathens should be required to open their ports and admit the civilizing influences of commercial nations. The idolatry, the despotism and exclusiveness of China and Japan should be knocked out of them, and if the war between these copper-colored nations could be made to accomplish such a result, it would be a blessing.''[63]

Debs might reject one form of zenophobic reaction, only to continue commitment to another. This basic contradiction, reflective of the tension he felt between the influence of the Terre Haute of his childhood and the new realities of corporate capitalism, ultimately limited his own critique of the new order during this period. Since the Philadelphia convention of 1885, the major emphasis in Debs's thoughts and actions focused on the development of a labor consciousness among working people. While always rooted in an understanding of the primacy of citizenship, Debs nonetheless perceived the need for working people to unite as working people in order to ensure their rights as citizens. His altered attitude toward the Knights of Labor, his emphasis on federation, and his occasional advocacy of a labor party all indicate this direction. Yet Debs never completely broke from the rather strong ideological formulations of his youth. He never severed his relations with the Democratic party until after 1894. Indeed, in 1892 as in 1888, he campaigned for the Democratic presidential candidate and retained a solid working relationship with Daniel Voorhees and Indiana's Democratic organization.[64]

More important, Debs retained his confidence in the ultimate harmony of interests of all citizens, and he remained capable of using this belief as a weapon against other workingmen. Attacked for his political views by two Connecticut lodges in 1891, Debs retorted by characterizing the brothers of Lodge 284 as stupid and mendacious, in league with the likes of Austin Corbin and Andrew Carnegie. Unconcerned with their refusal to solicit more subscriptions for the journal, he claimed he no longer needed them, for, he proudly asserted, under his tutelage the *Locomotive Firemen's Magazine* was famous throughout the nation, with a large readership of professional people—"lawyers, physicians, clergymen, educators, scientists.'' These readers would and were soliciting all the subscriptions necessary to maintain the growth and prestige of *his* magazine.[65] While in part personal pique, the ease with which Debs could jettison two lodges in this single instance dramatically defined the limits of his advocacy of a specific labor consciousness. Political principles had replaced sobriety as a test of comradeship. Yet in a critical way, Debs remained affected by the Terre Haute of his earlier years, even as he came to see that the values he thought characteristic of the era faced severe challenges.

In the January 1891 issue of the *Locomotive Firemen's Magazine* Debs shocked his readers with an announcement that, effective at the conclusion of his current term, he would resign both official positions he held within the Brotherhood since 1880. He stressed that while he had no disagreements with policy, the demands upon his time and health had become too strenuous after twelve continuous years. In a consciously cryptic comment he said that he was "determined to go into other business" but would remain in office until the September 1892 convention in order to give the Brotherhood ample time to decide upon a replacement.[66]

Considerable speculation arose over Debs's intention to pursue "other business." Gompers thought it might include journalism or the reform movement in general; others, that Debs was finally going to take advantage of a business or commercial offer. Both of these ideas proved to be inaccurate. Despite his disclaimer, Debs finally had decided that to continue his work with the Brotherhood would be self-defeating. The conservative majority seemed intractable, and the very craft basis of the railway men's organizations prevented rather than encouraged unity. Debs desired a completely new structure for the labor movement in order to offset the power of capital.

Debs had once hoped that federation would both resolve problems within the labor movement and eliminate all but an occasional tension between *"capitalists and workingmen."*[67] But the reverse now seemed more accurate. Recent strikes in New York and Texas indicated that railway management did not appreciate the efforts of a federated labor movement to defend itself.[68] And the expected labor unity did not occur. The Engineers, of course, remained apart, but those brotherhoods that had federated engaged in vicious factional fighting over craft jurisdiction and organizational autonomy. Rarely was the Supreme Council united in dealing with capital. Debs himself caught the brunt of this dissension at the Firemen's 1890 San Francisco convention, where he had suffered a thorough critique of his policies by the assembled delegates. So basic was this criticism that it compelled Sargent to devote a section of his report to Debs's defense.[69] With his political support ebbing and the national plan of federation tottering, Debs decided to begin anew his plan to unify railway men.

As if to confirm the actual reasons for Debs's resignation, the Supreme

Council completely disintegrated in the spring of 1891. Two of its members, the Brotherhood of Railway Trainmen and the Switchmen's Mutual Aid Association, engaged in a devastating factional fight over the right to organize yard workers on the Chicago and Northwestern Railway. After each group had successfully demanded that management dismiss selected opponents, the Supreme Council urged S. E. Wilkinson of the Trainmen and Frank Sweeny of the Switchmen to settle the dispute privately. But the intense ill-feeling between these associations, the result of past jurisdictional battles, prohibited such a peaceful settlement. Rather than talk with Sweeny, Wilkinson formed an alliance with the railroad corporation. He agreed to the wholesale firing of all workers, union and non-union alike, in the Chicago yards. In exchange, when management shortly rehired the work force, Wilkinson aided these executives in weeding out known members of the Switchmen's Association and replaced them with his members. What proved most confounding, as Debs stated in a signed editorial, was that the Trainmen "did not deny the alliance." A month later, the Trainmen were officially expelled from the Supreme Council, despite Debs's argument that the penalty was "injudiciously severe" as it punished the rank and file for the devious acts of their officers.[70] Despite formal assertions to the contrary, the Supreme Council no longer existed. The original critique of Walton and the Union Pacific men had proven an accurate prophecy.[71]

The subsequent Trainmen's convention severely tested Debs's contention that the membership was at odds with the grand officers. Not only did Wilkinson affirm his collusion with the railroad officials, but also the delegates, many acting on explicit directives from their lodges, overwhelmingly supported his conduct. They also rebuked the *Trainmen's Journal,* which had been highly critical of Wilkinson, and forced its editor, L. W. Rogers, to resign under pressure, accusing him of giving Debs undue influence over the journal's editorial policy.[72] Debs sought some solace in the conviction that the majority vote reflected the manipulative abilities of the grand officers "to obscure facts and warp judgements" and hoped that in time the rank and file of the Trainmen would repudiate that "crime of conspiracy and the infamy of scabbing."[73]

In January 1892 Debs found a more sympathetic audience for his views. More clearly the labor agitator than the grand officer, Debs was the keynote speaker at a massive labor rally in Chicago that had been called to expose and condemn the actions of the Trainmen. Speaking from the floor rather than the podium, as he did not feel "natural and comfortable, unless he is right on the ground floor with his brothers," Debs reminded the audience of his long trade union career. He recalled that he had organized the Trainmen's first lodge and had obtained commercial credit for the new organization on his personal note through McKeen's bank.

While the Trainmen's actions were despicable, Debs explained, they also proved again the need for labor unity. But, as that experience suggested, it was labor itself that created the most difficult barriers to unity. With growing anger, Debs pinpointed "this thing of caste that is creeping into labor organizations" as the major problem and insisted there was an alternative:

> If organized labor has any mission in this world, it is to help those who cannot help themselves. But what is organized labor in a great many ways trying to do? To cater to the power that oppresses them and resist the power that is trying to relieve them. . . . If we can get rid of that idea of caste in labor organizations; if we are capable of appreciating men according to their necessities, according to their honesty, we can establish an organization that will not only be a protection to the employees, but will be a guarantee to the officials that as long as they mete out justice they will never have a strike.[74]

The prolonged applause that greeted Debs's conclusion was gratifying. It affirmed that, as he more explicitly criticized labor's hierarchical structure, many workers, even some Firemen, would support him. This backing would be essential for the future. As his comments on caste made obvious, he had lost hope of reforming the older orders. But when Debs reasserted the need for some type of federated organization, he publicly announced for the first time that he might, in fact, intend to create just such a body to supersede the brotherhoods. At this turning point Debs reaffirmed his commitment to traditional American values. Caste feelings prevented men from seeing each other in their true light and thus tarnished and warped the meaning of manhood, individual dignity, and fraternity. If these might be restored, if the corporate model of work and workers might be overthrown—then not only would labor unity ensue but also Debs's long-cherished desire for harmony between employer and worker might be rekindled. While at times Debs teetered dangerously close to gazing back wistfully at a mythic past, the ideals and values he associated with his youth also formed the cutting edge of his opposition to the new corporate society.[75]

More immediately, however, this speech foreshadowed Debs's break with the Firemen, which occurred a few months later at the Cincinnati convention. Perhaps he had hoped that his attacks on caste within the labor movement in addresses such as this would eliminate the need to explain his resignation on the floor of the convention. He never relished public separations from friends and former associates, no matter how he had come to disagree with them, and this feeling intensified as he grew older. If so, Debs did not succeed, and he was forced to detail the actual reasons for resignation at the convention.

In one respect at least, Debs came to what he expected to be his last convention prepared to offer a thorough defense. After years of acrimonious debate, Debs reviewed in his yearly report the policy of the *Locomotive Firemen's Magazine*. He pointed to the substantial increase both in subscriptions and influence during the long course of his editorship and proudly defended his editorial positions toward the Brotherhood of Locomotive Engineers, federation, and the American Protective Association. He claimed, somewhat misleadingly, that under his tutelage the journal had always assumed that Firemen were workingmen and, as "laboring men have a fellow feeling for laboring men," this justified his comments upon the larger political issues. In conclusion, Debs affirmed the close ties he felt with many in the Brotherhood and, dismissing "all but pleasant memories," expressed his hope for the continued success of the order.[76]

When the time came for the floor debates over his resignation, Debs was conveniently ill (as he termed it, "physically prostrate incident to overwork and anxieties") and confined to his hotel room.[77] While hoping to avoid a direct confrontation—that would require a clarification of the "other business" to which he now intended to turn—Debs, in a sickbed interview, nonetheless indicated some of the more substantive reasons for his action. After noting the precarious condition of his health and his long years in office, he quickly passed to his actual reasons. "I don't expect to discount myself with organized labor," he told the reporter from the Cincinnati *Enquirer*, but "to continue in my present position would materially interfere with my plans for the future." He noted that "a life purpose" had been to organize all railway employees into one federated unit, but that this was impossible as long as workers were organized by class and craft. "Class organization is well enough," Debs argued, but it "fosters class prejudices and class selfishness, and instead of affiliating with each other, there is a tendency to hold aloof from each other." He specifically criticized the attitudes of the various grand officers who, in their jealous concern for craft autonomy, made federation "impracticable and impossible"; and he announced his intention to create a new organization among railroad workers "so all will be on an equality."[78]

Despite his direct criticism of all craft organization, Debs muted his specific differences with the Brotherhood and would have preferred to leave it that way. The actions of the delegates, however, forced him into a different posture. When the convention turned to the election of a secretary-treasurer, having already unanimously reelected Sargent and J. J. Hannahan, "the greatest scene of the convention" occurred. Delegates jumped to their feet, all demanding to be heard, and the chair lost any semblance of control. Slowly, amid the babble of voices, a common chant grew, until the over three hundred delegates proclaimed in unison that they wanted " 'Debs,' 'Debs,' 'Debs.' " Shortly after this demonstration, the convention rejected Debs's resignation and unanimously reelected him to the position of secretary-treasurer.

Debs then made a dramatic entrance onto the floor of the convention hall, which precipitated "the greatest of all demonstrations." When order was again restored, Debs rose to speak, "his face firmly set and shaking with pent-up emotion." He begged the delegates to accept his resignation. Again rebuffed, Debs announced that the action of the convention would now force him to explain. He was no longer "in harmony" with the Firemen, he told the delegates, and thus could not lead them. Pointing to their compulsory insurance program that provided minimal accident and death benefits—which fifteen years earlier he had declared the ultimate goal of the organization—Debs demonstrated how a narrow class perception had destroyed labor unity: "An order of this kind should be divorced from an insurance company . . . as thousands of men are expelled because they cannot maintain that branch of the order. When once expelled these men were stigmatized by Union men as non-Union men, or, as commonly termed, 'scabs,' thereby strengthening the opposition." The speech, as one reporter noted, "fell like a pall on the convention." The delegates were shocked, although many present had either been principals in or had closely followed the bitter fights of the past years. In the silence that followed his address, Debs nominated F. W. Arnold, a Chicago businessman since deposed as grand master in 1885, to succeed him as secretary-treasurer. Arnold was chosen over two other candidates, W. F. Hynes and W. S. Carter.[79]

The delegates' initial insistence on retaining Debs suggests how complicated was the relationship between them and their longtime leader. To an astonishing degree, Debs remained personally popular with the members despite the growing political tension. But this popularity also encompassed a certain ignorance. As their stunned reaction to Debs's convention speech suggested, few delegates understood the extent of the political differences that separated their order and Debs. In part, the delegates themselves were at fault, as they ignored obvious indications. But Debs also bore a certain responsibility. Rarely did he attempt to explain in detail the sources of his own altered attitude in the four years since Burlington. More the angry preacher than the patient organizer, Debs all too often saw opponents as sinners, and, in reaction to the thin line he himself had straddled for so long between his new ideas and the imperatives of his earlier years, he too easily relied upon insult and diatribe to convince them of their error. Even following his frank speech in Cincinnati, Debs's report of that convention in the *Magazine* omitted all reference to his actual reasons for resigning.[80] A poor teacher even as his public confidence and charismatic appeal grew, Debs remained uncomfortable at any public recognition of his own contradictions and was therefore unable to share his development with the rank and file in a nonantagonistic fashion. This was unfortunate. As Debs himself might have realized, had he but reflected on his own past decade, change came slowly, even fitfully, and the collective rank and file needed at least the time and opportunity that he had required.

Debs had intended to sever all official ties with the Brotherhood in Cincinnati. He found, however, that "after all, [I] could not entirely leave the task [I] had for so many years performed," and he accepted re-election as editor of the journal. But he demanded and obtained from the convention three important conditions. First, as editor, he would no longer be a member of the grand lodge and responsible for general policy. Second, the new secretary-treasurer would assume responsibility for the business affairs of the magazine, thus assuring Debs of the time for writing and speaking. Finally, Debs refused the proffered salary of $3,000, insisting it be no more than $1,000 per year. While remaining the editor assured him of an important national forum within the labor movement for his ideas ("in the *swim*, watching and noting the drift of events"), his preconditions freed him from any moral or practical commitment to specific activities. After almost eight years of growing tension between his obligations to his superiors and his own emerging ideas, he could now write a friend with deep relief that "while I am no longer numbered with *grand* officers, I shall continue to admire *grand* men in all of the orders."[81] Having asserted its almost sacred virtue for so long, Debs now took another major step toward exploring the previously clouded dimensions of his own manhood.

5

An Injury to One

Eugene Debs approached his work in 1893 with a buoyant contentiousness. His freedom from the Brotherhood of Locomotive Firemen allowed him to concentrate his considerable energies on building an industrial union for all railroad workers, and he remained confident of ultimate success. In politics, the recent presidential election encouraged Debs as well. Grover Cleveland, a Democrat who had criticized the use of troops to suppress the Homestead strike during the summer of 1892, had defeated Benjamin Harrison. Unalterably opposed to Harrison in any event, Debs now hoped that in the new president workers might find a friend in the White House.

There were some ominous signs, however. As the Homestead strike indicated, the industrial corporations persisted in their resistance to an organized, independent work force, and their persuasive example reached even into Terre Haute. In 1893 William Riley McKeen sold his Vandalia line to the Pennsylvania Railroad and ended any pretense of local control. Simultaneously, the Terre Haute Businessmen's Association, once primarily devoted to local boosterism, reorganized and adopted a strident anti-labor tone.[1] Nor was the condition of the economy promising in 1893. Early that year, the severe overcapitalization and unchecked speculation that had marked railroad investments for the past decade finally took their toll. With the financial failure of the Pennsylvania and Reading as the catalyst, seventy-four railroads declared bankruptcy that summer, and by December 600 banks and 15,000 businesses followed.[2] Not only would suffering be serious, but also Debs knew that such a downturn invariably resulted in efforts by employers to lower the wages and working conditions of labor. It had happened in 1877; he saw it again in the depression of 1883–85, which had led to the dramatic strikes by the Knights of Labor. In this context the establishment of a militant industrial union among railroad workers was of critical importance.

Discussion of a new organization for railroad workers had begun in 1891, although Debs did not become actively involved until June 1892. At first there was confusion as to the purpose of the organization. Some intended to revitalize the Supreme Council while Samuel Gompers privately hoped the discussions would lead to the affiliation of the various brotherhoods with the AFL.[3] By the time Debs joined the conferences, however, his purpose was clear. He intended to create an organization that would replace the brotherhoods, abolish craft divisions, and unify all railroad workers. When he was criticized for building a dual union that some saw as a fundamental attack on existing labor organizations in the industry, Debs responded directly. The combined brotherhoods had organized less than 25 percent of all railroad workers, he argued, and they showed no signs of improving their record. The only way to break down this narrow jurisdictional autonomy, Debs told his critics, was to create a competing union movement.[4] Yet Debs hoped to involve as many of the brotherhoods' officers as possible and, as he took control of the new organization, he invited the chiefs of all the brotherhoods to join the planning sessions.[5]

The first board meeting of the new organization, the American Railway Union, was held in Chicago in February 1893. Debs and F. W. Arnold unofficially represented the Firemen; George Howard, the Railway Conductors; W. S. Missemer and Sylvester Keliher, the Railway Carmen; and L. W. Rogers, the journal *Age of Labor*. Howard was elected chairman, but Debs set the tone. The purpose of the new organization, he explained, was to unite all railroad workers "into one, compact working force for legislative as well as industrial action." In light of the bitter feelings within and among the various brotherhoods, Debs emphasized the need for a patient campaign of education to encourage workers to explore their common interests and to obtain "a true understanding of what their rights are as employees."[6] The majority of the union's first board of directors were current or former grand officers of the existing brotherhoods, as were the newly elected national officers.[7]

Despite these vestiges of the past, the union's Declaration of Principles, presented and approved at the April board meeting, indicated the distance between the new union and earlier efforts. Written by Debs, it began with a severe and searching attack upon the principles and policies of the brotherhoods, particularly the "autocratic power" of the grand chiefs, their constant maneuvering for passes and privileges from railroad officials, and the complicated grievance procedures that so often diffused and shunted aside a railroad worker's basic problem.[8] While these criticisms were by now familiar, Debs did include some new points. He laid the blame for both railroad strikes and their defeats directly upon the brotherhoods. Since the brotherhoods existed primarily for skilled workers with steady work—steady enough at least to meet their dues and insurance payments regularly—by definition they excluded the majority of workers and thus contributed to the reserve labor pool that capital used so effectively during strikes. To counter this problem, made more serious by the current depression, Debs proposed a basic restructuring of the seniority system. He placed the American Railway Union on record as favoring the filling of vacancies "from the line of promotion [seniority] and from the unemployed in a ratio evincing due regard to the rights of both."[9] While vague as to specific implementation, this proposal alone would ensure the permanent opposition of the brotherhoods as it seriously threatened their organizational structure.

Debs argued in the declaration that the union's primary purpose was to protect members' "wages and their rights as employees." Lest he be misunderstood, however, he reasserted his belief that a strong unified labor movement would bring benefits to all in society. If "fair wages [were] the return for efficient service," Debs repeated as he had so often in the past, then "harmonious relations may be established and maintained . . . and the necessity for strike and lockout, boycott and blacklist, alike disastrous to employer and employee, and a perpetual menace to the welfare of the public, will forever disappear."[10] Industrial peace, Debs believed, could only be encouraged by a unified labor movement. When "the great body of railroad men" organized, he explained a year later, "more prudent counsel will prevail; the organization will be more conservative, and the chances for a strike largely reduced."[11]

In this attitude Debs echoed aspects of the Firemen's belief in the value of a conservative, hierarchical organization. But it would not be enough to retain the allegiance of the brotherhoods themselves. During the spring of 1893 Arnold simply stopped attending meetings. That June, a more open break developed with Missemer. Withdrawing from the board of directors, he charged that the union's only purpose was to supplant the brotherhoods. His membership, Missemer announced, now understood this and, citing a leaflet circulated nationally by the East St. Louis lodge, overwhelmingly rejected further cooperation with the American Railway Union.[12]

Missemer's charges momentarily dampened the enthusiasm of the union's leaders, but it was their private response that proved more telling. At the June board meeting Howard argued that Missemer had become unduly alarmed over the East St. Louis leaflet and suggested that the established practice of the brotherhoods should have been followed:

"Such matters would be given but little thought in older organizations," he explained, "and had the proper discipline been enforced at the start, no serious results would have been experienced." Debs continued Howard's analysis. "It was a mistake," he stated, "not to revoke the charter [of the East St. Louis local] in the first place and command the respect due the Grand Lodge." Such affairs, he noted, "require prompt and decisive action." Had that action been forthcoming, Debs assured the remaining directors that Missemer could have controlled the dissidents.[13] Debs and Howard were building a new union movement, based largely on their critique of the brotherhoods. Yet they did not hesitate to adopt as their model for handling rank-and-file movements the lessons they had learned in their own years with those brotherhoods.[14]

Despite these contradictions, public reaction to the new union was encouraging. Letters flooded the Chicago office from workers desiring information, organizers, and membership cards. P. J. McGuire, head of the Brotherhood of Carpenters and Joiners and a close associate of Gompers, was one of a number of national labor leaders who expressed interest and desired more information.[15] The less famous as well were active. James Hogan of Evanston, Wyoming, requested appointment as an organizer since he had already formed a local of over 100 members.[16] This enthusiasm continued into the fall of 1893, as letters from groups of railroad workers on a given line desiring to join en masse supplemented letters from individuals.[17] Many inquiries came from various brotherhood lodges, concerned with the possibilities of joint membership—as had happened a decade earlier with the Knights of Labor.[18] The continued excitement to the union's organizing circulars clearly indicated that many workers perceived the spirit of the American Railway Union in quite a different fashion than some of the union's formal practices might suggest. For these workers, as they built the union in their own communities, the most important fact about the Debs-led union was that it presented a viable alternative to the conservative approach of the brotherhoods. As W. S. Carter, a long-time opponent of Debs within the Firemen, bemoaned in January 1894, the Texas lodges with which he was in contact were restless and quite receptive to the new union.[19]

The reasons for this enthusiasm were evident to many. The union's retention of a hierarchical structure seemed less important to most than its affirmation of a unified industrial organization. Among western railway workers especially—the men of the Union Pacific, Southern Pacific, and the Santa Fe—the experience of the past decade had repeatedly shown them how divisive craft union organization could be. That they had often fought Debs during these years was now of little importance. This sense of urgency was heightened after a series of labor defeats during recent struggles with various corporations, and they watched apprehensively as popular opinion, reflected in the leading newspapers and magazines, adopted a strident anti-labor tone. More ominously, the state and federal governments had become more active in labor disputes. Troops had been used at Homestead and in the bitter miners' strike at Coeur d'Alene, Idaho. During the same time local police and state militia suppressed strikes and demonstrations of the unemployed in various locales throughout the country.[20] As a result, class antagonism and suspicion grew, and many workers felt that the corporation, with the government as an ally, was intent on securing their permanent degradation and destruction. Against this force many again questioned the soundness and effectiveness of the traditional organizations.

Within this context, then, Debs played an important role. His public stance against the brotherhoods, especially at the 1892 Firemen's convention, won him the praise of many western workers, for whom he became a symbol of a much needed defense of labor's liberty and manhood. In his speeches and editorials the charismatic qualities of Debs played a critical role in encouraging the enthusiasm that Carter deplored. In his person and in the purpose of the American Railway Union, railroad workers felt that they might finally find a leader and an organization both capable and willing to protect their jobs, families, and dignity. This millennial urgency that Debs projected, and that proved much more important to prospective members than any analysis of an internal hierarchy, was vividly captured by one new recruit. Responding to Carter's criticism, A. S. Dowling argued that Carter sought "to defend class organization and to discredit the efforts of Brothers Debs, Howard and Keliher to introduce through the American Railway Union the brotherhood of man."[21] Nothing less than this—the expectation that the new union would eliminate divisions within labor and transform the face of industrial America—motivated Debs himself.[22]

The first major test of the new union came in February 1894. The Union Pacific line was bankrupt, and the receivers for the federal district court ordered wages slashed for all workers across the system. In addition, federal Judge Elmer S. Dundy granted an injunction that forbade the men from striking or even meeting to discuss their reaction to a wage cut. Furious over the decision, Debs viewed it as a "deathblow to human liberty." He accused the courts and the corporations—"synonymous terms nowadays"—of being the "sappers and miners of constitutional liberty" and warned that the ultimate crisis was at hand: "The issue is upon us and I am in favor of forcing, not evading it. The time has come when we shall know whether this is a republic or a despotism. There is no difference between American and Russian slavery except that the former masquerades in a shroud of sovereign citizenship."[23]

American Railway Union men echoed Debs's belief. Reflecting the union's dramatic appeal to western railway workers, the columns of the *Railway Times* continually repeated this analysis. One regular contributor, Marie Louise, pinpointed the Civil War as the beginning of the growing collusion between the state and the corporation. She stressed that the depressions of 1873 and 1894 had helped the corporation to consolidate its position.[24] Another correspondent, N. R. Piper of Kenton, Ohio, also gave voice to this conviction. "If there is," Piper wrote, "any one thing more than another that has made a deep impression on my life, it was the cherished thought that I was a citizen of a free country. That I live in the grandest country the sun shines upon." But recently, he said, he had experienced the erosion of much of his national pride and witnessed among "the great common people" the fear "that serfdom awaited them in the near future." The resulting decline of patriotism had but one main cause, Piper argued, which was easily identifiable: "Courts are granting injunctions that leave about the same freedom that blacks enjoyed up to the civil war. There was a time that our government neither embarrassed nor restrained activities at any point. That time has passed. The power of the law is used to take from one man and to give another."[25]

Encouraged by such support, Debs attacked Dundy's decision in his speeches. In Cheyenne, Wyoming, for a directors meeting in late February, he repeated his charges concerning the loss of liberty and severely criticized the wage cuts as well. When, after a month of legal debate, Judge Henry C. Caldwell overruled Dundy and found for the union, Debs was jubilant. To the *Railway Times*, Caldwell had simply recognized that "the new [wage] schedule was calculated to arouse resentment in the breast of every self-respecting, intelligent and independent man in the service."[26] This decision reaffirmed for Debs and others in the union their peculiar optimism: despite perversions of liberty encouraged by the corporations, American values had not yet died. There were still men, even federal judges, who were willing to affirm an independent manhood and sense of fair play as central aspects of that liberty.

Just prior to Judge Caldwell's decision, the American Railway Union became involved in a dispute on another line that proved more serious. At the March directors meeting in Chicago, the board received two letters from workers on James J. Hill's Great Northern Railroad. R. M. Goodwin and J. C. Spence complained of deteriorating work conditions and an imminent wage cut, the third in less than eight months, that would reduce the average worker's salary to less than forty dollars a month. Since the cheapest monthly lodging in Butte, Montana—a major layover stop for Great Northern workers—was twenty-six dollars a month, strike sentiment was high, and they asked for assistance. The board ordered Hogan, a newly elected member, to travel to Minnesota "to take such action as in his judgement was to the best interests of the men and the order."[27]

Aware of this decision, Great Northern officials secretly ordered their managers to dismiss all union supporters. When he learned about this action, Debs informed the men along the line who then decided to strike, as one circular expressed it, in order to "see if we cannot break the chains that are being forced to reduce us, not only to slavery, but to starvation."[28] On 13 April the union informed C. W. Case, general manager of the Great Northern, that unless wages were restored to the level prior to the first cut and schedules and classifications made uniform, a strike would begin that noon, less than six hours away. Only when he received notice that the men had quit work did Hill respond. He then promised that any workers who faithfully remained on the job would be duly rewarded.[29]

Hill's appeal to the "faithful employees" was not only a public relations posture but also a serious attempt to destroy strike unity at the very outset. When the second 10 percent wage cut had been announced in January, both the Engineers and Firemen protested and had asked for arbitration. Hill acceded, and the final agreement, which both of the older brotherhoods accepted, called for a 9 percent cut! Hill now felt he could easily manipulate both P. M. Arthur and Frank Sargent and suspected that he might do so again in the current strike. In this belief he was aided by the brotherhoods themselves, as both the Engineers and Conductors publicly opposed the strike, and the Firemen attempted to persuade their members to return to work. Sargent did claim that he personally supported the strike but stated that, as the strike violated the Firemen's rules, he must oppose it. Despite this coalition, the men of the American Railway Union remained unified. For the first time in recent railroad history, neither the corporations nor the other brotherhoods succeeded in defeating a strike. The American Railway Union conducted "revival meetings" all along the line and, when faced with a direct choice between the brotherhoods and the new union, the men overwhelmingly followed Debs.[30]

When Debs arrived in St. Paul, Minnesota, on 18 April to take command of the strike, it was going well, spreading to new cities every day; the unity of the men of all crafts and levels of skill remained remarkable. From this position of strength, Debs and the other union officers met with Hill at his request a week after the strike began. Hoping again to undermine the workers' unity, Hill offered to send the whole matter to arbitration, which, as he defined it, would include the older brotherhoods as well. But Hill had simply not understood either the new situation or Debs. Rising immediately, Debs rejected Hill's offer and angrily told him that "if the other organizations represent the men, get them to set your wheels turning." The union's demands were clear, Debs noted, and he was "authorized to say that we will settle on these terms and no others." Debs then gave Hill a lecture on this new unionism, which emphasized how great was the distance between it and the practice of the brotherhoods:

This grievance is a universal grievance and all the men are united in this action. It will be to no avail to attempt to divide us into factions. If wages are not restored you can no longer have the services of the men. . . . They are convinced their demand is a just one. If their request is not complied with, they will, without regard to consequences, continue this struggle on the lines already laid down and fight it out with all the means at their command within the limits of the law. We understand your position; you understand ours.[31]

While Hill pondered these words, Debs and the other strike leaders were constantly active, holding meetings and encouraging the men. The Knights of Labor supported the strike, and in one meeting at St. Paul the union gained 225 new members.[32] Enthusiasm remained high, and the ranks continued unbroken. But Hill was active as well. On 19 April he telegraphed Richard Olney, the U.S. attorney general, to inform him of the strike and noted that it was "being conducted by men not in the company's employ."[33] On 28 April Hill telegraphed President Cleveland to request federal troops, claiming that the strike interfered with the United States mails and urged a "display of federal authority supported by troops."[34] Although the troops were not sent, along the line of the strike Great Northern officials, federal judges, U.S. marshals and attorneys—in complete disregard of the legal separation of their functions—joined in one orchestrated plea for federal intervention in support of Hill. As William McDermott, the U.S. marshal at Helena, Montana, explained to Olney after a series of arrests: "I have been disposed to be governed by the railroad companies, attorneys and U.S. Atty. here."[35] Debs's belief that the corporation perverted America's judicial tradition demanded no further proof.

Failing to obtain troops, Hill tried another tactic. He convened a meeting of the St. Paul Chamber of Commerce and invited Debs to present the union's position. Hill expected the chamber, which included such prominent business leaders as Charles Pillsbury, the grain magnate, to support him and repudiate the strikers. But following Debs's presentation, the chamber demanded that Hill and Debs submit the issues to an arbitration panel headed by Pillsbury, explicitly excluding the officers of the brotherhoods. Sensing the mood of the meeting, Debs quickly accepted and thus forced Hill to do likewise. In less than one hour the panel found in favor of the strikers and granted them 97½ percent of their wage demands. Although the issue of job classifications was postponed for further discussion, this was a startling victory that came even before many strikers knew the meeting was in session.[36]

Although dramatic and swift, the settlement was not without its own logic. One interpretation has suggested that the charismatic Debs, in his address before the Chamber of Commerce, was so persuasive that the assembled businessmen immediately saw the justice of his position.[37] While Debs could indeed be charismatic, it seems doubtful that moral suasion alone could sway the economic titans of the expanding Northwest. Men such as Pillsbury and Hill had made their fortunes through rational and systematic exploitation of the nation's resources and the labor of others and would not be moved by such appeals. Rather, a fortuitous sequence of events led to the quick settlement. Debs himself was important, as a new type of labor leader who refused to compromise behind closed doors. But Debs was even more important as a symbol. He stood for a group of strikers who had remained unified through the duration of the strike. Engineers and paint scrapers, firemen and switchers—all across the line the men resisted threats from the government's representatives, enticements from the company, and the active opposition of the brotherhoods to maintain the strike. This unity was the backbone of the strike and formed the one obstacle that Hill and his associates could not surmount. Debs encouraged that unity and helped maintain it, but he also drew his own strength from it.

Second, Pillsbury and the members of the Chamber of Commerce were not uninterested observers. They were the most powerful business group west of Chicago, and their business investments extended as far as Seattle. They all shared in common a reliance upon Hill's railroad for the success of their ventures. Pillsbury's grain could not reach St. Paul during the strike, nor could a merchant's goods arrive from Chicago. Business was at a standstill, and the region's bankers were restive; these competing interests broke down the unity of capital. As long as strike unity remained strong, the central position of the railroad in the local economy ultimately worked in favor of the strikers.

Nor was it surprising that public sentiment appeared to support the workers. Despite Hill's attempts, in the towns and villages dotting Minnesota, Montana, the Dakotas, and Idaho, local businessmen and merchants sympathized with their striking neighbors and extended credit for groceries and other necessities. W. C. Plummer, the federal land office agent at Minot, North Dakota, spoke for many when he stated in the waning days of the strike that local citizens "regard the men engaged in [the strike] the best men on earth. They are the life of the town, so far as Minot is concerned, and are related to everything that is respectable. The town had prospered on their earnings and the people want them to have living wages, and believe they are now too low."[38] The specter of local businessmen and farmers uniting with striking workers to oppose Hill and the monopolistic practices of the leading merchants and grain dealers frightened men such as Pillsbury. One strike sympathizer, in a letter to the Minneapolis *Union*, underlined that fear. The strike will help to unite workers and local businessmen, Thomas H. Lucas wrote, and together they "will demand the state ownership of the railways as the only possible permanent solution" to the problem of monopolistic control.[39] The growing influence of Ignatius Donnelly and the Populist party of Minnesota, which had endorsed the American Railway Union, strengthened Lucas's argument.[40]

Debs alone, then, did not produce the victory over the Great Northern. Yet it is true that his role was critical in the strike's success. His refusal to engage in private agreements with Hill, his commitment to the wishes of the rank and file, and his passionate advocacy of industrial unity elevated him to a new position among railway workers. Debs came to personify the American Railway Union and its efforts to develop an alternative to the corrupt policies of both the brotherhoods and the corporations. On a wider stage than ever before, working men of every description now repeated the chant—"Debs, Debs, Debs." An incident at the conclusion of the strike, quickly spread throughout the nation in newspapers and by word-of-mouth, dramatically captured the veneration Debs now received. As Debs recounted the story a few days later:

> In all my life I have never felt so highly honored as I did when leaving St. Paul on my way home. As our train pulled out of the yards the token of esteem, which I prize far more highly than all others, was in seeing the old trackmen, men whose frames were bent with years of grinding toil, who received the pittance of from 80 cents to $1 a day, leaning on their shovels and lifting their hats to me in appreciation of my humble assistance in a cause which they believed had resulted in a betterment of their miserable existence.[41]

As Debs and others understood, the praise and adulation heaped upon him was also an affirmation of his basic social vision. Now a leader in the battle to reverse the corporate revolution, the victory on the Great Northern portended even greater success. All the people, working in unison and dedicated to common goals, could indeed recover the power to assert their dignity and manhood. In no way was this basic aspiration of Debs more dramatically expressed than in the reception that greeted him on his return to Terre Haute on 3 May 1894.

As his train pulled into the depot, just a short distance from his residence, the assembled crowd roared in anticipation. Debs alighted from the coach, and over 4,000 of his neighbors and townspeople surged toward him, chanting and calling his name. Overwhelmed, he declined the offer of a carriage and instead walked with the crowd to the park near the Terre Haute House for the formal reception. When sufficient calm prevailed,

Samuel Huston, a local attorney soon to be elected district attorney for Vigo County, took the podium. He welcomed Debs home and praised his handling of the recent strike as representative of the basic values of their community. Looking over the crowd, Huston repeatedly noted that citizens of all classes within the Terre Haute community had gathered for the evening's celebration. His introduction complete, Huston gave the cheering crowd their neighbor and native son, Eugene Victor Debs.

When Debs began his talk, quiet fell upon the crowd. He told them haltingly that he had no words to express his appreciation and was overcome with emotion by this demonstration "on my return to my native city." Of the strike, he emphasized that the unity of the workers, who "stood up as one man and asserted their manhood," was the single most important cause of victory. Quickly passing over his role, Debs affirmed before his neighbors the importance of the American Railway Union and its intimate relationship to their shared values:

> The American Railway Union does not believe in force except in the matter of education. It believes that when agreements and schedules are signed there should be harmony between all. It believes and will work to the end of bringing the employer and employee in closer touch. An era of close relationship between capital and labor, I believe, is dawning, one which I feel will place organized labor on a higher standard. When employer and employee can thoroughly respect each other, I believe, will strikes be a thing of the past. . . . This strike is not without its fruit and will result in much good all along the line. I hope to see the time when there will be mutual justice between employer and employees. It is said the chasm between capital and labor is widening, but I do not believe it. If anything, it is narrowing and I hope to see the day when there will be none.

What is most striking in Debs's speech, on this the proudest evening of his career to date, was its tone of optimism. For Debs, the basic problem was not a system of economic organization but rather specific difficulties that might arise with a given corporate employer. In the end, he felt that he and Hill had come to respect each other and that this respect would both structure their future relations as well as offer a model for others. In an important fashion Debs perceived the Great Northern victory as an archetype, pointing toward an imminent industrial peace which itself was but an echo of the basic American archetype—the tradition embodied in the Declaration of Independence. Harmony, duty, manhood, and dignity—with the promise of this tradition once more powerfully rekindled, Debs embraced his community and exulted in the strength he derived from it:

What has occurred tonight seems to me like a dream, a revelation. You are too generous, honorable, magnanimous, and my heart rises to my lips in receiving this demonstration from you, my neighbors, from the people of my home, where I was born and have grown from childhood to manhood. A look into the recesses of my heart only can show you the gratitude I have no words to express. I can only assure you my eternal friendship and loyalty. With my heart on my lips, I thank you, my friends—honorable men, lovely women, little children. Had I the eloquence of an Ingersoll I could not express the happiness, the long life and success I wish you one and all. Once more, with gratitude trembling on my lips, I bid you all good fortune.[42]

With this celebration Debs returned home on terms consonant with his new understandings. Accepted and fêted for public positions at which he himself would have balked a short four years earlier, Debs gloried in his neighbors' acceptance of his dignity and manhood. A source of personal strength, he also saw in that relationship a model that could regenerate others across the breadth of the country.

The victory of the American Railway Union over Hill's Great Northern electrified railroad workers. In the new union they found, as Debs often repeated, the "only clear cut victory of any consequence ever won by a railroad union in the United States,"[43] and they flocked to the new organization. Approximately 2,000 new men joined each day in the weeks after the strike, and the union soon reached 150,000 members. This represented an enormous 3,000 percent increase in one year and placed the American Railway Union at the head of all railway organizations. The brotherhoods had a combined total of approximately 90,000, but this figure did not include losses due to the dramatic growth of the new union.[44] The revolution in sentiment, long brewing among the western railroad men, had finally found a structure for systematic and effective expression.

Not everyone in the labor movement viewed this development favorably. As might be expected, the heads of the brotherhoods attempted to prevent a major migration from their ranks. Debs and his allies threatened to change the face of labor relations and render obsolete the careful system of compromise and collaboration that the grand chiefs had developed as the foundation of their strength. Yet these men were in a difficult position. To attack Debs publicly in the days following the Great Northern strike would only encourage the rank-and-file revolt they feared. Nor could they hide the fact that they had accepted Hill's wage cut while Debs forced its reversal. Sargent's actions were not untypical; he and most of the brotherhood chiefs retained a certain public composure while they quietly dispatched emissaries to attempt to soothe the men and reassure railroad officials of their good intentions.[45]

Gompers also viewed the growth of the union with less than total pleasure. In his autobiography Gompers called the American Railway Union "the disruptive movement";[46] and in an important way the new organization did change his plans. Since 1888 Gompers had sought to recruit the brotherhoods, either individually or as a group, into the federation.[47] So insistent was he that, in the middle of his own bitter disagreement with the Knights of Labor, Gompers urged that the brotherhoods drop charges of scabbing against the Knights to allow for railroad worker unity.[48] In March 1894 he attempted another unity conference—significantly omitting the American Railway Union—which the brotherhoods postponed.[49] On 11 June, at the Knights' St. Louis convention, the conference finally convened. Brotherhood representatives attended, as did Gompers, McGuire, and Frank Foster for the federation. Differences in organization proved insurmountable, however, and the Knights' firm support for the Populist party evoked strong opposition from both Gompers and the brotherhoods.[50] But there was a more fundamental obstacle. As Gompers commented with chagrin, immediately following the conference the Knights joined forces with the American Railway Union. While he issued no public declarations condemning the new union, Gompers understood that the Debs-led union threatened the ideological foundations and practical structure of his organization.[51]

For different reasons, Debs also viewed the dramatic growth and influence of the American Railway Union with caution. Although elated, he felt that such startling growth might prove destructive. Perhaps remembering the experiences of the Knights of Labor in 1886–87, Debs feared that the energy and confidence of the new and untested members might force a strike before the union could solidify itself.[52] As a result, Debs found himself in a contradictory position during May and June 1894. Although the symbol of the new unionism, fêted and applauded for the Great Northern success, Debs publicly and repeatedly urged caution. The new union could not reverse every wrong immediately, he warned, and its future lay not in a series of strikes but rather in perfecting its organization. That achieved, capital of necessity would bargain in good faith.[53] Some 180 miles to the north of Terre Haute, however, at the Pullman Car Works outside of Chicago, a strike was even then developing that would severely test the new union as it would Debs's belief in the continued power of the community and the practicality of the idea of harmony in industrial America.

A manufacturer of the sleeping cars that bore his name, George Pullman had established his Car Works in 1881. In order to increase and control production, as well as to develop a paternalistic example for industrial labor relations, Pullman situated his plant at the center of a model town. He provided modern housing for his work force, churches for them to attend, water for them to drink, and cemeteries for their dead. In turn, Pullman deducted from their weekly wages rent and water charges, library fees, and grocery bills—the cost of these basic necessities unilaterally established by the corporation. During periods of economic prosperity, the plan almost succeeded, as high wages provided workers with an improved standard of living. Even during these times, however, many Pullman workers resented their employer's autocratic control.[54]

The immediate cause of the strike in the spring of 1894 was a severe wage cut ordered by the company. Since the previous August, wages had fallen on the average of 33 percent, and in some instances by as much as 50 percent. As one car builder with twelve years of experience at Pullman testified, his daily wages dropped from $2.26 to $1.03 in 1893 to an incredible $0.91 that spring.[55] During this same time the corporation did not reduce the cost of living for workers in the town. Food prices, rents, water, and gas rates—all remained stable or, in a few instances, increased. Jennie Curtis, herself an employee whose father had worked continuously for Pullman since 1884, stated the strikers' case simply and bluntly: "Mr. Pullman would not give me enough in return for my hard labor to pay rent for one of his houses and live."[56]

The wage cuts also agitated the deep resentment already present. As Debs suggested some months later, the strike was against "tyranny and degradation" as well as against the wage cuts.[57] Many workers complained that while the wage reductions prevented them from raising their families in proper fashion, the increasingly harsh treatment meted out by foremen and managers undermined their basic self-dignity. To work for Pullman, one employee suggested, was to be treated "worse than the slaves" had been in the South.[58] In a work force that was 27 percent American-born (and overwhelmingly of Anglo-Saxon heritage among the foreign-born),[59] the comparison was pointed and painful. Under pressure themselves from management, shop floor supervisors pushed workers unmercifully. The wage cuts, although cruel, might have been bearable, one woman worker argued, but for "the tyrannical and abusive treatment we received from our forewoman." A former worker herself, this supervisor "seemed to delight in showing her power in hurting the girls in every possible way" and would regularly "make you do a piece of work for twenty-five cents less than the regular price."[60]

It was in this context of anger and resentment, then, that the Pullman workers first heard of the American Railway Union's victory over Hill. Some two months prior to the strike, they had sought Debs's aid, and he had sent George Howard to help them organize. Taking strength from the recent success, on 10 May a committee of workers presented a list of grievances to Thomas H. Wickes, a Pullman vice-president, and received assurances that they would suffer no reprisals for the petition. Although Howard had from the beginning cautioned against a strike, the Pullman corporation forced the issue. On 11 May the company summarily fired three members of the committee that had presented the petition. As word spread through the plant, the work force, immediately and without exception, dropped their tools and struck. In asking for further support from the American Railway Union, these angry and oppressed workers placed Debs and Howard in a position they desperately wanted to avoid.[61]

While sympathetic, Debs carefully excluded the American Railway Union from formal support. But he and Howard did what they could to aid the Pullmen men and women by addressing strike meetings and raising relief funds. In an effort to duplicate the conditions of the Great Northern strike—and certainly to alleviate immediate suffering—Howard immediately requested assistance from the Civic Federation of Chicago, a middle-class group concerned with social problems and unified in their distaste for Pullman's manner and methods.[62] While the Civic Federation's efforts at arbitration were unsuccessful (Pullman refused to meet with them), they did provide the strikers with needed provisions. Other Chicagoans aided the strikers as well. The law firm of Mayor John Hopkins donated 25,000 pounds of flour and meat and established a medical clinic; the Chicago *Daily News* provided a rent-free office to coordinate relief efforts; Siegal, Cooper and Company gave another 200 barrels of flour. The active trade unions of Chicago supported the strikers fully, and the fire department collected almost $1,000 for the strike fund.[63]

Despite this impressive multiclass support, however, neither Debs, Howard, nor the Pullman workers were able to reproduce the conditions that led to victory in St. Paul. The circumstances were different, as the Pullman workers composed a largely self-contained unit without direct and obvious social and economic ties to the larger community. More important, in Chicago, in contrast to St. Paul, the railroad corporations were ready, even anxious, for the American Railway Union to enter the strike.

During the first two weeks in June the strike remained a local affair. The Pullman workers retained their unity while the corporation refused to negotiate. There matters stood until, on 12 June, the American Railway Union convened its first annual convention in Chicago. As Debs mingled with the delegates, he once again cautioned against hasty involvement in the strike. Money, supplies, organizers, speakers—all this and more Debs gladly supported, but he did not want to commit the union in any official capacity. The delegates, however, deeply moved by the personal testimony of Pullman strikers, rejected Debs's advice and voted to support a nationwide boycott of all Pullman sleeping cars. If the management of any line refused to detach those cars, the American Railway Union men would refuse to run the train.[64]

If the rejection of Debs's advice seems surprising, in retrospect it is understandable. The members of the convention, Debs as well as the delegates, had been deeply moved by the success of the Great Northern strike. It was not so much that they were now "hungry" for more strikes, but rather that it was their fundamental conviction that in this union they had found a way to turn back the predatory advances of the corporation. And their conviction was held with religious fervor. By restoring their own dignity and manhood, by asserting their individualism and self-respect, they would go far in revitalizing not only their lives but also the very life of the nation as well.

This messianic thrust, with implications beyond the immediate strike, was evident in even Debs's convention address. Amidst his call for "conservative propositions" and his warning of the "danger in extremes" in his opening speech, Debs spoke of experiences worse than strikes or wars. "When men accept degrading conditions and wear collars and fetters without resistance," Debs thundered, "when a man surrenders his honest convictions, his loyalty to principle, he ceases to be a man."[65] For Debs and many of the delegates, beyond the specific issues in this strike lay the larger task of regenerating American life and culture. This feeling, and not simply an uncontrolled emotional reaction to the plight of the strikers, motivated the delegates and led Debs to at first accede to their decision and then commit himself fully to the strike in the weeks that followed.[66]

When Pullman refused arbitration again, the executive board of the union ordered the national boycott of sleeping cars to begin on 25 June.[67] To the west of Chicago—along the Santa Fe, Southern Pacific, and Union Pacific—the boycott was remarkably successful. In city after city, when management refused to detach cars, railroad workers quit work and took the opportunity to protest their own impoverishment as well. Despite opposition from the brotherhoods, the boycott paralyzed the major western lines. Even in Terre Haute, a sympathy strike occurred. In this, the first strike Debs led that affected his native city, some 210 railroad workers (6 percent of the work force) attempted to disrupt rail traffic.[68] Across the nation the American Railway Union was so successful during the first week that the old Knights of Labor slogan, "An injury to one is the concern of all," seemed fulfulled, as yet another impressive display of labor unity spread throughout the country.

Not surprisingly, corporate leaders and their allies also understood the potent meaning of this unity. Few of them would have demurred from the New York *Times*'s description of the boycott as "in reality . . . a struggle between the greatest and the most powerful railroad labor organization and the entire railroad capital." The stakes in this strike were high: "Success in the Pullman boycott," the *Times* warned, "means the permanent success of the one organization through which it is sought to unite all employees of railroads."[69] If the newspaper analysis reflected Debs's intentions, it also explained the resistance from the railroad industry which would never accept a permanent industrial union among its workers.

Debs quickly discovered that the American Railway Union faced an opponent far more powerful than just Pullman. Twenty-four railroad corporations with terminals at Chicago, employing over 220,000 people, had formed a General Managers Association some years earlier. Their purpose was to minimize competition among the railroad corporations and to develop a compliant non-union work force under the direction of managerial "experts." In this strike, moreover, the association commanded impressive resources. Its members established committees to devise overall strategy, to implement day-to-day tactical decisions, to hire strikebreakers, and to coordinate these efforts with local, state, and federal authorities. Confident, well-prepared, and with seemingly unlimited resources, the association welcomed the involvement of the American Railway Union. In the aftermath of the Great Northern strike the association had decided that the time to force the issue was at hand.[70]

On 25 June the association met in Chicago to discuss the boycott announced by the union. Terming it "unjustifiable and unwarranted," the managers declared that any worker who refused to handle Pullman cars was subject to immediate dismissal. Two days later, as the strike grew, they appointed John Egan as full-time strike director. A former member of the association, Egan established an efficient command post in Chicago with access to railroad officials throughout the country. Simultaneously others were delegated to hire strikebreakers from eastern cities, a task eased by the depression and the old bitterness among labor organizations. Some of those hired as strikebreakers had been active in the Knights of Labor when that order struck the Gould system in 1886. Blacklisted for eight years, they now took revenge on those who, although at present strikers themselves, had originally obtained their positions by scabbing in 1886.[71]

Up to this point, the actions of the association did not differ significantly from earlier corporate responses to major threats to their autonomous control of production. More organized and powerful in association than as a single company, their methods remained familiar. Had the General Managers Association desired only to defeat a specific strike, the battle would have been fought on these grounds until its conclusion. But the managers had quite a different purpose in mind.

Although official recognition of the American Railway Union was never an issue in the strike,[72] the managers intended from the beginning to destroy the union and thus eradicate all militant unionism in the railroad industry. To achieve this, the association planned to involve the federal government fully and publicly as its ally, by claiming the strike hindered interstate commerce and prevented delivery of the mail. From the strike's inception the association cultivated a public atmosphere supportive of federal intervention. Its representatives themselves disrupted railroad traffic—stopping trains in transit and cancelling others before departure—and then used these disruptions on 2 July to justify their refusal to accept any more freight for shipment. The managers also found a valuable ally in Attorney General Olney. A corporation lawyer for thirty-five years, Olney retained close personal and professional ties with the major railroad executives and was himself a member of the board of directors for numerous lines, including the Chicago, Burlington and Quincy. Anything but objective, Olney became, in the words of one historian, "the supreme strategist in directing the forces of the government against the American Railway Union."[73]

Despite Debs's repeated instructions to strikers *not* to interfere with the mails, Olney and the association agreed to charge the strikers with that violation in order to involve the federal government directly. To implement the plan, the attorney general appointed Edwin Walker as the special government attorney in Chicago, which revealed early in the strike (30 June) how close the ties were between the association and the government. Walker was yet another corporation lawyer with extensive railroad interests who had but a week earlier represented the association. As Clarence Darrow complained, "I did not regard this as fair. The government might with as good grace have appointed the attorney for the American Railway Union to represent the United States."[74] But the point had been made. The federal government, in the persons of Grover Cleveland, Richard Olney, and the ubiquitous Walter Q. Gresham, currently secretary of state,[75] was hardly neutral. So close was this alliance that the association could confidently announce on 4 July that the strike and boycott no longer concerned them. "It has now become a fight between the United States Government and the American Railway Union and we shall leave them to fight it out."[76]

The approach Olney decided upon was simple and direct. In early July he asked Walker and Thomas Milchrist, the U.S. attorney for Chicago, to prepare an application for an injunction against Debs and the American Railway Union on the grounds that they interfered with the mails and hindered interstate commerce, thereby violating the Sherman Anti-Trust Act. On 3 July federal Judges William A. Woods and Peter S. Grosscup granted the injunction that, in effect, provided an omnibus bill of restrictions against the union. Forbidding Debs and his associates from even communicating with the union's locals, the injunction, if obeyed, would force the union to cease all operations immediately. Simultaneously,

Olney prepared to enforce the injunction by sending federal troops to Chicago. Despite the repeated public assurances from both the mayor of Chicago and Governor John P. Altgeld that local and state militia were sufficient to handle any violence, Olney found his excuse in a disturbance that occurred 2 July at Blue Island, Illinois, a town adjoining Chicago. When the federal marshal there wired him that his force was inadequate and requested troops, Olney presented the telegram to President Cleveland on the morning of 3 July as proof of the need for federal troops to enforce the injunction. Cleveland agreed, and by the evening troops entered the city.[77]

For the General Managers Association and its allies in the government, the injunction and the use of troops were two prongs of the same plan to decimate the railway labor movement. At issue was a unified labor movement challenging the unilateral corporate control of the work force—and neither the government nor the corporations intended to allow that threat to grow. Traditional American liberties were scorned, as Debs had frequently argued, for corporate interests dictated the actions of the executive branch and federal judges blatantly violated their code of ethics in their avidity to find in favor of the corporation.[78] The railroad managers had learned well the lessons of the Great Northern strike. Backed by the federal government with its special attorneys, 2,000 troops, and over 5,000 marshals, they avoided the divisions within the corporate business community that had plagued Hill. Never before had this collaboration been so public in character.[79]

In the manner of a self-fulfilling prophecy, the presence of federal troops incited the violence they were purportedly called to suppress. Whereas little violence occurred prior to 4 July, during the following week much railroad property was destroyed, and train service ground to almost a complete halt. On 8 July President Cleveland issued a proclamation against violence and ordered the troops to act decisively in suppressing the rioters.[80] In part at least, this violence stemmed from a fierce resentment directed at the presence of the troops. The men and women of Chicago, strikers and sympathizers alike, were incensed at being treated as common criminals by the government. Howard, himself a former Union soldier, testified that "the very sight of a bluecoat arouses their anger; they feel it is another instrument of oppression."[81]

Amidst this turmoil, and with far fewer resources than either the managers or the government, Debs attempted to direct strike efforts in this the most explosive labor struggle he had yet encountered. Wary of the threat of government intervention from the start, Debs repeatedly cautioned the striking men to obey the law, to refrain from violence, and not to interfere with the mails. Publicly he established a simple and quite limited tactical position for the union: "We want to win as becomes men; we want to win as becomes law-abiding citizens; we have got the right to quit in a body, and our rights end there; the railroad companies have the right to employ men to take our places; and their rights begin there, and we have no right to interfere."[82] Less than ten days after the strike began, however, the role of the railroad corporations and the federal government made it impossible to contain the strike within such a limited framework. Between the *agents provocateurs* hired by the corporations and the deep anger of working people toward the same corporations (an anger fed only recently by the Coxey agitation),[83] Debs and his directors found it difficult to control their ranks.

Even prior to the forceful entry of the federal government, the scope of the strike severely tested the organizational abilities of Debs and the young union. Their only prior experience had been a relatively local affair, involving but a single railroad. But the Pullman strike extended from Chicago to San Francisco, from St. Paul to Santa Fe and beyond into Texas, and in each instance local committees requested direction, support, and encouragement from the Chicago headquarters. As many of these members were new and unknown to Debs, such coordination proved difficult. With the Knights of Labor too weak to offer substantive support, the full burden fell upon the Chicago directors and most heavily upon Debs himself.[84] Locals across the country wired him for advice on boycott tactics, legal assistance, and organizing efforts. Simultaneously, Debs had primary responsibilities for overall strategy and for coordinating decisions with others in the labor movement.[85] Exhausted and overworked, Debs marveled that, in the days prior to the injunction, the strike continued to grow and at least a minimum of discipline prevailed.

The turning point came over the 4 July holiday. On the afternoon of the preceding day, the injunction placed the full legal power of the government at the discretion of the association. That evening troops entered the city. The following morning, Independence Day, Debs awoke in his hotel room and ambled toward the window. Immediately he cried for Theodore, who was still in bed, to come to the window. There, down on Jackson Street, the two brothers watched as federal troops stacked their arms in an adjoining courtyard. "Those fellers aren't militiamen," Debs exclaimed. "They're regulars, Theodore, they're regulars. Do you get that? Cleveland has sent the troops in."[86] At first, Debs welcomed the troops, hoping they would maintain order and thus allow the strike to proceed without violence.[87] But, on second thought, he understood that their presence marked a basic change: the troops were intended to enforce the injunction, and the American Railway Union now faced the almost certain prospect of direct conflict with the federal government. As he commented later, still somewhat shocked, the troops signaled the transformation of a strike against the railroad corporations "into a conflict in which the organized forces of society and all the powers of the municipal, State, and Federal governments were arraigned against us."[88]

The actions of the federal commander, General Nelson A. Miles, quickly bore out Debs's fears. Miles publicly expressed a bitter dislike of Debs and considered the strikers as rebels against government authority. Within hours after establishing a command post, General Miles demanded reinforcements and held the first of his many meetings with Egan. While Debs complained that such collaboration was "vulgarly out of place,"[89] he feared that, as the violence grew, the strike might turn into open confrontation between working people and their government. Accordingly on 6 July, "at the time the strike was at its very worst—at its zenith," Debs attempted to call it off. "Things," Debs felt, "were assuming too serious a phase, and . . . a point had been reached when, in the interests of peace and to prevent riot and trouble, we must declare the strike off." With the crisis at a point where "everything was at stake, where possibly it might have eventuated in a revolution," Debs and the members of the union's various committees drafted a proposal they would present to the association within the week. "We proposed," Debs later explained, "that we would declare the strike off on condition that they would take back the employees. We said, We do not ask you to recognize our organization; we do not ask you to recognize us; we simply say that this matter has become so serious that we ought to be patriotic enough to declare it off, and we are willing to meet you half way, by declaring it off . . . if you will simply take them back."[90]

That Debs never intended to lead a revolution in 1894 is quite clear from the whole tenor of his earlier career. When critical, Debs lashed out at the corporation for *its* revolutionary transformation of American society. Yet, Debs's appeal to patriotism in this instance ought not to be taken completely at face value. Confronted with certain defeat, he attempted to salvage what he could. If the men and women, in Chicago as throughout the country, might return to work without prejudice, they might yet fight another day. But if the American Railway Union was destroyed and its members blacklisted and hounded the rest of their working days, railroad unionism of any type would suffer a severe setback.

Paradoxically, this attempt at salvage led Debs to call for a general strike. At a conference he organized of Chicago's trade unionists on 8 July, Debs proposed a general strike to force Pullman and the General Managers Association to rehire the strikers on the terms Debs had outlined two days earlier. The delegates were generally supportive, but they voted to try arbitration one final time. If they did not reach a settlement with the Pullman corporation by the afternoon of 10 July, the general strike would start the following morning.[91] As was probably expected, the arbitration appeal failed—but so did the general strike. On the morning of 11 July, some union men, including members of the Knights of Labor, walked off their jobs. At most, however, 25,000 men, only a small percentage of Chicago's work force, joined the action. By this time, moreover, the situation had altered. On 10 July Debs and other officers of the union had been arrested on charges of conspiracy to obstruct interstate commerce and the mails, their offices ransacked, and their books and records confiscated by government agents. That demonstration of federal power caused some to re-evaluate their enthusiasm for the general strike. As important, however, was the position of the AFL.

After the conference on 8 July of Chicago's trade unions, the federation's affiliates in the city demanded that their president, Gompers, meet with them immediately to support their call for a general strike. Gompers opposed the strike, but, impressed with the seriousness of conditions in Chicago, he called a meeting for 12 July at the Briggs House to which he invited the executive board of the AFL and other national union officers, including representatives from the railway brotherhoods. Debs, released on bond following his arrest, also attended.[92] Whether Gompers planned the meeting for 12 July in order to ensure the defeat of the proposed general strike on 11 July is doubtful, but he did use the conference to achieve similar goals. Antagonistic to the very idea of the American Railway Union since its inception, Gompers plotted a course of action at the Briggs House meeting that, in his own words, "was the biggest service that could be performed to maintain the integrity of the Railroad Brotherhoods."[93] The key to this was the decision to invite the brotherhood chiefs. Although they were not affiliated with the AFL, had not been requested by the Chicago trade unionists, and were fundamentally hostile to the strike and to Debs, Gompers publicly recognized them as "men who were clothed with responsibility as well as authority" over railway workers. Completely dismissing the American Railway Union, Gompers insisted that these men approve any future plans as "they would know what action they could or could not take." Gompers proved quite willing to jettison the strikers to pursue his hope of attracting the brotherhoods to his organization.[94]

The final results of the Briggs House meeting were not surprising. With Gompers in the chair, the official statement, while avoiding direct public criticism of the union, called the strike "impulsive" and urged all members of the AFL engaged in sympathy strikes to return to work immediately. "A general strike at this time," the statement explained, "is inexpedient, unwise and contrary to the best interests of the working people."[95]

Even a decade later, Debs remained incensed at these words. He felt, accurately, that Gompers had opposed the new union from the start, and he agreed with some Chicago trade unionists that Gompers had been a traitor to the labor movement. Accusing Gompers of delivering "one of the final blows that crushed the strike," Debs concluded his indictment: "Mr. Gompers and his associates had far better stayed away. They not only did no good, but did great harm. The whole capitalist press exulted over the decision of Mr. Gompers and his colleagues, commended their conservatism and pointed to them as final proof that the strike should be broken and as complete justification for the brutal ferocity with which which they were maligning and outraging the strikers."[96] But while these charges had certain elements of truth, they were not completely fair to Gompers, and they presented Debs's own actions during the Briggs House meeting less than candidly.

When Debs met Gompers in Chicago that July, he privately told the AFL president that he favored a strong course of action. "I would make an injury to one in the cause of labor the concern of all," Debs stressed. "I would muster all the forces of labor in a peaceable effort to secure a satisfactory adjustment of our grievances, even if we had to involve all the industrial industries of the country."[97] Publicly, however, Debs himself refused to advocate such a course. Addressing the Briggs House meeting at an evening session on 12 July, Debs suggested that yet another committee attempt arbitration. If this again failed, then, he weakly stated, the general strike might proceed.[98] Since the proposed general strike would only enforce Debs's official statement conceding defeat on the major issues in the strike, it is not surprising that Gompers refused his support. To risk the possible existence of his organization in a cause already conceded was not, Gompers felt, reasonable: "To recommend to various labor organizations to strike in sympathy with the A.R.U. movement was unfair to those wage earners, as the A.R.U. confessed failure and that the strike was a lost cause. Such a course would destroy the constructive labor movement of the country."[99]

But other aspects of Debs's critique were valid. The fundamental differences between the two men concerning the nature of the trade union and its function in society, implicit in their experiences during the past decade, were finally and irretrievably acknowledged during the Pullman strike. Gompers, searching for stability within the labor movement and for its acceptance by the corporation, sought to create a movement based on business principles. While he hoped for the day when the "influences of the trade union movement" would "form the ethics of industry, society, and the state,"[100] he carefully structured his organization to accommodate as far as possible to corporate realities. Seeking the best possible situation for skilled workers, Gompers expressed little concern for the vast number of unskilled workers he ignored. For Debs, such a course was despicable. On calm reflection, Debs might possibly have understood why Gompers did not support the general strike in July 1894, but in no fashion could he approve Gompers's underlying reasoning. For Debs, the trade union movement was not merely a guide toward higher wages for a select handful of skilled workers. Its task was far greater, and he suggested as much when he discussed the implications of the Pullman strike:

> The great lesson of the Pullman strike is found in the fact that it arouses widespread sympathy. This fellow-feeling for the woes of others—this desire to help the unfortunate . . . should be accepted as at once the hope of civilization and the supreme glory of manhood. And yet . . . epithets, calumny, denunciation in every form that malice and mendacity could invent have been poured forth in a vitriolic tirade to scathe those who advocated and practiced the Christ-like virtue of sympathy. The crime of the American Railway Union was the practical exhibition of sympathy for the Pullman employees. Humanity and Christianity, undebauched and un-perverted, are forever pleading for sympathy for the poor and the op-pressed.[101]

This commitment to a "practical exhibition of sympathy" might well measure the distance between Debs and Gompers. For if Debs had learned one idea in the circuitous paths he had traveled since 1877, it was that an injury to one was indeed the concern of all. Debs might well have added that, for workers and nonworkers alike, this concept was central lest they preside over the dissolution of their society.

The results of the Briggs House meeting effectively ended the Pullman strike. Without substantive additional support from organized labor, the American Railway Union had no choice but to accept defeat. Neither for Debs nor his followers, however, did this indicate a return to more tranquil times. The General Managers Association moved to complete its intended destruction of railroad unionism, and Debs faced a series of legal and political repercussions stemming from the strike. In responding to these myriad pressures, Debs developed the major themes of his post-Pullman career.

The most immediate problem faced by Debs and the union membership was to provide for their legal defense. Throughout the country strikers faced charges of violating the injunction. With the union's funds exhausted, there was no money for lawyers or fines, and many served jail sentences.[102] This was true for Debs and the national officers as well. Arrested on 10 July on charges of conspiracy, Debs and the full board were re-arrested on 17 July—this time on charges of contempt of court for violating the original injunction. In an act of solidarity with the membership, they now refused bail and awaited trial in the Cook County jail. Released on their own recognizance on 25 July when Walker, now a member of the prosecution, became ill, Debs immediately returned to Terre Haute. Exhausted from the incessant activity of the past three months, he spent the next two weeks in bed.

In a brief trial in November 1894, before Judge Woods sitting without a jury, the directors of the union were found guilty of contempt. Debs was sentenced to six months in jail while the other directors received three months. After their appeals were denied, Debs and his associates reported to the Woodstock, Illinois, prison, some fifty miles from Chicago, early in January 1895. The following day, the more serious trial for conspiracy began before Judge Grosscup and a jury of twelve citizens. Debs and his attorneys, Clarence Darrow and S. S. Gregory, relished this opportunity and immediately attacked the prosecution, the General Managers Association, and the association's collusion with the federal government. Contrasting the secrecy and deviousness of the corporation with the public openness of the union, the defense ridiculed the charge of conspiracy. Pullman's refusal to honor a subpoena to testify only enhanced the defense's credibility. When a juror became ill on 8 February, the U.S. attorney and the judge recessed court, never to reconvene it. They had clearly lost the case—one report had the jury 11-1 for acquittal—but Debs's legal problems were far from over. He was temporarily released as his lawyers again appealed the contempt conviction. When again denied that June, Debs and the directors returned to Woodstock to complete their sentences.[103]

During the year following his arrests, when neither in court nor in jail, Debs gave his time and energy to prevent a total collapse of the American Railway Union. Touring the country constantly, Debs now accepted fees for his speeches in order to pay the union's debts and "to preserve free from blemish the name of that organization so dear to its members and so hated and feared by the railroads."[104] But all organizations among railway workers, even the brotherhoods, were in shambles. Over 8,000 firemen, more than one-third of the total pre-strike membership, either lost their jobs or ceased their affiliation with the organization to protect those jobs.[105] Most seriously hurt, of course, were the former strikers, brotherhood and American Railway Union men alike. The railroad corporations inaugurated an extensive and severe blacklist. When a worker asked for a recommendation from his pre-strike employer, he would receive the usual assessment of his technical abilities. A prospective employer then held the letter to the light after the applicant left the room. If the watermark showed a crane with its head cut off, the man had been active during the strike and was not to be hired. The decapitated crane caused untold suffering throughout the western half of the country.[106]

Yet at times it seemed that Debs's efforts might indeed revive the union. Publicly he repeated his assessment that "the prospects in the near future are very bright." When during a five-week period in 1895 an average of 130 new members enlisted per week, Debs saw that as a sign that "at heart the men are with us & they'll come to us soon."[107] But the problems were far greater than the available solutions. Not only were the corporations adamant, the blacklist effective, and many of the members in jail, but also the traditional problem of intralabor bitterness once again played a disruptive role. The AFL and the brotherhoods, of course, opposed the union's resurgence,[108] but there was even trouble within the American Railway Union. The men of the Great Northern, who participated in what was then Debs's greatest moment in May 1894, had given only lukewarm support to the Pullman strikers but a month later. The following year, when Hill planned to reduce wages again, they nevertheless applied to the union for support. Incensed, Debs instructed his brother not to forward any money: "We put up all the money we had for them in'94 and as soon as they got their pay raises they let the order go to the devil." Still furious, Debs later wrote his friend, F. X. Holl: "Were I guilty of such a crime I am inclined to believe I would commit suicide."[109]

This bitterness within the organization, compounded by the near total disintegration of the rank and file, made all but the most sanguine understand that there would be no revival of the American Railway Union. Further, for Debs, the dreamlike vision that had enveloped him as he stood before his townspeople in May 1894 and that seemed to fulfill his most basic hopes now lay shattered at his feet. The American Railway Union itself would not be the agent to reverse the trend of corporate control.

This disorganization, however, did not prevent Debs from engaging in a strenuous speaking schedule. While raising money to pay off debts, he also expanded his audience. He would always retain a special affinity for railway workers, but in the aftermath of the Pullman strike Debs became even more a national figure. Many who were not workers were drawn to him, affected by the force of his critique of the changes that had altered their lives as well. As Debs's private secretary commented in 1895, the just-completed tour was "the greatest campaign that has ever been made in the name of labor in this country. Farmers came for twenty miles, it is said, to hear him speak."[110] In the past Debs had been quite clear about the distinction between farmers and laborers and quite critical of the Populist party for confusing that difference. His thinking had changed, however. He spoke now not to organize a specific group of workers on a certain issue but rather to galvanize his multiclass audience to the dangers evident in the corporate revolution. This, too, he had done in the past, but always with some grounding within a specific labor context. After Pullman, however, Debs lost for the moment that concrete base rooted in working-class life and addressed a more amorphous, less defined audience. The Debs who had dismissed two lodges of the Brotherhood for their opposition to his political advocacy seemed to enjoy the new freedom. As he told his brother after a particularly exciting meeting in Milwaukee: "the ovation cannot be described. The audience was one of the most magnificent that ever congregated in Milwaukee. The vast hall was packed to the doors and hundreds turned away and not a soul of the 4000 people left till at 11 P.M. the last word of my two hour speech died on my lips. The uproar and enthusiasm that followed made it impossible to call for subscribers but I shall try this at other points."[111] Although certainly exhilarating, such meetings were a poor substitute for concrete organizing and apparently not always a successful source of funds, either.

As Debs became even more the public figure, the publicity altered his personal life as well. Never a modest man, his sense of his own importance expanded greatly during these years. To the wife of a friend who presented him with a portrait of himself, Debs vainly, if tactfully, explained that the photograph it was based on did not favor him and suggested two others as possibilities.[112] In a more serious manner, he developed an unrealistic sense of his own power to renew the union, the labor movement, and the very culture. He believed his own contributions indispensable and perceived the work of others as but supportive of his major efforts. The Buffalo local, Eugene told Theodore from Woodstock, "says that one speech there will surely give them 200 new members & I believe it." One speech, however, even one by Debs, was not a substitute for effective organizing.[113]

In his family life the period surrounding Pullman witnessed an intensification of familiar patterns. After initial concern over the depth and intensity of the vilification their son received in the press (which caused Eugene to reassure his aging parents that in being "simply true to myself" they need not "fear that I will dishonor the family traditions"),[114] Daniel and Marguerite offered consistent encouragement and support. On receiving a food basket from his mother and sister, Eugenie, the incarcerated strike leader proclaimed that "this sweet and tender devotion which is mother's soul and very life itself" produced in him new compassion "for all the race." Such support, however, also produced another reaction. "New aspirations leap from my soul," Eugene told Theodore. "By all the gods of all the ages I'll write my name at high water mark on the scroll of honor just in token of that love with which men are God-like and without which they are worse than savages."[115] Eugene returned to this theme in a more public fashion a year later. In a letter from Woodstock to the 1895 Labor Day rally in Terre Haute, he remembered how his mother's love revitalized him and hoped that the recollection of "this mood" in those present would "inspire renewed devotion to the interests of labor."[116]

The aid and encouragement Eugene received from his parents equalled the support his sisters provided, as they took time from their lives and families to aid him in many ways. But the brunt of this responsibility for the most famous sibling's pragmatic demands and emotional needs fell on Theodore's shoulders. Whether visiting at Woodstock or staffing the offices in Chicago or Terre Haute, Theodore continued in his role as his older brother's alter ego. At times Eugene could be quite imperious. In a letter reflective of many others during this period, Eugene told Theodore of his latest political alliances, outlined the theme of his most recent article, and demanded some postage stamps: "I must have these to mail out my acknowledgements, so hurry them along."[117] If Theodore ever felt resentment over his role, he never expressed it. Indeed, as did his sisters and parents, Theodore freely granted Eugene primacy within the family and sought in large measure the meaning of his own life in his brother's reflected image. Now son, now confidant, occasionally stern, and even paternal, Theodore understood that his brother's public career depended upon the intense dedication and unquestioning emotional support of the family. Eugene, too, acknowledged this. As he wrote one of his sisters from jail on his fortieth birthday: "The outer affairs of life are serious—it has been with me a perpetual struggle but it has also had its compensations. The inner life, the home life is the sustaining element. We must make this as beautiful as love and consistency can make it. We must *all* be in close touch, in warmest sympathy and vitalize and strengthen one another in every hour of trial."[118]

How stark was the contrast, then, between these close bonds and those with his wife, Kate? Eugene mentioned her only occasionally during this time and then most often as part of a formal litany recounting his family.[119] Over the past decade his own development had widened rather than narrowed their incompatibility. Separated by basic status differences, Eugene and Kate seemed to present a ludicrous contrast by 1894. With the nation's newspapers running headlines about the "Debs Rebellion" and his union financially bankrupt, Kate came to Chicago to comfort her husband. One reporter etched the tall, full-bodied woman as she approached the jail door: "She dresses well, and wears diamonds, a good sized stone in ear, and two separate sparklers of about a carat and a quarter each on her left hand."[120]

Following Pullman, Debs came home even less than before, usually only to recuperate from illness or to prepare for the next tour. With the exception of a visit to Woodstock, Kate remained at home.[121] She no longer tried to be his secretary and certainly not his companion during his feverish speaking schedule. As one somewhat hostile source said of her, she became a quite private person, seeing few neighbors and friends, concerned mainly with maintaining a largely empty house. To complicate matters even further, when the house was full, it was usually with Eugene's friends for whom Kate had little sympathy.[122]

Debs's national fame and notoriety thus reinforced earlier patterns in his life. His tendency to see himself as the eye of the hurricane—calm yet directing the drama that surrounded him—grew in vast proportions, as did his need for affirmation from family and friends. The pages of the *Railway Times*, a journal committed to the industrial organization of railroad men, became a vehicle for a cult of personality centered on Debs. During one three-month period in 1896, for example, more than a quarter of each issue highlighted his activities—a figure no other member or activity of the union even approached.[123] But the period after Pullman was not just one of applause and praise, with the expected opposition from the corporation's allies. Before he could turn full attention to new directions he had to resolve, finally and seriously, his long intricate relationship with the Brotherhood of Locomotive Firemen whose journal he still edited.

The encounter occurred at the Firemen's 1894 convention at Harrisburg, Pennsylvania. The recent Pullman strike dominated discussion, and Sargent devoted a major portion of his official report to an analysis of the American Railway Union. To the west of Chicago, Sargent noted, many lodges had violated their charters and joined the boycott, and the result was a seriously weakened Brotherhood. Of Debs, Sargent still claimed great respect and even friendship but thought him "foolish" and too easily influenced by disreputable elements within the organization. In defense of the Brotherhood's position, Sargent sharply reminded the delegates that during the Buffalo switchmen's strike in 1892, Debs himself had opposed a sympathy boycott. Deeply angry but publicly restrained, Sargent claimed that he was a better friend of labor "than the men responsible for this last conflict," and he urged the delegates to bar their members from joining any other railway organization. Although rarely criticized directly, it was clear that Sargent had launched a full attack upon Debs and his union.[124]

Three days later, Debs waited in an anteroom just off the convention floor. So deep was the antipathy toward him from these delegates—some of whom he had worked with for almost two decades—that for the first time in his experience before a labor convention a strong minority voted to refuse him floor privileges. When finally admitted, Debs made the most of the opportunity. He delivered a long, moving, and, at times, cutting defense of his past policy and action. In chilling tones he told the assembled delegates that he came not as a friend but rather "from a point of right and justice . . . to respond to all charges and innuendoes affecting my character." Debs insisted that the Firemen themselves must share responsibility for the current tension, as he had made quite clear at Cincinnati his disagreements with the order. In defending the American Railway Union, he issued a blistering attack upon the Brotherhood as a "class organization" that excluded a majority of unskilled workers. Federation, he continued, was another sham. How could it be other when a single grand officer possessed the "autocratic authority" to veto any strike? But the boast of being a true "class organization" even for skilled workers came under Debs's withering comments. No brotherhood met that goal, as each included men from the different railroad crafts: the Engineers had wipers among their members and about 45 percent of all Firemen were, in fact, railroad engineers. As this was the case, he demanded, "why not have an organization to represent all?" Finally, Debs remarked on the powerful concentration of capital and stated that the corporation used the divisions within labor to defeat working people. Knowing this, no longer could the Firemen or any other brotherhood take pleasure in their individual harmonious relations with a given railroad. Such relations, precisely because they were individual and thus excluded other working people, were *prima facie* evidence of collaboration with capital.[125]

In a poignant conclusion Debs examined his long association with the Firemen. He reviewed the sacrifices made, the opportunities rejected, and the honesty with which he had handled over $5,000,000 through the past years. He noted that his popularity had begun to wane at the 1890 convention at San Francisco but acknowledged the pride he felt in the support and affection shown him at the Cincinnati meeting. He dared any delegate to question his honesty or good intentions. With pain and anger, Debs then turned his attention to his home lodge, Number 16, in Terre Haute, where he had been a member since February 1875. Delegates from that lodge had strongly criticized Debs at the convention, questioned his leadership, and opposed his political involvements. Glaring down from the podium, Debs scornfully dismissed their complaints. "[I] probably missed six meetings" during the first ten years of the lodge's existence, Debs explained, and did "more for that lodge than a man can in a century." But he had long been disaffected. The lodge was now little more than a fraternal club, occupied with meaningless rituals and hazings and oblivious of the problems before labor. "I confess," he testily yet sadly concluded, "I seldom visit them now. I am opposed to such imitations. I saw men walking around with a rope around their necks and other senseless doings and I was opposed to it. I went home and read books."[126]

It had been less than five months since Debs's triumphant reception in Terre Haute at the conclusion of the Great Northern strike. Yet his expectations of harmony were destroyed, as even his home lodge desired to dissociate itself from Debs. Hurt and angry, he nonetheless ended on a different note, which indicated something of the direction of his future activities. The Pullman strike was a "spontaneous upheaval," Debs argued, a sign that "the French revolution will be repeated" unless dramatic steps are taken. The current depression, a premeditated "bankers' panic," was but the final proof of the necessity for labor's involvement in politics. "If we could but destroy the money monopoly, land monopoly, and the rest of them, all would be different." Since aversion to politics in the current era meant the destruction of labor, Debs proclaimed his desire for workers "to unify at the polls and vote for an independent people's party." Prophetically, Debs told the delegates, most of whom would give scant heed, that "there are questions I would like to see labor interest themselves in. Their conditions are like a cancer, you can cover it with a poultice but the cancer continues to spread. You must apply the knife and root it out if you expect relief." With that challenge, Debs left the podium. In the silence that greeted his words, he walked out of the hall, never again to address a convention of the Brotherhood of Locomotive Firemen.[127]

If no individual delegate stood to confront Debs following his speech, collectively they wasted little time in removing reminders of his presence. His longtime critic, W. S. Carter, won election as editor of the magazine, and the convention unanimously agreed, as "essential to the welfare of the order," to remove the national offices from Terre Haute. They quickly endorsed Sargent's prohibition of dual membership and reaffirmed their opposition to sympathy strikes. Old allies appeared in new garb. T. P. O'Rourke, once a critic from the "left" and a supporter of Debs's attack on the conservative Brotherhood policies,[128] understood the new tone. Chastened by Pullman, he altered his views, supported the majority, and became secretary of the grand executive board. Even J. J. Hannahan, who had been helpful during the strike, muted his opinions and was re-elected vice-master. While the exorcism proceeded, Terence V. Powderly and Gompers beamed approvingly from the dais.[129]

Strangely, the Harrisburg convention did not completely sever Debs's relationship with the Firemen. No longer an officer, he had written his final editorial, "Farewell to the Brotherhood," in November 1894. Yet Debs continued to pay his dues at least until December 1895.[130] Despite himself, Debs, at something of a loss after so many years of involvement, found the parting difficult. Throughout 1895 he peppered the magazine with letters and short articles defending his position. That September the new editor decided an official analysis of Debs's career with the order must appear, to end once and for all the continued debate and dissension. Until 1889, Carter wrote, Debs was "the most popular member" of the order whose "wishes and advice controlled, to a great extent, the legislation of the Brotherhood." In the years that followed, however, he became involved with other groups and ideas and seriously criticized the brotherhoods generally and the Firemen specifically. As a sign of Debs's essential untrustworthiness, Carter found it ironic that "the very things he condemns as President of the American Railway Union he approved as Grand Secretary and Treasurer of the Brotherhood of Locomotive Firemen."

Carter raised two major points. He contested Debs's condemnation of the Brotherhood for accepting passes from railroad corporations and Debs's critique of the order for failing to support the Pullman strikers. Of the first point, Carter simply stated that Debs had been a strong defender of the pass system while a grand officer. But Debs's comments on the strike drew a more pointed response. Carter rejected the claim that the Firemen had scabbed and argued that a majority of the rank and file refused to support the strike on their own initiative. Caustically he reminded Debs of his own role in 1886, when the Knights of Labor struck the Gould system and desired the support of the Firemen: "The Grand Officers of the Brotherhood, Brother Debs being one of them, sustained the Brotherhoods in ignoring District Master Workman Martin Irons' order to strike. Brother Debs did not brand himself as a scab; at least, not at that time." Carter saw no need to revise that policy a decade later.[131]

Carter's retorts were carefully chosen to focus attention on Debs's more vulnerable areas. It was common knowledge among railroad men, for example, that as late as December 1893, the directors of the American Railway Union applied for passes from the railroad. A common practice, and certainly no heinous crime, yet it remained a practice that Debs found difficult to admit.[132] Similarly, even after the Pullman strike, Debs tried to obtain a promotion for a U.S. army officer through his personal influence with Daniel Voorhees, Indiana's Democratic senator.[133] As Carter well knew, what Debs often presented as moral absolutes he as often violated out of regard for personal friendship or convenience. More embarrassing, however, was Carter's reference to Debs's role during 1886. While Carter would never admit that Debs's thinking had changed for valid reasons, his critique nevertheless perceptively caught Debs in one of his more fundamental contradictions.

As on other issues in the past, Debs was simply unable to discuss frankly the development of his own thought. The strange consistency in his career—the circuitous path that indeed had led him from 1877 to 1886 and now to 1894—remained obscured and clouded. Debs could and did preach with great power, but he frequently created barriers to exploring with others the meaning of shared yet different experiences. Carter he could never convert, nor Sargent either, but there were others. Perhaps the men of Vigo Lodge, who remained within the familiar confines of Terre Haute, might have been influenced. At the very least, his own process of "radicalization," as he would later call it, could have been presented more clearly for what it was—a critical response of American culture to a major transition within the society. But Debs could not, and Carter relied on this in his critique.

By 1895, then, Debs had dismissed each and every brotherhood as an effective labor organization. That left only the American Railway Union, now little more than a shell of its former self. Yet, as he told Henry Demarest Lloyd, "I am inclined to be optimistic." The "flagrant abuses" of corporate power were now well known, and the "emancipation and redemption of men from this thralldom" were foreseeable.[134] On the periphery of the labor movement for the first time in his life—paradoxically at the time his fame and reputation were greatest—Debs sought another way to maintain the struggle to preserve American culture. In his final speech before the Firemen he had indicated how he intended to accomplish this. He would "apply the knife" and "root out" that cancer of monopoly through a complete commitment to political action. Always the major focus of his public life, a resuscitation of American political culture through a defense of the independent citizen-producer became his primary emphasis in the battle he led to humanize industrial capitalist society.

6

What Is to Be Done?

LOOKING BACK AFTER some twenty-five years, Eugene Debs suggested that the direction of his activities since the Pullman strike had been determined by events. "The change from the economic A.R.U. to the political Social Democracy" had been "a matter of grim necessity, forced by the railroad corporations which waged relentless war upon the union and made its existence as a labor union impossible."[1] But this change was neither as dramatic nor as forced as Debs asserted. Throughout his career Debs had advocated political action and his last address to the Firemen continued that traditional emphasis. The years following Pullman did, however, force Debs to rethink, in some confusion, the meaning of that political commitment.

As the promise of Grover Cleveland the campaigner evaporated with the policies of Cleveland the president, Debs searched for a political alternative even as he built the American Railway Union. Through the winter of 1893–94, numerous midwestern papers, aware of his discontent, boomed Debs for the Populist party's nomination for governor of Indiana.[2] At the same time the *Railway Times* edged closer to an open endorsement of the Populist movement.[3] That March, to the accompaniment of the familiar chant "Debs, Debs, Debs," the president of the American Railway Union told Terre Haute's Populist party members that he now renounced his long association with the Democratic party. Declaring himself "an out and out People's [Populist] party man," Debs condemned the national banking system and argued there was little difference between either of the old parties.[4]

A similar tone marked the June convention of the American Railway Union. Debs delivered a blistering attack on the Cleveland administration and, in urging endorsement of the Populist party, insisted that only "the ballots of workingmen emancipated from the [old] parties" could force the "legislation which will lift workingmen to a higher plane of prosperity."[5] With great fervor, the delegates endorsed Debs's proposal, sadly noting that the traditional political parties, "like unto nearly everything else that we as good citizens have cherished, [have] been stolen, and [are] today locked up in Plutocracy's vault." With deep anger coupled with a strong faith, they asserted "that the hour has come when we should place it on record *that further loyalty to either is treason to RIGHT.*"[6]

Relations between this industrial union and the Populist movement remained quite close during 1894. Throughout the Midwest Pullman strikers frequently left their old brotherhoods and their accustomed political parties in the same motion.[7] This was particularly evident in Minnesota and Illinois, especially in Chicago,[8] and Debs repeatedly underscored this closeness during the fall of 1894. "While working for the A.R.U. we are all united upon the People's Party question," he wrote his friend F. X. Holl in October 1894. A month later one newspaper quoted Debs as stating "that it is hard to say where the agitation for a closer union of railway employees ends and the agitation for the People's Party begins."[9] This emphasis on political activity was not new but Debs's revised opinion of the trade union was.

"I will never again have any official connection with a strike," Debs proclaimed throughout late 1894 and 1895. If the recent experience taught one lesson, he explained, it was that the alliance between the corporation and the government was simply too strong to challenge on the economic front, especially as the violence that frequently resulted from such challenges turned American opinion against workers and strikes.[10] This turning point resulted from his new analysis of the meaning of the trade union under corporate capitalism. Against the power of a corporate-directed technology, Debs argued that the "trade unions will disappear and with them the trades as such." The linotype machine will replace the printer and even the locomotive fireman will become obsolete. Corporations will expand to "continental proportions and swallow up the national resources and the means of production and distribution." This long "night of capitalism will be dark," Debs warned, and against its power the trade union was feeble.[11] Stark as this analysis was, Debs never suggested that the struggle was over but rather pointed to the American political tradition as the ultimate source of strength.

The faith of Debs and his followers in the redemptive power of the ballot is, from a current perspective, simply staggering. They took the republican tradition seriously and stressed the individual dignity and power inherent in the concept of citizenship. While frequently vague over exactly how to transform their society, these men and women had no doubt but that, if the people united, the vitality of that tradition would point the way.[12] Too much should not be made over the absence of a detailed pragmatic program in 1894, as Debs and others understood that one only had to look at the revolutionary changes in America created by industry to pinpoint the major abuses. The development of a viable organization to channel the widespread discontent was of more immediate interest to Debs. This concern, and not simple "grim necessity," now motivated him, and even from Woodstock jail Debs eagerly anticipated his future role.

Wearing their convictions as badges of honor, Debs and the other directors of the American Railway Union surrendered to the authorities in June 1895 to serve out their prison terms. Debs insisted on a rigorous daily schedule. The men rose at six A.M. and, after breakfast and exercise, devoted the day to union matters and political affairs. As Debs wrote to a friend, "We have strict rules and no 'monkeying.' "[13] Debs also received numerous visitors, common working people as well as the more famous. To each he communicated, as one reporter noted during an earlier incarceration in 1894, his "peculiar personal magnetism" and "irrepressible optimism."[14] The sheriff of Woodstock, George Eckert, aided his famous prisoner in transforming the jail into a union office. Like Debs, Eckert was of Alsacian heritage and did all in his power to make the stay pleasant.[15]

While at Woodstock, Debs grew even more optimistic. To his father he predicted that the "whole plutocratic crew . . . are 'skating on mighty thin ice' " and proudly asserted his future role: "*I tell you*—You may rest assured that when the storm breaks I will be in it."[16] Jail not only failed to dampen his spirit but actually encouraged him. His incarceration proved to him the fragility of the system that jailed him, as it underscored its essential moral bankruptcy.

Then and in the years to come, the Woodstock experience emerged as the central mythic event of Debs's life. Journalists and novelists, untutored comrades and college-educated converts to Socialism—all came to see in that six-month sentence the origins of a fundamental change in Debs's life, in the history of their society, and, for many, in their own lives as well. "The Debs who emerged from jail was not the same man who had gone in," two sympathizers later wrote. "A new idea—that of socialism—was beginning to take hold of him."[17] Others as well, including adherents of almost every leftist tendency in twentieth-century America, understood this experience in similar terms. A legend grew of a dramatic conversion: that, in a flash of overwhelming insight, Debs understood the systematic problems with capitalism and the promise of Socialism and emerged from jail a changed and charged man.[18] Even Samuel Gompers, by 1895 a confirmed and bitter opponent, echoed these sentiments if from a different perspective. After Woodstock, he claimed, Debs "had lost all faith in the power of constructive work and became the advocate of revolt . . . the apostle of failure and later of secession."[19]

But the greatest promoter of this conversion theme—which found its archetype in the experience of Saul on to the road to Damascus—remained Debs himself. As the years progressed, he claimed that at Woodstock he discovered the reality of capitalism and accepted the mission of his life to preach Socialism. Prior to Pullman, Debs wrote in 1921, "I had heard but little of Socialism . . . [and] had yet to learn the workings of the capitalist system." But the strike changed that. "I was to be baptized in Socialism in the roar of conflict . . . in the gleam of every bayonet and the flash of every rifle *the class struggle was revealed*. This was my first practical lesson in Socialism." In jail, Debs continued, he pored over Edward Bellamy (whom he had earlier dismissed as a "Boston savant"), Lawrence Gronlund, W. H. "Coin" Harvey, Ignatius Donnelly, and especially Karl Kautsky, the German popularizer of Karl Marx. Into the heady mix, as Debs told the story, dropped Victor Berger, the Milwaukee Socialist leader, bearing as gifts the three volumes of Marx's *Das Kapital*. That gift, accompanied by an obligatory introductory sermon, was "the very first to set the 'wires humming in my system.' "[20]

In a 1924 interview Debs expanded on this theme. Then professing that he had been a Socialist even before Pullman, he stated that while at Woodstock he "decided to no longer resist the inevitable" and "accepted his mission."[21] That Debs himself deeply believed this account was indicated in a private letter written in 1925 to the man he felt most influenced him. Responding to Karl Kautsky's greetings on his seventieth birthday, Debs wrote: "I have always felt myself in debt . . . to your gifted pen for having opened my eyes to the light which guided me into the socialist movement. I was in jail, one of the immediate victims of capitalism, sitting in the darkness as it were, when your pamphlets first came into my hands and your influence first made itself felt in my life." Praising Kautsky for his "crystal-clear expositions," Debs wondered even then how anyone who read them could resist joining the Socialist movement.[22]

The Woodstock experience is critical in any evaluation of Debs's life and career. It remains the portal through which one understands the meaning of Socialism for Debs and other Americans in the decades to come. If the dramatic conversion did in fact occur, Debs's Socialist activity then marked a sharp break with the concerns and ideas of the first twenty years of his career. The conversion theme implicitly places Socialism outside the boundaries of traditional American political discourse and stresses its alien, if not subversive, character. It also provides an obvious critique of Debs's grasp of Socialist theory and an easy path to dismiss Debs and the movement he led. As such unlikely companions as Elizabeth Gurley Flynn and Daniel Bell have both noted—one sadly, the other with a certain derision—Debs's Socialism simply did not fit the intellectual categories of orthodox theory.[23] But perhaps the issue is neither Socialism's alien nature nor Debs's theoretical deficiencies, but the legend itself.

Debs celebrated his fortieth birthday in Woodstock jail. It would have been difficult, if not impossible, for him to reject in one moment the personal and cultural formulations of his earlier life. Further, other turns in his life had come not capriciously but from a continuing search to achieve certain consistent goals. The Woodstock experience, shorn of the mythic qualities with which the older Debs infused it, can help to explore the meaning of Socialism for this preeminent native son and through him for many other Americans as well.

If Pullman marked Debs's baptism into Socialism, it was not immediately evident. Testifying before the U.S. Strike Commission in 1894, Debs urged the substitution of the "cooperative commonwealth" for the wage system but resisted identification as a Socialist. "No sir; I do not call myself a socialist. There is a wide difference in the interpretation or definition of the term. I believe in the cooperative commonwealth upon the principles laid down by Lawrence Gronlund."[24] While Gronlund's principles might have served for some as a stepping-stone toward a more regular Marxism, for Debs they did not. Debs's understanding of the "cooperative commonwealth" remained as ill-defined and vague as the term Socialist, but, when pressed for a definition, he repeatedly placed that concept within the bounds of American political culture. He scorned the competitive system and demanded its overthrow by the ballot, as "every man is entitled to all he produces with his brain and hands."[25]

The religious underpinnings of American culture were also evident. Quoting the Socialist minister, George Herron, Debs argued that "Cain was the author of the competitive theory" while "the cross of Jesus stands as its eternal denial."[26] He relied on the poet Longfellow and not Marx or Kautsky in reasserting America's potential and again traced that promise to his culture's universal male suffrage.[27] But, he pondered on 4 July 1895 in Woodstock, this "most valued jewel" has been stolen from the people's "crown of sovereignty"—"can it be recovered or is it entirely lost?" With fervor and passion, Debs recalled his country's revolutionary tradition: "If the anniversary of the Fourth of July is devoted to arousing the American people to a realization of their great misfortune, if they will resolve to regain their liberties by renewing the pledge of the Fathers to perish or conquer, then Woods and WOODSTOCK JAIL may stand in the future monumental infamies, from which the people may go forth as did the revolutionary heroes from the infamous edicts of King George to regain their lost liberties."[28]

Although Debs now called his goal the cooperative commonwealth, it differed in few respects from the themes developed in his 1890 editorial, "Fraternization." Then, as in 1895, competition pitted itself against cooperation, and he invoked the religious element of American republicanism to justify his critique. Significantly, the millennial promise of the American tradition remained strong. "I have no sympathy with anarchy," Debs told a Chicago reporter from his jail cell, and "socialism is a broad term. I believe in every man having the opportunity to advance to the fullest limits of his abilities. I do not believe in the kind of socialism that measures everyone in the same mold."[29]

Substantively different in tone and circumstance, the final message nonetheless remained close to his earlier editorials. As Debs noted in a prison interview in the summer of 1895, he still believed "education, industry, frugality, integrity, veracity, fidelity, diligence, sobriety and charity"—the whole panoply of traditional Protestant virtues—essential to success, and he pointed to Lincoln as the classic American example. But present conditions presented serious new obstacles. Industrial capitalism, directed by giant national and multinational corporations, had so changed the structure of society that even adherence to these virtues resulted for many in poverty and degradation. To oppose this powerful counterrevolutionary impulse from business, Debs sought not to dismiss but to revive the power of those values.[30]

In pragmatic ways as well, Debs resisted even a nominal identification with the Socialist movement. A national figure, Debs was besieged with requests to lead or participate in various movements. But when the Socialist members of Chicago's trade unions offered Debs the leadership of a proposed Socialist industrial union, Debs ignored them. A Nebraska Socialist, W. L. Rosenberg, had a similar experience. Urged by Rosenberg to head an avowedly Socialist movement committed to a revolutionary transformation of America, Debs, from his jail cell, refused. "The first thing in order," he instructed Rosenberg, was "to unify all classes and schools of reformers" upon a common platform in order "to win at the polls and usher in the better day."[31] One of the more persistent requests came from Thomas J. Morgan, the Chicago labor activist, Socialist, and lawyer. In September 1895 Morgan accompanied Keir Hardie, the British Socialist and trade unionist, to Woodstock. Urging the formation of an International Bureau of Correspondence and Agitation to unite all favorable "to the establishment of the Industrial Commonwealth," Morgan asked Debs to head the group. As Morgan later wrote Henry Demarest

Lloyd: "I forced the results of our meeting into the following": Debs became president, Hardie, vice-president, and Morgan, secretary. But the results Morgan forced did not take. Rethinking his position, Debs refused Morgan permission to publicize the meeting and resigned from the bureau.[32]

The importance of Debs's resistance to adopting the Socialist label at this time is not merely of semantic interest. Ultimately, of course, he would embrace the term, but he would bring to it a meaning specific to his earlier career and profoundly rooted in his understanding of the American democratic tradition. The Pullman and Woodstock experiences do indicate a growing radicalization, but Debs took his inspiration from Jefferson and Lincoln and not from orthodox Socialist writers. Never had Debs's basic ideological vision found such forceful expression than in his oration upon release from jail in November 1895. There, rather than in the wistful strands of later legend, lay the themes that would inform his public career in the decades to come.

Debs's "Liberation Day" began early on the morning of 22 November. After breakfast with Sheriff Eckert's family, he had Theodore drive him through the small town to bid farewell to his friends of the past six months. By mid-afternoon, crowds had formed in the streets as the townspeople and surrounding residents arrived to view the ceremonies. At five o'clock that afternoon, a special train of six cars arrived from Chicago, jammed with bands, trade unionists, and supporters, to accompany Debs to the gala Chicago reception later that night. After much hugging, kissing, and joyous laughter, the crowd hoisted Debs on its shoulders and carried him to the train.

As the train approached the Chicago depot, an enormous roar rose from yet another crowd. In a pouring rain, over 100,000 people squeezed into Battery D at the station to greet the famous prisoner of Woodstock. After a great deal of exuberant confusion and shoving, a line of march formed, with Debs at the head surrounded by members of the city's trade unions, and the group proceeded to a speaker's platform. Somehow, amidst the cries and chants of "Debs, Debs, Debs," calm finally fell and the introductory speeches were given by, among others, Henry Demarest Lloyd.[33] After another sustained outburst, Debs rose to address the crowd. In his opening sentences he clarified for his audience his thoughts after six months in jail:

> Manifestly the spirit of '76 still survives. The fires of liberty and noble aspirations are not yet extinguished. I greet you tonight as lovers of liberty and as despisers of despotism. I comprehend the significance of this demonstration and appreciate the honor that makes it possible for me to be your guest on such an occasion. The vindication and glorification of American principles of government, as proclaimed to

the world in the Declaration of Independence, is the high purpose of this convocation.

Turning to his own recent legal difficulties, Debs asserted that he did not question the law or its administration but protested "the flagrant violation of the constitution." That document and the Declaration of Independence provided the evening's theme—"personal liberty, or giving it its full height, depth and breadth, American liberty." This traditional liberty, brought into the world by the founding fathers, had divine blessing. It was "countersigned by the Infinite—and man stood forth the coronated sovereign of the world, free as the tides that flo·v, free as the winds that blow." Into this sacred heritage, however, a serpent crept, "stealing the jewel of liberty from the crown of manhood." No longer can the American people sing, with Longfellow, of the glories of the "Ship of State"—the American Constitution, as "the poet wrote before the chart by which the good old ship sailed had been mutilated and torn and flung aside as a thing of contempt . . . before corporations knew the price of judges, legislators and public officials as certainly as Armour knows the price of pork and mutton." In the present age, a most secular one, "men with heads as small as chipmunks and pockets as big as balloons" now occupy the sacred public offices and gleefully accede to the corporation's reign. "What," Debs asked his audience, "is to be done?"

The lesson of the Pullman strike was clear. Against the perfidious alliance that undermined this tradition, working people were not defenseless. "They are not hereditary bondsmen. Their fathers were born free—their sovereignty none denied and their children yet have the ballot. It has been called 'a weapon that executes a free man's will as lightning does the will of God.' There is nothing in our government it can not remove or amend." That sacred fire, the very soul force of the Republic, the foundation of individual manhood, could be restored when "the people by the all pervading power of the ballot have repaired the old chart, closed the rents and obscured the judicial dagger holes made for the accommodation of millionaires and corporations, through which they drive their four-in-hands as if they were Cumberland gaps."

Debs ended his sermon—for that was what it was, replete with a recognition of sin and the source of redemption—on a most optimistic note. The people had the power within their grasp to right the wrongs of corporate society. For this child of the Enlightenment, leavened with liberal doses of religious perfectionism, the images of Christ, the founding fathers, and the people melded into one revered trinity. But the primal source, the sacred store of the nation's promise and duty, remained vital only if the people appealed to it. Concluding with a verse by the poet

James Russell Lowell, Debs urged his audience to embrace as their own the very core of that tradition:

> He's true to God who's true to man;
> whenever wrong is done.
> To the humblest and the weakest,
> 'neath the all-beholding sun.
> That wrong is also done to us,
> and they are slaves most base,
> Whose love of right is for themselves
> and not for all the race.[34]

In the final analysis Debs's speech at Battery D on the night of 22 November explains most profoundly his beliefs and commitments at the conclusion of his jail sentence, and he sought to galvanize the people in defense of these values. In Chicago, as in other meetings at Indianapolis and Terre Haute, the public response overwhelmed Debs, as the triumphal praise and exultation surpassed anything in recent memory. Even a private family dinner celebrating his return echoed this tone, as admirers nationwide wired statements for the toast.[35] Fêted and applauded, Debs seemed once again at the pinnacle of his career. Increasingly, Debs the individual became transformed for many into Debs the prophet, a symbol of nationwide discontent. As J. A. Wayland, later to be a close personal and political friend, wrote a week after Debs's release, the ovation owed less to the individual man than "to Debs the embodiment of resistance to tyranny, resistance to usurpation, to Debs the patriot." Debs "is a type of manhood to be honored. In all the ages of the world such men have been crucified, burned, hanged and murdered by the ruling powers of despotism such as now control this nation." But while suffering and oppression were the prophet's lot, Wayland confidently asserted that, as with others in the past, "when the future historian chronicles this period, the name of Debs will be a great central figure."[36]

This transformation of Debs from public individual to national symbol was inevitable and not without reason. Due to his recent activities, Debs served to focus and, after a fashion, to direct the anger many Americans felt. In turn, Debs also drew a strength from this role that largely accounts for his appeal over the coming three decades. But for Debs, as for many of his followers, only a thin line remained between the man and the symbol. While Wayland's analogy to Debs and the crucified Christ positioned Debs within the central Christian symbol for the first time, it certainly would not be the last. Others, including Debs himself, would repeat it in the years to come and this near canonization would create unforeseen problems. But for the moment Debs received it as confirmation of his mission.

In November 1895 two goals dominated Debs's thinking. While Debs was formally committed to rebuilding the American Railway Union, his activities centered more on raising money to pay creditors and assisting still blacklisted strikers. Second, Debs left jail publicly committed to the Populist cause in the coming national elections, and to this task he brought his vast energy and personal enthusiasm. As he informed Theodore just prior to his release, he intended to go *"among them old man as I never did before*. It will *be all business* with me from the 22nd on till my days are ended—and don't you forget it."[37]

Debs started a nationwide speaking tour at Ulrich's Hall in Chicago in January 1896. Despite his enthusiasm, he painted a gloomy picture of the immediate future. Technological progress was inevitable and even desirable, he argued, but the labor-saving machinery it created would result in increased unemployment and demand a major social readjustment. The trade unions "cannot supply the remedy for the ills of which the workmen complain," especially as they depend upon the permanence of the wage system for their very existence. It was precisely that system, Debs stated, that must be destroyed: "So long as one man depends upon the will of another or more often the whims and caprice of another for employment, he is a slave." Small businessmen faced a similar crisis, brought on by the corporate control of marketing and natural resources. The solution was apparent, if not necessarily imminent. As strikes were harmful and class warfare self-destructive, peaceful change through the ballot remained the most meaningful course open to Americans to regain their traditional rights and liberties.[38]

Debs repeated these basic themes throughout his tour. In Charleston, South Carolina, however—in the midst of his first southern tour since achieving national prominence—a reporter for the Charleston *Sun* raised the issue of Socialism. Would it not follow from his speech, the reporter asked, that if one man had two dollars and another six, the two ought to combine their resources so that each would have four. "By no means," Debs retorted. "If I had six dollars it would not, however, be right for me to prevent you from getting as much as I have because I have more money than you have." Debs stressed the corporate obstacles that prevented a greater equality in economic conditions, and, while still in the South, he also dismissed the "silver question" as central to Populism. The movement encompassed a more basic analysis of society, he explained, for "the great issue" concerns "a fairer distribution of the wealth. There is enough wealth here for all but it has been unfairly distributed."[39]

By spring 1896 the force of this agitation made Debs a spokesman for radicals within Populism and led many of them to declare publicly their support for Debs as the party's presidential nominee. While not a new cry—as early as March 1895 Debs had witnessed mass meetings proclaiming him the next president—he carefully kept his distance and repeatedly stated he would refuse any draft for political office.[40] Yet the boom continued. Newspapers across the country urged his nomination while Lloyd and other radical Populists privately worked for the same ends.[41] Debs was an attractive candidate, for many perhaps the most attractive within memory. In contrast with the views of Cleveland, Benjamin Harrison, and other recent major party candidates, Debs's proven commitment to basic American principles was a beacon for voters. As one paper stated when endorsing him, Debs was "firm and uncompromising in his advocacy of the rights of the working masses as against privileges for a class."[42]

In addition to Debs's attractive personal and political qualities, internal factional politics also recommended him to some Populists. Three major groups divided the movement. The Socialist contingent, easily the smallest of the three, rejected a simple reform platform in favor of a full commitment to Socialist principles. The other two groups, encompassing the majority of the membership, fought a basic battle for control of the movement. The "fusionists," who favored a close alliance with and even incorporation of their party into the Democratic party, restricted agitation to the question of the free coinage of silver. In contrast, the "middle of the roaders" rejected any alliance with the Democrats and sought to preserve a broader political analysis in the party's platform. This faction especially required a nationally recognized leader, as it was clear the fusionists would adopt as their candidate any even minimally sympathetic nominee of the Democratic party. On Debs's candidacy hinged the ability of many of his admirers to engage the fusionists for control of the movement.[43]

The battle for delegates between these two major factions dominated preconvention activity in the spring and early summer of 1896. By the time they convened in late July, moreover, the Democratic party had already nominated William Jennings Bryan, and this placed severe pressure on the "middle of the roaders." It was now essential for them to offer a viable national candidate to prevent the winnowing of the party platform. On the convention floor, Debs's supporters were busy. Lloyd delivered a sweeping indictment of fusion and free silver calculated to appeal to the antimonopolist sentiments of many delegates and especially to the southern Populists, who would commit political suicide, as he saw it, by fusing with the Democrats. A canvass of the state delegates on the third day of the convention indicated that Lloyd's efforts had borne fruit. In sixteen states a majority was pledged to Debs, and in six others there was strong sentiment for him. With at least one-third of the convention's delegates, his backers planned the nominating procedure. A southern congressman, M. W. Howard of Alabama, would place Debs's name in nomination, and the full delegations from Ohio, Illinois, Missouri, and Indiana would second it. Victory was by no means assured, but Lloyd, Howard, and their allies had solid reasons for optimism.[44]

In the middle of this excitement Debs wired Lloyd on the fourth day of the convention. "Please," the terse, one-line telegram stated, "do not permit use of my name for nomination."[45] His supporters were crushed. Lloyd, who knew all along of Debs's aversion to running but who had hoped that if Debs were nominated and strongly supported he would relent, was particularly despondent. Without another national candidate, Lloyd watched in frustration and despair as his faction lost any hope of controlling the movement. As the convention enthroned fusion and, in nominating Bryan, crowned free silver, Lloyd returned to Chicago convinced that Populism was "buried, hopelessly sold out."[46]

In one sense Debs's refusal to run indicated a certain consistency. But there was more to his refusal. Unknown to the delegates at the Populist convention, Debs had offered warm praise and congratulations to Bryan after his nomination by the Democrats two weeks earlier. Following Bryan's nomination by the Populists, Debs, but one day after his telegram to Lloyd, lavishly praised Bryan in yet another private letter. "In the great uprising of the masses against the classes," Debs wrote, "you are at this hour the hope of the Republic—the central figure of the civilized world. . . . The people love and trust you—they believe in you as you believe in them, and under your administration the rule of the money power will be broken and the gold barons of Europe will no longer run the American government."[47] For a man who had consistently broadened his understanding of Populism and who had rejected free silver as the central issue, it seemed a strange reversal.

Stranger still was Debs's role during the campaign itself. As he later explained, in 1896 "I was a populist in my party affiliations, and as Bryan was the nominee of my party I gave him my support."[48] And that he did. With the approval of the directors of the all but defunct American Railway Union, Debs urged all railroad workers to vote for Bryan. A vast difference existed between Bryan and the Democratic party, Debs's circular argued, and he stressed that he supported Bryan based on Bryan's endorsement of Populism.[49] But Debs's activities for Bryan extended beyond writing circulars. As Gompers refused to endorse Bryan officially,[50] Debs became the only labor leader of national importance who did. Although his trade union base was now minimal, Debs once again assumed the familiar role as the labor spokesman for a Democratic (albeit in this case a Democratic/Populist) candidate for the presidency.

In October 1896 Debs opened an extended speaking tour for Bryan. His themes were simple and direct, if somewhat contradictory with his earlier positions. In a speech at Hammond, Indiana, representative of others, Debs announced that "bimetalism is the only solution to the problem now staring us in the face, as to how to open the mills and factories to the work-ingman.'' Reviewing the past twenty years of strife and industrial conflict, Debs claimed that the gold standard, and it alone, was responsible for the current crisis: "Did not the great strike of '79 [*sic*], '86 and '94 occur under the gold standard, the standard your autocratic employers would have you vote again?'' In an obvious narrowing of his wider vision, Debs exhorted his audience to vote for Bryan and free silver ''to uphold your manhood, your honest principles, aid in the emancipation of the workingman [and] the salvation of the down-trodden laborer.''[51]

What makes this support of Bryan especially difficult to comprehend is that Debs had indicated earlier a broader critique of monopoly that reflected some familiarity with Socialism as well. In February 1896 Debs wrote Lloyd concerning an attack on Socialism that appeared in Tom Watson's newspaper, the leading southern Populist journal. "Mr. Watson has no rational conception of what 'Socialism' really is,'' Debs wrote and suggested that Watson's "tirade'' would neither injure its intended victims nor aid Populism.[52] Even on the eve of the Populist convention that July, Debs joined an effort to establish a ''co-operative civilization'' to replace capitalist society. The proposed group, ''one vast fraternal organization,'' scheduled its first meeting to coincide with the Populist convention. Given its wide-ranging reform platform, it was understand-able that many perceived this as an effort to replace the Populist party should the fusionists control the convention.[53]

In light of this persistent political inconsistency, the legend of Debs's conversion at Woodstock has little substance. But what are we to make of the actual Eugene Debs during 1896? As he tacked back and forth between different versions of Populism, with barely a public mention of Socialism, was he simply a naive leader thrust into national prominence but unable to function effectively under the pressure? Do these contradictions indicate a basic intellectual failing, a weak mind easily swayed? In part it is hard to avoid such conclusions, but by themselves they do not fully explain Debs's conduct. As he continued to search for an organizational vehicle for mass protest, Debs proceeded, for both political and personal reasons, quite carefully.

In the aftermath of the 1894 elections, which hardly resulted in a Populist sweep of the nation, Debs and the editors of the *Railway Times* nonetheless remained enthusiastic. The campaign had been an important learning experience for the movement, and they looked forward to 1896.[54] But working people did not flock to the Populist standard as they hoped, and the pressure to reduce the Populist critique to the single issue of free silver grew. Yet Debs, who himself had once endorsed free silver as the paramount issue, emerged from Woodstock with a broader understanding of Populism. He remained publicly committed to the movement, but its potential seemed less in 1896 than in 1894. But why did not Debs assume the leadership of the more radical Populists, announce for the nomination, and enter the St. Louis convention prepared to battle for every vote?

In personal terms such a struggle was contrary to his nature. Although he had given ample evidence of his ability for political infighting during his career, a closer look reveals an interesting pattern. Debs's most active involvement in the internal politics of the Firemen occurred prior to 1890, when his organizational support was greatest. As his opposition increased after 1890, he withdrew from an active role within the organization, only to harangue members in the pages of the journal. A similar pattern is evident in his political activity. Debs was full of hopes when he was elected to the Indiana assembly in 1885, but his optimism evaporated with his experiences on the various legislative committees. Rather than enter the fray, Debs withdrew and vowed never again to run for office. If Debs had given no evidence of his ability to maneuver within an organization, one might point to this as a rather odd trait for a political leader. However, he clearly had that ability, but his willingness to engage in organizational struggles closely reflected his own strength within the organization. As that strength ebbed with the Firemen, or when it never existed, as the freshman assemblyman discovered, his inclination to expose himself to possible defeat dramatically declined. Above all else, Debs needed people around him whom he trusted and from whom he could receive an embracing love that at times bordered on adulation. As he wrote from Woodstock, in a family context that mirrored many facets of his public attitude as well, "We must *all* be in touch, in warmest sympathy and vitalize and strengthen one another in every hour of trial."[55]

This complex of emotional needs clearly influenced Debs's public actions. As one who knew him commented, other leaders in the trade union and Socialist movements frequently encouraged in the rank and file a dependency on their leadership and position. But with Debs, "you knew he needed you."[56] Debs's ability to maintain close personal friendships with people he disagreed with politically further reinforced this tendency. While not true in every case, the conflicting demands of personal friendship and political debate often neutralized Debs. It was not surprising that he failed to appear at the Populist convention, for it continued a tradition begun at the 1892 Firemen's meeting. With few exceptions, whenever a convention threatened to involve him in serious and possibly antagonistic debate, he conveniently withdrew, claiming one or another ailment, and confined himself to his room. This posture enabled Debs to continue to appear as the lauded public figure even as it prevented his public contribution to the serious political questions under discussion.

But a final question remains. If a series of complicated reasons led Debs to avoid this struggle for the Populist nomination, how does one explain his private letters to Bryan or the peculiarly narrow campaign speeches he delivered? Not participating in the political infighting was one decison; obliterating a broad understanding of the issues, quite another. Ultimately Debs saw little alternative. Despite his disenchantment with the silver fad, the Populist party remained the only mass-based alternative to the values of industrial capitalism. To reject it could cause a devastating split and perhaps cost the election. And Bryan, from Debs's point of view, was certainly not the worst possible candidate. Bryan's power to move audiences—whether political delegates at the Democratic national convention or farmers in rural Nebraska townships—impressed Debs. If Bryan's base of support was in any meaningful way the people, then perhaps all was not lost, for, if elected, he would have to respond to their needs or face their anger.

Debs was neither a Socialist nor a confident leader of a popular movement in 1896. Politically naive, he lacked both a consistent analysis and a coherent program. But his commitment to Populism reveals another trait. Even in 1896 he saw in that movement a potent appeal to Americans that emphasized their culture's democratic promise. Within a year this appeal would form the core of his new commitment to Socialism. But in 1896 Populism had not fully run its course, and Debs was willing to temper his own ideas to support that movement in what proved to be its last serious campaign.[57]

William Jennings Bryan did not win the 1896 election. Although he carried twenty-six states to William McKinley's twenty-one, the Republican candidate captured the eight major industrial states with their commanding block of electoral votes.[58] Debs did not find these results surprising. The business community had gone to great lengths to intimidate workingmen in its employ, forcing them to join pro-McKinley organizations and threatening to close the factories if Bryan were elected.[59] But the elections did move Debs further along in another political direction. In letters to Lloyd and Berger in mid-December, Debs intimated that he had "plans for the future . . . a matter of importance," and he desired to consult with the two men soon after the new year. This cryptic message drew from Berger the chortle: "So writes Mr. Debs! What do you think about it?"[60]

Debs clarified his intent on 1 January 1897. In an open letter to the membership of the American Railway Union he announced that "the result of the November election has convinced every intelligent wageworker that in politics, per se, there is no hope of emancipation from the degrading curse of wage slavery." Scorning both traditional parties as captives of the corporation and briefly acknowledging the now prostrate body of Populism, Debs publicly embraced the cause of Socialism: "The issue is Socialism versus Capitalism. I am for Socialism because I am for humanity. We have been cursed with the reign of gold long enough. Money constitutes no proper basis of civilization. The time has come to regenerate society—we are on the eve of universal change."[61]

During the winter and spring of 1897 Debs engaged in a prolonged speaking tour in the western United States. He sought to explain the meaning of his Socialism and to build support for a merger between the remnants of the American Railway Union and the Socialist forces at the union's convention scheduled for Chicago that June. As he ingenuously suggested in May, events since the Pullman strike had justified the analysis and promise of the American Railway Union: as corporate power grew, the need for a new political party was obvious. But it was a particular type of Socialist party Debs advocated. The new group would be dedicated to a "grand co-operative scheme" that would enable people to "work together in harmony in every branch of industry." The nucleus of the movement, Debs explained, would settle in a western state, assume power through electoral politics, and then call for the "laborless thousands" to join them so that all might "enjoy 'life, liberty and the pursuit of happiness.' " From this frontier base, the new utopians would "rapidly overleap boundary lines" to occupy other states "in all directions until the old barbaric system has been destroyed and the republic is redeemed and disenthralled and is, in fact, the land of a free and happy people."[62]

As Debs explained his Socialist program, the more orthodox among his comrades shuddered, impatient with the call for yet another utopian scheme, and few corporate executives took the plan seriously. Yet to dismiss it so quickly missed its important meaning for Debs and his followers. First, Debs hoped that a colony would provide a haven for the many Pullman strikers who had been ruthlessly blacklisted since 1894. More critically, however, in invoking the model of a utopian community, the beacon light upon a hill demanding society return to its true values, Debs drew on the most basic of American archetypes. In tapping these deepest roots in the tradition of American radical protest, Debs kept before his audience with millennial fervor the evils of corporate society, and that urgency, in turn, reverberated widely in the consciousness of his listeners. For them as for Debs, the proposed organization was less a new venture than the continuation of the best of earlier protest movements. The moral imperative was the same, as was the intention to continue the political struggle. The forms might change, but the mission remained constant.[63]

Debs defended his program before the American Railway Union that June. He noted the opposition of some Socialists to colonization and to all efforts short of overthrowing capitalism. But he insisted that the suffering brought on by the long depression and the blacklist demanded attention. That "hunger and squalor [exist] in a land of fabulous plenty" gave clear proof that "the Almighty does not rule" in the councils of the nation. A cooperative effort was critical, he explained, especially as strikes have but "deepened the impression that the fight for independence has made [workers] still more dependent." In contrast, a Socialist cooperative would allow working people to "work out their own salvation, their redemption and independence . . . break every fetter, rise superior to present environments, and produce a change such as shall challenge the admiration of the world."[64]

Following Debs's speech, his program was quickly attacked by some delegates, including Daniel DeLeon and his Socialist Labor party. But the most influential critic was Berger. The growing Socialist party in Milwaukee stressed political action and had established a newspaper to carry its message. But it remained a local effort, with a few hesitant connections with Socialists in other cities. As Berger told Lloyd before the convention, the Milwaukee Socialist paper "has a political and social aim, but neither a social nor a political party—truly a queer position for a daily paper to be in." Urging quick action before "many well-meaning but somewhat 'hazy reformers' " became involved, Berger hoped that the convention's efforts would result in the formation of a Socialist organization solidly committed to conventional political action.[65]

During the June convention, Berger and his comrade, Frederich Heath, met nightly with Debs to urge him to disavow colonization and support the participation of Socialists in electoral activity. This Debs refused to do, but the new organization, named the Social Democracy of America, did support both programs. It urged all "honest citizens" to unite "to conquer capitalism by making use of our political liberty [and to] make democracy, 'the rule of the people,' a truth by ending the economic subjugation of the overwhelmingly great majority of the people." To ease the immediate suffering while the larger program unfolded, the party urged the use of "all proper means" to aid the unemployed, most prominently the establishment of a National Co-operative Commonwealth in a state to be selected.[66]

The differences that separated Debs and Berger on the issue of colonization remained important. Where Berger expressed a desire to outflank "hazy reformers," Debs expressed pleasure that all the "eminent reformers" planned to attend the June convention.[67] The action of the convention in selecting its officers reinforced this tension. Debs, of course, was elected chairman of the executive committee, but all of the officers of that committee (James Hogan, Sylvester Keliher, William Burns, and Roy Goodwin) were all former union officers deeply committed to colonization.[68] This, in effect, froze Berger's more orthodox Socialism out of the party's ruling circle.

Following the convention, Debs continued in his support of colonization, to Berger's increased discomfort. Debs wrote a well-publicized letter to John D. Rockefeller, in which he asked Rockefeller to "find it consistent with your own sense of social and patriotic obligation to join hands with us in our emancipating and enobling mission."[69] In a September circular to party locals Debs and Keliher requested people to donate $20 for the colonization committee's expenses; the next month Debs demanded that colonization "have the unwavering support of the entire membership."[70] Within party circles Debs was also adamant in his support of colonization. At a joint meeting of the Colonization Commission and the executive committee in December, which Debs chaired, his sole criticism of the commission was that it had stretched itself too thin by involvement in other affairs. Its task, he sharply reminded its members, was to obtain land.[71] Finally, in his opening speech at the 1898 convention of the Social Democracy, Debs boasted that, if given "10,000 men, aye, 1,000 in a Western state, with access to the sources of production," then he and they would alter the economic system of the country.[72]

There was one glaring inconsistency, however, in Debs's support of colonization. Speaking in Berger's Milwaukee stronghold shortly after the 1897 convention, Debs asserted that the Social Democracy did not depend upon colonization for its ultimate success. "It is a political movement," he insisted. "Were the colonization plan to prove a failure, it would not stop the Social Democracy movement." Comparing the new party to the formative days of the Republican party, he emphasized that its purpose was to abolish industrial slavery as the earlier party intended to abolish chattel slavery.[73]

That this speech occurred in Milwaukee was not surprising. Debs, still a political innocent, was being courted and pressured by both Berger and Lloyd. A strong faction led by Lloyd and the majority of the officers of the union favored colonization but opposed any political efforts. As Lloyd wrote Berger, there was little use in voting: "[The capitalists] will do the counting. And we can't shoot. They own all the guns."[74] Berger, of course, disagreed—and so did Debs—with any plan that would eliminate political action. But even as Berger met with Debs, Debs remained close with Lloyd. Despite the Populist convention fiasco, they had worked together to establish the Brotherhood of the Cooperative Commonwealth in 1896, and Debs unsuccessfully pressed Lloyd to direct colonization efforts in 1897.[75] In trying to balance the influence of Berger and Lloyd, Debs appeared confused, uncertain of his position on critical issues, struggling to unite deep irreconcilable differences.

While Debs's commitment to former union men strengthened his support for colonization,[76] this did not mean that Debs and Berger were political allies. Basic differences in ideology and temperament persisted. Berger was a powerful personality who, as Debs understood, felt he had no peer in the movement in ideological dispute. As he had at Woodstock, Berger frequently lectured Debs in 1897 and demanded, at times in front of others, that Debs acknowledge his more learned analysis. This clearly riled Debs. As he later explained, it was only when "I gave Berger to understand that I did my own thinking and that I would not be his lackey, nor allow him or anyone else to boss me" that he achieved some degree of independence.[77] While Berger needed Debs, an American-born spokesman of stature and importance, he wanted a properly coached Debs. In this struggle to define Debs's role in his first year in the Socialist movement lay much of the tension between the two men.

Beyond personal differences lay the critical question of the meaning and validity of a class analysis of American society. As Berger, Heath, and some of the Massachusetts members groped toward a more orthodox position, one that took Marx and Friedrich Engels seriously,[78] the majority in the party, including Debs, remained rooted in an older, classless vision of society. In an editorial in November 1897 the *Social Democrat* urged caution in preaching class consciousness, as it may "do mischief." It "is a good servant but a bad master. Socialism is something more than a mere labor question. It is a demand for equalizing of burdens and an equalizing of benefits throughout the whole society. Class consciousness for the laboring man is safe where it is made a part of a high moral demand in the interests of society as a complete organism and not of one class only." Noting that many earlier Socialist activists and thinkers, from Ferdinand Lassalle and Marx to John Ruskin and Karl Liebknecht, came from the middle class, the official paper of the party concluded: "An effective American Socialist Party must . . . make its campaign on the highest moral grounds. We must not make socialism obnoxious to the people."[79]

Wayland, editor of the popular *Appeal to Reason*, expressed this idea more succinctly. "There should be but one class of people," he wrote, "a working class, men and women doing useful things required for a high state of civilization."[80] But, as would be the case in years to come as well, Debs himself best expressed the gulf that existed between Berger's theory and a more traditional American approach. Speaking in Newark, New Jersey, he asked rhetorically, "What is Socialism?" His answer frustrated Berger: "Merely Christianity in action. It recognizes the equality in men."[81]

These tensions and disagreements exploded at the June 1898 convention of the party. The issue, as it had been all year, remained colonization, but fundamental differences concerning the role of class analysis and independent political action dominated discussion. Both sides began jockeying for position immediately. Berger, James Carey and Margaret Haile of Massachusetts, and William Mailly of Tennessee unsuccessfully sought to block the seating of delegates from twelve new Illinois locals, claiming their presence was simply an attempt to pack the convention with pro-colonization votes. The following day, 8 June, Berger's forces lost control of the rules committee but won a majority of seats on the important platform committee. Berger and Haile, both committed to political action, could outvote the pro-colonization third member, John F. Lloyd of Illinois.[82] Yet the ultimate control of the convention remained in doubt as many delegates reserved judgment while awaiting direction from the party's most famous member.

On the third day of the convention, Debs dramatically entered the debate on the future direction of the party and roundly attacked those who favored a rigorous class analysis. They were similar to the Socialist Labor party, he argued, which wielded a "class-conscious club" that more often than not "knocks [the worker] into unconsciousness." Embracing an older vision, Debs demanded that the delegates recognize that the "mission of the Social Democracy is to awaken the producer to a consciousness that he is a Socialist and to give him courage by changing his economic conditions." Affirming that he had "not changed in regards to our procedure," Debs reiterated his support for colonization and dismissed class theory as too narrow a doctrine to encompass the majority of current or potential American Socialists.[83]

Debs's speech electrified the convention. The colonizationists were exuberant, for control of the party now seemed assured. Berger, on the other hand, was depressed and probably furious. If Debs remained steadfast, Berger's influence would be minimal. While no detailed record exists of the caucusing that occurred that Thursday night following Debs's speech, it must have been extensive if previous experience was any precedent. Berger certainly met with Debs, and others might have as well. Whatever occurred that night, by Friday afternoon Debs's conduct suggested an important change.

Presiding over the convention, Debs remained neutral as the delegates hotly debated two reports from the platform committee. The majority report, signed by Berger and Haile, called only for immediate political action while Lloyd's minority report coupled a call for political action with support of colonization, a plan consistent with the original Declaration of Principles. The debate raged throughout the afternoon with first one side and then another gaining the floor. Debs moderated the exchange but himself was silent. At six o'clock, the delegates broke for dinner. When they reassembled later in the evening, Debs was conspicuously absent. Chairing the meeting in his place was Burns, a committed supporter of colonization. Although he was officially reported ill, resting at his hotel and unable to attend, Debs did send a brief message. To a shocked and stunned convention, Debs announced his support of Berger and Haile's majority report. As they recovered from this news, the majority of the delegates, ignoring Debs's almost incomprehensible reversal, endorsed John Lloyd's minority report by a 52–37 margin. With the vote lost but having retained Debs, the Berger forces bolted the convention to form a new group, the Social Democratic party. The split that Debs resisted was finally unavoidable.[84]

Despite Debs's deep distrust of Berger's version of Socialism, when he was forced to choose, he went with the Milwaukee leader. In part Debs simply did not trust the endorsement of political action by the pro-colonialists, perceiving it accurately as a ploy. In part, Debs's efforts to reconcile the two factions crashed against the shoals of Berger's resistance.[85] While Berger tempered his public criticism of colonization for political reasons, in private he remained adamant in his opposition. His barbed wit and commanding presence clearly had their effect on Debs, and ultimately the strike leader reneged on his expressed promise to his American Railway Union comrades. But Debs's actions on 9 and 10 June 1898 also indicate how confused and even rootless he was. The world of labor he understood from decades of intimate contact, but he had yet to ground himself in the world of Socialist ideology and politics. Insecure, with this confusion roughly rubbing against his image of national prominence, it was not surprising that Debs refused to confront the convention that Friday evening and stayed in bed. It was not his finest hour.

Beyond the specific issue of colonization, much remained unclear. Berger and Debs were tactical allies, but vast gulfs still separated them. If, as one historian has suggested, the 1898 convention marked the passing of "the last real vestige of utopianism in the American socialist political movement,"[86] it is not clear that this applied to Debs. Debs still questioned the emphasis on class consciousness as he continued to interpret political action within an older American moral tradition that placed ultimate hope in "the people" as citizen-producers. Even when he used a more orthodox Marxian language, it is difficult not to see Debs's meaning as derivative more from Edward Kellog, Gronlund, and an indigenous understanding of the labor theory of value than from Marx, Kautsky, or even Berger.[87]

After breaking, however awkwardly, with Social Democracy, Debs accepted election to the executive committee of the Social Democratic party. At an organizational meeting on 11 June, which Debs did not attend, the Berger-led group drafted a platform which argued that under capitalism "two distinct classes with conflicting interests" had developed: "The small possessing class of capitalists . . . and the ever-increasing large dispossessed class of wageworkers." The Social Democrats demanded the overthrow of capitalism and also included a series of immediate demands concerning nationalization of resources, legislation to improve working conditions, equality for women, and a program for farmers.[88] Debs had difficulty with the stark class analysis in the platform, but, given his attitude on the labor movement since Pullman, the new party's trade union plank produced even greater discomfort. The trade unions were "indispensable to the working people under the prevailing industrial conditions," the Social Democrats announced, and in the future they would be a vehicle in the eventual "abolition of the wage system." Party activists were urged to join unions in their trades but were specifically warned not to allow political differences among workers to prevent cooperation on economic issues. Endorsing strikes, boycotts, and the eight-hour day, the party strongly criticized the Socialist Labor party for its antagonism toward the AFL. Essentially the Social Democrat labor plank accepted without question the importance of the Gompers-led federation and prepared to establish as close a relation as possible with it, even as it claimed it might teach Gompers and his movement important lessons in Socialism.[89]

For the moment Debs publicly accepted the program. But others did not. Predictably, the Socialist Labor party was quite critical, as were Debs's former associates in the Social Democracy. The Chicago *Dispatch*, quoting anonymous friends of Debs, argued that while the split was a backward step for the movement it proved the "charge made by his enemies that if [Debs] cannot control, he will wreck any organization of which he is a member." Others, bitter and hurt over Debs's defection, characterized the new party as alien and by definition un-American: "This was really the point at issue. Should the old German Socialist methods, with its 'class-consciousness' club tactics, continue, or should American Socialist methods prevail?" Claiming a numerical victory, the *Social Democrat* announced that "American Socialist methods won."[90]

In reality, of course, Social Democracy lost. Its anti-political bias cost it support, and its plans for colonization proved impractical. Little of substance emerged during their year of work and, within a month after the 1898 convention, the Social Democracy no longer existed as a viable organization.[91] The basic cause for this decline, however, involved questions of personality rather than ideology. As their bitterness indicated, they no longer had their leader, the individual whom many had followed out of the brotherhoods into the American Railway Union, the man who had echoed their condemnation of " 'class-consciousness' club tactics." When Debs announced in the first issue of the *Social Democratic Herald*, ending all confusion about his contradictory role at the convention, that "the more I think of the outcome at Chicago, the more I am convinced that the wisest councils prevailed"—at that point the Social Democracy lost any hope for continued existence.[92] For Debs's position within the amorphous radical movement was paramount. Those who allied with the Pullman leader gained instant recognition. If nothing else, the criticism Debs received from the established press kept a group before the public eye. His leadership, of course, would not assure success, but without it, as the Social Democracy discovered, even survival was almost impossible.

At this point in his life, attracted more than ever before to orthodox Socialism, conflicting pressures and tensions nonetheless structured Debs's life. He had not altered his earlier views on class and in his speeches still called for a union of all citizens to oppose industrial capitalism. As the Social Democratic analysis, following Marx, expected capitalist development to compress all but the most wealthy and powerful into one oppressed class, Debs was able to sidestep for the moment this tension and even continue his appeal to multiclass audience. But the tension remained.

The Social Democratic labor policy created more immediate problems for Debs. Since 1894 he had argued the non-Marxist position that workers' economic organizations — the unions — could not compete with the political or technological power of the corporation. Its political power would direct public opinion while technology would render even skilled workers obsolete, and with them all unions. In sharp contrast with his new party's program, this emphasis had caused difficulties even before Debs left Woodstock. As plans formed for the celebration of his release, some members of the Socialist Labor party wrote to ask whether recent reports that he "advocate[s] the abolishment of Trade Union theories" were accurate. Upon Debs's response, the letter made clear, would rest the decision of the group to participate in the celebration. The response bristled with anger. Debs took offense at the request to define his position after twenty-one years of labor activity and "a sentence of six months for my fealty to the principles of the very Trade Unions which now propose to interrogate me." Although he denied the charge, Debs never did reconcile this assertion with his recent public statements. Instead, drawing on his position of prominence and a felt insult to his dignity, Debs dismissed the inquiry as an unwitting tool of the General Managers Association.[93]

But the questions did not cease. Debs's own statements during his speaking tours added to the impression. In Leadville, Colorado, during the bitter strike of the Western Federation of Miners in the spring of 1897, Debs told the miners that the "aims of organized labor . . . appeal for the sympathetic support of every good citizen." Calling the current strike "unfortunate," Debs noted that all strikes were "in the nature of a calamity." However, as he had told the American Railway Union's 1894 convention, in certain circumstances strikes were still necessary, for to refuse to permit them would result in a man's "being stripped of his manhood and independence without protest." Although he did not attack the miners' union, Debs did argue privately and publicly that only the ballot would ultimately resolve these conflicts.[94]

Embedded in this analysis lay a quite negative estimation of working people's ability to struggle against corporate power. Debs did not discern sources of resistance or even modes of survival in either the trade union, family or ethnic ties, religious identity, or cultural activities. "The last quarter of the century," he declared in 1897, "has so degraded American workingmen that there is hardly any spirit left in them."[95] So total was corporate power, he suggested a year later, that many workers, given an option between slavery and starvation, "choose" slavery and bow to their employers "because they have families depending upon them for support." In this way their fundamental obligations as men and citizens became "the occasion for their slavery and degradation."[96] But even where unions had organized, where men and women had rejected at least one level of that slave-like condition, Debs remained pessimistic. When miners in Illinois and Kansas won a new contract in 1899, Debs accurately argued that not only did widespread unemployment and exploitation remain, but he also then dismissed their gains as nearly meaningless:

> Oh miners, will you not open your eyes, and will you not use your brains to see and think for yourselves?
> You have won no victories worthy the name. You are slaves, every last one of you. . . . Arouse from your slavery, join the Social Democratic Party and vote with us to take possession of the mines of the country and operate them in the interest of the people . . . and then, and only then, will "glorious victories" have been achieved and you and your comrades be free and your families happy.[97]

Debs was not simply an obstructionist in this pessimism, although he clearly underestimated the power, vitality, and importance of specific worker struggles. His views flowed from an understanding of capitalist development. Looking back over half a century, Debs recalled a time when the workingman "controlled his own tools" and when "the boss worked with his men and their families associated together." Evoking memories of the Terre Haute of his youth, Debs felt that at that time "the laborer had no concern about his position. The boss depended upon him, and . . . the laborer's ambition was to run a little shop of his own and any time he could start out for himself."[98]

Now, of course, all was changed. Corporations and trusts ruled society and attempts to control or destroy them proved useless: "How are they going to do it? Can you compel men to compete against each other, to destroy each other's business?" Of course not, Debs retorted, for greed and self-interest clearly would dominate. But another possibility remained. Blending this Calvinist understanding of human nature with the unbridled optimism of turn-of-the-century progressive thought, Debs argued that nonetheless an inevitable pattern existed: "This, then, is the sequence of the progression of capital—the individual, the firm, the company, the corporation, the trust, and, last—the people, which is the only true and logical conclusion of the sequence."[99]

Debs's emphasis on the people as the culmination of a process of social concentration reflected a new theme evident only since his avowal of Socialism. Acquiring some familiarity with Socialist theory, Debs wedded an understanding of Socialism's historic inevitability with an exaggerated perception of corporate power. But in presenting in a kind of dialectical sequence the major oppressive force in society as the harbinger of liberation, Debs not only underestimated the value of the trade union but also bordered perilously close to the "paternalistic" view he had rejected in Bellamy some years before.

Yet the marriage never fully took. Quote as he might Marx, Engels, Lassalle, or Kautsky (with little acknowledgment of the differences among them),[100] the roots of his own social thought remained deeply enmeshed in a different tradition. As he complained to a Kansas mining audience in 1897, "at present individualism is a myth. Choice is out of the question. Opportunities are sealed against the individual."[101] Although a Socialist, Debs never embraced unequivocally that theory's determinism. Rather he consistently stressed the necessity for individual freedom of action. This in part also accounts for his attitude toward the trade union. It was not that the union movement was in any way alien but rather that trade union activity did not necessarily tap the deepest wellspring of American political culture. For Debs, that demanded an appeal to the individual's right to share fully in the value of his or her work, to participate equally as a citizen with others, and to rear his or her family accordingly. It lay, in short, in Debs's understanding of manhood.

By the late 1890s Debs felt that close organizational involvement with any trade union, indeed almost any organization, would impinge upon his freedom. Despite his Socialism, a fierce individualism fueled his core vision. "By remaining outside," Debs commented in 1898, "my opinions are my own and I can express myself without coming into contact with the narrow principles or theories of any order. If I stayed in I would be in the position of a hired hand."[102] In this instance, as in others, Debs's public statements uncannily reflected basic personal themes as well. Sensitive to Berger's tutelage, especially as it reminded him of past relations with William Riley McKeen and Frank Sargent, Debs remained nervously on guard against perceived challenges to his position and, in different ways, used both family and his public audiences as supports in his personal struggle. But precisely because his inner tension reflected larger social questions concerning the nature of manhood in corporate society, even this personal preoccupation served as a source of Debs's public appeal. For others, his vitality and power flowed from his ability to offer from within his own experience a politico-personal vision of how a citizen might live. At the heart of that vision stood the belief that even in a technological society there existed no need for "hired men."

This emphasis on the individual caused some negative reactions. Following the 1897 convention of Social Democracy, where Debs spoke of the futility of strikes, Louis Rogers, editor of the *Social Democrat*, exerted great effort to reassure workers that the party was not opposed to their cause.[103] Later that summer some delegates to a labor conference in St. Louis were livid with anger when Debs urged them to cease their attempts to unseat Gompers as president of the AFL, for Debs's attitude made clear that he held the trade unions almost a thing of the past. Most troublesome to his Socialist comrades, however, was his underlying reasoning. Wrapping himself "in the language of the revolutionary patriot," Debs intoned that he would "not part with my manhood." American liberties "cry aloud for protection, and my voice shall not be still. What I am doing is not for humanity, but to still the cry of my own conscience. The duty we owe is first to ourselves."[104] As one critic responded, "Debs flunked at the eleventh hour." In his unwillingness to endorse the trade union movement or to tackle Gompers, William Holmes thought that Debs "lacked the necessary backbone," almost wrecked the party, and "lost forever the confidence of many of the best men in the country."[105]

Yet this individualism lost Debs little of his appeal among the rank and file, most of whom had little knowledge of Socialist theory. During his two-month stay in Colorado with the Western Federation of Miners, speaking on behalf of their strike yet nonetheless critical of their efforts, neither the miners nor their president, Ed Boyce, contradicted him. At Leadville, a parade that preceded the mass strike rally had a large, almost lifelike statue of Debs marked "Our Leader" at the head of the column.[106] In West Virginia during a major coal strike in the summer of 1897, Debs was well received by the miners as he launched a multipronged attack upon the governor, the coal operators, and particularly the leaders of the United Mine Workers of America and the AFL.[107] "Why has not the Federation of Labor sent its men here," he demanded, and then he asked: "Where is Gompers?" Critical of national strike strategy, especially the refusal to organize the Baltimore and Ohio railroad workers who hauled the coal from the Monongahela district, Debs insisted the national unions fund an organizer to enter every mine in the district. He would not, he taunted to widespread applause, "accept the stigma of being a party to the failure of this strike unless my work is sympathized with."[108]

The strike was lost, but out of it grew another layer in the legend of Debs the labor martyr, giving his very health to the cause. As the journal *Motorman and Conductor* explained, Debs daily spoke at many meetings at various mining camps, and when once refused permission to use a grove of trees for their shade he addressed the miners for over two hours in the open road under a boiling sun. "But it was too much for human endurance. Debs reached his buggy, reeling under a sunstroke. . . . From that moment on he had to put on glasses, and he has never been the Debs he once was since that memorable afternoon."[109] By this point in his life, Debs had come to expect the demonstrative if misguided adulation due an "inspired evangelist of labor."[110] Rejecting any attempt by the labor or Socialist movements to make him a "hired hand," Debs presented himself as the sole arbitrator of disputes and demanded that his stature and public recognition silence critics. The other side of Debs's taunt to Gompers was a petty insistence that he be accorded primacy in whatever endeavors he undertook. Although his critique in this instance was valid, the line between personal privilege and political analysis was thin, one that he could and did easily confuse.

For Berger, his inability to influence Debs when they were apart was a persistent problem, most sharply evident in their disagreement concerning the relation between Socialism and the trade union movement. Berger's policy of "boring from within" the AFL to build Socialist strength essentially precluded a sustained criticism of Gompers. Indeed, Berger had been a *de facto* supporter of Gompers. Following the 1898 AFL convention, Berger criticized those Socialist delegates who had tried to unseat Gompers, for Berger felt that this action "weakened their strength as socialist propagandists." The Milwaukee leader also claimed to understand why Gompers refused to support the Socialist platform publicly: Gompers and other "leaders could not afford to get so far ahead of the members of the organization" as to lose them. To prove his point, Berger gleefully recalled a private conversation with Gompers at the convention in which Gompers referred to himself as a Socialist.[111] Berger's attitude greatly rankled Debs. His own critique of craft organization and trade union autonomy was clear, and he vividly remembered Gompers's presence on the podium as the Firemen's convention debated his right to floor privileges in 1894. Since then Debs had grown close to Boyce and other leaders of the Western Federation of Miners and encouraged them to leave the AFL.[112]

Yet Debs bided his time. His continued his independent tack, questioning the function of the trade union even while attacking Gompers on political grounds, but delivered no ringing denunciation of the Social Democrats' labor policy. When he was attacked at the 1897 AFL convention for "profiting" from the West Virginia strike, Debs restrained his anger.[113] Throughout these first years as a Socialist, Debs was careful not to break with his new comrades. Whether Berger's influence was ultimately effective or whether Debs himself trimmed his own opposition to avoid another party split is unclear. But his public record appeared tenuous during these years, and the deep disagreements over Socialist labor policy remained muted for a few more years.

Debs's role as a national spokesman for and symbol of those oppressed by corporate capitalism was not, however, in doubt. Whether in Leadville, Colorado, or Fairmont, West Virginia—or literally in the thousands of towns between[114]—Debs addressed both general audiences and meetings of workingmen and women on strike. Attracting large audiences in almost every instance, Debs relished the applause and praise. While the reasons for these triumphal tours were perhaps as diverse as the various audiences, certain common themes did appear. The publicity, fame, and response he generated derived less from either his advocacy of Populism or, after 1897, Socialism, than they did from his role in the Pullman strike. That strike, with the calling in of the troops, the use of the injunction, and the subsequent jailing of the union leaders, was the epochal event in turn-of-the-century America. It marked more clearly than other strikes or political struggles the intense battle to control the meaning of traditional American symbols and through them the direction of society. In his repeated references to it, as in his explanation of the meaning of Socialism, Debs continued to articulate the ideas that dominated his "Liberation Day" speech in Chicago. Liberty, he would stress at each stop in different fashion, was the theme; traditional republican values, the context; the present degradation of the people, the problem. Although an "outsider" by choice, this basic analysis kept him at the pinnacle of public attention and for many in America the embodiment of their deepest emotions and expectations.

It was not surprising, then, as the 1900 presidential election approached, that Debs remained the single most important personality in the fledgling Socialist movement. With a nationwide constituency that far exceeded formal party membership, Debs could and did claim a titular leadership of the movement. A Massachusetts Socialist spoke for many when he commented that Debs was "the historic figure around which, so far as persons are concerned, is gathered this movement."[115] Debs appreciated this as well. While he rejected any intention to accept the party's presidential nomination, he freely acknowledged that he held a special position within the party and "may be said to have been the 'father' of the movement."[116]

Ultimately, this view of Debs depended upon the increasingly mythic layers that surrounded interpretations of his life and career. In his and other accounts the complexity of his years in Terre Haute with the Firemen and, most recently, with the Populist party vanished from public discussion, to be replaced by a more heroic version. When, for example, Benjamin Harrison died in 1901, Debs again lashed out at his anti-labor activities and particularly stressed Harrison's deeds during the 1877 strike. Unlike earlier critiques of Harrison, however, Debs passed over his own role in 1877 and left the impression that then as now his working-class radicalism was consistent.[117] Such versions of his career had increased since Pullman and made it impossible for his comrades not to nominate him for president on the Socialist ticket. So powerful was Debs as a symbolic figure that without him there was little expectation of attracting a serious share of the electorate.

On the third day of the Social Democratic convention in March 1900, when the delegates turned their attention to selecting a presidential nominee, this motif found its first sustained and systematic expression. In placing Debs's name in nomination, Frederic O. MacCartney of Massachusetts luxuriated in the saga of the man's life. "In a dark epoch of strife a child was born," MacCartney began, "an epoch of strife between two great classes in society." In the midst of this titanic struggle this child, "from the earliest time he could take cognizance of the condition of the class into which he was born," developed his interests "in the destinies of his class. There was therefore the conjunction of the birth of a great movement with the birth of a great man." Over the following three decades, this child grew to manhood and "gave his life in consecration to his class and his kind." But then came the Pullman strike and the jail sentence at Woodstock. In a moment this child grown to manhood understood his true destiny. Evoking the full power of the prophetic Christian conversion experience, MacCartney offered as his candidate one who had not been found wanting in the crucible:

> When he entered the tomb, he had completed one cycle of his life. There it was that, like a John of Patmos, he had revealed to him a vision of the things that were to be, of the new kingdom, of the new era. There it was that there came to him a message which was the completion of the Pilgrim's Progress of labor. When he came forth from that tomb it was to a resurrection of life and the first message that he gave to his class as he came from his darkened cell was a message of liberty. He became the liberator. Then the inevitable movement and the man had met, and they were never again to be separated. He was still to continue to mold the movement and the movement was again to transform him into a liberator of his kind. . . . I therefore place in nomination the name of one whom we love, the peerless champion of labor, the knight errant of the new chivalry which will mean the emancipation of our land. I place in nomination the name of Eugene V. Debs.

MacCartney's oration concluded to wild applause. Bedlam reigned as the delegates cheered and whistled and pointed to the tall, somewhat gaunt figure sitting self-consciously on the floor of the convention. And well they might cheer Debs, as MacCartney's words assured them their pragmatic political needs would be fulfilled; and his speech also touched something else in their lives as well. Through MacCartney's version of Debs's life, these men and women also participated in a profound religious moment. Perhaps their sacrifices and trials were less well known, but they were no less real. Like him, they were forerunners of the desired and inevitable regeneration. The clarity of the conversion in Debs, the deep affirmation of a "resurrection of life" beyond the "tomb" encouraged and enheartened them. As each embraced more closely this vision, they found assurances that, as among the early Christians, their expectations and sacrifices were not in vain.

How stark, how in contrast to these jubilant eruptions Debs appeared as he rose to respond to the delegates' acclaim. Drawing himself erect, his body tensed, his face pinched, Debs tersely announced that he could not accept the nomination for reasons of health. At first the delegates did not believe they heard correctly: "For a few moments the profoundest silence prevailed, everyone present realizing how much to this man meant any other course, but all hoping the very silence itself was a herald of joy to come." As the realization grew that they had indeed understood, appeal after appeal was made, the one more florid, more desperate than the other. But through it all "the convention's choice, the choice of the visiting delegates, sat immovable as a statue." Finally, in confusion and some despair, the delegates adjourned until the following morning.[118]

During the night delegations continually visited Debs, urging that he reconsider. As in earlier gatherings, Berger and his associates closeted with him, argued with him, and ultimately wrought from him a reversal.[119] The following morning MacCartney again placed his name in nomination, and Debs, present on the dais, accepted the unanimous acclaim. In a brief acceptance speech Debs explained that the convention's "united voices" caused him to reconsider as "in your voice in behalf of Socialism there was the supreme command of duty."[120] Even his professed ambivalence ultimately served the legend as he once again demonstrated his willingness to sacrifice personal desire for the good of the movement.

MacCartney's perception that Debs and the movement he symbolized molded each other explains critical aspects of Debs's continued appeal. As others also knew, Debs was not a distant leader but rather one who needed the support and affirmation of his comrades. Unfortunately, his personal needs at times allowed him to accept such praise as MacCartney offered without correcting its obvious excesses. To this extent his prophetic call to regeneration suffered from his continued inability to teach what he had learned thoroughly and deeply. Even so, Debs's Socialist agitation marked an important turn in an older search to re-establish American rights and liberties.

In terms of Socialist theory Debs was closer to being a Lassallean than a Marxist in his advocacy of political action—but in reality he was neither. His appeal ultimately rested upon his ability to articulate and symbolize something of the severe dislocation experienced by all Americans in the transformation to industrial capitalism. If this new order demanded a rejection of the democratic tradition, if it required citizens to live without some control over their daily lives, then it must be rejected. For to live in that fashion was to live without basic dignity and that, as Debs often stated, signaled the death knell of the republic. These concerns dominated his Socialist career, and he drew strength from Americans even as he led them. To the extent that his appeal was successful, Eugene Victor Debs would help to keep alive for yet another generation a sense of the profound possibilities within their culture and within themselves.

III

SOCIALIST CITIZEN: 1901–1919

[The working class] must unite in one and the same industrial union and one and the same political party. And the union and the party must be managed and directed by themselves, *not from the top down, but from the bottom up.*

Eugene V. Debs, 1911

By 1900, the community of Terre Haute had completed its journey from a "straggling village" to a fully incorporated component of industrial capitalist society. Although the hopes for dramatic development no longer seemed plausible even to its most ardent boosters, Terre Haute had been thoroughly transformed. Most major industries, including the railroad, the iron works, the new large machine shop, and even the local streetcar company, were now owned by nonresident investors. Terre Haute's business elite traded their control of the local economy in exchange for favorable investment opportunities and in the process encouraged the expression of a sharper class awareness. As Eugene Debs grew into his role as a national symbol of resistance to this transformation, a new businessmen's group within Terre Haute formed that expressed this new consciousness. In the ensuing struggle between Debs and the business community during the 1902 streetcar strike, Debs learned again how far his city had changed since his early years as a native son.

Founded in 1902, the Citizen's Protective League made no pretense of serving a classless community of citizens. Under the leadership of William Riley McKeen, Herman Hulman, and Demas Deming, Jr., the league was anti-union from the start and prepared for industrial warfare. In its initial public statement, the league announced four primary goals. It intended to "discourage lockouts, strikes and opposing boycotts" in order to promote "the stability of business [and] the steady employment of labor." The league established a mediation commission under McKeen's direction and vowed to protect both its members and the community from all labor strife "by peaceable methods and conservative action." Finally, the league affirmed their members' "inalienable rights" to conduct business as its members desired, "without domination or coercion by any organized movements against such rights."[1]

The strike of Terre Haute's streetcar conductors in 1902 provided the league with its first opportunity to intercede in a local labor dispute. A bitter strike lasting three months, it began when the union asked for a reduction in the twelve-hour work day. The Boston-based Stone and Webster Corporation, through its local director, fired the leaders rather than negotiate, and the union asked Debs to direct the strike. Despite his experience as a labor and Socialist leader, Debs had never before directly confronted the leading figures in his hometown. Feelings ran high as Debs, criticizing the league's support of the eastern corporation, opposed men such as McKeen, Hulman, and a number of his brothers-in-law and nephews. Neither the presence of Debs nor the determination of the union proved powerful enough, however, and with the active public assistance of the league, Stone and Webster broke the strike.[2]

The streetcarmen's strike in Terre Haute marked an important transition for that community. In the Citizen's Protective League the city's workingmen and women found their longtime business and civic leaders pitted against them in open conflict that transcended the immediate dispute at stake. Now tied intimately to outside corporate interests, the business elite publicly pressed issues that, at the start of Debs's public career thirty years earlier, had been only whispered. The profession of harmony and the belief in a fluid social structure floundered on this more open class antagonism.

In turn, this transition provided the backdrop for Debs's Socialist agitation. In Terre Haute as throughout America a similar process occurred. In the nationwide struggle that emerged in the workshops, the neighborhoods, and at the ballot box to resist that transformation lay the larger meaning of Debs's Socialist appeal.

7

A Ripe Trade Unionist

EUGENE DEBS OPENED the 1900 Socialist presidential campaign before a large and enthusiastic Chicago audience in late September. Bringing it repeatedly to its feet in approval of his condemnation of capitalist society, Debs carefully orchestrated the response. The cooperative commonwealth, he explained in a modulated voice, would insure the dignity of each individual—the power of the citizen again would be dominant and the meaning of daily work rescued from the debasing control of corporate managers. Raising his pitch, he proclaimed Socialism the true patriotism, more in tune with the revolutionary heritage that formed the culture of his youth than the machinations of contemporary capitalists. In a resounding conclusion Debs implored the now hushed men and women before him to work fervently for and vote with the Socialist ticket as the ultimate salvation for themselves and their society.

But Debs's impassioned invocation of Socialism's promise belied the actual state of the young Socialist movement. Serious disagreements had divided the comrades since the preceding winter, when a dissident faction of Daniel DeLeon's Socialist Labor party, known as the Kangaroos and led by Morris Hillquit, Algie M. Simons, and J. Mahlon Barnes, had sought unity with the Berger- and Debs-led Social Democrats. The two groups had agreed to present a united presidential ticket, but intense ill-feelings remained between the factional leaders.[1] At the Social Democrats' convention in March 1900 many rank-and-file members of both groups wanted unity, and others supported union as an obvious tonic for the shaky condition of the Social Democratic party.[2] But the national leadership of both groups remained opposed. Debs, Victor Berger, and others

publicly recalled the repeated vituperative attacks made on them in the
DeLeonite press, which had claimed that their party contained every "ism
that leads away from the revolutionary path that alone means victory for
the working class."[3] Debs, too, argued against union.[4] The dissident
DeLeonites, he insisted, had had their training "in the bitter school of
bigotry and intolerance," and he demanded further proof of their good
faith. Until that was given, Debs urged his comrades to vote against unity.[5]

But political realities and rank-and-file sentiment thwarted the intentions of the Social Democratic leaders. The convention rejected Berger's
and Debs's obstructionism and established a committee to meet with the
Hillquit group to discuss plans for a merger. As most of the delegates
understood, there were no major ideological issues that separated the two
groups. Even Debs, responding to strong delegate pressure, altered his
position during the convention and supported the unity committee.[6]

Intent on preserving his own power and influence, Berger impeded
every effort of the unity committees to develop a common position, and he
enlisted Debs in the struggle, pressuring him to change his mind again; in
April Debs lamely announced that he was now "opposed to union because
I favor unity," a condition impossible "in the present strained situation."
Even his supporters found it difficult to accept this tortured explanation
and, amid rumors that he was but a soldier in Berger's army, Debs
asserted, to the disbelief of many, that the Milwaukee leader had not influenced his shift, which he attributed to a long internal struggle with his
conscience.[7] Berger, with Debs's help, was briefly successful. By May the
unity talks had collapsed, and Hillquit's supporters established their own
party, naming it the Social Democratic party, with headquarters in
Springfield, Massachusetts. Throughout the country, state and local
organizations split into hostile camps and a harsh struggle to control the
national candidates emerged.[8]

Although both factions had earlier approved the nomination of Debs
and his running mate, Job Harriman (an Indiana-born resident of Los
Angeles and a firm Hillquit ally), neither man could surmount the antagonism that resulted after the bitter struggles of the spring. Indeed the
men did not even always try. In August Harriman sarcastically referred to
his running mate as "the Giant," filled with self-importance and a
hindrance to the movement. Arguing that Debs's factional politics under
Berger's direction "were disgusting the members," Harriman privately
urged the immediate publication of "a neat little circular" attacking
Debs! Harriman then left the country for four weeks to attend the International Socialist Conference in France. Debs was equally sharp. He ignored
Harriman and refused to speak under the auspices of the Springfield
Socialists. It was not a promising beginning for the national campaign.[9]

Leaders of both factions soon limited their public attacks. The strong rank-and-file desire for union made them wary of alienating their supporters, and both groups shared a mutual dependence on the person of Eugene Debs. As had been true in the 1898 split, neither side in this controversy could hope for success or even continued existence if it lost Debs's commanding public support. Debs himself was conscious of this and, as the infighting abated, he clearly exulted in his position as the most prominent figure in the Socialist camp. The national tours, the crowds, the attention, and the adulation invigorated him—and let him ignore his awkward role within the party; he eagerly anticipated the coming campaign. While demanding, such tours were not new to him. During 1899 he had lectured continually for ten months, raising money for the American Railway Union debt and proselytizing for Socialism. The year 1900 brought no relief. In January Debs traversed Missouri, Iowa, Kentucky, Alabama, Georgia, Louisiana, and Texas; February found him in Florida and other southern states, and in March he was back in the Midwest and Southwest.[10] Even with no major tours scheduled after March, Debs was in frequent motion, attending meetings in Chicago, St. Louis, and New York.

This arduous schedule took its toll on this healthy man of forty-five, particularly since Debs slept upright on these long train trips, refusing to take a Pullman berth. When he arrived at his destination, moreover, he could rarely rest. His speeches averaged over two hours, and he was often exhausted, drenched in sweat, at their conclusion. Afterward there were meetings with comrades, efforts to organize trade unionists, and reunions with former co-workers from Brotherhood and Pullman days.[11] Debs was never one to refuse a drink, and these reunions were often joyous and prolonged; yet the following day's schedule was equally busy. Not surprisingly, after almost a year and a half of travel, Debs took to his bed in June 1900 with what he termed an attack of "rheumatism, the result of exposure and overexertion."[12]

Throughout the summer both Socialist factions expressed concern over Debs's health, for each understood the importance of his active involvement if the Socialists were to make a credible showing.[13] It was with some relief that these leaders watched a rested and energized Debs mount the Chicago platform in September to begin a six-week cross-country tour—the first truly national campaign of the American Socialist movement.

Despite the tireless efforts of Debs and Socialist comrades across the country, the results of the November elections were depressing. The total vote was under 100,000, and a state-by-state breakdown revealed but isolated pockets of Socialist strength. Only New York state gave Debs more than 10,000 votes, and no southern state except Texas returned more than 1,000 votes. Even at home in Terre Haute, Debs lost decisively.[14] A disappointed Debs claimed that the low vote reflected the "counting-out" by capitalist politicians of approximately 100,000 additional votes, but he predicted greater gains in the future. Berger was far more bitter in his postmortem analysis. Still waging the battle to prevent union, he blamed the low turnout on the "enforced political alliance" with the Springfield faction. Illogical and lacking evidence, Berger's assertions sparked yet another round of factional strife.[15]

In private Debs rejected both Berger's attack on the Springfield group and his own on capitalist politicians as sufficient explanations for the low vote. The results of the 1900 election forced him to confront the paradox that would stalk his career for the following twenty years. A radical native son whose efforts in the Pullman strike still stirred many Americans, Debs could and did attract large and diverse audiences. He influenced many who heard him. Yet a gulf remained between the size of the crowds and the final election results. Despite his powerful personal appeal and his presentation of Socialism as the fulfillment of traditional American culture, Debs and his comrades faced a barrier within that culture that hampered their organization. In a letter after the election to his brother Theodore, who was still the Chicago party's secretary-treasurer, Debs recounted the tumultuous meetings and demonstrations that marked his last swing through Indiana and Ohio: the meetings were "grand," "packed," "large," and "all that could have been expected." But the results were not. "Thus closes the campaign—and the results show that we got everything *except votes*. I am serene for two reasons: 1st. I did the very best I could for the party that nominated me and for its principles. 2nd. The working class will get in full measure what they voted for. And so we begin the campaign for 1904."[16]

Debs understood the broader dimensions of this problem only too well. During the campaign he wrote that the Socialist movement in America faced serious obstacles, in part because "it would be difficult to imagine a more ignorant, bitter and unreasoning prejudice than that of the American people against Socialism during the early years of its introduction" by European immigrants.[17] In 1902, still concerned with this problem, Debs consciously attempted to root Socialism in a specific American tradition. Focusing attention on the utopian Socialists of the antebellum era, with their peculiar mix of abolitionist fervor, communal living, and a grand and supremely individualistic literary culture, Debs claimed as precursors such men as Ralph Waldo Emerson, Horace Greeley, Henry David Thoreau, and William Ellery Channing. If the "dominant strain" of the Brook Farm utopian experiment was "emotional and sympathetic," Debs stated, "there was nevertheless a solid sub-stratum of scientific soundness in the undertaking."[18] Despite these appeals, most

Americans of all classes in 1900 remained hesitant to embrace the new movement. The association of Socialism with European class relations—a sordidness America long held it had eliminated—clashed abrasively with this society's comparatively higher wages for workers and its honored tradition of political rights. These election results only highlighted the disadvantageous position the Socialists occupied in 1900.

Yet these results did not devastate Debs and his comrades. In part, they realized that this was their first serious national campaign and that the bitter struggles within the movement had hampered their efforts. The question of party unity—perhaps the prime internal lesson the election taught the Socialists—demanded an immediate resolution. But there were other reasons to avoid despair and collapse. In contrast to Berger, Debs dismissed electoral victory as a primary goal. Debs was less concerned with the process of taking office than he was with the educational process of political campaigning. In 1900 Debs was not simply being churlish when he wrote Theodore that workers "will get in full measure what they voted for." Understanding only too well the deep hold of traditional political affiliations and how they formed a web of cultural and social attachments in both communities such as Terre Haute and in the neighborhoods of complex urban centers such as New York, Debs stressed the necessity of redoubling efforts in the future. His optimistic conclusion that the next campaign had already started reflected both an accurate appraisal of the problems Socialists faced and a continued commitment to the struggle.

Debs stressed another element in his emphasis on educational propaganda that remained a dominant theme throughout his Socialist years. In rejecting the mere accumulation of votes, Debs understood that the key to ultimate Socialist success was the profound transformation of individual voters. He repeatedly claimed that he desired no votes that resulted either from attractions to individual Socialist personalities or from a partial commitment to the Socialist program. The heart of his political work lay in demonstrating to the individual voter the necessity of transcending previous political and cultural consciousness, and he understood that no party functionary or political machine could substitute for that critical process. Socialist propaganda was obviously important in this context, but equally important was his understanding of capitalism itself. As he suggested to Theodore, there was a connection between those whom workers had voted for in 1900 and his own optimism concerning 1904. The task, Debs implied, was to make clear the contradictions between expectation and reality in American life, and capitalism itself, perceived by most American and European Socialists as inexorably causing the material impoverishment of a majority in society, would teach a critical lesson.

Debs did not simply ignore the 1900 results. Much as he had supported

Grover Cleveland in 1892 only to be disillusioned two years later, so, too, he foresaw a similar process for others in the post-1900 years. He also knew that nothing could substitute for the individual restructuring of one's own consciousness, for he believed that a meaningful collective salvation could only grow from such a process. Although he underestimated the power and versatility of capitalism, Debs remained even as a Socialist a committed native son, appealing to the humane ideal at the core of what was in practice often a sordid tradition.

The 1900 campaign was a beginning, but the Socialist movement needed to unite its various factions and form a coherent organization to proceed. The campaign had done little to soothe tension among the leaders, but the rank and file of each group derived a different lesson from the campaign. Angered at the leadership's posturing, Socialists in both Chicago and Boston organized impressive public meetings demanding an end to the dispute in the weeks following the campaign. Forced to respond but still intent on preventing unity, the leaders of the Chicago Social Democrats scheduled a party convention for January 1901. With Berger's approval, Debs dutifully announced on the eve of the convention that the convention's decisions on unity would reflect broad national support.[19]

Debs lied, allowing Berger and others to use his acknowledged national prominence in a petty organizational struggle. Debs knew that he, Berger, and others on the Chicago executive board had called the convention as part of their strategy to thwart rank-and-file sentiment for unity. In a series of what Debs called "deliberate" meetings that "went over the ground in detail," Debs participated with the others in establishing the agenda and tactics to deflect the support for union while they appeared to do exactly the opposite. By now Debs had become under Berger's watchful eyes an engaged factionalist, as intent as Berger to protect his own dominant and privileged position within the movement. As he wrote his brother in November 1900, "if there is any attempt to harmonize or placate *count me out*. We must go forward in our own lines & those who don't choose to fall in need not do so." Dismissing the Springfield faction, Debs showed little patience with those locals who refused to join either side: "Of the 'unaffiliates' and 'unattached,' I would not cater to them a damned bit. We have invited them to our convention and if they don't want to come let them stay out." Stressing that "our party has nothing to do with other parties," Debs noted that he had told Berger that if these tactics were altered he would "pull out & let the whole thing go." But, he grandly told Theodore, "I won't. *I'll* stick to the party through the gates of hell."[20]

Despite these machinations, Debs and Berger immediately lost control of the convention when it convened in January 1901. The internal condition of the party was so tenuous that unity appeared the only possible salvation. Since the preceding summer the Chicago party had lost one-third of its membership; its official paper, the *Social Democratic Herald,* suffered severe financial losses and the transparent factional tactics, juxtaposed to the Springfield Socialists' appeal to the rank and file, threatened even more serious erosion in the near future. Faced with overwhelming opposition from their own delegates, Debs and Berger, grasping at another request for a unity conference from the Hillquit forces, agreed to meet at Indianapolis the following July.[21] Although not intended, the convention's outcome did finally reflect rank-and-file attitudes and achieved broad national support.

With the question of unity settled, the major question before the July convention concerned the nature of the party's program. Specifically, the debate focused on whether to include such immediate demands as municipal ownership of utilities or election reform as part of the Socialist program. The Chicago faction heavily favored their inclusion. Declaring that "we are no longer a sect, we are a political party," these delegates insisted that American conditions, especially the nearly universal white male suffrage, demanded programs more specific than a call for the Socialist revolution. "We are after the American heathen," one delegate argued, "and anything I can do for him, regardless of the kingdom of heaven [i.e., the Socialist revolution], he is going to have." This opening toward reform appealed to Berger, then in the process of building a political machine to capture Milwaukee's municipal offices, and he defended the position rigorously from charges of opportunism and vote-catching.[22]

While a majority of the Springfield delegates, including Hillquit, also supported the inclusion of these demands, a significant group resisted. Algie M. Simons forcefully expressed the fear that such demands would blur all distinctions between Socialist and capitalist political parties and "take [Socialists'] attention from important things." Others were more apocalyptical and called for "only one immediate demand, and that the complete surrender of the capitalist class." After extended debate, a compromise solution offered by George Herron, which presented immediate demands as but a step to the full social revolution, passed by a decisive majority. Even Simons voted for it on the grounds of preserving unity.[23]

The other issues before the convention were settled quickly and with relative calm. St. Louis rather than Chicago became the site of the national office; a policy of greater state autonomy won over calls for a strong national executive board; and the delegates selected as their new name, the Socialist Party of America. Leon Greenbaum, a nondescript Socialist of only one year's standing in the movement but who had the advantage of having offended neither side during the long factional wars, found himself the party's new national secretary.[24] Hopeful that factional disputes now lay in the past, the united Socialist movement looked forward with high expectations to future struggles against capitalism.

Although Debs did not attend the convention, he applauded its actions and effusively shared its hopes. Proclaiming the convention "as a monument above internal dissension and factional strife," Debs approved the program and organization of the party. He even found a paragraph of praise for Greenbaum.[25] In that first flush of enthusiasm, it seemed that such hopes were justified. In the state and municipal elections of 1902, Socialists doubled their 1900 totals and won some local races. In the 1904 presidential campaign, the total vote again doubled as Debs and Benjamin Hanford, a New York printer, led the national ticket. In contrast with 1900, thirteen states, including Indiana, gave the Socialist ticket more than 10,000 votes, and in some states the increase over the first campaign was dramatic. New York, for example, tripled its vote; California quadrupled its; and Illinois increased its vote by more than seven times the 1900 total. Throughout the heartland of America, impressive percentage gains occurred in Iowa, Ohio, Kansas (an increase of almost 1400 percent), the Dakotas, and Minnesota. Even in the South, the weakest Socialist region, eight states now recorded more than 1,000 votes. Elated over this seemingly invincible mathematical progression, comrades throughout the country redoubled their efforts, more than ever convinced of the growing imminence of the Socialist revolution.[26]

During this same period formal party membership also grew. Less than 10,000 in 1900, the party could claim more than 23,000 dues-paying members by 1905. William Mailly's competent administration of the party also encouraged sanguine hopes. Mailly, who had succeeded Greenbaum in 1903, reorganized the national office and routed party speakers and organizers across America more efficiently.[27] While the party's most famous orator was not under Mailly's direction—Debs's need for money demanded that he tour either under his own auspices or those of a national lecture bureau[28]—Mailly's efforts greatly aided the vital and assertive Socialist movement throughout the country.

By 1905 the movement had come some distance from the bitter struggles that had marked its first national campaign. While unity did not eliminate all disputes (Berger's policy toward political campaigns and the party's relations with the trade union movement remained a litmus test for opposing Socialist tendencies), the movement appeared in far better health than at any time in the past. As it developed a solid organization and broadened its appeal, its ideology remained grounded in an understanding of American society's political and cultural traditions. While that caused more orthodox American Marxists such as Louis Boudin some discomfort, and provided many European comrades with moments of stunned silence, the instinctive and eclectic olio of natural rights, democratic thought, and Socialist theory indicated the potential the young Socialist movement possessed for overcoming the opposition to Socialism thought to be inherent in American culture.

As the movement grew and attracted a majority of American-born members,[29] the relationship of Socialism to American culture received continued emphasis. In the Southwest, the mercurial and innovative Julius Wayland published the *Appeal to Reason* at Girard, Kansas. The Indiana-born Wayland repeatedly hammered at the themes that Socialism was neither atheistic, anti-individualistic, nor foreign to American traditions. The paper's editorials affirmed time and again that "the revolutionary red, white and blue of our forefathers is good enough" as a symbol for American Socialists; and Wayland celebrated the growing number of Protestant ministers who joined the party as evidence of Socialism's native appeal. Wayland's most consistent theme, in what was once the most widely read of all Socialist periodicals, insisted that Socialism was fully compatible with American individualism.[30]

Herron also emphasized the essential unity of Socialism and individualism. A Protestant minister whose commitment to the Social Gospel brought him into the Socialist movement, Herron grounded Socialism in America's religious tradition. In campaign speeches for Debs and in numerous books and articles Herron focused on the "struggle of man for the possession and direction of his own life, for that self-ownership which is the soil and substance of all liberty." Raising the idea of individualism beyond the callous "glorified and independent individuality" of capitalist society, Herron argued that Socialism "should come to American life as the real and ransomed individualism. We should present Socialism as the co-operation of all men for the individual liberty of each man." Stressing the individual transformation of those who participated in the collective struggle, Herron also affirmed that he stood "vividly and intensely" on the movement's "class-conscious platform." But he cautioned against too particular an interpretation of that idea: "We are also achieving the emancipation of the masters of the working class," he insisted, "and of every man on the face of the earth."[31]

Debs shared this perspective, and it provided the basic continuity to his long public career. Capitalism, Debs told a Michigan audience in 1899, through its control of the means of production, would destroy the American family and thus undermine society itself: "When the American home falls the republic falls, and the brightest light that ever floated across the heavens of the nations goes out." On the stump or as the chairman of the 1904 Socialist platform committee, Debs repeatedly stressed that Socialism "makes its appeal to the American people as the defender and preserver of the idea of liberty and self-government, in which the nation was born." Through collective control of the means of production, Debs insisted, a democratic individualism might indeed be reborn. Against his perception of a destructive capitalist revolution, Debs pitted the prophetic promise of the Christian tradition and, amid appeals to Christ and Lincoln, relished the day when "the whole people will take the title-deed of Rockefeller's trusts and we will operate the . . . machinery of production and distribution."[32]

At times Debs did question whether the "idea of liberty . . . in which the nation was born" provided a sufficient ideological basis for the American Socialist movement. In a forceful 1901 Independence Day oration Debs wondered for the first time in public whether the values associated with the Declaration of Independence provided a potent critique of capitalism. Neither working people nor Afro-Americans had helped to draft that document, he noted, and he emphasized that the institution of slavery, so "in conflict with the spirit of the declaration," peacefully coexisted with it for nearly a century. He critically examined the founding fathers. They "had only vague conceptions of democracy," Debs told his audience, conceptions that were essentially limited to "themselves alone."

Here then was the precipice. If Debs replaced his earlier ideas with a class analysis, he would have to reject the values that had informed his public life to date and replace them with a new ideological vision that took its critical stance from outside American culture. This Debs refused to do. He found it impossible to entertain seriously any position that did not originate from within a broad American tradition. Appealing to an ideal even as he examined its flawed nature, Debs urged his audience to reject a narrow class analysis and encouraged both working and middle-class people to support the coming Socialist revolution. Imploring each class "to open their eyes and see the new light," Debs directed his listeners to the central meaning of that democratic tradition: "I like the 4th of July," he declared. "It breathes the spirit of revolution. On this day we affirm the ultimate triumph of Socialism."[33]

Debs persistently interpreted the Marxist concept of class in distinctly American terms. In an early Social Democratic party debate with Gustav Hoehn, a German immigrant Marxist and trade unionist, Debs defined the movement as meaning "simply a society of democrats, the members of which believe in the equal rights of all to manage and control [society]."[34] But in another context a year later, Debs argued differently. Despite a warm personal friendship, he rejected the attempts of Samuel "Golden Rule" Jones, a leading progressive and mayor of Toledo, Ohio, to enlist him in the nonpartisan movement. "I too," Debs wrote Jones in late 1899, "am for all the people, but the fact that confronts us is that government is dominated by a class in its own selfish interest and that this class must be dislodged. . . . I accept unequivocally the socialist theory that it is a class struggle and that we can only abolish class rule by conquering the capitalist class at the polls."[35]

The class struggle was real for Debs—he saw evidence of it throughout society—but he refused to interpret that evidence dogmatically. His apparent ignoring of trade union and workshop struggles contributed to his broad definition, but more fundamental was his insistence that to become a class-conscious Socialist one need not jettison the proud American political tradition. As he sought more clearly an integration of these two themes, he often appeared confused and contradictory. Yet in an odd way even Marxist theory proved quite malleable to this American adaptation, at least as Debs comprehended it. If it was predetermined that society would devolve into two classes—capitalists and workers—it made little sense to Debs to dismiss those petty bourgeois merchants or the professional men and aspiring entrepreneurs who were in the process, some more slowly than others, of discovering their impoverishment.[36] While the interpretations of the European Marxist revisionists coincided on this point, a far more indigenous influence affected Debs's own formulations.

Ironically, the optimism that permeated Debs's understanding of class formation relied on the continued development of the modern corporation for its success. If the corporation destroyed traditional values, Socialists could argue that the same corporation performed the task of preparing the way for the Socialist commonwealth. In a paradoxical twist the bitter enemy of earlier farmer and worker movements had become proof of Socialism's eventual triumph. As Simons presented the argument in 1906, corporate capitalism created the very platform for the workers' movement, a platform that saw "in the consolidation of ownership, in the organization of industries, in the trusts, in the concentration of wealth with its merciless inevitable onward movement, but a preparation for collective ownership and control."[37] The *Appeal to Reason,* in its usually pithy fashion, presented the argument in easily remembered fashion: "Socialism is not just a theory—it is a destiny."[38]

This sense of destiny, of inevitable progress toward an historically determined goal, provided Debs with an almost limitless source of affirmation in the direction of his political work. With confidence and enthusiasm he proclaimed that the "order of development" proceeded unerringly from the individual through the corporation to the trust—and then, at its ultimate resting place, the people.[39] But Debs's confidence owed less to Karl Marx than it did to a traditional American promise that saw in continued technological and material progress the very establishment of the Kingdom of God in America. As he pictured it in his first campaign speech in 1900, as that progression is accomplished, then all Americans will inhabit a familiar millennial landscape. "We live in the most favored land beneath the unbending sky. We have all the raw materials and the most marvelous machinery; millions of eager inhabitants seeking employment. Nothing is so easily produced as wealth, and no man should suffer for the need of it; and in a rational economic system poverty will be a horror of the past."[40]

Debs's presentation of Socialism took its strength during these years from his efforts to combine traditional concepts with newer understandings of economic theory, class formation, and technological development. Unorthodox and awkward at times, it nonetheless formed the basis of his wide appeal. For Debs, Socialism was the "ransomed individualism" Herron spoke of, and he upheld the promise even as he criticized the practice. Personal regeneration was always possible, Debs held, and he never doubted Wayland's explanation of the making of an American Socialist: "It is not what a man is forced to practice [i.e., his occupation] but what ideal he wants realized and works for that makes the Socialist."[41] In this fashion Debs attempted to span nineteenth-century ideals and twentieth-century reality in these early years as a national Socialist figure.

Debs's analysis also reflected traditional American themes in less attractive ways. Like other politically progressive thinkers, Debs was frequently blind to the inherent dangers of unlimited corporate development. His emphasis on the transfer of power to the people—as opposed to the elite who controlled the trusts—separated him from men such as Herbert Croly and even Walter Lippmann. But in that simpler age Debs never questioned whether the bureaucratic mechanisms necessary to direct a Socialist centralized economy would undermine the very individualism he intended to protect. Debs's view of the corporation also was far too sanguine. While he did not expect corporate leaders simply to give up power, his view of the transition to the Socialist commonwealth relied almost exclusively on victory at the ballot box. In this he dramatically underestimated the power of the corporation, as he did its adaptability. Corporate leaders themselves were engaged in a struggle to control the consciousness of their work force and would freely use any method—from the police power of the state to private profit-sharing programs—to achieve their goal. Against this broad power, Debs's reaffirmation of the political identity of all citizens proved less potent than he thought, especially as he still downplayed the importance of trade union organizing.[42]

But Debs's particular integration of Socialist theory with indigenous themes was, despite its obvious faults, far more appealing to Americans than any alternative at the time, or indeed since. His humanistic individualism with its demand for collective responsibility in structuring society and his call for a broad movement to oppose the current elite control of the political economy formed the social basis of his appeal to American-born and immigrant citizens alike. But before that battle might be won, divisive issues within the party needed to be faced.

The Socialist party had made great strides since 1900. Its organizational stability, active membership, and political appeal grew impressively, but Herron's comment that the party was "full of factional strife" remained accurate.[43] Differences among groups, in part derivative of the debate over immediate demands in 1901 and more broadly reflecting the vast regional variations in the movement's composition, continued to shape internal party life. Too amorphous to be yet termed firm ideological factions, these divergent tendencies nonetheless divided the party and established the major intraparty alliances for the coming years. Control of the national offices, the meaning of electoral activity, and relations with trade unions—disagreement over these issues fostered continued dissension.

These differences were evident in the extensive debate over immediate demands at the 1901 convention. Both Hillquit and Berger favored their inclusion, and for similar reasons. Without these demands, Hillquit argued, one could either "wait with folded arms the arrival of the revolution" or join the anarchists. Berger, on the other hand, pitted the "scientific Socialist" who supported the demands with the immature Socialist—"the disappointed Populist who has been led by his nose by free silver, free paper money and other free things."[44] Beneath the rhetoric a common theme united these former antagonists: each viewed the party in fairly traditional political terms. In building the Socialist movement the task was to run candidates for office who would win. To achieve this, a political party needed a broad platform. It made little difference to Hillquit whether his party's immediate demands mimicked those of the capitalist parties, since without these demands the other parties "will stand for progress and we for dreams."[45]

For Berger especially, his Socialist opponents (dubbed "impossibilists") represented a destructive force that threatened the unique position the Milwaukee Socialists occupied in that city's labor movement. An Austrian-born former schoolteacher who settled in Milwaukee at age twenty-two in 1882, Berger had not been present during the early years of the movement. When he assumed editorship of the pro-labor Wisconsin *Vorwärts* in 1893, however, he became a leading figure in an emerging labor-Socialist alliance with deep roots in Milwaukee's German immigrant community.[46]

Milwaukee's German population had grown steadily during the nineteenth century. The failed German revolution of 1848 brought many political refugees to the city, which was already over one-third German-born. Prospering in the economic boom during and after the Civil War, which encouraged a dramatic industrial development as the city tripled its population between 1870 and 1890, these immigrants soon competed with the Scotch and American-born citizens for control of the city's political and economic life. In this postwar period another wave of Germans arrived in Milwaukee who differed markedly from the '48ers. Primarily skilled workers, many of these later immigrants were active members of the German Social Democratic party who had migrated to escape the oppression of Socialists by Chancellor Otto von Bismarck. Although labeled revolutionaries by Bismarck, their concerns in Germany were less the immediate overthrow of the state than the gradual evolutionary development of a more socialistic society through parliamentary and trade union pressure. Highly class conscious, they were pragmatic and patient reformers whose political and cultural lives revolved around the *verein*, the German cultural club. Thus Berger's first important position was the presidency of the Southside *Turnverein* which, due to its political orientation, quickly became known as the "Red *Verein.*"

These skilled workers were from the first active in the labor movement and in American politics. In 1880 they formed a short-lived Milwaukee Trades Assembly and sent delegates to the founding convention of the Federation of Organized Trades and Labor Unions in November 1881. In politics the assembly stressed specific demands rather than an immediate Socialist revolution and, in 1882, eagerly joined with progressive middle-class forces to nominate for mayor John Stovall, the owner of the Cream City Iron Works who enjoyed a reputation for fair treatment of workers. Although Stovall won, the assembly soon disintegrated and, amidst a long, bitter struggle with the local Knights of Labor to control the city's labor movement, these workers established the Federated Trades Council in 1887. The council concentrated its efforts on organizing other skilled workers, encouraged close ties between local trade unions and their national offices, and affiliated with the AFL. In ignoring the growing unskilled work force, many of whom were new Polish immigrants, the council followed the example of both Gompers and their own earlier experiences. Craft organization of skilled workers dominated the German movement, and in Milwaukee the overlapping membership in the local unions and the *vereins* created a formidable ethnic barrier for non-German workers.

In 1894 the council formed an alliance with Berger's small Socialist group, the local Populist movement, and the Socialist Labor party to field a slate of candidates in the municipal elections. Although the alliance was unsuccessful, the possibilities of such a union remained attractive to Berger's Socialists (the majority of whom were skilled trade unionists themselves) and the council. With the collapse of Populism after 1896 and the withdrawal of most trade unionists from the Socialist Labor party in reaction to its efforts at dual unionism in 1895, relations between Berger's forces and the council became closer. A common ideology and shared ethnic identity encouraged this commingling, and in December 1899 the newly elected executive board of the council consisted solely of Socialists, among them Berger as a representative of Newspaper Writers Local 9. This alliance proved beneficial to both groups. Between 1904 and 1910 eighteen Socialist unionists went to the state legislature, where they supported bills favorable to workers. The 1910 election of Emil Seidel as mayor gave Milwaukee its first pro-labor administration. Similarly, the election of Berger to Congress that same year brought national attention to and created a national forum for labor's concerns. If the alliance ignored unskilled workers and interpreted its professed Socialist vision pragmatically, it also represented a rare example of intimate labor-Socialist cooperation in America. Formed in a specific ethnic and industrial context, it was precisely this delicate relationship that Berger sought to protect when he attacked those Socialists who advocated a more aggressive revolutionary position.

Egocentric and vain, filled with a sense of his own importance, Berger had an essentially unattractive personality, and his nearly insatiable appetite for power within the Milwaukee and national Socialist movements has often obscured, both then and since, an understanding of the social basis of the Socialist political machine he helped to create. Ideologically conservative and in practice wedded to the AFL through his alliance with local labor, Berger represented one experience in the diverse regional pattern that constituted the American Socialist movement. When Berger endorsed Edward Bernstein's revisionist Marxism in 1901 and specifically celebrated the evolutionary principle that was its cornerstone, self-identified Socialist trade unionists of the city hailed his announcement—not Republican and Democratic voters. In Milwaukee, to come to Socialism without advocating a revolutionary transition while maintaining close ties with the established labor movement was to achieve the best of all possible worlds.[47]

The opponents to Berger's Socialism were not the mad-eyed anarchists of his imagination. Nor did they necessarily dismiss the relevance of political work. They were not, however, "Milwaukee Socialists." In spite of Herron's compromise resolution in 1901, these differences continued to grow, and by 1903 Hillquit wrote his wife from a national committee meeting in St. Louis that he, Berger, Barnes, and others were "always fighting together" in intraparty disputes.[48] Essentially these differences reflected an enormous cultural gap that divided the party into distinct regional groupings. The eastern party leaders—mainly professional men, frequently immigrants themselves who were keenly interested in the European theoretical Marxist debate—little understood the dirt farmers of Oklahoma or the lumberjacks of Washington and Oregon. August Claessens, a New York Socialist, discovered this to his dismay when he was talking to miners in Kingman, Arizona. After his talk a miner approached him and disagreed that it was necessary to read to become a Socialist. " 'All a fellow needs to know,' " Greely Clack suggested, " 'is that he is robbed.' " For Claessens, the contrast between this miner and the fierce debaters in New York's Union Square, where comrades fought "about the dialectical, historical, materialistic, economic deterministic, Marxian analyses of the exploitation of workers," was sharp and almost insurmountable.[49]

On specific issues, moreover, the tension grew even more obvious. Ever protective of his own position and influence, Berger harshly attacked Wayland's *Appeal to Reason* in 1904 as "a menace to the movement." He claimed that Wayland's promotional schemes undercut the less solvent Socialist press, accused Wayland of exploiting his work force, and attributed to the Kansas publisher "visions of empires."[50] What was left unsaid, of course, was that the *Appeal*'s growing influence posed a direct challenge to Berger's *Social Democratic Herald*. A difficult man personally, of whom his wife once complained that he "undertook to remake me according to the pattern he thought a wife should be,"[51] Berger felt that his professed theoretical ability allowed him to treat comrades in a similar fashion.

Berger's conduct in the 1905 Milwaukee city elections greatly clarified these opposing tendencies within the party. Rather than run a Socialist slate in the judicial elections, Berger urged his adherents to support the Republican candidate, whom he endorsed as a "liberal, upright man." Although Berger was but following the Milwaukee tradition, he received bitter criticism from Socialists of many persuasions. Mailly, anything but an "impossibilist," warned other moderate Socialists that "the dissatisfaction with opportunism and Bergerism is national in scope" and would seriously split the party if not checked. From Kansas, the *Appeal* demanded Berger's removal from the national executive committee and warned him "that fusion, compromise, and political trading will not be tolerated." In April the Socialist local in Crestline, Ohio, formally requested a national referendum to remove Berger from office, and by July enough locals had seconded the demand to submit it to the party membership.[52]

While few defended Berger's endorsement of the Republican candidate, many Socialists agreed with Hillquit that "a spirit of tolerance" was necessary. Debs, in a public letter of support, went a step further. Acknowledging Berger's error, Debs nonetheless defended him as an exemplary Socialist whom all might emulate: "In every secret fibre of his being he is a Socialist," Debs wrote of Berger. "Impulsive by nature, hotblooded to fireness, his judgement may at times go wrong, but never his ardent loyalty and passionate love for the Socialist movement." Despite this impressive coalition of support, Berger only narrowly won the party referendum by 500 votes out of almost 9,000 cast.[53] The growing number of anti-Berger Socialists knew practically, if not always theoretically, the difference between their political action and what they termed Berger's fishing for votes.

Debs's role in the dispute is odd. He supported Berger and only a few months earlier had tried to "make up for past remissness" by praising Hillquit.[54] Yet Debs had such important disagreements with both men that many anti-Berger comrades regarded him in 1905 as the natural leader of their faction. Debs's relations with Berger were further strained in early 1906 by the Milwaukee leader's sharp retort to Debs's rousing, emotional defense of three officials of the Western Federation of Miners who were accused of the murder of a former Idaho governor. Referring to Debs as "our wellmeaning, but injudicious friend," Berger expressed pleasure that most of the press had not picked up Debs's article, "Arouse, Ye Slaves," from Wayland's paper. The few that did, he happily noted, dismissed it with reference to Debs's known fondness for drink, a reference Berger insisted left him "doubly vexed."[55] Debs was furious. In a private letter he stressed that "certain tendencies" in the "Milwaukee situation," if unchecked, would result in the "collapse of the local movement," and he looked forward to the time when the national party would be "strong enough to sweep the little bosses, dictators and disrupters into the gutters where, if they have any mission, there would seem to be the place for them to fulfull it."[56] Others were more public in their anger toward Berger. The *Appeal* condemned Berger for catering to middle-class voters in attacking Debs, and A. L. Smith, a national committee member from Louisiana, called for Berger's expulsion from the party.[57]

Yet Debs refused to lead a public fight with Berger. He consistently claimed that he was "entirely too much engrossed in the work" of agitation to involve himself, and he regretted that Socialists "waste so much of their time and substance in factional fighting."[58] Some have suggested that Berger and Hillquit maneuvered Debs into this stance to isolate him and his more radical ideas from the membership.[59] But so powerful was Debs's public appeal among the rank and file that this theory remains doubtful. Others have suggested that Debs hesitated, due to Berger's early efforts to instruct him in Socialism.[60] A more probable explanation, however, lies with Debs himself and his view of his role in the development of American Socialism. As Debs's attitude increasingly indicated, his differences with Berger were not minor. "Bergerism" clashed with Debs's Socialist vision in important ways, but Debs approached the edge of this battleground only in private. In public he presented his own analysis but always stopped short of a sustained critique of other Socialists. While he did fear the effects of a factional fight on the party, open factional fighting also threatened him. Debs was still self-conscious in the presence of such confident theorists as Berger and Hillquit and doubted his ability to carry an argument intellectually. But to enter the battle would also demand that he relinquish the symbolic role of father he had assumed for the whole movement and face as brother and peer the criticism of other Socialists. This possibility jarred abrasively with his own self-image and inner needs. In his role as national spokesman and symbol for the movement, Debs was politically effective while he basked in the praise and devotion he required. Open breaks with other leaders of national importance could turn sour the response of many audiences to him. It was to protect his status, so tied to his personality, that Debs ultimately resisted such struggles. He was not isolated by others but rather chose not to lead publicly a more coherent radical faction within the movement.

Instead, Debs let his own actions speak for themselves. As he more successfully integrated traditional American themes with a clearer analysis of class consciousness, Debs rethought his previous evaluation of labor organizing. This, in turn, led him to the founding convention of the Industrial Workers of the World (IWW) and into basic yet publicly restrained opposition to the Socialist position on the trade unions expressed by Berger and Hillquit.

The Socialist party's official labor policy, first developed at the 1898 Social Democratic convention, remained essentially unchanged throughout the first decade of the twentieth century. Party activists were urged to join the union of their trade, to fight the creation of dual unions in competition with the AFL, and to understand that the party and the union were two separate arms of the same movement. Socialists might "bore from within" the AFL to augment their strength, but the official policy warned comrades not to allow political activity to disrupt the functioning of the union.[61] Yet this approach did not prohibit all criticism of the AFL. As the American delegate to the International Socialist Congress in 1904, Hillquit could inform that meeting that Socialists were taking "every proper opportunity to preach the gospel of Socialism" and where necessary to criticize those "conservative and incapable leaders" of the AFL.[62] Berger, even as he persisted in efforts to influence Gompers, became more openly critical of the AFL leader's continued silence concerning Socialism.[63]

But these Socialist hopes for a stronger influence within the AFL, based essentially on the Milwaukee model, were severely shaken at the AFL's 1903 Boston convention. Fearful of the growing Socialist strength within the organization, Gompers ended dramatically any expectations that he would encourage Socialism, slamming Socialists and Socialism in a direct, brutal attack. "I want to tell you, Socialists, that I have studied your philosophy; read your works upon economics . . . both in English and in German—have not only read but studied them . . . I have kept close watch upon your doctrines for thirty years; have been closely associated with many of you and know how you think and what you propose." His credentials established, Gompers then demolished any lingering hopes for cooperation that Berger and others might yet retain. "I know, too, what you have up your sleeve. And I want to say that I am entirely at variance with your philosophy. I declare it to you, I am not only at variance with your doctrines, but with your philosophy. Economically, you are unsound; socially, you are wrong; industrially, you are an impossibility." The Socialist program in the AFL convention went down to defeat by more than a five to one margin.[64]

Berger was furious. In a prominent editorial he attacked Gompers for his conservativism in opposing Socialism and the industrial organization of workers. So incensed was Berger that he even criticized the idea of trade union autonomy (whereby no other union could make jurisdictional or political demands on another), which was the basis not only of the AFL but also of Berger's skilled immigrant Socialist constituency. Over time Gompers became, in Berger's estimation, "one of the most vicious and venomous enemies of Socialism and progressive trade unionism in America."[65] Yet the Milwaukee leader and his supporters never seriously explored their own suggestions concerning the industrial organization of workers or their critique of trade union autonomy. Instead, they consistently opposed attempts to build an alternative to the AFL. At both the 1908 and 1910 party conventions, Berger led the fight against resolutions that would have broadened the party's trade union plank to emphasize the need to organize the unorganized, unskilled workers who comprised the majority of the American working class.[66]

Debs found this policy toward unskilled workers distasteful. He had long known the inadequacy of craft organization and felt that union men wasted time in attempting to influence Gompers, especially in light of the AFL leader's close association with the National Civic Federation, a coalition of major capitalists dedicated to industrial harmony. For Socialists who scurried after the elusive Gompers, Debs had even less sympathy.[67] Moreover, emphasis on political action remained prominent in his thought. To the 1902 Western Federation of Miners convention he argued that if it was important for workers to organize economically to realize "a class identity," then "it is vastly more important that they shall combine on the political field, where they are absolutely invulnerable." Two years later, before the United Mine Workers' convention, Debs again inferred that trade union matters were of less long-term importance than concentrated political activity.[68]

However, Debs's emphasis on political action in these speeches no longer reflected the full scope of his thought. Although he still emphasized political agitation, Debs had, by late 1904, dramatically revised his opinion of the trade union, especially the industrial union. He now reaffirmed the value of the union as a defense for working-class interests. And he had come to see the organized industrial workers' movement as an indispensable ally to Socialist agitation. After almost a decade as a Socialist, Debs had finally integrated his traditional emphasis on democratic rights with an institutionally rooted class analysis. This approach enabled him to avoid the "class-conscious club" that had so long disturbed him in some interpreters of Marxism, even as he broadened and strengthened his commitment to the American political tradition. A Socialist need not choose between democratic rights and the class struggle, Debs discovered, for, in a mature industrial society, itself organized in hierarchical fashion, the fulfillment of that very democratic promise demanded a thorough restructuring of the economic arena. To ignore this interdependence would insure the ultimate irrelevance of the political tradition itself.

Central to this re-evaluation was Debs's relationship with the Western Federation of Miners. Founded in 1893, the origins of the union reflected the bitter and prolonged class warfare in the western mine fields. The first union in the region was formed in 1864 in the fabled Comstock Lode area of Nevada. The miners of Gold Hill, Nevada, built an industrial union (which did, however, exclude the Chinese) to oppose a reduction in wages, demanded a closed shop, and swore an oath to fight, in "acquaintance with our fellows," "the tyrannical oppressive power of capital." Over the next two decades, as highly capitalized and technologically sophisticated corporate efforts transformed the nature of mining throughout the West, the Gold Hill miners' constitution remained a model for others. In 1878 the Butte (Montana) Workingmen's Union organized with the intention of including not just miners but *all* workers in every occupation in Butte. This proved too cumbersome organizationally, but when the Butte Miners Union emerged in 1885 its leaders encouraged other workers to affiliate with the Knights of Labor. By 1890 this industrial union of miners, with branches throughout the western states, represented the strongest opposition to corporate mine owners in the region.[69]

The union played an important role in the workers' lives. The primary defense against exploitation by employers, the union also served as a focal point for political agitation. There was yet another function. Often living in mining camps dominated by the corporation, the miners found in their union hall a cultural and political sanctuary for themselves and their families. Parties, weddings, and funerals were held there, and many halls possessed a well-stocked library that included Socialist, Knights of Labor, and Populist papers and pamphlets. The absence of the union could mean a bleak existence, as a fifteen-year-old novice miner discovered in 1884 at the Ohio mine, some sixty miles from Winnemucca, Nevada. "In the front room bunks were ranged," Bill Haywood later recalled, but "there were no chairs, no tables, no furniture of any kind other than a desk and the stuff belonging to the men."

The experience of these miners had made them militant, class-conscious industrial unionists, but by the late 1890s few were Socialists. The class struggle was violent, they had learned, more often fought with the cartridge box than at the ballot box. Yet the Western Federation did not simply dismiss political work. Among the leaders and to a lesser extent the rank and file, Union Labor, Populist, and Socialist candidates frequently received strong support. In the Colorado election of 1892, for example, the successful Populist candidate for governor, Davis H. Waite, received impressive support from miners, and his use of state power to check corporate violence during the Cripple Creek strike of 1894 suggested to all the importance of political action. As Ed Boyce, president of the Western Federation, noted in 1897, workers could either "fight with the sword or use the ballot with intelligence," depending on circumstances. It was precisely at this juncture that these western miners influenced Debs. His three-month stay with Boyce in 1897 forced him to begin to re-evaluate that earlier dismissal of union work—although it took time for this to be reflected in Debs's public statements. Debs enthusiastically approved the withdrawal of the Western Federation from the AFL in 1897 and a year later again applauded as these miners and other western workers created the Western Labor Union. The new union, as Boyce explained, intended to organize "the local unions and get them all into municipal unions, then . . . into the various state unions and assemblies, from which we could organize an interstate or western union." With Debs's support, the Western Labor Union adopted the original Butte Workingmen's Union program on a regional scale.[70]

A two-fold critique of Gompers united Boyce and Debs. Both men rejected the AFL's emphasis on skilled workers, trade union autonomy, and involvement with the National Civic Federation. Second, both agreed that Gompers's attempts to bar political agitation from the labor movement encouraged the continued subservience of workers toward their employers. For Boyce and especially for Debs, strong economic organization by workers demanded a political voice for its fulfillment. As Debs and Boyce continued to influence each other, their fruitful interchange held great promise for American Socialists and labor activists alike. This became quite apparent in 1902. At the annual Western Labor Union convention, strong sentiment existed to transform that union into the American Labor Union, which would explicitly and directly challenge the AFL by organizing eastern workers. Although almost two decades old, AFL officials feared that their organization might be seriously weakened in the ensuing struggle. Important AFL-affiliated unions, the Brewery Workers and the United Mine Workers of America in particular, contained forceful elements opposed to AFL policies, and a creditable showing by a new national union might win these factions majority support within their organizations. In an attempt to forestall such action, Gompers sent Frank Morrison, his national secretary-treasurer, to address the Western Labor Union convention.

Morrison's speech created exactly the opposite reaction to what Gompers wanted. With an amazing lack of tact, Morrison condemned both past organizing efforts and the proposed new union and vowed that the AFL would continue to oppose the "contention and disruption" that the miners caused the labor movement. Distorting the historical record, he compared these western workers with the Knights of Labor in what he argued were similar efforts in dual unionism. In his conclusion, a misplaced conciliatory effort, he referred to his audience as "the most progressive trade unionists in America" but insisted they bring their ideas into the AFL or face a prolonged conflict.[71]

It was with some pleasure that Debs followed Morrison to the podium. Debs pointedly reminded the AFL representative that, during the 1880s, it was his organization and not the Knights of Labor that practiced dual unionism. In a blistering critique of AFL policy, Debs stressed the importance of creating a national industrial union structure. Gompers's affiliation with the National Civic Federation was not merely a philosophic problem, he explained, for in numerous recent strikes that organization had actively worked to undermine worker strength—as Gompers remained silent. Debs attributed the conservative policy of the United Mine Workers to its national leadership's close ties with Gompers and excoriated both the AFL and the Civic Federation for their roles in the ongoing coal strike. The AFL was moribund, he exclaimed, but to the delegates before him he offered an alternative course: "We are going to begin right here! We are going to begin right now in this Western country . . . I want the trade unions to organize thoroughly and to assert their rights upon the economic field and to do all they can to keep them there. I ALSO WANT THE TRADE UNIONISTS AS SUCH TO STAND TOGETHER UPON A POLITICAL PLATFORM!"

Defining a Socialist as "a 'ripe' trade unionist," Debs offered concrete proposals. He urged the delegates to create the American Labor Union, with a national rather than regional jurisdiction, and excitedly predicted that many eastern workers, angered over AFL policy, would respond. Debs dismissed the expected charge of dual unionism. Not until there came "a divorce between Samuel Gompers and Marcus Hanna [of the National Civic Federation]," Debs declared, could union with the AFL even be considered. Not surprisingly, the delegates followed Debs's advice and, with the Western Federation of Miners at its core, founded the American

Labor Union. In one of its first acts, the new union declared itself in favor of Socialism.[72]

Debs's speech in 1902 marked an important juncture in his search for an integrated understanding of the relationship between a democratic philosophy and the Socialist theory of class struggle. But within the Socialist party the speech produced intense debate. Max Hayes, the Cleveland Socialist trade unionist, dismissed the new union's declaration for Socialism as the result of the undue influence of Debs and the Reverend Thomas Haggerty, the Socialist Catholic cleric. Algie M. Simons and Gustav Hoehn were also critical. But the major criticism came from the National Committee of the Socialist party itself. In the semiannual report the committee attacked unnamed comrades who sought to unify political and union work and censured them for opposing official party efforts to build Socialist strength by "boring from within" the AFL.[73] Debs was quick to respond. In a long article he attacked those Socialists who would dismiss "the young, virile class-conscious union movement of the West" in favor of "the 'pure and simple' movement of the East." To oppose the American Labor Union, he insisted, solely because it was a dual union left Socialists no alternative but to support the Gompers–Hanna alliance. Perceiving "a radical fundamental difference" between the eastern and western regions of the country, Debs argued that western workers were "far enough advanced" to insist on "class-conscious political action" and thus deserved strong Socialist party support.[74]

As Berger had in another context, Debs's role in this dispute further defined divisions within the party. For Harriman and Hillquit, the emergence of the American Labor Union posed two dangers. The new union not only opposed official party policy toward the AFL but also, as Harriman wrote in 1903, western Socialists "will endorse the ALU hoping by that means to control the party as against the east." For its part, the *American Labor Union Journal* dismissed those who came to Socialism "by the kid glove route." A study of the "materialist concept of history," the *Journal* argued in 1904, was less important in the making of a Socialist than the knowledge that "he is being robbed, degraded and starved." This comrade, "to whom wage slavery is not a theory but a fact," had little patience with further dalliance with the AFL. This debate dominated the 1904 party convention where, after some struggle, Berger, Hillquit, Hayes, and others successfully thwarted a full discussion of industrial unionism and the relation between political and economic action.[75]

Amidst this tension a group of western labor leaders and party members issued a call in November 1904 to about thirty industrial unionists and/or Socialists to meet in Chicago in January 1905 to discuss the creation of a national revolutionary labor union. The delegates decided to establish an industrial union committed to the class struggle with no official connection to any political party and announced a general convention in June 1905 to form the new union, the Industrial Workers of the World (IWW). Unable to attend the January meeting, Debs fully and publicly supported the resolutions.[76]

Although invited, Berger and Hayes refused to attend the January meeting. Criticizing the proposed IWW, Berger argued that the problem with the AFL was less its leaders than the rank and file, who continually elected them to office. Ignoring the issue of organization in the industrial unionists' critique, Berger dissociated the Socialist party from any responsibility and pointedly claimed that Debs acted solely on his own. Privately Berger was even sharper. Claiming that he had "been charged with heresy" by some IWW supporters, he vowed to confront Debs directly. "I will go and see Debs personally next week," Berger wrote Hillquit in March 1905. "He must come out immediately and come out in a decided and unequivocal manner [against the IWW] or there will be war. If Debs stays with that crowd, he will land them some prestige for a little while, but I am also sure that will be the end of Eugene V. Debs."[77] Whether or not Berger confronted Debs, the results could not have pleased him. When the founding convention of the IWW opened in June in Chicago, Debs was one of the over 200 delegates in Brand's Hall.

"Fellow workers," William D. Haywood announced in opening the convention, "this is the Continental Congress of the working class. We are here to confederate the workers of this country into a working class movement that shall have for its purpose the emancipation of the working class from the slave bondage of capitalism." The object of the organization, Haywood announced, was "to put the working class in possession of the economic power, the means of life, in control of the machinery of production and distribution, without regard to capitalist masters." The AFL "is not a working class movement." Its by-laws prohibit blacks, most immigrants, and unskilled whites from membership: "What we want to establish at this time is a labor organization that will open wide its doors to every man that earns his livelihood either by his brain or his muscle." Stressing again the "purpose of placing the supervision of industry in the hands of those who do the work," Haywood scorned those, whether from capital or labor, who still espoused a harmony of interest between the two classes. "There is a continuous struggle between the two classes," he concluded; recognizing this, the IWW has "but one object and one purpose and that is to bring the workers of this country into the possession of the full value of the product of their toil."[78]

The applause that greeted Haywood's remarks established the tone for the first days of the convention. It was a heady, exciting time, as delegate after delegate rose to condemn the AFL, its pro-capitalist leadership, and other "labor fakirs"—perceiving at the convention the very forces that would soon replace that moribund organization. And the contrasts among the delegates seemed to reinforce the sense of unity. From the West came the embattled leaders of the Western Federation and the American Labor Union, some of them but recently released from jail for their support of the 1904 Cripple Creek strike. Joining them was Algie M. Simons, the University of Wisconsin graduate, devotee of Frederick Jackson Turner, and editor of the *International Socialist Review*. Daniel DeLeon, leader of the Socialist Labor party, was a fully accredited delegate and had the unusual experience of being warmly praised by Debs from the convention floor. Lucy Parsons, widow of one of the Haymarket martyrs, spoke eloquently on behalf of women workers and provided a dramatic visual continuity with earlier dedicated labor organizers; Mary (Mother) Jones's very presence recalled the current need for continued organizing drives. In short, the convention united many conflicting tendencies within the militant labor movement and held out the hope that their common commitment to revolutionary industrial unionism would permanently overcome past difficulties.

Debs's speech to the convention embodied these hopes and revealed the distance he had traveled from the not-so-distant days when he rejected further labor organizing. Surveying the present labor movement, Debs accused it of being under the control of capitalists and pointed to the recent string of lost strikes as proof that the AFL was bankrupt. Dismissing the charge of dual unionism—"we might as well have remained in the Republican and Democratic parties and have expected to effect certain changes from within"—Debs found common ground with DeLeon. Although "sound in its economics," Debs nonetheless argued that the Socialist Labor party "does not appeal to the American working class in the right spirit." Its opposition to fakirism has often resulted in fanaticism, Debs stated, but he declared that in the proposed new organization "there is a middle ground that can be occupied" by all factions "without the slightest concession of principle."

Quite consciously, Debs commented that this attitude represented a major change for him. In embracing DeLeon and an industrial union dedicated to undermining the AFL, Debs found himself "breaking away from some men I have been in very close touch with, and getting in close touch with some men from whom I have been very widely separated. But no matter," he announced, "I have long since made up my mind to pursue the straight line as I see it." With these words Debs served notice to Berger and his allies within the party how fundamental was his disagreement with their trade union position. But precisely because he was Debs, formed from experiences at some distance from both Berger and Haywood, Debs

concluded his speech, and his decade-long search, with a firmer integration of the twin poles of revolutionary political and economic action: "If
this work is begun properly, it will mean in time, and not a long time at
that, a single union upon the economic field. It will mean more than that;
it will mean a single party upon the political field [great applause]; the one
the economic expression, the other the political expression of the working
class; the two halves that represent the organic whole of the labor movement."[79]

In not mentioning the Socialist party by name, Debs, sensitive to the
disagreements submerged beneath the general enthusiasm, prefigured the
convention's compromise position on political activity. The committee on
the constitution, heavily represented by Western Federation and
American Labor Union delegates, asserted the permanency of the class
struggle and urged workers to unite on the political as well as the industrial
fields. But it also insisted that the revolution would only occur when
workers "take hold of that which they produce by their labor through an
economic organization of the working class, without affiliation with any
political party." Paradoxically, this view reflected aspects of the Socialist
party's own relationship with the AFL, but in this new revolutionary context it seemed confusing. Simons called the report "almost ridiculous,"
while Clarence Smith, secretary-treasurer of the American Labor Union,
condemned it as mere "toadyism to three different factions in this convention": the industrial unionists who dismissed political work, the political
Socialists, and the anarchist element. Smith was right. The western
delegates, through the Western Federation, dominated the convention,
and by 1905 few supported continued political action. The nearly continuous bitter strikes of recent years and the open collusion between mine
owners and state and federal politicians had convinced them that the election of a governor such as Waite was the rare exception and not the rule in
a capitalist-dominated political system. But to appease those Socialists
such as Debs who insisted on continued political work, the western leaders
held back and supported the resolution, even though it tried to unite fundamentally contradictory views. It would not be long before the sanguine
hopes that the convention had thus solved a basic problem proved illusory.[80]

The June convention caused immediate trouble among Socialists. While
Debs praised the new organization, Simons warned of increased tension
from its Socialist opponents. Mailly, the national Socialist party secretary,
hoped that factional disputes might be avoided, especially as the party came
to understand the difference "between endorsing an organization
and . . . supporting an organization in a fight with the capitalist class."[81]
Hope as he might, Mailly knew his distinction was not understood by
many. As Hayes reported a year later, many Socialist locals were deeply
divided over support of the IWW and some, such as the one in Cincinnati,

had formally split over the issue. Similar tension existed in many AFL locals. In large part Hayes blamed Debs for this tension, complaining that Debs's current speeches stressed the general strike more than political action. The Socialist leader, Hayes commented, no longer exhibited "his infectious enthusiasm for political action."[82]

What worried these Socialists was not the revolutionary rhetoric of the IWW—that, they felt, would have little sustaining appeal to American workers—but rather the very real organizational threat the industrial union presented to the AFL and to Socialist policy. The core of the IWW, as of the American Labor Union before it, remained the Western Federation of Miners. With approximately 27,000 members concentrated in the trans-Mississippi West, the Western Federation organized the miners into a strong militant union. The attitudes of these men, hardened in vicious class warfare, were almost incomprehensible to the skilled trade union Socialists of Milwaukee, and their example was important to other workers as well. Many scorned political activity and therefore the Socialist party, and they had nearly total contempt for Gompers and his AFL.[83] The Socialist defenders of the AFL would have been concerned enough over the Western Federation, but they regarded the changing relations between that union and the UMWA as even more dangerous.

Founded in 1890 with a militant biracial membership organized along industrial lines, the UMWA affiliated with the AFL early in its history. It was not a smooth marriage. Within the union there existed a strong Socialist faction, and individual locals frequently countermanded both their own national officers and the policy of the AFL. Relations with the Western Federation also were not easy. Prior to 1902 the western union organized coal as well as metalliferous miners, and the two unions frequently clashed over jurisdictional disputes. Even after the Western Federation stopped organizing coal miners, the battles continued, and more than one Western Federation local found itself raided by UMWA organizers.[84] John Mitchell, president of the UMWA after 1899, aggravated relations further. Born in the coal fields of Illinois to Scotch-Irish Presbyterian parents in 1870, this former member of the Knights of Labor rose swiftly in the hierarchy of the union. While Mitchell could be quite impressive on the stump before a strike audience, his actions, especially during the 1902 Pennsylvania anthracite strike, greatly angered UMWA militants. In October, during the sixth month of that strike, Mitchell engineered acceptance by a miners' convention of arbitration by the National Civic Federation. Not only were his own members angry, but also Mitchell antagonized both Western Federation leaders and Debs, who had warned against arbitration. By 1904 relations had not improved. Debs, closely associated with the Western Federation leaders, repeatedly attacked Mitchell's endorsement of harmony as a proper guide to labor-capital relations.[85]

In 1905 two events occurred that suggested a possible new relationship between the two unions. Although still a minority, the oppositional caucus within the UMWA gained support in protest of Mitchell's handling of a bitter Colorado strike. Robert Randall, president of a UMWA local, accused Mitchell of intentionally settling a strike of coal and metalliferrous miners, so that only his members won any concessions, and of then withdrawing all support from the Western Federation strikers. Although Mitchell forced Randall from office, this fight clarified the factions within the union.[86] The second event was the creation of the IWW. Its sharp attack on craft organization, trade union autonomy, and the AFL's anemic defense of strikers found many supporters within the UMWA. Structurally, moreover, the creation of the IWW established an organizational framework through which the two miners' unions might amalgamate. If the dissidents did gain control over the union and withdrew from the AFL, the new national union would offer a ready home.

It was precisely this possibility that frightened Socialists such as Berger and Hayes. Were the miners' unions to unite, it would encourage others in the same direction. This not only could fatally weaken the AFL, but also it would reduce to insignificance their faction's role within the Socialist party. Berger and his allies had pointed to unions such as the UMWA as proof of the correctness of the "boring from within" tactic: it might be slow and suffer an occasional defeat, but an oppositional nucleus was forming in the AFL. But, if the UMWA left and united with the IWW, what importance would Berger or Hillquit have in a movement dominated by Haywood, Debs, and other western radicals? Conversely, this prospect excited the Western Federation and segments of the UMWA, especially in Illinois. For its part, the Western Federation worked hard to overcome past tension. When William Trautmann, secretary of the IWW, bitterly attacked Mitchell and the UMWA leadership in 1906, the editor of the Western Federation's journal, the *Miners' Magazine,* attempted to repair the damage. While he did not support Mitchell's policies, John O'Neill wrote to the Socialist UMWA officer, Adolph Germer, "it seems to me that the anarchy of capitalism at the present time furnishes a subject which should command all the attention" of labor organizers.[87] A similar tone dominated the Western Federation's organizing efforts. Following the formation of the IWW, requests from UMWA locals in Illinois, Kansas, and Colorado to affiliate inundated the Western Federation. Carefully the western leaders refused to organize miners already in the UMWA. Their efforts were "directed entirely to organizing the unorganized men, who are employed in and around the mines and mills in the Western states," one official explained. Not insignificantly, this policy also prevented bitter

Eugene V. Debs Foundation, Terre Haute.

Eugene Victor Debs (second from left), with his brother Theodore (far left) and Steven M. Reynolds (second from right).

Cunningham Memorial Library, Indiana State University, Terre Haute.

The painting crew of William Riley McKeen's railroad in 1870. Seated, far left, with his can of paint, is fourteen-year-old Eugene Debs.

Herman Hulman's business on Main Street, downtown Terre Haute in the late 1880s.

Vigo County Historical Society, Terre Haute.

Vigo County Public Library, Terre Haute.

William Riley McKeen, president of the Vandalia
Railroad and Debs's first employer.

Herman Hulman, Terre Haute's wholesale grocer
and Debs's employer and friend.

Vigo County Public Library, Terre Haute.

Eugene V. Debs Foundation, Terre Haute.

HON. GRAFTON F. COOKERLY
AND E. V. DEBBS

Will address their fellow citizens on the issues
of the day, on

FRIDAY, AUGUST 30TH 1878,

At 7 1-2 O'CLOCK P. M.

AT FREEZE'S GROCERY,

COR. THIRTEENTH & CHESTNUT STS

All are invited, irrespective of former party
affiliations.

A Democratic Ward Club will be formed immediately after the Speaking.
By Order of Committee.

Debs spoke on political issues even before he held public office, as witness this Democratic party poster.

Cunningham Memorial Library, Indiana State University, Terre Haute.

Eugene V. Debs, age thirty-nine, on the eve of the Pullman strike.

Eugene V. Debs Foundation, Terre Haute.

Socialist party campaign poster, 1904.

"Debs talks to us with his *hands*, out of his *heart*." On the stump at a Socialist picnic in Knoxville, Tennessee, 1905.

Cunningham Memorial Library, Indiana State University, Terre Haute.

Perkins Library, Duke University, Durham.

These American Socialists accompanied the three-car "Red Special" through the Midwest in the campaign of 1908.

Eugene V. Debs Foundation, Terre Haute.

Eugene Debs at Canton, Ohio, June 16, 1918.

Some of the 21,000 citizens of Terre Haute who signed the petitions for Debs's release from jail in 1921. In the background is Baur's drugstore, originally owned by Kate Debs's stepbrothers.

Eugene V. Debs Foundation, Terre Haute.

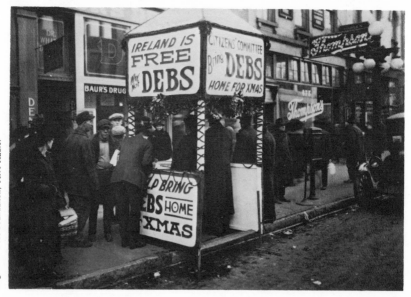

Eugene V. Debs Foundation, Terre Haute.

Eugene Debs accepting the 1920 Socialist party nomination. Otto Branstetter is fourth from right, and James Oneal is on the far right.

Eugene and Theodore embracing on Eugene's release from the Atlanta Federal Prison, December 1921.

Eugene V. Debs Foundation, Terre Haute.

Lilly Library, Indiana University, Bloomington.

"You seem always to have been in my heart and life." Eugene on Mabel Dunlap Curry.

Cunningham Memorial Library, Indiana State University, Terre Haute.

Family portrait taken on the porch of the Debs home in Terre Haute, September 1925. Seated, from left, are Theodore Debs, his wife Gertrude, and Katherine and Eugene Debs. The man in the rear is Howard Debs Selby, a nephew.

Eugene V. Debs Foundation, Terre Haute.

Debs standing before the Atlanta Federal Prison, at his release on December 24, 1921.

jurisdictional battles with the UMWA and deprived Mitchell and his supporters of an opportunity to discredit dissidents in their own ranks.[88]

Western Federation leaders were also active in attempting to unite the two unions. The executive board of the union broached this subject in 1906 and proposed a joint meeting of both unions' executive boards at that year's IWW convention.[89] At the 1907 UMWA convention opposition to Mitchell was stronger than ever before, and sentiment for union with the IWW was widespread. The following year Haywood, just released from an Idaho jail, addressed the UMWA convention and pleaded for unity between the two unions: "It will be impossible for the smelting companies to operate their smelters [if unity is achieved] because the coal miners will not mine coal to be used as scab smelters."[90] Debs was active behind the scenes in these attempts to unite the two unions. Inexplicably, however, he refused to cancel speaking engagements in 1909 and 1910 to address the UMWA convention, despite his knowledge that the pro-unity forces needed every supporter on hand.[91]

Ultimately, the attempts at unity failed. The UMWA remained affiliated with the AFL, and the dissidents never achieved majority support within the union. Further dissension racked the Western Federation. A bitter struggle in 1906 and 1907 eventually led to the union's withdrawal from the IWW, which left the IWW without a significant union base and the Western Federation without a national affiliation. In 1911 the Western Federation reapplied for membership in the AFL, and was accepted by Gompers. From this vantage point, the Socialist critics of the "impossibilists" appeared at least partially accurate when they criticized the reliance upon resolutions in favor of Socialism by Western Federation leaders instead of extended agitation among the rank and file. Despite the bitter experience these miners suffered at the hands of industrial capitalism, the rank and file was never as consistently radical as such leaders as Boyce or Haywood.[92]

But in the years immediately following the founding of the IWW, this was not at all clear. Gompers, for one, nervously kept a watchful eye on the new organization through a paid informant and delivered repeated attacks on the IWW and Western Federation in an attempt to defuse its potential influence.[93] The Socialist opposition was also wary and feared disruption if the two miners unions united. While individual Socialists would switch positions over the coming years (Simons and Debs are two prominent examples), the intraparty struggle over the IWW's relations with the labor movement and the relative merits of the IWW versus the AFL provided a continuous point of reference that contributed to the hardening of factional disputes during the next decade.

His fervent support for industrial unionism and his newfound integration of political activity with an aggressive class analysis marked the distance between Debs and Berger or Hillquit in their understanding of Socialism. As Debs argued in 1905, during a nationwide tour on behalf of the IWW, the choice was "between the A.F. of L. and capitalism on one side and the Industrial Workers and Socialism on the other. How can a Socialist hesitate in his choice for an instant?"[94] Yet even during this period, an exciting and fruitful time for Debs, a certain tendency among his new allies worried him. When, in 1903, the militant Socialist leaders of Colorado sought to expel from the party a group of Socialist ministers (among them Carl D. Thompson, J. Stitt Wilson, and Franklin H. Wentworth) for opposition to the leadership's revolutionary tactics, it was Debs, and not Berger, who came to the ministers' defense:

> The trouble with some men is that they must "judge" other men and "condemn" them if they don't conform to their contracted ideas. They talk about "revolutionary Socialism" and "opportunism"; these and a few other stock phrases complete their vocabulary. . . . Such men may organize a sect, but never a party; they may mean well, and usually do, but they are too fanatic and intolerant to develop a great movement. The worst of all is that they imagine themselves "revolutionaries." They are in fact quite the reverse; such influence as they have is wholly reactionary.[95]

As Debs developed a more holistic vision as a Socialist, he remained firmly committed to building a movement that reflected American political realities. A party, not a sect, was his goal and this consistent concern would, a few short years after Haywood's stirring address that opened the 1905 convention, lead Debs to dissociate himself from both the IWW and Haywood.

In speech after speech, as Debs outlined the destructive impact of a harsh factory discipline, low wages, and dangerous working conditions on American workers and their families, he seemed to draw on a private well of understanding that gave his critique its tone of personal urgency. Although Debs had not labored for his livelihood since the 1870s, when he traded the fireman's shovel for the city clerk's pen, the development of capitalism intimately affected his adult family life nonetheless. The sure confidence that suffused his formal Episcopal wedding to Kate in 1885—asserted even more strongly in their expensive eastern honeymoon—did not survive the ascendency of the new order. As Debs moved further into opposition, the social bonds that had at first united the young couple collapsed, and personal feelings proved inadequate to sustain a close relationship. In many ways Debs had come to think of his wife by 1900 in more formal terms, deserving fond memories and due a certain loyalty—but no longer at the core of current passions and involvements.

Never deeply introspective concerning such relations, Debs's reserved Victorian sensibilities prevented him from discussing even with close friends the nature of his marriage. But his actions implied more than he consciously admitted. The Debs home on North 8th Street became a stopover for him, where he might recover from the strain of his travels. Following the 1904 campaign, for example, Debs returned home exhausted and remained in bed "for several weeks." Still bedridden in January, he told his friend, James Whitcomb Riley, that he suffered from "nervous exhaustion," marked by "the most violent and incessant headaches that mortal ever suffered" and predicted that "it will take some time to overcome." During the sickness Kate attended him, nursed him, and acted as a stern guard against the constant stream of visitors and comrades who appeared on the porch. Predictably, as Debs recovered, he itched for the road and in February resumed his travels.[96]

Debs's activities during 1907 suggest the nature of the relationship between him and Kate as each approached full middle age. A year not marked by a presidential campaign, the pattern is also typical of these years. Debs began 1907 recuperating from a severe "rheumatic attack," which had prevented him from leaving immediately for Girard, Kansas, and the offices of the *Appeal to Reason*. After consulting a specialist in Cincinnati, however, Debs went to Girard without Kate and lived there through the spring, using that community as a home base for his travels. Sick and exhausted by early summer, he returned to Terre Haute and to his bed, where he stayed confined for more than six weeks. Recovered by September, he began a western tour which returned him to Terre Haute for a short Christmas layover—after which he immediately began an eastern tour that occupied him until February 1908.[97] Capping this odyssey, Debs spent a major portion of the spring and summer months of 1908 at Girard, returning home briefly in September before starting on an arduous presidential campaign aboard the "Red Special."[98] Kate's participation in her husband's life, personally as well as publicly, was fairly circumscribed. She was rarely with him when he felt healthy and fit.

While sufficient evidence to evaluate the medical basis of Debs's multiple illnesses does not exist, it is difficult to avoid the impression that many were emotional rather than physical in nature. With certain exceptions—a throat illness, for example, which resulted in an operation at the Mayo Clinic in 1910[99]—Debs's doctors often could find no illness to cure. They prescribed rest and on occasion special diets. Beyond that, as Debs himself once stated, "the most skillful doctors in our city have been unable to overcome" the ailment.[100] As with many other men and women reared with middle-class aspirations in late nineteenth-century America, Debs used illness as an emotional escape from the pressures of his life. Whether in a hotel room in New York during a tour, surrounded by concerned comrades, or at home, attended by the dutiful Kate, Debs periodically created for himself a haven from the world where he might bask in the devotion and uncritical attention of others.[101]

This need structured Eugene's relationship with Kate. The distance evident between them during the Pullman strike—when Kate visited her husband in jail wearing diamonds—had not lessened in the intervening years. At times he sought to express affection, but the language remained stilted and formal. "To Kate," he wrote in 1907, "The flower of my soul." On occasion, his letters home reflected a warmer tone. "Love and Kisses from the sweet honeymoon days of nearly twenty-five years ago," he wrote Kate from Pittsburgh in 1910. But on the actual anniversary in June of that year, Debs was on the road, far from Kate and Terre Haute.[102] Bound by formalities and lacking the "infectious enthusiasm" that permeated his relations with comrades and other family members, Eugene desired little more than Kate's careful observance of her formal duties.

For her part, Kate had long separated her life from his. Turning more inward, her concerns revolved around her family, especially her mother and nephew who lived with her. But her husband's activities affected even this domain. Feeling awkward as the wife of a revolutionary Socialist and isolated as an unaccompanied female in Terre Haute society, Kate withdrew even from her circle of friends and remained more and more within the confines of her own house. Never publicly critical, even in private she presented the best possible face. To a friend she explained that while her husband was not home for their twenty-fifth wedding anniversary, her mother had returned from visiting relatives "so the day was a day of joy." A few months earlier, commenting on her husband's preparations for the tour that would keep him away on their anniversary, Kate attempted to protect her marriage's public face: "This is the one trying thing about his work. The home life of which he is so fond has to be largely sacrificed. But it also has its compensations and we must bear it as cheerfully as we can." Infrequently, a more bitter tone crept into her letters that reflected a repressed but pervasive anger. Writing to Grace Brewer in late 1910, Kate complained of the length of yet another tour Eugene and George Brewer, an editor at the *Appeal to Reason,* had embarked on. "I had hoped and understood that such *long* trips were things of the past," she protested and stated that while her husband would rarely complain her reality was quite different: "I know what a let down there is after he gets home and how he suffers and how I have to take care of him to get him in readiness for the next dose." Citing his age and physical condition, Kate tried to reclaim her husband, now age fifty-five, for the last years of their lives.[103]

But this would not occur. Despite her assertions to the contrary, Eugene was not fond of "the home life," at least as Kate understood it. Rather, when Debs apothesized the family, his personal reference point remained his parental family. In contrast, his relation with Kate was simply not that important. "Having reached the zenith of my power," Debs wrote his parents in 1905 to thank them for the "world of comfort" their love provided: "No matter how sorely we may be tried if love floods in at the windows and abides with us . . . this earth is paradise through all pain and tears and to the very end."[104]

Although Debs understood his parental home as "the sustaining element" in his own life,[105] he continued to attribute to each parent somewhat different qualities. On his father's eighty-second birthday in 1902, Eugene wrote that "no boy, living or dead, ever had a better father," for Daniel "set a truer example of honesty, manliness and all other virtues that crown the true man" than anyone else.[106] Powerful as this tribute was, Eugene saw in his mother's influence the source of "whatever good there is in me and whatever I have or may accomplish."[107] Of his mother, little more of a specific nature could be said. Her influence was so encompassing, her direction of the affective family life so intense that her oldest son would write at age forty-four that "there is not a page of our memory, not a tablet of our hearts, that is not adorned and beautified by acts of her loving care."[108] In the face of such feeling, there remained little room for Kate.

The distinction Debs made between his parents—the attribution of the more public virtues to his father while reserving the deepest inner qualities for his mother—reflected his attitudes toward women in general. In certain contexts, Debs's position on the role of women was quite progressive. He defended the Women's Department when he edited the Firemen's magazine and a decade later supported both female suffrage and women's right to wear "bloomers" if they so chose. As a Socialist he supported Josephine Conger-Kaneko in her efforts to build a women's Socialist press. At times, Debs seemed to understand the mythos that had long justified women's oppression. Welcoming equality between husband and wife in 1895, Debs foresaw "a land redeemed from a form of slavery" begun when "old father Adam played the role of sneak" and blamed Eve for the original sin: "From that day to the present, woman has suffered the penalties of ostracism by the lords of creation, the masculine moiety of the human family."[109]

But another aspect of Debs's thought concerning women also influenced his public attitudes and dominated his private images. When Debs proposed the cooperative colony in 1897, he explicitly eliminated women from early membership in favor of "able-bodied men" to perform the rough work. The arrival of women, however, would signal the "first great impetus toward speedy success." Further, when Debs defended women's suffrage he did so from a particular image of women's essential role: "I

firmly believe every social condition will be improved when women vote,"
he argued in 1898. "They have more integrity and honor than men. A
woman's vote cannot be bought by a glass of whiskey."[110]

This duality in Debs's vision of men and women, reflective of so much
of nineteenth-century culture, remained fundamental to his perception. In
a 1917 pamphlet he praised men for their "masterful activity" in the world
from ancient Greece to modern industrial society but chided them for accepting oppression in face of their evident collective power. Even in oppression, however, men were active while women presented different
qualities: "But if the hand of man is strong to do, the hand of woman is
greater still, because it is softened and skilled to comfort and heal."[111]
Three years later he expanded this theme: "If man, the titan, makes the
world big, woman, the enchantress, makes it beautiful. . . . Man may
make the nation, but the woman does more—she makes the home
. . . woman [is] guardian of the sacred fire. Should she fail, earth
would return to the stone age. . . . It was woman who invented all the
arts, from agriculture to weaving, from architecture to music. It is
woman's voice that bears the soul in prayer and hymn towards higher
things."[112]

The force of these comments is striking. In attributing to women the
central core of human existence, and by implication revealing the inadequate reality beneath the assertive male's public mask, the sixty-five-year-
old Debs testified to the dominant personal theme in his life. From his early days in Terre Haute through his voluminous writings to and about his
parents as an adult, Debs consistently pictured women as more sensitive,
more spiritual, and, despite their social position, more dominant than
men. Similarly, as a young man searching for work in East St. Louis in
1874, Debs questioned his manly qualities and during his long life never
satisfactorily answered those questions for himself. Rather, he focused his
attention on women's presumed nature, idealized their assumed collective
virtues, and thus maintained the comfortable dimensions of his own emotional dependency. This was the personal source of his nearly constant
private and public examination of manhood, and this paradoxically
strong assertion of dependency established the context for the insistent
demands made on comrades throughout his Socialist career. It also
clarifies his relationship with his wife. By personality and background,
Kate simply could not meet the emotional demands of her husband. His
incessant dependency clashed with her reserve, her sense of propriety, and
her expectations of a husband. To the extent that she nurtured him when
sick, she fulfilled a portion of those needs. But Debs required a more intense relationship than this, one strong enough to contain his dependency
yet supple enough to release him back into the world. His brother,
Theodore, filled that role to near perfection.

Theodore's life was finely tuned to that of his older brother's. He himself relinquished financial security for his family in order to serve Eugene's career. In exchange, Eugene contributed to their support from his lecture fees throughout his Socialist career.[113] As secretary, book-keeper, advance man, and closest confidant to Eugene, Theodore became his brother's political eyes and ears—at times to the dismay of comrades who found it difficult to approach Eugene directly.[114] Beyond these actions, however, Theodore performed a far more critical role for his brother. Constantly willing to sacrifice his desires for his more famous brother's well-being, Theodore was the emotional bedrock upon which Eugene depended. Alternately a parent in attitude, a lover in emotional intensity, and a younger sibling in deference, Theodore molded his life to his brother's needs. In 1911 the sacrifice that maintained that commitment became clear to a number of Socialist friends.

In that year the alleged immoral conduct and forced resignation of J. Mahlon Barnes as secretary-treasurer rocked the Socialist party. Because of his identification with the Berger-Hillquit faction, the party's trial of Barnes became the battleground for the larger fight between the hardening left and right tendencies within the movement. Frank Bohn, of the left wing, proposed Theodore as Barnes's replacement. He argued, in words he knew would appeal to Theodore, that if the left "simply allow[s] matters to drift on as they are, never caring for the organization of the Party, then we shall be guilty of disregard for the best interests of the Movement." Further, Bohn stated, Theodore's candidacy already had the support of many leftist Socialists, including Charles Kerr, Mary Marcy, and Haywood.[115] A week later Bohn wrote Eugene that Haywood specifically wanted Theodore and argued that the party needed his brother's revolutionary principles and strong personal character so that the right could not "make use of [the office of secretary-treasurer] for any purpose they may have in mind."[116] But Theodore refused, his reasoning clear, if anguished:

> I positively cannot accept the nomination and no one knows what it costs me to make this decision. I cannot go into details. It would do no good . . . there are personal reasons for my position which I cannot publicly explain and which would probably not be understood if I did. To refuse any service to the party is justifiable only on the ground of rendering a greater service by doing so, and that is the guiding and controlling principle in my present situation. I am sorely tried in making this decision but there is no other alternative under the existing circumstances.[117]

For Theodore, the deeply woven ties that bound him to Eugene demanded that his "greater service" in aiding the movement through his brother preempt not only other party needs but often his own desires as well.[118]

Despite Theodore's fears of public misunderstanding, some comrades did comprehend this relationship. E. A. Brenholtz, of Turnersville, Texas, praised Theodore for "a greatness of soul which appreciates itself and its capabilities perfectly, and yet stands aside, and assists the loved one in the appointed lifework."[119] Eugene also acknowledged his brother's devotion. He understood, as one admirer phrased it, that if he were the light then Theodore was "the tower which helps to hold him up and let him shine."[120] Following his mother's death in 1906, when Eugene felt that "the light had gone out of the world,"[121] he increasingly talked of his younger brother in terms previously reserved only for his mother. In a birthday note in 1908 Eugene wrote his brother that "no mortal has ever had a dearer brother, a more loyal pard, a sweeter soul, a more perfect ministering angel than you have been to me and I love you with all the holy power that one soul can love another."[122] Theodore now became the central sustaining element in Eugene's life: "He is by far the better part of me. He is and does the things for which I get the applause."[123]

Following their mother's death, Eugene made Theodore the central female symbol for his life. He was, Eugene wrote to David Karsner, "the noblest brother that ever brothered a brother," and added: "You know that Theodore has all his life been a big sister to a little brother in me."[124] To Mabel Dunlap Curry, whose own life would be intimately interwoven with Debs's during his last decade, he explained that Theodore "should have been born a woman. He has the heart of a mother. Many and many a time he saved me." Specifically, he recalled the 1908 campaign, when he spoke for sixty-eight consecutive days from the caboose of the "Red Special." Following an exhausting speech, Theodore "stripped me naked, put me in a bath with just the right temperature and then rubbed me till my flesh was all aglow . . . and that's only one of a thousand things he did for me for which I love him as devotedly as a mother does her first born."[125]

Although the specific images fluctuated—Eugene was in turn younger sibling, child to Theodore's maternal role, and then mother himself—the separation of male and female function remained and allowed Eugene his particular freedom from the world. Theodore comprehended this symbolism as well. Responding to Brenholtz's praise of his devotion to Eugene, he demurred yet revealed the very core of the relationship between these two brothers: "If I possessed or could attain such perfectly beautiful heights as you attribute to me, I would feel that I had inherited all the divine love of a mother whose whole life was a continuous denial that her children might enjoy."[126]

In Theodore and a few other comrades Debs found the relationships he required and he proceeded with his work. However complex and tortured his emotional life may at times have been, it was precisely this vulnerability in him, this ability to use his own contradictions in what was often an unconscious communication with audiences, that proved to be an important base of his public appeal. His lack of inner confidence and his dependent nature often manifested itself before audiences as an interest in and concern with their individual welfare. And indeed, in large part, it was, for Debs was not the only American confused over the contrast between their public presentation of self and the inner doubts and fears of a generation in transition.

Recuperated after a stay at North 8th Street, Debs departed again on another presidential campaign in 1908, after his own fashion addressing these concerns and the more specific issues of Socialist policy and direction.

8

The Working-Class Republic

COMRADES ACROSS THE COUNTRY anticipated magnificent results in November 1908. In the midst of a period of tremendous excitement and growth Socialists applauded the unrest and challenges to traditional capitalist authority that pervaded the country. Within the labor movement the IWW attracted great attention, but radical sentiment also grew in the more established unions as well.[1] In popular culture Upton Sinclair's sharply drawn novel, *The Jungle* — an exposé of the meat-packing industry and of the inherent oppression of workers under capitalism—won a vast audience, as did the novels and stories of Jack London, the fervent California Socialist. During these years two Socialist periodicals, the *Appeal to Reason* and *Wilshire's Magazine,* each averaged circulations of 250,000 and repeatedly hammered at the basic contradictions of American capitalism.[2] Throughout the country a vigorous Socialist press emerged, not only in New York and Milwaukee, but also in such communities as Benton, Missouri, Myton, Utah, and Charleroi, Pennsylvania.[3] The activities of such progressive muckrakers as Ida Tarbel and Lincoln Steffens further increased this excitement. While most Socialists would distinguish between their movement and the progressive impulse—and particularly noted the limited critique of capitalism that most reformers offered—they nonetheless welcomed the agitation. "Socialism is either an evolutionary science or it is no science at all," one sympathizer wrote in 1905, and many saw in the progressive yeast future Socialists waiting to rise above the inadequate reformist movement.[4]

The condition of both the party and the movement fired Socialist hopes, too, especially as it suggested the ability of Socialists to contain the conflicting tendencies already evident. From a base of less than 10,000 members in 1901, the party doubled that figure by 1904, increased it another third by 1906, and in 1908 had over 41,000 dues-paying members in over 3,000 locals.[5] The social composition of the members was also encouraging. While middle-class professionals tended to dominate the party's governing councils, a party canvass of members in 1908 indicated a different orientation for the rank and file. Two-thirds of those who responded—approximately one-sixth of all members—listed themselves as workers; and over 60 percent of these workers were skilled members of the various trades. Although still small, the party had a solid and vital working-class core.[6]

The Socialist movement—those who sympathized with the Socialist critique and, where eligible, voted for Socialist candidates, but who failed to take out a party card—also grew during these years, although less evenly than the party itself. After doubling the votes over past elections in both the 1902 congressional campaign and the 1904 presidential contest, the Socialist total declined by nearly 30 percent—from over 400,000 to under 300,000—in the 1906 state and local elections.[7] While some argued that the losses reflected the factional antagonisms of recent years, most party members took a more sanguine view. Various reform movements temporarily attracted the voters, they argued, and thus drained Socialist strength. William R. Hearst's municipal ownership party undercut the Socialist ticket in New York, and other progressives distracted voters in Toledo, Cleveland, and Chicago. But they felt that as reformism ran its course and the limitations of its analysis became more apparent, the Socialist movement could only grow in strength. In the meantime, Socialists could take comfort that amid all the reform excitement they retained a solid committed group of voters.[8] The sharp attacks of such capitalist politicians as Theodore Roosevelt encouraged this optimism. Estimating their strength from their opponents' fears, many Socialists found in Roosevelt's attention to the movement further proof of their own imminent success.[9]

In this mood the delegates to the Socialist convention gathered in May 1908 to nominate their presidential ticket. Although a majority of party members favored drafting Eugene Debs for the third consecutive time, it was not clear that he would accept. Citing his health and his desire for a fresh choice as standard-bearer, Debs wrote in March that he had "discouraged the use of my name and am still hoping that it will not be presented to the convention." Artfully, however, Debs left the door ajar, noting that "there is nothing in the line of duty that I would not do for the party."[10] The status of Bill Haywood complicated the pre-convention jockeying. Recently released from prison and acquitted on charges of murdering the former governor of Idaho, Haywood had immense popularity, and many wanted him as their candidate, especially if Debs chose not to run. Party leaders, however, opposed Haywood and his brand of Socialism, and the feeling intensified after Haywood completed an eastern speaking tour that spring. Debs attempted to soften the criticism and explained that if Haywood gave some poor speeches, no one could always be at his best. But he reassured the comrades on one point. Haywood did not want the nomination and would, like Debs, accept it only from a "sheer sense of duty to the party. He himself told me this and I am sure in all sincerity for Haywood does not dissemble."[11] But by the opening of the convention the opposition eliminated Haywood as a serious candidate.[12]

In a certain sense, then, the process of nominating the Socialist candidate was open for the first time in party history. Quickly, those who disagreed with Debs on industrial unionism sought to fill the breach. Morris Hillquit worked for James Carey's candidacy; Seymour Stedman nominated Algie M. Simons, who had recently resigned as editor of the *International Socialist Review*. When Victor Berger rose to nominate Carl D. Thompson, a Socialist minister and Berger ally, tension filled the hall and Berger acknowledged it: "It is my fate to do unpopular things," he began. Presenting himself as the power behind Debs, Berger told the delegates that "I did an unpopular thing fifteen years ago when I succeeded in getting Comrade Debs into the Socialist movement. I did an unpopular thing twelve years ago when I did my very best to start the old Social Democracy together with Comrade Debs. I again did a very unpopular thing by splitting that party at the time they stood for colonization."[13] Berger's speech angered Debs and had little effect on the delegates.

Elected to the Indiana delegation, Debs was in Chicago but not on the floor of the convention, which caused Hillquit to comment "that may perhaps be a political move, and not a bad one."[14] From the floor, however, Debs's supporters conducted a well-organized campaign. Nominated by P. H. Callery of Missouri, his seconds quickly met their opponents' objections. They declared that Debs's health was fine and the political opposition from certain comrades unfounded. "Eugene V. Debs is the embodiment of the American proletarian movement," Frank P. O'Hare of Oklahoma proclaimed, and even John Spargo of New York defended him, noting that his "mistakes . . . have done him more credit than the right things that many other people have done."[15] But the invisible hand of Debs decided the debate. As in the past, he remained apart from the center of controversy but followed the proceedings carefully and influenced the outcome through others—in this case, by releasing a private letter to Ben Hanford for a public reading to the delegates. His health, Debs averred, was robust, and, although he had "no desire to run for office" and maintained his "positive prejudice against the very thought of holding office," his final paragraph threw wide open the door to his candidacy. "To obey the commands of the Socialist party," Debs reminded the delegates, "I violated a vow made years ago that I would never again be a candidate for political office. My whole ambition—and I have a good stock of it—is to make myself as big and as useful as I can, as much opposed to the enemy and as much loved by our comrades as any other private in the ranks. You need have no fear that I shall shirk my part in the coming campaign. I shall be in condition, and I hope there will be no good ground for complaint when the fight is over."[16]

Against the power of Debs's still invisible presence—against the imagery of this acknowledged leader offering himself as but a private—Berger, Hillquit, and their allies had little chance. While Berger held his Wisconsin delegation for Thompson, Hillquit lost complete control of his New York comrades. In the ensuing stampede, Debs received 159 votes to 14 for Thompson and 9 for Simons.[17]

Despite the attempt to block Debs's nomination, Socialists enthusiastically united behind the Debs-Hanford ticket. Max Hayes, the Cleveland Socialist and trade unionist, predicted a minimum of one million votes, and some thought he was too conservative.[18] For his part, Debs saw in the reception tendered him on his return to Girard, Kansas, after the convention a providential omen. Greeted and fêted by "the people of Girard, regardless of party, creed or color," Debs thought he "caught a glimpse of the fine, sweet, beautiful, *human* society *that is to be.*"[19] Intending to capitalize on the widespread anticipation, J. Mahlon Barnes, the campaign manager, raised funds for a three-car railroad train to enable Debs to tour more extensively than ever before. Dubbed the "Red Special," between late August and 2 November, election day, it carried Debs and his entourage—including a brass band and a baggage car filled with literature—to more than three hundred communities in thirty-three states. Haywood was but one of numerous nationally known Socialists who joined for part of the tour, and all along the way local comrades would board for a stop or two, or even overnight.[20]

At almost every stop a powerful excitement animated the crowds. In downstate Illinois two working-class Irish women listened from the edge of the crowd while Simons spoke. Reportedly, one asked the other, " 'An is that Debs?' The other replied, 'Oh no, that ain't Debs—when Debs comes out you'll think it's Jesus Christ.' "[21] In Glenwood Springs, Colorado, a recent bride of sixteen attended Debs's lecture from the caboose of the "Red Special" with her husband and mother. Twelve years later she recalled the importance of that event for her in a letter to Debs: "I had never heard of the class struggle," Mae Bishop remembered, "and I did not know that there was such a thing as the Socialist party in the world.

I listened to your lecture . . . and after the meeting I lingered and asked you questions." That experience began her radicalization, and that of her husband and mother as well. Still in the movement, she thanked Debs for helping her "to start out in the right direction at such an early age."[22]

In small towns as in the large mass meetings in New York, Chicago, and Milwaukee, Debs's speeches crystallized opposition to corporate capitalism and legitimized for untold numbers of Americans their individual anger that grew out of their daily work experiences. At the height of his powers, Debs aided others to understand the connection between their personal circumstances and the larger social reality.

Given these efforts, the final result, an increase of only 18,000 votes over the 1904 total, was discouraging. In their post-election explanations some Socialists pointed to the influence of Samuel Gompers who, after twenty-two years of political neutrality, had publicly supported the Democratic candidate, William Jennings Bryan. Others suggested that the current depression had forced many workers to "tramp" to find work, and these men failed to meet the residency requirements for voting. But the most accepted Socialist interpretation stressed the changing nature of American politics. Both traditional parties had drafted reform platforms in 1908, it was argued, in an attempt to undercut recent Socialist gains. This, comrades suggested, was proof of Socialism's potency, and they found a silver lining in the dismal results: the party now knew the extent of the committed Socialist support among Americans. As they had before, Socialists claimed that the various reform movements would yet run their course—perhaps more slowly than they had hoped—and encouraged each other to rededicate themselves in the next local and state campaigns.[23]

Yet the gap remained. The final results confused Debs. He took pleasure in the growing strength in the West and Southwest (states that accounted for almost 30 percent of the national Socialist vote in 1908),[24] but the larger picture was discouraging. If, as he had often stated, "what 'the people' want they take,"[25] it was now less clear what exactly it was they wanted. Nonetheless, as he recovered his health from the exhausting campaign, Debs determined to return to the podium with his forceful presentation of Socialism.

Debs's appeal as a Socialist agitator had many sources. He remained the "hero of Woodstock," whose advocacy of American democratic values reverberated widely in the consciousness of his audience. But the Socialist Debs then merged a class analysis of American society with his keen understanding of citizenship. His sharp critique of corporate capitalism transcended reformism, as it did the mere desire to return to a less complicated past, for at root he demanded the transfer of power from the corporate elite to those who produced society's wealth. It was this Debs, the

Socialist citizen who helped evolve an indigenous democratic Socialism, that drew the crowds and the attention throughout a long career.

As a speaker, Debs was a compelling and commanding force. In an era given to long orations, his speeches often lasted two or more hours—but rarely did he bore an audience. His long, thin body pulsated with energy; his outstretched arms, extensions of that inner force, implored, emphasized, and above all embraced; the veins in his head bulged with concentration, and his eyes, piercing yet loving, seemed to acknowledge each individual in the audience. His voice ran a gamut of tones: mock whisper to normal conversation to full stentorian power. Yet from all accounts it was rarely forced or theatrical. His appeal, most frequently described by contemporaries as evangelical,[26] transcended at that moment factional disagreements and led each in the audience to glimpse a different social order.

Heywood Broun, the sensitive cynic of 1920s journalism, sensed Debs's magnetism. "I'm told," Broun reported, "that even those speeches of his which seem to any reader indifferent stuff, took on vitality from his presence." One "hard-bitten Socialist" confessed to Broun his confusion about this power. Deeply opposed to "sentimental flummery"—to calling others comrades, to rhetorical excesses and imprecise theory—as he considered it "a lot of bunk," the man was confounded in Debs's presence: "But the funny part of it is that when Debs says 'comrade' it is all right. He means it. That old man with the burning eyes actually believes that there can be such a thing as the brotherhood of man. And that's not the funniest part of it. As long as he's around I believe it myself."[27]

Debs did not simply confirm his audiences' preconceptions but rather, as on the question of racial prejudice, frequently challenged their basic assumptions. While not free of contradictions himself, Debs called upon both party comrades and workers to reaffirm and strengthen their dedication to liberty for all. Among American Socialists, as throughout the society, racial equality was not strongly defended. By 1913 there were few blacks in the party and little energy devoted to organizing them. The party's state secretary for South Carolina explained why: "It would not be wise to permit negroes to join white locals. The race prejudice is so strong here that such a practice would endanger the entire movement."[28] At their best, American Socialists held that black oppression was but a part of the larger class question and deserved no special attention. This position they consistently reaffirmed at party conventions between 1901 and 1919.[29] Girding that formal analysis, however, was a different set of assumptions. "As a race," Charles Dobbs publicly asserted in 1904, "the negro worker of the South lacks the brain and backbone necessary to make a Socialist."[30] Party secretary William Mailly urged the Georgia Socialist Eliza Frances Andrews to exploit the Democratic party's claim to protect white workers from black rule but quickly assured Andrews that he did not intend to imply "that the black or yellow races are not inferior to the white race."[31] A decade later, a Texas comrade wrote Carl D. Thompson, director of the party's Bureau of Information, for statistics on miscegenation, "especially in the 'Democratic' strongholds." The fear of racial equality "kept me out of the party for a long while after I became class conscious," Arch Lingan explained, "and I am anxious for data along the line mentioned for some of my old 'Democratic' friends." Incredibly, Thompson replied that he had no figures but desired them and asked Lingan to forward any information he possessed.[32]

While there were important examples of biracial unity among Socialist dock workers in New Orleans and Philadelphia, timber workers in Louisiana, and numerous miners in locals in the coal regions,[33] Berger reflected the pervasive party attitude. "There can be no doubt that negroes and mulattoes constitute a lower race," Berger told his comrades in 1902. Arguing that the "Caucasian and indeed even the Mongolian" were more civilized "by many thousands of years," Berger appealed to the crudest racial stereotypes to clinch his argument: "The many cases of rape which occur whenever negroes are settled in large numbers prove, moreover, that the free contact with the white has led to further degeneration of the negroes, as of all other inferior races."[34]

Along with most Socialists, Debs shared a class analysis of racial prejudice but had shorn it of much of the violent racism that motivated other comrades. Somewhat blindly, he argued in 1903 that "there is no 'Negro problem' apart from the general labor problem" and expressed the hope that even in the South racial prejudice would soon evaporate.[35] In another article that same year Debs insisted that the party had "nothing specific to offer the negro, and we cannot make special appeals to all the races. The Socialist party is the party of the working class, regardless of color—the whole working class of the whole world."[36]

To a certain degree, this one-dimensional analysis covered Debs's own racial prejudice, formed in the anti-black atmosphere of south-central Indiana. Even into his sixties, Debs relished dialect jokes and praised the humorist Eugene Field for his large repertoire of racial and ethnic stereotypic stories.[37] Equally important, as an early Socialist leader Debs continued to accept a form of white supremacy in his political thought. In 1898 he opposed the American annexation of the Philippines, Cuba, and Puerto Rico—while welcoming the absorption of Hawaii—on essentially racial grounds. Mimicking the worst of the American tradition, Debs explained to a Midwest newspaper: "I think that was entirely proper and in perfect keeping with the constitution of the United States. In the first place it was the desire of the natives of Hawaii to become citizens of the United States through annexation. They are composed in a degree of Caucasians, and they already have a government established. Then Honolulu is a coaling station for the United States, and this government must need protect itself in this regard."[38]

But this racial jingoism does not completely represent Debs's attitudes. As the leader of the American Railway Union, he forcefully and publicly insisted in 1894 that the union abolish the color line. Defeated by the rank and file, Debs often reminded his audiences in later years that the exclusion of black workers "was one of the factors in our defeat."[39] During his career Debs also addressed the larger cultural issues at the core of white-black tension. Accused of encouraging the closer proximity of "debased" black males and "pure" white women by advocating the organization of blacks into the party, Debs addressed the myth of the black male rapist directly: "Whence came he? Not by chance. He can be accounted for. Trace him to his source and you will find an Anglo-Saxon at the other end. There are no rape-maniacs in Africa. They are the spawn of a civilized lust."[40] That same year, 1904, he attacked Thomas Dixon's popular racist novel, *The Leopard's Spots*, for its assumptions that "one race was created to be the bondsmen of another race"; twelve years later he condemned D. W. Griffith's painfully ugly racist movie *Birth of a Nation*.[41]

By the 1920s Debs's understanding of American race relations led him to a fundamental critique of white American culture itself. He castigated the double standard that allowed white men to abuse black women with near impunity while black men, merely suspected of such activity, often were lynched without trial. Racism created in America "a false and pernicious civiliation," Debs told his audience, and were Christ to return, "the Galilean Carpenter would . . . scorn and lash the pharisees who profess to be his followers while . . . they exercise their despotic and damnable [racial] dominion."[42]

Although never free of elements of racial feeling, Debs's attitudes clearly changed over the course of his career. But even earlier, when his understanding was more attuned with the Indiana of his youth, Debs's actions frequently confronted trade unionists and Socialist comrades with direct challenges to their practice of racial exclusion. During his tours of the South Debs often refused to speak before segregated audiences. In Montgomery, Alabama, in 1900 Debs forced the manager of the hall to permit Afro-Americans to attend. In appearances that same year at Columbus, Macon, Savannah, and Atlanta, Georgia, as in Birmingham, Alabama, Debs either demanded that Afro-Americans be allowed in or insisted on an end to segregated seating *within* the hall. In all these speeches Debs directly criticized the white trade unionists who organized the meetings for excluding blacks from the union.[43] With a basically inadequate analysis—how could Afro-Americans simply be part of the larger labor question when most white workers refused to work or organize with them?—Debs's actions nonetheless frequently confronted comrades with a stark demand that they reconsider their position. A true native son, Debs offered in himself an example of possible change within basic areas of American culture. Debs's witness was instructive, even if some in the Socialist movement failed to notice.

Important as it was, the question of equality did not occupy the greater part of Debs's attention. His central message focused on expanding and strengthening the self-perception of America's white workingmen and women. In a fashion inconceivable only sixty years after his death, Debs hectored these men and women in speech after speech and urged them to realize the profound potential each possessed. "I would have you understand," Debs insisted, "that within yourselves there is all that is necessary to develop a real man. So much of what there is within you is latent, undeveloped." While corporate capitalism clearly encouraged this condition through its degrading work discipline and corruption of the political process, Debs told workers that they also were at fault. Their passive compliance to authority actively aided their own enslavement.[44]

At the core of Debs's appeal lay a spirited defense of the dignity of each individual. Traditional, in that it stemmed from his earlier understanding of manhood, this message also reflected his more acute realization of the nature of class relations in mature capitalist society. Debs encouraged his audiences to discover the dual nature of such terms as manhood and dignity, much as he himself had two decades earlier. Referring to the fliers for factory employment that advertised for "hands," Debs urged all working people to resist such insulting definitions. "Think of a hand with a soul in it," Debs told one audience, and prodded them to consider the relationship between individual self-respect and a new collective identity: "A thousand heads have grown for every thousand pairs of hands, a thousand hearts throb in testimony of the unity of heads and hands, and a thousand souls, though crushed and mangled, burn in protest and are pledged to redeem a thousand men."[45]

The worker, Debs told a Kansas trade union audience in 1908, has under capitalism nothing but his labor. Capital owns the means of production, and the worker, more dependent than ever, must find a buyer for his labor. But "can you boast of being a man among men" in this context? Of course not: "No man can rightly claim to be a man unless he is free. There is something godlike about manhood. Manhood doesn't admit of ownership. Manhood scorns to be regarded as private property."[46]

This emphasis on manhood, the central theme in Debs's personal and public life, had at least two important consequences. First, his consistent use of the term excluded women from attention in his analysis of capitalism. It was not that he did not know that women worked but rather that he perceived the impact of industrial society on American culture from a traditional male vantage point. While effective before audiences that included women, Debs saw women as subsidiary to his main concerns, in orbit around and tangential to the leading actors in this drama, their fathers, husbands, and brothers. Their place was really in the home, one can almost hear Debs say, and his continuous use of manhood as the linchpin of his analysis reveals his basic understanding of "the women's question." Far more than he could publicly admit, Debs hinged his analysis of capitalism on a reassertion of traditional paternal authority, despite the fact that neither his parental nor his own marital relations followed this pattern.

But within these limits, Debs's appeal was quite powerful. His emphasis on manhood and the potential for a more holistic self-image, presented in his insistence on the harmony of the head and the hand, structured his analysis of class in capitalist society. For American workingmen reared in a culture that emphasized their primacy within the family, the dignity and responsibility of their common citizenship, and the self-esteem derivative from their craft, Debs's use of manhood held great cultural and political meaning in the face of capitalism's attack in all three spheres. Through a complex evolution, Debs had discovered the essential dual aspect in his culture's tradition: the American Revolution was not a static event, embossed in marble and praised each July. Its essential meaning demanded a prophetic call to each succeeding generation to renew and reinterpret that heritage. Debs did successfully combine this tradition with a pointed class analysis. The vastness of the country's resources meant that America, perhaps alone among all nations, "should be free from the scourge of poverty and the blight of ignorance." That it was not, Debs noted some years later, was in part but not solely the responsibility of capital: "The kingdom of heaven so long prayed for, has been set up here on earth," Debs argued. The millennium lacked but the active realization by its citizens.[47]

The Debs who preached at his full powers during these years rarely romanticized working people or his Socialist comrades. On occasion overly rhetorical, he persistently confronted his audiences with their own responsibility for the erosion of liberty and exhorted them to struggle to recapture their heritage. "He begged his hearers not to accept his conclusions," one Georgia paper commented in 1900. "But he implores you to study as he has studied."[48] The relation between this individual responsibility and an engaged collective identity remained an important theme. A decade later, before a Utah audience, he gave that understanding classic expression:

> I am not a Labor Leader; I do not want you to follow me or anyone else; if you are looking for a Moses to lead you out of this capitalist wilderness, you will stay right where you are. I would not lead you

into the promised land if I could, because if I could lead you in, some
one else would lead you out. YOU MUST USE YOUR HEADS AS WELL AS YOUR
HANDS, and get yourself out of your present condition.[49]

Debs understood more clearly than most Socialists the particular ambivalence of American working people. Increasingly treated as "hands,"
these men and women did come to occupy a distinct class in American
society. Yet they resisted a conscious identification of themselves as a
working class. Ethnic and religious differences played a part in this, but
even more important was the tradition of political equality with its over-
riding individualistic emphasis.[50] Debs knew this, in large part from his
own experience, but he directly and at times brutally demanded that his
audience confront the aggressive collective implications of these traditions.

At the sight of a "two-by-four boss," Debs told a strike rally in
Philadelphia in 1908, many working people "tremble and take off your
hat. You are looking for some one to make an excuse to for being on
earth." The workingman, he prodded, "is so easily satisfied. He is strongly inclined to be content. Give him a miserable job; a two-by-four boss to
wield the hunger whip over him; and a place to sleep and enough to eat to
circulate his blood and keep him in working order, and his ambition is
satisfied." From his understanding of manhood, Debs attempted to offer
these workers, who were then bickering over whether to call a sympathy
strike in support of the striking streetcarmen, a vision beyond their isolation: "This world only respects as it is compelled to respect, and if you
working men want to be respected you have got to begin by respecting
yourselves. Get out of the capitalist parties. You do not belong there. You
are in an environment that taints you, corrupts you, reduces you. All these
affiliations are calculated to strip you of your manhood, reduce you to a
condition where you are ashamed of yourself."[51]

Following the speech, Debs and some comrades drove to New Jersey.
Along the way, Debs gave an extemporaneous speech, "fit," he said, "for
Walt Whitman." For at least one in this small audience, the speech was a
revelation. As Joseph Cohen remarked many years later, it "was entirely
different from the Socialist propaganda speech which he had just
delivered in Philadelphia. [It was] an apostrophe to Democracy, a
superlative prose poem."[52] But in an important fashion Cohen misunderstood Debs and his "Socialist propaganda." Debs's belief in
democracy, in a specific American tradition which stressed the dignity of
each individual citizen, never wavered even as he advocated a collective
class analysis. For without that understanding of the individual citizen,
the class struggle became a forced theory, disembodied from and in tension with the deepest currents in the culture and in himself.

Rooted in this analysis, Debs resisted any temptation to find a short cut to the Socialist assumption of power. In 1910, for example, he argued that if Socialists could "have the power to govern now, we would say 'no.'" Such a development would "precipitate a catastrophe," he stated, for "the people are not yet ready. They must be further educated. They would not know what to do with their freedom if they had it." What was true of the people was also true of his comrades, for "even the socialists are not ready."[53] Patterning himself after generations of Protestant preachers, Debs emphasized the centrality of individual conversion in constructing a collective identity. At times as pessimistic as any Calvinist divine in his prognosis, Debs remained essentially optimistic. His faith and his despair met in the individual before him in the audience. In that person lay another opportunity to touch the soul, to point to the unity of heart and hand, and thereby to insist again that active engagement and willingness to struggle formed the center of the democratic tradition itself.

For many Americans, Debs's political message and personal qualities were attractive. Debs was able, in the words of J. A. Wayland, to reach "the deep-hidden good that is in every creature."[54] For "Mother" Ella Bloor and Alexander Trachtenberg, both important members of the Communist movement after World War I, Debs was the evangelist possessed of a "wonderful personal magnetism" who "always tried to convert" his audience.[55] To James P. Cannon, the Kansas-born leader of the American Trotskyist movement, Debs was "an ever-present influence" who drew from his audience a response quite unlike any other public figure. As Robert Hunter, the conservative Socialist from Terre Haute, attempted to explain to Lincoln Steffens, Debs was "a preacher, a Luther or a Calvin, rather than a political leader. He [was] a man who has dedicated his life to a cause, and put aside many years ago all questions of expediency, of policy, and of compromise."[56] This power was evident. Once, while addressing Chicago's Polish Federation, Debs held the large crowd captive, moving them to tears and wild applause during the course of his two-hour speech. Perplexed, as the majority of the audience understood little or no English, Debs asked a bilingual comrade to inquire how this was possible. One Polish Socialist responded quite simply: "Debs talks to us with his *hands*, out of his *heart*, and we all understood everything he said."[57]

Yet the familiar disparity remained. Despite his personal and political appeal, Debs's ability to attract audiences always exceeded the political support he and the movement received. To some this suggested that his political analysis had less meaning than his personal appeal. As one sensitive if critical New Orleans reporter commented after Debs spoke in that city, he was "an ill-balanced man, a dreamer," with "the gift not of wisdom but of epigram." Yet the audience reaction was perplexing. Working people had packed the hall: the "old grizzled man with a long

white beard, and the venerable air of a prophet, with face and hands
seamed and seared with toil''; the "young mechanic, evidently dressed out
in Sunday best''; the "day laborer, with inevitable heavy forward droop
of shoulder.'' All listened with intensity and applauded with passion, but
the reporter did not think that they had just become Socialists: "One left
the building with the feeling that it was not what the man had said but what
he was that carried away his hearers.'' Stumbling toward an explanation,
he suggested that "it was not so much that they cared for what he said, but
that they cared that he cared for them—if this does not confuse the
point.''[58]

At times Debs echoed this analysis. When a new acquaintance commented after a speech that the audience "all seemed to love you,'' Debs
responded: "They love me because they know I love them.''[59] On occasion
blinded by his own power with audiences, Debs never lost, as did the New
Orleans reporter, an appreciation of the basic political symbolism that
gave his wide appeal its basis. From Woodstock to a later jail term at
Atlanta Federal Penitentiary during and after World War I, Debs remained
the most visible and dynamic opponent of the new corporate order, and
the large audiences he drew indicated the extent of the unrest among working people. But the task of transferring that response into more concrete
channels was difficult. As Debs frequently noted, a worker too often insisted on remaining in the old parties because "his father . . . and his
grandfather belonged to that party.''[60] Sensitive to the continuing importance of that politico-cultural force in working people's lives, Debs's own
brand of Socialism pointed to the continuity in the changed allegiance he
advocated.

Unlike any other Socialist of his era, Debs transcended the ethnic and
geographical differences that separated working people. In the Southwest,
for example, he elicited dramatic responses from poor tenant farmers and
coal miners. He had lived among them and knew their hopes and expectations; and his Protestant temperament and revivalistic fervor poignantly
addressed their anger and frustration as those hopes went unfulfilled.[61]
Immigrants, and perhaps especially Jews, enthusiastically received him.
"Deps, Deps, they called him,'' a Yiddish-speaking comrade remembered. He embodied "the hopes and the zeal of the foreign-born for
social and economic change'' in this new alien society. "His words made
men cry, even when they were not fully understood, and working class
women would present him with bouquets—my mother would do that
when she went to his meetings—and worry about his health.''[62] Charney
Vladeck, general manager of *The Forward,* New York's Socialist Yiddish
daily, caught the essence of Debs's appeal. Explaining why pictures of
Debs plastered the walls of Jewish immigrant homes alongside such traditional Jewish figures as Sir Moses Montefiore and the Rabbi of Lubawich,

he wrote: "Debs was the liberator, the first who had come from the ranks of the American workers, holding out his hand and saying, 'I am your brother.' They had respect and admiration for radicals of their own race. But they worshipped Debs."[63]

Even among non-Socialists Debs held a unique power. As a young teenager in Worcester, Massachusetts, the playwright S. N. Behrman remembered wandering into a Debs meeting. Sitting almost under the podium, Berhman watched, entranced, as the "tall and angular" speaker "leaned far over the edge of the platform, as if to get close to each of his listeners. His arms reached out, as if to touch them." Although he remembered none of the specifics of Debs's speech, decades later Behrman asserted that the experience "gave to all my later life an orientation it would not otherwise have had." It was less Debs's specific argument than "the overwhelming impression that Debs' personality made on me. Most of all, I remember his intensity and what seemed to me to be his quivering sensitiveness to pain." As he grew older, Debs became for Behrman his "standard of reference" for all politicians who sought his allegiance: others "fulminated against gold and tariffs and refractory Cabinet members . . . [but] they were not stripped, as was Debs, of everything but the spirit of humanity."[64]

But Debs's success as a Socialist agitator had other sources than his powerful personal appeal. Debs was no Socialist Midas, turning into comrades all whom he touched. Rather, his effective agitation crystallized for many the meaning of Socialism because the analysis Debs presented echoed their own daily experience. A rampant industrial capitalism, aggressively in search of ever greater profits, was ultimately responsible for the growth of the Socialist movement.

Between the Civil War and World War I America matured as an industrial society and became the leading industrial nation in the world. This expansion spurred the emergence of a new understanding of the relationship between the federal government and American citizens. The Civil War had greatly broadened Washington's power in such areas as taxation and military draft. Further, during the Civil War the partnership between this new, more centralized government and the business community first assumed its modern form.[65] But for Americans without access to board rooms or Washington agencies, the ultimate effects of this alliance were less desirable. In the factory and on small individual farms throughout the land, the crux of this relationship involved the question of class control. Industrial capitalism would replace the power and dignity of the idea of citizenship with the concept of the "hand"—hundreds and thousands of them to fill the slots created by the expanding economy.

This question of class affected Americans nationwide, but in different ways. The Milwaukee Socialists in the skilled trades had adjusted more thoroughly to the structure of the new order and now sought out its pressure points; miners to the west and south of Milwaukee were engaged in a battle for physical survival. Immigrants presented yet another experience. In large part unskilled and unfamiliar with American society, they possessed neither citizenship nor the vote and thus sought other ways to protest and alleviate their conditions. In the southwestern states yet another variant of Socalism grew during these pre–World War I years. Conventional Socialist wisdom held that as farmers owned land and employed hired help, they held different and antagonistic interests from wage workers. But, Debs proclaimed in 1914, these southwestern Socialists exhibited a firm "class conscious enthusiasm" that granted them full status in "the revolutionary movement of the working class."[66]

As early as 1901 Wayland noted in the *Appeal to Reason* that while "the farmer is often held up as an example of manly independence," in reality "he has no say so as to what he is to get for his labor any more than the veriest wage slave that lives." Natural disasters might wipe out his investment but a more consistent threat was the economic system in which the farmer sold his produce: "Should he have a good crop, he must take what others are willing to give him for it."[67] Although the national party did not recognize farmers' demands until after 1910, salesmen for *Appeal to Reason* and Socialist organizers throughout the Southwest organized an effective agitation. By 1912 the Southwest had the fastest growing regional Socialist movement. Despite the relatively low population density, it accounted for 12 percent of the national Socialist vote for Debs.[68] Two years later the Oklahoma Socialists, then second only to New York state in official party membership, captured 21 percent of the gubernatorial vote and elected Socialists to several municipal offices.[69] Clearly a new wind blew across the southwestern plains.

Two major reasons account for the transformation of these predominantly rural and small-town citizens. First, the changing pattern of land ownership after 1900 dramatically altered the consciousness of these men and women. In 1890, a year after the last great land sale in the territory, less than 1 percent of all farmers in Oklahoma were tenants working for another man. A decade later over 43 percent leased their land, and by 1910 54 percent—over 100,000 farm families—worked the Oklahoma land for someone else.[70] In Texas and Kansas a similar pattern occurred.[71] To farmers reared in a culture of "manly independence," these figures were ominous. The severe disadvantage they faced when competing with local land speculators or the large "bonanza farms" owned by industrial corporations resulted in a growing number of bankruptcies. There was no innate "shame" to tenant farming but, by 1910, the belief of these farmers in mobility was seriously shaken as tenancy increased, and fewer and fewer farmers made the transition to owners.[72]

Political realities in tenant farm country followed this economic pattern. The large landowners, or the managers who represented them, dominated local and state politics, influenced the press, and frequently had substantial economic investments in regional industry, commerce, and banking. This power they did not hesitate to use. When the tenants on absentee owner Tom Padgitt's farm in Coleman County, Texas, struck for better conditions in 1908, Padgitt and his resident manager immediately mobilized merchants and artisans in the neighboring town of Leadlay to cut off credit to the tenants and had the local sheriff evict the tenants identified as Socialists. When Padgitt and his wife arrived at their 12,000-acre farm from their home in New Mexico, he praised his manager and declared that the battle in Coleman County was but a part of the nationwide struggle against "red agitation."[73] Many tenants, however, as they experienced this tightened class structure, formed organizations to channel their protest. Combining a radical democratic anger with an indigenous adaptation of popular Marxist thought, these men and women were attracted to the Socialist movement.[74]

If the prospect of building a regional movement of farmers disturbed the more orthodox Socialists, the second major source of southwestern Socialism was more familiar. At the center of the agricultural wrapper that encased this movement lay a core of blue-collar workers. Strongest among the UMWA locals in Kansas, Arkansas, and Oklahoma, this Socialist influence grew with the region's urban development and industrial concentration. A blue-collar belt existed across the agricultural heartland with strong ties to the radicalized farmers.

The creation of this proletariat occurred over a thirty-year period. With the development of the railroad repair yards and freight depots, a working class emerged that was organized during the 1880s by the Knights of Labor. During the dramatic strikes of 1885-86 these workers challenged their employers' power and actively sought alliances with small farmers and local businessmen. By 1900 the lumber industry as well was contributing to this development. National corporations dominated the industry and sought to impose a factory-style work discipline in the rural areas of Texas, Arkansas, and Louisiana. But it was the coal mines that gave the greatest impetus to the creation of this working class. Mines were from the first a corporate venture requiring a large capital investment, and mine operators employed a multi-ethnic and racial work force in the hope of undermining worker unity. But throughout the Southwest, however, the miners organized into the UMWA and embraced its militant industrial unionism that included men of all races and nationalities. In Pittsburgh County, Oklahoma, Sebastian County, Arkansas, and Crawford County,

Kansas, strong UMWA locals united the miners, conducted successful job actions, and voted Socialist. British, Italian, and Slavic miners joined with other Americans to elect Socialist union and municipal officials in mining communities throughout the region.[75]

Despite its rural image, the Southwest contained an important working-class element that possessed a strong class awareness. Kansas miners in 1902, for example, supported a strike by union motormen on the interurban trolleys; a few years later Oklahoma miners aided the streetcarmen's strike in Oklahoma City.[76] Fighting the transformation of the region, these workers discovered shared grievances with tenant farmers, and together they presented a formidable force that challenged the bid for control of the region by the large landowners, bankers, and industrialists.

Into this changing reality came the effective agitation of the Socialist party itself. The party grew because its leaders sensitively understood and articulated the concerns and the culture of the region's mining and farm families. National leaders—Debs, Mother Jones, Kate Richards O'Hare —drew tremendous responses. But even more important were the *Appeal to Reason* salesmen, local ministers, union organizers, and rural farmers who lived in the Southwest and built the party and the movement.[77]

The most successful approach used by these local organizers in this region was the Socialist encampment.[78] First introduced in Grand Saline, Texas, in August 1904, these week-long meetings put the historic form of the religious revival to new but not so different purposes. Drawing farmers from miles around, encampments gathered thousands and thousands of farmers to hear Socialist talks, to enjoy Socialist dramatic skits, and to visit among themselves. They gave these men and women, as one Socialist noted, "the greatest opportunity of their lives for a good time." The encampment, he suggested, was also a tremendous opportunity for Socialist agitation: "It is the drawing power of the socialist message, combined with the amusement features, that makes these mid-summer gatherings universally popular. The encampment is the greatest single agency at our command for reaching the great mass of political sinners in the South."[79] The encampments, like the revivals, were held in summer when the crops were "laid by" but also "when the shadow of the drought becomes darkest."[80] This perennial sense of urgency surrounding nature and its power reinforced the concern many felt about their own economic condition. "When there is almost a total failure of crops," a former resident of Colorado City, Texas, wrote in 1913, the families of migrant workers and tenant farmers were forced to "lead a gypsy life, much like 'tramps.' "[81] This combination of conditions made the encampment a brilliant and effective innovation for Socialist organizing.

The encampment was not just a technique borrowed from local culture and put to a different purpose. The center of Socialist strength in the

Southwest lay in the small towns and adjoining rural areas, and it shared its appeal with fundamentalist religious sects. In 1906 over 86 percent of all Baptists, Methodists, Disciples of Christ, and United Brethren in the Southwest lived outside the principal cities.[82] To a surprising extent, conservative religion and native Socialism meshed rather than clashed, their commingling eased by a pervasive sense of urgency over the fundamental evil people experienced in their society and in their daily lives. The encampments' biblical images—the basic linguistic symbol of the culture—challenged economic oppression, and southwestern Socialists boasted of one comrade who had "scarcely a peer in Texas as an authority on the Biblical viewpoint" of Socialism.[83] Ministers and lay people alike joined the movement and found that Socialist doctrines "link fine with the teachings of Christ."[84]

The religious tone that permeated this Socialist movement did not negate the growing class awareness—but it did interpret that consciousness in a particular cultural context. The crisis in people's lives, as in their society, was no mere intellectual problem. Rather, as H. Richard Niebuhr has suggested, it fostered "a revolutionary temper" and a belief that "life is a critical affair" and forced each to confront "the necessity of facing the ultimate realities of life." This religious force, never confined to Sunday sermons but rather the primary cultural expression of daily experience, emphasized revival and rebirth from the suffering of human existence. In this fashion "newness of life" gave renewed urgency "to the idea of the Kingdom of God on earth."[85] This convergence of religious and secular millennialism generated a powerful social critique. A common religious impulse provided moral principles—the "notion of right"[86]—to denounce capitalism; the democratic tradition provided the context through which class anger found expression; and deteriorating social conditions supplied the impetus for anger and action. As one Milton, Oklahoma, Socialist wrote the U.S. attorney general in 1912, protesting the arrest of the editorial board of the *Appeal to Reason:* "Christ was crucified by the same class of men . . . and for no other reason than the teaching of truth to the 'mob' that it might be better prepared to protect itself from the arrogant servants and the commercial pirates of the world. . . . O, no," A. P. Folsom concluded, explaining his social philosophy, "I am not an anarchist, neither was Christ, Luther, Washington, Jefferson and Lincoln."[87]

In the Southwest this powerful combination of religious impulse and prophetic Socialism generated a popular, broad-based critique of capitalism. Far different in expression and social origin than the Milwaukee Socialist movement, these southwestern Socialists countered the distrust of their movement by eastern comrades with the words of their national hero, Eugene Debs: "I have met many of the farmers down your way," Debs wrote the Oklahoma and Indian Territory Socialist organizer in 1906. They "were revolutionary to the heart's core, and furnished the very best material for the party movement."[88] Self-conscious of their cultural traditions and painfully aware of their current circumstances, these Socialists forged from their roots a basic attack on capitalism that expressed their new, sharp class awareness.

The Southwest was not the only region where the results of industrial development and effective local organizing built a strong Socialist movement. In many of the towns and smaller cities in the Midwest major changes in regional agricultural and industrial production precipitated new social relations among former neighbors. Class lines became clearer as conflicting interests emerged and altered the texture of people's daily lives. Like Terre Haute decades earlier, St. Marys, Ohio, experienced its introduction to industrial capitalism on a relatively small scale. But unlike Terre Haute, the citizens of St. Marys elected a strong Socialist administration to counter the power of regional capitalism.

Located in rural Auglaize County, eighty miles northwest of Columbus, St. Marys seemed an unlikely candidate for electoral success. As the surrounding county, this small city of under 6,000 in 1910 was inhabited by American-born citizens, the majority of whom lived in single family dwellings and sent many of their children to local schools at least through age fourteen.[89] Despite this appearance of stability, both the city and the county experienced an important transformation between 1890 and 1910 that laid the basis for Socialist agitation. In these years the rural population of Auglaize County declined as a changing social structure propelled individuals to the small cities. Between 1900 and 1910 the number of owner-operated farms decreased by almost 12 percent, and the tenant farm population grew by almost 20 percent. In the city even sharper contrasts appeared. Although St. Marys ranked seventy-third in the state in the value of its manufactured products, the sixty men who controlled local industry in 1900 formed a dominant elite whose emergence generated class divisions. Immediately underneath these manufacturers was a group of forty-four salaried officials and clerks—white-collar employees who managed the city's industry and whose average yearly salary approached $900 per year. Beneath them were the wage workers. While the available records do not allow a careful analysis by skill and occupation, the less refined comparison that is possible is revealing. Of the 453 wage workers, all over age sixteen, who were employed in 1900, the 410 men averaged wages of $447 per year, just about half that of the white-collar employees. The forty-three working-class women fared worse, with an average yearly pay of but $209.[90]

In this context the Socialist movement grew. With only seven members in 1910, these comrades published a newspaper—with the help of a

Socialist cooperative printing plant in nearby Findlay, Ohio—and counted 112 members a year later. Entering a full slate of candidates in the November 1911 municipal elections, these Socialists ran an energetic campaign that included a speech by Haywood at an October rally. To everyone's surprise the Socialists swept the election, winning the mayoralty, most of the city's other executive offices, and the seven positions on the city council. The thirty-year-old mayor, Scott Wilkens, who had left the farm eight years before to work at the post office, received 48 percent of the vote in a three-way race.[91]

Even before this startling victory, the strength of the movement in St. Marys and other midwestern communities attracted national attention. Frank Bohn, a left-wing Socialist, applauded the comrades in June 1911 but remained somewhat uneasy as he felt their origins were less influenced by Socialist theory than by the recent social change in the community. In a long report following his organizing tour of the Midwest, Bohn perceptively caught the tone and substance of this transformation even as he bemoaned the absence of firm theoretical foundations. "The social distinctions in the small towns are now much more clearly marked than formerly," he noted. If in earlier years the "large degree of social equality" followed from the very structure of community values, from the citizens' "manner of living, their ideas and the education of their children, all this is now changed." In St. Marys the new high school caters to the "better people"; the new industrial leaders, riding through town in their automobiles, no longer stop to talk with other citizens; and the electric wires, gas pipes, and sewer lines are installed only in the better neighborhoods. In a fashion alien to past experience one man's poverty and another man's wealth are "known to the whole community." As a result, "the old time American workingman is very much embittered." He sees "men he has known from boyhood"—and knows "are 'no better than he is' "—reaping new benefits from his labor. In contrast, his own "condition is becoming steadily worse."

Beyond this, though, Bohn had misgivings. At first, Bohn thought, this nascent comrade tended to blame himself for failing to grasp the opportunities he held were open to all. Contact with the Socialist movement expanded his understanding, but, in contrast with the worker in the larger urban centers, Bohn argued that "the necessity of revolutionary theory and practice" remained unclear:

> The point of departure in the reasoning of the man in the small town is usually as regards his conception of government. . . . In the small town the worker is bred to be both religious and patriotic. When his living conditions have deteriorated, when he sees his children denied the opportunities that would make their life easier than his, and after he has seen several local politicians grow rich through town and coun-

ty graft—then he is ready for a larger view of life. Its form is usually bitter enmity towards the wretches who have debased "his country" and its government.

For Bohn and other Socialists, this deficient grasp of Socialist theory explained "the tremendous hold" of the *Appeal to Reason*: "Its editors comprehend perfectly the psychology of the American-born worker and specifically the worker in the small town. The *Appeal to Reason* comes into the home of this man and he begins to sweat from anger." Inadequate by itself, Bohn hoped that this process initiated "the first act in the making of a revolutionist."[92]

Bohn understood the effects of industrial capitalist development, but he and others remained condescending toward the new party members. Embarrassed by "religious and patriotic" sensibilities, Bohn was surprised by Mayor Wilkens's class-conscious administration. In one of his first official acts, Wilkens visited a machine shop where some workers had been laid off for refusing to work Saturdays. Urging the men to organize a union and offering them the city council chambers for a meeting, the Socialist mayor of St. Marys promised them that if they struck, the city would protect their rights and, in the event of violence by company-hired thugs, he would swear in strikers as deputies.[93]

Like other Socialists with a national audience, Bohn misunderstood the basic social foundation of his own movement's appeal. In the person of Debs, in the vibrant movement in the Southwest, and in communities such as St. Marys, religious belief and a deep-rooted patriotism did not inhibit the growth of a strong class awareness. That awareness developed within a specific political and cultural context that provided it with a most powerful ally: through these men and women and their specific traditions a class analysis—so at odds with the dominant ideology of individualism—entered American culture and its political discourse with a power and force otherwise unimaginable. Misunderstood by many, that mixture of biblical appeal, democratic ideology, and growing class awareness was the great strength of the Debsian Socialist movement and remains today its most potent legacy.

Support for Debs's contention that class relations now structured American society was evident in urban industrial areas as well. In Reading, Pennsylvania, for example, a diversified industrial city with over 70 percent of its adults engaged in working-class occupations, Reading's workers were American-born, a high percentage were church members, and a substantial number owned their own homes. The city's population grew by 65 percent between 1890 and 1910, reflecting the influx of rural people from surrounding Berks County; simultaneously its central industrial base shifted from the production of machines to textiles, especially hosiery. The opposition of employers to the union movement and the effective leadership of James Maurer, Andrew Bower, and J. Henry Stump provided the context in which the Socialist movement grew. A major force in the city, Socialists elected aldermen, mayors, and state representatives into the 1930s.[94]

A similar process occurred in Schenectady, New York, where in 1911 the Socialists elected a mayor, eight of thirteen aldermen, and a state assemblyman. Between 1900 and 1910 that city's population increased by 130 percent, in large part due to the dramatic expansion of its two major employers: General Electric and American Locomotive. With a predominantly American-born constituency — although Schenectady Socialists had a high percentage of Irish men among their leaders—these skilled and semiskilled workers voted the Socialist ticket.[95]

Despite important differences, a common theme united these two urban Socialist experiences. In each city Socialist electoral success relied on working-class support. In Schenectady the skilled machinists, organized in the International Association of Machinists, backed the Socialists, and the party drew firm support throughout the working-class wards. While the middle-class minister, George R. Lunn, became that city's first Socialist mayor, half of all victorious Socialist candidates in 1911 were machinists and members of their union.[96] In Reading, with a higher proportion of semi- and unskilled workers than other cities with Socialist electoral victories, the alliance between the Socialists and trade unionists was even stronger and of longer duration. From its founding in 1900, Reading's Federated Trades Council supported (if unofficially) the Socialist movement. An overwhelming majority of its delegates were members of the party, and through effective organizing in union halls, cultural associations, and even church socials—as well as through traditional Socialist meetings—they consistently recorded votes for the Socialist ticket far in excess of the party membership. Not only was the Socialist electoral strength drawn ''consistently and with increasing intensity'' from the working-class wards but so were its candidates for office. Between 1910 and 1935, 85 percent of all those nominated for office by Reading Socialists held working-class jobs. Although different in expression and experience from their Oklahoma comrades, as they were in important ways from the Milwaukee Socialists as well, workers in Reading, Schenectady, and other industrial communities created Socialist movements of varying strengths that depended upon working-class people for support and expressed in indigenous terms a class analysis of American society.[97]

This critique of industrial capitalism, organized around a clear class awareness, had deep and powerful roots among Americans. Integrated in different fashion with democratic ideology, trade union practice, and earlier political and religious traditions in the specific locale, this

American expression of class nonetheless created a vigorous response in opposition. The differences among the regional movements were obvious; they would continue to cause bitter conflict within the party; and they required a firm but sensitive national leader to bridge the disagreements. But this should not obscure the fact that the Socialist movement's appeal rested on a realistic assessment of American society and culture.

It was this foundation that supported the platform from which Debs spoke. As he had decades earlier, a growing number, if still a minority, of Americans now questioned the revolution in their political traditions, cultural values, and daily work experience engineered by industrial capitalism. Hesitantly and at times awkwardly realigning their long-held individualism with a new collective identity, they provided the Socialist movement with its greatest local and national electoral successes in 1911 and 1912.[98]

After the discouraging 1908 campaign, the growth of the Socialist party was impressive. Official party membership doubled between 1909 and 1911 and increased another 40 percent in 1912, when the party achieved its highest recorded membership, almost 118,000 activists. The off-year elections also pointed to the renewed health of the movement. In 1910 Socialist party candidates for state and local office attracted nearly 700,000 voters, and in 1911 seventy-four cities and towns elected at least one Socialist mayor or major city official. From Schenectady, New York, to St. Marys, Ohio, from Coeur d'Alene, Idaho, to Berkeley and Watts, California, Socialist officials assumed office and utilized what power they possessed in support of local working people. Nowhere, Bohn proclaimed, were the results "unworthy of our cause. Everywhere our fundamental position was emphasized." Looking forward to "1912—The Beginning of an Epoch," Bohn predicted that with the capitalist parties on the defensive the comrades would move "through this wilderness of crooked paths" and possibly capture more than two million votes in the presidential election.[99]

Fermenting just beneath this surface unanimity, however, basic differences remained concerning the applicability of the Socialist class analysis and relations with the AFL and IWW. The struggle to control the party apparatus and thus the political direction of the Socialist movement in America intensified between 1908 and 1912. To a large extent, these tensions reflected the tremendously diverse nature of the American movement and the contrasting regional experiences with industrial capitalism. Although Haywood, Berger, and Wayland all appealed to the working class, each envisioned a vastly different movement. In important ways these leaders and others, such as Hillquit in New York, Maurer in Pennsylvania, and Max Hayes in Ohio, could not rise above their specific contexts to reach the common ground at the core of their different Socialist commitments. In Debs, however, the party possessed a comrade of unparalleled national stature who, through his incessant travels, was intimately familiar with most of the regional movements. With friends in each faction and armed with a deep belief in the power of a democratic working-class Socialist movement, Debs's leadership qualities would undergo a critical test in these four years.

The opening round in the renewed factional strife began innocently enough in early 1909. Writing in the *International Socialist Review*, William English Walling criticized Keir Hardie's Independent Labour party of Britain for relying on the skilled workers, "the aristocracy of labor," for its electoral support. Walling argued that industrial development and worker consciousness were more advanced in America and that to limit the labor activity of the party to the skilled workers was in effect undemocratic. A month later, Robert Hunter responded and suggested that Walling misunderstood the British party. Arguing that the combination of Socialists and skilled trade unionists in Britain represented an alliance and not a fusion (and thus preserved independent Socialist principles), Hunter characterized Walling's position as "contrary to socialist tactics." In the same issue the *Review* sided with Walling and argued that an American labor party would flounder on the conservative reefs of official trade union ideology.[100] There the matter rested, an exchange reflecting basic tensions in the Socialist movement that remained more theoretical than immediate, until the following November.

On 19 November Algie M. Simons wrote Walling a letter from Toronto, where he was attending the annual convention of the AFL. Simons was impressed by the number of former Socialist party members present as delegates and depressed by their reasons for leaving the party. He argued that the party was divided between intellectuals and the "never works" (i.e., the IWW impossibilists) and that this condition kept "the actual wage-workers" from remaining in the party. To remedy this situation, Simons proposed the creation of an American labor party along British lines, closely aligned with Gompers and the AFL. He urged the simplification of Socialist party machinery in order to appeal "directly to the union men," ignored the unorganized majority of American working people, and demanded that his faction "drive from our own ranks" those "who are seeking to raise rebellion against every person whom they cannot use for their purposes." In a closing appeal Simons informed Walling that his party faction—and he specifically named Hillquit and John Spargo among them—already had "preparations under way to bring about an internal [party] revolution" and desired Walling's cooperation. Walling decided that political concerns outweighed the claim of friendship, and he privately circulated and then published Simons's letter in the *Review*. The battlelines of a major party dispute now formed with greater vigor than ever before. Petulantly and somewhat tardily, Spargo chastised Simons for his tactical blunder: "Surely," the national executive committee member wrote, "you ought to be careful as to whom you write, even intimating our plans!"[101]

Reaction to the airing of Simons's letter was swift. Debs denounced the plan and argued that the party "has already CATERED FAR TOO MUCH to the American Federation of Labor."[102] Rose Pastor Stokes, the immigrant Socialist married to a Connecticut Socialist millionaire, condemned the plan as "nothing but a desire to get into office. . . . Since we cannot win the entire A.F. of L. to the revolutionary position, these comrades think it would be an advantage to come down to the narrow position of the A.F. of L."[103] Her husband, J. G. Phelps Stokes, also was critical, and Socialist locals in New York City and elsewhere denounced Simons, Berger, and Hillquit.[104]

But those who shared Simons's views were also active. Hillquit argued that, while the "prime object" of the party was to organize the working class politically, "it has so far not succeeded in doing so." Therefore he would support a "bona-fide workingmen's party . . . organized . . . on a true workingmen's platform" and insisted that the party would have to do so also. Berger was, as usual, both more vindictive and more pragmatic than Hillquit. Dismissing his opponents as "impossibilists" who, if successful in discrediting his faction, "would even try to paralyze us where we have worked successfully," Berger urged Hillquit and Spargo to concentrate on the coming election of a new national executive committee. He suggested a list of candidates "whom we want to see elected" and instructed Hillquit to use his influence in New York, as he would in Milwaukee, to direct the Socialist press accordingly.[105]

The issues in this dispute were fundamental: who was to control the party and how would it respond to the continued resistance of many workers to Socialism. For Berger, Hillquit, and their allies, the answer to the first question was obvious. Their professed theoretical superiority and control of strong local Socialist movements based on skilled unionists meant *they* were the answer. The second point went to the heart of the matter. Like Berger and Hillquit, Simons actively resisted the growing "lumpenproletarian" influence in the party, which he equated with the IWW and their supporters. Focusing solely on the organized skilled craft unionists, Simons argued that, although he had been quite critical of the AFL in the past, "I am forced to recognize that it comes much nearer to representing the working class than the S.P., and unless we are able to shape our policy and our organization so as to meet the demands and incarnate the position of the workers, we will have failed in our mission."[106]

For Debs, such a course was despicable and stupid. Socialists who advocated a policy of accommodation with Gompers exchanged their principles for the "dirtiest Tammany tricks." Their reward, Debs wrote in anger, was "being puked on in return by" Gompers. "Berger's performances in this connection," Debs told Hunter, "have been disgraceful and contemptible beyond words." To Debs, the sight of Socialists, "alleged revolutionary leaders," joining forces with the AFL was "absolutely inexcusable" and the crassest form of class collaboration. Debs understood far more clearly than other party leaders the resistance to Socialism by American workers but stressed that these collaborative attempts merely compounded the problems facing Socialists: "It is this very thing that confounds and confuses the rank and file, muddles the situation and makes our already difficult task next to impossible." Demanding that the movement retain its fundamental principles even as it adapted to specific American conditions, Debs declared for "clear cut action and uncompromising principles. I do not propose to try to win the intimidated rank and file of the A.F. of L. by publicly pandering to their corrupt bosses."[107]

The labor party dispute further solidified internal party divisions.[108] As both Simons's and Debs's responses make clear, the question of Socialist labor policy remained the most critical issue before the members. Control of the party apparatus therefore assumed great importance, as each side jockeyed to influence the outcome on a related series of issues. Immigration policy, for example, was a source of major disagreement. At the 1910 party congress, a majority of the committee on immigration (Berger, Ernst Untermann, and John Wanhope) approved a resolution calling for the "unconditional exclusion" of all Oriental workers. Reflecting the AFL's position, this resolution argued that as America was already afflicted with its own racial problems the continued immigration of Asian workers would weaken labor. After long debate a substitute motion passed that favored exclusion but removed the overt racial reference. This resolution, introduced by Hillquit and approved by a slim margin (55–50), evoked an angry response from Debs. Speaking on behalf of those Socialists opposed to close relations with the AFL, Debs called the resolution "utterly unsocialistic, reactionary, and in truth outrageous." Drawing clearer the lines that divided the party, Debs termed the resolution's supporters "subtle and sophisticated defenders of the civic federation unionism" and proclaimed his refusal "to sacrifice principle for numbers and jeopardise ultimate success for immediate gain . . . [and] to turn my back upon the oppressed."[109]

Debs was assuming a leadership role among the revolutionary democratic Socialists within the American movement. Although he had allowed his membership in the IWW to lapse, without comment, in 1908, Debs still proclaimed the necessity of industrial unionism. Such organizing efforts broke through the narrow confines of AFL policy and focused primary attention on the majority of American industrial workers who possessed neither skill nor craft. Attempts to replace the older craft unions were a waste of time, Debs argued, and instead he emphasized the unique possibilities inherent in the very structure of industrial unions. These unions, he now understood, were based upon the "mutual economic interests of all workers [in an industry] and the solidarity arising therefrom." Therefore industrial union organization presented a clear path to democratic Socialist political action. If the trade or craft union based its existence on "the prevailing industrial system," the industrial union, democratically controlled and rooted in a solidarity among workers, had for its goal both improved conditions and the "ultimate abolition of the existing productive system, and the total extinction of wage servitude." Advising comrades to "bore from within and without" the old unions, Debs saw the industrial union movement as "laying the foundation and erecting the superstructure of the new revolutionary economic organization, the embryonic industrial democracy."[110]

Early in 1911 Debs went a step further and directly linked his advocacy of industrial unionism to internal party disputes, especially to the question of democratic governance of the party. In a perceptive and at times caustic article, "Danger Ahead," Debs applauded the recent 1910 electoral gains but cautioned against an infatuation with municipal Socialism. There were votes in 1910 "obtained by methods not consistent with the principles of a revolutionary party," Debs wrote, and he warned that this "spirit of bourgeois reform" could "practically destroy [the party's] virility and efficiency as a revolutionary organization." But there were those in the party, the unnamed "vote-getters," who encouraged this trend and used Socialist propaganda "as a bait for votes rather than as a means of education." In an obvious reference to Berger's Milwaukee practices as well as to the recent labor party controversy, Debs condemned those who would "join hands with reactionary trade unionists in local emergencies and in certain temporary situations to effect some specific purpose." To elect local officials, "here and there, where the party is still in a crude state will inevitably bring trouble and set the party back," Debs argued, and he warned his Socialist adversaries: "Voting for socialism is not socialism any more than a menu is a meal."

"Of far greater importance," Debs insisted, "than increasing the vote of the Socialist party is the economic organization of the working class. . . . Socialism must be organized, drilled, equipped and the place to begin is in the industries where the workers are employed." Without this effective economic base, working class "political power, even if it could be developed, would but react upon them, thwart their plans, blast their hopes, and all but destroy them." Integrating class analysis and democratic ideology with a newfound power, Debs again pointed to the democratic industrial union movement as the foundation of a meaningful Socialism. Such a movement would prepare "the workers, step by step, to assume entire control of the productive forces when the hour strikes for the impending organic change. . . . Organized industrially . . . [workers] will just as naturally and inevitably express their economic solidarity in political terms and cast a united vote for the party of their class."[111]

"Industrial unionism," Debs wrote a month later, "is the structural work of the co-operative commonwealth, the working class republic."[112] In these articles Debs all but declared open public war on Berger, Hillquit, Spargo, and their allies. Spurning his knowledge of the important regional differences within the movement, Debs held that there was but one path to the Socialist revolution and strongly implied that it was no accident that the same party bosses who retarded the growth of a democratic Socialist movement were also most closely affiliated with the AFL. Buoyed by the dramatic IWW free-speech fights as well as by that union's first attempts to organize immigrant steel workers at McKees Rocks and New Castle, Pennsylvania, Debs somewhat impulsively sought to reduce the diverse movement to a single model. His critique of party bosses was discerning, and his understanding of the structural differences and contrasting orientations of craft and industrial unionism was perceptive. Yet his enthusiasm overwhelmed him, and he lost sight of the delicate balance that would allow him to press his critique while stopping short of dismissing his opponents.

In private Debs went further than even his sharp public attack. "If the socialist movement tolerates a boss, be it Berger or Jehovah," he wrote Carl Thompson late in 1910, "it is false to its professed principles and the lightening should strike and will strike it just as certain as we invite it." Debs vowed that he would soon "face Berger" on this issue "before the delegates of a convention, or better still, the rank and file," and in the process he revealed just how consistent were the concerns that motivated his own sense of self. "I discovered [Berger's] true nature long ago," he told Thompson, "but I was indulgent with him to the verge of cowardice. I have heard him talk to Fred Heath in a room full of people as I would not talk to the mangiest cur, and Heath took it all meekly and without protest, and Berger took it for granted that it was his right to exact such servile and debasing obeisance from comrades. He tried it on me," Debs remembered, "but there he struck a snag":

> I yielded and submitted until self-respect moved me to call a halt, and I did. Berger was determined that I had no right to differ with him and insultingly commanded me to act the part of a lackey to him, and then our relations came to a very sudden end. I told him that I was a

man and a socialist, that I would permit neither man nor god to boss
or dictate to me in the vulgar spirit that moved him to turn purple as
he tried to bulldoze me into docile subjection to him as he had done to
so many other comrades.[113]

In contrast, Debs offered his vision of a Socialist leader and, not insignificantly, his perception of his own role in the movement: "The true
leader uses all his power, not to rule others, but to impart the power and intelligence to them to rule themselves."[114]

Debs's opportunity to "face Berger" was not long in coming. At the
party's national convention in May 1912, the delegates renominated Debs
for the fourth time as their presidential candidate. But the selection of
Debs was more fractious than ever before, as Berger and Hillquit organized 40 percent of the voting delegates for their candidates, Emil Seidel
and Charles E. Russell, respectively.[115] Publicly, at least, this opposition did
not upset Debs, but Hillquit's actions toward the close of the convention
did. Implying that he spoke with the unanimous approval of both the National Executive Committee and the convention's Committee on Constitution, Hillquit moved that J. Mahlon Barnes, the former national secretary
whose forced resignation in 1911 had caused many to look to Theodore
Debs as a replacement, be appointed campaign manager. Given the seemingly impeccable recommendations (the national committee at this time
included both Haywood and Kate Richards O'Hare as well as Hillquit)
and the late hour, Barnes's appointment was approved.[116]

As news of the appointment spread, furious reaction ensued from the
rank and file. Although Barnes had been forced from office in 1911, for
fathering a child by Jean Keep and then refusing to acknowledge his
responsibility, many comrades remained angry at that conduct and at the
actions of Hillquit, Berger, Spargo, Hunter, and Seymour Stedman who,
in a vicious party trial, attempted to portray Keep as the guilty person.[117]
Debs shared this anger,[118] but the internal struggle for democratic control
of the party remained paramount for him and his allies. For, it was soon
discovered, Hillquit had lied when he stated that Barnes had the
unanimous approval of two major Socialist committees. Compounding
the offense, Hillquit then enlisted Berger, Spargo, and others to pressure
the official stenographer to doctor the convention proceedings to
eliminate his reference to unanimous support. Unabashedly, Hillquit
decided to weather the storm. He and Berger inhabited a world of
predominantly professional, middle-class party leaders and possessed little patience for and less interest in the majority of their "untutored" comrades. As New York Socialist Bertha Howe wrote to a friend, Hillquit
"says 'Hillquitism' can only mean normal socialism, since anti-
Hillquitism means something very like Anarchism, or words to that
effect."[119]

In a remarkable series of letters to Fred D. Warren, editor of the *Appeal to Reason*, Debs discussed the implications of the dispute over Barnes. "My mail," he wrote in June 1912, "is loaded with threats and protests about the Barnes affair." Some party locals resolved to stop paying dues to the national office; others refused to contribute to the coming campaign; "and numberless others declare that they will not vote the ticket unless Barnes is removed." Pointing to the "official machine" of the party bosses as the basic issue, Debs told Warren "that machine has got to be smashed if the party is not to be wrecked" and vowed to release a statement that would, by naming "those who are responsible," force the issue: "They think my lips are gagged on account of my position [as presidential candidate] but if I permitted the party to be utterly disrupted by my cowardly silence I would be a traitor indeed to the thousands of good comrades who trust me."[120] Yet less than a week earlier, in a face-to-face meeting with both Berger and Hillquilt, Debs contained his anger and issued no protest as the majority of national officials refused to remove Barnes from the campaign.[121]

A month later, in another long letter to Warren, Debs recounted the insistent attacks by both Berger and Hillquilt on the *Appeal* at the last convention. A week later, following an editorial in which Berger accused Debs of egotism, Debs exploded. "I will have something to say to that gentleman after the campaign is over," Debs wrote. "I have been silent under his insults a good many times for the sake of the party . . . but [I will] tell a few truths about Berger the Boss and the bully that will put him right before the comrades." Although Debs had changed his mind and decided to wait until after the campaign, he proposed to Warren a united effort to "fight the machine that is now throttling the party." With his oratory combined with the *Appeal*'s circulation, Debs argued that the rank and file would flock to "us in the fight against machine politicians, boss rule and [for] a truly democratic socialist party."[122] As Debs noted to another friend the same day, since the Berger-Hillquit alliance "could not defeat me . . . it could and did," through the Barnes appointment, "get control of my campaign as it did four years ago, and it is not an accident that since the machine has been set upon destroying me, or at least my influence, my campaigns have been managed by those who did all in their power to defeat my nomination."[123]

Debs's expressed willingness to conduct a major factional fight was a dramatic reversal for him—and an indication of the depth of his personal and political disgust over the direction of the party. But Warren saw the situation differently. On 8 August he wrote Debs that he would not put the *Appeal* at his disposal in the fight against Berger and Hillquit. In part the paper, already in deep financial difficulty,[124] could lose needed subscribers if it engaged in such a fight. But Warren's reticence went deeper: "I am willing to follow you, dear Gene, to any lengths in fighting for a better system," but if Debs continued with his plans "then we will have to part company. . . . It is not necessary for me to tell you, Debs, that I love you as no other man on earth," but "to see you dissipate your energy in the hopeless task of keeping the socialist party straight" pained Warren. "To me the socialist movement is everything and the socialist party but a means to the accomplishment of our ends." Reflecting the power and indigenous roots of the southwestern movement, Warren told Debs of a recent speech before a large Socialist audience, "all revolutionaries," where no one expressed to him after the talk "the slightest interest in the Barnes controversy or the other questions which agitate socialist party officialdom."[125]

Debs was stunned that his old friend refused to join him. Sadly, he acknowledged that Warren was right—Debs and the *Appeal* must part ways after the campaign—but Debs vowed to start his own paper to carry the fight. Debs agreed with Warren's analysis of the party and the Socialist movement but warned him not to "forget that the party is the necessary instrument and if it is corrupted the movement is betrayed and defeated."[126] A series of letters followed, which altered neither man's position, and after the campaign the two had a pleasant time when Warren visited the recuperating Debs in Terre Haute. But the moment had passed.[127]

Debs's handling of the Barnes controversy reveals the central weakness of his leadership. He knew this was no minor dispute, and he understood his critical role as a national leader of the opposition to dictatorial and anti-Socialist internal party policy. Yet, as he always had in the past, he found a reason to delay the fight: "This is a different statement," Debs noted when he announced he would not insist on Barnes's resignation, "than the one I had first intended." Now Debs simply supported a national referendum on the question, held that September during the campaign. Not surprisingly, Barnes was retained as manager, if only to insure campaign continuity.[128]

The effects of a more vigorous struggle, had Debs decided to undertake it, are difficult to determine. While his fear of splitting the party was real, other options were available. Had Theodore Debs agreed to run for Barnes's position in 1911, and had his brother publicly pressed a discussion of the relationship of Barnes's appointment in 1912, democratic socialism, and industrial unionism, the effect upon the party and the movement might have been immense. Taking control of the national party apparatus from those exclusively committed to a narrow, AFL-orientated policy, while striving to preserve a place for them within the party, could have greatly enhanced the effectiveness of the Socialist movement. Most important, such a course would have made possible friendlier relations with the IWW. This, in turn, might have checked the excesses of the IWW, especially concerning "direct action," and have prevented a final split between the IWW and the Socialist party. But the two brothers did not. As Eugene told Warren, "parting company with Theodore . . . I cannot do." Neither would he publicly "face Berger." Inevitably, then, the movement splintered, and Debs found himself siding with his long-time party enemies.[129]

In January 1912 a strike in Lawrence, Massachusetts, momentarily held the promise of binding together the various factions that were rending the Socialist party. Sparked by a group of Polish female textile workers who quit their looms when they received an unannounced wage cut, the strike broadened the following morning. On Friday, 12 January, a large contingent of Italian workers left their jobs at the American Woolen Company, damaged machinery on their way out, and went from mill to mill along the Merrimack River, urging workers in other factories to join their strike. By nightfall over 10,000 textile workers—of both sexes, all ages, and numerous nationalities—had quit work. Lawrence braced for its most dramatic labor conflict.

A spontaneous, angry response to the latest corporate insult, the Lawrence strike was nonetheless not without organization. The skilled workers had their union, the United Textile Workers of America, but it was generally ineffective and refused to organize the large numbers of unskilled immigrants from eastern and southern Europe. The Socialist party, too, had a small local in Lawrence, but its focus remained centered on the Lawrence Central Labor Union, and its organizers had made little inroads within the diverse immigrant community. Even before 1912, however, the local leaders of the IWW had organized these workers. Conscious of the way in which ethnicity divided working people, the Lawrence IWW recruited organizers from every major ethnic group, who brought its message of militant industrial unionism into church fairs, socials, and cultural activities. As most of these men and women could not vote—many knew very little English—this agitation spoke pragmatically and directly to their sharpest needs. These local organizers also did not dismiss the more conservative local unions. Louis Picavet, a French-Canadian textile worker and member of IWW Local 20, followed Debs's policy of working with the older unions even while building a strong IWW movement. Under such direction, the influence of the local, if not its formal membership, grew impressively, and in August 1911 its members conducted a series of slowdowns and wildcat strikes throughout the industry.[130]

The 1912 strike lasted eight weeks. Despite the ethnic differences, the presence of the state militia, and a brutal police attack on striking families at the train depot on 24 February, the textile workers remained united.

Contrary to their public image, in part the result of their own loose talk, national IWW leaders who came to Lawrence counseled against violence and supported specific demands to be obtained through negotiation with the mill owners as the goal of the strike. As Haywood noted at the time, employers could not "weave cloth with the bayonets" of the soldiers. All the workers had to do was to withdraw their labor, keep their hands in their pockets, and wait out the bosses. By mid-March they won their four major demands, and the victory was hailed throughout the country.[131]

Within the Socialist movement this triumph had a stunning effect. After years of growing tension and open, bitter hostility, it seemed as if the two major tendencies within the movement had finally discovered the path to cooperation. The IWW emphasis on "direct action"—which rejected both political work and often traditional organizing efforts—no longer appeared an issue, as both sides worked together effectively. Lawrence Socialists were active in the strike, and the national party gave over $18,000 to the strike fund. Socialists throughout New England and from New York City and Philadelphia arrived to lead the exodus of strikers' children to other cities to avoid the hunger, lack of heat, and potential violence in strike-torn Lawrence. Even Berger, now a U.S. Congressman and for many years the bitterest opponent of the leftist Socialists, cooperated. He demanded and obtained a congressional investigation of the strike and, as the *International Socialist Review* stated proudly, "Congressman Berger worked hand in hand with Haywood and gave invaluable assistance in exposing . . . the hypocritical pretenses of the tariff-protected mill owners." The example of such an alliance between two enemies, and of the way in which the Socialist party fully supported the IWW-directed strike, led the *Review* to state that the Lawrence battle "is only a beginning. Its importance lies in the fact that winning tactics have been discovered and have already received the virtual endorsement of the Socialist party of America. Industrial Unionism is no longer an untried theory. Henceforth its progress will be swift and sure."[132]

This enthusiasm marked the first days of the Socialist party's May convention as well. When the labor plank for the first time in party history called special attention to the needs of the unorganized, unskilled immigrant workers and urged all unions to abolish "artificial restrictions" on the membership, the left and the right in the Socialist movement appeared to clasp hands. Tom Hickey, the Texas-based organizer of tenant farmers, did just that as he hugged Job Harriman, a particularly bitter personal enemy for the past fifteen years. But it was Haywood who captured the importance of the moment. As both a national officer of the party and a leader of the IWW, Haywood symbolized the fundamental differences within the movement. But in 1912 he told the delegates with great enthusiasm that, with this new labor policy, "I can go to the working class, to the eight million women and children, to the four million black men, to the disfranchised white men . . . and I can carry to them the message of Socialism.'' Haywood again endorsed political action but noted that, as many of his followers did not possess the vote, the party's approval of industrial unionism would allow Socialists to organize all workers ''at the machine so that they could carry on production after capitalism has been overthrown.'' With a great smile and his broad frame spread wide as if embracing the audience, Haywood stated that he could now ''shake hands with every delegate in this convention and say that we are a united working class.''[133]

But such was not the case. Those Socialists who favored industrial unionism and opposed the policy of unilateral support of the AFL misread the meaning of the new labor plank. The recent experience at Lawrence notwithstanding, Berger, Hillquit, and their allies remained deeply antagonistic toward Haywood and the IWW. And Haywood himself fueled this anger. In the middle of the Lawrence strike, the *International Socialist Review* published a major speech that Haywood gave in New York in which he goaded his Socialist opponents, using all of the rhetorical weapons available, including personal insult. While formally approving political action, Haywood, in a pointed reference to Berger, stated that he would rather workers could elect a factory superintendent than a Congressman. Haywood dismissed Socialist lawyer Hillquit, claiming ''for all the ages agone,'' lawyers ''have been the mouthpieces of the capitalist class.'' The IWW leader then told his New York audience of the major lesson he took from his experience in the western mines: ''I despise the law,'' he decried, ''and am not a law-abiding citizen. And more than that, no Socialist can be a law-abiding citizen. When we come together . . . to overthrow the capitalist system, we become conspirators then against the United States government.'' Finally, Haywood termed ''coercion'' as the best method of achieving the transition to industrial Socialism and specifically attacked all union workers who agree to a contract with capitalism: ''The trade unionist who becomes party to a contract takes his organization out of the columns of fighting organizations,'' Haywood declaimed. ''He removes it from the class struggle and he binds it up and makes it absolutely useless.''[134]

Haywood's speech crystallized opposition to him and the IWW. Direct action, Haywood's talk made clear, would not only mean organizing at the point of production among unskilled immigrant workers without the right to vote, but also it would demand, through its scorn of political action and praise of illegal activities, a frontal attack upon both the Socialist party and any labor union not affiliated with the IWW. Despite the recent cooperation at Lawrence, Haywood dismissed all who refused to follow his approach. He had come to believe too many of his own press clippings.

The one-eyed hero of the wild west, more at home in the bordello than the drawing room, could not pass up the opportunity to taunt the "effete Socialists" of the nation's major city.

But Debs also shared the blame for the final rupture. One effect of his inconsistent role as a party leader was to encourage Haywood in his irresponsible rhetoric. With the national party firmly controlled by bitter opponents, Haywood thought, wrongly but understandably, that the Socialist party would be of no help to him. Debs's failure to act had another consequence as well. Since Debs relinquished any attempt to influence the IWW, his inaction left him no choice but to side with Berger and Hillquit in their successful effort to expel Haywood and his supporters from the party.

Debs's disagreements with Haywood were severe and nearly total. In the same issue of the *Review* that carried Haywood's speech, Debs insisted on the necessity of developing tactics "adapted to the American people and to American conditions." Debs agreed that as capitalist laws were prejudicial to working people they should have little reverence for them, but he would not "make an individual lawbreaker of myself." Debs understood in Haywood's platform plastique—that stressed sabotage and "direct action" by workers at the point of production—"the tactics of anarchist individuals and not of Socialist collectivists." Terming these measures "reactionary, not revolutionary," Debs concluded they played directly "into the hands of the enemy": secrecy and stealth "cannot make for solidarity," would open the movement to *agents provocateurs*, would totally sunder the Socialist movement, and leave those left "responsible for the deed of every spy or madman."

Most important, Debs insisted that Haywood's conception of workers was false. American workers "are law-abiding," Debs stated, "and no amount of sneering or derision will alter that fact. Direct action will never appeal to any considerable number of them while they have the ballot and the right of industrial and political organization." Had the topic not been so painful, Debs might have also asked Haywood to explain why the rank and file of the Western Federation of Miners, the very mythic origins of Haywood's presentation of self, had recently voted to re-affiliate with the AFL.

Toward the conclusion of his long article, Debs reaffirmed the intimate connection between industrial unionism and Socialism, proclaimed his "faith in proletarian political power and in the efficacy of political propaganda as an educational force in the Socialist movement," and made a fateful decision. Looking ahead to the May party convention, Debs hoped that that meeting would "place itself squarely on record . . . against sabotage and every other form of violence and destructiveness suggested by what is known as 'direct action.' " This statement remained Debs's sole pre-convention comment on the most explosive issue that gathering faced.[135]

At the convention Haywood's joy at the prospect of what he termed "a united working class" quickly turned to bitterness. On the day following the adoption of the labor plank, the delegates took up a proposed constitutional amendment that would expel "any member of the party who opposes political action or advocates sabotage or other methods of violence as a weapon of the working class." The final struggle had begun. E. H. Merrick of Pennsylvania immediately moved to strike the motion and noted that continued discussion of it would destroy the unity and harmony that prevailed but a day before. Marguerite Prevey of Ohio also opposed it, as did Tom Hickey. But they were in the minority. When Berger took the floor and equated the IWW by name with the anarchism of Johann Most, he could almost smell the victory over the "impossibilists" that he had long worked for. Merrick's motion was defeated, 191–90, and the battle was over. For the first time since 1901 the party was unable to contain its divergent elements. It would not, however, be the last time basic issues were resolved in that fashion.[136]

Following the convention, Debs expressed second thoughts concerning the new section of the party constitution. Writing in the *Review* in July, Debs noted that he would have rather reduced "to the minimum the offenses punishable by expulsion from the party" and, while opposed "to anarchist tactics," he instead "would have the party so declare itself on moral ground." In a private letter a month later to Berger, Debs disagreed with the Milwaukee leader's assessment of the "immediate danger from the alleged anarchist element" but favored after the election "a thorough housecleaning . . . and the expulsion from the party of any who prefer violence to the ballot."[137] If Debs was beset by contradictions, others were far clearer. Adolph Germer, an official in both the party and the UMWA, stressed that the primary task facing the party was "to set Haywood outside . . . so that we would not be required to bear the responsibility of his idiotic tactics." Carl Thompson, replying to Helen Keller's appeal in support of Haywood, asked whether she would choose "the Paris Commune or Schenectady" as the model for the Socialist commonwealth. Even British trade unionist Keir Hardie chimed in, calling Haywood a "bounder" and expressing thanks that "all of his type on this side remain outside the Party."[138]

Not surprisingly, the national referendum sponsored by the New York State Socialist party to recall Haywood from the National Executive Committee for his speech in New York won handily. Haywood received less than one-third of the votes cast and carried only ten state organizations, all but Tennessee and West Virginia (which he won by three votes) in the far West or Southwest.[139] Nor did the dispute stop there. Between 1912 and

1913 the party lost almost 23,000 members, the great majority as a result of this fight.[140]

Although many Haywood supporters were now outside the party, bitter antagonism remained. In March 1913 Debs referred to the IWW as "an anarchist organization in all except in name" and now firmly supported the party's "decided stand" against the group and its leader: "I think you know there is a very wide difference between the kind of political action Haywood advocates and the kind I advocate, even if we do happen to use identical words." A year later, Debs was venomous in his opposition. At Lawrence, Akron, and elsewhere, he argued, a simplistic emphasis on direct action coupled with bombastic rhetoric, careless organizing, and a desire to grandstand for the assembled reporters had resulted in devastating defeats for working people. These workers "were most basely betrayed, sold out and treacherously delivered to their enemies by the IWW Judases." Debs distinguished between industrial unionism and the "sabotage and direct action" the IWW encouraged and warned the labor movement to deal sharply with "this base and treacherous gang . . . when it projects itself into a local disturbance with professions of loyalty to labor upon its lying lips and treason to labor in its venal heart." [141]

Despite an isolated attempt to heal the wounds incurred in this fight, Debs remained angry.[142] The collapse of the IWW in Lawrence in 1913, and with it the rollback of the gains the strikers had won, fueled his anger. Debs blamed Haywood and other IWW leaders for eliciting and then misusing the deep commitment, sacrifices, and energies of these workers.[143] But it was Debs's experience in the 1912–13 West Virginia miners' strike that confirmed all of his worst fears concerning the nature of IWW organizing drives. The local miners, with the belated support of their state and national officials, struck in May 1912 when the coal operators in Kanawha County refused to sign a contract. The operators raised a private army to suppress the miners and the sympathetic governor, William E. Glasscock, declared martial law and sent in the state militia that September. As the strikers armed to defend themselves, the appeal of the IWW grew, especially as the Socialist party offered little initial aid. Arrested under the provisions of the martial law in February 1913, Mother Jones wrote a friend of her many "brave boys" currently in jail and bitterly protested the attitude of the Socialist party: "If Victor Berger or Hilford [Hillquit] or any of those or of their Jesus's was in here what a howl would go up. . . . The dear well fed socialists . . . can tell us what they are doing in the Balkan war or something that kind," but they "overlook the horrors at home."[144]

At first, Debs echoed Mother Jones's feelings. Following his appointment to a special party committee (along with Germer and Berger) to investigate the strike in May 1913, Debs wrote Germer that the party's delay was unconscionable: "Had it been Berger and Spargo in the bullpen instead of Mother Jones and John Brown," the national office "would not have waited."[145] When Debs arrived in West Virginia, however, the situation was even more complicated than he had thought. A newly elected governor, Henry Hatfield, had rescinded the martial law edict and promised the Socialist committee that UMWA and Socialist organizers would no longer be harassed by state troops. Under orders from the national party to attempt to repair relations with the UMWA, Debs was horrified at the antagonism that existed between the two groups. Socialists in the mine fields scorned the UMWA and advocated immediate insurgency by armed groups of miners; many openly endorsed the IWW. As one state Socialist leader told a group of Holly Grove miners in 1912, he had "become in recent years almost what they call a 'Haywoodite.' Some of my friends in the state say I must be removed from office because I believe in direct action." "Gentlemen," Harold Houston retorted, "I believe in action that gets results, and as Bill Haywood says, 'The more direct, the better.' " That this would stand in West Virginia and the nation as the primary contribution of the Socialist movement to the defense of one of the few unionized coal fields in the whole state incensed Debs. That these Socialists also undermined one of the few progressive industrial unions in the nation added to his fury.[146]

When the committee's report appeared, a storm of protest arose from the West Virginia militants. They accused Debs especially of selling out their cause, of heeding more the governor's promises than his comrades' experience, and of ignoring their needs in order to curry favor with "corrupt" national UMWA officials.[147] As descriptions of Debs's motivation or even of the unintended results of his report, these accusations are false. But for Debs they did mark the distance between his advocacy of industrial unionism and that of Haywood and those West Virginia Socialists who endorsed him. The attacks on the UMWA, the praise of direct action, and the loose talk of social revolution against the armed power of the state were at best infantile, destructive concepts to Debs. It was not that one should never attack an established union—Debs's record on that, even in relation to the UMWA, was quite clear. Rather, as he wrote to John Brown, it was "entirely a matter of tactics. . . . The way to keep reactionary trade union officials where they are is to attack them as Merrick has been doing and their followers adhere to them all the more closely." Directly blaming the Socialists for the angry responses from the UMWA leaders and even from the rank and file, Debs asked Brown "how could the U.M.W. men help but hate socialists if Merrick is a fair representative of the feeling of socialists toward their union? . . . The tactics they are pursuing in their mad denunciation of everything U.M.W., good, bad, and indifferent, are utterly suicidal and destructive all around."

Arguing that many West Virginia Socialists were "just enough for political action to cloak their anarchy," Debs feared that "the spirit of the Chicago I.W.W.ism" would destroy all organizations it touched, including the UMWA. "From my crown to my footsoles I am an industrial unionist," Debs reminded Brown, but "I am not an industrial anarchist." To attack the UMWA as Socialists did in West Virginia was "a suicidal, asinine and destructive act," performed "to the delight of the mine owners." Concluding his long letter, Debs etched the issue sharply: "You will find that sooner or later you will have to take your stand wholly with the Chicago I.W.W.ites or against them," for they will leave you with little choice.[148]

Following the expulsion of the IWW, the best opportunity in Debs's career to unify the Socialist movement and to re-orient the labor movement along industrial lines passed. Although Debs would continue to urge the unification of the Western Federation of Miners and the UMWA, increasingly there was less and less response from either Socialists or miners.[149] It would not be until a generation later, during the Great Depression, that a powerful industrial organization emerged.

The concerted efforts of employers nationwide helped to prevent this unity. From Terre Haute to Telluride and beyond, Citizens Protective Associations formed with the express intent of eliminating any union activity, even of the most moderate type. The judiciary, as in the late nineteenth century, was a most helpful ally. Injunctions appeared on corporate demand to break strikes and jail strikers, and the AFL reeled under the impact of two U.S. Supreme Court decisions that threatened its very existence.[150] As was so evident during the Pullman strike in 1894, corporate managers had easy access to state and federal troops and in the aftermath of Lawrence in 1912, Leadville and Butte in 1914, and numerous other strikes, it was working people who gathered at the grave, buried their dead, and sifted the ashes of their torched union halls and offices.

But Socialists also bore responsibility for this disunity. Berger and Hillquit consistently clung to their narrow approach to labor, even in the face of opposition from their own supporters. In Milwaukee, for example, delegates and members of the unions affiliated with Berger's own Federated Trades Council refused in 1905 to support the position of the Wisconsin State Federation of Labor, which condemned the newly founded IWW. Sixty percent of the delegates to the council looked forward to the IWW's development, and during the debate they argued that many of their members did as well. But it was Berger and the leaders of the council, using the enormous local economic and political power they possessed, who forced these skilled workers to rescind their vote and support the resolution.[151] Trailing after a bankrupt policy and following it with such severe blinders that they could not perceive important changes in the culture and attitudes of working people, Berger, Hillquit and their allies stringently limited Socialist options.

Debs's motivation differed from Berger's, but he, too, contributed to this condition. The power and force of his analysis after 1905 had its deepest roots in the call to fraternity among working people that in 1890 marked the turning point in his relations with the Brotherhood of Locomotive Firemen. Debs's fervent articulation of the mutual necessity of internal party democracy, unified industrial organization, and aggressive political agitation indicated the rich potential of a Socialist movement sensitive to American conditions. As Debs argued in 1911, "The union and the party must be managed and directed" by workers themselves—"*not from the top down, but from the bottom up.*"[152] While not even Debs expected his speeches to effect an immediate change, he did intend them to mark the path to be taken and to redirect his party's efforts toward that goal. This he failed to accomplish, in large part due to his own deficiencies as a national leader.

It would be tempting to suggest that Debs's commitment to a democratic process inhibited him from using his position of prominence to influence more directly the resolution of these issues. But this was not the case. As his correspondence suggests, he both understood the basic differences within the party and the need to air them publicly. This, despite repeated private declarations to the contrary, he refused to do. Yet it is these private declarations—especially to Warren and Thompson during 1910, 1911, and 1912—that contain the personal sources of Debs's persistent inability to confront such opponents as Berger. The tone of the letters over the years follows a consistent cyclical pattern: direct attacks on Berger, his dictatorial methods, and Socialist theory lead to a firm conviction to "face Berger" and confront him within the party. Invariably, some weeks or months later Debs backs off, claiming one or another party responsibility prevents him, at the moment, from entering the fray. Predictably, however, he points to another time in the near future when the circumstances will be right and the enemy engaged. But that time never comes as this cycle repeats itself. Beneath this maneuvering is Debs's anger at Berger. In part it is overtly political. In large part it is also personal and is at times indistinguishable from fear.

Throughout these letters Debs repeatedly refers back to his early Socialist years when Berger demanded Debs accept his tutelage. From Woodstock in 1895 through the contradictory directions Debs took under Berger's prodding during the negotiations that led to Socialist unity, Debs followed Berger while he seethed internally. Finally, as he told both Warren and Thompson, he privately confronted Berger and claimed his own manhood.[153] Not coincidentally, that confrontation marked the decline of their political relationship. As Debs aligned himself with labor movement militants, he created his own synthesis of Socialist theory and American values that differed in substance from Berger's.

Yet Berger retained a remarkable hold on Debs. More than a decade later, Debs recounted his "moment of manliness" vis-à-vis Berger with the immediacy of a far more recent event. While his continued anger had political roots, his letters also reveal that the basis of that anger remained a fear of Berger. As he had from their first association, Debs felt inadequate before Berger's formidable personality and seeming theoretical brilliance. Never one who relished conflict in personal terms, Debs feared that in a battle with Berger he would appear the fool. Worse yet, in such a battle, resolved perhaps through a national referendum, Debs might lose—the "machine" Debs decried was no mere figment of his imagination—and this possibility also checked Debs. As he had since his years with the Firemen, Debs avoided conflicts that would test his power with the rank and file. His own dependency on the recognition of his honored and special position cautioned him, if unconsciously, in such contexts.

Debs was more comfortable in the role of a national figure of importance, and his lack of leadership in serious disputes had important effects. By not helping to create more favorable relations between the party and the IWW, Debs inadvertently encouraged Haywood and his supporters to further excesses. The issue of direct action still separated Debs from the IWW, but the persistent hostility of Socialist leaders to any policy that deviated from their official commitment to the AFL created an insurmountable barrier to a more fruitful discussion. More poignantly, this lack of leadership left Debs personally and politically in the embrace of Berger. "Furthermore," Debs wrote his old nemesis in August 1912 in reference to the Barnes affair, "I favor putting an end to Hillquitism, which has become synonymous with bossism. In addition to his desire to be a dictator extraordinary, Hillquit . . . in many other ways has conclusively proved himself to be the proverbial bull in the china shop. When the term of the New York attorney, as a member of the Executive Committee, expires, I strongly favor his retirement to the ranks where he can do fully as much good and infinitely less harm than in his present capacity."[154] This latest sally of Debs's could only have caused Berger to chortle.

It was not as if Debs had no other options, but this attempt to enlist one longtime enemy to battle another, all the while suppressing his awareness of the close personal and political relationship between his two antagonists, seems pathetic. Debs might have insisted that the very diversity of the Socialist movement demanded, given a firm commitment to internal democracy, a multiplicity of tactical approaches. He might have followed his own advice and demanded room within the party to "bore from within and without" the established trade unions. This would have given the industrial unionists the opening they required while acknowledging the importance of Berger's own organizing efforts. Further, in any open, principled fight over internal party democracy, even Berger and Hillquit would have been hard pressed to defend their autocratic role. Moreover, what options did Berger and Hillquit have? Had Debs called Berger's bluff to bolt the party, he might have discovered just how shallow a bluff it was. Berger needed the national movement for his own sense of importance and as the arena to display his theoretical virtuosity. More important, as Berger had understood since 1896, the Milwaukee leader needed Debs—as did Hillquit and every other national leader. Debs was, in the public image, *the* national Socialist movement. An American-born radical with a powerful appeal to Americans of different class and ethnic backgrounds, Debs could bridge the regional differences and represent a unified and diversified Socialist movement.

But Debs refused. Fearful of exposing his own prestige to possible criticism and woefully insecure before the vaunted intellectual pretensions of other party leaders, Debs desisted. It was with an almost audible sigh of relief that he took to the road to start the 1912 campaign and to assume the more comfortable mantle as the embodiment of the Socialist spirit. Above the fray, checkmated by his desire to remain there, Debs reveled in the tremendous reception he received on the campaign trail and in the voting booth that November.

9

Arise, Comrade Debs

THE SEVEN YEARS BETWEEN the campaign of 1912 and the return to peacetime "normalcy" following World War I were eventful years for both Eugene Debs and the Socialist movement. Despite the encouraging election results in 1912, the movement reeled time and again during these years from repeated shocks to its system. The continued struggle to define the meaning of industrial unionism took its toll, but other issues were more threatening. The regional nature of the Socialist movement, reflecting both the uneven development of American industrial capitalism and the vast ethnic and religious heterogeneity of American working people, remained an obstacle to national party unity. The effects of World War I heightened these tensions. The capitulation of European Socialists to the nationalist fervor in their respective countries in August 1914 and their consequent denial of international working-class solidarity not only provided the bodies of male workers for the trenches but also undermined the faith in Socialism's inevitability worldwide. The entry of the United States into the conflict in 1917 deepened the problems for American Socialists. Much like a last minute reprieve, however, the Bolshevik Revolution late in 1917 seemed at first to restore hope in Socialism's ultimate victory. Yet the effect of this external event on the American movement was quite the opposite. Birthed in the social upheaval of a war-torn land, the Russian Revolution proved to be unexportable, but not before attempts to do just that ravaged the American Socialist movement.

For Debs, these were perhaps the most trying years of his Socialist career. The battle over the IWW was but a prelude to the bitter factional strife these years would bring. The twin issues of war and revolution would force him to draw on his deepest resources in efforts to maintain both his faith in Socialism and the semblance of a national Socialist organization. Beyond these specific issues, moreover, a deeper, more profound crisis awaited Debs. The reaction of American workers and of his comrades in the movement to these dramatic events compelled him to confront the meaning and relevancy of his life's work, and this inner struggle contrasted sharply with his public confidence. For, as in the past, it was to Debs that comrades of all factions turned in search for a national symbol who might embody the cause. But the years of travel finally caught up with him. Frequently sick, he suffered three serious collapses during these years and was often paralyzed in spirit and body.

In 1912, however, none of this was evident. Indeed, the optimism that fueled Debs and his supporters seemed for once justified as greater numbers of Americans than ever before anticipated pulling the Socialist lever in the November elections.

In June 1912 Debs opened his campaign in Riverside Park, Chicago. Following a nearly total collapse the preceding spring, Debs had been under the care of an osteopathic physician at Girard,[1] but his energy and intensity were evident as he brought the crowd to its feet time and again. "The workers have never yet developed or made use of their political power," he told them. Unable for so long to break from the hold of the traditional political parties, many now, "disgusted with their own blind and stupid performance," rejected all political activity, including Socialism. But, Debs insisted, the Socialist party is "organized and financed by the workers themselves as a means of wresting control of government and of industry from the capitalists and making the working class the ruling class of the nation and the world." Attempting to maintain a balance between the viciously contending factions within the party, Debs both defended the party's endorsement of immediate demands, since the Socialist revolution "cannot be achieved in a day," and warned all to "never for a moment [mistake] reform for revolution and never [lose] sight of the ultimate goal." Debs stressed the need for a "revolutionary industrial unionism" that would enable workers to develop "their latent abilities [and] their knowledge" to prepare them "for mastery and control of industry."[2]

A month later in Milwaukee, before a giant rally in Pabst Park, Debs adjusted the tone of his speech. Emphasizing the appeal of the Socialist party in contrast to the traditional parties, he spent much of the talk attacking the Progressive party candidate, Theodore Roosevelt. Only toward the end did Debs raise potentially divisive issues. Urging the Milwaukee workers to form "closer and closer . . . bonds of economic and political solidarity," Debs weaved praise of Victor Berger with an endorsement of industrial unionism and a fervent defense of Joseph Ettor and Arturo Giovannitti, IWW organizers on trial for murder as a result of their activities during the Lawrence textile strike. *"Comrades,"* Debs concluded, striking the theme of unity once again, *"this is our year."*[3]

Across the country, Debs elicited great hopes. He remained, one western comrade remarked, "the greatly beloved Comrade of old and the entire trip is a continuous ovation." Further east, the process of capitalist development that aided the 1911 Socialist victory in St. Marys, Ohio, appeared to spread. Before the campaign one small businessman and poultry farmer in Custar, Ohio, wrote the U.S. attorney general a bitter letter. He had not voted once in the past decade, U. E. Loy informed George W. Wickersham, "just because there was no difference in the 2 old Parties, nothing to vote for, except Pools and Monopolies. . . . But thank god, there is going to be a change, and it is coming fast to; and you can bet, that us Farmers out this way, and there are quite a few of us, are going to do all we can to get the other man ediguated [*sic*] to Socialism, and we are making scores of them too." Throughout that state the "Ohio Yell" boomed the message and mixed campaign fervor with a wry factional message:

> Ripsaw, ripsaw, ripsaw, bang!
> We belong to the Gene Debs' gang.
> Are we Socialists? I should smile!
> We're Revolutionists all the while.[4]

In New York City Socialists hosted a massive rally that drew 22,000 people to Madison Square Garden. After rousing speeches by Debs, gubernatorial candidate Charles E. Russell, and others, the pitch of excitement gripped even those on the platform. Russell impulsively hugged and kissed Debs, who responded enthusiastically. They then both embraced Lucien Sanial, the aging former leader of the Socialist Labor party. It was, as Debs noted at the start of the campaign, "a year with supreme possibilities."[5]

The results of the 1912 election met these expectations. The Socialists doubled their 1908 total as nearly 900,000 Americans marked the Socialist column. Impressive alone, these figures contained additional significance as well. The Socialist vote in 1912 constituted 6 percent of the national presidential vote. Far short of a majority, this percentage, however, did mark the highest level ever recorded by a national Socialist candidate, and it confirmed for many that Socialism was emerging as a powerful political force in American society. Roosevelt's presence in the campaign made this argument especially convincing. Many of his supporters were thought to be Socialists-in-the-making, and it was not inconceivable that, four years hence, the Socialist percentage of the national vote might again double.

Even Woodrow Wilson, the Democratic candidate, ran on a reform platform of sorts. When the inadequacies of both the Progressive and Democratic party programs became obvious, Socialists argued, former supporters would flock to the Socialist party. Although less impressive than 1911, local Socialist electoral success in 1912 encouraged this analysis. Eight more cities elected Socialist officials, and an additional twenty Socialists took seats in their state legislatures.[6]

After years of struggle and difficulty, the Socialist moment of exultation was sweet indeed. But a closer analysis of these results would have revealed a need for caution. In 1912 the trans-Mississippi southern and western states accounted for almost one-third of the national Socialist vote and constituted the most vital and energetic regional section of the party. An examination of the leading state Socialist organizations in 1904 and 1912 (both years that witnessed a doubling of the vote over the preceding national election) suggests the specific dimensions of this shift. Third in 1904, Ohio led the nation in 1912 with over 90,000 Socialist votes and increased its share of state ballots cast from 3 to 8 percent. Supportive of the leftist faction in party disputes, many Ohio comrades agreed more with Socialists in the West than with those in Wisconsin.[7] New York, second in 1904 (and first in 1908), dropped to fifth in 1912, with 4 percent of the state's ballots. Given Berger's domineering national presence, the Wisconsin results were most revealing. Fifth in 1904, the Wisconsin Socialists ranked ninth in 1912. While they increased the percentage of the total vote from 6 to 8 percent, the small increase reflected a decline of 12 percent in all ballots cast in 1912. The Socialist vote did not increase dramatically. Concentrated in specific Milwaukee wards, these comrades achieved a certain local electoral success but by 1912 lacked the vigor of other state Socialist movements.

Outvoting Wisconsin were states with whom Berger had little in common. Oklahoma placed sixth in 1912, doubling both its Socialist vote and its percentage of the popular vote (from 8 to 16 percent) over 1908, that state's first presidential election. Washington state, thirteenth in 1904, now ranked seventh. A center of leftist agitation and IWW activity, Washington Socialists tripled their 1904 totals and doubled, from 6 to 12 percent, their portion of the popular vote. Fourth in both 1904 and 1912, California Socialists nearly tripled their vote in 1912 as they increased their share of all ballots cast from 8 to 12 percent. Even Indiana, never a center of Socialist strength, pulled ahead of Wisconsin in 1912 with almost 37,000 votes and raised its popular percentage from 2 to 6 percent.[8]

The Indiana vote remained something of an aberration, but the regional shift in Socialist voting strength was not. Western and southwestern Socialists lived at the cutting edge of the class struggle. In the mines of Montana, Minnesota, and Utah, the forests of Washington and Oregon, and the tenant farm regions of Texas and Oklahoma, demands for better conditions, union recognition, and on occasion the right to exercise traditional political liberties encountered fierce opposition and in places a brutal and violent repression directed by resident managers and the local business community in alliance with police and state militia officials. In contrast, Socialists in more settled areas, while often engaged in bitter struggle, discovered a wider range of possible accommodation with capitalism. A Washington lumberjack had little immediate understanding of or sympathy with his New York Jewish comrades as they approved the famous 1910 "Protocol of Peace," which brought Socialist trade unionists and garment industry employers together on a joint arbitration board.[9] This uneven pace of industrial development and basic ethnic and religious differences kept the movement off-balance, with different regions somewhat out of step with each other in their understanding of capitalist reality and Socialist strategy.[10]

This shifting geographical division within the movement aggravated tensions among Socialists, especially as national leadership remained essentially in eastern Socialist hands. When, in 1913, Kate Richards O'Hare, an Oklahoma Socialist popularly identified with the left, won election over opposition from Berger and Morris Hillquit to the International Socialist Bureau, Berger scoffed in disgust. "She will make [the Socialist party] ridiculous," he wrote Hillquit, "but by doing so she will just represent the exact state of our American movement." Charles Maurer of Pennsylvania also deplored the Socialist consciousness of many, especially the western comrades who had enthusiastically supported Bill Haywood. While a few possessed "a fair conception of the class struggle," the majority, Maurer thought, "have a very superficial knowledge of Socialist fundamentals. These are the dangerous members."[11] Debs sought to bridge this growing gap and remind all of the great victory they had won in 1912. Stressing the need to "unite for our common good," he suggested in 1913 that the two major factions that emerged from the Haywood battle, " 'the reds' and 'the yellows,' " shared basic principles. The Socialist party was weak and misguided in a number of ways, he wrote, but it remained "the most vital force in the class struggle" and thus required support: "It is only when we unite and work together in the true spirit of socialism that we can do the best and overcome the worst there is in us."[12]

Such appeals, however, were made in vain, and Socialist party membership began to decline. More than 22,000 members left the party between December 1912 and December 1913, another 2,500 during 1914, and over 4,000 in 1915. On the eve of Wilson's preparedness campaign, the program that eased America into World War I, the Socialist party counted less than 80,000 members.[13] The strength of the broader movement also seemed suspect. In the 1914 off-year elections the Socialist vote plummeted nationwide. Wisconsin dropped 22 percent from 1912, Washington and California 25 percent, and Illinois, Michigan, and Pennsylvania over 50 percent. A comparison of the results in 1910 and 1914, both non-presidential election years, also did not prove encouraging. While New York elected Socialist Meyer London to Congress, the Ohio vote fell by 18 percent, Pennsylvania by 25 percent, and Wisconsin by 33 percent.[14]

Some sought to explain this turnabout with reference to actions the party might have taken. Factional opponents in the Haywood fight, for example, blamed each other, and charges of toadyism toward the AFL clashed with countercharges of IWW impossibilism. Another influential analysis emphasized capitalism's fearful reaction to Socialism's recent success. In St. Marys, Ohio, for example, Mayor Scott Wilkens found that local industrialists used every means possible to hinder his administration. Deprived of control of the police, the city's employers hired thugs to disrupt meetings of organizing workers and then paid the legal fees when they were arrested. Employers refused to bond the Socialist city treasurer and fired elected Socialist officials and their public supporters. Local bankers used every possible excuse to foreclose on the mortgages held by these Socialists. Not surprisingly, the movement in St. Marys soon petered out, unable to defend itself against the onslaught.[15]

But questions of party tactics and leadership or capitalist repression, while important, did not fully explain the Socialist predicament. Had Debs worked more systematically within the party to assure a place in the broad Socialist movement for the IWW, it is not at all clear that the ultimate results would have been any different. Debs and his comrades still had to face their marginal appeal among American workers, skilled or unskilled, organized or not. Even in 1912, when Socialists captured one-third of the vote in their continuing effort to unseat Samuel Gompers as president of the AFL, those ballots did not indicate a corresponding high level of rank-and-file support of Socialism. Similarly, while repression of Socialists had an effect, the absence of widespread and sustained protest against such actions suggests something of the limits of Socialism's appeal. The cause of the Socialist decline, embedded in the very heart of their 1912 success, lay rather in the perception of American political traditions held by working people themselves.

The expectation that reform movements would develop Socialist voters over time, an attitude shared by Socialists and Roosevelt alike,[16] proved misguided. While Socialist candidates profited from the reform unrest, the majority of voters who did break from the traditional parties stopped short of the Socialist ticket. In California, for example, the working-class wards in both San Francisco and Los Angeles shifted toward the Progressive party, and especially its U.S. Senator, Hiram Johnson, between

1910 and 1914. But the majority stopped there and felt no contradiction between their status as workers and their refusal to pull the Socialist lever.[17] The attraction to reform varied in workers' wards nationally, but nowhere was there a simple equation between a reform tendency and ultimate Socialist advocacy. Further, it must be remembered that many workers never even broke from the traditional parties. As one Clay County, Indiana, Socialist coal miner mourned decades later, remembering his hero: "Poor old Debs! . . . The people wouldn't vote for him the way they should have. He told people the truth, but they went on voting Democrat and Republican."[18]

Many Socialists never delved deeply into this apparent contradiction, preferring instead to repeat the belief that a Socialist victory was inevitable. But some did. In his 1917 report to the party Adolph Germer, a former mine worker and then the party's national secretary, sought a more thorough explanation. Quickly passing over the effect of the party's own factional disputes, Germer argued that the American political system itself, evidenced in the continued support it received from workers, had proven far more adaptable than Socialists had previously considered. The politicians of the old parties had successfully adjusted their rhetoric and even, to an extent, their programs to demands for reform without losing control. The assumed connection between reform and Socialism was becoming, therefore, highly debatable.[19]

Germer attempted to retain hope with appeals for renewed effort, but he unwittingly echoed the more pessimistic 1906 view of H. G. Wells. Impressed and disturbed by the "boss system of American politics," Wells thought that it nonetheless remained the only alternative to direct corporate control. Ultimately, in exchange for political loyalty, this system provided a series of essential services especially to the working class and immigrant poor of the cities. In the power of that alliance, Wells suggested, "resides the impossibility of socialism in America—as the case for socialism is put at present." Wells pushed his perceptive analysis further. The nature of this alliance was one critical support for the broad ideological hegemony that permeated American culture. Socialists might appeal to American values and emphasize, as Debs did continually, the collective responsibility at the heart of the American experiment. In times of crisis Socialism might well have its appeal. But even among workers it would remain an alien concept for most, an idea tainted by its European origins and perceived as contrary to American ideals. Following Alexis de Tocqueville, an earlier European critic of America, Wells also understood that the majoritarian democracy that characterized American society allowed for little sustained dissent. As another British observer noted a few years before Wells, the "unpopularity of Socialism in the United States, when presented under that name, is greatly to be regretted."[20]

If America's ideological atmosphere was not encouraging to Socialists, the limited successes they did achieve compounded rather than eased the problem they faced. In a remarkable letter to Carl Thompson in 1913 Walter Lippmann, the former secretary to Socialist Mayor George Lunn of Schenectady, explored the problems and pitfalls of municipal Socialist efforts. "The road to Socialism may be in our theoretical text-books," Lippmann warned, but "there is nothing inevitable about the tactics of to-day and tomorrow." Briefly reviewing his break with the Lunn administration, he argued that in Schenectady and nationally the problem with municipal Socialism "can be stated quite simply on one very important issue: The economic policy of the administration." In Schenectady as elsewhere Socialists came to power in 1911 supported by important segments of the working class, in large part on the promise not to raise taxes. This essentially reformist policy seriously undercut any hopes for a true Socialist administration, Lippmann commented, for at the core of that tax policy was an inability to effect even a modest distribution of wealth. "On the crucial question of whether the administration would cut deeper into the returns on privilege," Lippmann concluded, "Schenectady said no. And because of that, political action in Schenectady must be ineffective." Sensitive to the elastic boundaries of American politics, Lippmann thought the greatest problem faced by Socialists was to remain "clearly distinguished from progressives." Given the success of reformist measures to both to middle-class and working-class voters, he urged Socialists "to work at once to map out a set of immediate demands far more radical than anything the Progressives had accepted. If the reformers could go that far, it was clearly our business to move ahead." The Socialist vote would be smaller, Lippmann argued, but purer. But if the movement could not distinguish itself from reform, he predicted, it would prove that "our magnificent pictures of the future are the idle dreams of incompetent men."[21]

Lippmann sharply caught one horn of the American Socialist dilemma. He soon solved it for himself by leaving the party for the Progressive movement, but the problem remained for his former comrades. Even where a Socialist ticket achieved electoral success with important working-class support, the attraction to reform measures remained. How to present Socialism to a society at once individualistic, anxious over emerging class distinctions, and yet resistant to a permanent class consciousness, continued as the paramount problem of Socialism. As the power of the traditional political symbols persisted, some Socialists saw a solution in Lippmann's call for "far more radical" action. Already evident in the battle with Haywood, this tendency, which as a Socialist Lippmann explicitly disavowed, ultimately assumed that workers were far more revolutionary than they were. In the hands of leftist critics and the increasingly militant immigrant Socialist organizations of the Finns, Russians, and Slavs, this call for radical action led to a deification of the Russian Revolution in 1917, a final sundering of the Socialist movement in 1919, and a continued inability to comprehend American reality.

But there was no simple alternative course. The vast ethnic and religious heterogeneity of the country worked to reinforce the sense of Socialism as "un-American." While exploitation was often severe, many immigrants nonetheless viewed American conditions favorably when they were contrasted with their immediate European pasts. American industry had a pronounced labor shortage during much of the late nineteenth and early twentieth centuries, and consequently wages were high relative to Europe. This, in turn, encouraged a belief in the potential for opportunity. These conditions did not prevent immigrants or American-born workers from engaging in serious labor struggles, but they did contribute to the signal unwillingness of the majority of American workers to consider a fundamental restructuring of their society. It was not so much that America was the proverbial promised land but rather that in the promise of America lay a path to a modicum of success. This expectation permeated the culture and affected native and immigrant alike, much as it had influenced Debs's own development.

Neither Debs nor his comrades were able to resolve this dilemma. Debs's integration of American thought with Socialist theory remains the most attractive strand within twentieth-century America's radical tradition. With pride Debs frequently identified himself as "a citizen, a working man." Yet he constantly encountered working-class American citizens who embraced those same terms but gave them a meaning antagonistic to Socialism. Debs understood that he was engaged in a struggle to define the social meaning of these terms, and his references to the founding fathers, the abolitionists, Populists, and other American dissenters sought to place his understanding within an indigenous historical context. Socialist agitators did not act alone, these repeated references implied, but rather proudly stood with and acted in the memory of those earlier dissenters who represented the best of an American tradition.

But Debs and American Socialists of all persuasions found themselves outflanked by men such as Wilson, Roosevelt, and scores of lesser known editorialists, politicians, and pundits. Repeatedly these people argued that Socialism was "un-American" and pointed to a "New Freedom," a "New Nationalism," or some other new entity as the solution to the unrest in American society. In this struggle for cultural hegemony Debs and his supporters were simply overpowered. The majority of Americans, and the majority of American working people, rejected Socialism as "un-American." That this label was fraudulent, as applied to the Debsian Socialist movement, is obvious, but the combined influence of the Wilsons and the Roosevelts, greatly aided by a political culture that saw in American institutions as they were the promise of the future, dominated the battle for cultural hegemony. In a society that instinctively termed any critical dissent "un-American," American Socialists had a problem with image from the beginning.

Leftist critics in Debs's time and since have suggested that his particular adaptation of Karl Marx and American political thought was reformist and have argued that this lack of orthodox Marxism in large part accounts for the failure of Socialism in America. Others have merged this critique with an analysis of the repressive capabilities of the corporate-governmental alliance. Yet in each instance the supporting assumptions are questionable. As Debs frequently noted, American workers were not, merely as a result of their relationship to the means of production, *ipso facto* revolutionary or possessed of even a rudimentary class consciousness. As he himself had learned, and as others did as well at Pullman, Coeur d'Alene, and in the Oklahoma farm country, the task of affirming a collective identity in a culture that boasted of its individualistic mores was difficult indeed. Debs and his comrades broadened, for a time at least, the boundaries of political discourse and ignited for many a renewed critical understanding of America's traditions. But despite the very stark class formation that accompanied industrial capitalism, the recognition of that development—the emergence of a corresponding class awareness—proved to be anything but inevitable. Debs's ability to stand within the "patriotic and religious" culture that Frank Bohn mistrusted and from that source to emphasize the reality of class in America marks the potency of his agitation, even as it simultaneously records the power of the dominant ideology.

In a fundamental way neither Debs nor the American Socialist movement failed. That they were not victorious is evident, but in an important fashion both Debsian Socialists and later interpreters posited the wrong question. Failure assumes the possibility of success, but that was never a serious prospect for the Debsian movement. Had Debs, for example, fought with greater determination to carve a place within the party for the IWW, the effects could have been important and perhaps have strengthened the tenuous relations that existed between the party and American workers. But it would not have been a prelude to revolution. As Debs repeatedly stated in his best moments, there was no shortcut to political or economic power, especially given the influence of the dominant culture on working people themselves. As all Americans would rediscover during World War I, their society was not a tolerant one. Rather, as conservative Appellate Court Justice Learned Hand wrote in 1920, "it is a country where you are expected to conform and if you don't you are looked on with suspicion."[22]

This was the reality that Socialists and radicals encountered. Although their faith in the inevitable emergence of class consciousness blinded many to the very complex and conservative society they faced, in their struggle rather than solely in the outcome lies the greater part of the movement's continued relevance. As the concluding segment of a long struggle that spanned numerous movements and many decades during the emergence of a mature industrial capitalist system, Debs and his comrades sought to recall their fellow citizens to the best in their common tradition. In their courage, if not always their programs, these men and women gave to those who would follow a powerful example.[23]

Debs finished the 1912 campaign in poor health. The many years on the road had taken their toll on the fifty-seven-year-old Socialist leader. Known to comrades across the country as a heavy drinker who enjoyed raucous reunions, prolonged conversations, and occasional visits to a brothel while maintaining an intense speaking schedule, Debs appeared visibly weakened in the years after 1912.[24] Although frequently bedridden, Debs tried to address the major problems of the growing war hysteria and the party's response as first Europe and then America plunged into world war.

Debs took to his bed immediately following the campaign. While the election results were encouraging, a telegram he received from Girard, Kansas, a week later obliterated any joy he felt. On 10 November 1912, after returning home from a movie, J. A. Wayland, former editor and still publisher of the *Appeal to Reason*, committed suicide by shooting himself through the mouth. Stunned and devastated, the ailing Debs was too sick to travel to Girard to deliver the funeral oration. Along with comrades across the nation, however, he tried to understand why Wayland took his life. It was common knowledge that Wayland had been deeply depressed for over a year since his wife had been killed while riding in a car he drove. But for Debs and others, Wayland's brief suicide note remained troubling. "The struggle under the competitive system is not worth the effort," Wayland wrote in his last editorial. "Let it pass." Personally and politically Debs found it an ominous finale to the most successful Socialist campaign in American history.[25]

Despite his adherence to special milk diets to purge his system and continued osteopathic treatment in Terre Haute, Debs's health remained fragile through the spring and summer of 1913. In September a complete physical and emotional collapse forced Debs to cancel another western tour. Instead, he went to Estes Park, Colorado, on 1 October and remained at the sanitarium there until late November.[26] It took Debs over a month to realize just how sick he was. He told Theodore in mid-November that he now understood that "had I waited a year longer [to recuperate] I would have been a wreck beyond repair."[27]

But the mountain air, the healthy food, the physical exercise, and the spa's social activities rejuvenated Debs. At a friend's cabin after dinner one night, a makeshift band formed and played such favorites as "Turkey in the Straw," "Marching through Georgia," "Arkansas Traveller," and "When Johnny Comes Marching Home." For Debs the evening was a sheer delight. Dressed in corduroys and boots and with a fresh pipe dangling from his lips, Gene "laughed and clapped my hands with the enthusiasm of a kid. It was an old fashion treat to warm the heart . . . and make old men boys again." Soon after this evening Debs left Estes Park to visit friends in Denver. While there he spoke to a strike meeting of miners and did not return to Terre Haute until just before Christmas. At that point, he wrote Hillquit, he felt he needed six more weeks of quiet before returning to his work full time. "My life would be reduced to but a few days," he confessed to Hillquit, "if it were not for socialism and for the little use I may be to the movement."[28]

After this confrontation with his own mortality, Debs characteristically ignored the lessons it might have taught. In part, he was driven by economic needs that could only be met by touring. But as he also admitted to Hillquit, he felt restless and depressed over prolonged absences from the public platform. With his ties to the *Appeal* broken by the dispute with Fred Warren and with Wayland's suicide, Debs gladly accepted in early 1914 a good financial offer to tour for the *National Rip-Saw*, a St. Louis-based Socialist paper that included Kate Richards O'Hare, Oscar Ameringer, and Phil Wagner on its staff. In February he began his first tour under the *Rip-Saw*'s auspices and quickly fell back into his old patterns. Long speeches night after night, spiced with reunions with comrades and friends, followed by the incessant travel—it was all familiar. In Texas that September, for example, Debs rose at 2:30 A.M. to catch his train and changed cars at 5:00 A.M. to arrive at his destination in mid-morning. Leaving that afternoon, he switched cars five more times in order to reach Pittsburg, Kansas, in time for an evening meeting the following day. As he still agreed to travel to rural areas as well as major cities, rail transportation was frequently his most comfortable mode of travel. Following a meeting in Pocatello, Idaho, in 1915, the nearly sixty-year-old Socialist leader traveled seventeen miles "over almost impossible roads" by carriage to the train spur that would take him to his next meeting at Burley, Idaho—only to find that the train had already left.[29]

Increased physical strain was not the only new element in these tours. The internal party battles had created a subtle change in Debs's speeches as well. Debs now muted his criticism of other party leaders, although he remained disturbed by the direction of the party. He still advocated industrial unionism and urged the Western Federation of Miners and the UMWA to unite and leave the AFL, but even he sensed that the moment had passed. "It was plain," a Seattle Socialist noted in 1915 following Debs's routine endorsement of industrial unionism, that "he was only speaking figuratively and not with the intention of attempting to break up the present unions." A year later, when pressed by the editor of *La Parola Proletaria*, the Italian Socialist Federation's leftist weekly, to specify whether his continued insistence on industrial unionism should lead Socialists to join the IWW, create a new industral union, or work within the AFL, Debs rejected all three alternatives. Somewhat limply, he talked of the necessity of educational agitation among workers to encourage industrial unionism. The Haywood dispute had taken its toll.[30]

Instead, Debs emphasized a critique of capitalism that stressed the inevitability of Socialism while it avoided specific reference to divisive issues. "The trouble is that the Republican, Democratic and Progressive parties are but the subdivisions of the capitalist system," he told a Nashville crowd in 1914. Of the four major parties in the 1912 campaign, Debs reminded his audience, only the Socialist party had doubled its vote over 1908. "You may hasten Socialism," he insisted, "you may retard it, but you cannot stop it. It is inevitable." But Debs knew that the party had serious difficulties in 1914. Socialism was still "unpopular in America," he told his Nashville supporters, "because a new idea is always an unwelcome intruder. . . . It takes a man of great moral courage to step from a majority into a minority." Appealing to his most deeply held cultural symbol, Debs explored the historical context of that moral courage. The American Revolution "was started by men who refused to drift with the majority . . . but in the pages of history the names of George Washington, of Thomas Jefferson and of Patrick Henry will always shine resplendent." This example of struggle against overwhelming odds encouraged him, for despite the difficulties he believed "the logic of capitalism" was daily increasing the ranks of the Socialist movement.[31]

In August 1914 the outbreak of World War I forced Debs to address another issue that threatened to destroy his basic optimism. The war dealt a savage blow to hopes for international Socialist and worker solidarity. In Germany, France, Britain, and throughout the continent, European Socialists voted for military appropriations, defended nationalism, and encouraged their members to enlist in their nation's army. With America not yet a belligerent, Debs could avoid for a time such decisions, but he worried about the effects the obvious American sympathies for the Allies would have on the Socialist movement. "Despotism in autocratic Russia, monarchic Germany and republican America," he wrote in 1914, "is substantially the same in its effect upon the working class."[32] Trying to shore up his American comrades, who were stunned by the denial of the "inevitable march" of international Socialism by the Europeans, Debs supported efforts to present to President Wilson a plan to end the hostilities.[33]

In his speeches during 1914 and early 1915 Debs focused his audience's attention on the curtailment of democratic freedoms that war hysteria would induce and repeatedly condemned the capitalist nature of the war. In a concise summation of many speeches, Debs wrote that he had "no country to fight for; my country is the earth; I am a citizen of the world." Stressing the class nature of the struggle, Debs exclaimed: "I am not a capitalist soldier; I am a proletarian revolutionist. . . . I am opposed to every war but one; I am for that war with heart and soul, and that is the world-wide war of the social revolution. In that way, I am prepared to fight in any way the ruling class may make necessary, even to the barricades."[34] While Debs's embrace of violent resistance remained rhetorical (as it had in his stirring 1906 defense of Haywood, Charles Moyer and George Pettibone, "Arouse Ye Slaves"),[35] his perception of the difficulties ahead for Socialists, and for all Americans, led him to redouble again his own efforts.

Debs's mounting of the barricades—or the platform—would have to wait. In 1915 America was not at war, but, even if it were, Debs's role would have been minimal. In the spring of that year he suffered his second major collapse in less than two years. Bedridden for over six weeks with painfully torn leg muscles, congestion, and physical exhaustion, Debs relied on "large doses of morphine" to keep him "from going frantic." So critical was his condition, Theodore wrote, "that his doctor asked for a conference. He suffered terribly. It was the first time I ever heard him groan." In mid-June Eugene appeared stronger but remained at a sanitarium to rebuild his broken health.[36]

Somewhat recovered by fall, Debs resumed a limited schedule of speaking engagements—but now he zealously guarded against further depleting his strength.[37] More and more he stayed home in Terre Haute, but this enforced domesticity did not significantly alter the relationship with his wife. Although the scope of his travels was far more circumscribed than in the past, Debs's relative good health propelled him "on the road" and away from North 8th Street once again. Daily he went to the office he and Theodore maintained on Main Street, answered correspondence, and wrote articles. Whether at home or the office, he received a continual flood of visitors from near and far. As long as Debs was in town, they were assured of a hearty reception. Particularly galling to Kate's sensibilities was her husband's habit of encouraging local friends, bar owners, brothel operators, and restaurateurs to visit on the front porch. One such friend, Anthony Rieber, a restaurant owner whose mistress was a famous madam who ran "The Bucket of Blood" (a nearby brothel catering to working-

class men), remembered that "Gene never reprimanded me for my participation in the life of the demi-monde and we exchanged many ribald
jokes" concerning Terre Haute's extensive "Red Light" district. While
Debs "did jump on me all spraddled out" for supporting the Democratic
party (his mistress's uncle was the party boss for the district), Rieber
recalled that Debs must have "had some intimate experiences with the
habitues of the demi-monde," for he had so many good friends among
them. The only thing that might have upset Kate more than Rieber's
presence on the porch was her husband's return visits to the bars and
brothels of his friends.[38]

Debs's frequent bouts with sickness and pain kept him at home, but they
did not silence his pen. In 1916, with the war fever growing, Debs worried
about the state of the party. "For some years," he noted, there had been a
tendency "to obscure the class character of the party to make it more ac-
ceptable to the middle class."[39] With few illusions about the revolutionary
potential of American workers, Debs nonetheless maintained his long-held
belief that Socialist agitation must point the way toward a stronger collective identity and eschew mere vote-getting techniques. The specter of war
underscored his concern. Despite this belief, it was impossible for Debs to
consider another presidential campaign as the effort would have killed
him. But he felt that the crisis was stark, that the class war was "raging
with unusual intensity," and that his place was at the battlefront. The
comrades, he felt, expected this of him. He was the central American symbol of resistance to capitalism, and frequently they reminded Debs of his
responsibilities. "Let your voice go, go everywhere, in every town and
city, go to the heart of all the workers," Carlo Tresca wrote from jail in
1916 during the bitter Mesabi Range strike in Minnesota. In his first attempt to write in English, this Italian-born IWW organizer ignored past
factional differences and struck at the heart of the matter: "Help, Gene!
You are the heart, the brain of the worker in America and your voice is the
voice of labor. Not make difference what will be, in this fight, the consequence for me and my fellowworkers in cell, arise, comrade Debs, arise the
workers and let them realize the necessity of the stand, one for all and all
for one."[40]

Debs never considered running for president in 1916, and the Socialist
party nominated Allan Benson in his place. But deeply moved by appeals
such as Tresca's—especially since they reflected his own vision of his
political role—Debs agreed to run for Congress from the Fifth District of
Indiana. Covering six counties, the Fifth was a heterogeneous area. Surrounding the major city of Terre Haute were nearly 10,000 coal miners
organized into the UMWA; a rural population of over 24,000; noticeable
concentrations of Germans and Italians; and, in Hendricks and Putnam
counties, a dominant Quaker influence. Debs campaigned with great

energy, toured the district in an auto caravan, and attracted national attention. For the party, it was an important race. As Noble Wilson, Debs's campaign manager, explained, "This is a national fight. 'Gene will be as much the representative of the working class of the nation as he will of the Fifth District of Indiana." The party sent nationally known speakers into the district, as well as such international luminaries as James Larkin of Ireland and Madame Aleksandra Kollontai of Russia. Debs ran a good race but finished a distant second to his Republican opponent.[41]

It was during this campaign or in the months immediately following that Debs and Mabel Dunlap Curry began their intense decade-long relationship. A native of Franklin, Indiana, Mabel Curry was the mother of three children. Her husband, Charles, had been a professor of English at Indiana State Normal in Terre Haute since before 1900. The Currys resided a few blocks from the Debs home, and they knew each other socially to some extent, for in 1916 Charles Curry, a political conservative, publicly praised Debs's personal character while carefully avoiding any endorsement of his neighbor's political position.[42]

Exactly how Debs and Mabel Curry first met remains unknown, but clearly she was attracted to him, and vice versa. An energetic public advocate for women's suffrage, Curry was an accomplished speaker on the Chautauqua circuit nationally and throughout Indiana. While she emphasized the suffrage question, she also addressed the nature of women's role in marriage, birth control, and other related issues. In addition she spoke on rural life for Purdue University's Farmers' Institute. Curry was a strong, feisty woman possessed of keen intelligence, sharp wit, and an ability to laugh at herself. Plump, almost matronly in appearance, she was a warm friendly person and an effective speaker.[43] This, of course, stood in contrast with Kate who had joined her husband in the final 1916 election parade largely to quell local rumors that she did not love her husband enough to attend his meetings.[44]

By the summer of 1917 the relationship between Gene and Mabel was well established. Theodore and his wife, Gertrude, were aware of it, encouraged it, and helped the two to meet. Whenever Debs left Terre Haute to speak, he stood on the caboose platform as the train slowed at the crossing visible from the Curry house, and he doffed his hat in silent good-bye in that brief moment. For Debs, Mabel Curry possessed the qualities he had long searched for and found neither in his wife nor in temporary assignations throughout his career. "You seem always to have been in my heart and my life and I can not think of a time when you were not with me," he wrote Mabel during this period. I "love you with tenderest regard, and deepest reverence, and all the passionate devotion man can have for the rarest, loveliest and most beautiful of souls. I am reaching for you this morning, my precious love, with both arms and all my heart. The love I bear you can never be told in words." In Mabel, Eugene found the woman he sought since shortly after that June morning in 1885 when he selected a mate who conformed to his current expectations even as he embarked on a far different and less conventional career.[45]

As the other woman, Mabel's public role was circumscribed, and she suffered great anxiety when Eugene, during the summer and fall of 1917, succumbed to his third physical collapse since 1913. Theodore thought this was "the most serious" of the three and left his brother "pretty nearly sapped of his vitality."[46] During his long recuperation in a sanitarium at Boulder, Colorado, propriety kept Mabel from visiting, and they relied on letters to Theodore to maintain contact. Knowing Eugene's nature, and taking a long, confident view of their relationship, Mabel encouraged Eugene as he grew strong to seek female companionship. But he refused. "I've no heart for it. I did not even take that walk I wrote you about and now the dear lady is gone. I have not taken a walk with other than men since I've been here—*not once*." Instead, Eugene explained that he spent much time alone, in his room or on the lawn, "writing and dreaming of the lover that has my heart and that I'm [desiring] to see with an insistence that has admitted of no other companionship."

In these long letters to Mabel, Eugene offered specific advice on political questions as well as his professions of love. Urging her not to attend a suffragist conference in New York, controlled by "the war lords and their vassals," he also cautioned Mabel against public identification of herself as a Socialist. While a militant Socialist woman was to address that conference, she was included purposely to attract other Socialists. "But it's different, entirely different with you. You are supposed to be first & last a 'suf' & to plead with the regulation meekness and mildness for 'votes for women!' " Rather than express her true feelings, and face an angry public reaction to the acknowledgment of her crypto-Socialism, Eugene urged her to avoid the conference: "You would be as sadly out of place in it as I would be in a coca cola campaign for the national beverage."[47]

His health, her politics, and their geographical separation presented one set of problems. But as their love deepened, its very intensity caused a more serious problem, for both Mabel and Eugene were already married to others. To most close friends, Eugene said nothing of his feeling for Mabel. Turning down an invitation from Henry and Elizabeth Vincent to continue his recuperation at their home after leaving Boulder in November 1917, Debs painted a glowing if false picture of his home life: "I have been so long away and am now so happy to be at home where Mrs. Debs, my Katherine, is doing everything in her own loving way that can be done to get me back to myself again."[48] With their relationship long since channeled along formal and structured paths, Eugene sought to protect Kate from gossip and further hurt but faced few other conflicts concerning her.

For Curry, however, the situation was more complicated. In contrast to Gene, Mabel's relationship with her spouse had been until recently quite vital, despite a growing tension over her public activities. Her love for Debs, and their mutual desire to consummate that love, produced great tension and anxiety in her, as these feelings clashed with her marital obligations. In a series of letters to Eugene that have not been preserved but whose themes appear in his letters to her, Mabel wrote of the pain this conflict caused her and wondered whether as a man Eugene felt it as deeply as she. In response Eugene recognized her "agonizing ordeal and tragic struggle in which all was at stake" and reaffirmed that he would never cease his love for her. But his reaction to "the situation"—as both termed the cause of her tension—was quite revealing.

"Although I frankly admit to being ashamed to confess it," Debs wrote that men are not as sensitive as women in this regard. "They certainly ought to be, but it is biologically impossible, I think, for in the elemental grossness of their male nature they can't be as sensitive as women about anything. My reason for this conclusion is that I *feel* that it is and must be so." Echoing his understanding, now almost four decades old, of Helen Jeffers, the Terre Haute woman attracted to the firemen of Vigo Lodge, Eugene told Mabel that "woman in her very nature is immeasurably more emotional, refined, gentle, sensitive and sympathetic than man can possibly be." He acknowledged that their relationship had caused Mabel to suffer "far more in the last few years than I have for the very reason of your being more sensitive, more delicately strong, in a word for being a *woman*, and being fated for some indescribable reason to suffer accordingly." But Debs was quick to note he was not insensitive to Mabel's suffering. He emphasized his attempts to share her "pain and agony" even as he recognized his failure, as any man must. "But I can at least understand *your* situation and your feeling *perfectly so*," he assured Mabel, "and appreciate . . . the chasity of spirit and body and the integrity of soul which makes 'duty' so difficult and repugnant in such a situation."[49]

Eugene's letters did not resolve the cause of Mabel's tension, but they probably did ease her burden somewhat. In contrast to her husband, Gene placed Mabel on a pedestal, gloried in her presumed superior nature, *and* applauded and encouraged her in maintaining an aggressive, if circumspect, role in the world. As part of this encouragement Eugene gradually introduced her to Socialist comrades, especially women, with whom Mabel shared common interests. A few were also informed of the special relationship between the two. Introduced by letter to Rose Pastor Stokes in 1917, Mabel anxiously awaited the time when the two women might sit "face to face. *His* 'lovers' are all mine," she wrote Stokes, "and I want to put my arms about you as I know he does."[50]

Ultimately neither Eugene nor Mabel took any action to end their respective marriages. For Eugene, the distant relationship with Kate notwithstanding, his sense of protection toward her and concern with public image apparently checked any serious consideration of divorce. Mabel was far more receptive to the idea but the weight of the advice from both Debs brothers, and her own sense of responsibility and propriety, checked her as well. "Gene and Theo have both given me the same advice," she told Rose Pastor Stokes in 1919, " 'Do not squash anything.' It is because my husband is such a fine kind man—his position is so enviable—my three daughters are superb. Gene and I would have been living together by this time had it not been for this very situation. His wife and my husband cannot be hurt and humiliated for the sake of our happiness."[51]

Weighing their love with the commitments of a lifetime, Debs and Curry surmounted this personal crisis only to face an even more serious public one. Their relationship grew and deepened during the years that witnessed America's passage from a partisan neutral to an active belligerent in World War I, which, in turn, served as a midwife to the Russian Revolution in 1917. Despite his alternate bouts of sickness and his intense involvement with Mabel, these events dramatically affected Debs as they did the whole American movement. Once again the call came, and he responded. With resolve and considerable pain, Debs mounted the platform to address his fellow citizens.

When President Wilson severed diplomatic relations with Germany in February 1917, the last step before a formal declaration of war, the leadership of the Socialist party was in serious disarray. Since 1914, when European Socialists had embraced nationalism, the debate over that conduct had caused another round of factional struggle within the American party. Attempts to present a manifesto on "disarmament and World Peace" in 1915 had caused severe disagreements. In the aftermath of this debate, and amid the growing patriotic hysteria of 1916 and 1917, party members such as William English Walling, J. Phelps Stokes, Charles Edward Russell, and Algie M. Simons publicly resigned from the party to support the war effort.[52]

Although these defections helped legitimize the avid prowar stance taken by Gompers, they did not debilitate the party. Allan Benson, the Socialist presidential candidate in 1916, joined the prowar Social Democratic League of America,[53] but neither he nor the other prowar Socialists had large personal followings within the party. Indeed, between 1916 and 1919 party membership rose and reversed the post-1912 decline.[54] For many Americans, Socialist Joseph Labadie noted, the war was "not at all popular." They saw no reason for risking their lives or those of their sons in a conflict they believed was backed by American corporate interests. In farm communities and in urban working-class neighborhoods, opposition to the war was so widespread that in 1917 the White House provided the initial funding for Gompers's prowar Alliance for Labor and Democracy. On an earlier tour of the upper Midwest, Debs told Frank O'Hare that "farmers and their families have come from a hundred miles around" to hear his Socialist antiwar speech. "And they are red to the core."[55]

In reality, of course, these farmers were anything but "red to the core." While some were members of the party, the majority opposed the war from a radical conviction that stopped short of Socialism. But in other segments of the Socialist movement, being "red to the core" was fast becoming the litmus test of true Socialist consciousness. Overwhelmed by European events between 1914 and 1918, competing Socialist factions sought to dominate the party and the movement and seemed at times anxious to expel those considered deviant. As this battle involved the rank and file as well as the national leadership, its effects were of far greater importance than the defection of the prowar Socialists.

In a November 1914 speech at New York's Cooper Union Hillquit established the early dimensions of this struggle by defending the German Social Democrats for their support of the war. "National feeling," Hillquit argued, "stands for existence primarily, for the chance to earn a livelihood. It stands for everything we hold dear—home, language, family and friends. The working man has a country as well as a class. Even before he has a class." In many ways Hillquit's speech provided insight into the collapse of the prewar European Socialist movement, but his unqualified support of the Socialist capitulation to nationalist feeling produced a firestorm of protest.[56]

From Florence, Italy, where he now resided, George Herron called himself "sick unto death" over the "moral failure" of the German comrades and strongly objected to Hillquit's position. Prophetically Herron warned Algernon Lee, editor of the socialist New York *Call* and a Hillquit ally, that their current policy "will result in the very divisions and disasters that you wish to avoid."[57] Walling, like Herron then still opposed to the war, bitterly rebuked Hillquit in the left-wing journal, *The New Review*. Pressing an attack on "nationalistic" Socialists worldwide, Walling proposed to start by expelling Hillquit from the American party.[58] Although the New York leader proclaimed his innocence of either revisionist Socialism or pro-German sympathies, many simply did not believe him.[59]

As in other disputes, Berger shared many of his friend's perceptions. Widely suspected of pro-German sympathies (Louis B. Boudin ridiculed Berger in 1917 as "just an ordinary, everyday, somewhat boisterous German Imperialist"),[60] Berger also defended the German Social Democrats and urged the adoption of their policy in America. In 1916 Berger proposed a compulsory national service that would emphasize military and industrial training of American youth as the proper Socialist response to the preparedness campaign. A national protest resulted, and a motion to remove the Milwaukee leader from party office narrowly failed. Undaunted, Berger happily wrote to Hillquit a few months later that he expected the continued British naval defeats to undermine Allied confidence and prepare the way for revived Socialist participation in the peace settlement. Confidently, if unrealistically, Berger told his friend that "while Marxism and its prophets may be lost, eclectic Socialism will attain more strength than Marxism ever could."[61]

Understandably, Hillquit kept his friend's letter from reaching a wider public. But it was impossible to hide the actions of Milwaukee's Socialist mayor, Daniel Hoan, during that summer of 1916. Approached by a Citizens Committee to head a parade termed "A Patriotic Demonstration," Hoan agreed with the nearly unanimous support of the city's Socialist officials and the party's County Central Committee. As the national press broadcast the message that a Socialist mayor supported a "Military Preparedness Parade," Hoan and Berger came under increased attack. Responding to a query from Debs, Hoan attempted to explain the distinction between a military parade and a patriotic one in that summer of intense prowar propaganda. The mayor acknowledged that capitalist-controlled "demonstrations . . . are hypocritical and more or less disgusting," but sought nonetheless to defend his position. "I submit that careful [thought] will lead any thinking socialist to the conclusion that every socialist is imbued with a genuine patriotic spirit, and that we are devoting our lives to make this nation a better place in which the men who toil may live, as well as displaying an international patriotism. . . . I feel," Hoan concluded, "that it is surely preferable, rather than scoff at the word patriotism, to seize upon it and make it a word to express our ideas and popularize our [thoughts]."[62]

Debs exploded at the servile concept of citizenship advocated in Hoan's letter. "Socialists are not required to demonstrate their patriotism for the benefit of the capitalist class," Debs instructed Hoan in a private letter. "The socialists of Milwaukee who are responsible for this perversion of principle may think it good vote-catching politics, but in my opinion it is an insult to militant socialism." Barely containing his fury, Debs tied "such vote-seeking, office-hunting political practices" to the past factional disputes that led "hundreds of red-blooded socialists to quit the party in disgust," and he drew a clear distinction for Hoan to ponder: "If marching in capitalist parades to prove that we are patriots" becomes a test of party loyalty, "then I shall deny that I am a socialist."[63]

Debs was not forced from the party, but the intraparty tensions continued to mount. When Meyer London, the lone Socialist Congressman, voted for war appropriations in April 1917, Seymour Stedman wrote London of the intense hostility of many comrades. Acknowledging "the terrific pressure and public sentiment which must have surrounded you," Stedman commiserated with London because "it makes it double hard where a person is born in another country." Nor did Hoan's official conduct during the war ease this tension. As his private secretary wrote the national office of the party, the mayor rejected an antiwar stance and instead elected to "execute and carry out the laws of the United States." In pursuit of this brand of patriotism and to "protect the interests of the worker," Hoan placed Milwaukee Socialists on local draft boards, the City Council of Defense (which, among other patriotic actions, protested the increased black migration into the city), and fully endorsed the Liberty Bond drives.[64]

As Hoan's actions and Stedman's comments suggest, a shrill war cry marched hand-in-hand with a renewed insistence on loyalty and "pure Americanism" across the land. Organizations such as the American Defense Society and the American Protective League, each founded and maintained by wealthy conservatives, militarists, and professional men who received substantial corporate donations for their work, mixed together an intense, narrow patriotism with a bitter animus against immigrants, aggressive workers, and all radicals and Socialists. In the enormous preparedness parade in New York in 1916, for example, all participants marched under the banner "Absolute and Unqualified Loyalty to Our Country." In communities throughout America, but perhaps especially where a large German population existed, the meaning of this slogan was made pointedly clear. Immigrants and sons and daughters of immigrants were forced to kiss American flags publicly, donate heavily to the war effort, and affirm their Americanism repeatedly—or face beatings, destruction of property, and, on occasion, murder. Theodore Roosevelt was but one of many Americans who advocated shooting any German-American thought to be disloyal.[65] In the ensuing madness America not only girded itself for war but also completed important steps in a basic cultural transition. In a land of vaunted individualism, the corporate-directed insistence of patriotism on demand not only suppressed dissent but also was encouraged as the very fulfillment of that nineteenth-century ideal. In the process the cultural face of corporate America drew more sharply into focus.

The majority of Socialists, however, did not capitulate to this patriotic fury, nor did they nurse pro-German sympathies. American-born agitators such as Debs, Kate Richards O'Hare, Haywood, and the less famous rank-and-file members persisted in their opposition to the war and its Socialist supporters. Among the newer immigrants who joined the party after 1912, moreover, the majority scorned the position of Berger and

Hillquit as they fervently applauded news of revolutionary developments in Europe. This new immigrant influence grew enormously during the war years and reflected a far different experience than that of earlier immigrant Socialists. Unlike the Milwaukee trade unionists who supported Berger, for example, the newer immigrants were largely unorganized, unskilled workers in basic industries in eastern factories and western mines. Too recently arrived to possess the vote, they tended to disparage Socialist political action and gravitated instead toward revolutionary industrial unionism. More important, many of them arrived in the United States with extensive political and economic experience with industrial capitalism. A significant number of Jewish immigrants had participated in the 1905 Russian Revolution, an event that reflected the increased proletarization of these former artisans and small traders. Post-1900 Finnish immigrants also reflected this change. Many had participated in their own 1905 revolt against the tsar and in a later 1906 uprising as well.[66]

This migration of radicalized industrial workers from Russia, Finland, Poland, and other eastern European countries continued until 1914. In America oppressive work conditions frequently reinforced their radical orientation. As one historian of Jewish immigrants has suggested, "Russian and American capitalists proved to be the unwitting marriage brokers or *shadkhens,*" between these immigrants and the Socialist movement.[67] Where earlier immigrants heard in the American Socialist movement "language which meant to us that we were regarded as human beings with human rights," as Joseph Schlossberg later recalled,[68] the newer immigrants heard different words. Hardened in class warfare and retaining the political perspectives of their respective European experiences, many heard in the party's pronouncements less a welcome than a defense of those who would undermine orthodox Socialist theory.

The ethnic institutions these immigrants maintained reinforced their European orientation. Among Jews, political radicalism in America drew essential nurture from a complex web of institutions and traditions brought over from Europe. The persistence of the Bund, the working-class Socialist organization founded in Vilna in 1897, the widespread use of the more popular Yiddish (and not Russian or Hebrew) as the language of agitation, and the integration of political and social activities in the fraternal orders and *landsmanshaften*, societies of workers from the same European community, helped preserve their European understanding even as it contributed to their American isolation.[69] Nor were Jews unique. The large Finnish Socialist communities in both central New England and the Great Lake states were each centered in the culture life of the immigrants. The ubiquitous Finnish Socialist hall was simultaneously the focus of political activity and a social meeting place, and it frequently housed the first efforts at cooperative stores. For many Finns, the Socialist hall replaced the church and served, much as the church did in a different context, to encourage a radical Finnish national consciousness in America.[70]

Ever sensitive to European developments, these immigrant radicals organized themselves into separate foreign-language federations within the American party. Two of the earliest, the Finnish and the Italian, existed by 1906. By 1913 seven others formed, including the Jews, Poles, and Hungarians. In 1915 the Russian Federation organized and affiliated with the party.[71] It was not hard for these immigrant radicals to oppose the national Socialist leadership, and many would have even if they had been more aware of American conditions. In addition to specific issues concerning the war, both Berger and Hillquit were widely known for their support of immigration restriction. That this would have prevented many of these newer immigrants from coming to America was not lost on them. Further, Hillquit's New York electoral campaigns consistently denied their very real ethnic dimension in favor, the revisionist leader paradoxically claimed, of a more orthodox Socialist analysis—an approach many found condescending. At bottom, however, the Berger-Hillquit version of Socialist trade union policy represented the major problem. "I know very well," Hillquit wrote the secretary of the New York local in May 1914, "that the unorganized workers are just as much entitled to redemption through Socialism as their organized brothers." But their lack of union organization made them difficult to "reach," and Hillquit insisted on emphasizing agitation with organized workers despite his awareness that "the vast majority . . . are either unthinking or reactionary." Hillquit's analysis ignored immigrant cultural institutions and amounted to a dismissal of his new Socialist comrades—and they understood it precisely in that way.[72]

Standing in sharp contrast to Berger's Milwaukee constituency and to some of the organized garment workers in Hillquit's New York movement, these immigrant radicals directed their federations with almost complete autonomy from the national party. During the war years their growth was phenomenal and accounted for much of the national party's statistical increase. In 1917 the federations comprised 35 percent of all party members. Two years later that figure had risen to 53 percent. Within specific organizations the increase was dramatic. The Russian Federation, with but 792 members in early 1918, reported almost 4,000 members a year later. A force to be reckoned with in the party, these leftist immigrants, in alliance with a portion of the American-born Socialists, took the lead in forming what they considered to be a true revolutionary movement in America that would have no room for the Bergers and Hillquits.[73]

As the increased immigrant strength reflects, European events (and to a lesser extent domestic anti-immigrant activity and racial oppression) created an apocalyptical climate among the left that blurred their vision and misled their efforts.[74] The long European war had ignited deep unrest throughout the continent. Especially in Russia and Germany, the working-class men who filled the respective trenches grew angry over the slaughter of their comrades, the political chicanery of their governments, and the oppressive conditions their families experienced at home. As this revolutionary discontent grew, even political exiles basked in its reflected glory.

In New York Leon Trotsky, well-known as a participant in the 1905 revolt, cut an impressive swath among leftist immigrant Socialists. Arriving in New York from Spain on 13 January 1917, within twenty-four hours Trotsky helped create the left-wing journal, *The Class Struggle*, and simultaneously pronounced judgment on the American Socialist movement. With the exception of Debs, the Russian revolutionary concluded, American Socialist leaders were similar to the salesman "who supplements his commercial activities with dull Sunday meditations on the future of humanity." Hillquit specifically was attacked as "the ideal Socialist leader for successful dentists." Overwhelmed by the presence of a "real" revolutionary of Trotsky's stature (despite his lack of knowledge of American conditions) and encouraged by his support of their analysis, the growing left wing was ready for what Vladmir Lenin would later call infantile leftism. The February Revolution in Russia, which brought Alexander Kerensky to power and overthrew the tsar, intensified these emotions and focused attention ever more firmly on Europe. As Trotsky and other Russian exiles left for home intending, they told the awe-struck Socialists who remained, to complete the process of Marxian revolution, the mystique of immediate revolutionary victory swept the American left.[75]

The Bolshevik Revolution in November 1917 convinced many on the left that all that stood between them and the establishment of American soviets was a purge of conservative leaders and the restructuring of the party on proper revolutionary principles along the Russian model. So intense was this excitement and so consumed were they by European events that few caught the paradox in one immigrant Finnish comrade's explanation of how Finnish events encouraged his involvement in American revolutionary movements. The passionate concern he and other Finns had with their native land stemmed not only from their international Socialist consciousness, he stated, but also from the belief that, as the crisis was further advanced and "our cause at present has a considerably stronger foothold" there than in America, Finland might be a model for Americans. But an American revolution required support in New York, Omaha, and San Diego and not Turku, Finland.[76]

Anticipating a major struggle, the Socialist party convened its emergency convention in April 1917 to draft a response to Wilson's proclamation of war against Germany. Berger and Hillquit were present, but they no longer dominated the proceedings. Instead, Charles Ruthenberg of Ohio and Pat Quinlan of New Jersey, each a revolutionary industrial unionist, and Boudin, Hillquit's New York nemesis who represented the leftist faction organized around the journal, *The Class Struggle*, played far more dominant roles. After intense debate and numerous amendments and minority reports, the delegates overwhelmingly approved the majority report of their Committee on War and Militarism. Written by Hillquit, the report bound the party to a "continuous, active, and public opposition to the war," the draft, and private and public funding of the war effort. It promised "vigorous resistance" to repressive measures against radicals and workers, "consistent propaganda" against militarism, and "a campaign of education among the workers to organize them in strong, class-conscious, and closely unified political and industrial organizations." Alone among the world's major Socialist parties, the American party had taken a firm stand against the war.[77]

At first glance it appeared that, almost miraculously, American Socialists had healed their major disagreements overnight in order to present a united front in the crisis. But such was not the case. In the sessions prior to the drafting of the final report, Berger and others strongly defended the German Socialists and worked to have John Spargo, who had already resigned from the party to support the war, appointed to draft the final version. This, and the national leadership's successful deflection of demands to proscribe Meyer London for his support of military appropriations, convinced many leftist Socialists that neither Berger nor Hillquit signed the majority report with conviction. Hillquit did not believe it, Boudin wrote, and would not honor it: "I know that this sounds like accusing a party leader of dishonesty. But I cannot help making that accusation."[78] In a certain way the criticism was accurate. Certainly Berger signed the report out of frustration. As German military fortunes declined and the patriotic fury continued, Berger searched for a way to save the party from the reaction he feared would come. In this, however, both he and Hillquit were more isolated than ever before, as the defection of the prowar Socialists had deprived them of their staunchest allies in previous party fights. Berger was under pressure from his trade union supporters, many of whom had already joined the Alliance for Labor and Democracy, outmaneuvered, and outvoted at the convention; his reaction is instructive in the light of past factional battles: when his bluff was firmly called, he backed down and remained, however awkwardly, with the national movement.[79]

Despite the seeming unity, the party remained racked by serious disagreement on the meaning of revolutionary action, on the importance for Americans of European developments, and over the contrasting evaluations of the honesty, integrity, and perceptiveness of each side's opponents. Desperately in need of a unifying force, comrades across the country, facing arrest, deportation, and a vicious violence orchestrated by federal government agents, instinctively looked toward Terre Haute and their one, truly national, Socialist leader.

Eugene Debs did not attend the party's convention, although he did approve of the stand it adopted. He was sick that April, "barely able . . . to stand on [his] feet."[80] During that spring and summer, his spirits remained low and his physical condition caused him frequent severe pain. Then, toward the end of summer, he suffered his third major collapse and entered a sanitarium. To Mabel he wrote of the restorative effects of the mountain walks on his body and soul and encouraged her to maintain her equilibrium amidst "these terrible days." He suggested that she "see Theo as often as you can" both to ease her pain at their separation and for mutual political support.[81] Debs's physical revival proved temporary, however, and the following spring found him bedridden again. He "is not yet well enough," Theodore wrote David Karsner in March 1918, to maintain his correspondence and must "be cautious against straining too much until his strength is once more restored."[82]

Debs's physical condition, albeit serious, was not the sole cause of his depressed spirits. As he viewed his country and his comrades from his bedroom window, all appeared in shambles. With a thoroughness he never anticipated, federal marshals corraled radicals of every nationality, faction, and ideological persuasion, and U.S. district attorneys freely interpreted a vague Espionage Act, passed in 1917, to win indictments and convictions on charges of treason and antiwar activity. Not to be outdone, local patriots in the Arizona mining community of Bisbee, working in close association with state officials, "captured" over 1,200 IWW copper miners, the majority of whom were American-born citizens, loaded them into cattle cars with minimal provisions, and deported them into the New Mexico desert. In Butte, Montana, during the same summer of 1917, Frank Little, an antiwar IWW organizer, was dragged from his bed, tortured, and then lynched by local vigilantes. Less violent but no less disturbing was the arrest of such comrades as Kate Richards O'Hare, Rose Pastor Stokes, Emma Goldman, Alexander Berkman, Berger, Germer, and countless others. Closer to home, the Vigo County Council for Defense caused the discharge of a Terre Haute schoolteacher for her Socialist party membership, attacked German–Americans on the streets of Debs's "beloved little community," and invaded private homes to commandeer and then burn publicly all German language books. In that community where "all were neighbors and all friends," a Socialist coal miner was lynched for refusing to buy a Liberty Bond.[83]

The depression of the Socialist spirit was endemic. "This big game is over [and] we never won a hand," the usually buoyant Bill Haywood wrote John Reed from jail in 1918. "The other fellow had the cut, shuffle, and deal all the time." With mordant humor, Haywood continued: "Personally we didn't lose much, just a part of our life. That is all, some of us as high as twenty years."[84]

Equally depressing was the condition of the Socialist movement. It was bad enough that Russell, whom Debs had so effusively embraced before 22,000 comrades in New York during the 1912 campaign, now presented himself as the representative of "the real American Socialist movement." On an official American mission to the Kerensky government in the summer of 1917, Russell informed one Russian crowd that their February Revolution had greatly altered American Socialist attitudes toward the war, for Russia was no longer an autocracy.[85] Of little importance within the American movement at that time, Russell's ideas gained adherence in the aftermath of the November Bolshevik Revolution. With the tsar overthrown and the Bolsheviks enthroned in Russia, some, including Berger, Meyer London, and other New York Socialists, thought it possible to support openly the "war for democracy." Under the guise of aiding their Russian comrades, these American Socialists sought to escape the intense repression the official antiwar stance had brought on all Socialists. Debs spurned this approach as little different from the nationalism of the German Social Democrats. Instead, he issued a call in May 1918 for a new convention to revise, in light of recent events and according to the principles of international Socialism, certain planks in the 1917 St. Louis platform. The non-Socialist press suggested that this meant that Debs as well had become a prowar Socialist and, as the New York *Daily News* imagined, the party was "buzzing with dissension" as a result. Debs angrily issued another statement, which affirmed his opposition to capitalist war.[86]

This active involvement momentarily lifted Debs's spirits, but the deeper depression remained. All had changed in such a short time. The old *Appeal to Reason* molted and became the *New Appeal* under Emmanuel Haldeman-Julius and endorsed the prowar Social Democratic League. Debs condemned the new position. "You will not have long to live," he wrote former Girard comrade, Louis Kopelin, "to see that the Appeal has committed suicide." Other news was also disheartening. Fred Warren, who had said in the summer of 1916 that he had "lost all hope of the Socialist Party being able to do anything of real value for the working class," retreated to a utopian Socialist community in Fallon, Nevada. There he was joined by other former *Appeal* staffers, Lincoln Phifer and Eli Richardson, and by Phil Wagner, Debs's former editor of the *National Rip-Saw*. During that dismal winter of 1917–18, there was but one sure ray of hope—and that occurred thousands of miles away.[87]

At first the Bolshevik Revolution brilliantly illuminated the leaden sky over the American Socialist movement. To the leftists, it affirmed the accuracy of their analysis and propelled them further in their quixotic search for an American equivalent. But many of their opponents took heart as well. Although Hillquit questioned aspects of Bolshevik theory and doubted the revolution's ability to maintain power, he relished the revolutionary disruption of international power politics and felt the Russians had given Socialists everywhere hope. The national headquarters of the party issued a proclamation declaring that the Bolsheviks had "inspired the working classes of the world with the ideal of humanity's supremacy over class rule" and concluding, "We glory in the achievement and inevitable triumph."[88]

For immigrants, and perhaps especially those who were not yet committed leftist activists, the November revolution was a critical event. As Joseph Freeman, a young Russian Socialist-immigrant living in Brooklyn, recalled, the Bolsheviks restored for him a Socialist faith seriously undermined by the conservative tactics of Berger and Hillquit. For Freeman and for countless other immigrants, this restoration far transcended simply political theory. The Socialist movement was a path out of their European past into the American present. The movement was a cultural force of tremendous importance, and the contradictions perceived within it concerning the war had essential personal meaning. As Freeman explained, "But if you questioned socialism, where were you? How painfully you had struggled against the superstitions of the vanished village, against the barriers of the American ghetto, to achieve a rational explanation of the world, something to guide your actions. But if the socialists whom you revered supported a capitalist war, what meaning did the world have? You could not go back to the religion of your grandfather, or to the naive illusions about an ideal Jewish state in Palestine." The Bolshevik Revolution allowed Freeman and countless others to avoid that "frightfully lonely life." Instead, as did many American-born Socialists, they "concentrated [their] hopes on the Russian Revolution in direct proportion as American socialism became more confused."[89]

From his sickbed in Terre Haute, Debs applauded as well. Russia under the tsar had long served as a symbol of the worst despotism and of the direction corporate capitalism was leading America. Now it was a joy indeed to savor that unexpected event, and Debs saw in the reversed symbolic position of the two nations lessons for American comrades. The Russian Revolution is "the soul of the new-born world," he proclaimed early in 1918. "Verily, the last are now the first and the world's most pitilessly plundered and shamelessly exiled have become the world's revolutionary redeemers and supreme liberators." His enthusiasm appeared limitless: "We stand or fall," he wrote Rose Pastor Stokes, "by

Russia and the revolution—the whole program clear-cut from start to finish." As he would express it a year later, in an article in *The Class Struggle*, "From the crown of my head to the soles of my feet I am a Bolshevik and proud of it. 'The Day of the People' has arrived!"[90]

Uplifting and encouraging though it was, the Bolshevik success nevertheless found Debs still ailing and frequently confined to his bed. As the sixty-three-year-old Socialist leader inched his way into the spring of 1918, his enforced passivity grated more and more. All around him his comrades were in jail and the movement in turmoil while he remained at home. The misrepresentations in the press, the queries of comrades, and the beatings and jailings of both close friends and unknown supporters moved Debs to plan a tour of Indiana and neighboring states for June. But beneath these concerns lay a deeper one. Since 1900, when he acknowledged his role as the " 'father' of the [Socialist] movement,"[91] Debs had occupied center stage among his comrades and supporters. It was to him that they looked in a crisis, and it was his unique power they relied on, as had Carlo Tresca in 1916, to fire their own imaginations and convince the doubters. Debs, too, had come to depend on this conception of his role. So intertwined had become his vision of himself with his public career that his comment to Hillquit in 1914—that his life would not long last if it were not for his use to the movement—had an intense personal meaning. Still in pain, but unable to remain any longer at North 8th Street, Debs took to the road to deliver what would become the most famous protest speech of its time.

Fully expecting, even anticipating, his arrest, Debs spoke numerous times during the first two weeks of June without attracting the notice of the authorities. On 15 June he arrived in Canton, Ohio, to address the state convention of the party. The leftist faction dominated the Ohio movement, and three of its leaders were then in jail in Canton, charged with obstructing registration for the draft. The next day, when a group of Socialists arrived to take Debs to the meeting, he insisted first on visiting Ruthenberg, Alfred Wagenknecht, and Charles Baker in jail. After a brief but intense meeting, Debs walked the short distance to Nimisilla Park where he would speak. With the help of comrades he eased his way through the cheering crowd of over 1,000 people and laughed along with them as Marguerite Prevey ridiculed the reports that Debs had become a prowar Socialist. When Prevey finished, Debs rose, walked to the front of the wooden bandstand, and faced the crowd.

"Three of our most loyal comrades," Debs intoned, pointing to the nearby jail, "are paying the penalty for their devotion to the cause of the working class." They have discovered, as many others had as well, the danger, "in a country fighting to make democracy safe in the world," of exercising their "constitutional right of free speech." The bodies of the three men were locked up, Debs suggested, but not their souls—and neither was "the Socialist movement." The moral courage that would accept jail, if necessary, for principle remained the essence of the Socialist belief: "There are many who seek refuge in the popular side of a great question. As a Socialist, I have long since learned to stand alone. . . . When I rise it will be with the ranks, and not from the ranks." Those in the movement who are "weak and cowardly," who lack the fiber to endure "the revolutionary test" will "fall away . . . disappear as if they had never been." In their place "in this crucial hour" others "are writing their names in fadeless letters in the history of mankind."

"They tell us," Debs reminded his audience, "that we live in a great free republic; that our institutions are democratic; that we are a free and self-governing people. This is too much," he bitterly noted, "even for a joke. But it is not a subject for levity." It was, rather, "an exceedingly serious matter." At stake was the very vitality of the meaning of citizenship. With a war-induced influence broader than ever before, corporate leaders "are today wrapped in the American flag [and] shout their claim from the housetops that they are the only patriots." They "have their magnifying glasses in hand" and scan "the country for evidence of disloyalty, eager to apply the brand of treason to the men who dare to even whisper their opposition." Yet Debs found reason to take heart. "Every time they strike at us," he affirmed, "they hit themselves. . . . They help us in spite of themselves. Socialism is a growing idea," he insisted, "it is coming, coming, coming all along the line," and he shared the meaning of that "expanding philosophy" in his own life. "It has given me my ideas and ideals; my principles and convictions," Debs explained as he leaned across the crowd. "It has taught me how to serve—a lesson to me of priceless value. It has taught me the ecstasy in the handclasp of a comrade . . . to multiply myself over and over again; to thrill with a fresh born manhood; to feel life truly worth while"; and to embrace "every member of the working class without an exception [as] my comrade, my brother and sister."

"Our hearts," Debs asserted, as the audience cheered wildly, "our hearts are with the Bolsheviki of Russia [who] by their incomparable valor and sacrifice added fresh lustre to the fame of the international movement." Precisely because of this triumph, however, the movement in America would face further persecution, for capitalists as well as Socialists understood that "the truth alone will make the people free." In this struggle to influence the consciousness of citizens, the risks were severe but the possible results vast. But in an era of mad, patriotic conformity, it was important to recall again "the minorities who have made the history of the world. . . . We, who are here today, are under infinite obligations to them because they suffered, they sacrificed, they went to jail . . . in their struggle to leave the world better for us than they found it for themselves. . . . The only way we can discharge that obligation is by doing the best we can for those who are to come after us."

Ultimately the central issue, as always for Debs, revolved around the individual. At this midpoint in the speech, Debs had shared with his audience something of his own motivations and reminded them that, despite appearances, they did not stand alone. It was now time to reach through the audience, to those individuals before him and to those who would later read his words, and touch what Debs saw as the core of the Socialist commitment. Talk of inevitability might be encouraging, but Debs knew that the struggle depended upon each individual. "Join the Socialist Party," he proclaimed. "You cannot do your duty by proxy. You have got to do it yourself and do it squarely." Then "you will know what it is to be a real *man* or *woman*. You will lose nothing . . . but you will find something of infinite value, and that something will be yourself. And that is your supreme need," Debs told Americans, "to find yourself—to really know yourself and your purpose in life."

Debs never quite allowed that a majority of his fellow citizens could define that purpose in essentially private ways that excluded others. The meaning of the American tradition, reinterpreted in an era of sharp class warfare, was so real to him that it precluded such a possibility. Since the 1880s, the examples of Thomas Paine, Thomas Jefferson, John Adams, William Lloyd Garrison, and others had served as his essential political guide, and he remained adamant in the belief that if he could see and understand, so could others. His faith, increasingly out-of-step even in his day, appealed to the best in an often sorry history. As he concluded his speech, invoking Abraham Lincoln, defending the IWW, and reaffirming the necessity of industrial unionism, "the forerunner of industrial democracy," to enable workers to control their "own jobs . . . own labor and be free men instead of industrial slaves," Debs returned to the message that had structured his entire public career. "Socialists," he quietly explained, have a "duty to build the new nation and the free republic. We need industrial and social builders. . . . We are all pledged to do our part. We are inviting—aye challenging you in the name of your own manhood and womanhood to join us and do your part . . . [to] proclaim the emancipation of the working class and the brotherhood of all mankind."[92]

As the thunderous applause that greeted his speech pealed across Nimisilla Park, the thin, tired Socialist leader and his hoarse yet chanting audience shared an intense religious moment, reflections of which would touch Socialists throughout America. He had said nothing he had not said many times before and had referred to the war but once. But the very ritual of his repetition in the face of the most extensive repression the nation had experienced to that time prepared the altar for the sacrifice. The gaunt man with the burning eyes had affirmed the commitment of his comrades by giving of himself as best he knew and fulfilled, by his own definition, the obligations of true manliness. In that very act Debs served notice to his country, as he had in 1894, that to resist oppression was at least as much a part of the American tradition as compliance with the dictates of corporate leaders. In the process he provided Socialists everywhere with the moral encouragement to continue the struggle.

Socialists were not the only members of the crowd that day. The U.S. attorney for northern Ohio, E. S. Wertz, had stenographers recording Debs's words as well. Taking offense at Debs's defense of the IWW and critical remarks about corporate and government leaders, Wertz sent a copy of the speech to the Justice Department in Washington for an opinion on the advisability of prosecuting Debs. After discussing it for three days, department officials, including Attorney General Thomas W. Gregory, discouraged the proposed prosecution. "Parts of the speech," the Justice Depatment opinion stated, "taken in connection with the context, bring the speech close to, if not over, the line, though the case is by no means a clear one. All in all the Department does not feel strongly convinced that a prosecution is advisable."[93]

If his superiors in Washington feared the negative publicity of a failed prosecution, Wertz had more confidence in his grand jury. Disregarding Washington's advice, he obtained a federal grand jury indictment in Cleveland against Debs on 29 June, charging the Socialist leader with ten violations of the Espionage Law as enacted in 1917 and amended in 1918. Arrested the following day in Cleveland, Debs spent the night in jail—his first since 1895—until Prevey and a Cleveland comrade posted the $10,000 bond. Trial was set for 9 September before Judge D. C. Westenhaver in Cleveland.[94]

Following the example of political prisoners the world over, Debs demanded that his lawyers not contest the charges, now reduced to two.[95] He had given the speech and would stand by it. After a two-day parade of prosecution witnesses, who could only attest that indeed Debs had given the speech, Wertz rested his case at 11 o'clock on 11 September. On Debs's instructions, so did his lawyers. After a short recess, Debs returned to address the jury himself. "Gentlemen," he announced, "I do not fear to face you in this hour of accusation." Admitting the specifics of the prosecution's case, he objected only to Wertz's insinuation that he favored violent revolution: "That is not true. I have never advocated violence in any form." Carefully covering the same ground as at Canton, Debs applauded the courage of his jailed comrades, pleaded "guilty to the charge" of supporting the Bolshevik Revolution, and condemned capitalist exploitation in general and war profiteers in specific. But his basic message to the jurors and to those Americans beyond the courtroom encompassed a stirring defense of American liberty as the cornerstone of American Socialism.

"Washington, Paine, Adams—these were the rebels of their day," Debs reiterated. "At first they were opposed by the people and denounced by the press. . . . And if the Revolution had failed, the revolutionary fathers would have been executed as felons. But it did not fail. Revolutions," he noted with pleasure, "have a habit of succeeding when the time comes for them." From Paine and Adams, Debs invoked the memory of America's abolitionists, of Elijah Lovejoy, murdered for his beliefs in 1837 just as some "I.W.W. in our day," and of Wendell Phillips, Garrison, Gerrit Smith, and Thaddeus Stevens. "You are teaching your children," Debs pointed out to the jury, "to revere their memories, while all of their detractors are in oblivion." Yet those who act in their memory today face a more savage persecution. In the tradition of these earlier patriots, Debs proclaimed his patriotism and his "love [for] the flag as a symbol of freedom." He believed, "however, in a wider pariotism" as well, one international in scope, and dedicated to the human brotherhood that will replace "the capitalist-competitive system in which we live."

Returning to the specific charges, Debs defended his right of free speech under the Constitution, sarcastically quoted Wilson's 1912 campaign speeches in support of that right, and ended on a stark note: "Gentlemen, I am the smallest part of this trial. . . . There is an infinitely greater issue that is being tried in this court, though you may not be conscious of it. American institutions are on trial here before a court of American citizens."[96]

The following day the jury found him guilty as charged, and Judge Westenhaver set Saturday, 14 September, for sentencing. Arriving in court that morning, Debs rose and made his final statement in the case. Affirming his "kinship with all living beings," Debs expressed the crux of his Socialist humanism in words that would be remembered even decades later. "While there is a lower class, I am in it; while there is a criminal element, I am of it; while there is a soul in prison, I am not free." Incisively he recalled that he "could have been in Congress long ago" but instead "preferred to go to prison." He asked "for no mercy . . . for no immunity" but rather again asserted that capitalist ideology was not the sole definition of citizenship. Pointing to the struggle between "greed . . . and the rising hosts of freedom," Debs found hope even in those dark days, "for the cross is bending, the midnight is passing." With the impassive judge staring down at him, Debs concluded his speech and unconsciously revealed just how consistent his own goals had remained. As he had at Battery D in Chicago, twenty-three years earlier in November 1895, this Socialist citizen called on the poet Lowell to carry his essential message:

> He's true to God who's true to man;
> whenever wrong is done.
> To the humblest and the weakest,
> 'neath the all-beholding sun.
> That wrong is also done to us,
> and they are slaves most base,
> Whose love of right is for themselves
> and not for all the race.[97]

With that, Debs told the judge, "I am prepared to receive your sentence." The judge was prepared to give it. Acknowledging Debs's sincerity and courage, Westenhaver still condemned those "within our borders who would strike the sword from the hand of this nation while she is engaged in defending herself against a foreign and brutal power." He then sentenced Debs to ten years in jail.[98]

The Canton speech and Debs's addresses to the jury and the judge electrified Socialists throughout America. Widely reprinted and even more widely quoted, Debs's words gave a demoralized movement a new focus and rallying point. If he had said nothing new, the circumstances of the speech and the ensuing prosecution gave it a more trenchant meaning than the bare sentences themselves suggested. The image of the sixty-three-year-old leader risking jail for principle sparked Socialists everywhere. Letters poured into Terre Haute praising Debs and testifying to the effect his words had. An editor of a leading leftist journal suggested that "the Socialist Party of America had found a leader, a leader who was able to unite all shades and all factions, all groups and all opinions into one, because he represented the spirit of the International."[99] Events would soon show, however, that this was far too optimistic an evaluation.

Somewhat overwhelmed, Debs gently dismissed much of the fulsome praise. "That in the recent trial I stood where every loyal comrade was in duty bound to stand," he wrote Ruth LePrade in late September, "entitles me to no such generous recognition."[100] Notwithstanding his protestations, Debs clearly relished the praise and the effect his actions seemed to have on his comrades. But his protest served another purpose as well. Referring to his "simple duty to the party," Debs told Algernon Lee that his deeds were "almost contemptible" when compared with those of "Lenin, Trotsky, Liebknecht [and] Luxembourg"—and by inference elevated himself into just such a class.[101] Lenin's strident 1918 address to American workers reinforced this perception. Debs, the Russian leader declared, was "one of the best loved leaders of the American proletariat." Characterizing the Terre Haute native as "a fearless man," Lenin expressed no surprise at the jail sentence, for Debs was one of "the true internationalists, the real representative of the revolutionary proletariat."[102]

One form of praise did rankle, however. Many called their hero "the grand old man" of the movement. Meant as a term of endearment, Debs bristled when he heard it: "I am trying my best to be a man," he snapped in a fall 1918 speech, "but I am neither grand nor old. . . . The spirit within me and the soul of me, the spirit and soul of socialism, are a sure guarantee against 'old age.' "[103] But more serious problems demanded attention. Most immediately, Debs had to find a way to support himself, Theodore, and their office expenses. Most of the Socialist presses had been suppressed, and Debs had few outlets for articles. Further, the terms of bail while appealing his conviction limited his travels to Terre Haute and the court's area of jurisdiction in northern Ohio. But the major influenza epidemic of 1918 cancelled plans for a tour of twenty communities in the district. Despite a $50 a week stipend from the party over and above its aid for his legal defense, Debs was more than $1,500 in debt by March 1919.[104]

Personal difficulties aside, the state of the movement commanded his greatest attention. The war ended in November 1918, but the repression of radicals and labor agitators continued, as both government agents and organizations of businessmen-patriots continued their guardianship of American communities. This, in turn, falsely encouraged many leftist Socialists to believe that, as in pre-1917 Russia, the repression indicated the weakness of the government and the strength of the workers and demanded of them fulfillment of their role as the revolutionary vanguard. As these currents nearly swamped the movement, the Russians issued a call for the formation of a Third International to replace the now defunct Second International that had dominated the prewar years. With the Russian revolutionaries as the worldwide leaders, the call formalized the pattern that would allow events unrelated to America to consume the attention and reactions of the American left. Accompanied as it was by the full prestige of the world's only successful Socialist revolutionaries, the January 1919 call was uncritically accepted by many. But for Americans, at least, it nonetheless remained an odd document. Its condemnation of European "Social patriots" the American left interpreted as justification to purge all who disagreed with their analysis, thereby completing the destruction of a vision of a diverse American movement. Even odder, moreover, was the social analysis the Russians presented. Terming the current period one "of the dissolution and ruin of the whole capitalist world," the Russians demanded of Socialists in every country encouragement of "mass action of the proletariat going as far as open conflict with arms in hand" in order to establish "the dictatorship of the proletariat" to "aim at the immediate expropriation of capitalism and the suppression of private property and . . . its transfer to the proletarian state." Concluding their call with specific invitations to Socialist organizations in each country to participate in the International, the Russians so honored three American groups; the IWW, the Socialist Labor party, and the "left of the American Socialist Party (tendencies represented by Debs and the Socialist Propaganda League)."[105]

Thoroughly unrealistic, this call, with its promise of an immediate worldwide millennium, propelled the left to increased activity and confirmed for many, if not most, the necessity of ridding the party of reformist elements. With the proposed purge the final obstacle to revolutionary action by the workers would be removed.

Debs at first shared much of this sentiment. Overwhelmed again, as he had been during the 1912 party struggles, by the subtle intricacies of Socialist ideology and factional nuance and not a little impressed by the signal position Lenin and other "real" revolutionary leaders accorded him, he lent his considerable prestige to the left wing. In the February 1919 issue of *The Class Struggle*, which contained Louis Fraina's demand to organize a formal left wing and expel all reformist leaders, the editors announced that Debs had agreed to join them as a member of the editorial board: "Comrade Debs has accepted the invitation of *The Socialist Publication Society*," the editorial read, "to serve in this capacity as he feels that he is in full accord with the policy of *The Class Struggle*." In the same issue Debs's lead article, "The Day of the People," condemned reformist leaders, declared that "the people *are* ready for their day," and issued his famous statement that he was a Bolshevik "from the crown of my head to the soles of my feet." So enthusiastic was Debs and so clear the editorial that no one could doubt that Debs fully shared the leftist position.[106]

Later that month Debs explained his position again to Julius Gerber, secretary of the New York City local currently fighting an attempted leftist takeover. "I am in sympathy with the radical tendencies in our party," Debs informed Gerber. "There needs to be a change in many things." The specific changes he called for, however, underscored his ideological innocence and revealed how complete was his emotional response to the Russian Revolution and his presumed role in its American version. Pointing to the party's attitude toward "the Gompers scabbing and strikebreaking unions," Debs attempted to integrate that consistent theme in his work with the recent cataclysmic events in Europe: "We have got to take a clean cut stand in favor of revolutionary industrial unionism," he preached. "We have to get completely away from Scheidemannism [the German Social Democratic leader who supported the war] and what it stands for and plant ourselves squarely on uncompromising ground both economically and politically." Disdaining the factional struggle currently destroying the New York local ("I have no time for that sort of business"), Debs retorted to an earlier letter from Gerber that the New York comrade "need have no fear that [my] heart is going to mislead me as to the essential facts of the situation." About the only solace Gerber might draw from Debs's letter was his opposition "to splitting the party," as he believed "the changes that are necessary can all be made and should be made within the party."[107]

A month later Debs reiterated this position in the first issue of a new monthly, *The Illinois Comrade*. Stressing the need for "sound and efficient organization . . . to take advantage of the unprecedented opportunities created by the war," Debs wallowed in the revolutionary fantasy that the Russian example and the effects of the war had critically weakened capitalism in America as in Europe. With "hundreds of thousands" of Americans already unemployed, with strikes occurring everywhere, and with returning soldiers discontent, Debs argued that the moment was at hand: "Comrades, the call comes to us all in this hour of supreme importance to . . . do everything that in our power lies to face fitely [*sic*] and worthily the duties and responsibilities which the impending revolution imposes, and to supplant the present criminal and corrupt system of capitalism with the working class republic."[108] It was a dramatic reversal for the Eugene Debs who had long held that American workers were essentially law-abiding and would only proceed step by step toward a democratic Socialist republic.

The contrast between the demoralized American movement and the euphoric Russian experience obviously accounts for much of the reaction by Debs and the left. The American Socialists had faced a programmed repression as well as indiscriminate violence and had little to show for it. Even worse, they felt themselves dismissed as insignificant by their revolutionary European comrades. Beyond this, however, other factors affected Debs personally. A sick and depressed Debs had consciously planned the speaking tour that had led to Nimisilla Park. As much as he wanted to revive the movement, he wanted to revive himself, to cap his career, as it were, with a final clarion call of resistance.[109] That he did do, but events overtook him and he found himself unable, in the winter and spring of 1919, to separate fact from fiction. Indeed, it is quite possible that during the spring powerful visions of personal prominence and public affirmation influenced again this leader who so consistently questioned his own inner worth. Debs was sick again, and facing a very real ten-year jail term; his actions suggest both the power of the revolutionary mystique as well as a personal desire to go to jail, if need be, as the leader of an imminent revolutionary movement that in his wildest fantasy might liberate him, the very incarnation of the movement itself. A grand vision, but the reality proved far more painful for both the movement and Debs.

On 10 March 1919 the U.S. Supreme Court unanimously upheld Debs's conviction and sentence. Speaking for the court, Justice Oliver Wendell

Holmes rejected Debs's argument that the indictment violated his right of free speech. **Seymour Stedman then filed a petition for a rehearing,** which the court denied at the end of March.[110] Jail loomed ever closer, but not before a strange intercession for clemency was made by a group of pro-war former Socialists. Although Debs had greeted the court's decision with the scornful comment that "it is good for, at least, a million Bolshevist recruits in this country," Charles Edward Russell and Allan Benson, along with Frank Walsh, a noted lawyer and Wilson supporter, petitioned Attorney General A. Mitchell Palmer for clemency for Debs and other political prisoners. From the Paris Peace Conference, Wilson cabled his private secretary, Joseph Tumulty, that he would be "willing to grant a respite in the case of Eugene V. Debs and the others . . . but I doubt the wisdom and public effect of such an action." He instructed Tumulty to confer with Palmer and to "let me know the result of the conference before I act."[111]

Palmer was adamant in his opposition to any clemency. Debs's "attitude of challenging and defying the administration of law," he wrote Wilson, "makes it imperative that no respite of clemency be shown at the present time." Ohio's U.S. Senator Atlee Pomerene made the point even clearer: "Since the decision of the Supreme Court [Debs] has preached Revolution, urged the establishment of Soviets in this Country . . . and spoke[n] of the Bolshevists in the most glowing terms." Fearful of such agitation and unaware that Palmer had already decided against clemency, Pomerene pressed the point: "Any attempt to show Debs leniency now will be attributed to a spirit of weakness on the part of the Government. . . . Let Debs pose as a martyr if he will . . . it will not do one half the harm to the principles of the American Democracy that will result from exercise of misguided leniency."[112]

With Palmer's opposition the sacrificial ritual begun at Canton reached its painful, if bloodless, conclusion. The object of the sacrifice, however, was by now confused and despondent. Publicly, Debs pressed his new political faith with fervor during February and March and played to the hilt his assumed revolutionary stance. His private feelings were a different matter. To Mabel Curry he wrote that February: "I don't know why but I feel dreadfully depressed—I want to get away from everybody. The comrades are kind as they can be and I am trying hard not to let them know what is in my heart. There's an awful loneliness has gripped me—I want you, dearest, need you here . . . your comfort and strength and inspiration." With jail closing in on him, the reality of the separation from his "dearest Mabel" could no longer be postponed. As Curry had written three months earlier to Rose Pastor Stokes, "*No one* knows as I know what just a *year* [in jail] would do! The separation [from me] would kill him. *This I know.*"[113] Beyond this, it is also possible that Debs's depression stemmed from an awareness that not only was the revolution not imminent but also that the movement itself was on the verge of its most bitter and final internal struggle. If so, he kept the feeling to himself, sharing it neither with Mabel Curry nor his comrades.

On Tuesday, 8 April, Debs was taken sick again with an attack of lumbago and a painful inflammation of the nerves. He remained in bed until that Friday when, according to Mabel Curry, the telephone call came from Wertz ordering him to promptly surrender himself at Cleveland. At one o'clock that afternoon, Debs left his bed to spend the next five hours with Mabel and, for a part of that time, with Theodore as well. They would not see each other again before Gene left for jail. Debs planned to take the evening train on Saturday to Cleveland, and Mabel, too distraught to receive her lover's customary tip of the hat at her crossing, instead walked in a strange part of town as the train left. Terribly sad, she was also bitter at the fate that kept her from Eugene at the end while his wife, whom she felt was emotionally incapable of experiencing even a tenth of her anguish, accompanied him to the depot. But propriety demanded that distance, and neither Eugene nor Mabel would violate that imperative. On that note the revolutionary leader went to jail.[114]

Debs achieved a portion of what he desired. He was, once again, as in 1894, the preeminent symbol of American resistance to corporate capitalism. If not fêted in quite the same way as before, he nonetheless took great pride in his dedication to principle. In achieving this, Debs also put to rest, for a moment, his own inner fears of becoming the "grand old man" of the movement and gently dismissed as such. He had proved his manhood once again, proved to himself his worth, and this pride would sustain him in the difficult years ahead. But that thin line that had stalked Debs's career since his days in the Brotherhood of Locomotive Firemen, which had confused personal needs and political judgment, returned to haunt him now with a vengeance. His personal depression, the state of the movement, his own vanity as a purported revolutionary leader—all had contributed to his unrealistic analysis of the meaning of the Bolshevik Revolution for Americans during 1918 and 1919. Shortly, Debs would re-emphasize themes more consistent with his earlier agitation. But not before his analysis helped (even though he probably could not have prevented it) to set the stage for the final rupture of the Socialist movement.

Debs's journey to jail suggested the basic problem. From Terre Haute on Saturday night, to Cleveland Sunday morning, to Youngstown that afternoon and on to the penitentiary at Moundsville, West Virginia, that evening, this working-class hero was carried toward his sentence by willing union labor men, organized into the various brotherhoods that Debs himself had helped create more than four decades earlier. As Debs noted, "Most of them [were] wearing the button of their craft in their hats."[115] For some, this deeply hurt: "I am ashamed," E. A. Brenholtz wrote Theodore, "ashamed beyond all words."[116] Shame aside, it ought not to have been surprising. Debs's Bolshevik agitation made little sense to most American workers. More pointedly, the symbol of union men taking Debs to prison denoted the persistent gap that had structured his career: his personal appeal among workers, while never unanimous, vastly outdistanced his political support. As Debs himself knew, Gompers and other labor leaders were not the sole obstacles. Rather, it was the rank and file who rejected, for myriad reasons, Debs's proposed transformation of American society.

On 8 April 1919 one such worker wrote the attorney general, after Palmer's opposition to clemency for Debs had become public. "I am a working man and a citizen," Ralph C. Reed noted, "and believe Debs should get what is coming to him . . . so now let him take his with others like him."[117] The meaning of citizenship and of work remained the central issue, and the contrast that persisted between his and Reed's understanding of those terms caused Debs no little pain as he reviewed his life's work from his jail cell.

A RADICAL'S LEGACY: 1920–

The trials and privations, the defeats and discouragements, the pains, punishments and persecutions were all good for me; they were all needed in my life and I thank whatever gods there be for them all.

The darkest days have brought me the most light; the severest trials have had the richest rewards, and the bitterest defeats have given me my only victories.

I would not omit a single item from the record, nor blot out a single experience, but if I did I should wish it to be the most joyous one rather than the bitterest of them all.

Eugene V. Debs, 1926

When Eugene Debs began his journey to jail, Terre Haute was still a small diverse manufacturing community, "an industrial island in an agricultural sea," as *Fortune Magazine* labeled the city some years later. Terre Haute remained insignificant for both the regional and national economy, yet the class feeling that permeated the community's leading families during the 1902 streetcar strike did not therefore ease. The major scandal that erupted following the 1914 election revealed new aspects of how the "best people" dominated this small but complex city.[1]

Political contests had always been hard fought affairs in Terre Haute, but none was so rough as the election of Don Roberts as mayor in 1910. Roberts built a machine within the Democratic party that relied on an alliance with the bordello owners, drug dealers, and assorted criminals who gave the city its low reputation. With their aid Roberts and his ward bosses routinely voted the dead, stuffed ballot boxes, and intimidated the opposition at election time. Following the 1914 Congressional elections, however, the U.S. district attorney indicted Roberts and 109 other Terre Hauteans for defrauding the federal government. The Terre Haute citizens who publicly supported the accused included Frank McKeen, the son of William Riley, now in charge of the family business, as well as other major businessmen who had formed the Citizens' Protective League in 1902. They posted bond for Roberts and others under indictment.[2]

The ensuing grand jury investigation suggested that McKeen and his compatriots were less concerned with the question of justice than in protecting the strong but quiet alliance that had long existed between the profiteers of the "demi-monde" and the more respected residents of the city. Under Roberts, property in the center of the business district had been assessed at 25 percent of its true value while residential property (in a city where over 60 percent of the residents owned their homes) was regularly assessed at a rate between 60 and 75 percent. The exception to this residential assessment was in those parts of Cherry and Ohio streets, in the second ward, that housed Terre Haute's "best people." The resulting tax schedules for the leading families were thus dramatically low: Riley McKeen paid taxes on less than $5,000 of real property; Demas Deming, Jr., on less than $7,000, and Herman Hulman on less than $6,000. In other ways as well, this alliance between the politicians and the "best people" was quite profitable for each side.[3]

Yet open class conflict did not accurately describe social relations in this small city during the first decades of the twentieth century. During Riley McKeen's funeral in February 1913, the city's streetcar workers stopped,

"with bowed heads uncovered," in honor of the man who had so effectively helped to break their strike a decade earlier. This observance was, of
course, encouraged by their employers and was not spontaneous, but
neither did the men refuse to give the formal homage. Terre Haute's trade
unions had grown in numbers but not in militancy, and many workers continued to hold community leaders such as McKeen in some regard, despite
their obvious anti-union bias.[4]

Debs shared these feelings as well. In 1917, for example, he joined his
old employer, Hulman, in a series of private discussions concerning the
world war. While Hulman failed to convince Debs to support Woodrow
Wilson's war efforts, both men fervently reaffirmed their deep friendship
and respect.[5] Some years later, over 21,000 Terre Haute citizens (approximately one-third of the town's total population) petitioned for Debs's
release from the federal penitentiary.[6] Terre Hauteans could at times be
quite vindictive, as Schubert Seebree discovered when forced from the
city, unable to find employment, following his 1918 campaign as the
Socialist Congressional candidate.[7] But even many of the older business
leaders retained a special regard for Debs. Nationally Debs was a leader in
the class struggle, but in Terre Haute, despite his efforts to organize local
unions, he remained the native son even into his final years.

In the fall of 1925, Gene and Kate, strolling in the cool evening after dinner, passed the old mansion of Chauncey Rose, now rotted and crumbled,
awaiting final demolition. Pausing before the house, they spotted two of
Rose's old trunks amid the debris. Swept with a melancholy for the spirit
of his youth, a disturbed and agitated Debs returned home to write a letter
to the local paper. "Chauncey Rose did more for Terre Haute than any
other man living or dead," Debs wrote of the city's major mid-nineteenth-
century entrepreneur. "Rose built the first railroad into Terre Haute, and
devoted his entire fortune to the growth and development of the city and
the prosperity and welfare of the people." Angry at this defilement of
Rose's memory, it was the condition of the worn and battered trunks that
etched Debs's feeling, "trunks that, no doubt, in crossing the eastern
mountains knew the stage coach, the ox-cart and the old canal in their
pilgrimage . . . that shared the pioneer life of the Wabash Valley, its
heroism and hardships, as well as its romance, its simplicity and beauty."
That these relics of an earlier time—symbols of the conquest of nature, of
manhood tested and victorious, which evoked waves of adolescent dreams
and memories—that these should be scorned and neglected caused the
deepest pain. With sad anger, Debs concluded his letter: "This is
predominantly a business age, a commercial age, a material and in a larger
sense a sordid age, but the moral and spiritual values of life are not wholly

ignored by the people. Sentiment, without which men are lower than savages, is still rooted in and flowers in the human soul and makes possible the hope that some day we shall seek and find and enjoy the real riches of the race."[8]

10

A Species of Purging

"Organize! Educate! Agitate!" Eugene Debs proclaimed as he entered jail in April 1919. Urging his comrades to "reach your fellow workers with the socialist viewpoint," Debs offered a final message to his American supporters: "Tell my comrades that I entered the prison doors a flaming revolutionist, my head erect, my spirit untamed and my soul unconquered."[1] Stirring sentiments, but the reality of prison life and the enforced long hours spent meditating on the state of the party and its relation with American working people would create over time quite different emotions.

At first, however, Debs's prison term seemed almost pleasant. The warden at Moundsville, Joseph Z. Terrell, was quite kind. He assigned his famous prisoner to light duty in the prison hospital, waived regulations that required specific approval for every book or magazine, and allowed Debs liberal visiting privileges. While Debs himself asked for no favors, Terrell's actions, as had Sheriff George Eckhart's at Woodstock almost a quarter of a century earlier, eased his initial adjustment.[2] So, too, did the reception Debs received from the other convicts. His famous statement that "while there is a soul in prison, I am not free" had preceded him, and many inmates expressed admiration for this man who chose on principle to live among them. As a result, Debs's first days in prison were "busy, in fact rushed." His fellow prisoners, Debs wrote his brother ten days after entering jail, "almost 900 of them, nearly all seem to want to see me & chat with me . . . every time they have a chance." Some said they had heard him speak and with them Debs quipped: "I hope that isn't why [you're] here." Two black prisoners were especially solicitous. They "do everything for me," he explained to his brother whose place they now took, and "are as gentle as if I were a nursing infant. How far sweeter they are than some of their vaunted white 'superiors.' "[3]

Energized by this relatively easy adjustment, Debs sought to maintain active involvement with events beyond Moundsville. As he had twenty-five years earlier, he peppered his letters to Theodore with demands and directions concerning correspondence, future plans, and even reminders to his longtime office manager of where certain material was filed. In his personal affairs as well, Debs tried to sustain a sense of power and immediacy. Overjoyed that Mabel Curry had become Theodore's office assistant, Debs asked his brother to "be good to her in every way you can" and specifically requested Theodore share his letters first with Mabel before sending them on to Kate. At times, however, these attempts to influence the lives of others from prison had ludicrous results. Concerned that Kate felt isolated, as she rarely ever visited the Terre Haute office, Eugene asked Theodore to visit her with his wife and daughter and also requested that Mabel "see her [as] often as she can." Eugene had explained to Kate that a "warm friendship" existed between Mabel and himself and thought that this would explain Curry's visits. But Kate was not as insensitive as Mabel assumed or Eugene himself believed. So cold was Mabel's reception when she did visit Kate that she vowed never to return. "You know," she wrote to Rose Pastor Stokes, "what a dear idealist he [Debs] is. He thinks *no one* could help loving me. But they *can!*"[4]

Debs's cheery countenance—he told Morris Hillquit in May that he was "all right, and Tomorrow is already dawning"[5]—probably would not have survived the long sentence served even under these favorable conditions. But this he never discovered. Early in June 1919 an aide to Attorney General A. Mitchell Palmer ordered Terrell to prepare to transfer Debs to the maximum security penitentiary at Atlanta, Georgia. On 13 June, with but a few hours notice, Debs began his journey to Atlanta in secrecy, speeded along as before by union men. The transfer incensed Theodore. "The liberal and humane treatment Gene was receiving at Moundsville," he wrote Adolph Germer, "got on the nerves of Palmer, the Quaker, and the director of half a dozen corporations that are bilking the public." To Joseph Cohen, Theodore insisted that the transfer to "a southern hell-hole" was purposively intended "to completely shatter his health . . . and thus accomplish in that way what they dare not in another."[6]

Theodore's anger, aggravated by the secrecy of the move and the absence of an official explanation, was nonetheless misdirected. His brother's transfer to Atlanta was less the result of a conscious plot than a little considered effect of the protracted negotiations between federal and state officials concerning the financing of federal inmates in state prisons.[7] But Theodore's worry about Gene was real. The climate in Georgia was more taxing and the prison far more structured than Moundsville. Normal prison regulations now confined Debs to his cell for a larger portion of the day, visiting privileges were curtailed, and he was allowed to write but one letter, a single sheet, per week, and then only to an approved list of family members. Debs was denied access to all Socialist literature and was forbidden to keep the voluminous letters that poured in each week from unapproved correspondents. While not completely isolated, these restrictions did prevent Debs from closely following the factional struggles during 1919 and 1920.[8]

The changing nature of Debs's prison experience was not noticed by most of his supporters. They were aware, of course, of the shift to Atlanta, but he remained to them less a suffering individual than a profound symbol of resistance to oppression whose very imprisonment became their encouragement. One Oklahoma lawyer compared him to "the Nazarene Carpenter," inasmuch as Debs had "taught us continually, during the last twenty-five years, to Love one another and not to shoot one another." The comparisons to Christ were pervasive, and Debs's role as a catalyst in the conversion of others was a dominant theme. Praising Debs's "wonderful self-denial American spirit," a Colorado supporter prayed for more men and women "who will be like you, crucified by men for the truth you preach." From a Brooklyn veteran, a self-confessed former "rabid militarist" and "Socialist hater," came a sentimental if deeply felt poem that honored the fundamental role Debs played in his conversion. Una Augusta Joiner sent a long letter that recounted the rural poverty and isolation of her Oklahoma family, the continued effect of Debs's visit in 1915 to their home, and the inspiration he still provided them. Redoubling her efforts for Socialism, Joiner fervently hoped that her family's efforts "will give us the opportunity to prove our worthiness to be your comrade."[9] One of the more poignant letters came from a Mrs. H. Benson of Grand Rapids, Michigan. Sixty-two years of age in 1920, Mrs. Benson had just voted for the first time in her life and had cast her ballot for the imprisoned Socialist leader. Sorrowful that even many "workingmen can't see," she wrote to share with Debs "something of the love that is expressed by those who *do* think." Hoping for eventual success of "Socialism, or whatever it may be called when it comes," Mrs. Benson affirmed that then "there will be no *wars* for we will be living nearer to Christ's teachings and as you have been likened to Him, because of your gentleness . . . may you still bear out to the world His likeness and may he bless you so abundantly with His Wonderful love that you cannot contain it."[10]

In more public forums as well, an explicit comparison of Debs to the crucified Christ became the dominant motif. "Stand here with me," John G. Stilli wrote during the summer of 1919 in the *Illinois Comrade*, "and tell me this, who is this man I see this morning on his way to Calvary—tell me that? And tell me this—tell me what crime did 'Gene Debs commit?'' Contrasting the attitude of American Christian bishops with that of Debs and other radicals, Stilli mocked: ''Christianity used to go to jail regularly. Jesus evidently expected as much.'' But now only radicals went ''while the bishop of Christ presides at the board of trade banquets or at the victory dinner.'' To an Ohio minister, Debs was the ''Social Savior . . . the vicarious victim of Society's sins, and his life is a continual crucifixion.'' Stressing Debs's public role as ''a priest of humanity,'' the Reverend Walter Hurt praised what he termed Debs's basic belief that man is able to ''work out his own salvation.'' Debs, he stated, ''believes every human being is better than his environment.''[11]

The figure of Christ was not the only symbol used to explain the meaning of Debs's imprisonment. Indeed, from the lips of Victor Berger, Hillquit, and many of the left-wing immigrants, it would have sounded quite foreign for both religious and cultural reasons. But for the many who did employ it, the comparison was no mere rhetorical device. The destructive effects of industrial capitalism spurred a profound religious revival in turn-of-the-century America, which pitted ''old fashion principles . . . with the amoral tendencies'' of the new order. Emphasizing ''the need of a new birth,'' as Timothy L. Smith has suggested, these older values were neither anachronistic nor misguided. Rather, in decided contrast with the boastful promise of linear social progress embraced by capitalism and, in a different context, by orthodox Socialist theory as well, these values drew their ''real strength from the common ideas of sin and forgiveness, love and duty, death and resurrection, which have been handed down from father to son and mother to daughter from generation to generation.''[12] A source of tension within the Socialist movement, this religious impulse simultaneously marked a major source of opposition to industrial capitalism.

This concentric circle of suffering and redemption structured Debs's core vision of the world. Throughout his career his speeches had followed the tradition of the Protestant jeremiad, and he never shied away from publicly acknowledging his understanding of the continuity in spirit between Christ and ''John Brown, Abraham Lincoln or Karl Marx.'' Debs's Christ, he wrote in 1917, was ''the martyred Christ of the working class.'' A ''pure communist'' who instructed his disciples to sell their possessions and live communally, this Christ ''organized a working class movement . . . for no other purpose than to destroy class rule and set up the common people as the sole and rightful inheritors of the earth.'' Christ, too, suffered ''the most farcical trial,'' but for three centuries following his crucifixion ''the movement he had inaugurated, fired by his unconquerable revolutionary spirit, persisted.'' Ultimately coopted by the ruling class, ''the dead Christ was [then] metamorphosized from the master revolutionist who was ignominiously slain, a martyr to his class, into the pious abstraction, the harmless theological divinity who died that John Pierpoint Morgan could be 'washed in the blood of the lamb.' " But for Debs and countless others, the example remained: Christ's love for the poor and his ultimate sacrifice "made forever holy the dark tragedy of his death, and gave to the ages his divine inspiration and his deathless name."[13]

Throughout his prison term, both at Moundsville and Atlanta, the example of Christ provided Debs with a constant source of encouragement. On the walls of each of those cells he hung no pictures of Karl Marx, Russian Bolshevik leaders, or his American comrades. Rather, as he awoke each morning, Debs stared at the contorted visage, crowned with thorns, of the crucified Christ. To Debs, that image represented the essential meaning of his own life and symbolized as well his understanding of the motivation of many of his comrades.[14]

But, like Christ, Debs had to suffer first before he might become a "divine inspiration" to the world. If before his incarceration he felt that he had already "given my life to the working class and its struggles drop by drop, and almost to the last atom of my strength,"[15] Debs discovered at Atlanta that even more would be required. In part, these trials were physical in nature. He entered prison in poor health a few months short of his sixty-fourth birthday. While he was not required to perform hard physical work at Atlanta, the climate, the confinement, and the regimentation of prison life continued to take its toll. Debs lost weight, had bouts of anxiety that kept him from sleep, and pined for those invigorating days of recuperation in Colorado. Although he tried to keep his condition from his family, and especially from Kate to whom he sent optimistic letters, Mabel Curry knew differently. In his notes to her, often secreted out in a packet of mail sent to Terre Haute, and during her visit to Atlanta in the summer of 1920, Debs confided his true condition. "He has been quite ill," Curry wrote David Karsner in November 1920, "ill and depressed. . . . But he has fooled his family *all* right."[16] As the prison sentence dragged on into 1921, Debs's physical condition continued to deteriorate. Theodore reported after a December 1921 visit that "Gene says he feels good . . . but there is a weariness in his voice that denotes the loss of vitality. How much recuperative power that is still available only time can tell."[17]

Beyond his physical condition, Debs's enforced separation from Curry caused both considerable anguish. Busy with preparations for her daughter's nineteenth birthday party in 1920, Mabel found the time to write a long letter to her "favorite convict." That designation tickled Eugene, but he also understood Curry's underlying feelings: "I know you don't enjoy the holidays and parties," he wrote in response, "and that

you only celebrate for others until you can celebrate my release."[18] Their
separation at times drove him to despair. "Sometimes the maddening
thought forces itself upon me that I shall not see you again," he wrote
following a particularly despondent mood. "But the reaction follows
swiftly, and must, or I would lose my sanity." Yet it was a difficult act of
faith he made. "Now and then there are flashes of vision, but so much I see
through a glass darkly. I can do little here," he acknowledged after more
than a year in jail, "but screw my courage to the sticking point, and that I
have done. . . . But I want you. My heart cries for you, aches for you, and
will not be still."[19]

Periodically depressed by this separation, Debs fought to retain his
belief that "our day . . . will come because it *must* come." After two
years in jail, and almost nine months since Mabel's visit, he affirmed that
"during that period of absence, trial, suffering and agony, our beautiful
love, divine in its perfection, had grown steadily stronger, defying time
and fate." Not surprisingly, however, his image of Mabel, and of all
women, remained true to the duality that had dominated his life. Despite
his pain, Eugene professed that Mabel had suffered more than he. But as
he had so often in the past with his comrades and with Mabel, he made her
experience a mirror through which to view himself better and in the process to become again the center of attention and concern. "You have inspired in me a greater, tender love than you know, and through its eyes I
can see the infinite grace of your spirit and the incomparable beauty of
your soul. What a truly wonderful little woman you really are. . . . You
are my wonderful lover, and my heart longs and reaches for you." As he
noted in an earlier prison letter, her very suffering inspired in him "the
reverence and admiration for all things beautiful."[20]

Mabel Curry understood clearly the deep insecurity in Debs's sense of
self that the isolation of prison intensified. She gladly accepted her role in
Debs's nearly daily struggle for emotional survival and lovingly responded
to his comments concerning her pain with words Debs most needed to
hear. On the second anniversary of his incarceration, she wrote him "that
never did a mortal pay more bravely nor more uncomplainingly for his
ideals than you have done. The two years have been long and tragic for us
all but they have [augmented] your stature as a *man* and your integrity as a
humanitarian." Hoping her letter found him thinking of his eventual
release, Mabel promised that he would "find nothing but devotion here
and the warmest hands and heart ready to receive you."[21]

Alone in his cell, Debs tried to maintain the positive note of Mabel's letters. Terribly lonely on his first Thanksgiving in Atlanta, he insisted to
Theodore (and not incidentally to himself) that he "never had the moral
strength and spiritual assurance I have to-day" and never felt "more free,
never more victorious." Two years later, facing his third Thanksgiving

dinner at Atlanta with no release in sight, he asserted again his determination: "The real me, *the man within*, they can't touch," he wrote his brother. "I am simply paying my dues to the cause."[22]

Debs kept as busy as possible at Atlanta. As at Moundsville, he was assigned to work in the prison hospital where the duty was light and the opportunity for talk with fellow prisoners ample. Debs frequently mediated disputes between regular prisoners as well as factional arguments among the political prisoners. But as in the two other penitentiaries where he had resided, Debs's greatest influence came from the daily conversations he had with the ordinary working-class prisoners. As he himself later noted, he recognized in these men a common brotherhood and took strength from them even as he encouraged them in their troubles. As one convicted thief wrote a friend, "The other prisoners loved him." Describing himself as anything but "an 'Idealist' " who found it impossible to "believe in any such theories," this convict yet proclaimed "that Gene Debs is a real man. . . . Indignities and insults have been heaped upon him because he has taken the part of the ignorant, downtrodden and oppressed in prison." Although locked in his cell fourteen hours a day, Debs spent the remaining time actively and constantly involved with the prison population and became something of a legend among the men. He even affected the prison guards, the infamous "screws" who dominated daily prison life. Sometime after Debs's release, Carlo Tresca, the Italian anarchist and former IWW organizer, found himself in Atlanta convicted of criminal obscenity for publishing a birth-control advertisement. Driven hard by the guards for his political and sexual views, Tresca's life changed dramatically after he received a letter from his friend Debs. He was given lighter duty and the constant harassment ceased, Tresca explained to a friend, because, as one guard expressed the feeling, " 'No friend of Gene Debs does a stroke of work in this jail.' "[23]

Despite these relationships with other inmates, prison life took its toll. Debs found he could not escape the persistent self-doubt that stalked his soul. His repeated assertions that he would not allow his isolation—which he likened "to suffocation and being buried alive"—to "touch my spirit" took on a forced quality after more than a year in jail. That his own sanity, as he had termed it, demanded such assertions he knew, but more frequently than he acknowledged his spirit was deeply depressed. As he looked from his prison cell, he saw the movement he had led for so long rent by fratricidal anger while all of the factions were as isolated politically as he himself was then physically from the daily concerns of the majority of American working people. Further, from that same prison cell he watched as the society to which he had devoted his life's work, in an effort to compel it to uphold its deepest ideals, conducted a furious purging of dissidents and radicals of all persuasions. In arresting these men and women, suppressing their publications, and deporting those of foreign birth—all in the years following the armistice that ended the war—American society paid little homage to even the most basic of democratic rights. As he watched in enforced inactivity, Debs's personal and political despondency merged to create the most profound depression he had ever experienced.[24]

"I had a strange dream last night," Gene wrote Mabel from Atlanta. "I was walking by the house where I was born—the house was gone and nothing left but ashes. All about me were ashes. My feet sank in them and my shoes filled with them. With much effort I struggled through. I stopped to brush the ashes from me. A man came along and pointed out that my clothes were tattered. I wandered on and found a secluded spot. Weary and sad I sat down to read." At this point in the dream, he heard music and dancers appeared. "Mr. Curry and Clarence Royce [a Terre Haute lawyer and friend] were there together, but were not dancing. You were dancing with a man I did not know or could not recognize. . . . You were unusually beautiful in a lovely gown as you stood beside your partner, but you seemed pale and not merry as the others. I was glad to be unobserved." Suddenly the dancers disappeared, but the dream continued: "Some one sat beside me and held my hand. It was you." At that moment, he recounted, "I awoke. Outside it was thundering and lightening and rain was falling. I did not go to sleep again—The house was gone—and only ashes—Ashes!"[25]

Desolate, depressed, and drained of energy, Debs confronted the demonic ferociousness of his doubts. Beyond Mabel's love nothing else had escaped the pervasive sense of destruction. In the ashes of his dream, he feared, lay the meaning of his life's work.

The depression that enveloped Debs in prison had many sources, but none was more entrenched than the pain he felt as he examined the Socialist movement's weak ties with American working people. As was his tendency, he saw this central political issue now in quite personal terms. "Down South here I am impressed today with the ironies of fate," he wrote on Labor Day 1920. Recalling his efforts to organize southern workers, even urging them immediately after the Pullman strike to apply for AFL charters, and remembering his attempts on behalf of the black worker, "demanding that he be unionized the same as the white worker," Debs felt he had little to show for his decades of work. "Well, today union labor is celebrating in the South—it has become exceedingly respectable (as long as it eschews the wicked radicals), is patronized by politicians and preachers and professors . . . and there isn't one among them who knows or cares that I am here, and not one of the union speakers who would dare mention my name." With a bitter bravado, he sought to adjust to that painful reality: "It is all clear to me, and right, as things now go. I have not the least fault to find. It could not have been otherwise, and I would not have it otherwise. I am where I was ticketed to and started for, and I thank God I reached my destination without being sidetracked. I had the satisfaction of being brought here, every foot of the way, by union men, not by scabs, and what more could I ask?''[26]

But sardonic parody could not erase the oppressive sense of failure. While Debs was never able to eliminate these doubts, he did take solace, in this, the starkest crisis of his life, in the cycle of death and rebirth that had for so long drawn the circumference of his vision. He found that inner strength to persevere in reflections on his own manliness and in the examples of others who had preceded him in that lonely path.

"As to the struggle with self," he confessed to Theodore from prison, "it is not a lack of frankness or fairness I wish I could tell you about it, but I can't even tell myself. I don't know the *why* of it. It is a sort of mental and spiritual reaction and at times it comes with pitiless severity. It is not new," Debs explained, recalling the fabric of his life, "save in degree. I suppose it is because I *see* the heights I must *feel* the depths, and they precisely correspond in extent. There are moments when all the ecstasies of the soul are mine and others when I see all that is darkest . . . and in the struggle to escape that ensues I feel myself undergoing a species of purging by fire as if I had that in me that sinned against my soul and indicted my manhood. I think Lincoln must have known something of this when he said that if there was anyone in purgatory who suffered more than he did he pitied him. During these periods of moral pregnancy and travail," Debs continued, "for such they are, it seems to me that my heart is the very heart and center of all the sadness and sorrow, all the pain and misery, and all the suffering and agony in the world. I don't know why it is so. I only know that deep melancholy is so completely a part of me, and I have been so often under its chastening influence, that it has become sacred to me, and costly as it is, I should not wish it taken out of my life.''[27]

His years in Atlanta Federal Penitentiary took the measure of Debs. His health and his separation from Mabel, Theodore, and other comrades depressed him, and vindictive punishments by Palmer, such as cutting off all visiting and mailing privileges just before the Wilson administration left office, added to his isolation.[28] But these trials paled before the private struggle Debs waged during these years. Never very introspective, the circumstances of prison prevented him from burying his doubts in renewed bursts of activity. The prospect that there was "nothing left but ashes" tormented Debs and nearly broke his spirit.

But it did not. In the Christ at Gethsemane Debs discovered more profoundly than ever before a spiritual brother whose own life was proof of the possibilities of rebirth and resurrection. In the "failure" of his career lay much anguish, but in the final analysis Debs's very confrontation with that pain allowed him to live with it. As he relived his life from his jail cell, he reaffirmed the outlines of his larger analysis. The malaise of industrial capitalism, as much spiritual as material, had transformed American society. It was evident in the altered meaning of citizenship, in the demeaned value assigned to an individual's work, and, most important, in the undercutting of the power of manhood and, as he had recently come to suggest, womanhood as well. Debs continued to "weep over the stark tragedy of the working class," as he wrote from prison in 1920. Their "poverty . . . misery . . . [and] despair" oppressed him just as their resistance to his particular synthesis of aggressive democratic thought, class awareness, and prophetic Christian symbolism continued to perplex and confuse.[29]

Yet Debs found renewed hope. In this the autumn of his life, he readjusted again to the recognition that the transformation he so deeply searched for would not be imminent, even as he found a sustaining meaning in the power his example and that of his comrades might have for those yet to come. Less sure, if no less intense, Debs looked forward to resuming his activities upon his release. With the Socialist party in splinters all about him, however, not even Debs could refuse again to engage in the party's factional disputes.

On 13 April 1919, the day Debs arrived at Moundsville, the factional struggle in New York reached a turning point. During the winter and early spring, the left wing had organized itself into an independent organization, issued a manifesto of principles, distributed its own membership cards, and collected its own monthly dues. On Sunday, the 13th, at a meeting of the party's state committee in Albany, the Hillquit forces retaliated. A motion by David P. Berenberg, which carried by a vote of 24-17, committed the state Socialist organization to recall the charter of any local that affiliated with the leftist Socialists. In immediate terms the vote meant that over 4,000 Socialists in various leftist locals were subject to expulsion. Beyond that, the resolution signified that the traditional party leadership had decided to contest the left in each and every local. The final split of the movement was now assured.[30]

When the left scheduled a national conference for New York that June, the traditional leaders of the Socialist party realized that their opponents intended to capture the party. As the spring elections for national office indicated, moreover, the left's chances were quite good. Led by the foreign-language federations, leftist candidates captured twelve of fifteen seats on the National Executive Committee and four of five of the international delegates. Never sensitive to issues of internal party democracy, the outgoing National Executive Committee, a majority of whom opposed the left, simply declared the recent elections invalid on the spurious grounds that too few members had voted and that the language federations had voted as a bloc. The May meeting of the committee also expelled the federations, consisting of over 20,000 members, and, for good measure, the state organization of Michigan for its proposed revision of the state constitution that would outlaw any call for immediate demands by Socialists. All in all, more than 26,000 members were expelled without a hearing.[31]

The response to this dictatorial action from Socialists across the country was swift. Literally hundreds of letters poured into the national office protesting the absence of internal party democracy and condemning "boss rule." Predictably, the secretary of the Jackson (Michigan) local was quite bitter: "We do not accuse you of treason to Socialism," M. V. Brentmasser wrote. "We know that you were never socialists."[32] From Warren, Ohio, J. F. Denison, a party member since 1898, expressed disgust over the expulsions and placed the origins of the current dispute in the struggle over Bill Haywood. In 1912 the "reds" favored " 'political and direct action' combined" and the "yellows *political action only*," Denison recalled, and he argued that the growth in the left by 1919 had stemmed from the IWW belief in "the necessity of the solidarity of the working class in 'mass action.' " So, Denison concluded, "this party fight started seven years ago has come to a showdown. The *reds* are now undoubtedly in the majority . . . [and] I am on the 'Left' side where I was seven years ago as a *Red*. This is Marxian, as I read it."[33] Although the Bolshevik Revolution also played a key role in the formation of the Socialist left, Denison was correct to see echoes of the IWW in the left's calls throughout 1919 for immediate revolutionary action. Unaware of the intricacies of Bolshevik ideological disputes and still free of direct Russian influence on their movement, the American left interpreted the current battle over revolutionary strategy in terms of earlier struggles.

So did the left's Socialist opponents. Harry L. Arnold, of Xenia, Ohio, supported the national office and suggested that since 1912 "things have not seemed to be going right." Following the recall of Haywood, Ohio's Socialist leaders gave, he thought, little emphasis to industrial organizing. As a result, they themselves were recalled from office and replaced by a leftist slate.[34] While Socialist opponents of the left considered the labeling of the party leadership as pro-war "Schneiderman's" unjust and ridiculous,[35] their anger over the expulsion of the federations was also expressed in terms of older disputes. "We do not believe," Mary M. Dawson, secretary of the Columbus (Kansas) local wrote in the summer of 1919, "that the NEC, or any other party official has the right, under the constitution of the party, to exercise disciplinary powers over the membership." Insisting that such power resided solely in the rank and file, she reminded Germer that "only on that theory can the Socialist party be kept *safe for Democracy*."[36]

Throughout the summer of 1919, as Debs adjusted to Atlanta's debilitating climate, the battle raged within the party. Accusations were hurled back and forth, and the old issues of industrial unionism and internal democracy became, for a moment, inextricably intertwined with a religious belief in the imminence of the American revolution. The wave of strikes that swept the country in coal, steel, and textiles fueled this fervor. The Seattle general strike, which led to worker control of the city for a few days, and the bitter strike of the police in Boston, defeated only when Governor Calvin Coolidge mobilized the national guard, encouraged in many leftist partisans the belief that America hovered on the brink of its revolutionary moment. To anyone dedicated to discovering the revolutionary potential of the masses, it now seemed evident.

Yet the left itself was not unified. Disagreement arose over the proper tactical approach to the Socialist party. Doggedly following their understanding of their Russian heroes, about a third of the organized left bolted the national conference in New York that June. They refused to accept the majority position that sought to capture the Socialist party and instead insisted on the immediate formation of a competing American Communist party. They argued that Lenin and Trotsky always valued ideological purity over a mathematical majority and proudly proclaimed that the Russian leaders never compromised with factional opponents. Three separate tendencies now existed within the decimated Socialist movement: a discredited national leadership still controlled the Socialist party; the leaders of the foreign-language federations remained intent on forming a Communist party; and another leftist group, composed of immigrants and a majority of the American-born left wing, were officially committed to commandeering the Socialist party.[37]

All three tendencies clashed in Chicago in late August. At the Socialist national convention the old leadership remained in control and, with the help of Chicago's police, physically expelled delegates whose credentials they challenged. John Reed, the famous Bolshevik sympathizer whose paean to that revolution, *Ten Days That Shook the World*, had helped create the American mystique of Bolshevism, was the most prominent individual ejected by the police. Soon, however, he was joined by many others, including the entire California delegation. While the Communist party birthed itself in another hall, Reed, along with Marguerite Prevey, Alfred Wagenknecht, and Charles Baker, created the Communist Labor party. Although the two Communist parties would eventually merge in May 1921, at the direction of the leaders of the Communist International (Comintern), the 1919 split did reinforce an important guideline for future American radicals. Ideological purity assumed a theological importance, and the formation of competing splinter groups or, conversely, attempts to crush these same groups became the *sine qua non* of revolutionary integrity. As Max Eastman wrote in 1919 of the "mood, not [the] conscious intent," of the immigrant leaders of the left, they sought to organize "a Russian Bolshevik church, with more interest in expelling heretics than winning converts." They held "a pretty fixed opinion that although Americans must perforce be admitted to the church they must not be admitted in such numbers as to endanger the [Slavic Socialist] machine's hold upon the dogmas and the collection box." Given the tepid welcome American workers extended the left, the purging of erstwhile comrades in pursuit of theoretical purity became a major if misleading sign of continued political relevance.[38]

The Socialist party fared little better following 1919. A discredited national leadership attempted to direct a fractured party. The war, its domestic repression, and the factional struggles greatly reduced the membership rolls, and those who remained, party secretary Otto Branstetter noted in 1921, "are doubtful of ourselves and our own ability." Few retain "any faith in the Party," he informed Debs, and "nobody wants to do anything through the Party."[39] This depressing condition sharply limited the influence of the party's analysis even when it was accurate. With the exception of a decreasing handful of the faithful, few Americans were concerned with James Oneal's incisive critique of the left's infatuation with Russia. "You live in a reflected world," Oneal retorted while debating Robert Minor over the question of affiliation with the Comintern. Echoing Debs's 1912 response to Haywood, Oneal pressed the issue: "You have thought nothing out. You have not analyzed the situation in the United States. You don't know the American proletariat. You don't know its psychology. You don't know its history." Attacking the very heart of the left's position, Oneal argued that, rather than tottering, American capitalism concluded the war more powerful than before and thus America was "the last place to expect a huge mass movement."[40] But few listened, and the party's lack of credibility produced only catcalls from their leftist opponents.

Through the bars of his cell Debs watched as the party he had led for so long nearly disintegrated. During his first months in prison he received contrary impressions from his two closest confidants. Theodore regretted that the split came at a time when government repression was intense and noted archly that in Indiana at least he had not heard of any organized leftist movement. Mabel Curry, on the other hand, thought during the spring of 1919 that the left was "absolutely right." The national leadership was bankrupt, she told Rose Pastor Stokes, and, in a classic sentence, Curry expressed the emotional power of the Russian example on American radicals: "The revolution in Russia has been a university course for all radicals who wish to know the way."[41] Following the August conventions, however, even Curry tempered her enthusiasm.

During the winter and spring of 1919–20, Debs remained publicly silent while he tried privately, as far as he could, to urge all factions to reunite. Following a prison interview with Debs in January 1920, Socialist attorney Samuel Castleton informed Hillquit that Debs agreed with Hillquit's analysis of the split and felt as Hillquit did "that all differences are reconcilable." For his part, the New York leader thought that Debs was "the only man in the United States who could bring about a satisfactory reconciliation."[42] Theodore, too, agreed with this evaluation, although he was quite doubtful that a reunification was possible, for "the wounds are deep." Both Debs brothers, however, expressed hope that the rank and file would not follow their leaders and would demand unity in order to present the strongest ticket in the coming fall elections. To further this effort, Debs agreed that spring to accept the Socialist party's presidential nomination for the fifth time. It was the first time in American history that a federal convict ran for the presidency of the United States.[43]

In contrast with his past conduct, Debs now agreed to try to mediate the bitter dispute from his jail cell. On 15 April 1920, Germer, Castleton, and Karsner journeyed to Atlanta to confer with Debs and Joseph Coldwell, a Rhode Island political prisoner who represented the left wing. As a result of the conference Karsner and later Mabel Curry traveled throughout the Midwest and especially Ohio in an effort to establish a basis for reunification, using Debs's proposed presidential campaign as the healing symbol. Two weeks later Karsner reported mixed results. The Communist Labor party, Prevey had told him, would support Debs fully, but it was not clear that this would lead to a united movement. Further east, the results were depressing. Socialist party leaders in New York, especially Algernon Lee and Julius Gerber, adamantly rejected any attempts at reconciliation and angrily attacked Karsner and indirectly Debs for even attempting such an effort. Indeed, the "old line leaders" of the party, Karsner reported, did not even want Debs as their candidate. About the leaders of the Communist party Karsner remained silent, as there was no hope for public expressions of support from them. Despite these results, Karsner encouraged Debs not to alter his plans concerning the nomination. Referring to the "regrettable . . . split in the the party in 1912," he reminded the imprisoned leader that he had nonetheless doubled his vote that year over 1908. "You are the only man in the United States who can speak for us, dear Gene, and I urge you to do it."[44]

Debs was nominated for the presidency at the Socialist party's May convention. As had been true so many times in the past, without Debs the Socialists would attract little national attention, and even those who opposed Debs saw little choice. But the nomination did not ease the tension between these Socialist leaders and their candidate. Attempting to retain his fervor for the Bolshevik revolutionaries while simultaneously offering himself as a symbol of potential unity—all from a jail cell where he lacked the detailed information concerning the ongoing debate—Debs's attitude continued to antagonize Socialist leaders.

In a letter to Karsner in late April—later widely published in the Socialist press—Debs reacted to Karsner's efforts as his representative. "There is no fundamental difference," he explained, "between the great majority of the rank and file of the three parties." Blaming all sides for the mistakes made that resulted in the split, Debs stressed that "I personally know most of the members of all these factions" and believed them "equally eager to serve the cause." He predicted that in a "united front" centered on his candidacy lay "the greatest opportunity ever presented to us since the day we were organized." The left saw in the ejection of five Socialist assemblymen from the New York state legislature for their party affiliation validation of their scorn for political action in capitalist society. Debs, however, argued that the illegal action of that state's elected officials "has shaken the whole country." It was not an impressive letter. Debs's political analysis and enthusiastic exhortation suffered from his obvious ignorance of recent intraparty debates. While leaders of the left remained impassive, the leaders of the Socialist party grew livid with anger over Debs's assertion that they, too, were at fault. His message to the upcoming convention—that it "be strong and stand firm; clear-sighted and avoid compromise"—was interpreted by many as support for the left.[45]

Debs's conduct following his nomination furthered this impression. In an interview in the Atlanta *Georgian*, Debs proclaimed himself "a radical" and explained that his major fear "has always been that I might not be radical enough. In my own party, I always led the minority, but I hope to lead a united Socialist party to the polls this fall." Concerning the internal fighting, Debs took it as "a good, healthy sign, the radicals keep the conservatives from giving away too much to popularize the movement." In a reference that could only antagonize the "old line leaders," Debs explained that was exactly what had happened with the Populist party in 1896. The leadership, "by pandering to more conservative elements . . . lost the radical support of their party, which became the Socialist party." To Berger, Hillquit, and other longtime Socialist leaders, the analogy was obvious, even if Debs's presentation of his own history was misleading.[46] When a Socialist committee arrived at Atlanta to offer Debs the nomination formally, federal prisoner 9653 continued with his criticism of their policy. He took them to task for refusing to vote for unconditional affiliation with the Third International and repeated the detailed criticisms Prevey had "suggested and *more*. . . . There will be all kinds of comment & I will be denounced," Gene wrote his brother, "but

I'll stake my life I made no mistake. I followed the inner light that God put there to guide through dark places and it has never led me astray and never will."[47]

Less than a month later, however, Debs had cause to reconsider this divine inspiration. Responding to his criticism of the party, Hillquit wrote Debs a long detailed letter that contained an occasional sharp rebuke. Referring to "the superficial critic" who might think the party platform conservative, Hillquit defended its "systematic omission of our favorite Marxian terminology" on the grounds that such language remained incomprehensible to most Americans: "I am now more convinced than ever that in order to get our message across we must divorce ourselves from the worship of phrases, and talk the plainest possible English." Insisting that this did not mean the abandonment of the class struggle, Hillquit also confronted Debs's criticism of the party's reservations concerning affiliation with the Third International. "Like you," Hillquit wrote, "I am a determined and enthusiastic supporter of the Soviet Government of Russia." But Hillquit insisted on a distinction between that government and the International. He refused "to take every dictum that comes from Moscow" or to "abdicate my own judgment" concerning American conditions. "The Communists of Russia have done certain things which their own desperate conditions have probably forced upon them," Hillquit argued, but when "they attempt to elevate such actions into a general and universal maxim of Socialist conduct in all countries, I must refuse to accept it." Specifically, Hillquit pointed to the International's invitation to the IWW, its insistence on the "dictatorship of the proletariat" as the only revolutionary model and, most heatedly, to the International's ban on Socialist groups in Europe and most recently the American party "and your humble servant in particular."[48]

Despite the basic differences that had long separated them, Debs was greatly affected by Hillquit's letter. Ignoring Hillquit's consistent criticism of both leftist Socialist and Communist factions—which Debs himself had often led in the past—Debs instructed his brother to tell Hillquit that he now understood that many of his—Debs's—criticisms were made without sufficient information and expressed special interest in Hillquit's analysis of the question of affiliation with the International. Debs further instructed his brother to state that, even if certain small disagreements remained, he heartily agreed with Hillquit's basic position. This new tone in Debs's comments became public almost immediately following a June 1920 visit from Kate Richards O'Hare. Recently released from jail herself, O'Hare brought from Atlanta Debs's new campaign theme. He "deplored the recent differences," she reported, but emphasized that " 'this is no time for divisions.' " Attesting to the sincerity of "some of my most dear friends" in the Communist and Communist

Labor parties, O'Hare quoted Debs as insisting that they were nonetheless "mistaken in their tactics, and they will discover that the Socialist party is best adopted for emancipating the American working class." Three months later, Debs was even more specific. " 'The Moscow program would commit us to a policy of armed insurrection,' " William Feigenbaum reported Debs as stating. " 'It is outrageous, autocratic, ridiculous.' "[49]

This abrupt turnabout in part reflected Debs's isolation in prison. Since he responded as he did with incomplete information, his comments frequently caused angry reactions from one or another of the factional opponents which, in turn, caused him to re-evaluate his earlier statement. To avoid this predicament in the future, Debs told Karsner in August 1920 that he would make no formal announcement until he had ample time to study the issues involved.[50] But as his interviews with O'Hare and Feigenbaum made clear, his basic analysis had already undergone an important change. Throughout his Socialist years Debs had frequently criticized party policy. Contrary to his claim, he never led in any consistent fashion the Socialist minority, but he had symbolized for many a commitment to a democratic, egalitarian movement. From that perspective his infatuation with the Russian Revolution and his advocacy, during 1918 and 1919, of the imminence of American soviets, contradicted the beliefs of a lifetime. While many of the nuances of Marxist theory remained incomprehensible and seemingly unimportant to Debs and other comrades in those heady years, Debs did find himself unequivocally aligned with some rather odd bedmates. In the calls for armed insurrection and massive direct action, Debs supported for this moment the very position he had so forcefully rejected in 1912. The Russian tonic proved quite powerful, especially as few American Socialists ever thought their comrades would come to power anywhere in the world. After years of adjusting to the wilderness, the riches of the banquet table overwhelmed them.

In jail, however, Debs's fantasy of the working class liberating him died a painful if rather quick death. How could he maintain that hope when working people did not protest in significant numbers his incarceration and union men conducted him to jail? Further, as the internal fighting grew more intense, even Debs in his isolation began to sense that many factional leaders were more intent on purging dissidents than approaching workers. As a result Debs decided by the August interview with Karsner that, when his announcement did appear, he would offer it "as a member of the socialist party, as an ordinary servant in the ranks. I am not a leader of the party," Debs persisted in believing, "and have never wished to be. I have never wanted to exploit myself, and it would be self-exploitation if I presumed to tell the party what it should do."[51]

In this somewhat subdued tone Debs approached the 1920 campaign.

He, of course, could not tour the country, but prison officials did allow him a weekly press release. While not an effective replacement for his presence, Debs made the most of the opportunity. "I would rather have a man think and vote against me than vote like a sheep," he argued in one release and proceeded to attack corrupt union officials who, in alliance with capitalists, encouraged that ovine attitude. He urged workers to remember the "trail of blood along the track of centuries" that marked their common existence. Vote, he implored, with the passionate awareness that stems from the recognition that "you are still exploited and starved and degraded" and that looks to the future "that is to see your class free and your cause crowned with victory." But not even Debs fully believed his words any longer. In his last statement of the campaign he claimed that he was immune to further disappointment. "The [election] result will be as it should be," he declared fatalistically. "The people will vote for what they think they want, to the extent that they think at all, and they too will not be disappointed." Struggling with a pervasive depression that would reduce his life's work to ashes, he continued: "The people can have anything they want. The trouble is they do not want anything. At least they vote that way on election day." As he searched for some basis to affirm his life's work, Debs concluded with a personal reflection that addressed more his pain than it did the political situation: "If the earth and all it contains is not for the people, not a handful of them, but all the people, then there is certainly a mighty mistake somewhere that needs the Almighty's correction."[52]

The results of the election did little to lift Debs's depression. Although he topped his 1912 total, the 919,000 ballots cast for convict 9653 did so only barely, and his share of the national vote dropped from 6 to 3 percent. There was some solace to be gained from the protest that nearly one million Americans registered against the repression of radicals. But, as in the past, the majority of these men and women were not necessarily committed to a Socialist program. The gaunt visage of "old Gene Debs" drew them, and they applauded his principled stand in defense of traditional American liberties and somewhat secondarily his Socialist convictions. But even this homage did not relieve Debs's sense of despair. "I *knew* when the election was over and the pressure removed," Curry wrote Karsner that November, "he would go to pieces and he *did.*" Caged in prison, each month of confinement draining him further, Debs sank deeper into depression. Besieged on all sides with demands that he formally enter the factional disputes, he withdrew further into himself. "Gene can't stand many more months," Mabel wrote Upton Sinclair after the election. "He is constantly seeing such harrowing sights—and such drafts are being made on his sympathies that I know it is 'eating in.' "[53]

As winter slowly gave way to spring in 1921, concern for the fate of Debs and the other political prisoners intensified. The radical movement, encompassing all three organized parties, remained weak and marginal despite the rhetorical expectations, and the anti-radical repression had further dispersed and isolated these men and women. For some, especially those in the IWW, Haywood's flight to the Soviet Union in April 1921 to avoid his jail term represented the depressed state of the movement. Long a symbol of the militant working-class movement whose integrity and commitment, if not always his tactics, were widely acknowledged, Haywood's desertion of his IWW comrades and the many other radicals in jail greatly demoralized those who remained. As one former supporter angrily stated two years later, "If Bill ever comes back to the United States, he will be met at the dock by a direct action committee of the I.W.W., who will leave very little for the government to do." Oddly enough, the one source of hope came not from the radical movement itself but rather from the new administration of Warren Gamaliel Harding. During the campaign Harding had supported amnesty for political prisoners, based on individual case-by-case review. As Debs explained his hopes to Branstetter in 1921, Harding, in contrast with Wilson, "showed a decent disposition towards the political prisoners."[54]

Reflecting fundamental political differences, the amnesty movement was anything but unified. Former pro-war Socialists such as Algie M. Simons wrote personal appeals on Debs's behalf, which cited his health and the assertion that, in contrast to Berger and others, Debs "was bitterly anti-German." Norman Thomas, the New York Socialist minister who, in his youth, had been Harding's newspaper boy in Marion, Ohio, twice visited his former customer in 1921 to plead for Debs. Samuel Gompers organized a Committee for Amnesty that spent as much time fighting those radicals still active as it did working for the release of political prisoners. The Socialist party viewed these efforts with some concern. Speaking for the leadership, Branstetter repeatedly argued that Gompers's motives were not to be trusted. Further, he stated, care needed to be exercised when working with other radicals as well, for many of them, he felt, were willing to "sacrifice" Debs for the sake of the other political prisoners. As Branstetter made clear, the Socialists' primary concern was to secure Debs's release, regardless of the fate of the other prisoners.[55]

In late March Harding's attorney general, Harry M. Daugherty, charged by the president to review the file of Debs and other political prisoners, issued an unusual order. He informed the warden at Atlanta to place Debs on a train, alone and unguarded, for a trip to Washington. Debs spent a day with Daugherty and other administration officials and favorably impressed them. Although word of the conference and its unusual circumstances leaked out, Debs obeyed Daugherty's stricture about disclosing their conversation to anyone. Not even Mabel was informed of the discussion. This development, however, greatly excited Debs and his supporters, and many, including Debs himself, now argued against a planned demonstration and picket line around the White House. Hopes that he might be released on Independence Day collapsed in the face of an organized opposition from the newly founded American Legion. Debs's depression, one shared by his close comrades, was profound. By that fall, hoping to create a public atmosphere to encourage Harding, Mabel, Theodore, and other comrades renewed plans for a Washington demonstration. Backed by petitions totaling more than 300,000 signatures and with 700 organizational endorsements, a group of supporters picketed the White House on 15 November.[56]

The renewed activity did not lighten Debs's depression. As the hopes of the spring evaporated in the heat of the American Legion's protest, Debs prepared for a longer stay in Atlanta. Following a visit with him, Prevey tried to ease his tense and tired mood. Reminding him that he and Harding shared at least one thing in common, an enjoyment of the motion picture star, Tom Mix, she jokingly assured Gene that "the president will appreciate your desire to see Tom. Some day, dear Gene, we shall see Tom do his stunts and you can laugh all you want." But Debs was not then in a laughing mood. In October he issued a series of instructions to Theodore that had all the markings of a man grimly battening down the hatches as a major storm approached. He no longer wanted anyone to visit him, and he told his brother to inform as many comrades as possible to stop sending him packages or letters. Debs even proscribed Theodore's correspondence, demanding letters only when absolutely necessary and then as brief as possible. For his part, he announced he would write Theodore only spare and infrequent letters in the future. Isolated and depressed, Debs felt that contact with the outside would only increase his sense of impotence and preferred instead to preserve his strength for the essential private battle to survive. "There are no bars and no walls for the man who in his heart is free," Debs told his brother, "and there is no freedom for the man who in his heart is a slave."[57]

Debs's depression did not alter his political position. Repeatedly, he insisted to the Socialist leadership, he forbade any special pleading for himself at the expense of other political prisoners. He rejected any suggestions that he accept a release conditioned on the promise to cease future political activity. Debs succinctly provided Theodore with his nonnegotiable position: "I either go out a man as I came in or I serve my term to the last day."[58]

But Debs did not have to serve his full sentence. Responding to a growing public pressure, Harding announced on 23 December 1921 that Debs and twenty-three other political prisoners would have their sentences commuted to time already served on Christmas Day. Debs was informed the following day and immediately began his bittersweet preparations for his departure. As elated as he was to have won his release without requesting a pardon and in the company of at least a portion of the other political prisoners, Debs felt a deep sadness at leaving his friends and fellow prisoners of the past three years. During the most severe personal crisis of his life, the convicts at Atlanta had stood by him, encouraged him, and reminded him in his most desolate days of the potential that each individual possessed. In turn, Debs had befriended many of them. As one prison-mate, Sam Moore, remembered some years later while still in the penitentiary: "God what would I not give for those old days those happy days, those miserable days back again. As miserable as I was I would defy fate with all its cruelty as long as Debs held my hand, and I was the most miserably happiest man on earth when I knew he was going home Christmas."[59]

On Christmas afternoon Theodore and a group of Socialist comrades met Debs at the gates of Atlanta Penitentiary. As they joyfully and tearfully embraced and fervently kissed one another, a low rumbling in the background intensified. Warden Fred Zerbst, in violation of every prison regulation, had opened each cell block to allow the more than 2,300 inmates to throng to the front of the main jail building to bid a final goodbye to their friend. Turning away from the prison, Gene started down the long walkway to the parked car. As he did, a roar of pain and love welled up from the prison behind him. With tears streaming down his face, he turned and, hat in hand, stretched out his arms. Twice more, as he walked to the car, the prisoners demanded his attention. Twice more he reached to embrace them. At the car, a terribly thin and drained Debs offered one final good-bye and quickly entered.[60]

Union men might have smoothed his journey to jail, but Debs remained the only American who could evoke such love and admiration from this primarily working-class prison population. One of his first actions upon release again suggested why Debs was so loved. On the way to the train that would take him to Washington and an interview with the president, Debs removed from his wallet the five dollar bill prison regulations provided each released prisoner. With a short note, he sent it to the committee working for the release of Bartolomeo Vanzetti and Nicola Sacco, two working-class Italian immigrant anarchists accused of murder by a Massachusetts court. There would not be another American radical like him for some time.[61]

Following a brief, pleasant interview with Harding, who simply desired to meet this famous prisoner, Debs began his journey back to Terre Haute. As it had more than a quarter of a century earlier, his native city marked his return from jail with a gigantic demonstration. A crowd estimated at over 25,000, considerably swelled by a massive influx of Clay County miners, met Debs's train as it pulled into the depot at eight o'clock on the evening of 28 December. Stepping off the train, Debs was lovingly grabbed by comrades, hoisted on their shoulders, and carried to the wagon that would lead the procession—the very same wagon that had led the procession on his return from Woodstock in 1895. Men fought for the honor to harness themselves to the lead ropes that would propel their leader through the streets of Terre Haute. Exhilarated despite his exhaustion, Debs tried to respond to the cries and shouts of the crowd, but its intensity simply overwhelmed him. Slowly the men pulling the wagon inched their way through the densely packed streets, traveling the short distance from the depot to Debs's house at 451 North Eighth Street. Waving for a final time, Debs left the wagon and walked up the steps of his front porch for the first time in almost three years.[62]

As powerful and moving as this greeting was, the shouts had barely died when far more troublesome issues confronted the weakened sixty-six-year-old Socialist. The preceding April, the Communist party initiated a direct attack on Debs for his failure to join it. Referring to him as "this sincere and mistaken old man," an editorial in the journal, *The Communist*, argued that Debs's revolutionary commitment had "burned itself out, and he now associates with those whose role will be that of the hangmen to the proletarian revolution in America." Claiming that Debs refused to grasp "the hand which Lenin extended," Louis Fraina, the editor, continued his magical incantation of revolutionary phrases to condemn Debs. "Poor old Debs," he wrote, "straining his weak eyes in the direction of the red vanguard of the revolution, sinks deeper and deeper into the swamp of social-democratic reform. His once heroic figure will grow smaller and smaller as the proletariat reaches ever higher and higher heights." In a final snide comment, referring to Debs's journey to Washington to meet with the attorney general, Fraina stated: "Debs has gained his liberty and lost his revolutionary soul."[63]

As vicious as the editorial was, it only equalled the tone that dominated all discussion between Socialists and Communists. All the factions knew, however, that Debs's public endorsement remained the prize, and they besieged Debs to announce for their group with an intensity greater than when he was in jail. Even members of the Communist party swallowed their official analysis and appeared on Debs's porch, although Fraina himself remained too busy with revolutionary politics in Moscow before various international Communist commissions to bother much about events in Terre Haute.[64]

Immediately after New Year's Day 1922, Oneal, the former Terre Haute steelworker, led a committee from the Socialist party to see Debs. Rumors abounded as to Debs's ultimate attitude, and the group sought assurances that James Maurer's impression following a fall 1921 interview "that the 'impossibilists' have not succeeded in fooling" Debs had not changed. Debs gave them that assurance. Whatever his disagreements with the Socialist party he would not abandon it and, he added, he found himself in sharp disagreement with many of the positions the left had taken. But Debs stressed that at this time he spoke confidentially and, as Theodore repeated in a telegram to Oneal after the meeting, he was not well enough to defend his position in public debate. In an attempt to deflect the demand that he enter the debate, Gene and Theo suggested that the party emphasize amnesty for all political prisoners and relief for the Russian famine as its major priorities that spring.[65]

In a February article Debs stressed those concerns and suggested that egocentric desires of the leaders of all factions had greatly contributed to the dispute. He also stated that, when his health permitted, he would issue a full and detailed account of his position.[66] But rather than quieting the clamor, Debs's article seemed to have fanned it. Throughout February and March a constant parade of unannounced and uninvited visitors knocked on his door, each insisting on an audience, as individually all felt they possessed critical insight and information concerning the political struggle. The mail brought even more requests. Finally, in late March Debs snapped, and Branstetter, a persistent but by no means unique petitioner, bore the brunt of Debs's accumulated anger. "You cannot seem to understand that I am sick and worn and that I have not had the ghost of a chance to rest since I got out of the penitentiary. The visitors come every day," Debs complained, "and most of them have grievances or troubles to tell me about or want something done. I have just had two hours with a communist. Another is waiting for me." His house, he sharply explained, was in disarray, the result of long overdue repairs; his wife sick, "on the verge of utter nervous prostration"; and he himself was a full thirty pounds underweight. Yet "you and those you speak for insist that I must declare myself and of course declare myself your way."

Somewhat unfairly, Debs maintained this bitter tone as he discussed the current political context. "When I entered prison," he reminded this party leader, "there was a united party. When I came out it had been torn to pieces. I had nothing to do with it." Implying that the party officials wanted Debs to declare his stance in order to relieve the party of the disastrous tension these same officials helped to create, Debs recalled for Branstetter that he still held membership in the Socialist party "and that ought to signify that I have not turned against the party as has been intimated." But neither could he then, without further information, uncritically endorse the party: "You recite the outrages perpetuated by the communists upon the Socialist party," he bluntly stated, "but unfortunately the outrages were not confined to one side."[67]

Debs and Branstetter ultimately reconciled the tension between them and reasserted the affection they held for each other. But the events of that spring convinced Debs that, contrary to what he had hoped upon his release, it would be impossible to devise a plan to reunite the contesting branches of the radical movement.[68] Each day brought further distressing news. The same day Debs wrote Branstetter, he received a letter from Maynard Shipley, a California Socialist and personal friend, informing Debs that he and his wife had left the party as it was now nothing more than "the ally of petty-bourgeois reform organizations." Debs's response to his friend, that "in the larger and truer sense you and I are always in the same party and the same movement," was an increasingly inadequate comment on the larger political issues.[69]

Through the spring and summer Debs nonetheless remained silent, carefully editing the articles Karsner prepared for publication under his name to avoid further controversy.[70] His health remained poor, and the constant demands made by comrades further weakened him. That July Debs entered the Lindlahr Sanitarium in Chicago, a natural cure treatment center run by the Seventh Day Adventists. The visitors, however, still streamed to his door, and within two weeks Theodore successfully demanded that his brother switch to another branch of the center in Elmhurst, some fifteen miles outside of Chicago.[71]

While this change helped Debs secure needed rest, his own actions created obstacles to a more complete recuperation. Responding to news reports of the impending execution by the Soviet government of Russian revolutionaries opposed to aspects of the Bolshevik regime, Debs cabled his one-time enthusiastic admirer, Lenin: "I protest with all the civilized people in the name of humanity against the execution of any of the Social Revolutionaries or the unjust denial of their liberty," he told the Russian leader. "Soviet Russia can set an example by refusing to follow the practices of worldwide czardom and should uphold the higher standards we seek to erect and profess to observe." The response from the American comrades was predictable. Communist supporters barraged Debs with protests and demands for a retraction; Socialists applauded and asked for an even broader statement. Although the doctors refused many visitors permission to see their patient, Debs was kept quite busy with this new correspondence.[72]

In other ways as well Debs disregarded his doctor's orders. As he grew stronger, he actively sought out old friends and comrades with whom he could disregard politics and enjoy himself. In August, for example, Debs signed himself out and had a long rollicking evening with Carl Sandburg and Sinclair Lewis at Sandburg's Chicago home. Drinking until the early hours of the morning, Debs confessed the next day that he "had to break written sanitarium rules" out of respect for the demands of friendship![73] Equally important to him was his relationship with Mabel Curry. In New York with her husband that summer, Mabel and Eugene exchanged long letters (possibly through Karsner, who was quite aware of the relationship[74]). When Mabel returned home that fall, they continued to profess their love and on 5 November, Eugene's sixty-seventh birthday, Mabel sent him a box of taffy she made herself, each piece of which contained a small love note. Debs "wept over" the gift and told Mabel that the little messages "contained the line, the word my heart has been hungering for and I have almost been dying for these days and weeks." Gene confirmed plans for Mabel to visit the following week and promised her a special treat. A friend had given as a present "a quart of rare old home made wine and I'm going to save it till you come and then we will have a birthday drink together."[75]

But the enjoyment of friends and visits from Curry did not ease the political demands made on Debs. Feeling more rested than he had in years despite his occasional carousings, Debs prepared his long-awaited statement on the factional strife, which he released through the national headquarters of the Socialist party on 2 October 1922.

"At the time I entered prison," Debs reminded current and former comrades, "the Socialist Party, though shaken violently in the general upheaval and shattered by the fierce and relentless persecution its anti-war attitude had precipitated upon it, was still a united party." Stressing the pain he felt at seeing comrades who were "once standing at elbow-touch" now "pitted against each other in bitter fratricidal strife," Debs explained that prison censorship and concern for his own health had prevented him from speaking out earlier. Now having studied the issue "as best I have been able to," Debs was prepared to announce his decision—but not before he once again claimed that he spoke "for myself only and for no one else" and rejected in advance any importance to his views beyond that accorded to any comrade in the ranks.

"I have arrived at the definite conclusion," Debs informed the American radical movement, "that my place in the future as in the past is in the Socialist Party, and in its ranks and beneath its banner I shall continue to serve the working class and the social revolution." Recalling the party's formation twenty-five years earlier, "a child of the American Railway Union," Debs understood no reason "why I should desert the Socialist Party now":

I have spent the better part of my active life in its service and why should I now turn upon it and rend it; seek to tear down, destroy what I have devoted all these years of struggle and persecution helping to build? I admit that the party has made mistakes and that it is not to-day what I would like to see it, but the same would be true of any other party I might join. If the Socialist Party is not the revolutionary work-ingclass party it should be, it can be made so, but if it is held that this is impossible then how is it possible to achieve that result with the same material, the same comrades, the same ultimate aims, merely adopt-ing another name and marching under another banner?

As Debs's argument strongly implied, he was no longer infatuated with the Russian example and considered the fine points of ideology largely ir-relevant to American conditions. Pointedly, however, Debs moved beyond this dismissal of arcane ideological disputations. Noting the com-mon agreement among all for political and economic organization of the working class, he approached in public the edge of his own inner doubt: "If after twenty-five years of the best effort at our command we should confess that we have failed and that we cannot make the Socialist Party the true political expression of the class struggle, then I should have to con-clude that the same melancholy failure would mark our efforts to build up such a party under any other name."

A powerful statement of a confirmed personal faith anchored in the previous twenty-five years of agitation, Debs's press release was also more than that. The prewar movement had had a great viability, he suggested, and had made important inroads on the consciousness of Americans. Despite the current conditions, he refused to believe that the moment had passed and urged the comrades in each faction to unify and broaden the movement once again. On the critical question of affiliation with the Comintern, Debs continued his insistence that all radicals understand American conditions first. The bitter ideological fighting on this point was unfortunate, and Debs hoped that it would soon disappear so that all Socialists worldwide might present a united front. Until that time, however, he urged the American movement to "hold aloof" and affiliate with no international Socialist organization. Instead, American Socialists should "give our time and energy to the reconstruction of our shattered party. That will occupy us fully for a time and once we have a party of power and standing there will be no trouble about affiliation."

Finally, Debs sought to clarify his attitude toward the Russian Revolu-tion. Without ever referring to his telegram to Lenin, which had caused such an angry reaction from American Communists, he restated his un-qualified support of the Bolshevik Revolution and praised Lenin and Trotsky for leading "the historic beginning of the international revolution that is destined to sweep capitalism and militarism from the face of the earth." It is to be hoped, he proclaimed, that "the Soviet government is the beginning of the self-government of the people throughout the world."[76]

If Debs had serious hopes that his statement might unify the radical movement, they soon collapsed. Leaving the sanitarium in late November, Debs returned to Terre Haute and kept his peace as the left attacked him for his position. Over Christmas 1922 he suffered another severe attack of lumbago and remained bedridden for more than two weeks. Stronger the following February, Debs left for Chicago where he would spend three weeks speaking in public for the first time in four years and meeting with party officials to devise programs that might revitalize the Socialist movement.[77] It was during these Chicago meetings that Debs encountered left-wing hecklers for the first time since the dissident Firemen on the Union Pacific fought him in 1890. He confronted them in Chicago, he told Theodore, and forced them to "keep silent." In Butte, Montana, that September Debs privately met with a group of Communists who had, he felt, "done all they could to smash the Socialist party." Their conference, he told Theodore, resulted "in a very plain & pointed interview" while the public meeting "was a marvel of harmony & enthusiasm—not a communist there."[78]

Despite this clear record, leaders of the Communist movement throughout 1923 and 1924 still sought to enlist Debs's support. Debs and William Z. Foster, a former syndicalist, leader of the 1919 steel strike, and now a major official in the Communist party, engaged in a long exchange of letters in the summer and fall of 1923. Foster's group, the Trade Union Educational League, sought to organize a Communist party caucus within the International Ladies Garment Workers Union in New York. When the union expelled the Communist agitators, Foster asked Debs to intercede on their behalf, even though the ILGWU remained the one firm basis of trade union support for the Socialist party. Foster's attempt ended with some bitterness on Debs's part.[79] Similarly, the Communist party published a pamphlet in 1924 addressed to Debs and other "honest workers" in the Socialist movement. The pamphlet defended the recent Communist tactic of going underground from the criticism of Debs and other Socialists and called for a united labor party of all dissident groups. The appeal had little effect. As Theodore had written some months before—in words that had his brother's endorsement—of the secret underground convention of the Communist party at Bridgeman, Michigan, in 1922: "For the life of me I cannot understand how men or women with intelligence more than that of a moron could be caught up or take a part in such opera-bouffe. But they did."[80]

The Communist party's 1924 call for united electoral efforts by all liberals and radicals set the stage for Debs's last serious political struggle. Originally the Communists hoped to work through the Minnesota Farmer-Labor party, a state third-party organization with strong ties to certain labor unions, to establish the basis of a national third party movement. The party had ceased its underground tactics and hoped that its public support of progressive U.S. Senator Robert La Follette of Wisconsin for the presidency would broaden its support. But shortly before the June 1924 convention that would nominate La Follette, the senator announced that he would refuse to accept it. La Follette and the other elected officials involved wanted nothing to do with a movement so identified with the Communist party in the public mind. In this La Follette was encouraged by representatives of the Conference for Progressive Political Action (CPPA), who desired him to run for the presidency with their backing. Founded in 1922, the CPPA had the active support of a number of labor leaders and Socialists and was especially strong among railroad brotherhoods who had emerged from the war greatly strengthened. In addition to its anti-Communist orientation, the CPPA also opposed the Farmer-Labor party's efforts to create a viable third-party organization on the local, state, and national levels. They intended to run a candidate for president more to pressure the traditional parties than in an attempt to supplant one of them. But so bitter was the Socialist feeling toward the Communists that even this critical difference carried little weight, and the party officially endorsed La Follette's candidacy on the CPPA ticket. Despite their blinding hatred of the Communists, the Socialists were right in this instance. For, after six months of actively promoting a united front policy, the Communist party changed its view dramatically in late May 1924. Returning home from a pilgrimage to Moscow, Foster announced that the Russian leaders had decided that the American party's approach was in error: neither La Follette nor a united front policy was to be endorsed. Ironically, La Follette's withdrawal saved the Communists public embarrassment, as they swiftly nominated Foster to lead their ticket that November.[81]

Despite his long hostility to both the railroad brotherhoods and to such political fusions, Debs endorsed the Socialist party's alliance with the CPPA. In a telegram to the party's 1924 convention, Debs approved the alliance, warned against a factional split, and simultaneously urged the delegates "to hold the Socialist party intact, adhere rigidly to its principles and keep the red flag flying." Two weeks later he was more enthusiastic: "There is no compromise in going with the working class when it breaks with the old parties," Debs announced in an interview while recuperating again at Lindlahr. "It is our duty to march with our brothers in this struggle and by local co-operation show that we can work together in the labor party which should be organized next January."[82]

Debs's endorsement of La Follette marked the final break between the Socialist leader and his former comrades now in the Communist movement. Speaking for the Communist party, Foster bitterly attacked Debs and drew from him a sharp retort. In supporting La Follette until the last moment the Communists themselves, Debs reminded Foster, sought to do what they now attacked others for having accomplished. Suspicious and bitter over the Communist party's fluctuating principles, Debs admitted that he could be wrong and pointedly underscored one of his major disagreements with Communist practice: "*Having no Vatican in Moscow to guide me,*" he sarcastically told Foster, "*I must follow the light I have, and this I have done in the present instance, as I always have in the past.*" Foster responded with equal hostility: Debs had "winked" at the Socialist party's support "of many reactionary policies" and in supporting La Follette had, "by that action, definitely [left] the camp of revolutionaries and [went] over to the opportunists and petty bourgeois reformists." Recalling Debs's praise of Lenin some years earlier, Foster ended with an angry rebuttal to Debs's reference to the "Vatican in Moscow," the Comintern: "In your letter, you sneer, in orthodox yellow-Socialist fashion, at our affiliation with the institution that incorporates the very soul of Leninism, the Third International."[83]

With these revolutionary phrases the Communist party leaders ceased their efforts to influence Debs. But they kept Debs in the wings and after his death found a way in which they could resuscitate him for their own purposes. Debs became a John the Baptist, the precursor to such party leaders as Foster, Charles Ruthenberg, and Earl Browder. Debs's Leninist "deficiencies" resulted from both historical accident—due to his age and weakened condition he was unable to absorb the lessons of Leninism—and from the ability of the Hillquits and Bergers to manipulate him. In this way the Communist movement attempted to retain links with the tradition Debs represented, for, after the ideological and rhetorical bombast had evaporated, Debs and the movement he symbolized remained the most potent oppositional force in twentieth-century America.

The continued sniping between Socialists and Communists in the postwar years provided a false sense of vitality for each side. As each party receded further and further in the consciousness of American workers, the bitter factional attacks couched in revolutionary ritualistic phrases allowed each for the moment to perceive themselves as central actors on the American political stage. Wrapped as they were in a subculture that honored theoretical accuracy over the evidence of experience, the leadership and increasingly the rank and file of these now decimated movements turned inward with a vengeance. Attacking former comrades or, for the Communists especially, experiencing the continued repression by government agents became a visible sign of life. But the hoped-for resurrection of a vibrant opposition emerged neither from internal purging nor from attention paid the left by government agencies and their informers. Debs sensed this deeper crisis even as some of his closest Socialist comrades suggested that he was now part of the problem and not, as he had been in the past, a symbol of the solution.

At first Debs greeted his return to the podium with great fervor. Throughout 1923 his letters to Theodore and other comrades reflected his joy at resuming a public role again and receiving the enthusiasm of comrades and supporters who came to applaud the former convict. "The movement is being set afire in our tail," he wrote his brother from Rochester, New York, in May 1923. "The party is reorganizing in great shape." This hope was shared by others as well. State secretaries of the party vied with each other to obtain Debs's presence. Birch Wilson, the Pennsylvania secretary, had already arranged for three meetings in January 1924 but wanted a minimum of eight to ten more for February. Debs could revive the movement, many Socialist party officials felt, as no other person could. But as the tone of Wilson's letter suggested, this focus on Debs contained a rather desperate quality. No longer the national symbol of a broad and varied Socialist movement, the sixty-eight-year-old Debs was increasingly asked to become a Socialist Midas and to singlehandedly reverse the fortunes of the movement.[84]

This, of course, was impossible. As the various attempts at fusion politics suggested, nationwide a distinctly Socialist movement was in tatters. One comrade informed Branstetter that "not even Debs could rebuild the socialist party in Oklahoma at this time."[85] The endorsement of La Follette in 1924, and Debs's hope that it would lead to a labor party after the election, dramatically etched the contrast between the pre- and postwar movement. In 1910 Debs, William English Walling, and others had argued against a labor party on the grounds that it would at best duplicate and more probably supplant the Socialist party itself. In 1924, however, they were willing to grasp at any prospect that might encourage the development of such a labor party. Yet even these results were disappointing. La Follette gained almost five million votes but less than 900,000 were Socialist. Moreover, even that figure overestimated Socialist strength, as in a number of states, especially California, La Follette did not have a separate place on the ballot and thus all his votes were recorded as Socialist.[86]

As Debs's initial enthusiasm wore off, he, too, began to sense the magnitude of the problem. The condition of the party was "critical," he wrote in 1925. A year later, he told Theodore that a revived and virulent Klu Klux Klan had almost prevented him from speaking in Cincinnati. Two years earlier, following Debs's first post-jail speaking tour, August Claessens noted that in contrast with the continuously declining membership of every leftist group, only the Klu Klux Klan seemed to prosper. Evaluating Debs's recent tour, Claessens had depressing news for readers of the *Socialist World*. The audiences were large, but even Debs was "getting but few of these people to join our party," Claessens informed them. "If Gene Debs cannot arouse his audiences out of their indifference and insufferable apathy, then quite certainly the rest of our speakers and organizers cannot expect better luck."[87]

Claessens's critique of the "indifference and insufferable apathy" of Debs's audiences was unfair. But he and other comrades were not simply being churlish when they published such evaluations. Rather they chose the one course open to them. The results of Debs's tours were evident to anyone who desired to know—party membership remained low, morale was fractured, and active working-class support was negligible. But if the audiences were not to blame, then perhaps Debs was—but no Socialist was willing to explore this possibility in public. Debs's sacrifices had been too great and his commitment too profound for his comrades to criticize him publicly, however gently, in his last years. Further, such an analysis would force many to confront the prospect that throughout the movement there existed no sure touchstone for eventual resurgence.

In private correspondence, however, party leaders were more frank. "It is my unfortunate lot to say 'no' to Gene to more suggestions than all the rest of the people he is associated with in party work," Bertha Hale White, the party's national secretary, wrote Hillquit in June 1925. Debs still maintained that he could draw enormous audiences, White ruefully explained, and interpreted poor attendance to a lack of effort on the part of local organizers. From her vantage point, White perceived a far different reality: "We have never been able to arrange a second meeting for Gene in the past three years that was not a bitter disappointment to him. What he does not realize is that his imprisonment is an old story and he is not the drawing card he once was." Recounting a recent conversation with Debs, White told Hillquit that she had told Debs directly that "the old speeches will not do. . . . I made it as emphatic as I could, saying his old speeches were familiar to every person who would be at his meetings and he must even change his phrasing." This the seventy-year-old Debs found impossible to do, and even many Socialists complained to the national office. "Gene's psychology is all wrong," White argued, reflecting the immense alterations in the Socialist movement since the war; "the old Appeal days and methods are of the past. We have to find a real force to make the paper [*American Appeal*] what we want."[88]

Decades later a Debsian Socialist recalled the pain of Debs's last public years. When J. A. McDonald first heard Debs speak in 1908, he was deeply moved by Debs's vision and, as had been true for so many others, that experience marked a turning point in his life. Still a Socialist in 1925, McDonald eagerly attended a Debs meeting but encountered a weakened, aged leader whose words and demeanor lacked any semblance of their former force and vitality. "Had the lecture been delivered by anyone other than Debs, many in the audience would have walked out before the conclusion," McDonald remembered. "But it was Debs and they remained."[89]

To be considered no longer a "real force"—to retain audiences out of the memory and respect for his past power—was a new and bitterly confusing experience for Debs. His prison sentence had done more than merely weaken him physically. Those years marked a critical division in the movement and in Debs's role in it. The government repression and the vicious and destructive factional fighting created deep malaise among former and current comrades and led many to question even the meaning of earlier Socialist successes. Characteristically, however, Debs himself refused to explore this new mood, and his speeches reflected this lack. He might recognize the depressed state of the movement,[90] but he could neither confront the reasons for it nor, in his many letters during these years, acknowledge his own altered status. As late as February 1926 he argued that the demoralized and dispersed condition of the American movement "can not last in the face of the almost universal advance of the Socialist movement."[91]

Never very introspective, Debs struggled to maintain his public face during these last years and consequently sought to drive from his consciousness the fear all was indeed but ashes. More desperately in need of public affirmation than ever before, he could neither relinquish the platform nor engage in a fundamental, public examination of his and the movement's history. Inexorably, however, the years themselves propelled this public man to a final private confrontation with himself.

Debs never regained his health following his term at Atlanta. After his stay at the Lindlahr Sanitarium in 1922, his speaking tour that spring and summer left him exhausted. Bedridden for most of the winter and spring of 1923–24, Debs re-entered Lindlahr for another four months in early summer. Throughout 1925 his health remained fragile, and he spent much of that winter in bed as well. This time Kate, too, fell sick, overwrought with grief at the death of her sister, and in March 1926 the Debses left for a Bermuda vacation so each might recuperate—their first prolonged vacation together since their honeymoon over forty years earlier.[92]

During these bleak years, Debs remained close to Mabel Curry, but it proved difficult for them to spend much time with each other. Mabel could not always travel to the sanitarium in Chicago and, as she had discovered some years earlier, she was not welcome in the Debs house. When his health permitted, Gene and Mabel did attempt to schedule their separate speaking engagements so that they might meet each other during their travels.[93] But even this proved difficult. Resuming their letters, Gene continued to affirm his love for Mabel and attempted perhaps, in his own indirect fashion, to accept the incompleteness of their relationship. Throughout his jail sentence Debs repeatedly claimed that "our day must come." Yet the post-jail years found them separated more than ever before. Writing Mabel of a mutual female friend's sexual promiscuity (which she justified with a philosophy of free love and psychoanalytic theory), Gene condemned her practice as "repellant from a truly moral point of view" and explained his attitude in words that applied to his relationship with Mabel as well: "It is true that nothing is more sensitive to love than freedom but it is equally true that freedom *voluntarily* imposes its own restrictions and joyously sets its own bounds to safeguard the [gift] of priceless value in its keeping."[94]

Gene and Mabel never narrowed the distance that structured their relation, and it is not at all clear that he desired to do so. The obverse of his insistent, lifelong need for public affirmation was an equally intense inability to recognize his own inner self or to share that with others. He shared more with Mabel than with any other woman and yet, amid his passionate avowals of love, Debs remained most often physically and emotionally removed. Debs had more male friends, yet even Theodore, his closest confidant, never violated the boundaries his older brother erected around himself. On occasion, as during the crisis at Atlanta, Debs himself lowered these barriers for a moment. When they were replaced, however, not even Theodore would think of disturbing them.

Yet throughout his life Debs continually touched individuals in the most personal way. He might need the podium to distance himself, but others responded as if he were a most intimate friend. Even in the post-jail years, when his speeches were flat and his mind and body frail, flashes of this power remained. In his articles and speeches Debs continually reminded Americans that the jails were filled with political prisoners and urged them to renew efforts to obtain their release. In 1923 one such prisoner wrote Debs of the profound influence of his life and work. "You and I belong to different schools of socialism," Bartolomeo Vanzetti noted from his prison cell in Charlestown, Massachusetts. "But you are my Teacher. I do not vote," the anarcho-syndicalist explained, "but I would trust unto you the sacrest and dearest things of life. . . . I am positive that if a minority would follow your practical example the reality of to-morrow would be above the dreams of many dreamers."[95]

The realization of those dreams would have to wait until another time, for another movement, and perhaps another leader. Debs left Bermuda rested but caught a cold on the rough return voyage that he was unable to overcome. Through the summer of 1926 he was again frequently in bed and grew progressively weaker. That September, in order to test the belief that Debs and other political prisoners had lost their citizenship, Theodore helped his brother from his bed and took him to the Terre Haute City Hall to register to vote for the November elections.[96]

Some days later, on 20 September, Theodore brought Eugene once more to Lindlahr in the hope that its nature cure would help his brother regain his strength. He left Lindlahr but one time, bundled in heavy blankets against the sharp October air, for a short drive in the sun. On 15 October Debs suffered a massive heart attack and lapsed into a coma. For five days he lay unconscious, his eyes closed, his long limbs slack and feeble. On 20 October 1926, his limp body cradled on either side by Theodore and his sister, Emma, Eugene Victor Debs died.[97]

Theodore and Emma escorted their brother's body home to Terre Haute. Among the mourners who greeted the train was Percy Head, president of the Central Labor Union that Eugene had helped organize many years before. Softly but firmly, he requested of Theodore a final sacrifice: "You will have to give him to us for a while, Theodore. You know he belongs to us."[98]

On Friday, 22 October, the body of Debs lay in state in the bare auditorium of Terre Haute's Labor Temple. Throughout the day thousands of men and women from Indiana and from across the nation came to pay their final homage and to draw their final inspiration. His body was moved during the night to the front parlor of his home on North Eighth Street; the procession past his body continued on Saturday morning. Standing to the side of the casket was the Debs family: Theodore, his wife Gertrude, and their daughter, Marguerite; his sisters, Emma Debs Maillaux and Marie Debs Heinl and her children, Robert and Fred. As each mourner passed, someone in the family had at least a word of shared grief for them, the famous as well as the unknown. Kate, his wife of forty-one years, remained upstairs.

At two o'clock, funeral services were held on the front porch of the Debs house. The participants—Norman Thomas, Morris Hillquit, Victor Berger, William Cunnea, and Seymour Stedman—were all practiced speakers, but their words that day were inadequate. There was little to be said. In the hearts of the individuals in the massive crowd on the street mingled memories of the man who now lay before them. He had been able to touch them and to lead untold numbers of them to a new understanding of themselves and their society. But now he was dead, and the fervent words, evocative, tearful memories, and demands for "delayed monuments of metal and stone" were perhaps ritually necessary but nonetheless inadequate. "His real moment," one friend wrote Theodore, "lives in the hearts that beat with saddened cadence this week; hearts which dare hope because our 'Gene raised their eyes to the sun."[99]

Epilogue

OVER THE COURSE of his long public career Eugene Victor Debs did focus the eyes of many toward the sun. The specific content of his message to Americans changed dramatically in the years between his first political speech before the Firemen's national convention in 1877 and his last years as a Socialist, but a certain consistency persisted. Throughout Debs appealed to and searched for the rich, latent power he saw in each individual, and in himself. His public life was a continuous sermon, a call for rebirth and regeneration that achieved greater force and urgency as he understood the broader dimensions of the crisis his society faced. Powerfully suited to his own personality, this preacher's stance enabled Debs to touch his fellow citizens with a power and immediacy that has rarely been equalled.

Yet an equally persistent disappointment stalked Debs's efforts. He could lift eyes to the sun but had less success in influencing Americans, even those stirred by his vision, to accept his specific program. As he moved into the American Railway Union, he left many Brotherhood men behind; in time he left a portion of these men as well when he joined forces with Victor L. Berger. As a Socialist, he was never able to convince a majority of workers to jettison their traditional political loyalties. His efforts to organize workers into industrial unions were but partially successful in his own time, while the party he had devoted such energy to was, at his death, demoralized and nearly destroyed. This passionate preacher was a poor teacher whose inability to examine his own political odyssey detracted from his effectiveness and helped create the tremendous despondency of his last years. But Debs's Socialist agitation occurred within the confines of a highly individualistic, increasingly conservative, and rapidly maturing capitalist society and culture. That he and his comrades were as successful as they were in such an inhospitable climate remains far more significant than their final tally of votes.

Whatever his shortcomings as a teacher and political leader, large numbers of Americans accorded Debs a position of great importance. The man and his message were one. Debs's own struggles with the meaning of such traditional values as manhood, duty, citizenship, and work reflected the experience of many in that generation in transition. As the nation traveled its tortuous path to a developed industrial capitalist society, those older values encountered a fundamental challenge from a corporate revolution that ultimately required not citizens but "hands" to staff its factories. The challenge was simultaneously private and public and produced a crisis of culture, which was also a crisis of meaning for individual men and women. In his ability to fuse the personal and the political, Debs personified a more holistic vision that affirmed the older moral values while accepting, even welcoming, technological innovation and economic progress. Debs was a unique, powerful personality whose public image often obscured his own personal anxieties and conflicts. But to many Americans he symbolized his generation's protest against industrial capitalism. His personal qualities assumed political importance and his agitation touched the hearts and affected the lives of real people. "I tell you one thing," Bartolomeo Vanzetti wrote Theodore Debs a month before his execution by the Commonwealth of Massachusetts. "Since my mother death very few women gave me a sense of mothernal love and protection as the one I felt in Gene's presence, and no other man."[1]

Debs was no mere hero, however, hovering above the crowd, beyond reach, revered, and thus easily dismissed. His public power rested in part on personal qualities and in part on political ideas and programs, but his importance transcended both, for the critical fact was that for many Americans Debs embodied *their* experience and *their* social protest. In this fashion the life of Debs had meaning for his audiences, and it has meaning for the generations since, beyond its personal qualities. Three aspects of his story bear special mention as his society enters its third century of national life.

First, Debs remains the classic example of an indigenous American radical. He was not born a Socialist, and he did not reject American values when he became one. The son of a petty-bourgeois shopkeeper, Debs's life as it unfolded revealed an organic unity, and his transitions from grocery clerk to Brotherhood official to Democratic politician to labor leader and Socialist remain years after his death believable and instructive. Perhaps more prominently, but no less powerfully, than many others of his era, Debs came to understand the complex character of the American democratic tradition and publicly fought to define America's cultural symbols anew in the changed context wrought by industrial capitalism. In so doing he reminded all Americans that active engagement occupied the center of their national traditions. His life was a profound refutation of the belief that critical dissent is somehow un-American or unpatriotic. His contemporaries saw in the life of this native son not only an affirmation of the struggle for justice but also a deep grounding of that battle in a distinctly American experience.

Debs was not just an amorphous radical. Between the Chicago, Burlington and Quincy strike in 1888 and the founding of the Industrial Workers of the World in 1905, Debs, in consort with many of his comrades, developed a credible integration of traditional values with a perceptive analysis of the class basis of industrial capitalist society. In a process of growth he claimed owed more to a dissenting American tradition than to Socialist or Marxist thinkers, Debs offered an understanding of contemporary experience and presented with great force the imperative to create a society of political and economic equality, the democratic egalitarian society he called "the workers' republic." Resistant to ideological disputations and at times, as in 1918-19, given to unrealistic assessments, Debs at his best brought an understanding of class into the center of American political discourse. Unlike many radicals then and since, Debs rejected a concept of class or a vision of Socialism based on determinism. He had vivid experience with the reality of class division and class conflict, and he saw their broad social effects all around him. Nevertheless, he rarely lost sight of the need for each individual to recognize that reality and act on that recognition. Precisely because this understanding of class emerged from his experience, Debs understood that a commitment to the class struggle was neither unpatriotic nor irreligious. On the contrary, Debs maintained that such a commitment was the very fulfillment of the basic democratic promise of American life and the values manhood, duty, and citizenship that sprang from it. Far more than any other national figure in twentieth-century America, Debs sought to integrate the political and economic themes of American culture in his message and his life. That effort remains his most potent legacy.

Debs's specific labor work embodies his final major contribution. His incessant organizing and lifelong commitment to working people are impressive by themselves, but the development of his understanding of the proper trade union structure was equally significant. If in 1885 he saw the Knights of Labor as dangerous to social harmony and a year later ignored the formation of the American Federation of Labor, his attitudes soon changed. Class realities in corporate America led him first to suggest and then to advocate the industrial organization of all workers in a given industry, a development evident in the American Railway Union during the great Pullman strike of 1894. His belief in the power of such organizing led him to re-evaluate his understanding of the trade union and to his involvement in 1905 with the Industrial Workers of the World. But Debs did not stop there. As an organizing tool the industrial union held great power but, as Debs developed that concept in speech after speech, it also provided him with the concrete vehicle through which American workers might further merge their political and economic concerns. In the decade following his death, that tradition found new expression in the Congress of Industrial Organizations, and it remains an important, needed source of inspiration and experience even today.

Ultimately, of course, Debs and his comrades did not transform the face of corporate America. Often blinded by a sanguine optimism and, with Debs especially, frequently lacking in strong, consistent leadership, Socialists and their organizations stumbled to a painful, ambiguous conclusion in the years following World War I. The cultural hegemony that girded their society proved more powerful than they had expected. The economic crises and continued immiserization they predicted did not occur in their lifetimes. Yet Debs's fear that there was "nothing left but ashes" was not accurate. The story is not complete and the final conclusion has not yet been written. As Studs Terkel has recently noted, "There are signs, unmistakable, of an astonishing increase in the airing of grievances: of private wrongs and public rights. . . . A long-buried American tradition may be springing back to life. In a society and time with changes so stunning and landscapes so suddenly estranged, the last communiques are not yet in."[2]

Rather than ashes, the life of Eugene Victor Debs may instead be represented by the phoenix, the symbol of regeneration and rebirth even in the midst of tragedy—a constant reminder of the profound potential that yet lives in our society and in ourselves.

Notes

Abbreviations

OA   Oscar Ameringer Papers, Archives of Labor History and Urban Affairs, Wayne State University, Detroit, Michigan

WPA   Works Progress Administration File, Vigo County and Terre Haute, Cunningham Library, Indiana State University, Terre Haute

LBB   Louis B. Boudin Papers, Butler Library, Columbia University, New York City

GGB   George and Grace Brewer Papers, Archives of Labor History and Urban Affairs, Wayne State University, Detroit, Michigan

LB   Lewis Browne Papers, Lilly Library, Indiana University, Bloomington

SGLB   Samuel Gompers Letterbooks, Library of Congress, Washington, D.C.

VLB   Victor L. Berger Collection, Milwaukee Public Library, Wisconsin

MB   Meta Berger Papers, Wisconsin State Historical Society, Madison

MB   Marion Butler Collection, University of North Carolina Library, Chapel Hill [cited as MB (Chapel Hill)]

TDSB   Theodore Debs Scrapbook, Fairbanks Memorial Library, Terre Haute

AC   August Claessens Papers, Tamiment Institute, New York University

JEC   Joseph E. Cohen Papers, Tamiment Institute, New York University

GC   George Caylor Papers, Tamiment Institute, New York University

GC   George Caylor Papers, Wisconsin State Historical Society, Madison [cited as GC (Madison)]

LC   Lewis Corey Papers, Butler Library, Columbia University, New York City

LLC   Labor and Laboring Classes File, Fairbanks Memorial Library, Terre Haute

JRC   J. Robert Constantine, Personal possession, Terre Haute

SC   Samuel Castleton Papers, Tamiment Institute, New York University

WFD   Walter F. Dietz Papers, Louisiana State University Library, Baton Rouge

JMD   John M. Dickey Papers, Lilly Library, Indiana University, Bloomington

CSD   Clarence S. Darrow Papers, Library of Congress, Washington, D.C.

TD   Thomas Dowling Papers, Indiana State Library, Indianapolis

EVD   Eugene V. Debs Collection, Tamiment Institute, New York University

EVD	Eugene V. Debs Papers, Houghton Library, Harvard University, Cambridge, Massachusetts [cited as EVD (Harvard)]
CE	Charles Ervin Papers, Tamiment Institute, New York University
ME	Max Eastman Papers, Lilly Library, Indiana University, Bloomington
WE	William Edlin Papers, Yivo Institute, New York City
MXE	Max Ehrmann Papers, Lilly Library, Indiana University, Bloomington
DF	Eugene V. Debs Collection, Debs Foundation, Terre Haute
EF	Eugene V. Debs Collection, Fairbanks Memorial Library, Terre Haute
EGF	Elizabeth Gurley Flynn Collection, Wisconsin State Historical Society, Madison
NF	Nicholas Filbeck Papers, Lilly Library, Indiana University, Bloomington
PPF	Political Prisoner File, Department of Justice, National Archives, Washington, D.C.
AG	Adolph Germer Papers, Wisconsin State Historical Society, Madison
GG	George Gloss, Personal possession, Boston
JG	Jean Gould Papers, Archives of Labor History and Urban Affairs, Wayne State University, Detroit, Michigan
PG	Poets Garden Collection, Doheny Library, University of Southern California, Los Angeles
IAH	Isaac A. Hourwich Collection, Yivo Institute, New York City
BH	Bolton Hall Papers, New York Public Library
DH	David W. Henry Papers, Indiana State Library, Indianapolis
GDH	George D. Herron Papers, Tamiment Institute, New York University
FH	Frederic Heath Collection, Milwaukee County Historical Society, Wisconsin
IH	Indiana History Collection, Lilly Library, Indiana University, Bloomington
MH	Morris Hillquit Papers, University of Wisconsin, Madison
MH	Morris Hillquit Papers, Tamiment Institute, New York University [cited as MH (Tamiment)]
INH	Eugene V. Debs Papers, Indiana Historical Society, Indianapolis
PH	Powers Hapgood Papers, Lilly Library, Indiana University, Bloomington
RH	Robert Hunter Papers, Lilly Library, Indiana University, Bloomington
DWH	Daniel W. Hoan Collection, Milwaukee County Historical Society, Wisconsin
RGI	Robert Green Ingersoll Papers, Library of Congress, Washington, D.C.
DJ	Department of Justice, Central Files (Year Files), National Archives, Washington, D.C.
DJ	Department of Justice, Subject File, 77175, National Archives, Washington, D.C. [cited as DJ (Subject)]
DJ	Eugene V. Debs File, Bureau of Prisons, Washington, D.C. [cited as DJ (Bureau of Prisons)]
H-J	Emmanuel Haldeman–Julius Papers, Lilly Library, Indiana University, Bloomington
SMJ	Samuel M. Jones Papers, Toledo–Lucas County Public Library, Toledo, Ohio
DFK	David F. Karsner Papers, New York Public Library
MWK	May Walden Kerr Papers, Newberry Library, Chicago
AL	Algernon Lee Papers, Tamiment Institute, New York University

HDL   Henry Demarest Lloyd Collection, Wisconsin State Historical Society, Madison

GL   George Lutzai Collection, Archives of Labor History and Urban Affairs, Wayne State University, Detroit, Michigan

JL   Joseph Labadie Collection, Special Collections, University of Michigan, Ann Arbor

ML   Meyer London Papers, Tamiment Institute, New York University

EVL   Eugene V. Lux, Personal possession, Seattle, Washington

GWL   George Washington Lambert Papers, Indiana Historical Society, Indianapolis

EM   Edwin Markham Papers, Tamiment Institute, New York University

WEM   William E. McLean Papers, Indiana Historical Society, Indianapolis

L-M   Labor-Management Documentation Center, M. P. Catherwood Library, Cornell University, Ithaca, New York

TM   Thomas Mooney Papers, Bancroft Library, University of California, Berkeley

REN   Robert E. Nye Papers, Wisconsin State Historical Society, Madison

JO   James Oneal Papers, Tamiment Institute, New York University

GHP   George H. Purdy Papers, Indiana Historical Society, Indianapolis

JP   Juliet Peddle Papers, Indiana State Library, Indianapolis

DJP   Department of Justice, Central Files (Special Section), Political Prisoners, National Archives, Washington, D.C.

SLP   Socialist Labor Party Collection, Wisconsin State Historical Society, Madison

JOP   John Panzer Collection, Archives of Labor History and Urban Affairs, Wayne State University, Detroit, Michigan

SPP   Socialist Party Papers, Perkins Library, Duke University, Durham, North Carolina

SP   Socialist Party Collection, Milwaukee County Historical Society, Wisconsin

SP   Socialist Party–Social Democratic Federation Collection, Milwaukee Public Library, Wisconsin [cited as SP (Library)]

CBQ   The Burlington Archives, Newberry Library, Chicago

CER   Charles Edward Russell Papers, Library of Congress, Washington, D.C.

OHR   Oral History Research Project, Butler Library, Columbia University, New York City

JR   John Reed Papers, Houghton Library, Harvard University, Cambridge, Massachusetts

SMR   Steven Marion Reynolds Papers, Indiana Historical Society, Indianapolis

RR   Railroad File, Fairbanks Memorial Library, Terre Haute

JWR   James Whitcomb Riley Papers, Lilly Library, Indiana University, Bloomington

ES   Emil Seidel Papers, Milwaukee Public Library, Wisconsin

ES   Emil Seidel Papers, Milwaukee County Historical Society, Wisconsin [cited as ES (H.S.)]

IS   Eugene V. Debs Collection, Indiana State Library, Indianapolis

DJS   David J. Saposs Collection, Wisconsin State Historical Society, Madison

LS   Lincoln Steffens Papers, Butler Library, Columbia University, New York City

AMS　　Algie M. and May Wood Simons Papers, Wisconsin State Historical Society, Madison
JPS　　J. G. Phelps Stokes Papers, Butler Library, Columbia University, New York City
RPS　　Rose Pastor Stokes Papers, Yale Univesity, New Haven, Connecticut
SS　　　Seymour Steadman Papers, Tamiment Institute, New York University
SS　　　Seymour Steadman Papers, Wisconsin State Historical Society, Madison [cited as SS (Madison)]
US　　　Upton Sinclair Collection, Lilly Library, Indiana University, Bloomington
AT　　　Alexander Trachtenberg Papers, Wisconsin State Historical Society, Madison
FT　　　Frank Tannenbaum Papers, Butler Library, Columbia University, New York City
HT　　　Horace Traubel Papers, Library of Congress, Washington, D.C.
NT　　　Norman M. Thomas Papers, New York Public Library
PT　　　Mrs. Philip Taft Papers, Tamiment Institute, New York University
RST　　Robert S. Taylor Papers, Indiana State Library, Indianapolis
RWT　　Richard W. Thompson Papers, Lilly Library, Indiana University, Bloomington
RWT　　Richard W. Thompson Papers, Indiana State Library, Indianapolis [cited as RWT (Indianapolis)]
EU　　　Ernst Untermann Papers, Milwaukee County Historical Society, Wisconsin
ISU　　Eugene V. Debs Collection, Cunningham Library, Indiana State University, Terre Haute
MHV　　Mary Heaton Vorse Papers, Archives of Labor History and Urban Affairs, Wayne State University, Detroit, Michigan
MV　　　Morris Vinchevsky Papers, Yivo Institute, New York City
MRV　　Mill Records, Vigo County, Indiana Historial Society, Indianapolis
JAW　　James A. Woodburn Papers, Lilly Library, Indiana University, Bloomington
FDW　　Fred D. Warren Papers, Lilly Library, Indiana University, Bloomington
WEW　　William English Walling Papers, Wisconsin State Historical Society, Madison
HW　　　Harry Weinberger Papers, Yale University, New Haven, Connecticut
JMW　　John M. Work Collection, Wisconsin State Historical Society, Madison
RW　　　Ryan Walker Papers, Lilly Library, Indiana University, Bloomington

Notes to Part I

1. Oneal, "Debs Turns Seventy," 4. See also Robert Hunter, another native of Terre Haute and Socialist comrade of Debs, to Lincoln Steffens, 6 July 1908, LS.
2. EVD to Karsner, 6 Dec. 1924, DFK.
3. EVD to Theodore Debs, n.d. [1908], ISU.

Notes to Chapter 1

1. Quoted in Holliday, *Indiana Methodism,* 222.
2. E. Peddle to M. Peddle, 18 Apr. 1851, JP.
3. Beste, *The Wabash,* II: 94–96.
4. From an article written by Bayless Hanna in 1883 of Terre Haute society on the eve of the Civil War, quoted in Oakey, *Greater Terre Haute,* I:158–59. Hanna was Terre Haute's representative to both the State Assembly and Senate during the 1860s and in 1870 was elected attorney general of Indiana.
5. "Robert Hunter's Memories," chs. 1, 19, RH.
6. William E. McLean Notebooks, no.9 [1899], WEM.
7. Wiley, "Methodism in Southeastern Indiana," 10, 12.
8. Iglehart, "Life and Times of John Schrader," 2, 127.
9. Abbott, "Reminiscences," 207; Phillips, *Indiana in Transition,* 2–6.
10. Holliday, *Indiana Methodism,* 142; Carmony, *Brief History of Indiana,* 61–62; Carmony, "The Hoosiers and Their Heritage," 3–14.
11. J. R. Wheelock to Sarah Patten, 20 June 1834, quoted in Kuhns, "Congregationalism in Indiana," 348–49*n.*
12. Stott, *Indiana Baptist History,* 177ff. Dowling is quoted in Holliday, *Indiana Methodism,* 227, 233–34.
13. Sweet, *Circuit-Rider Days,* 31.
14. Cox, *Settlement of the Wabash Valley,* 50.
15. Abbott, "Reminiscences," 206.
16. Condit, *History of Early Terre Haute,* 82–83.
17. Marty, *Righteous Empire.*
18. Beste, *The Wabash,* I:205–6.
19. Cox, *Settlement of the Wabash Valley,* 159.
20. Wright, "Political Institutions and the Frontier," 32–33.
21. Terre Haute *Express,* 14 Sept. 1899; *Souvenir Volume;* Ginger, *The Bending Cross,* 4.
22. Theodore Debs to Emma Debs Maillaux, 13 Dec. 1926, ISU.
23. Ginger, *The Bending Cross,* 5–6; Brommel, *Debs,* 13–14; Terre Haute *Tribune-Star,* 13 Sept. 1970; Bradsby, *History of Vigo County,* 729.
24. Bradsby, *History of Vigo County,* 729.
25. "The Two 'Genes': A Talk with Debs," *Illustrated Buffalo Express,* 26 Apr. 1896; Maude Bell, "Debs at Elmhurst," *Debs Magazine,* 2 (Jan. 1923), 6, 14; Ginger, *The Bending Cross,* 9–10; EVD to Theodore Debs, n.d. [1908], ISU.
26. *Twelfth Annual Report of the Terre Haute Public Schools,* 29. See also Sidney Mead's discussion of the public schools as the prime inculcator of a "religion of democracy" in his *Lively Experiment,* 66–71.
27. The Terre Haute Common Council on 7 May 1855 established the school system for all of the town's children "provided, however, it is expressly declared and understood that nothing in this ordinance contained shall be so constructed as to permit any Negro or mulatto person or child to attend any

said school or receive instruction therein." Quoted in A. R. Markle, "Free
School System First Came to Terre Haute in May of 1855," Terre Haute
Tribune, 10 Aug. 1947. For a brief discussion of Indiana's laws toward Negro
education see Litwack, *North of Slavery*, 115, 151. On the establishment of a
Negro school in Terre Haute see *Twelfth Annual Report of the Terre Haute
Public Schools*, 30–32.

28. *Twelfth Annual Report of the Terre Haute Public Schools*, 87.
29. Terre Haute *Evening Gazette*, 29 Mar. 1879; EVD, prison note, n.d., Debs
    Miscellany Folder, ISU; Brommel, *Debs*, 16–18.
30. Darrow, *Farmington*, 58–60, 67.
31. EVD, "The Story of a Convict," n.d., DFK. On the influence of Hugo, see
    Katherine M. Debs's remarks in "Here is the Mighty Debs," New York
    World, 12 July 1894.
32. *Twelfth Annual Report of the Terre Haute Public Schools*, 23–25; see one of
    the earliest clippings in the Debs Scrapbook, untitled, n.d., Reel 283, I:4–5
    (Tamiment Institute microfilm edition).
33. Carmony, *Brief History of Indiana*, 62; Starr, *Industrial Development of In-
    diana*, 41, 86, 92.
34. Quoted in Daniels, *Village at the End of the Road*, 66–68.
35. Jobson, *America and American Methodism*, 289.
36. Cox, *Settlement of the Wabash Valley*, 153–54; Condit, *History of Early
    Terre Haute*, 157; Oakey, *Greater Terre Haute*, I:142; Reed, *Encyclopedia of
    Biography of Indiana*, I:76–78; Burke, "Chauncey Rose," 1–6; Jordan, *Na-
    tional Road*, 80, 95; interview with Mrs. Dorothy Clark, Terre Haute, Ind., 18
    Apr. 1974.
37. Burke, "Chauncey Rose," 9–10; Roll, *Colonel Dick Thompson*, 75, 133.
38. *Biographical History of Eminent Men of Indiana*, ch. 8, 40–42, 54–58; Reed,
    Encyclopedia of Biography of Indiana, I:25–28, II:296–98; Finley, "Quaker
    Pioneer in Indiana," 36; Roll, *Colonel Dick Thompson*, 124; Ridgley, "Terre
    Haute during the Civil War," 38.
39. A full year before the road was finished, Rose already contemplated its suc-
    cess and made plans to hire additional engineers. Rose to Charles Peddle, 7
    June 1851, IH.
40. Burke, "Chauncey Rose," 8.
41. *Ibid.*, 18–44.
42. Reed, *Encyclopedia of Biography of Indiana*, I:78–82; Condit, *History of
    Early Terre Haute*, 143–44.
43. Dunn, *Memorial and Genealogical Record*, 186–90; *Biographical History of
    Eminent Men of Indiana*, ch. 8, 35–38; Reed, *Encyclopedia of Biography of
    Indiana*, II:296–98. On the role of the State Bank of Indiana as a training
    ground for Terre Haute's future leaders, see Oakey, *Greater Terre Haute*,
    I:194.
44. Richard W. Thompson to Barnabas Hobbs, 20 Oct. 1870, RWT; Terre Haute
    Evening Gazette, 17, 24 Mar. 1888; Terre Haute *Star*, 19 Feb. 1913; Oakey,
    Greater Terre Haute, I:207–8; Ingalls & Company, comps., *Advantages and
    Attractions of Terre Haute*, 35–42.
45. Chandler, *Visible Hand*, chs. 4–5, especially 133–37, 148–59.
46. Henry C. Gilbert, "The Terre Haute and Richmond Railroad," n.d., RR;
    Phillips, *Indiana in Transition*, 231; Ridgley, "Indiana during the Civil
    War," 41; Reed, *Encyclopedia of Biography of Indiana*, I:80. Reed places the

date of McKeen's lease at 1863, but this is too early, as he did not buy the line until 1869.

47. Balsley, "Indiana Iron from Native Ore," 366; Bradsby, *History of Vigo County*, 484; Cutshall, "Terre Haute Iron and Steel," 239; Ingalls & Company, comps., *Advantages of Terre Haute*, 7; Hassam, *Terre Haute*, 19, 33.

48. Material for this section was compiled from the following sources: Esarey, *History of Indiana*, III:488; Oakey, *Greater Terre Haute*, I:142, 157, 198, 240-41; Condit, *History of Early Terre Haute*, 58, 110-11, 133-36, 143-44; Seeds, ed., *Republican Party of Indiana*, 118-19; Dunn, *Memorial and Genealogical Record*, 186-90; Cumback and Maynard, eds., *Men of Progress*, 352-54; Reed, *Encyclopedia of Biography of Indiana*, I:1-8, 76-82, 397-98; II:25-28, 163-64, 296-98; *Biographical History of Eminent Men of Indiana*, ch. 8; Hassam, *Terre Haute*, 13.

49. Hassam, *Terre Haute*, 61.

50. Coleman, *Debs, a Man Unafraid*, 1-3; Karsner, *Talks with Debs*, 78-79.

51. EVD to "My Dearest Father and Mother," 12 Sept. 1904, ISU; Karsner, *Talks with Debs*, 80-81.

52. Theodore Debs to Henry T. Schnittkind, 24 May 1929, ISU. The "other causes" mentioned were epidemics that killed four of the ten children born to Marguerite Debs.

53. Karsner, *Talks with Debs*, 80-81.

54. R. E. Boyer to Theodore Debs, 21 Oct. 1926, ISU.

55. EVD to "Dear Parents," 29 Sept. 1874, ISU.

56. EVD to Louise Debs, 3, 8 Oct. 1874, ISU.

57. EVD to "Dear Parents," 29 Sept. 1874, ISU.

58. Enclosed in letter of EVD to Louise Debs, 8 Oct. 1874. For a later expression of similar sentiments, see EVD to Theodore Debs, 27 Jan. 1876, both in ISU.

59. Coleman, *Debs, a Man Unafraid*, 28; Ginger, *The Bending Cross*, 12-13, 15.

60. Terre Haute *Tribune-Star*, 13 Sept. 1970; Bradsby, *History of Vigo County*, 729.

61. Terre Haute *Evening Gazette*, 6 Sept. 1888; 10 Apr. 1889.

62. Record Books, Vigo Lodge No. 16, Brotherhood of Locomotive Firemen, 3 vols., I:1-11 (hereafter cited as Record Books).

63. EVD to Louise Debs, 3 Oct. 1874, ISU.

64. Cutshall, "Terre Haute Iron and Steel," 239-44.

65. Indiana State Board of Agriculture, *A General Description of Indiana, including its Climate, Agricultural and Mineral Resources, Manufactures, Transportation, Population, Education and Statistics*, as reprinted in *Senate Report 693*, I:503-5.

66. Cutshall, "Terre Haute Iron and Steel," 244.

Notes to Chapter 2

1. *Proceedings of BLF*, 1882, 8. The journals of proceedings of the annual conventions of the BLF were published for the years 1874 to 1885; subsequent proceedings were published more regularly. The full citations for these journals are in the Bibliography; in the notes the abbreviated citations will be: *Proceedings of BLF*, followed by the year.

2. *House Document 29*, 76.

3. *Proceedings of BLF*, 1882, 14-15.

4. Bellah, "Civil Religion in America," 168-89. For a more pessimistic evalua-

tion of this tradition, see McWilliams, *Fraternity*, and Bellah himself in *Broken Convenant*.

5. *Senate Report 1261*, I: 688–89.
6. *Ibid.*, 218–19.
7. *Ibid.*, 8–9.
8. EVD, "Stray Leaves from the Notebook of a Labor Agitator," *The Comrade*, 3 (June 1904), 187. Also of interest is EVD, "Serving the Labor Movement," *The Call*, 1 Oct. 1922, 1–2.
9. Both Kopelin, *Life of Debs*, 9, and Karsner, *Debs, Life and Letters*, 120–21, present this version; Morais and Cahn, *Gene Debs*, 14, state that EVD was so excited by the idea of organizing that he paid from his own pocket the initiation fee of half the charter members. Ginger (*The Bending Cross*, 21–22) and Coleman (*Debs*, 28) ignore these points, as they do the possibility of Debs's personal ambition, and stress rather Debs's boredom with his clerk's job.
10. Record Books, I:1–11.
11. *Ibid.*, 12–13 (4 May 1875).
12. *Locomotive Firemen's Magazine*, 2 (Mar. 1878), 115–17 (hereafter cited as *LFM*).
13. *Ibid.*, 1 (Dec. 1876), 2.
14. *Ibid.*, 1 (Nov. 1877), 381; Record Books, I, II.
15. The first comment is from L. M. Holloway of Alliance, Ohio, and is in *LFM*, 1 (Apr. 1877), 149–50; Debs's comment is in *ibid.*, 1 (Aug. 1877), 269–71.
16. *Ibid.*, 2 (Oct. 1878), 441–42.
17. Debs's letter is in *ibid.*, 2 (Feb. 1878), 83–85.
18. See the leaflet announcing the meeting for 30 Aug. 1878, DF.
19. Record Books, I:34–35 (18 July 1875).
20. *Ibid.*, II:74 (2 Oct. 1881). This attitude was not uncommon in the labor movement. In San Francisco the District Council of Painters, the first union in that city to establish free medical and hospital care for members, provided coverage for all illness and injury, on or off the job, "excepting such difficulties or illnesses as may arise from venereal diseases or vicious habits." *Organized Labor,* 7 Apr. 1906.
21. Record Books, I:176 (13 Apr. 1879).
22. *Ibid.*, I:49 (26 Aug. 1875). Debs was chairman of this meeting and the motion carried unanimously.
23. *Ibid.*, I:87 (17 Feb. 1876). See also the meeting of 22 Nov. 1877 (I:143) for an account of the expulsion of one member, M. Ganey, for selling liquor.
24. *Ibid.*, II:112 (9 July 1882); II:114 (23 July 1882).
25. *Ibid.*, II:13 (28 Sept. 1879). The man in question, Brother Snodgrass, later apologized and was allowed to re-enter. See the meeting of 26 Oct. 1879 (II:15).
26. *LFM*, 3 (Jan. 1879), 17–18.
27. *Proceedings of BLF*, 1882, 8–9.
28. Record Books, III:98 (27 Apr. 1885); III:104 (8 June 1885); III:108–9 (13 July 1885); III:151 (14 June 1886).
29. Quoted in Foner, *History of the Labor Movement*, I:468–70.
30. Quoted in Duss, *Harmonists*, 184–86. For an account of the strike nationwide, see Bruce, *1877*.
31. *LFM*, 1 (Aug. 1877), 274–76. In March the *LFM* supported the Engineers' strike on the Boston and Maine line, arguing that it was "brought about by the conspiracy refusing to pay the men an honest price for their labor." Those

who refused to strike were considered to be "thus violating their obligation to God and man." *Ibid.*, 1 (Mar. 1877), 106.

32. Gresham, *Gresham,* 1:407.
33. In 1881 Debs stated that the only way the Brotherhood became involved in the strike was "through the power usurped by one of our grand officers." *LFM,* 5 (June 1881), 169–71.
34. Ware, *Labor Movement,* 45.
35. EVD, *American Movement,* 83–84.
36. Bureau of the Census, *10th Census: Report of Statistics of Manufacture,* 418, 440, 449, 506. On the reaction to the wage cuts see *LFM,* 1 (July 1877), 238. For slightly different estimates see Bruce, *1877,* 46, and Boyle, *Railroad Strikes,* 9.
37. Terre Haute *Express,* 23 July 1877. Workers in another small midwestern community, Newark, Ohio, also swore off liquor prior to striking. See Bruce, *1877,* 127. This is in distinct contrast with the attitude of workers in the larger urban centers such as Chicago or Pittsburgh.
38. Terre Haute *Express,* 25 July 1877; Gresham, *Gresham,* 1:404; Martin, *Great Riots,* 365.
39. Terre Haute *Express,* 25 July 1877.
40. *Ibid.,* 26 July 1877.
41. *Ibid.,* 27 July 1877. After communication with other strikers at St. Louis and Effingham, Ill., the Terre Haute strikers decided to allow only mail trains through. *Ibid.,* 28 July 1877.
42. *Ibid.,* 25, 26 July 1877. For a discussion of cooperation across classes during early industrial labor struggles, see Gutman, "Worker's Search for Power," 38–68.
43. Terre Haute *Express,* 29 July 1877; Gresham, *Gresham,* 1:392, 398.
44. Gresham, *Gresham,* 1:399.
45. *Ibid.,* 400; Terre Haute *Express,* 30, 31 July 1877. On 1 Aug., Miller and three other strikers were arrested on federal charges of contempt of court by order of Judge Gresham. At the Indianapolis trial they were defended by Judge A. B. Carlton of Terre Haute, while Charles W. Fairbanks, brother of Terre Haute's mayor, assisted the prosecution. McKeen was chief prosecution witness. The defendants received sentences ranging from thirty days to six months. Terre Haute *Express,* 2 Aug. 1877; Gresham, *Gresham,* 1:403.
46. Thompson to Col. Thomas A. Scott, 5 Aug. 1877, RWT. In the strike's wake, a number of midwestern Republicans, including McKeen, Thompson, and Gresham, discussed capturing the 1880 Republican presidential nomination for Ulysses S. Grant, as they felt the need for a strong military president for expected future labor unrest. See Thompson to William Dennison, 29 May 1880, RWT; Gresham, *Gresham,* 1:408.
47. Gompers, *Seventy Years,* 1:383.
48. Terre Haute *Express,* 9 Sept. 1877.
49. The only mention of the strike in the lodge records notes that on 1 Aug. regular business was suspended to discuss "the late strike," at which time the resolution was passed supporting Sayer and Miller. Record Books, 1:138 (1 Aug. 1877).
50. Quoted in *LFM,* 1 (Oct. 1877), 354–56. The convention adopted a complicated procedure for grievances, which tried to avoid any hint of a potential strike. On presentation of a grievance, the local lodge would decide whether "under the existing circumstances the management is justified in its action."

If not, a committee would meet with the company; if that failed, the Grand Lodge would review the issue and visit the company if necessary. If this, too, failed of resolution, the Grand Lodge would retire to secret session "and determine upon future action." *Proceedings of BLF*, 1877, 39. Such a procedure made strikes next to impossible and, more important, located the power to call strikes solely with the national officers.

51. Coleman, *Debs*, 42.

52. On the early lodge elections, see Record Books, I:53 (12 Sept. 1875); I:90 (9 Mar. 1876); I:115 (13 Aug. 1876); I:135 (27 June 1877); I:139 (26 Aug. 1877). Also see *LFM*, 1 (Jan. 1877), 63.

53. *Proceedings of BLF*, 1877, 5, 28; *LFM*, 1 (Nov. 1877), 381.

54. Ware, *Labor Movement*, 52.

55. Hesseltine, *Third-Party Movements*, 51–52. For an account of Ignatius Donnelly, whose tumultuous political career as a Republican Congressman (1862–68), Liberal Republican advocate (1871–72), and Independent party leader in Minnesota (1872–76) epitomizes part of this movement, see Ridge, *Donnelly*, chs. 8, 9. Destler examines the Anti-Tariff League and the Liberal Republican movement from the perspective of Henry Demarest Lloyd, a future ally of Debs's, in *Lloyd*.

56. Weinstein, *Prelude to Populism*, 230–32; Hesseltine, *Third-Party Movements*, 52–54. The repeal of the Resumption Act by Congress after the 1878 elections depleted the movement's strength as did the gradual absorption of labor's position by the Democratic party. See Thornbrough, *Indiana in the Civil War Era*, 313. For a discussion of producer ideology, see Montgomery, *Beyond Equality*, 14ff.

57. Stewart, "Populist Party in Indiana," 337.

58. Thornbrough, *Indiana in the Civil War Era*, 292–312.

59. *Ibid.*, 312. See also the entries in William McLean's notebooks, especially no. 6, for examples of this veteran Democratic campaigner's pro-labor rhetoric (WEM).

60. Indianapolis *Sentinel*, 5 Aug. 1888, as quoted in Burley, "Campaign of 1888," 37. Phillips, *Indiana in Transition*, 2–6, 46–48, argues that with the Republican victory in 1896 Indiana began to identify with the industrial East rather than, as under the Democrats, with "the perennially discontented agricultural west." Thornbrough suggests that, following the unprotested 1880 nomination of the anti-Greenback Indiana banker, William H. English, as the Democratic vice-presidential candidate, the Democratic infatuation with the money question in Indiana ceased and "a political era had ended." *Indiana in the Civil War Era*, 317.

61. Thornbrough, *Indiana in the Civil War Era*, 258ff.; Bradsby, *History of Vigo County*, 402; Ginger, *The Bending Cross*, 27.

62. Karsner, *Debs, Life and Letters*, 122.

63. Terre Haute *Evening Gazette*, 29 Mar. 1879.

64. *Ibid.*; on the nominating contest, see the editions of 17, 18, 22, 27 Mar. 1879; on Debs's relation with Harper, see Ginger, *The Bending Cross*, 29–32.

65. Terre Haute *Express*, 7 May 1879. Crofts ran third with 1,054 votes while Ross received 1,444.

66. Bradsby, *History of Vigo County*, 445. Havens polled 2,022 votes.

67. *LFM*, 3 (June 1879), 178; Terre Haute *Evening Gazette*, 29 Apr. 1879.

68. Terre Haute *Express*, 7 May 1879.

69. Mullen contested and lost an 1876 lodge election to Debs; Record Books, I:90 (9 Mar. 1876).
70. Terre Haute *Express*, 3 Sept. 1879. For the development of this controversy, see the issues of 24, 31 Aug. 1879.
71. The Greenback candidate received exactly the same number as EVD in ward one—198 votes.
72. Terre Haute *Express*, 7 May 1879; Bureau of the Census, *Ninth Census*, I: 130, 309; *Tenth Census*, I: 418, 449. On black votes see the testimony of A. B. Carlton and John Lamb, *Senate Report 693*, I:18-20, 149-56.
73. One example of how this emphasis on harmony and community, while formally disavowing class differences, bordered on ideological control by the upper class occurred in the 1884 campaign. During a parade in support of Thomas Hendricks, the Democratic vice-presidential candidate and former Indiana governor, forty-eight of Hulman's employees marched as a group, all carrying long brooms as a symbol of their employment. Hulman, of course, was a major Democratic party figure in Terre Haute. One wonders at the extent of the coercion, overt perhaps but more likely simply woven into the fabric of social life, that produced such a seeming unity. Terre Haute *Evening Gazette*, 25 Oct. 1884.
74. Ginger, *The Bending Cross*, 29.
75. In this election Debs outpolled Republican J. W. Barnett by a thin margin, 2,460-2,222. But he again gained more votes than the successful candidate for mayor. Bradsby, *History of Vigo County*, 446; untitled clipping, Kate Metzel Debs Scrapbooks, DF.
76. In addition to having a close political relationship with Democrats such as John Lamb and William McLean, Debs also referred to Bayless Hanna, a prominent Republican, as a friend. EVD to Robert Ingersoll, 26 Jan. 1882, RGI.
77. Coleman, *Debs*, 73.
78. *Ibid.*, 72.
79. *Ibid.*, 63-66.
80. On the county convention, see untitled clipping, Kate Metzel Debs Scrapbooks, DF. On his Congressional future, see another untitled clipping in the Scrapbooks, dated Minneapolis, Sept. 1885; "Eugene V. Debs," *American Railroader*, Sept. 1885, EVD Scrapbooks, reel 283, vol. 4, 1 (Taminent Institute, microfilm edition).
81. Terre Haute *Evening Gazette*, 9 Sept. 1884. For Debs's prominence within the party, see the issues of 6, 20 Aug., 6 Oct. 1884.
82. On the Democratic platform, see Foulke, *Indiana General Assembly*, 2ff. Indiana Republicans stressed arbitration but offered few specific proposals for labor. See the leaflet collection, IRP.
83. Terre Haute *Evening Gazette*, 7 Nov. 1884; Bradsby, *History of Vigo County*, 413; *Brevier Legislative Reports*, 23: appendix 17, 38.
84. Terre Haute *Evening Gazette*, 16 Jan. 1885.
85. *Brevier Legislative Reports*, 23: appendix 77.
86. Debs's three minor bills concerned public building bonds, licensing of vending merchandise, and an amendment to a bill encouraging agriculture. *Ibid.*, 22:342, 344. The bill to grant women suffrage won a majority (45-43) but lacked a constitutional majority (51). The anti-discrimination bill lost 43-40. *Ibid.*, 22: 35; 23: 184. The legislature did pass a bill entitling all races

to equal access to public accommodations; see Phillips, *Indiana in Transition*, 23.

87. *Brevier Legislative Reports*, 22: 71; Terre Haute *Evening Gazette*, 20 Jan. 1885.
88. *Brevier Legislative Reports*, 23: 132.
89. *Ibid.*, 23: 69, 88; Coleman, *Debs*, 84–85.
90. Coleman, *Debs*, 84–85; Ginger, *The Bending Cross*, 42–44; Morais and Cahn, *Gene Debs*, 25.
91. Derthick, *National Guard*, 16–17. Also of interest is Gephart, "Politicians, Soldiers and Strikes," 89–120.
92. On the Gould strike, see Foner, *History of the Labor Movement*, II: 50ff.; Allen, *Great Southwest Strike*. On other Knights' strikes before the Gould and for an account of the reaction to the public endorsement of strikes by the Knights on 1 Jan. 1884, see Ware, *Labor Movement*, 132–44.
93. Foulke, *Indiana General Assembly*, 16. Foulke was a Republican state senator.
94. *Brevier Legislative Reports*, 22: 304–5, 336.
95. Terre Haute *Evening Gazette*, 10 Jan. 1885. Some unemployed workers, declaring they were sick of charity and desired regular work at decent wages, formed "The Laboring Men's Organization" to press their demands.
96. *Ibid.*, 24 Apr. 1888.
97. Coleman, *Debs*, 60–61; see also Debs's final speech to a Brotherhood convention, *Proceedings of BLF*, 1894, 503–4.
98. EVD, "Serving the Labor Movement"; Dorothy J. Clark, "Terre Haute's First Labor Union," Terre Haute *Tribune-Star*, 22 Feb. 1959; Ginger, *The Bending Cross*, 38–39. It would be important to know more of Debs's association with McGuire, as it was his first known contact with an avowed Socialist. No adequate biography exists on McGuire and the most serious account of his career, Christie, *Empire in Wood*, makes no mention of the Terre Haute local.
99. EVD, "Serving the Labor Movement"; EVD, "Stray Leaves," 187; EVD, "Revolutionary Encampments," *The National Rip-Saw*, Sept. 1914, 12.
100. Kopelin, *Life of Debs*, 9.
101. Gompers, *Seventy Years*, I: 215–18; Foner, *History of the Labor Movement*, I:518–19; Phillips, *Indiana in Transition*, 340n.
102. The figures are from the federal census of 1880 as quoted in Phillips, *Indiana in Transition*, 338.
103. Thomas N. Taylor, "The Interests of Organized Labor," n.d., LLC.
104. Much of the material from this section is taken from the *LFM*. Debs became assistant editor in January 1879 and editor-in-chief in August 1880. In 1890 he claimed that from August 1880 on he assumed complete control of the magazine and wrote or approved each editorial. *LFM*, 14 (Jan. 1890), 36. See also McMurry's discussion of the *LFM* as "a personal organ for the propagation of his [EVD] opinions" in *Burlington Strike*, 35.
105. *LFM*, 6 (Jan. 1882), 16.
106. *Ibid.*, 6 (Mar. 1882), 128.
107. *Ibid.*, 7 (Jan. 1883), 23.
108. See the mention of Debs's defense of hard work against genius in a Terre Haute debate, where he argued that the example of "Michael Angelo and Cicero" proved genius "a non-entity." *Ibid.*, 4 (May 1880), 154.

109. *Ibid.*, 7 (Mar. 1883), 122–23.
110. *Ibid.*, 6 (Apr. 1882), 170–171.
111. *Proceedings of BLF*, 1880, 14.
112. *LFM*, 4 (Nov. 1880), 347; Ginger, *The Bending Cross*, 31.
113. *LFM*, 5 (Feb. 1881), 56.
114. Record Books, II: 63 (8 May 1881); *Proceedings of BLF*, 1882, 16–17.
115. *LFM*, 7 (June 1883), 253–54.
116. *Ibid.*, 8 (June 1884), 339–42, emphasis added.
117. *Ibid.*, 6 (Sept. 1882), 406.
118. *Ibid.*, 3 (Jan. 1879), 17–18.
119. At the 1879 convention the delegates voted unanimously to "ignore" strikes and endorsed arbitration. *Proceedings of BLF*, 1879, 40.
120. *LFM*, 5 (June 1881), 169–71.
121. The editorial appears in *ibid.*, 8 (May 1884), 277–82. Debs's public acknowledgment of his "mistake," which makes no mention of Pettibone, is in *ibid.*, 8 (Nov. 1884), 665. For the convention fight, see *Proceedings of BLF*, 1884, 21–22, 147.
122. *Proceedings of BLF*, 1884, 124–27.
123. *LFM*, 7 (Nov. 1883), 492–93.
124. *Ibid.*, 7 (Jan. 1883), 24.
125. *Ibid.*, 8 (May 1884), 277–82.
126. *Ibid.*, 7 (Apr. 1883), 161.
127. Ginger, *The Bending Cross*, 35.
128. "The Most Enjoined Man in the World," St. Louis *Chronicle*, 1 Sept. 1900.
129. Quoted in untitled clipping (Philadelphia, Sept. 1885) in EVD Scrapbooks, reel 283, vol. 1:36–39 (Tamiment Library, microfilm edition).
130. Record Books, II:75 (9 Oct. 1881); II:141 (24 Sept. 1882).
131. EVD to "Jennie," 17 Oct. 1881, ISU.
132. Kate Richards O'Hare, "Home to Kate," *The National Rip-Saw*, Nov. 1921, 3; Reed, *Encyclopedia of Biography of Indiana*, II:163–64.
133. John Erskin Hankins, "Katherine Metzel Debs," untitled clipping, DF; Oakey, *Greater Terre Haute*, I:436; II:540–41; Beckwith, *Vigo and Parke Counties*, II:317. See also the letter of Steven M. Reynolds to his wife describing the expensive decor and prices of the Terre Haute House, 2 June 1889, SMR.
134. O'Hare, "Home to Kate," 5.
135. *LFM*, 9 (Aug. 1885), 477; Record Books, III:3 (27 July 1885); Ginger, *The Bending Cross*, 44.
136. Ginger, *The Bending Cross*, 52–54. Debs's salary was more than three times the average annual salary of even many highly skilled railroad workers.
137. *Ibid.*, 61–64. Ginger's informant, Kate's half-brother's wife, says that Kate was the sterile partner, *ibid.*, 463. EVD once explained how he compensated for this lack of family, in one of his few public references to it: "We have no children; I spend much of my time with children; I love them." St. Louis *Chronicle*, 1 Sept. 1900.
138. Ginger, *The Bending Cross*, 43–44.
139. Ridgley, "Terre Haute during the Civil War," 5.
140. Ginger, *The Bending Cross*, 13; *Souvenir Volume*.
141. John Spargo, "The Reminiscences of John Spargo," 210–11, OHR.

Notes to Chapter 3

1. Buchanan, *Labor Agitator*, 11–12.
2. Quoted in Garraty, *New Commonwealth*, 109. For a broad analysis of these developments, see Wiebe, *Search for Order*; Chandler, *Visible Hand*.
3. Commons, ed., *History of Labour*, II:361; Garraty, *New Commonwealth*, 128–29. Also of interest is Haber, *Efficiency and Uplift*.
4. Commons, ed., *History of Labour*, II:368; Ware, *Labor Movement*, 139–40.
5. *John Swinton's Paper*, 12 Apr. 1885, quoted in Ware, *Labor Movement*, 140.
6. Commons, ed., *History of Labour*, II:368–70; Ware, *Labor Movement*, 140–44.
7. Ware, *Labor Movement*, 144–45.
8. Quoted in Foner, *History of the Labor Movement*, II:54; see also Commons, ed., *History of Labour*, II:370–75.
9. McMurry, *Burlington Strike*, 34–35.
10. EVD, "A Grand Brotherhood," untitled Philadelphia newspaper, 22 Sept. 1885, in EVD Scrapbooks, reel 238, vol. 1:36–37 (Tamiment Library, microfilm edition).
11. *Proceedings of BLF*, 1885, 171–72.
12. *Ibid.*, 197ff.
13. *LFM*, 8 (Aug. 1884), 467–69.
14. *Ibid.*, 8 (Nov. 1884), 661–62.
15. *Ibid.*, 9 (Apr. 1885), 222–25.
16. *Ibid.*, 9 (Feb. 1885), 89–91.
17. *Ibid.*, 9 (Dec. 1885), 726–29; see also *ibid.*, 11 (Apr. 1887), 546–47.
18. *Ibid.*, 10 (Apr. 1886), 206–7; see also his critique of P.M. Arthur's speech on labor, *ibid.*, 10 (Feb. 1886), 70–71.
19. *Ibid.*, 10 (Apr. 1886), 193–200.
20. *Ibid.*, 10 (May 1886), 266–67 (emphasis added). This connection between "absolute independence" and white Americans on one hand, and unmanly dependency and American Indians on the other, was an important theme in nineteenth-century America and served as one support of an intricate sociopsychological justification of a policy of Indian extermination. See Rogin, *Fathers and Children*.
21. *LFM*, 10 (June 1886), 326–29. Debs's emphasis on the "Americanism" of this personal liberty was not lost on either Gompers or the rank and file of the Cigar Makers Union, many of whom, as Gompers himself, were immigrants.
22. Gabriel, "Evangelical Religion," 37; see also Gutman, "Protestantism and the American Labor Movement," 79–118.
23. For references to Hugo, see *LFM*, 8 (Feb. 1884), 76. Debs quoted a section from Henry George's *Progress and Poverty*, which was quite critical of industrial development and ended with a somber biblical warning: "The promised land flies before us like a mirage. The fruits of the tree of knowledge turn as we grasp them to apples of Sodom that crumble at the touch." *LFM*, 9 (Feb. 1885), 96–97.
24. *LFM*, 9 (Feb. 1885), 91–95.
25. *Ibid.*, 9 (Oct. 1885), 615–17.
26. *Ibid.*, 10 (Jan. 1886), 7–8.

27. *Ibid.*, 10 (July 1886), 394–97.
28. *Ibid.*, 10 (Nov. 1886), 641–43. Debs also pointed out that foreigners owned over twenty million acres and urged political action to prevent such accumulation in the future.
29. *Ibid.*, 9 (May 1885), 283–85.
30. *Ibid.*, 9 (June 1885), 343–46. Debs suggested that in war "the truth is often cloven down," but argued that the relative moral justice of either side was of less importance than the final results. Thus he supported western imperialism in both Indo-China and the Sudan and invoked Christian symbols in his defense because "a vast region [will be] redeemed from the thralldom of barbarianism." *Ibid.*
31. *Ibid.*, 10 (Apr. 1886), 203–5.
32. *Ibid.*, 8 (Dec. 1884), 725–27; see also his editorial, "Education," in the issue of 9 (Mar. 1885), 161–62.
33. Karsner, *Talks with Debs*, 148–49. For a more contemporary example of Debs's attitude, see Robert G. Ingersoll to EVD, 2 Feb. 1881, DF. A different if incomplete analysis of Debs's religiosity is presented by Currie, "Religious Views," 147–56.
34. Socialist leader Morris Hillquit once called Gompers "the most class-conscious man" he had ever met; William Z. Foster, the Communist leader, argued during his "boring from within" period that the AFL's insistence on obtaining more economic demands from capital was "directly anti-capitalist." Hillquit's is the more perceptive of the two views. See Reed, *Labor Philosophy of Gompers*, 25, 57.
35. See the letters of Theodore Debs to Karsner, 17 Jan. 1919, 19 May 1922, DFK.
36. Gompers, *Seventy Years*, I:416.
37. Taft, *A.F. of L.*, 8; Roe, *Juggernaut*, 34; McGuire, "American Federation of Labor," 39. Selig Perlman suggests that the Terre Haute conference was called to start a rival organization to the Knights of Labor. This is misleading, although it was the desire of some of the delegates. Commons, ed., *History of Labour*, II:318. See also Ware, *Labor Movement*, 243–45.
38. *Report, First Annual Session of the Federation*, 14–15. See also Taft, *A.F. of L.*, 9–10.
39. *Report, First Annual Session of the Federation*, 3, 4ff. The resolutions covered child labor, apprentice laws, the eight-hour day, a mechanics lien law, curtailment of foreign, especially Chinese, immigration, and the adoption of a protective tariff. See Taft, *A.F. of L.*, 12–13.
40. Quoted in Taft, *A.F. of L.*, 10; see also Kaufman, *Samuel Gompers*, chs. 1–6.
41. Gompers, *Seventy Years*, I:229–30.
42. Ware, *Labor Movement*, 92; Taft, *A.F. of L.*, 10.
43. *Report, First Annual Session of the Federation*, 16–17; Taft, *A.F. of L.*, 11.
44. *Report, First Annual Session of the Federation*, 16–17; Foner, *History of the Labor Movement*, I:520; Taft, *A.F. of L.*, 11–12; Commons, ed., *History of Labour*, II:322–24.
45. Ware, *Labor Movement*, 248.
46. McGuire, "American Federation of Labor," 40–41.
47. Gompers, *Seventy Years*, I:75–82.
48. For an excellent discussion of producerism, see Montgomery, *Beyond*

Equality, especially chs. 1, 5; also of interest is Destler, *American Radicalism*, 25–27.

49. On this strike, see Ware, *Labor Movement*, 145ff.; Allen, *Great Southwest Strike*; Foner, *History of the Labor Movement*, II:83–86. On Haymarket, see David, *Haymarket*.
50. *LFM*, 10 (June 1886), 331.
51. *Ibid.*, 10 (May 1886), 257–61.
52. *Ibid.*, 10 (June 1886), 356–57, 10 (July 1886), 426.
53. *Proceedings of BFL*, 1886, 38–39. In August 1887 EVD could still express regret at the resignation of William Kerrigan, general manager of the Missouri Pacific during the strike, for he had always "enjoyed the confidence and regard of his employes." *LFM*, 11 (Aug. 1887), 491.
54. *LFM*, 10 (June 1886), 372.
55. *Ibid.*, 331.
56. Des Moines *Leader*, 12 July 1886, quoted in *LFM*, 10 (Aug. 1886), 489. For a similar response from a paper in the middle of the strike, see the Parsons (Kans.) *Sun*, n.d. [Apr. 22, 1886] as quoted in *LFM*, 10 (June 1886), 372. The *Sun* states approvingly that EVD and Sargent condemned the strike.
57. *LFM*, 11 (Jan. 1887), 11–13.
58. *Ibid.*, 3.
59. Terre Haute *Evening Gazette*, 25 June 1888, 24 Apr. 1889; EVD, "More Park" (typed), ISU.
60. Terre Haute *Evening Gazette*, 26 May, 6 Sept. 1888, 10 Apr. 1889. Both Theodore and John Heinl, Eugene's brother-in-law, were members of the local Knights of Pythias. As a member of its drill team, Theodore marched behind "the silk flag of the McKeen rifles" in a contest at Cincinnati. See *ibid.*, 26 May, 12 June 1888.
61. In 1889 Daniel Debs was listed among the town's wealthier citizens according to the taxes he paid. With an assessed property value of $8,500, he was not among the top twenty individuals but was clearly wealthier than most. Along with Daniel, three of the Baurs and Heinl were also listed as leading property holders and taxpayers. Collectively, then, Debs's family, through both blood and marriage, occupied a secure if secondary niche in the town's economic hierarchy. See *ibid.*, 30 Mar. 1889.
62. Ginger, *The Bending Cross*, 31; interview with Marguerite Debs Cooper, niece of EVD, 31 Mar. 1974, Terre Haute.
63. EVD to Theodore Debs, 8 July 1895, ISU.
64. Terre Haute *Evening Gazette*, 28, 31 July, 30 Aug. 1888.
65. *Ibid.*, 16 Aug. 1888. Following his brother, Theo was also active in Democratic politics, serving as treasurer of the Young Men's Democratic Club. See *ibid.*, 14 Aug. 1888.
66. *Ibid.*, 29 Oct. 1888. It is interesting that throughout this speech, EVD made no mention of McKeen, although he was a prominent Republican, a local supporter of Harrison, and had opposed the strikers in 1877.
67. *LFM*, 11 (May 1887), 264. The full stanza reads: "And, say in business, where's as clean / A record now as Rile' McKeen?— / E a more purely daily walk / In railroad er in racing stock? / And search the earth from end to end / And where's a better all around friend / Than Eugene Debs?—a man that stands / And jest holds out in two hands / As warm a heart as ever beat / Betwixt here and the Mercy Seat!" In later years Debs's supporters usually quoted only those lines directly referring to him, thus muting the real

meaning of his life during these years. See Ginger, *The Bending Cross*, 54; Le Prade, ed., *Debs and the Poets*, 40.

68. The Firemen struck the Brooklyn Elevated Company in 1887. Although it lost, Debs pointed with pride to the support it received from the mayor of Brooklyn. This was also the first strike called with official Brotherhood sanction. See *LFM*, 11 (Sept. 1887), 513-15; *Proceedings of BLF*, 1888, 40-41.

69. McMurry, *Burlington Strike*, 38-44; see also EVD's editorial against classification, *LFM*, 10 (Sept. 1886), 513-15. For an example of the antagonism between EVD and Arthur see EVD's editorial "Labor and Capital," *LFM*, 10 (Feb. 1886), 70-71.

70. On the Brotherhood of Locomotive Engineers' early history, see Stevenson, "Brotherhood."

71. McMurry, *Burlington Strike*, 40.

72. *Ibid.*, 15-17.

73. *Ibid.*, 92-94.

74. Terre Haute *Evening Gazette*, 6, 7 Jan. 1888; Commons, ed., *History of Labour*, II:474-75.

75. McMurry, *Burlington Strike*, 75, 80; *Proceedings of BLF*, 1888, 45.

76. Interview in the Chicago *Herald*, n.d., reprinted in Terre Haute *Evening Gazette*, 1 Mar. 1888. See also the report of EVD's speech at Easton, Pa., just prior to the strike for similar sentiments in the Terre Haute *Evening Gazette*, 27 Feb. 1888.

77. *Proceedings of BLF*, 1888, 49-50; McMurry, *Burlington Strike*, 107.

78. *Proceedings of BLF*, 1888, 50; McMurry, *Burlington Strike*, 108. The eastern grievance chairmen had refused to attend the Chicago meeting.

79. *Proceedings of BLF*, 1888, 50; McMurry, *Burlington Strike*, 113.

80. Terre Haute *Evening Gazette*, 16 Mar. 1888.

81. McMurry, *Burlington Strike*, 116-28; Gresham, *Gresham*, I: 409-16.

82. On Arthur, see EVD, "The Strike that Should Have Been Won," *Call Magazine*, Apr. 1918, 3; Sargent's explanation is in *Proceedings of BLF*, 1888, 50-51; EVD's attitude is discussed in Gresham, *Gresham*, I:416.

83. Terre Haute *Evening Gazette*, 16, 20 Mar. 1888; *Proceedings of BLF*, 1888, 51; *ibid.*, 1890, 99.

84. Terre Haute *Evening Gazette*, 28 Feb. 1888; Buchanan, *Labor Agitator*, 306-8; Ware, *Labor Movement*, 89; McMurry, *Burlington Strike,* 92-94.

85. Buchanan, *Labor Agitator*, 308-10; McMurry, *Burlington Strike,* 95; Terre Haute *Evening Gazette*, 2, 3 Mar. 1888.

86. Terre Haute *Evening Gazette*, 24, 28 Mar. 1888; McMurry, *Burlington Strike,* 98, 138-41.

87. Report of Informant number 1, 25 June 1889, file 33 1880, 9.81, CBQ. EVD's prediction proved accurate. The Burlington banned the Engineers after the strike and did not allow another lodge to reorganize until 1903, after Arthur had died. See Stevenson, "Brotherhood," 195ff.

88. *Proceedings of BLF*, 1888, 41-70; *ibid.*, 1890, 73-101.

89. *Ibid.*, 1890, 101.

90. EVD, "The Strike that Should Have Been Won," 3.

91. Daniel Debs to Emma Debs Maillaux, 12 Mar. 1888, ISU.

92. EVD, "The Strike that Should Have Been Won," 3.

93. *LFM*, 12 (Apr. 1888), 242-46.

94. *Ibid.*, 251-52. Two years earlier, EVD had attacked a Louisiana governor's

speech at an Engineers' convention on the same grounds. See *ibid.,* 10 (Jan. 1886), 8–9.

95. This theme was frequently mentioned during the strike. In a fund-raising circular of 10 Apr. 1888, sent to all lodges, Debs and Sargent suggested that the members appeal to the middle class in their respective communities for support in their fight against "corporate injustice. There are merchants and business men who have the welfare of society at heart and who know when workingmen are fairly paid, society is the gainer—that the business pulse beats more healthfully and their prosperity is assured, and it is known that hundreds of such men stand ready to give upon proper solicitation." *Proceedings of BLF,* 1888, 63–64.

96. *LFM,* 12 (May 1888), 335.

97. Quoted in Robbins, *Railway Conductors,* 110.

98. *LFM,* 12 (May 1888), 325–28.

99. *Ibid.,* 12 (July 1888), 482–83.

100. *Ibid.,* 13 (Jan. 1889), 11–12.

101. *Ibid.,* 12 (July 1888), 484–86.

102. *Ibid.,* 12 (June 1888), 406–8. For an earlier and perceptive view of EVD's development during this time, see Shannon, "Debs, Conservative Labor Editor," 357–64.

Notes to Part II

1. On Terre Haute's strike activity, see U.S. Commissioner of Labor, *Third Annual Report,* 168ff., and *Tenth Annual Report,* I: 258ff.

2. O'Neal, *Terre Haute's Shame,* 10–12; Hilton and Due, *Electric Interurban Railways,* 55; Blackburn, "Interurban Railroads of Indiana," 221–79, 400–464.

3. Oakey, *Greater Terre Haute,* I: 231; Terre Haute *Evening Gazette,* 10 Mar. 1888.

4. Terre Haute *Evening Gazette,* 7 May 1889.

5. *Ibid.,* 13, 17 May, 20 June 1889; Oakey, *Greater Terre Haute,* I: 228–29. For the analysis of M. H. Butler, of the Knights of Labor, see Terre Haute *Evening Gazette,* 5 June 1889.

6. Oakey, *Greater Terre Haute,* I: 228–29; Drummond, "Terre Haute," 64–66; Hubbard, ed., *Book of Indiana,* 489.

7. See O'Neal, *Terre Haute's Shame*; Blackburn, "Interurban Railroads of Indiana."

8. Daniel Debs to Emma Debs Maillaux, n.d. [ca. 1888], ISU.

9. Terre Haute *Evening Gazette,* 19 Dec. 1887, 6, 30 Jan. 1888.

10. For a more detailed discussion of Terre Haute's workers in the decade following the 1877 strike, see Salvatore, "Railroad Workers and the Great Strike of 1877," 522–45.

11. Terre Haute *Evening Gazette,* 29 Mar. 1889.

Notes to Chapter 4

1. EVD, "Fraternization," *United Labor* (Denver), 9 Aug. 1890.

2. See John Winthrop, "A Model of Christian Charity," in *U.S. Colonial History Readings and Documents,* ed. David Hawke (Indianapolis, 1966), 96–97.

3. On this bitter dispute, see *Proceedings of BLF*, 1884, 104; *ibid.*, 1885, 194–95; *LFM*, 10 (Dec. 1886), 712, 13 (Jan. 1889), 6-7, 13 (Apr. 1889), 299–300; 14 (Jan. 1890), 39–41; McMurry, "Federation," 74–75; Stevenson, "Brotherhood," 184ff. Vigo Lodge condemned the BLE's exclusionary action as "contrary to the Spirit of our American Government which we hope will live forever." Record Books, III:134 (28 Dec. 1885).

4. *LFM*, 10 (Feb. 1886), 110.

5. Stevenson, "Brotherhood," 182–83; EVD, "The Education of Locomotive Engineer-Men," *Locomotive Engineering* (Jan. 1892), 13.

6. *LFM*, 12 (June 1888), 410. See also his editorial, "Equality of Conditions," where he extends this analysis in another attack on the aristocracy of labor. *Ibid.*, 12 (Sept. 1888), 653–54.

7. See *Switchmen's Journal*, 3 (July 1888), 104–5, 3 (Aug. 1888), 149–50.

8. *Proceedings of BLF*, 1888, 9–10, 11–13, 349–50.

9. *Ibid.*, 351; the interview with EVD in the Terre Haute *Evening Gazette*, 22 Sept. 1888. Unfortunately, there is no specific record of the voting on any of these issues.

10. EVD gave a stirring speech before the Brakemen's convention, and, although it was not yet a labor organization (it would endorse strikes in 1889), it voted to support federation. For accounts of the speech see Terre Haute *Evening Gazette*, 19 Oct. 1888; and the speech of W. P. Kennedy, president of the Brotherhood of Railroad Trainmen, 5 Nov. 1955, SPP (National Subject File).

11. Gompers to Arthur, 9, 17 Oct. 1888, SGLB.

12. Informant number 1, Report to Pinkerton Agency, 21 Oct. 1888, file 33 1880 9.31, CBQ.

13. Informant number 1, Report to the Pinkerton Agency, 19 Oct. 1888, file 33 1880 9.31, CBQ; McMurry, "Federation," 77–78.

14. EVD shared these attitudes with Gompers, who had criticized the Engineers' refusal to federate as an action "unworthy of their grand organization." Gompers had been active during 1889 in supporting conferences of railway men in an effort to unify them; he even went so far as to urge that the charges of scabbing against the Knights of Labor be dropped so that they might also join. See *Railroad Trainmen's Journal*, 7 (Jan. 1890), 11–12; Gompers to Executive Council, AFL, 7 Feb., 7 Sept. 1889, SGLB.

15. *Switchmen's Journal*, 4 (May 1889), 2; 4 (July 1889), 97–98; *LFM*, 13 (July 1889), 627–29.

16. *LFM*, 13 (July 1889), 585–86.

17. See *Switchmen's Journal*, 4 (Feb. 1890), 438–39; McMurry, "Federation," 79–80, for a discussion of these two plans.

18. *LFM*, 13 (Dec. 1889), 1090–91.

19. *Ibid.*, 13 (Dec. 1889), 1091–93, 14 (Feb. 1890), 135–36, 14 (Mar. 1890), 236.

20. See *Switchmen's Journal*, 4 (Feb. 1890), 433–36, 4 (Apr. 1890), 531–33; *Railroad Trainmen's Journal*, 7 (Feb. 1890), 67–68, 7 (May 1890), 259–66, 7 (July 1890), 390–92, 400–404.

21. *LFM*, 14 (Mar. 1890), 238–42.

22. *Ibid.*, 251–52.

23. *Ibid.*, 252–54.

24. *Ibid.*, 14 (June 1890), 546–47.

25. *Ibid.*, 547–50.

26. *Ibid.*, 14 (Feb. 1890), 144–48, 14 (Apr. 1890), 341–43, 14 (May 1890), 437, 14 (June 1890), 550, 557.
27. Robbins, *Railway Conductors*, 44–46; *LFM*, 14 (May 1890), 436, 14 (June 1890), 534. Howard's career is interesting as it indicates the loose sense of class that many railway men's leaders adopted at this time. Howard had held almost every possible position on a railroad, from brakeman to general superintendent. At the time of his election in 1889, he was master of transportation and general superintendent for the Mackey railroad in southern California. In welcoming his election, EVD reprinted letters of tribute from D. J. Mackey as an indication of Howard's qualifications and to demonstrate the career success of this self-made man. In 1893 Howard joined EVD in directing the American Railway Union. See *LFM*, 13 (Nov. 1889), 1000; McMurry, "Federation," 80. Some years later Howard explained this attitude: "Railroad men," he suggested, "as a general thing are clannish; they want to associate with railroad men and it don't matter if one of them is discharged and goes into other business like the grocery business, he still likes to affiliate with railroad men and likes still to be considered a railroad man." See *Senate Executive Document No. 7*, 15.
28. *Railroad Trainmen's Journal*, 7 (July 1890), 414–15; *LFM*, 14 (Aug. 1890), 708–9.
29. *LFM*, 14 (Aug. 1890), 695–704, 716.
30. See the letter of T. P. O'Rourke, *ibid.*, 15 (Mar. 1891), 251–53; *Railroad Trainmen's Journal*, 7 (Oct. 1890), 597–99.
31. *LFM*, 15 (Mar. 1891), 240–42; EVD, "Fraternization."
32. For Walton's letter, see *LFM*, 14 (Jan. 1890), 12–13; on the Brotherhood of Telegraphers, *ibid.*, 14 (Aug. 1890), 708–9.
33. Informant number 1, Report to the Pinkerton Agency, 25 June 1889, file 33 1880, 9.81, CBQ.
34. See EVD's signed statement, "An Open Letter to P. M. Arthur, Esq.," *LFM*, 14 (Jan. 1890), 39–41, and his comments on the BLE and Federation, *ibid.*, 14 (Dec. 1890), 1116.
35. *Ibid.*, 13 (Apr. 1889), 330–31; see also, for example, the letters with EVD's response in *ibid.*, 13 (Oct. 1889), 911–24.
36. *Ibid.*, 14 (Jan. 1890), 47–51.
37. *Ibid.*, 14 (Mar. 1890), 243–45.
38. See the resolutions of Lodge 284, New Haven, *ibid.*, 15 (Feb. 1891), 134–38; Lodge 285, Hartford, *ibid.*, 15 (May 1891), 442–43. This was not the first time that EVD was criticized for being too political in his editorials. In September 1887 fireman O. A. Dosskey objected to EVD's emphasis on a labor party and argued that it was the task of neither the editor nor the Brotherhood "to solve labor problems on political-economical questions." *Ibid.*, 11 (Sept. 1887), 548. See also the letter of "Sprague," who complained of the increasing centralization of power within the Grand Lodge. *Ibid.*, 10 (Mar. 1886), 167.
39. *Ibid.*, 13 (May 1889), 392–94.
40. *Ibid.*, 14 (Mar. 1890), 196–98. See also his editorial, "The Common Laborers," *ibid.*, 14 (Apr. 1890), 293–94, as well as his admonition to Gompers and Powderly to cease their bickering and unify their forces, *ibid.*, 14 (Aug. 1890), 705.
41. *Ibid.*, 16 (Sept. 1892), 779–80, 13 (Nov. 1889), 965–66, 16 (May 1892), 387–89.

42. *Ibid.*, 14 (Apr. 1890), 291–93.
43. *Ibid.*, 13 (Sept. 1889), 780, 14 (Feb. 1890), 100–104, 18 (May 1894), 468–70.
44. *Ibid.*, 15 (July 1891), 624–25, 15 (Dec. 1891), 1064–66, 16 (May 1892), 441–43, 17 (Sept. 1893), 733–37.
45. *Ibid.*, 17 (Sept. 1893), 740–43.
46. *Ibid.*, 18 (May 1894), 470–71.
47. Gompers to Sargent and EVD, 30 Aug. 1890, to McGuire, 22 Oct. 1891, to EVD, 31 Oct., 29 Nov. 1892, to McGuire, 28 Nov. 1892, SGLB.
48. *LFM*, 14 (May 1890), 385–89, 18 (Feb. 1894), 144, 14 (Jan. 1890), 43–44, 15 (Mar. 1891), 250; see also Gompers, *Seventy Years*, I: 391–93.
49. *LFM*, 13 (Mar. 1889), 206–7.
50. For examples, see *ibid.*, 17 (Apr. 1893), 267–71, 18 (Feb. 1894), 149–51, 18 (Apr. 1894), 405.
51. See *ibid.*, 14 (May 1890), 447, 14 (June 1890), 544–45, 14 (July 1890), 579. EVD had supported women's equality earlier, too. In a July 1886 BLF meeting at Kansas City EVD argued that he "could not see why it was that women did not receive the same compensation for the same work performed, as a man." While some firemen would have objected to that, it is possible that EVD's support of women's equality *within* the family caused much of the opposition in 1890. See the letter of William Piercy and W. C. Haverstrick in *ibid.*, 10 (Aug. 1886), 484; see also *ibid.*, 18 (Mar. 1894), 282–85.
52. *Ibid.*, 13 (Apr. 1889), 289–91, 17 (Nov. 1893), 904–5.
53. *Ibid.*, 13 (Oct. 1889), 905.
54. *Ibid.*, 15 (Apr. 1891), 301.
55. *Ibid.*, 16 (June 1892), 531.
56. On the BLF's attitudes toward blacks, see *Proceedings of BLF*, 1888, 351; Informant number 1, Report to the Pinkerton Agency, 24 Oct. 1888, file 33 1880 9.31, CBQ. At times, this issue also caused difficulties between the firemen and engineers. One fireman, "Benn," complained in 1887 that many engineers desired black firemen because they could intimidate the blacks to do work a white fireman would consider below his dignity. *LFM*, 11 (Sept. 1887), 546–47, 15 (Mar. 1891), 244.
57. See Higham, *Strangers in the Land*, especially ch. 6.
58. In 1891 EVD asserted that he favored free speech on all issues except where it concerned sexual mores. He would have "no free speech Satans in American Eden homes; no square foot of American soil defiled by the advocates of polygamy; no brothel beasts, advocating free love." *LFM*, 15 (Apr. 1891), 306–07. On religious freedom, see *ibid.*, 15 (Nov. 1891), 1029–30.
59. *Ibid.*, 15 (May 1891), 399–400.
60. *Ibid.*, 17 (Mar. 1893), 179–86.
61. Higham, *Strangers in the Land*, 62–63, 80–87; Higham, *Send These to Me*, ch. 3; *LFM*, 18 (Mar. 1894), 280–82.
62. *LFM*, 18 (Apr. 1894), 396, 18 (June 1894), 607–10.
63. *Ibid.*, 18 (Oct. 1894), 979.
64. See EVD to F. X. Holl, 11 Mar. 1892, 22 Aug. 1894, SC.
65. *LFM*, 15 (Feb. 1891), 134–38.
66. *Ibid.*, 15 (Jan. 1891), 43–44.
67. *Ibid.*, 13 (Nov. 1889), 1022–23.
68. *Ibid.*, 14 (Sept. 1890), 803–5; McMurry, "Federation," 83.

69. *Proceedings of BLF*, 1890, 141–43.
70. [Sheahan], *Grand Lodge*, 1–3, 6–11; *LFM*, 15 (June 1891), 534–38, 15 (Aug. 1891), 711–15; McMurry, "Federation," 84–86. For Theodore Debs's views see Theodore Debs to J. A. Phillips, 4 Apr. 1937, ISU.
71. At the 1892 convention Sargent stated that the BLF would work in an ad hoc manner on future grievances until a formal national federation was re-established. He pointedly dismissed any attempt to revive the system plan of federation. *Proceedings of BLF*, 1892, 112–13.
72. *LFM*, 15 (Sept. 1891), 835–36, 15 (Nov. 1891), 1032. Rogers immediately established a new labor journal, the *Age of Labor,* which EVD endorsed. See *LFM*, 16 (Jan. 1892), 44.
73. EVD to E. E. Clark (grand chief, Order of Railway Conductors), 17 Nov. 1891, L-M.
74. *LFM*, 16 (Feb. 1892), 154–62. In 1889 Wilkinson presented EVD with a medal for his aid to the Trainmen and called him "the godfather of our order." Terre Haute *Evening Gazette*, 3 Jan. 1889.
75. What ultimately prevented EVD from "looking backward" and becoming irrelevant to his society was both his sensitive understanding of the pain working people lived with under industrial capitalism and his unabashed and enthusiastic endorsement of the technological inventions so important to the development of capitalism. Debs tried to find a way to "translate" the older values without precisely rejecting those developments that offered such potential for alleviating human misery. For EVD's views on technology dur-ing the early 1890s, see *LFM*, 14 (May 1890), 385–89, 14 (Oct. 1890), 871–73, 15 (June 1891), 483–85.
76. *Proceedings of BLF*, 1892, 288–93.
77. *LFM*, 16 (Oct. 1892), 902. This was the first time that EVD had not been ac-tive in a BLF convention, but it also began a custom that would last throughout his Socialist career. Whenever serious personal or ideological disagreements developed at future conventions, EVD usually found a way either to avoid the convention completely or to be confined to his room with one ailment or another—to emerge only when a decision had been reached. However, from his sickbed EVD frequently tried to influence the debate through press interviews and instructions to delegates who supported his position on a given question.
78. Cincinnati *Enquirer*, 20 Sept. 1892.
79. *Ibid.,* 22 Sept. 1892; *LFM*, 16 (Oct. 1892), 902–7.
80. *LFM*, 16 (Oct. 1892), 902–7.
81. EVD to E. E. Clark, 10 Oct. 1892, L-M; *LFM*, 16 (Oct. 1892), 905–7.

Notes to Chapter 5

1. Phillips, *Indiana in Transition*, 231; Reed, *Encyclopedia of Biography of In-diana*, I: 80.
2. Faulkner, *American Economic History*, 503–5.
3. In his autobiography, Gompers claimed that he was approached first by George Howard and that he discouraged him, for the plan would "under-mine the railroad brotherhoods." Howard, Gompers states, then claimed he would approach Debs whom Gompers felt would also refuse. However, Gompers probably rewrote history here. Philip Foner, using now unavail-able correspondence, writes that Gompers "encouraged Howard to organize

an industrial union of railroad workers which would be brought into the A.F. of L." Gompers, *Seventy Years*, I:404–5; Foner, *History of the Labor Movement*, II: 254–55.

4. See EVD's statement in the *Railway Times*, 2 Feb. 1895.
5. Boyle, *Railroad Strikes*, 58.
6. *American Railway Union, Proceedings of Executive Board* (carbon copy), 8 Feb. 1893, ISU (hereafter cited as *Proceedings, ARU*, followed by meeting).
7. *Proceedings, ARU*, 11–17 Apr. 1893.
8. *Declaration of Principles, ARU*, 6–8.
9. *Ibid.*, 9–10, 13.
10. *Ibid.*, 11–12.
11. *Senate Executive Document 7*, 172.
12. *Proceedings, ARU*, 21 June 1893; Painter, *Fifty Years*, 50ff.
13. *Proceedings, ARU*, 21 June 1893.
14. In other ways as well the formal structure of the ARU paralleled that of the brotherhoods it was intended to replace. The union's constitution concentrated power in the president who, with a majority of the directors, would "decide all questions and appeals." The grievance procedure—a cause of great friction in the past—also followed the example established by the grand chiefs. After filing a grievance, a member relinquished any active role in its outcome. Power to resolve the conflict or to call a strike resided in the national officers, and neither the individual grievant nor his co-workers and local union leaders could influence that decision. See *Constitution of the American Railway Union*, 10, 15. See Howard's defense of this "respectful, business-like manner" in the *Railway Times*, 15 Feb. 1894.
15. See *Proceedings, ARU*, 24 May 1893. Howard was delegated to respond to McGuire.
16. *Ibid.*, 21 June 1893.
17. *Ibid.*, 12–13 Dec. 1893.
18. The ARU allowed and even encouraged this. See Boyle, *Railroad Strikes*, 57.
19. *LFM*, 18 (Jan. 1894), 61–65.
20. Foner, *History of the Labor Movement*, II: chs. 14, 15; Yellen, *American Labor Struggles*, ch. 3; Dulles, *Labor in America*, ch. 10.
21. *Railway Times*, 15 Feb. 1894.
22. See EVD's discussion of this as presented in Coleman, *Debs*, 106.
23. *Railway Times*, 15 Feb. 1894; Ginger, *The Bending Cross*, 101–2.
24. *Railway Times*, 1 June 1894; see also the issues of 15 Feb., 1 Mar. 1894.
25. *Ibid.*, 6 Apr. 1894.
26. *Ibid.;* Ginger, *The Bending Cross*, 102.
27. *Proceedings, ARU*, 13–14 Mar. 1894; Ginger, *The Bending Cross*, 103; *Debs: His Life, Writings and Speeches*, 8. An account terribly biased in favor of Hill is found in Holbrook, *Hill*, 126–27.
28. *Debs: His Life, Writings and Speeches*, 8.
29. *Ibid.*, 8–9.
30. *Railway Times*, 1 May 1894; St. Paul *Globe*, 2 May 1894; Ginger, *The Bending Cross*, 103–4; *Debs: His Life, Writings and Speeches*, 9; Boyle, *Railroad Strikes*, 48–52.
31. *Railway Times*, 1 May 1894; *Debs: His Life, Writings and Speeches*, 9–10; Ginger, *The Bending Cross*, 104. For a different and somewhat fanciful account, see the typed manuscript of F. X. Holl (n.d.), SC.

32. *Railway Times*, 1 May 1894.
33. Hill to Olney, 19 Apr. 1894 (1894, B. 763), DJ.
34. Hill to Cleveland, 28 Apr. 1894 (1894, B. 762), DJ.
35. McDermott to Olney, 27 Apr. 1894 (1894, B. 763), DJ; see also J. E. Cronan (U.S. marshal, Grand Forks, N.D.) to Cleveland, 28 Apr. 1894, and James H. Forney (U.S. attorney, Moscow, Idaho) to Olney, 22 May 1894 (1894, B. 762), DJ. One federal judge, temporarily covering the Minnesota judicial district, dissented from this crescendo. Judge Walter H. Sanborn noted in a telegram to Olney that no court order had been violated and that the strikers were allowing all mail trains to pass. Sanborn to Olney, 28 Apr. 1894 (1894, B. 763), DJ.
36. *Debs: His Life, Writings and Speeches*, 11; Ginger, *The Bending Cross*, 105–6.
37. Ginger, *The Bending Cross*, 105–6.
38. St. Paul *Globe*, 1 May 1894.
39. As quoted in *Railway Times*, 1 May 1894.
40. Ridge, *Donnelly*, 335.
41. Terre Haute *Express*, 4 May 1894. For a slightly different version, see Ginger, *The Bending Cross*, 106; Painter, *That Man Debs*, 17.
42. EVD's speech is reprinted in *Debs: His Life, Writings and Speeches*, 10–12; on the reception and Huston's address, see also Terre Haute *Express*, 4 May 1894, and *Railway Times*, 15 May 1894.
43. Quoted in Painter, *That Man Debs*, 17.
44. Foner, *History of the Labor Movement*, II:258; *Senate Executive Document 7*, 138; Boyle, *Railroad Strikes*, 51.
45. See the report of Sargent on the ARU in *Proceedings of BLF*, 1894, 297–321.
46. Gompers, *Seventy Years*, I: 283.
47. Gompers to Arthur, 9, 17 Oct. 1888, to Sargent and EVD, 30 Aug. 1890, SGLB.
48. Gompers to Executive Council, AFL, 7 Feb., 7 Sept. 1889, SGLB.
49. Gompers to McGuire, 23 Mar. 1894, SGLB.
50. Gompers to McGuire, 7 May 1894, SGLB; Taft, *A.F of L.*, 90–93.
51. Gompers, *Seventy Years*, I:283.
52. See EVD's testimony in *Senate Executive Document 7*, 129; *Railway Times*, 15 July 1894.
53. *Senate Executive Document 7*, 172.
54. For a detailed discussion of the town's history, see Buder, *Pullman*; Carwardine, *Pullman Strike*; Lindsey, *Pullman Strike*, chs. 2–4.
55. Carwardine, *Pullman Strike*, 80–82.
56. Letter of Curtis in *ibid.*, 75–78.
57. *LFM*, 18 (Aug. 1894), 760–62.
58. Carwardine, *Pullman Strike*, 80.
59. Of the foreign-born, 22 percent were Scandinavian by birth; 13 percent, German; 12 percent, British or Canadian; 11 percent, Dutch; 6 percent, Irish; "Latins and others" comprised the remaining 14 percent. See Carwardine, *Pullman Strike*, 98.
60. *Ibid.*, 77.
61. See Howard's testimony in *Senate Executive Document 7*, 7; Carwardine, *Pullman Strike*, 33–37.

62. The group included Lyman Gage, Mrs. Potter Palmer, and Jane Addams, among other civic leaders.
63. *Senate Executive Document 7*, 8; Carwardine, *Pullman Strike*, 42–44; Boyle, *Railroad Strikes*, 56–57.
64. For an excellent account of the convention, see Lindsey, *Pullman Strike*, 126ff.
65. *Proceedings, First Quadrennial Convention, ARU*, 4–5 (incomplete copy at Tamiment Institute).
66. It was also true that EVD did not control the convention. Despite similarities to traditional brotherhood practice, by 1894 the ARU was quite democratic, at least in regard to white members. (When EVD introduced a proposal at the convention to abolish the color line, the official newspaper gleefully reported that, although EVD was the "ablest leader of the age," the defeat of the proposal proved that theirs was a democratic organization! *Railway Times*, 2 July 1894. The delegates voted instead to form an auxiliary group "for the benefit of colored men" and recommended it "have the hearty support and sympathy of the regular union." No such group was ever formed. *Ibid.*, 15 July 1894. For an earlier discussion of race, see *Proceedings, ARU*, 12–13 Dec. 1893.)
67. *Proceedings, ARU*, 25 June 1894.
68. *Ibid.*, 30 June 1894; Foner, *History of the Labor Movement*, II:264; U.S. Commissioner of Labor, *Tenth Annual Report*, I: 258ff.
69. New York *Times*, 27 June 1894, as quoted in Lindsey, *Pullman Strike*, 136.
70. Lindsey, *Pullman Strike*, 114–18.
71. *Ibid.*, 137–40.
72. *Railway Times*, 15 July 1894.
73. Lindsey, *Pullman Strike*, 142–43, 148.
74. *Ibid.*, 147–55; Darrow, *My Life*, 61.
75. Gresham, who had been a federal judge during both the 1877 and 1888 strikes, was active in the Pullman strike deliberations. As secretary of state, he attended the daily cabinet meetings to discuss strike developments. His wife claimed that in alliance with Secretary of War Daniel S. Lamont Gresham played an important role in composing the stern orders for General Nelson Miles. Gresham, *Gresham*, I:416–19; Lindsey, *Pullman Strike*, 190.
76. Lindsey, *Pullman Strike*, 144.
77. EVD specifically ordered that the mail trains were not to be interfered with as long as the Pullman cars were detached. Lindsey, *Pullman Strike*, 158–71; *Senate Executive Document 7*, 175. The text of the injunction is reprinted in *ibid.*, 179–80. For the reaction of Illinois officials, see Lindsey, *Pullman Strike*, 179–202. The telegrams between Altgeld and Cleveland are reprinted in Coleman, *Debs*, 133–41.
78. See, for example, the telegram of federal Judge James H. Beatty to Olney, 18 July 1894: "The *railroad strikers and the lawless of Coeur d'Alene* [Idaho] are under control, but I do not think it desirable to withdraw the troops until the discharged union employees cease to be a menace to new, non-union employees" (1894, 762), DJ.
79. *Senate Executive Document 7*, xviii–xix; Lindsey, *Pullman Strike*, 167–69.
80. See EVD's testimony in *Senate Executive Document 7*, 150–51; Lindsey, *Pullman Strike*, 203ff.
81. *Senate Executive Document 7*, 39–40.
82. *Ibid.*, 140–41.

83. See McMurry, *Coxey's Army*; Vincent, *Commonweal.*
84. Boyle, *Railroad Strikes*, 61.
85. *Proceedings, ARU,* 3, 4, 7 July 1894.
86. Coleman, *Debs*, 132.
87. Lindsey, *Pullman Strike*, 174–75.
88. *Senate Executive Document 7*, 145.
89. *Ibid.,* 144–45, 339; Lindsey, *Pullman Strike*, 174. See also Cooper, "The Army as Strikebreaker," 187–94.
90. *Senate Executive Document 7*, 145–46.
91. Lindsey, *Pullman Strike*, 223–24; Foner, *History of the Labor Movement*, II:270–71.
92. Gompers to EVD, 5 July 1894 (telegram), to McGuire, 9 July 1894, SGLB; *Senate Executive Document 7*, 154. The two brotherhood representatives were P. H. Morrissey of the Trainmen and Arnold of the Firemen.
93. Gompers, *Seventy Years*, I:414.
94. See Gompers's testimony in *Senate Executive Document 7*, 195, 198. Gompers artfully played off the brotherhoods against the ARU in his account of the strike in Swinton, *Striking for Life*, 301–2.
95. Lindsey, *Pullman Strike*, 226–27; Foner, *History of the Labor Movement*, II:271–75; Swinton, *Striking for Life*, 313–14. The text of the conference's resolution is reprinted in Gompers, *Seventy Years*, I:411–13; see also *Senate Executive Document 7*, 192–93.
96. EVD to Peter Damm, 22 Apr. 1905, ISU. See also Karsner, *Talks with Debs*, 60–61.
97. *Senate Executive Document 7*, 154–55.
98. Lindsey, *Pullman Strike*, 226–27.
99. *Senate Executive Document 7*, 191–92; Gompers, *Seventy Years*, I:411.
100. See the testimony of Gompers in *Senate Executive Document 7*, 200–201, 205.
101. EVD, "Labor Strikes and Their Lessons," in Swinton, *Striking for Life*, 324.
102. For a discussion of post-strike finances, see *Proceedings, ARU*, 28 Aug., 18, 21 Sept. 1894.
103. For a more detailed discussion of these trials see *Debs: His Life, Writings and Speeches*, 23–39; Lindsey, *Pullman Strike*, 280–305; Ginger, *The Bending Cross*, 152–67.
104. EVD to Morris Vinchevsky, 4 Apr. 1901, MV.
105. Boyle, *Railroad Strikes*, 46.
106. F. X. Holl to W. A. Love, n.d., EVD. For slightly different versions, see Boyle, *Railroad Strikes*, 59; Estes, *Railway Employees United*, 16.
107. EVD to Directors, ARU, 29 Oct. 1895, to Theodore Debs, 10 Nov. 1895, ISU.
108. This did not prevent Gompers or the AFL from contributing some money to the legal defense fund, however.
109. EVD to Theodore Debs, 5 Nov. 1895, ISU; to Holl, 16 May 1895, 24 Mar. 1896, SC.
110. L. P. Benedict to Henry Demarest Lloyd, 12 Mar. 1895, HDL.
111. EVD to Theodore Debs, 9 Jan. 1896, ISU. For another example of this attitude see EVD to Theodore Debs, 15 Nov. 1895, ISU.
112. EVD to Holl, 18 July 1895, SC.
113. EVD to Theodore Debs, 15 Nov. 1895, ISU.

114. EVD to "My Darling Parents," 16 July 1894, ISU; untitled clipping, "Is Popular at Home," 19 July 1894, TDSB.
115. EVD to Theodore Debs, 4 Nov. 1895, ISU.
116. As quoted in *Railway Times*, 16 Sept. 1895.
117. EVD to Theodore Debs, 10 Sept. 1895, ISU.
118. EVD to "My Darling Sister," 5 Nov. 1895, ISU.
119. See, for example, EVD's speech at the 1894 Firemen's Convention, *Proceedings of BLF*, 1894, 504.
120. "Here is the Mighty Debs," New York *World*, 12 July 1894.
121. During this period I have been able to find only one mention of Kate accompanying Eugene. In November 1894 Kate, her mother, and Debs toured Illinois. See untitled clipping, 1 Nov. 1894, TDSB. When Kate died in 1937, her stepbrothers sold the house on North 8th Street and burned all of the files and correspondence that filled the attic. Reportedly voluminous, this material certainly would have shed more light on Debs's life and probably Kate's as well. Interview with Marguerite Debs Cooper, 31 Mar. 1974, Terre Haute.
122. Interview with Marguerite Debs Cooper, 31 Mar. 1974, Terre Haute.
123. See the *Railway Times* from 15 Jan. through 1 Apr. 1896.
124. *Proceedings of BLF*, 1894, 297–321, especially 303, 318–21.
125. *Ibid.,* 499–503.
126. *Ibid.,* 503–4.
127. *Ibid.,* 504–5.
128. See O'Rourke's letter in *LFM*, 17 (Feb. 1893), 173–74.
129. See EVD to Holl, 9 May, 29 Aug. 1894, SC; *LFM*, 18 (Nov. 1894), 1079–81.
130. EVD to Holl, 28 Nov. 1894, SC; to Theodore Debs, 27 June, 10 Sept. 1895, ISU; *LFM*, 18 (Nov. 1894), 1078.
131. *LFM*, 19 (Sept. 1895), 808–10. In a later issue Carter erroneously argued that to join the ARU would commit the brotherhood to accepting Negroes as members, a policy few favored. *Ibid.,* 19 (Nov. 1895), 997.
132. See *Proceedings, ARU*, 12–13 Dec. 1893. For earlier examples of EVD's endorsement of this policy, see EVD to Holl, 10, 24 May 1890, SC.
133. EVD to Holl, 11 Mar. 1892, 22 Aug. 1894, SC.
134. EVD to Lloyd, 24 July 1894, HDL. For other expressions of optimism see EVD to Holl, 16 Jan. 1895, SC; to Theodore Debs, 8, 13 Aug. 1895, ISU.

Notes to Chapter 6

1. EVD to Karsner, 8 Oct. 1922, DFK.
2. *Railway Times*, 15 Feb., 1 Mar., 2 Apr. 1894.
3. "Politics and Political Parties," *ibid.,* 1 Mar. 1894. See also the editorial, "Labor and the Ballot," in the same issue, which endorses political activity and urges the worker to "divest himself of his party tag" in order to "vote his individual sentiments as becomes a free man."
4. *The American Non-Conformist* (Indianapolis), 22 Mar. 1894. See also Coleman, *Debs*, 152. On Populism in Terre Haute and Indiana see Phillips, *Indiana in Transition*, 34–35; Gresham, *Gresham*, II: 659; Stewart, "Populist Party in Indiana," 352–53.
5. *Proceedings, First Quadrennial Convention, ARU*, 8ff.
6. Reprinted in *Railway Times*, 2 July 1894.
7. Scharnau, "Morgan," 229; *The Searchlight* (Chicago), 14 June 1894. After

the strike, a group of 500 blacklisted Pullman workers and their families arrived in Blakeley, Ala., to start a single-tax colony modeled after the principles of Henry George. Clearly the strike, the union, and EVD's agitation threatened traditional political activity. See the *Southern Mercury*, 29 Nov. 1894.

8. Ridge, *Donnelly*, 335; Scharnau, "Morgan," 241–43; Goodwyn, *Democratic Promise*, 418.

9. EVD to Holl, 3 Oct. 1894, SC; untitled clipping, 1 Nov. 1894, TDSB. EVD was optimistic about Populism's potential and told Henry Demarest Lloyd that it would come to power in a "resistless rush." Nonetheless, in order to rebuild the ARU, EVD at times refused to speak under Populist auspices. See EVD to Lloyd, 15 Aug. 1894, HDL; to Holl, 8 Dec. 1894, SC.

10. See the *Christian Evangelist* (St. Louis), 16 Aug. 1894; Chicago *Times-Herald*, 1 Sept. 1895; EVD, "Political Lessons," *Railway Times*, 1 Mar. 1895.

11. *Railway Times*, 1 Aug. 1895. See also the editorial, "Machinery's Mission," *ibid.*, 7 Apr. 1898.

12. *Ibid.*, 1 Mar. 1894.

13. EVD to Holl, 18 July 1895, SC. For examples of how EVD conducted union business from jail, see EVD to Theodore Debs, 10 Sept., 5, 15 Nov. 1895, ISU.

14. Untitled clipping, 23 July 1894, TDSB.

15. EVD to "My dear old Pards" [parents], 8 Jan. 1895, ISU.

16. EVD to "My dear old Comrade," n.d., ISU.

17. Morais and Cahn, *Gene Debs*, 54.

18. See *Debs: His Life, Writings and Speeches*, 13; Kopelin, *Life of Debs*; Flynn, *Debs, Haywood, Ruthenberg*. Neither Ginger, *The Bending Cross*, nor Quint, *American Socialism*, suggest this, however.

19. Gompers, *Seventy Years*, I: 415–16.

20. On Donnelly, see EVD to Holl, 9 July 1895; on Gronlund, EVD to Holl, 24 Mar. 1896, 31 May 1897, SC; on Harvey, EVD to "Kude" [Theodore], 3 July 1895, ISU; EVD, "What Labor's Battle Taught Me," *National Rip-Saw*, Nov. 1921, as reprinted in the New York *Call*, 6 Nov. 1942.

21. Painter, *That Man Debs*, 72–73.

22. EVD to Kautsky, 4 Dec. 1925 (copy), ISU.

23. Bell, *Marxian Socialism*; Flynn, *Debs, Haywood, Ruthenberg*.

24. *Senate Executive Document 7*, 170; *Railway Times*, 15 Sept. 1894.

25. EVD, "Our First Great Need," *Co-operative Age* (St. Paul), n.d. [1895], EVD Scrapbooks, Reel 283, vol. I: 166, and see also his "The Problem of Labor," untitled clipping, n.d. [June 1895], EVD Scrapbooks, Reel 283, vol. I: 214–16 (Tamiment Institute, microfilm edition); EVD, "Labor," Cincinnati *Enquirer*, 30 June 1895; *Railway Times*, 2 Apr. 1896.

26. "Eugene V. Debs in the Pulpit," *American Non-Conformist*, 2 Apr. 1896.

27. EVD, "New and Old," *Railway Times*, 15 May 1895.

28. EVD, "In Prison," *ibid.*, 15 July 1895.

29. EVD, "Fraternization"; "Hopkins Used Debs," Chicago *Times-Herald*, 1 Sept. 1895.

30. *Railway Times*, 15 July 1895.

31. See the *Eight-Hour Herald* (Chicago), 9 Nov. 1895; Rosenberg's and Debs's letters are reprinted in *Socialist Labor* (Lincoln, Neb.), 14 Sept. 1895. On Rosenberg, see Paulson, *Radicalism and Reform*, 61.

32. Morgan to Lloyd, 6 Sept. 1895, HDL. In an earlier letter to Lloyd, Morgan had written: "Why not link the honest and enthusiastic friends of 'collectivism' or liberal Socialism, or Cooperation (what's in a name anyhow) you know what I mean. This thought is in the atmosphere of radical reform, Debs is wrestling with it in Woodstock jail, Doerrant carries it with him to Europe and its runs from one end of my pen to you in your summer house. We of the English-speaking race must be up and doing." Morgan to Lloyd, 18 July 1895, HDL. Given the ideological imprecision of Morgan, an avowed Socialist, exactly what Debs was "wrestling with" is open to question. See, too, Scharnau, "Morgan," 265.
33. Lloyd's speech is reprinted in his book *Men, the Workers*, 179–93.
34. The account of EVD's arrival in Chicago is taken from *Debs: His Life, Writings and Speeches*, 45–49, which also contains EVD's speech at Battery D, 327–44.
35. *Railway Times*, 2 Dec. 1895; J. B. Maynard to Daniel Debs, 20 Nov. 1895, ISU.
36. Wayland, *Leaves of Life*, 36–37; for other examples of these themes see the letter of an Indiana ARU member and the poem of a Mississippi member in *Railway Times*, 15 Feb., 15 June 1895, respectively.
37. EVD to Theodore Debs, 15 Nov. 1895, ISU.
38. EVD's speech is reprinted in *Railway Times*, 15 Jan. 1896.
39. Reprinted in *ibid.*, 16 Mar. 1896; untitled clipping, 12 May 1896, TDSB.
40. In a letter to his parents from Portland, Oreg., EVD noted the "talk about a boom for President" and proudly told them that they "will see this whole country come to the porch demanding my nomination." EVD to "My darling Parents," 22 Mar. 1895, ISU; Quint, *American Socialism*, 236.
41. *Railway Times*, 1 Feb. 1896; Scharnau, "Morgan," 273; Quint, *American Socialism*, 232–36. Morgan, a friend of Lloyd, refused to join in these plans. He doubted the Lloyd wing would capture the Populist convention, but, even if it could, he would be opposed: "I am a Socialist, cannnot be known or understood as anything else, and as such even the Radical P.P.'s [People's party] think my work on their behalf should be unseen and unheard." Morgan to Lloyd, 6 July 1896, HDL.
42. Cleveland *Citizen*, as quoted in *Railway Times*, 1 Feb. 1896.
43. Goodwyn, *Democratic Promise*, ch. XV ; Koenig, *Bryan*, 211–19.
44. Koenig, *Bryan*, 205–15, 246; St. Louis *Union Record*, 25 July 1896; Goodwyn, *Democratic Promise*, 464–66. Many in the radical Texas delegation refused to support EVD due to his well-known opposition to the racist and xenophobic American Protective Association; see St. Louis *Union Record*, 25 July 1896, and the discussion in ch. 4.
45. EVD to Lloyd, 25 July 1896 [telegram], HDL.
46. Woodward, *Tom Watson*, 301; Quint, *American Socialism*, 236–37.
47. Koenig, *Bryan*, 205, 246.
48. EVD to Morris Vinchevsky, 4 Apr. 1901, MV.
49. *Railway Times*, 1 Aug., 15 Sept., 1 Oct. 1896; Burlington (Ia.) *Hawk-Eye*, 19 Aug. 1900. EVD claimed in a letter to the chairman of the Populist party's executive committee that the circular "has created a great stir in railroad circles." EVD to Marion Butler, 14 Sept. 1896, MB (Chapel Hill).
50. Gompers's circular is reprinted and critically evaluated in *Railway Times*, 1 Aug. 1896; on Gompers and Bryan, see also Koenig, *Bryan*, 246–47.
51. *Railway Times*, 2 Nov. 1896.

52. L. P. Benedict to Lloyd, 7 Jan. 1896; EVD to Lloyd, 1 Feb. 1896, HDL.
53. *Railway Times*, 1 July 1896. Aware that their efforts might be seen as an attempt to supplant the Populist movement, the group, in a note accompanying the call, stressed that this was not a new political party but a united front of all opposed to monopoly.
54. *Ibid.*, 15 Dec. 1894.
55. EVD to "My Darling Sister," 5 Nov. 1895, ISU.
56. Interview with a former Socialist who knew EVD and wishes to remain anonymous, Oct. 1973.
57. For an excellent discussion of the potential of Populism, see Goodwyn, *Democratic Promise*, especially 523–24. His discussion of Debs, Darrow, and other Populist radicals and their support for Bryan in 1896 has been helpful.
58. Koenig, *Bryan*, 251–52.
59. *Railway Times*, 1 Oct. 1896.
60. EVD to Lloyd, 12 Dec. 1896; parts of EVD's letter to Berger, and Berger's comment, are contained in a letter from Berger to Lloyd, 14 Dec. 1896, HDL.
61. *Railway Times*, 1 Jan. 1897; "Debs Hails Socialism," Chicago *Record*, 1 Jan. 1897; Ginger, *The Bending Cross*, 193–94; Quint, *American Socialism*, 281–82; see also EVD to Vinchevsky, 4 Apr. 1901, MV.
62. EVD, "It is Coming," *Railway Times*, 1 May 1897.
63. For EVD's later understanding of this continuity, see *Appeal to Reason*, 6 Sept. 1902; Atlanta *Georgian*, 14 May 1920. For testimony of former Populists who joined the Socialist movement see *Appeal to Reason*, 7 Dec. 1901, 19 July, 27 Sept. 1902, 6 May 1905; *The Rebel*, 20 Mar. 1915; Bedford, *Socialism and the Workers*, 3. Mary E. Lease's olio of Populist politics, evangelical Christian religion, and avowal of Socialism is recorded in an undated, untitled clipping, IAH. The editors of the *Railway Times* affirmed that in endorsing Socialism neither they nor EVD rejected Populist principles; see the issue of 15 Feb. 1897.
64. For EVD's speech see *Railway Times*, 15 June 1897. On EVD's sensitivity to the suffering of blacklisted ARU members, see Ginger, *The Bending Cross*, 179–81.
65. Berger to Lloyd, 3 Feb. 1897, HDL.
66. Social Democracy of America, *Constitution*, 5; *Social Democrat* [successor to *Railway Times*], 1 July 1897.
67. EVD to Holl, 31 May 1897, SC.
68. Quint, *American Socialism*, 294.
69. For EVD's letter, see *Sunday Chronicle* (Chicago), 20 June 1897.
70. *Social Democrat*, 23 Sept., 7 Oct. 1897.
71. Social Democracy of America, "Minutes, Joint Meeting National Executive Board and Colonization Commission, Social Democracy of America, 12 December–14 December 1897" [carbon], 4, ISU.
72. *Social Democrat*, 16 June 1898; Quint, *American Socialism*, 312–13.
73. *Social Democrat*, 15 July 1897.
74. Destler, *Lloyd*, 425.
75. For EVD's relation with Lloyd, see EVD to Lloyd, 10 Dec. 1894, 27 Aug. 1895, 10 July 1897, 7 Jan. 1899, HDL; Destler, *Lloyd*, 382. In each instance EVD praised Lloyd's books. Lloyd, however, refused appointment to the Colonization Commission because the Social Democracy refused to unite with the Brotherhood of the Co-operative Commonwealth.
76. See Ginger, *The Bending Cross*, 194–96.

77. EVD to Ryan Walker, 5 Aug. 1912, RW.
78. But even here the Massachusetts's members were primarily old Populists whose platforms reflected that movement; see Bedford, *Socialism and the Workers*, 3.
79. *Social Democrat*, 11 Nov. 1897. For other examples, see the letter of W. C. Green, of Orlando, Fla., who suggested that the proper symbol for Social Democracy was the Christian cross, 24 Feb. 1898; from Dr. Jay E. Fox, of Columbus, Ohio, who saw in the party a defense of traditional American rights, 24 Mar. 1898; and from A. Allen Noe, of Houston, Tex., who stressed that the party represented a "New Declaration of Independence . . . declaring that all men should be born free," 7 Apr. 1898.
80. *Social Democrat*, 17 Mar. 1898.
81. *Ibid.,* 4 Nov. 1897.
82. Social Democracy of America, "Proceedings, First Annual Convention Social Democracy of America, 7 June-11 June 1898," ISU, 6, 16 (hereafter cited as "Proceedings, SDA"); Quint, *American Socialism*, 311–12.
83. *Social Democrat*, 16 June 1898.
84. "Proceedings, SDA," 77–83; *Social Democratic Herald*, 9 July 1898; Quint, *American Socialism*, 314–16.
85. See, for example, EVD, "The Social Democracy," *New Time*, Aug. 1897, 79.
86. Quint, *American Socialism*, 318.
87. On Kellogg and the labor theory of value, see Destler, *American Radicalism*.
88. *The Social Democratic Party of America*, n.p.; *Social Democratic Herald*, 9 July 1898; Quint, *American Socialism*, 293, 319–22; Kipnis, *American Socialist Movement*, 59–64.
89. The party's trade union policy is reprinted in *Social Democratic Herald*, 9 July 1898. For a discussion of Socialist trade union strength that inadvertently reveals the essential Socialist weakness, see Laslett, *Labor and the Left*.
90. Chicago *Dispatch*, 11 June 1898; *Social Democrat*, 16 June 1898; Quint, *American Socialism*, 316.
91. *Social Democratic Herald*, 9 July 1898.
92. *Ibid.,* 9 July 1898; see also EVD, "The Future," *ibid.,* 16 July 1898.
93. EVD's letter is reprinted in *Debs: His Life, Writings and Speeches*, 42–45. For an interpretation that accepts EVD's analysis at face value, see Ginger, *The Bending Cross*, 175.
94. *Railway Times*, 1 Mar. 1897; see also EVD, "To the Hosts of the Social Democracy of America," *Social Democrat*, 2 Sept. 1897.
95. See EVD's speech at St. Louis Labor Conference against Government by Injunction, *Social Democrat*, 2 Sept. 1897.
96. EVD, "Arouse, Ye Slaves," *Social Democratic Herald*, 29 Oct. 1898.
97. *Ibid.,* 2 Sept. 1899.
98. Interview with EVD in *The Press* (Ottumwa, Ia., 14 Dec. 1898), reprinted in *Social Democratic Herald*, 24 Dec. 1898.
99. *Social Democratic Herald*, 23 Sept. 1899.
100. See EVD, "The Growth of a Year Pressages Success," *ibid.,* 1 July 1899.
101. From a speech at Pittsburg, Kans., reprinted in *Social Democrat*, 14 Oct. 1897.
102. *Social Democratic Herald*, 8 Oct. 1898.
103. *Social Democrat*, 19 Aug. 1897; Quint, *American Socialism*, 296.
104. *Social Democrat*, 2 Sept. 1897.
105. Holmes to Joseph Labadie, 15 Nov. 1897, JL.

106. *Railway Times*, 1 Mar. 1897.
107. Chicago *Dispatch*, 17 July 1897; the resolution of the Cleveland Central Labor Union in support of EVD's position is reprinted in Cleveland *Citizen*, 7 Aug. 1897.
108. Nashville *Banner*, 6 Aug. 1897; untitled clipping, "Debs Discouraged," 22 July 1897, EVD Scrapbooks, Reel 283, vol. II: 126–27 (Tamiment Library, microfilm edition).
109. *Motorman and Conductor*, July 1898, reprinted in *Social Democratic Herald*, 6 Aug. 1898.
110. See the comment of the Columbus (Ohio) *Evening Press*, reprinted in *Social Democrat*, 19 Aug. 1897.
111. Seymour Steadman, "The Federation and Socialism," *Social Democratic Herald*, 31 Dec. 1898.
112. Dubofsky, *We Shall Be All*, 61–67.
113. EVD to Mother Jones, 28 Jan. 1901, Mother (Mary) Jones Papers, Historical Society of Pennsylvania, Philadelphia.
114. During one eight-month period in 1899, EVD was on tour for all but two months, criss-crossing the country, although on this tour he spent little time in the South. *Social Democratic Herald*, 29 Apr.–30 Dec. 1899.
115. *Ibid.*, 6 Jan. 1900.
116. *Ibid.*, 25 Nov. 1899.
117. *Ibid.*, 30 Mar., 13 Apr. 1901. In the same vein is EVD's account of his life, "Stray Leaves," 187–89. Compare these accounts with his 1888 critique of Harrison, before his neighbors in Terre Haute, which frankly acknowledges his lack of suppport for the 1877 strikers. See Terre Haute *Evening Gazette*, 29 Oct. 1888.
118. *Social Democratic Herald*, 17 Mar. 1900; Indianapolis *News*, 9 Mar. 1900.
119. An anonymous party member quoted Berger as saying that night that he would visit EVD as "I have some personal influence with Debs." *Social Democratic Herald*, 7 Apr. 1900.
120. *Ibid.*, 17, 24 Mar. 1900.

Notes to Part III

1. Citizens' Protective League, *Address*, 2–4; Terre Haute *Evening Gazette*, 28 May 1902.
2. O'Neal, *Terre Haute's Shame*, 12–14; Blackburn, "Interurban Railroads," 269; EVD to Theodore Debs, 2 Feb. 1902, ISU.

Notes to Chapter 7

1. Hillquit, *Loose Leaves*, ch. III; Hillquit, *History of Socialism*, 294–310; Quint, *American Socialism*, 332–43; Scharnau, "Morgan," 304–8. The delegates voted fifty-five to one, with three abstentions, for unity. See *Social Democratic Herald*, 10 Feb. 1900. A sympathetic treatment of Daniel DeLeon, head of the Socialist Labor party, is found in Seretan, *DeLeon*.
2. Theodore Debs, "Report of the National Secretary-Treasurer of the Social Democratic Party," 1 Mar. 1900, 34, ISU.
3. Socialist Labor Party, *Daniel DeLeon*, II: 82. For EVD's reaction, see EVD to Morris Vinchevsky, 4 Apr. 1901, MV.
4. EVD to Vinchevsky, 2 Dec. 1899, MV.

5. EVD, "On Unity," *Social Democratic Herald*, 20 Jan. 1900; EVD, "The Issue of Unity," *ibid.*, 21 Apr. 1900.
6. "First Annual Convention, Social Democratic Party," *ibid.*, 17 Mar. 1900; Quint, *American Socialism*, 345–47. The committee consisted of Berger, Heath, Seymour Steadman, and Margaret Haile, all anti-union; James Carey, John Chase, Gustave Hoehn, William Butscher, and William Lonergan, all pro-unity.
7. EVD, "The Issue of Unity," *Social Democratic Herald*, 21 Apr. 1900. For a reaction to EVD by one who favored unity, see William Mailly to Hillquit, 24 Apr. 1900, MH. Some Socialists also claimed that EVD was less the "soldier" to Berger than a peer desirous of protecting his position. See Butscher to Hillquit, 1 Aug. 1900, MH; Butscher to W. G. Hapgood, 13, 28 Aug. 1900; Butscher to J. Mahlon Barnes, 9, 27 Sept. 1900; Butscher to Simons, 13 Aug. 1900; Butscher to Harriman, 7 Aug. 1900; Butscher to Morgan, 17 Sept. 1900, all in William Butscher Letter-Press Books, SPP; Morgan to Lloyd, 25 Oct. 1900, HDL; Scharnau, "Morgan," 310–19.
8. On this dispute see *Social Democratic Herald*, 12, 19 May, 2 June, 11, 25 Aug. 1900; and the following articles in the same paper: Margaret Haile, "The Fusionists Reject Political Co-operation," 2 June 1900; EVD, "No Organic Unity Has Been Effected," 21 July 1900; Haile, "Cause of Socialism is Disgraced in Massachusetts," 28 July 1900.
9. Harriman to Hillquit, 18 Aug. 1900; see also Harriman to Hillquit, 20 Aug. 1900, MH; and Butscher to W. E. White, Butscher Letter-Press Books, SPP.
10. *Social Democratic Herald*, 1899, 1900.
11. *Ibid.*, 20 Jan., 10 Mar. 1900.
12. EVD to Steven M. Reynolds, 6 June 1900, SMR; *Social Democratic Herald*, 23 June 1900.
13. Butscher to E. T. Tucker, 9 Aug. 1900, Butscher Letter-Press Books, SPP.
14. "Socialist Vote for President," n.d., General Records, SPP; *Social Democratic Herald*, 17 Nov., 1 Dec. 1900.
15. EVD, "The Progress of the Social Revolution," *Social Democratic Herald*, 1 Dec. 1900. Berger's analysis is in *ibid.*, 10 Nov. 1900.
16. EVD to Theodore Debs, 9 Nov. 1900, ISU.
17. EVD, "Outlook for Socialism in the United States," *International Socialist Review*, I (1 Sept. 1900), 130.
18. EVD, "The Socialist Movement in America," *Social Democratic Herald*, 26 Apr. 1902.
19. EVD, "The Approaching Convention," *ibid.*, 12 Jan. 1901.
20. EVD to Theodore Debs, 9 Nov. 1900, ISU.
21. Kipnis, *American Socialist Movement*, 102–4.
22. "Proceedings of Socialist Unity Conference," comments of F. MacCartney, 137–38, Berger, 143–45, G. Goebel, 163, SPP.
23. *Ibid.*, 121, 165–69, 174–75. For the record of the roll call on immediate demands, recorded by faction and by individual delegate, see *ibid.*, 242–48.
24. *Ibid.*, 442; *Social Democratic Herald*, 17 Aug. 1901; *International Socialist Review*, II (Sept. 1901), 283–86; Kipnis, *American Socialist Movement*, 105–6.
25. *Social Democratic Herald*, 17 Aug. 1901; "Comrade Debs is Pleased," *The Worker* (New York), 11 Aug. 1901.
26. Kipnis, *American Socialist Movement*, 162–63; Hillquit, *History of Socialism*, 310–11; F. X. Holl to EVD, 21 May 1904, SC; "Socialist Vote for

President,'' General Records, SPP. See also John Spargo, "Ben Hanford,'' *The Comrade*, I (Nov. 1901).

27. *The Party Builder*, 13 Dec. 1913; Mailly to Rev. Thomas J. Hagerty, 4 Mar. 1903, to Walter T. Mills, 13 Feb. 1903, Mailly Letter-Press Books, SPP. See also "Socialist Profiles: William Mailly,'' *The New Leader*, 18 Mar. 1933.

28. Theodore Debs to J. B. Barnhill, 23 June 1904, JL; Alfred Flude to Steven M. Reynolds, 28 Apr. 1911, SMR. EVD continued to help support his brother's family and to repay the debts of the Pullman strike.

29. See *International Socialist Review*, II (Sept. 1901), 283–86.

30. *Appeal to Reason*, 26 Apr. 1902, 3 Aug. 1901. For additional letters of Socialist Protestant ministers, see *ibid.*, 30 May 1896, 18 May 1901, 16 Nov. 1901, 12 Apr., 19 July 1902, 14, 21 Apr. 1906. On the essential compatability of Socialism with prophetic American Protestantism, see *ibid.*, 2 Nov. 1901, 8 Feb. 1902, 8, 15 Oct. 1904. Wayland is discussed in detail in Quint, "Julius A. Wayland,'' 585–606. See also the letter of A. W. Ricker in *Appeal to Reason*, 14 June 1902; Algie M. Simons, "Socialism and Individuality,'' *ibid.*, 7 Jan. 1905.

31. Speech of Herron, Chicago, 6 Jan. 1901, reprinted in *ibid.*, 19 Jan. 1901. See also Herron, *Day of Judgement*, 24, and Dombrowski, *Christian Socialism*, 182–84; "Proceedings of Socialist Unity Conference,'' 3–8, SPP. See also the account of Herron's speech in Chicago, where he and EVD shared the platform to open the 1900 presidential campaign, in Quint, *American Socialism*, 135–36, and Herron, *Why I Am a Socialist*.

32. EVD, "Labor and Liberty,'' Saginaw (Mich.) *News*, 6 Feb. 1899; *Appeal to Reason*, 29 Oct. 1904; *Evening Capital News* (Boise), 2 Nov. 1910. See also Fergus *Globe* (Fergus Falls, Minn.), 15 June 1906; New York *Times*, 14 Jan. 1911; Utica (N.Y.) *Press*, 7 Apr. 1910.

33. EVD, "The Mission of Socialism Is As Wide As the World,'' *Social Democratic Herald*, 13 July 1901.

34. EVD, "Social Democracy,'' *ibid.*, 8 Oct 1898. For the issues in this debate, see the letters of G. A. Hoehn, 26 Nov. 1898, and Sumner F. Claflin, 19 Nov. 1898, and EVD, "Arouse, Ye Slaves,'' 29 Oct. 1898, all in *ibid.*

35. EVD to Samuel M. Jones, 8 Dec. 1899; see also EVD to Jones, 24 July 1899, and Jones to EVD, 29 Nov. 1899, 25 Sept. 1900, SMJ. EVD publicly criticized Jones while praising Marx and Engels in his article, "The Growth of a Year Pressages Success,'' *Social Democratic Herald*, 1 July 1899.

36. See EVD, *Unionism and Socialism*, 21–22, and his *Socialist Party*, 21; *Evening Capital News*, 2 Nov. 1910; EVD, "The Social Democratic Party's Appeal,'' *The Independent*, 13 Oct. 1904, 839–40.

37. Simons, *Class Struggles in America*, 63–64. See also Simons, *Man Under the Machine* and *Philosophy of Socialism*.

38. *Appeal to Reason*, 28 Apr. 1906.

39. EVD, "The Workers and the Trusts,'' clipping, n.p., Sept. 1899, in EVD Scrapbooks, Reel 283, vol. 4: 131 (Tamiment Library, microfilm edition).

40. See EVD's speech at Chicago, 29 Sept. 1900, typed copy, ISU. In this speech EVD neither recognized that corporate capitalism might adjust to these conditions and thus "impede'' that inevitable progression nor, despite his experiences in 1894, did he indicate any appreciation of the role of the state in this transformation.

41. *Appeal to Reason*, 20 May 1905. See also Wayland's comment in *ibid.*, 19 Apr. 1902.

42. See, for example, EVD, "Workers' Vote," Minnesota *Union Advocate* (St. Paul), 30 Aug. 1901. For a discussion of Socialism and scientific management see Haber, *Efficiency and Uplift*, 150ff.
43. Herron to Lloyd, 9 Dec. 1900, HDL.
44. "Proceedings of Socialist Unity Conference," comments of Hillquit, 129-30, Berger, 143-45.
45. "Proceedings of Socialist Unity Conference," 131; see also Holzman, "Socialists in Milwaukee," 68, 82.
46. The discussion of Berger, Milwaukee, and the Socialism that developed there is taken from the following accounts: Gavett, *Labor Movement in Milwaukee*, 27, 32-99; Holzman, "Socialists in Milwaukee," 5-34, 58-64, 67; Korman, *Industrialization, Immigrants, and Americanizers*, 16-40, 52, 67. A valuable analysis of the first wave of German immigration can be found in Wittke, *Refugees from Revolution*. David Montgomery, *Workers' Control*, 70, discusses the social meaning of reformist Socialism.
47. *Social Democratic Herald*, 12, 19 Oct. 1901; Shannon, *Socialist Party of America*, 21-24. For Hillquit's early comments on Bernstein, see "Proceedings of Socialist Unity Convention," 129.
48. Hillquit to Vera Hillquit, 30 Jan. 1903, MH.
49. Claessens, *Didn't We Have Fun*, 38-40. For other expressions of this contrast, see the letters of Mailly to Russell C. Massey, 17 Feb. 1903, to John M. Work, 4 Mar. 1903, and to A. W. Ricker, 14 July 1903, Mailly Letter-Press Books, SPP; and *The Rebel*, 1, 15 May 1915.
50. *Social Democratic Herald*, 13 Aug. 1904.
51. Meta Berger, "The Autobiography of Mrs. Victor Berger," 14, MB.
52. Kipnis, *American Socialist Movement*, 183-84; Mailly to Algernon Lee, 24 Aug. 1905, AL; *Appeal to Reason*, 6 May 1905; see also *International Socialist Review*, VI (July 1905), 51, VI (Aug. 1905), 115. The *Review* attacked Berger but opposed his expulsion.
53. Kipnis, *American Socialist Movement*, 184-85; *Social Democratic Herald*, 1 July 1905.
54. See EVD to Hillquit, 31 Dec. 1904, MH.
55. Victor L. Berger, "They Cannot Repeat 1886," *Social Democratic Herald*, 28 Apr. 1906.
56. EVD, Theodore Debs to Isadore Ladoff, 23 May 1906, IS. See also EVD to Elbert Hubbard, 13 Apr. 1906, EVD.
57. *Appeal to Reason*, 19 May 1906; Elizabeth Thomas to Hillquit, 15 Aug. 1906, MH. Two years later this tension erupted again in public, when Lincoln Steffens jointly interviewed Berger and Debs on whether business would receive compensation after the Socialist revolution and subsequent nationalization of major industry. See *Everybody's Magazine*, Oct. 1908, 455-69; EVD to Hillquit, 21 Aug. 1908, MH; to Steffens, 21 Sept. 1908, LS.
58. EVD to Adolph Germer, 13 Apr. 1903, AG; to Charles Erwin, 14 Mar. 1908, CE.
59. Trachtenberg, *Heritage of Gene Debs*, 12-13; Flynn, *Debs, Haywood, Ruthenberg*, 14-15.
60. Miller, *Victor Berger*, 42n41.
61. *Social Democratic Herald*, 9 July 1898.
62. Socialist Party of America, *Report of the Socialist Party; International Socialist Review*, IV (June 1904), 756.
63. *Social Democratic Herald*, 31 May 1902.

64. Gompers, *Seventy Years*, I: 397; *The Independent*, 26 Nov. 1903.
65. *Social Democratic Herald*, 21 Nov. 1903; penciled comment in Berger's hand in the margin of Harriman to Berger, 2 July 1912, SP.
66. See *National Convention, 1908*, 28–32; *National Convention, 1910*, 278–89. In 1912 the party reversed the decision, declaring itself in favor of industrial unionism and stressing the importance of organizing the unorganized. See *National Convention, 1912*, and ch. 8 herein.
67. *Social Democratic Herald*, 21 Nov. 1903; EVD, "Shall We Have Peace?," *ibid.*, 1 Feb. 1902.
68. See EVD, "Pleads for Socialism," *ibid.*, 7 June 1902; EVD, "Plain Talk to the Miners," *ibid.*, 6 Feb. 1904.
69. Lingenfelter, *Hard Rock Miners*, 3–30, 35–45, 49, 56–64, 90, 183–94; Jensen, *Heritage of Conflict*, 4–16, 25–53, 72–95; *Senate Document 122*, 69–105.
70. Lingenfelter, *Hard Rock Miners*, 128–33, 143; Haywood, *Bill Haywood's Book*, 22; Jensen, *Heritage of Conflict*, 39, 47–53, 61, 65; Suggs, *Colorado's War*, 15–16; Dubofsky, *We Shall Be All*, 30–34; untitled clipping, EVD Scrapbooks, Reel 283, vol. 2: 19 (Tamiment Library, microfilm edition).
71. *Proceedings, American Labor Union*, 40–42.
72. *Ibid.*, 42–47; *Social Democratic Herald*, 14 June, 12 July 1902; *American Labor Union Journal*, 3 Sept. 1903.
73. Max Hayes, "World of Labor," *International Socialist Review*, III (July 1902), 56; Simons, "Socialism and the Trade Union Movement," *ibid.*, III (July 1902), 46–49, and Hoehn, "The American Labor Movement," *ibid.*, III (Jan. 1903), 406–11. See also *ibid.*, III (Oct. 1902), 227.
74. EVD, "The Western Labor Movement," *ibid.*, III (Nov. 1902), 257–62; see also EVD, "An Up-to-Date Labor Class Movement," *Social Democratic Herald*, 23 Aug. 1902.
75. Harriman to Hillquit, 10 Mar. 1903, MH; Hillquit was attacked as "a smooth, slippery kind" by Clarence Smith, secretary-treasurer of the American Labor Union, in *American Labor Union Journal*, 12 Feb. 1903. See also *ibid.*, 26 May 1904; Kipnis, *American Socialist Movement*, 157–59.
76. Brissenden, *I.W.W.*, 60–67; Dubofsky, *We Shall Be All*, 76–80.
77. Victor Berger, "A Timely Warning against Unwise Action," *Social Democratic Herald*, 21 Jan. 1905; Berger to Hillquit, 27 Mar. 1905, MH.
78. IWW, *Founding Convention*, 1–2.
79. *Ibid.*, 142–47.
80. *Ibid.*, 224, 229–30. For the full debate, see *ibid.*, 224–44; Brissenden, *I.W.W.*, 92–96; Dubofsky, *We Shall Be All*, 83–85.
81. See EVD, "The Industrial Convention," *International Socialist Review*, VI (Aug. 1905), 85–86; Algie M. Simons, "The Industrial Convention," *ibid.*, 76–77; Mailly to Hillquit, 17 Mar. 1906, MH.
82. Hayes, "World of Labor," *International Socialist Review*, VI (Jan. 1906), 434–35, VII (July 1906), 54–57.
83. Suggs, *Colorado's War*, 15–16, 25–28.
84. *Ibid.*, 16; Glück, *Mitchell*, 19–20; Western Federation of Miners, *Proceedings, 1906*, 214.
85. Glück, *Mitchell*, 1–19, 34–53, 96–136; EVD, "Plain Talk to the Miners," *Social Democratic Herald*, 6 Feb. 1904; EVD, "The Fate of the Coal Digger," *ibid.*, 23 April 1904; EVD, "A Shameful Affair," *ibid.*, 2 July 1904. See also EVD to Germer, 4 Mar. 1904, SC; *American Labor Union Journal*, 5 May 1904.

86. Glück, *Mitchell,* 169–78.
87. O'Neill to Germer, 24 Mar. 1906, AG.
88. Western Federation of Miners, *Proceedings, 1906,* 5, 124–26, 223–24; James Kirwan to Germer, 18, 27 Aug. 1906, AG; the quote is from Kirwan to Germer, 11 Dec. 1907, SC. See also Hayes, "World of Labor," *International Socialist Review,* VIII (Jan. 1908), 437. There was also some sentiment in favor of joining the IWW among West Virginia coal miners. One Kanawha County miner wrote that the Western Federation made a more "spirited fight for the defense of their persecuted members" than the Mitchell-led national office of the UMWA. See *Voice of Labor,* June 1905.
89. Kirwan to Germer, 18 Aug. 1906, SC.
90. Glück, *Mitchell,* 200–201, 216–18.
91. EVD to Germer, 25 Jan. 1909 [telegram], AG; EVD to Germer, 15 Dec. 1909, SC.
92. See Hayes, "World of Labor," *International Socialist Review,* III (July 1902), 56; Simons to Louis B. Boudin, 18 Oct. 1906, LBB; Notarianni and Stipanovich, "Immigrants, Industry, and Labor Unions," 1–15.
93. Dubofsky, *We Shall Be All,* 87, 93–96.
94. Quoted in *ibid.,* 96.
95. EVD, "The Crusaders," *American Labor Union Journal,* 19 Feb. 1903.
96. *Social Democratic Herald,* 7 Jan. 1905; EVD to Steven M. Reynolds, 19 Jan. 1905, SMR; EVD to Riley, 3 Jan. 1905, JWR; Theodore Debs to Germer, 7 Mar. 1905, SC. See also EVD to Reynolds, 6 June 1900, 30 May 1904, SMR.
97. Kopelin, *Life of Debs,* 42; EVD to Holl, 30 Sept., 23 Dec. 1907, SC; Theodore Debs to Germer, 5 Sept. 1907, AG; Theodore Debs to Holl, 8 Nov. 1907, SC; EVD to Algernon Lee, 9 Dec. 1907, EVD.
98. Theodore Debs to Holl, 21 Nov. 1908, SC.
99. EVD to Reynolds, 2 Apr. 1906, SMR; Kate Debs to Fred D. Warren, 2 Aug. 1910, FDW.
100. EVD to Riley, 3 Jan. 1905, JWR.
101. See Mailly to EVD, 31 Oct. 1904, SMR; J. Mahlon Barnes to Hillquit, 13 Oct. 1908 [telegram], MH. On the social meaning of these illnesses, see Haller and Haller, *Physician and Sexuality.*
102. EVD to Kate Debs, 9 June 1907, n.d. [19 Feb. 1910], Kate M. Debs Scrapbooks, DF; Kate Debs to Grace Brewer, 10 June 1910, GGB.
103. Kate Debs to Grace Brewer, 10 June 1910, 24 Apr. 1910, GGB, 11 Oct. 1910, DF. Before his death, Ned Bush, then curator of the Debs Foundation, informed me that before Grace Brewer died he had corresponded with her concerning letters in her possession from Kate Debs. While some were sent to the foundation and others to Wayne State University in Detroit, Bush understood that Brewer retained and/or destroyed certain letters in which Kate discussed her marriage and her disappointments more frankly.
104. EVD to "My Dearest Dandy and Daisy," 25 May 1905, to "My Dearest, Most Beloved Parents," 4 Nov. 1905, ISU.
105. EVD to "My Darling Sister," 5 Nov. 1895, ISU.
106. EVD to "My Dearest Father," 2 Dec. 1902, ISU.
107. *The Illustrated Buffalo Express,* 26 Apr. 1896.
108. EVD, *Tribute of Love,* 5.
109. EVD, "Current Topics," *Railway Times,* 1 Oct. 1895; Winnifred Harper, "Eugene V. Debs," *Coming Light* (San Francisco), Aug. 1898; EVD to

Conger-Kaneko, 8 June 1911, DF; EVD, "The Coming Woman," Minneapolis *Tribune*, 28 July 1895.
110. Dorothy Richardson, "Women in Debs' Colony," Milwaukee *Sentinel*, 25 July 1897. For Socialist women's protest of this decision, see the letters of Ella Reeve Ware, 3 Feb. 1898, and Imogene C. Fales, 5 May 1898, both in *Railway Times*; also Harper, "Eugene V. Debs."
111. EVD, *Debs Trilogy*, 8–13, 18.
112. EVD, *Woman*.
113. EVD to Theodore Debs, 2 Feb. 1902, ISU; interview with Marguerite Debs Cooper, 31 Mar. 1974, Terre Haute. See also the series of letters from EVD to Theodore during April-May 1908 (ISU), from Girard, Kans., where EVD frequently mentions a "draft enclosed" and notes that although he does not have much, he does not want Theo and his family to want for anything.
114. Roger Baldwin, "Recollections of Debs," JRC. One of the organizers of the *New Review*, desiring the approval of EVD, complained: "How to reach Debs is puzzling to me. If I write to Girard, the letter will be forwarded to his brother, and that would end it." Herman Simpson to Louis B. Boudin, 8 Sept. 1912, LLB.
115. Bohn to Theodore Debs, 25 Sept. 1911, ISU.
116. Bohn to EVD, 3 Oct. 1911, ISU.
117. Theodore Debs to Bohn, 7 Oct. 1911, ISU.
118. Theodore's daughter, Marguerite Debs Cooper, suggested a similar interpretation, saying that her father "idolized Gene and wouldn't leave him." Interview with author, 31 Mar. 1974, Terre Haute.
119. Brenholtz to Theodore Debs, 13 Feb. 1912, ISU.
120. James Larkin Pearson to Theodore Debs, 3 Apr. 1924, ISU.
121. EVD, prison note, n.d., Miscellany File, ISU.
122. EVD to Theodore Debs, 15 Aug. 1908, ISU.
123. EVD to Karsner, n.d. [9 Sept. 1922], DFK.
124. EVD to Karsner, 11 Sept. 1922, DFK.
125. EVD to Curry, n.d. [prison note?], ISU.
126. Theodore Debs to Brenholtz, 20 Feb. 1912, ISU.

Notes to Chapter 8

1. See Laslett, *Labor and the Left*; Montgomery, *Workers' Control*.
2. Hillquit, *History of Socialism*, 353.
3. Weinstein, *Decline of Socialism*, 94–103.
4. William English Walling, "An American Socialism," *International Socialist Review*, V (Apr. 1905), 577.
5. *The Party Builder*, 13 Dec. 1913; John M. Work, "Report of National Secretary, 1913," SPP; Hillquit, *History of Socialism*, 352.
6. Hillquit, *History of Socialism*, 354–55.
7. Kipnis, *American Socialist Movement*, 170.
8. *Ibid.*, 167–68; Hillquit, *History of Socialism*, 348.
9. Shannon, *Socialist Party of America*, 5.
10. EVD to Charles Ervin, 14 Mar. 1908, CE.
11. John M. Work, "Glances at My Life," ch. 3, p. 48, JMW; Charles Dobb to Hillquit, 29 July 1907, MH; EVD to Ervin, 14 Mar. 1908, CE.
12. Hillquit to Vera Hillquit, 8 May 1908, MH.

13. Socialist Party, *National Convention, 1908*, 148–50, 152; *International Socialist Review*, VIII (Jan. 1908), 435.
14. Hillquit to Vera Hillquit, 8 May 1908, MH.
15. Socialist Party, *National Convention, 1908*, 146–48, 150.
16. *Ibid.*, 151–52.
17. *Ibid.*, 160–61; Hillquit to Vera Hillquit, 14 May 1908, MH.
18. Max Hayes, "The World of Labor," *International Socialist Review*, VIII (June 1908), 788–91.
19. EVD to Theodore Debs, 17 May 1908, ISU.
20. Hillquit, *History of Socialism*, 350–51; Terre Haute *Tribune*, 3 Nov. 1908.
21. Work, "Glances at My Life," ch. 3, p. 54, JMW.
22. Bishop to EVD, 8 Jan. 1920, ISU.
23. Kipnis, *American Socialist Movement*, 214.
24. See "Socialist Vote for President," General Records, SPP.
25. EVD, "Socialism's Steady Progress," *American Labor Union Journal*, 26 Feb. 1903.
26. See *The Toiler* (Terre Haute), 24 Aug. 1900; Robert Hunter to Lincoln Steffens, 6 July 1908, LS; Trachtenberg, *Heritage of Gene Debs*, 23.
27. Broun, *It Seems to Me*, 35–39.
28. "Negro Membership in the Socialist Party," General Records, SPP. The one exception was in the mining districts of Kentucky, where, due to the UMWA's long-standing policy of racial equality, local Socialists "found no objections to negroes in the party." Walter Lanfersiek to Carl D. Thompson, 17 May 1913, SPP.
29. "Proceedings of the Socialist Unity Conference," 102–14, 361–75, 445–46, SPP; "Minutes of National Convention, Socialist Party, 31 August to 5 September 1919" (mimeo), 45, SPP. See also the report of the National Executive Committee's refusal to appoint a national organizer for the black community. *The Party Builder*, 21 May, 14 June, 19 July 1913.
30. "The Farmer and the Negro," *International Socialist Review*, IV (Apr. 1904), 614.
31. Mailly to Andrews, 21 Apr. 1903, Mailly Letter-Press Books, SPP.
32. Lingan to Thompson, 27 Sept. 1913, Thompson to Lingan, 2 Oct. 1913, SPP.
33. Ameringer, *If You Don't Weaken*, 218–19; Green, *Grass-Roots Socialism*, 204–28; Gutman, *Work, Culture and Society*, 121–208.
34. Berger, "The Misfortune of the Negro," *Social Democratic Herald*, 31 May 1902. On the question of race and class, see Simons, "The Negro Problem," *International Socialist Review*, I (Oct. 1900), 204–11.
35. EVD, "The Negro Question," *Social Democratic Herald*, 25 July 1903. Twenty years later, Debs's view that "the Negro question" was subsidiary to the larger class question had not changed. See EVD, *Negro Workers*, 12.
36. EVD, "The Negro in the Class Struggle," *International Socialist Review*, IV (Nov. 1903), 260. See also EVD, "The Negro Question," *American Labor Union Journal*, 9 July 1903.
37. EVD, *Riley, Nye and Field*, 14.
38. Interview with EVD in *The Press* (Ottumwa, Ia.), reprinted in *Social Democratic Herald*, 24 Dec. 1898.
39. *Railway Times*, 2 July 1894; EVD, "The Negro Question," *Social Democratic Herald*, 25 July 1903; EVD, *Negro Workers*, 8–9.
40. EVD, "The Negro and His Nemesis," *International Socialist Review*, IV (Jan. 1904), 397.

41. *Social Democratic Herald*, 13 Aug. 1904; Ross D. Brown (a black Indiana Socialist) to EVD, 16 Jan. 1916, Mrs. I. B. W. Barnett (president of the Negro Fellowship League, Chicago) to EVD, 17 Jan. 1916, ISU. Two years later EVD publicly supported W. E. B. Du Bois and was quite critical (if at times erroneously) of Booker T. Washington. See EVD, "The Negro: His Present Status and Outlook," *The Intercollegiate Socialist*, Apr.-May 1918, 11–14.

42. EVD, "Black Persecution," *American Appeal*, 20 Feb. 1926.

43. *Social Democratic Herald*, 24 Feb., 10 Mar. 1900; Jacksonville (Fla.) *Metropolis*, 17 Mar. 1911; EVD, *Negro Workers*, 7–8. On the importance EVD placed on organizing southern workers see William Mailly to EVD, 27 Mar., 26 June 1903, Mailly Letter-Press Books, SPP; EVD, undated prison note, "Monday, A.M. 6th, Labor Day!," Debs Miscellany Folder, ISU.

44. EVD, "Speech at Toledo, Ohio, 27 November 1918," Box 700, section 5, p. 10, DJ (Subject).

45. EVD, "A Thousand Hands to One Head," Camden (N.J.) *Labor*, 8 Jan. 1905.

46. EVD, *Unity and Victory*, 27–28; the speech was originally given before the Kansas AFL Convention, 12 Aug. 1908, at Pittsburg, Kan.

47. EVD, *Growth of Socialism*, 12; EVD, "A Message to the Children," reprinted in EVD, *Labor and Freedom*, 83, 89.

48. Augusta (Ga.) *Herald*, 12 Feb. 1900.

49. *Plain Talk* (Salt Lake City), 29 Oct. 1910; see also Norfolk (Va.) *Landmark*, 27 Mar. 1911.

50. This contributed to the slowness of Socialists' organizing efforts; see Robert Rives La Monte, "Socialist Respect for Capitalist Law," *International Socialist Review*, XII (Feb. 1912), 503.

51. EVD, "The Forbidden Speech," untitled clipping, 11 Oct. 1908, EVD.

52. Cohen to Irving Stone, 11 Mar. 1945, as quoted in George N. Caylor, "Brother Joe, Fragmentary Chapters for a Life of Joseph E. Cohen," 68, GC (Madison).

53. Undated [1910], untitled clipping, Mrs. Henry Vincent Scrapbooks, JL.

54. Kopelin, *Life of Debs*, 40.

55. Bloor, *We Are Many*, 50–53; Trachtenberg, *Heritage of Gene Debs*, 23; see also *The Toiler* (Terre Haute), 24 Aug. 1900.

56. Cannon, *Ten Years of Communism*, 250–53; Hunter to Steffens, 6 July 1908, LS. See also John L. Elliot, "Eugene V. Debs, The Man," *The Standard*, Dec. 1926, 104–6.

57. EVD to "Dearest," undated [1922–23], GG. For an earlier description of a similar experience see Hunter to Steffens, 6 July 1908, LS.

58. New Orleans *Item*, undated clipping [Mar. 1911], EVD; see also Charleston *News & Courier*, 23 Mar. 1911.

59. Work, "Glances at My Life," ch. 7, p. 9, JMW.

60. EVD, *Socialist Party*, 7; EVD, *Unity and Victory*, 12, 19–20.

61. Green, *Grass-Roots Socialism*, 153–62.

62. Frank Donner, untitled manuscript, JRC.

63. Quoted in Allen, ed., *Adventurous Americans*, 330.

64. Behrman, *Worcester Account*, 75–78.

65. See Chandler, *Visible Hand*; Frederickson, *Inner Civil War*.

66. Quoted in Green, *Grass-Roots Socialism*, 298.

67. *Appeal to Reason*, 9 Mar. 1901. For other discussions of the farmer and especially his cultural isolation and his relationship to Socialist agitation see

the issues of 26 Jan., 2, 16 Mar. 1901; Algie M. Simons, "Socialism and Farmers," *Appeal to Reason*, 28 June 1902.

68. Figures computed from "Socialist Vote for President," General Records, SPP. When combined with the votes of the Socialists in the western states, the two regions accounted for over 30 percent of the national Socialist vote.
69. Shannon, *Socialist Party of America*, 34; Green, *Grass-Roots Socialism*, 290–91; Weinstein, *Decline of Socialism*, 116–18.
70. Carver, ed., *Rural Economics*, 525–26; National Resources Committee, *Farm Tenancy*, 94.
71. National Resources Committee, *Farm Tenancy*, 92, 95; Carver, ed., *Rural Economics*, 525–26; *The Rebel*, 3 Apr. 1915; *Platform and Campaign Book, Okla. Socialist Party*, 39–45; Green, *Grass-Roots Socialism*, 240–41.
72. Carver, ed., *Rural Economics*, 525–28; Bizzell, *Green Rising*, 238; Green, *Grass-Roots Socialism*, 69–72; *The Rebel*, 3 Apr. 1915.
73. *The Rebel*, 3 Apr. 1915. In 1910 the average Texas farm was 138 acres, far below the size of Padgitt's holdings. See Carver, ed., *Rural Economics*, 632.
74. On the Texas-based Renters' Union see Carver, ed., *Rural Economics*, 532–34; T. A. Hickey, "The Land Renters Union in Texas," *International Socialist Review*, XIII (Sept. 1912), 239–44; *The Rebel*, 9 Jan., 6 Feb., 20 Mar., 17 Apr. 1915. On the Oklahoma Farmers Emancipation League see *The Rebel*, 16 Jan., 13 Feb., 13 Mar. 1915. Green perceptively explores these and other groups in *Grass-Roots Socialism*, chs. 5–8.
75. Allen, *Great Southwest Strike*, 25, 68–87, 145–47; Allen, *East Texas Lumber Workers*, 24, 30–31; Green, *Grass-Roots Socialism*, 197–204, 208–27, 247; McWhiney, "Louisiana Socialists," 315–36; Weinstein, *Decline of Socialism*, 116–18.
76. *Appeal to Reason*, 20 Sept. 1902; *The Rebel*, 19 June 1915. See also *Appeal to Reason*, 4 Oct. 1902.
77. Green, *Grass-Roots Socialism*, ch. 4.
78. See the statement of Pat Nagle, Oklahoma's premier Socialist organizer among tenant farmers, in *The Rebel*, 3 July 1915.
79. "The Socialist Encampment," *The Southern Worker* (Huntington, Ark.), Apr.–May 1915; Oles Stoter, "Conducting Socialist Encampments," n.d. [1914], SPP; Ameringer, *If You Don't Weaken*, 263–64.
80. "10th Annual Socialist Encampment at Grand Saline, Texas, August 18–23, 1913," clipping in Texas folder, SPP; Webb, *Great Plains*, 375; Ameringer, *If You Don't Weaken*, 263–64.
81. Mr. and Mrs. E. E. McKee to Ethelwyn Mills, 12 Mar. 1913, SPP.
82. Niebuhr, *Social Sources of Denominationalism*, 183.
83. *The Rebel*, 20 Mar. 1915.
84. *Ibid.,* 5 June 1915; see also the issues of 30 Jan., 29 May 1915.
85. Niebuhr, *Kingdom of God*, 26–27.
86. Gutman, *Work, Culture and Society*, 87–88.
87. Folsom to Attorney General George W. Wickersham, 18 Feb. 1912, Box 699, section 1, DJ (Subject); see also EVD, "Revolutionary Encampments," *The National Rip-Saw*, Sept. 1914.
88. EVD to J. E. Synder, reprinted in the *Appeal to Reason*, 2 June 1906.
89. U.S. Bureau of the Census, *Thirteenth Census*, vol. 3: *Population*, 402, 424; vol. 8: *Agriculture*, 321, 330; Roseboom and Weisenburger, *Ohio*, 372; Howe, *Historical Collections of Ohio*, I: 303–4.
90. Bogue and Beale, *Economic Areas*, 914; Howe, *Historical Collections of*

Ohio, I: 302; *Complete Gazetteer*, 2355; U.S. Bureau of the Census, *Twelfth Census*, vol. 1: *Population*, 636; vol. 8: *Manufactures*, 691, 726–27; U.S. Bureau of Census, *Thirteenth Census*, vol. 3: *Population*, 366, 402; vol. 8: *Agriculture*, 321, 330.

91. Frank Bohn, "The Socialist Movement in the Middle West," *Revolt*, I (3 June 1911); "Victory at St. Marys, Ohio," *International Socialist Review*, XII (Dec. 1911), 376–77.

92. Bohn, "The Socialist Movement in the Middle West."

93. "A Revolutionary Mayor," *International Socialist Review*, XII (June 1912), 832.

94. Stetler, *Socialist Movement in Reading*, 6–19, 37–39; Maurer, *It Can Be Done*, 139ff.; Pratt, "Jimmie Higgins," 141–56.

95. Hendrickson, "Tribune of the People," 72–74.

96. *Ibid.*, 73; Montgomery, *Workers' Control*, 70, 73.

97. Stetler, *Socialist Movement in Reading*, 12, 43–44, 59, 93, 134.

98. For a discussion of immigrant Socialists, see ch. 9 herein.

99. *The Party Builder*, 13 Dec. 1913; "Immense Socialist Gains," *International Socialist Review*, XI (Dec. 1910), 364; Frank Bohn, "To-Day's Victory and To-Morrow's Battle," *ibid.*, XII (Dec. 1911), 363–65; Weinstein, *Decline of Socialism*, 116.

100. Walling, "Laborism versus Socialism," *International Socialist Review*, IX (Mar. 1909), 683–89; Hunter, "The British Labor Party, A Reply," *ibid.*, (Apr. 1909), 753–64; "Editor's Chair," *ibid.*, 801.

101. "A Labor Party," *ibid.*, X (Jan. 1910), 594–606; Spargo to Simons, 29 Nov. 1909, SPP.

102. "A Letter from Debs," *International Socialist Review*, X (Jan. 1910), 609.

103. Rose Pastor Stokes to Steven M. Reynolds, 26 Nov. 1909, SMR.

104. J. G. Phelps Stokes to Hillquit, 2 Dec. 1909, MH; Walling to EVD, 14 Dec. 1909, 12 Feb. 1910, to Fred D. Warren, 26 Feb. 1910, WEW; to Louis B. Boudin, 12 Mar. 1910, LBB.

105. Hillquit to J. G. Phelps Stokes, 3 Dec. 1909, Berger to Hillquit, 6 Dec. 1909, MH; to Simons, 6 Dec. 1909, SPP.

106. Simons to Walling, 1 Dec. 1909, form letter from Walling to numerous individuals, 26 Nov. 1909; see also Arthur Bullard to Simons, 26 Jan. 1910, SPP.

107. EVD to Hunter, 2 Feb. 1910, ISU. See also Walling to Boudin, 12 Mar. 1910, LBB.

108. See, for example, Charles H. Kerr to Boudin, 11 Mar. 1910, 5 Apr. 1911, Bertha Howe to Boudin, 17 June 1911, LBB. Also relevant is EVD's letter in *Revolt*, I (13 May 1911).

109. *National Convention, 1910*, 75ff.; "A Letter from Debs on Immigration," *International Socialist Review*, XI (July 1910), 16–17; Kipnis, *American Socialist Movement*, 282–87. For an earlier statement on immigration by Hillquit, see his article, "Immigration in the United States," *International Socialist Review*, VIII (Aug. 1907), 65–75.

110. EVD, "Industrial Unionism," *International Socialist Review*, X (Dec. 1909), 505–8; EVD, "Industrial Unionism. A Letter to Tom Mann," *ibid.*, XI (Aug. 1910), 90–91.

111. EVD, "Danger Ahead," *ibid.*, XI (Jan. 1911), 413–15.

112. EVD, "The Crime of Craft Unionism," *ibid.*, XI (Feb. 1911), 467.

113. EVD to Thompson, 26 Nov. 1910, ISU; Dubofsky, *We Shall Be All*, 198–209.

114. EVD to Thompson, 29 Nov. 1910, ISU. See also EVD to Grace Brewer, 13 Nov. 1911, DF; to Fred D. Warren, 8 Jan. 1910, FDW.
115. *National Convention, 1912*, 138–40.
116. Kipnis, *American Socialist Movement*, 408.
117. William Cunnea, E. M. Winston, and Bernard McMohn to EVD, 11 June 1912, R. H. Howe, T. J. Morgan, and Harvey P. Moyer to EVD and to Emil Seidel, 1 July 1912, ISU; *Revolt*, II (2 Sept. 1911).
118. See EVD to Ernest Untermann, 24 Nov. 1911, ISU.
119. Kipnis, *American Socialist Movement*, 409–10; Howe to Boudin, 22 July 1912, LBB; John M. O'Neill to Berger, 14 Aug. 1911, SP.
120. EVD to Warren, 19 June 1912, FDW.
121. Work, "Glances at My Life," ch. 5, pp. 14–15, JMW.
122. EVD to Warren, 27 July, 5 Aug. 1912, FDW.
123. EVD to Ryan Walker, 5 Aug. 1912, RW; Miller, *Victor Berger*, 49.
124. See EVD to Warren, 23 July 1912, FDW.
125. Warren to EVD, 8 Aug. 1912, FDW.
126. EVD to Warren, 11 Aug. 1912, FDW.
127. See EVD to Warren, 19 Aug., 19 Nov., 2 Dec. 1912, Warren to EVD, 16 Aug., 15 Nov. 1912, FDW.
128. EVD, "Statement of Presidential Candidate," n.d. [July 1912], ISU. It was reprinted in *International Socialist Review*, XIII (Aug. 1912), 167–69. See also Kipnis, *American Socialist Movement*, 410. In contrast with this public position, see EVD's private letter to Barnes, 2 July 1912, ISU.
129. EVD to Warren, 23 July 1912, FDW. See also Theodore Debs to Germer, 15 Mar. 1911, AG, for Theodore's refusal to become party secretary despite his fear that the trial of Barnes had generated "warring factions" that grew "more fierce as the days go by."
130. Dubofsky, *We Shall Be All*, 227–35.
131. *Ibid.*, 235–53.
132. *Ibid.;* Thompson to Warren, 26 Mar. 1913, and "Socialist Party Contributions to Strike Funds," n.d., National Subject File, SPP; "Victory at Lawrence," *International Socialist Review*, XII (Apr. 1912), 679.
133. *National Convention, 1912*, 100, 195.
134. Haywood, "Socialism, the Hope of the Working Class," *International Socialist Review*, XII (Feb. 1912), 461–71. Hillquit's rejoinder is in "Report of Discussion Meeting under Auspices of Local New York, Cooper Union, 11 January 1912," MH (Tamiment). For a discussion of the misunderstanding of the labor plank by pro-IWW socialists see Oneal, *Sabotage or Syndicalism*.
135. EVD, "Sound Socialist Tactics," *International Socialist Review*, XII (Feb. 1912), 481–86.
136. Oneal, *Sabotage or Syndicalism*, 26; *National Convention, 1912*, 122–36.
137. EVD, "This Is Our Year," *International Socialist Review*, XIII (July 1912), 16–18; EVD to Berger, 10 Aug. 1912, ISU.
138. Germer to Hunter, 23 Dec. 1912, AG; Helen Keller, "A Call for Harmony," *International Socialist Review*, XIII (Feb. 1913), 606; Thompson to Keller, 22 Feb. 1913, SPP; Hardie to Germer, 14 Feb. 1913, AG.
139. "Results of Referendum D, 1912," Weekly Bulletin, Socialist Party (mimeo), 1 Mar. 1913, General Records, SPP.
140. [Adolph Germer], "Report of Executive Secretary [to] Emergency National Committee," 6–7, SPP.
141. EVD to Walling, 5 Mar. 1913, ISU; EVD in *The American Socialist*, as

quoted in "Editorial," *The New Review*, III (Sept. 1914), 550–52. For other indications of this continued fighting, see "Washington State Convention," *International Socialist Review*, XIII (May 1913), 813; Grace Silver, "National Committee Meeting, Socialist Party," *ibid.* (June 1913), 877–80; Robert Wark, "To the Minority," *The Party Builder*, 6 Sept. 1913. The issues of *The Party Builder* for 7 and 14 June 1913 also contain detailed discussion about Haywood, the IWW, and the referendum.

142. See EVD, "Let Us Build," *The Party Builder*, 9 Aug. 1913.

143. Buhle, "Debsian Socialism," 263–64. For dissenting views see Dubofsky, *We Shall Be All*, 256–58; Leinenweber, "American Socialist Party," 1–4.

144. U.S. Senate, *Paint Creek District*, I:21, 49, 199, 483–508; II: 1988–89, 2050, 2092–99; Jones to Mrs. Maude Walker, 27 Apr. 1913, H-J. See also Cometti and Summers, *Thirty-Fifth State*, 523–24.

145. EVD to Germer, 14 May 1913, SC.

146. See Barkey, "Socialist Party in West Virginia," 143–45; Weinstein, *Decline of Socialism*, 34–35. Houston is quoted in Barkey, 113.

147. See Fred Merrick, "The Betrayal of West Virginia Red Necks," *International Socialist Review*, XIV (July 1913), 18–22; Edward H. Kintzer, "Reconstruction in West Virginia," *ibid.*, 23–24; W. H. Thompson, "Strike 'Settlements' in West Virginia," *ibid.*, 87–89.

148. EVD to Brown, 26 June 1913, ISU. See also the comments of one Socialist UMWA miner who also attacked the West Virginia leftist Socialists in John K. Hildebrand, "Constructive Unionism in the Mining Industry," *International Socialist Review*, XIII (July 1912), 69–70. For a narrative of the strike see Fetherling, *Mother Jones*, 85–103. For an interpretation that uncritically accepts the leftist Socialist analysis, see Corbin, "Betrayal in the West Virginia Coal Fields," 987–1009.

149. EVD to James Oneal, 9 May 1914, JO.

150. See Karson, *American Labor Unions*.

151. Gavett, *Labor Movement in Milwaukee*, 102–3.

152. EVD, "Labor's Struggle for Supremacy," *International Socialist Review*, XII (Sept. 1911), 141–43.

153. See EVD to Thompson, 26 Nov. 1910, ISU; to Warren, 5 Aug. 1912, FDW.

154. EVD to Berger, 10 Aug. 1912, ISU.

Notes to Chapter 9

1. See the letters EVD to Theodore Debs, 21, 26, 27 Apr., 18 May 1912, ISU.

2. EVD, "Political Appeal to American Workers," 16 June 1912, 5–6, 12, EVD.

3. EVD, "The Fight for Freedom," reprinted in EVD, *Labor and Freedom*, 152–67. For a similar speech in St. Louis in late June see St. Louis *Post-Dispatch*, 30 June 1912.

4. Ellis B. Harris, "Debs in the West," *International Socialist Review*, XIII (Oct. 1912), 351–52; Loy to Wickersham, 15 Jan. 1912, Box 699, Section 1, DJ (Subject); "The Ohio Yell," *International Socialist Review*, XII (June 1912), 832.

5. New York *World*, 30 Sept. 1912; EVD, "A Year With Supreme Possibilities," *Appeal to Reason*, 13 July 1912. See also EVD to Grace Brewer, 17 Aug. 1912, EVL; EVD, "This Is Our Year," *International Socialist Review*, XIII (July 1912), 16–18.

6. "Socialist Vote for President," n.d., General Records, SPP; Weinstein, *Decline of Socialism*, 116–18.
7. In Ohio 43 percent of those who voted opposed Haywood's recall in 1912. See "Result of Referendum D, 1912," Weekly Bulletin, Socialist party (mimeo), 1 Mar. 1913, General Records, SPP.
8. Figures compiled from "Socialist Vote for President," n.d., General Records, SPP; Schlesinger, *American Presidential Elections*, III: 2046, 2131, 2242. Of the sixty-eight Socialists elected to state legislatures between 1900 and 1913, thirty-six, or 53 percent, won victory in Wisconsin, and a majority of these represented Milwaukee wards. An additional fourteen were in Massachusetts. See [Carl D. Thompson ?], "Socialist Representatives in State Legislatures," n.d. [1913], General Records, SPP.
9. See Stolberg, *Tailor's Progress*, 17, 91; Dubofsky, *When Workers Organize*. It is useful to contrast the history of this "Protocol" with EVD's call for armed defense by western miners to understand the enormous regional differences within the movement. See EVD, "The Gunmen and the Miners," *International Socialist Review*, XV (Sept. 1914), 161–62.
10. In a letter written in 1945, Kate Richards O'Hare noted that in the South Socialism "had to be expounded in King James Bible words and quotations"; in the Midwest, in "the language of Populism and Greenbackism"; in urban centers, "we based our appeal on the organized labor movement and the hopes and aspirations of emigrants [*sic*]." These regional differences caused severe problems in her view: "New York was a world apart. The Socialist movement [there] was based entirely on European concepts; Hillquit and his clique never knew that the Hudson River was not the West boundary of the United States, with some colonies in Chicago and Milwaukee. They were never American and never had the slightest conception of American psychology and political theories." O'Hare to Samuel Castleton, 16 Sept. 1945, SC.
11. Berger to Hillquit, 23 Oct. 1913, MH; *The Party Builder*, 20 Sept. 1913.
12. EVD, "The Need for Organization," *The Party Builder*, 5 July 1913; EVD, "Let Us Build," *ibid.,* 9 Aug. 1913.
13. [Adolph Germer], "Report of Executive Secretary [to] Emergency National Committee," 6–7, SPP.
14. "Decrease in the Socialist Party Vote," *The New Review*, IV (Mar. 1915), 176–78.
15. Frank Dawson, "St. Marys Fighting Mayor," *International Socialist Review*, XIII (June 1913), 874–76.
16. McNaught, "American Progressives," 510–11.
17. Shover, "Progressives and the Working Class Vote," 260–73.
18. Lawson Shull, "My Memories of Eugene Debs," June 1965, JRC.
19. [Germer], "Report of Executive Secretary [to] Emergency National Convention," 7, SPP.
20. Wells, *The Future in America*, 131–32; Sidney Webb as quoted in McNaught, "American Progressives," 509.
21. Lippmann, "On Municipal Socialism," 184–86, 190–91; see also Lippmann to Graham Wallas, 31 July 1912, as quoted in McNaught, "American Progressives," 513.
22. Hand to Wallas, 17 Jan. 1920, as quoted in McNaught, "American Progressives," 518–19.

23. For a discussion of the "failure" of Socialism from many different historical and political perspectives, see Laslett and Lipsett, *Failure of a Dream*.

24. See George Caylor to Harry Golden, 26 Aug. 1960, Golden to Caylor, 30 Aug. 1960, GC. Roger Baldwin remembered that he and Kate Debs discussed EVD's drinking at least once after 1921; Kate termed it "an old habit she deplored." Baldwin, "Recollections of Debs," JRC. The incident at the bordello is retold in John Spargo, "The Reminiscences of John Spargo," 203ff., especially 209, OHR. One elderly Debsian Socialist who desires anonymity remembered that as a young man his task was to conduct EVD to his New York meetings. He frequently picked up EVD at a Greek restaurant in New York's Greenwich Village—EVD had a fondness for Greek wine—and he could not recall a time when EVD was without female companionship when he arrived. For this young Socialist, EVD was a hero, and he asked no questions even as he frequently had to sober EVD up before the talk.

25. See EVD to Fred D. Warren, 19 Nov. 1912, FDW; Wayland, *Wayland's Undelivered Address*, 19–21; Vincent, *The Editor*, 26–27, 35–47, for the attempts of comrades to explain the suicide; Brewer, *The Wayland I Knew*; Kopelin, *Life of Debs*, 47; Fred D. Warren, "J. A. Wayland and the 'Appeal to Reason,' " *American Socialist*, Mar. 1957, 12–15.

26. Warren to EVD, 16 Aug. 1912, EVD to Warren, 3 Jan., 8 Sept. 1913, FDW. See also Theodore Debs to Grace Brewer, 3 Oct. 1913, DF; *The Party Builder*, 11 Oct. 1913.

27. EVD to Theodore Debs, 12 Nov. 1913, ISU.

28. EVD to Theodore Debs, 2 Oct., 7 Nov. 1913, ISU; to Hillquit, 20 Dec. 1913, MH.

29. Theodore Debs to Grace Brewer, 19 Jan. 1914, DF; *The Party Builder*, 7 Mar. 1914; EVD to Theodore Debs, 26 Sept. 1914, to Llewelyn Lloyd, 14 Apr. 1915 [telegram], ISU.

30. Seattle *Union Record*, 30 Jan. 1915; EVD to V. Bussy, 2 Sept. 1916, ISU.

31. *Labor Advocate* (Nashville), 20 Mar. 1914.

32. Quoted in "American Socialists and the War," *The New Review*, III (Oct. 1914), 615.

33. See Thompson to EVD, 23 Dec. 1914, SPP; EVD to Allan Benson, 22 Mar. 1915, ISU; Theodore Debs to Germer, 16 Aug. 1915, AG; Walter Lanfersiek to Hillquit, 23 Dec. 1915, MH.

34. EVD, "Even to the Barricades," *Rebellion* (New Orleans), Dec. 1915, 37.

35. For another example of this rhetorical violence in which, in defense of Mexican revolutionists imprisoned by the American government, EVD threatened "*to incite an insurrection*" and "place myself at the head of it," see EVD to Warren, 1 Feb., 1 Mar. 1910, FDW; EVD, "The Murder of Magen," n.d. [1922], DFK.

36. EVD to Warren, 18 May 1915, FDW; Theodore Debs to Germer, 3, 14 June 1915, SC.

37. See EVD to Frank P. O'Hare, 31 Dec. 1915, ISU.

38. Rieber to William K. Alderfer, 2 Feb. 1960, General Files, Wisconsin State Historical Society, Madison. See also Karsner, *Talks with Debs*, 116–17, 132–39.

39. Quoted in Ginger, *The Bending Cross*, 334–35.

40. EVD, "The Class War and Its Outlook," *International Socialist Review*, XVII (Sept. 1916), 135–36; Tresca to EVD, n.d. [18 Sept. 1916], ISU.

41. H. Scott Bennett, "Will Eugene V. Debs Sit in Congress?," *International*

Socialist Review, XVII (Sept. 1916), 144–45; Noble C. Wilson, "Help Elect Debs," *ibid.*, 167; Ginger, *The Bending Cross*, 334–38. A disturbing note in the campaign for EVD was the presence in the coal districts of Mother Jones on behalf of Woodrow Wilson and the incumbent Democratic senator, John Kern. Kern had been responsible for her release from jail during the 1913 West Virginia strike prior to EVD's arrival. In part Jones was repaying a favor and in part, although she was a committed labor organizer, Jones never fully supported the Socialist ticket in any election. See Fetherling, *Mother Jones*, 152–54. For another interpretation see Corbin, "Betrayal in the West Virginia Coal Fields," 1006–7.

42. Theodore Debs to Ruth LePrade, 13 Apr. 1923, PG; J. H. Hollingsworth, "Eugene V. Debs, What His Neighbors Say of Him," clipping, n.d., 7, EVD.
43. Curry, *Woman with a Message*.
44. Ginger, *The Bending Cross*, 336–37.
45. On their good-byes from the train, see Curry to Rose Pastor Stokes, 19 Apr. 1919, RPS; EVD to "My precious Love," Fri. (Group I); "Ura" [EVD] to "Most precious Love," Tues. 24th (Group I), GG. I consulted this collection, consisting of some forty-five letters—the majority from EVD to Curry—while they were in the possession of George Gloss, owner of the Brattle Street Bookstore, Boston. He had discovered them when he purchased the estate of Rosalie Goodyear, a member of the rubber family and a close friend and confidant of Curry. Goodyear was also a friend of EVD's. See Goodyear to Theodore Debs, 18 Mar. 1945, ISU; Goodyear to ?, n.d., GG. The great majority of these letters are undated, and frequently EVD used special designations to identify both himself and Curry. The most common is Ura for himself and Juno for Curry. Through internal evidence it is possible to date these letters according to three periods: Group I, the pre-jail years (1917–Apr. 1919); Group II, the jail years (Apr. 1919–Dec. 1921); Group III, the post-jail years (Jan. 1922–Oct. 1926). Where possible, I will note the month and/or year as well as the group. I am deeply indebted to George Gloss for allowing me access to these letters. He valued comradeship and scholarship above possible financial loss.
46. Theodore Debs to Joseph E. Cohen, 12 Nov. 1917, JEC.
47. EVD to "My Dearest Comrade," Group I (1917), GG.
48. EVD to the Vincents, 24 Nov. 1917, Vincent Scrapbooks, JL.
49. "Gene" to "My precious Love," Group I; see also "Ura" to "My beloved," Tues., Group I, GG.
50. Curry to Stokes, n.d. [1917], RPS.
51. Curry to Stokes, 19 Apr. 1919, RPS.
52. Socialist Party, "Disarmament and World Peace," n.d. [1915], General Records. For the debate see "Minutes of National Executive Committee Meeting, 14 December 1914, Peace Program," General Records; Hillquit to Carl D. Thompson, 6, 18, 20 Jan., 9 Feb . 1915, Thompson to Hillquit, 13, 21 Jan., 2, 11 Feb. 1915, Charles E. Russell to Thompson, 15 Jan. 1915, Allan Benson to Thompson, 19 Jan. 1915, Simons to Thompson, 20 Jan. 1915, all documents and letters in SPP. Also valuable is Cantor, "Radical Confrontation," 223.
53. Ironically, Benson was nominated in 1916 largely as a result of a series of articles condemning war preparations. See Weinstein, *Decline of Socialism*, 125. Benson and his running mate, George Kirkpatrick, received less than

600,000 votes. On Benson's membership in the league, see Walling to Emmanuel Haldeman-Julius, 25 July 1918, H-J.

54. On membership figures, see [Germer], "Report of the Executive Secretary [to] Emergency National Committee," 6–7; "Membership List, January-April 1917"; "Membership List, January-April 1919," General Records, SPP.

55. Labadie to Henry Boll, n.d. [1918], JL. On resistance to the war see Gaston, *Nonpartisan League*, 175ff.; Garin Burbank, "Disruption and Decline of the Oklahoma Socialist Party"; Green, *Grass-Roots Socialism*, 345–95; Peterson and Fite, *Opponents of War*, chs. 3–6. John Spargo, a co-founder of the alliance, recounts Wilson's role in "The Reminiscences of John Spargo," 266, OHR. EVD's letter is quoted in Ginger, *The Bending Cross*, 332–33.

56. Quoted in William E. Walling, "The Remedy: Anti-Nationalism," *The New Review*, III (Feb. 1915), 77–83. See in the same issue "Some New Socialist Principles," 108ff.

57. Herron to Lee, 4 Oct., 3 Nov. 1914, 18 Feb. 1915, GDH.

58. Walling, "The Remedy: Anti-Nationalism."

59. See, for example, Hillquit to Henry Hyndman, 31 Dec. 1914, MH.

60. Boudin to Harry W. Laidler, 5 June 1917, LBB; Spargo, "The Reminiscences of John Spargo," 200–202, OHR.

61. Miller, "Socialist Party Decline," 407–9; Berger to Hillquit, 3 June 1916, MH.

62. Hoan to EVD, 15 Aug. 1916; see also EVD to Hoan, 11 Aug. 1916, DWH.

63. EVD to Hoan, 17 Aug. 1916, DWH. For similar sentiments, when EVD refused to join with Upton Sinclair in the latter's prowar position, see EVD to Sinclair, 12 Jan. 1916, US.

64. Steadman to London, 23 Apr. 1917, ML; P. G. [Paul Gauer] to Thompson, 15 Jan. 1918 [carbon], DWH.

65. Higham, *Strangers in the Land*, ch. 8.

66. Liebman, *Jews and the Left*, 29–31, 133–206; Kostiainen, *Finnish-American Communism*, 30–31; Gedicks, "Radicalism among Finnish Immigrants," 12–16.

67. Liebman, *Jews and the Left*, 588; Ollila, "From Socialism to Industrial Unionism," 170–71. For the concentration of immigrants in specific industries, see Eckler and Zlotnick, "Immigration and the Labor Force," 97, 100.

68. Joseph Schlossberg, "Interview," 6–7, and see also Pauline Newman, "Interview," 29ff, OHR; Liebman, *Jews and the Left*, 451, 474.

69. Liebman, *Jews and the Left*, 135–206, 355ff.

70. Kostiainen, *Finnish-American Communism*, 26–37; Passi, "Fishermen on Strike," 89–102; see also Smith, "Religious Denominations as Ethnic Communities," 207–26. On Italian radical efforts, see Fenton, *Immigrants and Unions*, 160–75.

71. Kostiainen, *Finnish-American Communism*, 31; Fenton, *Immigrants and Unions*, 176; John M. Work, "Report of National Secretary," n.d. [1913], SPP; Weinstein, *Decline of Socialism*, 183.

72. Kostiainen, *Finnish-American Communism*, 37–43; Ollila, "From Socialism to Industrial Unionism," 157–71; T. E. Latimer, "Executive Committee Rule," *International Socialist Review*, XV (Feb. 1915), 481–84; Fenton, *Immigrants and Unions*, 176–85; Goren, "Portrait of Ethnic Politics," 236;

Dubofsky, "Success and Failure of Socialism in New York City," 365–66; Hillquit to Julius Gerber, 8 May 1914, MH (Tamiment).

73. Leinenweber, "American Socialist Party," 18; Weinstein, *Decline of Socialism*, 182–83. Weinstein argues with some force that the formal organizational life of the left wing did not coalesce until spring 1919. While there is some truth to this, Weinstein downplays the persistent ideological struggles engendered by the debate over industrial unionism. This then allows him to argue that wartime repression by American authorities and a false consciousness (i.e., the "Bolshevik mystique") on the part of radical immigrants were the major causes of Socialism's failure. The thrust of Section III suggests a far different interpretation of both the specific point concerning the federations and the larger issue of the meaning of Socialism in America.

74. Dubofsky, "Success and Failure of Socialism in New York City"; for a leftist attack on Hillquit's campaign, see Dannenberg, *Reform or Revolution*. On the repression of radicals, see "The I.W.W. and the Socialist Party," *International Socialist Review*, XVIII (Oct. 1917), 205–8; Preston, *Aliens and Dissenters*.

75. Trotsky, *My Life*, 270–74; Deutscher, *Prophet Armed*, 241–43.

76. On the question of the "Bolshevik mystique," see Weinstein, *Decline of Socialism*, chs. 4, 5. The unidentified Finnish Socialist is quoted in Leinenweber, "American Socialist Party," 20. For an analysis of the split within the Finnish Federation on the question of revolutionary tactics, see Kostiainen, *Finnish-American Communism*, 58–112.

77. "Proceeding of Emergency Convention of the Socialist Party of America. At St. Louis, 1917," SPP; Conlin, *American Anti-War Movements*, 68–73.

78. Boudin to Harry W. Laidler, 5 June 1917, LBB; Boudin, "The Emergency National Convention of the Socialist Party," *The Class Struggle*, I (May-June 1917), 42–47; Leslie Marcy, "The Emergency National Convention," *International Socialist Review*, XVII (May 1917), 665–69. In 1915 a national party referendum approved, by a vote of 11,041 to 782, the penalty of expulsion for any Socialist legislator in America who voted for war credits. Trachtenberg, ed., *American Socialists and the War*, 21.

79. Gompers, *Seventy Years*, II: 377–86; Maurer, *It Can Be Done*, 231ff.; Stetler, *Socialist Movement in Reading*, 77–78. For a different evaluation of the party's antiwar stance see Cantor, "Radical Confrontation," 222–28.

80. EVD to Bruce Rogers, 9 Apr. 1917, to Germer, 11 Apr. 1917, ISU.

81. "Gene" to "Dearest of Comrades," Wed., Group I (1917), GG.

82. Theodore Debs to Karsner, 14 Mar. 1918, DFK.

83. For an overview of this repression see Peterson and Fite, *Opponents of War*, chs. 6–9; on the IWW, and specifically Bisbee and Butte, see Dubofsky, *We Shall Be All*, 376–93; Preston, *Aliens and Dissenters*, ch. 4; on Terre Haute, see Ginger, *The Bending Cross*, 351–52. For EVD's reaction, see EVD, "The I.W.W. Bogey," *International Socialist Review*, XVIII (Feb. 1918), 395–96; EVD, "The Indictment of Our Leaders," leaflet, Apr. 1918, EVD. Also relevant is Caroline A. Lowe to Elizabeth Gurley Flynn, 20 Mar. 1919, EGF.

84. Haywood to Jack Reed, 1 Sept. 1918, JR.

85. Simons to Alexandra Kollontai, 15 May 1917, and untitled manuscript of Russell's address at Pavlovsk-Voksal, 30 June 1917, CER. These prowar former Socialists also tried to influence immigrant Socialists, especially in New York City, but had little success. See William Edlin to Walling, 20 Apr.

1917, Walling to Edlin, 7 June, 25 Aug. 1917, Gompers to Edlin, 25 Mar. 1918, WE.

86. EVD, "A Personal Statement" (mimeo), n.d. [May 1918], ISU; New York *Daily News*, 17 May 1918; EVD to Steven M. Reynolds, 25 May 1918, SMR; Ginger, *The Bending Cross*, 349–53. But a month earlier EVD seemed somewhat confused. In a private letter to Germer he noted that the Bolshevik Revolution and Germany's attempts to reduce Russia "to a HOHENZOLLERN vassalage has created a tremendous change of sentiment throughout the world which we cannot afford to ignore." He then endorsed the resolutions of the recent London meeting of the Inter-Allied Labor and Socialist Conference. Germer agreed with EVD with one exception: he reminded EVD that the conference had enthusiastically endorsed all allied military efforts. EVD to Germer, 8 Apr. 1918, Germer to EVD, 18 Apr. 1918, ISU. Hillquit's qualified support for American war efforts can be found in his letter to *The New Republic*, 1 Dec. 1917, and in the critique of Hillquit by Louis B. Boudin, "St. Louis and After," *The Class Struggle*, II (Jan.–Feb. 1918), 126.

87. L. [Ludwig Lore], "Spargo, Simons and Private Kopelin," *The Class Struggle*, II (Sept.–Oct. 1918), 500–502; EVD to Kopelin, 14 Dec. 1917, ISU; Shepperson, *Retreat to Nevada*, 66–68, 164–65. For an analysis of the effect of the *Appeal*'s new position on the Oklahoma movement, see Green, *Grass-Roots Socialism*, 373–74.

88. Hillquit to Job Harriman, 30 Apr. 1918, MH; Socialist Party, "Proclamation on Russia," 4 Feb. 1918, SPP.

89. Freeman, *American Testament*, 77–78, 100.

90. EVD, "The Soul of the Russian Revolution," included in letter to Karsner, 30 Mar. 1918, DFK. (The draft was written at least a month earlier.) EVD to Stokes, n.d., RPS; EVD, "The Day of the People," *The Class Struggle*, III (Feb. 1919), 3–4. See also New York State, *Revolutionary Radicalism*, I: 555.

91. See note 118, ch. 6.

92. EVD, *Canton Speech*, reprinted in EVD, *Writings and Speeches of Eugene V. Debs*, 417–33.

93. John Lord O'Brien to Wertz, 20 June 1918, Box 700, DJ (Subject). A longer section of this opinion is quoted in Shannon, *Socialist Party of America*, 115.

94. Karsner, *Debs, Life and Letters*, 14.

95. EVD was ultimately charged with a "willful attempt to cause or incite, insubordination, mutiny, disloyalty and refusal of duty with the military forces of the United States" and to "obstruct and attempt to obstruct the recruiting and enlistment service of the United States." *Ibid.*, 24.

96. The official transcript of EVD's address to the jury is reprinted in *ibid.*, 23–44. EVD's autographed copy of the transcript can be found in DFK.

97. EVD's speech to the judge is reprinted in *ibid.*, 48–54.

98. *Ibid.*, 54–55.

99. L. [Lore], "Eugene V. Debs," *The Class Struggle*, II (Dec. 1918), 622–24.

100. EVD to LePrade, 30 Sept. 1918, PG.

101. EVD to Lee, 10 Oct. 1918, EVD. See also EVD to Joseph E. Cohen, 20 Sept. 1918, JEC; EVD to John Reed, 21 Sept. 1918, EVD (Harvard).

102. Lenin, *Letter to American Workingmen*, 9–10.

103. EVD, *Fight for Liberty*, 4.

104. Theodore Debs to Upton Sinclair, 6 Nov. 1918, US; EVD to Horace Traubel, 6 Dec. 1918, HT; Germer to Hillquit, 22 Mar. 1919, MH.

105. Reprinted in New York State, *Revolutionary Radicalism*, I: 418–19. Founded

in 1915, the league was a center of leftist agitation and dominated by Lettish immigrants in Boston. Louis Fraina, an Italian-born radical and central figure in the left faction, edited the league's paper, *Revolutionary Age*. See Weinstein, *Decline of Socialism*, 184–85; Louis Corey [Louis Fraina], "Outline of Autobiography," LC.

106. For EVD's article and the editorial, see *The Class Struggle*, III (Feb. 1919), 1–4. Others disagreed with EVD. Boudin resigned from the journal in September 1918 to protest its simplistic application of Bolshevik theory for Americans. See *ibid.*, II (Sept.–Oct. 1918), 492.

107. Unsigned [EVD] to Gerber, 27 Feb. 1919 [carbon], SC. The final page and signature are missing. However, it is typed on Theodore Debs's stationery and datelined Terre Haute; internal evidence, especially in the first paragraph, removes any doubt but that the writer is EVD. On the New York fight, see Germer to Hillquit, 22 Mar. 1919, MH; Weinstein, *Decline of Socialism*, 192–96.

108. EVD, "Our Opportunity," *The Illinois Comrade*, I (1 Mar. 1919).

109. See the comments of friends who saw EVD just prior to the June 1918 tour: Oneal, "Debs Turns Seventy"; Ehrmann, "Reminiscences of Max Ehrmann," 254; George Goebel, as quoted in Brommel, "Pacifist Speechmaking of Debs," 148. See also Darrow, *My Life*, 69; Nearing, *Debs Decision*, 14–15; Ginger, *The Bending Cross*, 352–53.

110. The court's decision is reprinted in full in Karsner, *Debs, Life and Letters*, 237–42. On the appeal see Morris H. Wolf to Steadman, 29 Nov. 1918, SS. (Both men were EVD's lawyers.) Nearing, *Debs Decision*, 38–47.

111. For EVD's response to the court, see Karsner, *Debs Goes to Prison*, 3. On the clemency petition, at first erroneously attributed to EVD, see Terre Haute *Tribune*, 3, 8 Apr. 1919; Wilson to Tumulty [received], 3 Apr. 1919 [cable], Box 699, Section 4, DJ (Subject). A similar petition had been made a month earlier by William Henry, state secretary, Socialist party of Indiana, in his letter to Wilson, 15 Mar. 1919, Box 699, Section 4, DJ (Subject).

112. Palmer to Wilson, 3 Apr. 1919, Pomerene to Palmer, 5 Apr. 1919, Box 699, Section 4, DJ (Subject).

113. "E–" to "My own dearest," Sat. Noon, Group I (1919), GG; Curry to Stokes, 18 Nov. 1918, RPS.

114. Terre Haute *Tribune*, 13 Apr. 1919; Curry to Stokes, 19 Apr. 1919, RPS. Both Ginger, *The Bending Cross*, 384, and Karsner, *Debs, Life and Letters*, 58, placed the call from Wertz on Saturday and not Friday as did Curry.

115. Quoted in Engdahl, *Debs and O'Hare*, 17.

116. E. A. Brenholtz to Theodore Debs, 1 Jan. 1920, ISU. See also Engdahl, *Debs and O'Hare*, 4; Robins, *War Shadows*, 19–20; EVD, undated prison note, "Monday, A.M. 6th. Labor Day!," Miscellany Folder, ISU.

117. Reed to Palmer, 8 Apr. 1919, Box 699, Section 4, DJ (Subject).

Notes to Part IV

1. "Oh, The Moonlight's Fair Tonight along the Wabash," *Fortune*, XIX (May 1939), 78.

2. O'Neal, *Terre Haute's Shame*, 34.

3. *Ibid.*, 1–8.

4. Indianapolis *Star*, 21 Feb. 1913.

5. Hulman to EVD, 13 June 1917, ISU.

6. Ginger, *The Bending Cross*, 408.
7. Shubert Sebree, "Gene Debs—My Beloved Comrade," 10, JRC.
8. Terre Haute *Tribune*, 9 Sept. 1925.

Notes to Chapter 10

1. See "The Last Message of Debs," *Illinois Comrade*, I (1 Apr. 1919); Engdahl, *Debs and O'Hare*, 17.
2. Karsner, *Debs, Life and Letters*, 75–77; EVD to Karsner, 22 Apr. 1919, DFK.
3. EVD to Karsner, 15 May 1919, DFK; to Theodore Debs, 22 Apr. 1919, ISU.
4. EVD to Theodore Debs, 21, 22 Apr. 1919, ISU; Curry to Stokes, 16 May [1919], RPS.
5. EVD to Hillquit, 3 May 1919, MH. Hillquit also sent $100 to Theodore to help with office expenses; see Theodore Debs to Hillquit, 5 May 1919, MH.
6. T. J. Spellacy (assistant attorney general) to Terrell, 5 June 1919, DJ (Bureau of Prisons); Theodore Debs to Germer, 20 June 1919, SPP; Theodore Debs to Cohen, 21 June 1919, JEC.
7. Karsner, *Debs, Life and Letters*, 105–9.
8. Theodore Debs to Rosalie Goodyear, 25 July 1919, GG.
9. John T. Cooper to EVD, 21 Dec. 1920; Mrs. J. H. Carter to EVD, 29 Mar. 1921, ISU; Henry Da Silva, "A Birthday Greeting to Eugene Debs" [poem], included in a letter of Theodore Debs to Karsner, 12 Dec. 1921, DFK; Joiner to EVD, 5 Nov. 1921, ISU.
10. Benson to EVD, 7 Dec. 1920, ISU.
11. John G. Stilli, "Debs and Christianity," *Illinois Comrade*, I (1 July 1919), 1–2; Hurt, *Debs, an Introduction*, 18–20, 42.
12. Smith, "Historic Waves."
13. EVD, *Jesus*. See also EVD's letter to a Michigan prisoner, reprinted in *The Rebel*, 9 Jan. 1915.
14. The picture of Christ EVD had in his prison cell can be found in DFK.
15. EVD to Bruce Rogers, 9 Apr. 1917, ISU.
16. Curry to Karsner, 28 Nov. 1920, DFK; to Upton Sinclair, 7 Nov. 1920, US.
17. Theodore Debs to Gertrude Toy Debs, 22 Dec. 1921, ISU.
18. "B. and the Vision" [EVD] to "My dear Comrade," Sat. evening, June 4, Group II (1921), GG.
19. "Ura" to "My most Beloved," Tues., 19th, Group II (1920 or 1921), GG.
20. "Ura" to "My beautiful Love," Mar. 28, Group II (1921), "Ura" to "My own beloved," Mon. 9th, Group II (May 1921), GG.
21. Curry to "My Very dear Comrade," 11 Apr., Group II (1921), GG.
22. EVD to Theodore Debs, 27 Nov. 1919, EVD, prison note, 9 Sept. 1921, Debs Miscellany Folder, EVD to Theodore Debs, 25 Oct. 1921, ISU.
23. Joseph M. Coldwell to Winnie Branstetter, 18 July 1920, EVD to Branstetter, 9 Dec. 1920, SPP; EVD, "Behind Prison Walls," July 1922, DFK. The story of the prison thief is told in a letter by his friend, Rachel H. Minshall, to Oswald F. Villard, 22 Nov. 1920, EVD (Harvard). Tresca's experience is retold in Max Eastman, *Heroes*, 31.
24. Untitled prison note, dated 1921, Debs Miscellany Folder, ISU. On the Palmer raids, see Preston, *Aliens and Dissenters*, 180–237.
25. Untitled, undated prison note, Group II, GG; on Clarence Royce, see Esarey, *History of Indiana*, III: 488.

26. Untitled prison note, "Monday, A.M. 6th. Labor Day!" [1920], Debs Miscellany Folder, ISU.
27. Untitled, undated prison note, Debs Miscellany Folder, ISU. A portion of it is reprinted in Coleman, *Debs*, 320-21.
28. On the suspension of EVD's privileges, see Fred Zerbst to Palmer, 14 Feb., 3 Mar. 1921, Box 700, section 7, DJ (Subject); Lucy Robins to D. S. Dickerson, superintendent of prisons, 24 Feb. 1921; Dickerson to Robins, 28 Feb. 1921, DJ (Bureau of Prisons). The protest of Georgia's Senator-elect, Tom Watson, once a Populist colleague of EVD's and now a rabid racist and antiradical, is in the Atlanta *Georgian*, 25 Feb. 1921.
29. Untitled prison note, "Monday, A.M. 6th. Labor Day!" [1920], Debs Miscellany Folder, ISU.
30. Draper, *American Communism*, 156. See also Maurice L. Paul to Elsie Heller Ehret, 13 May 1919, New York State Records, SPP, for an example of the left's organizing tactics.
31. Draper, *American Communism*, 157-58; Weinstein, *Decline of Socialism*, 196-201; Howe and Coser, *American Communist Party*, 35-36.
32. Brentmasser to "The Insignificant Seven" [National Executive Committee, Socialist party], 25 July 1919, SPP.
33. Denison to Germer, 17 Aug. 1919, SPP.
34. Arnold to Germer, 29 July 1919; see also T. H. Coxe to Otto Branstetter, 12 July 1919, SPP.
35. John W. Ellison to Germer, 29 July 1919; see also E. J. Hewit [secretary, Ashtabula, Ohio, Socialist party local] to Ohio Socialist party, 12 Aug. 1919, Ohio Records, SPP.
36. Dawson to Germer, 7 July 1919, SPP.
37. For a more detailed analysis of these issues, see Howe and Coser, *American Communist Party*, 28-40; Draper, *American Communism*, 156-75; Weinstein, *Decline of Socialism*, 201-15.
38. On the 1919 convention, see Germer to David Shannon, 14 July 1950, AG; "Minutes of the National Convention, Socialist Party," 31 Aug. to 5 Sept. 1919 [mimeo], 12, 32-33, General Records, SPP; Draper, *American Communism*, 176-96; Max Eastman, "The Chicago Conventions," *The Liberator*, Oct. 1919, 15.
39. Branstetter to EVD, 4 Apr. 1921, IS.
40. Oneal and Minor, *Resolved*, 8, 19.
41. Theodore Debs to Karsner, 26 Apr., 14 May 1919, DFK; Curry to Stokes, 16 May [1919], RPS.
42. Castleton to Hillquit, 10 Jan. 1920, Hillquit to Castleton, 30 Jan. 1920, MH.
43. Theodore Debs to Karsner, 19, 30 Mar., 10 Apr. 1920, DFK; Theodore Debs to Cohen, 1 Apr. 1920, JEC; EVD to Karsner, 30 Apr. 1920, DFK.
44. Karsner, untitled mss., 14 Apr. 1920, DFK; Karsner to EVD, 27 Apr. 1920, ISU. (A copy of this letter is in DFK.) "B. and the Vision" [EVD] to "My dear Comrade," Sat. evening, June 4, Group II (1921), GG.
45. EVD to Karsner, 30 Apr. 1920, DFK. The letter was reprinted in *Socialist Review*, June 1920, 15-16.
46. Atlanta *Georgian*, 14 May 1920; see also New York *Times*, 30 May 1920.
47. EVD to Theodore Debs, 1 June 1920, ISU.
48. Hillquit to EVD, 30 June 1920, MH. See also Hillquit's keynote speech at the 1920 convention in Harry W. Laidler, "The Socialist Convention," *Socialist Review*, June 1920, 28-29.

49. Theodore Debs to Hillquit, 12 July 1920, MH; "Kate O'Hare Visits Debs," *Socialist World*, I (July 1920), 8–9; Feigenbaum, "Debs to the Socialist Party," *Socialist World*, I (Oct. 1920), 16–18.
50. Karsner, "Interview with Debs," transcript, Aug. 1920, DFK.
51. *Ibid.*
52. EVD, "Look Out for Your Leaders" [press release] and "Last Press Release," SC.
53. Curry to Karsner, 28 Nov. 1920, DFK; to Sinclair, 7 Nov. 1920, US.
54. Dubofsky, *We Shall Be All*, 459–60; *Debs Magazine*, II (Jan. 1923), 11; EVD to O. Branstetter, 9 Apr. 1921, IS.
55. Simons to Colonel Guy D. Goff, 28 Mar. 1921, Box 700, section 7, DJ (Subject); Swanberg, *Norman Thomas*, 82–83; Robins, *War Shadows*, 40, 92ff.; O. Branstetter to Bertha H. White, 8 Dec. 1921, SPP.
56. Ginger, *The Bending Cross*, 407–9; Curry to Karsner, 4 Apr. 1921, DFK; EVD to O. Branstetter, 9 Apr. 1921, IS; Kate Debs to Grace Keller, 17 June 1921, EVL; Curry to Oswald G. Villard, 25 July 1921, EVD (Harvard); Theodore Debs to Ruth LePrade, 18 Aug. 1921, PG; O. Branstetter to Harding, 26 Oct. 1921, SPP; New York *World*, 16 Nov. 1921.
57. Prevey to EVD, n.d. [1921], EVD to Theodore Debs, 25 Oct. 1921, ISU.
58. EVD to O. Branstetter, undated prison note [1921], to Theodore Debs, 25 Oct. 1921, ISU.
59. Ginger, *The Bending Cross*, 413–14; Moore to Cohen, 9 Jan. 1927, JEC. See also Rachel H. Minshall to Villard, 22 Nov. 1920, EVD (Harvard); Eastman, *Heroes*, 31; Schorer, *Sinclair Lewis*, 456.
60. Ginger, *The Bending Cross*, 414. In the film *Eugene Debs and the American Movement* (Cambridge Documentary Films) this powerful and moving scene of EVD's departure from prison has again been made available to audiences. One of the few pieces of motion picture footage of EVD still extant, the film incorporates newsreel footage of EVD walking down the path from prison.
61. EVD to Sacco-Vanzetti Defense Committee, 25 Dec. 1921, DFK.
62. Ginger, *The Bending Cross*, 417–19; *Debs Magazine*, I (Dec. 1921-Jan. 1922), 6, 14.
63. *The Communist*, Apr. 1921, 12. See also Maurer, *It Can Be Done*, 252, for a discussion of the Communist party as the instigator of the "grand old man" theme in an attempt to explain EVD's refusal to join the party.
64. See Draper, *American Communism*, 252–58.
65. Maurer, *It Can Be Done*, 252; Theodore Debs to Oneal, 6 Jan. 1922 [telegram], JO. See also Theodore Debs to Karsner, 15 Feb. 1922, DFK.
66. EVD, "The World is Waiting," *Debs Magazine*, I (Feb. 1922), 4.
67. EVD to O. Branstetter, 25 Mar. 1922, IS.
68. O. Branstetter to EVD, 29 Mar. 1922, EVD to O. Branstetter, 30 Mar. 1922, IS.
69. EVD to O. Branstetter, 25 Mar. 1922, IS; De Ford, *Up-Hill*, 191.
70. Theodore Debs to Karsner, 25 Mar. 1922, DFK.
71. Theodore Debs to Cohen, 8 July 1922, JEC; EVD to Karsner, 12 July 1922, Theodore Debs to Karsner, 29 July 1922, DFK.
72. Karsner to EVD, 27 July 1922, EVD to Karsner, 30 July 1922, Theodore Debs to Karsner, n.d. [1 Aug. 1922], DFK; *The Call*, 27 July 1922. For EVD's response to Communist party criticism, which not only defended his telegram but also attacked "the communists with but few exceptions" for ignoring him and other political prisoners, see EVD to J. Louis Engdahl, 9 Aug. 1922, IS.

73. EVD to Karsner, 23 Aug. 1922, DFK; Schorer, *Sinclair Lewis*, 340–41.
74. See Curry to Karsner, 30 Apr., 4 Nov. 1920, DFK.
75. EVD to Karsner, n.d. [24 July 1922], to Curry, n.d., enclosed in letter of Curry to Karsner, 14 Sept. 1922, to Karsner, 23 Sept. 1922, DFK; to Theodore Debs, 5 Nov. 1922, ISU; "Gene" to "My dearest Love," 5 Nov. 1922, Group III, GG.
76. EVD, "Review and Personal Statement," press release, National Office, Socialist party, 2 Oct. 1922 (copy in DFK).
77. Theodore Debs to Karsner, 3, 12 Jan. 1923, DFK; Theodore Debs to Sinclair, 9 Jan. 1923, US; Theodore Debs to Cohen, 19, 26 Feb. 1923, JEC.
78. EVD to Theodore Debs, 5 Mar., 8 Sept. [1923], ISU.
79. See EVD to Foster, 12 Sept., 8 Oct., 8 Nov. 1923, Foster to EVD, 22 Sept., 7 Nov. 1923, ISU.
80. Pepper, *Underground Radicalism*; Theodore Debs to Cohen, 26 Feb. 1923, JEC. On the Bridgeman convention, see Draper, *American Communism*, 363–75.
81. Gieske, *Minnesota Farm-Laborism*, 86–92; Weinstein, *Decline of Socialism*, 274–78, 290–323; Draper, *American Communism and Soviet Russia*, ch. 5, esp. 113–18.
82. "Minutes of National Convention, Socialist Party, Cleveland, July 6–8, 1924," *Socialist World*, V (July 1924), 9–15; Chicago *Socialist*, 19 July 1924. See also EVD, "A Supplementary Word," *Socialist World*, V (July 1924), 5–6.
83. EVD to Foster, 23 July 1924, reprinted in *New Leader*, 22 Oct. 1933; Foster to EVD, 30 July 1924, ISU. For Foster's account, see his *History of the Communist Party*, 211–24.
84. EVD to Theodore Debs, 18 May [1923], ISU; Wilson to O. Branstetter, 8 Nov. 1923, State of Pennsylvania Records, SPP.
85. John Hagel to O. Branstetter, 6 Aug. 1923, PT.
86. Weinstein, *Decline of Socialism*, 323. On attempts to organize a labor party in Pennsylvania, "provided that the candidates, in all cases, run on the tickets of the Labor Party and Socialist Party only," see *American Appeal*, VII (1 Jan. 1926).
87. EVD to Sinclair, 24 Oct. 1925, US; to Theodore Debs, 31 Mar. 1926, ISU; Claessens, "The American People and the Socialist Party," *Socialist World*, IV (Dec. 1923), 10–11.
88. White to Hillquit, 8 June 1925, George Kirkpatrick to Hillquit, 19 Nov. 1925, MH.
89. McDonald, "The Fighting Debs," JRC.
90. EVD to White, 29 June 1925, ISU.
91. Quoted in *American Appeal*, VII (20 Feb. 1926). For a more incisive view see Hillquit's analysis in the same issue.
92. On EVD's illnesses see Theodore Debs to Karsner, 28 Nov. 1923, 1 Mar. 1924, EVD to Karsner, 19 July, 29 Sept. 1924, DFK; Theodore Debs to Faith Chevaillier, 10 Mar. 1924, 15 Dec. 1925, 4 Feb. 1926, PG; Painter, *That Man Debs*, 155–56.
93. "Gene" to "Dearest," Thursday, A.M., Group III (1922), GG.
94. "Gene" to "Dearest," Thursday, Group III (1924?), GG.
95. Vanzetti to EVD, 29 Sept. 1923, ISU.
96. *American Appeal*, VII (18 Sept. 1926). EVD did not lose his citizenship, although as a convicted felon there was some question concerning his eligibili-

ty to vote. He died before the November election that would have resolved the issue. See Hillquit's legal opinion in *ibid.,*, 24 Apr. 1926.
97. Theodore Debs to Oscar Baur, 21 Dec. 1927, ISU.
98. *American Appeal*, VII (30 Oct. 1926).
99. Marcet Haldeman-Julius, "Funeral," 3–16, and Guy Bogart to Theodore Debs, 22 Oct. 1926, ISU.

Notes to Epilogue

1. Vanzetti to Theodore Debs, 22 July 1927, ISU.
2. Terkel, *American Dreams*, xxv.

Bibliography

Manuscripts

The collections consulted are listed in the guide that precedes the notes. While each collection has something of value, certain of them are indispensable for a study of Eugene V. Debs. The archives at the Cunningham Library, Indiana State University, Terre Haute, is the richest repository of Debs material. Spanning the whole of his life, the nearly 5,000 letters in the collection provide essential material on Debs's personal and public life. The Debs Foundation, located in Debs's home in Terre Haute, has a selection of letters and memorabilia, and it contains the Record Books of Vigo Lodge. The Fairbanks Memorial Library of Terre Haute is an important source for local history and the files of local newspapers. The numerous collections at the Tamiment Institute, Bobst Library, New York University, and at the Wisconsin State Historical Society, Madison, are also invaluable for a study of Debs and the Socialist party. The single most important collection for a study of the party, however, is at the William R. Perkins Library, Duke University, Durham, N.C. This collection contains the records of the national office and the reports of state secretaries and organizers from every region in the nation.

Unfortunately, when Katherine Debs died in 1937, members of her family destroyed the voluminous correspondence of Eugene and Theodore Debs that had remained in the attic since Debs's death in 1926. Informants have suggested that this material was particularly important for an understanding of Debs's pre-Socialist years and especially his trade union organizing during the 1880s. Collections at the Lilly Library, Indiana University, Bloomington, and the Indiana State Library and the Indiana Historical Society, both in Indianapolis, help offset this loss. Finally, the relatively small collection of letters between Debs and Mabel Dunlap Curry are critical for this study. I again thank George Gloss of the Brattle Street Book Store, Boston, for allowing me to read them while in his possession.

Government Documents

Indiana. *Brevier Legislative Reports Embracing Short-Hand Sketches of the Debates and Journals of the General Assembly of the State of Indiana, Regular Session of 1885 and Special Session of 1885,* compiled by W. H. Drapier. 2 vols. Indianapolis, 1885.

New York. *Revolutionary Radicalism: Its History, Purpose and Tactics, with an Exposition and Discussion of the Steps Being Taken and Required to Curb It; Being the Report of the Joint Legislative Committee Investigating Seditious Activities, Filed April 24, 1920, in the Senate of the State of New York.* 4 vols. Albany, 1920.

United States. Bureau of the Census. *Ninth Census of the United States.* 3 vols. Washington, D.C., 1872.

————. *Tenth Census of the United States.* 22 vols. Washington, D.C., 1883.

————. *Twelfth Census of the United States.* 12 vols. Washington, D.C., 1901–3.

————. *Thirteenth Census of the United States.* 11 vols. Washington, D.C., 1913.

United States. Commissioner of Labor. *Third Annual Report, 1887. Strikes and Lockouts.* Washington, D.C., 1888.

————. *Fifth Annual Report, 1889. Railroad Labor.* Washington, D.C., 1890.

————. *Tenth Annual Report, 1894. Strikes and Lockouts.* 2 vols. Washington, D.C., 1896.

United States. 45th Cong., 3d Sess., House Miscellaneous Document 29. *Investigation by a Select Committee of the House of Representatives Relative to the Causes of the General Depression in Labor and Business, Etc.* Washington, D.C., 1879.

————. 46th Cong., 2nd Sess., Senate Report 693. *Report and Testimony of the Select Committee of the United States Senate to Investigate the Causes of the Removal of the Negroes from the Southern States to the Northern States.* Washington, D.C., 1880.

————. 48th Cong., 2nd Sess., Senate Report 1262. *Report of the Committee of the Senate upon the Relations between Labor and Capital, and Testimony Taken by the Committee.* 5 vols. Washington, D.C., 1885.

————. 53rd Cong., 3d Sess., Senate Executive Document 7. *Report on the Chicago Strike of June–July, 1894, by the United States Strike Commission, Appointed by the President, July 26, 1894, under the Provisions of Section 6 of Chapter 1063 of the Laws of the United States Passed October 1, 1888, with Appendices Containing Testimony, Proceedings, and Recommendations.* Washington, D.C., 1895.

————. 55th Cong., 2nd Sess., Senate Report 591. *Carriers Engaged in Interstate Commerce and Their Employees.* Washington, D.C., 1898.

————. 58th Cong., 3d Sess., Senate Document 122. *A Report on Labor Disturbances in the State of Colorado, from 1880 to 1904, Inclusive, with Correspondence Relating Thereto.* Washington, D.C., 1905.

————. 63rd Cong., 1st Sess., Senate Committee on Education and Labor. *Hearings, Conditions in the Paint Creek District, West Virginia.* 3 vols. Washington, D.C., 1913.

Newspapers and Journals

American Appeal (Chicago), 1926–27.

American Labor Union Journal (Butte, Mont.), 1902–4.

Appeal to Reason (Girard, Kans.), 1896–1917.

Brotherhood of Locomotive Firemen's Magazine (Terre Haute), 1876–95.

The Class Struggle (New York), 1917–19.

The Coming Nation (Girard, Kans.), 1910–11.

The Comrade (New York), 1901–5.

Debs Magazine (Chicago), 1921–23.

International Socialist Review (Chicago), 1900–1918.
The Melting Pot (St. Louis), 1913–20.
New Occasions (Chicago), 1897.
The New Review (New York), 1913–16.
The New Time (Chicago), 1897–98.
The Party Builder (Chicago), 1912–14.
Railroad Trainmen's Journal (Galesburg, Ill.), 1890.
The Railway Times (Terre Haute), 1894–97.
The Rebel (Hallettsville, Tex.), 1912–17.
Revolt (San Francisco), 1911–12.
Social Democrat (Chicago), 1897–98.
Social Democratic Herald (Chicago, Milwaukee), 1898–1913.
The Socialist World (Chicago), 1920–25.
The Switchmen's Journal (Chicago), 1888–90.
Terre Haute *Evening Gazette*, 1875–96.
Terre Haute *Express*, 1875–85.
Terre Haute *Tribune*, 1908–26.
Voice of Labor (Chicago), 1905.

Books, Articles, and Pamphlets

Abbott, Lyman. "Reminiscences. A Mid-Western Parish during the Civil War." *The Outlook*, 23 Sept. 1914, 203–20.
Abell, Aaron I. "The Reception of Leo XIII's Labor Encyclical in America, 1891–1919." *Review of Politics*, VII (Oct. 1945), 464–95.
Adams, Frederick B., Jr. *Radical Literature in America*. Stamford, Conn., 1939.
Advantages of Terre Haute, Ind., as a Point for the Manufacture of Iron. Terre Haute, 1870.
Aldred, Guy A. *Convict 9653: America's Vision Maker*. Glasgow, Scotland, n.d.
Allen, Devere, ed. *Adventurous Americans*. New York, 1932.
Allen, Ruth A. *East Texas Lumber Workers: An Economic and Social Picture*. Austin, 1961.
_____. *The Great Southwest Strike*. Austin, 1942.
Alley, John. *City Beginnings in Oklahoma Territory*. Norman, Okla., 1939.
Ambler, Charles Henry. *West Virginia, the Mountain State*. New York, 1940.
American Federation of Labor. *Industrial Unionism in Its Relation to Trade Unionism*. Washington, D.C., 1912.
American Labor Union. *Proceedings of the Fifth Annual Convention . . . Held at Denver, Colorado May 26th to June 7th, 1902*. Denver, 1902.
American Railway Union. *Constitution*. Chicago, 1893.
_____. *Declaration of Principles, Embracing All Classes of Railway Employes*. Chicago, 1893.
_____. *Proceedings, First Quadrennial Convention*. Chicago, 1894.
Ameringer, Oscar. *Communism, Socialism and the Church: An Historical Survey*. Milwaukee, 1913.
_____. *If You Don't Weaken—The Autobiography of Oscar Ameringer*. New York, 1940.
_____. *Socialism for the Farmer*. St. Louis, n.d.
_____. *Socialism: What It Is and How to Get It*. Chicago, 1913.
Amsden, John, and Stephen Brier. "Coal Miners on Strike: The Transformation

of Strike Demands and the Formation of a National Union." *Journal of Interdisciplinary History*, VII (Spring 1977), 583–616.

Appeal to Reason. *Appeal Answers to Questions about Socialism*. Girard, Kans., 1914.

———. *An Evening in Girard*. Girard, Kans., 1908.

———. *Wayland's Undelivered Address*. Girard, Kans., 1913.

Balsley, Howard L. "Indiana Iron from Native Ore." *Indiana Magazine of History*, XLV (Dec. 1949), 353–68.

Baritz, Loren, ed. *The American Left: Radical Political Thought in the Twentieth Century*. New York, 1971.

Bastian, Robert W. "Architecture and Class Segregation in Late Nineteenth-Century Terre Haute, Indiana." *Geographical Review*, LXV (Apr. 1975), 166–79.

Beckwith, H. W. *History of Vigo and Parke Counties*. Chicago, 1880.

Bedford, Henry F. *Socialism and the Workers in Massachusetts, 1886–1912*. Amherst, Mass., 1966.

Behrman, S. N. *The Worcester Account, Early Reminiscences*. London, 1954.

Bell, Daniel. *Marxian Socialism in the United States*. Princeton, 1967.

Bellah, Robert N. *The Broken Covenant: American Civil Religion in Time of Trial*. New York, 1975.

———. "Civil Religion in America." In Russell E. Richey and Donald G. Jones, eds., *American Civil Religion*. New York, 1974.

Bellamy, Edward. *Plutocracy or Nationalism—Which?* Boston, 1899.

Benson, Allan L. *The New Henry Ford*. New York, 1923.

Berkman, Alexander, and Emma Goldman. *Deportation: Its Meaning and Menace*. New York, 1919.

Beste, J. Richard. *The Wabash: Or Adventures of an English Gentleman's Family in the Interior of America*. 2 vols. London, 1855.

Bestor, Arthur. *Backwoods Utopias: The Sectarian Origins and the Owenite Phase of Communitarian Socialism in America, 1663–1829*. Philadelphia, 1970.

A Biographical History of Eminent and Self-Made Men of the State of Indiana. Cincinnati, 1880.

Bizzell, W. B. *The Green Rising*. New York, 1926.

Blackburn, Glen C. "Interurban Railroads of Indiana." *Indiana Magazine of History*, XX (Sept. 1924), 221–79; (Dec. 1924), 400–464.

Bloomfield, Maxwell H. *Alarms and Diversions: The American Mind through American Magazines, 1900–1914*. The Hague, 1967.

Bloor, Ella Reeve. *We Are Many*. New York, 1940.

Bockstahler, Oscar L. "Contributions to American Literature by Hoosiers of German Ancestry." *Indiana Magazine of History*, XXXVIII (Sept. 1942), 231–50.

Bogardus, Frank Smith. "Daniel W. Voorhees." *Indiana Magazine of History*, XXVII (June 1931), 91–103.

Bogue, Donald J., and Calvin L. Beale. *Economic Areas of the United States*. New York, 1961.

Bohn, Frank, and Father Thomas McGrady. *The Catholic Church and Socialism*. Chicago, n.d.

Bolino, August. "American Socialism's Flood and Ebb." *American Journal of Economics and Sociology*, XXII (Apr. 1963), 287–301.

Boyle, O. D. *History of Railroad Strikes*. Washington, D.C., 1935.

Bradsby, H. C. *History of Vigo County, Indiana with Biographical Selections.* Chicago, 1891.

Braverman, Harry. *Labor and Monopoly Capital: The Degradation of Work in the Twentieth Century.* New York, 1976.

Brewer, George D. *The Fighting Editor, or Warren and the Appeal.* Girard, Kans., 1910.

_____. *The Rights of the Masses.* Chicago, n.d.

_____. *The Wayland I Knew.* Girard, Kans., n.d.

Brissenden, Paul F. *The I.W.W. A Study of American Syndicalism.* New York, 1957.

Brock, Peter. *Pacificism in the United States from the Colonial Era to the First World War.* Princeton, 1968.

Brommel, Bernard J. "Eugene V. Debs: The Agitator as Speaker." *Central States Speech Journal* (Fall 1969), 202–14.

_____. *Eugene V. Debs: Spokesman for Labor and Socialism.* Chicago, 1978.

_____. "The Pacifist Speechmaking of Eugene V. Debs." *Quarterly Journal of Speech*, LII (Apr. 1966), 146–54.

Brotherhood of Locomotive Firemen. *Journal of the Proceedings of the First Twelve Annual Conventions of the Brotherhood of Locomotive Firemen from 1874 to 1885, Inclusive.* Terre Haute, 1885.

_____. *Journal of Proceedings of the Thirteenth Annual Convention.* Terre Haute, 1886.

_____. *Journal of Proceedings of the First Biennial Convention (Fourteenth Convention).* Terre Haute, 1888.

_____. *Journal of Proceedings of the Second Biennial Convention (Fifteenth Convention).* Terre Haute, 1890.

_____. *Journal of Proceedings of the Third Biennial Convention (Sixteenth Convention).* Terre Haute, 1892.

_____. *Journal of Proceedings of the Fourth Biennial Convention (Seventeenth Convention).* Terre Haute, 1894.

Broun, Heywood. *It Seems to Me, 1925–1935.* New York, 1935. Reprinted from the New York *World*, 23 Oct. 1926.

Bruce, Robert V. *1877: Year of Violence.* Indianapolis, 1959.

Bryan, William Jennings. *The First Battle.* Chicago, 1896.

Buchanan, Joseph R. *The Story of a Labor Agitator.* New York, 1903.

Buder, Stanley. *Pullman, an Experiment in Industrial Order and Community Planning, 1880–1930.* New York, 1974.

Buhle, Mari Jo. "Women and the Socialist Party, 1901–1914." *Radical America*, IV (Feb. 1970), 36–55.

Buhle, Paul. "Debsian Socialism and the 'New Immigrant' Workers." In William L. O'Neill, ed., *Insights and Parallels: Problems and Issues of American Social History.* Minneapolis, 1973.

_____. "Intellectuals in the Debsian Socialist Party." *Radical America*, IV (Apr. 1970), 35–58.

Burbank, David T. *Reign of the Rabble. The St. Louis General Strike of 1877.* New York, 1966.

Burbank, Garin. "Agrarian Radicals and Their Opponents: Political Conflict in Southern Oklahoma, 1910–1924." *Journal of American History*, LVIII (June 1971), 5–23.

_____. "The Disruption and Decline of the Oklahoma Socialist Party." *Journal of American Studies*, VII (Aug. 1973), 133–52.

Burke, William Maxwell. *History and Functions of Central Labor Unions.* New York, 1899.

Burley, R. C. "The Campaign of 1888 in Indiana." *Indiana Magazine of History,* X (June 1914), 30–53.

Cady, John F. *The Origin and Development of the Missionary Baptist Church in Indiana.* Franklin, Ind., 1942.

Calverton, V. F. "Eugene Debs and American Radicalism." *Common Sense* (July 1933), 10–13.

Cannon, James P. *The First Ten Years of American Communism.* New York, 1962.

———. "The Revolutionary Heritage of Eugene Victor Debs." *Labor Defender* (Dec. 1926), 210–11.

Cantor, Milton. *The Divided Left: American Radicalism, 1900–1975.* New York, 1978.

———. "The Radical Confrontation with Foreign Policy: War and Revolution, 1914–1920." In Alfred F. Young, ed., *Dissent: Explorations in the History of American Radicalism.* DeKalb, Ill., 1968.

Carmony, Donald F. *A Brief History of Indiana.* Indianapolis, 1966.

———. "The Hoosiers and Their Heritage." In Donald F. Carmony, ed., *Indiana, a Self-Appraisal.* Bloomington, 1966.

Carver, Thomas Nixon, ed. *Selected Readings in Rural Economics.* New York, 1916.

Carwardine, Rev. William H. *The Pullman Strike.* Chicago, 1973.

Chandler, Alfred D., Jr. *The Visible Hand: The Mangerial Revolution in American Business.* Cambridge, Mass., 1977.

Chaplin, Ralph. *Wobbly: The Rough and Tumble Story of an American Radical.* Chicago, 1948.

Chatfield, Charles. "World War I and the Liberal Pacifist in the United States." *American Historical Review,* LXXV (Dec. 1970), 1920–37.

Chicago Federation of Labor. *The Causes of Industrial Panics in the United States.* Chicago, 1903.

Christie, Robert A. *Empire in Wood: A History of the Carpenters' Union.* Ithaca, N.Y., 1956.

Citizens' Protective League. *Address. Constitution, By-Laws and List of Members.* Terre Haute, 1902.

Claessens, August. *Didn't We Have Fun!* New York, 1953.

———. *Eugene Victor Debs: A Tribute.* New York, 1946.

Clemens, G. C. *A Primer on Socialism.* Terre Haute, 1900.

Coleman, McAlister. *Eugene V. Debs, a Man Unafraid.* New York, 1930.

Cometti, Elizabeth, and Festus P. Summers. *The Thirty-Fifth State: A Documentary History of West Virginia.* Morgantown, 1966.

Commons, John R., ed. *History of Labour in the United States.* 2 vols. New York, 1918.

———. "Karl Marx and Samuel Gompers." *Political Science Quarterly,* XLI (June 1926), 281–86.

Condit, Blackford. *The History of Early Terre Haute from 1816–1840.* New York, 1900.

Conger-Kaneko, Josephine. *Woman's Slavery: Her Road to Freedom.* Chicago, n.d.

Conlin, Joseph R. *American Anti-War Movements.* Beverly Hills, 1968.

_____. *Big Bill Haywood and the Radical Union Movement.* Syracuse, N.Y., 1969.

Cooper, Jerry M. "The Army as Strikebreaker—The Railroad Strikes of 1877 and 1894." *Labor History,* 18 (1977), 179-96.

Corbin, David A. "Betrayal in the West Virginia Coal Fields: Eugene V. Debs and the Socialist Party of America, 1912-1914." *Journal of American History,* LXIV (1978), 987-1009.

Cox, Sanford C. *Recollections of the Early Settlement of the Wabash Valley.* Lafayette, Ind., 1860.

Cumback, Will, and J. B. Maynard, eds. *Men of Progress. Indiana.* Indianapolis, 1899.

Cummins, Cedric C. *Indiana Public Opinion and the World War (1914-1917).* Indianapolis, 1945.

Currie, Harold W. "The Religious Views of Eugene V. Debs." *Mid-America,* LIV (1972), 147-56.

Curry, Mabel Dunlap. *The Woman with a Message.* Terre Haute, n.d.

Cutshall, Alden. "Terre Haute Iron and Steel: A Declining Industry." *Indiana Magazine of History,* XXXVII (1941), 237-44.

Dacus, J. A. *Annals of the Great Strikes in the United States. A Reliable History and Graphic Description of the Causes and Thrilling Events of the Labor Strikes and Riots of 1877.* St. Louis, 1877.

Daniels, Wylie J. *The Village at the End of the Road. A Chapter in Early Indiana Railroad History.* Indianapolis, 1938.

Dannenberg, Karl. *Reform or Revolution, or Socialism and Socialist Politics.* New York, 1918.

Darrow, Clarence S. *Farmington.* Chicago, 1904.

_____. *The Story of My Life.* New York, 1934.

David, Henry. *The History of the Haymarket Affair.* New York, 1963.

Debs, Eugene V. "Address." *Searchlight Library,* I (Nov. 1894).

_____. *The American Movement.* Terre Haute, 1904.

_____. "Confederation of Labor Organizations Essential to Labor's Prosperity." *American Journal of Politics* (July 1892), 63-71.

_____. *Debs: His Life, Writings, and Speeches.* Chicago, 1908.

_____. *The Debs Trilogy: Man, Woman, Child,* edited by Lincoln Phifer. New York, 1917.

_____. *The Fight for Liberty.* Chicago, n.d. [1918].

_____. *The Growth of Socialism.* Chicago, n.d.

_____. *Jesus, the Supreme Leader.* Girard, Kans., n.d.

_____. *Labor and Freedom. The Voice and Pen of Eugene V. Debs,* edited by Phil Wagner. St. Louis, 1916.

_____. *The Negro Workers.* New York, 1923.

_____. *Pastels of Men,* edited by Frank Harris. New York, 1919.

_____. *Remarks at the Reception and Banquet of Hulman & Company.* Terre Haute, 1893.

_____. *Riley, Nye and Field.* N.p., 1914.

_____. "Robert G. Ingersoll." *American Journal of Politics* (Feb. 1893), 198-202.

_____. "The Social Democratic Party." *The Independent,* 23 Aug. 1900, 2018-21.

_____. "The Social Democratic Party's Appeal." *The Independent,* 13 Oct. 1904, 835-40.

———. *The Socialist Party and the Working Class.* Chicago, 1904.

———. *Tribute of Love to His Father and Mother.* Terre Haute, 1899.

———. *Unionism and Socialism.* Terre Haute, 1904.

———. *Unity and Victory.* Chicago, 1910.

———. *Walls and Bars.* Chicago, 1973.

———. *Woman . . . Comrade and Equal.* Girard, Kans., n.d.

———. *Writings and Speeches of Eugene V. Debs,* with an introduction by Arthur M. Schlesinger, Jr. New York, 1948.

———. *You Railroad Men.* Chicago, n.d.

De Caux, Len. *Labor Radical: From the Wobblies to CIO.* Boston, 1970.

De Ford, Miriam Allen. *Up-Hill All the Way: The Life of Maynard Shepley.* Yellow Springs, Ohio, 1956.

DeLeon, Daniel. *Woman's Suffrage.* New York, 1911.

———, and Eugene V. Debs. *Industrial Unionism.* New York, 1921.

De Leon, David. "The American as Anarchist: Social Criticism in the 1960s." *American Quarterly,* XXV (Dec. 1973), 516–37.

Derthick, Martha. *The National Guard in Politics.* Cambridge, Mass., 1965.

Destler, Chester McArthur. *American Radicalism, 1865–1901.* Chicago, 1966.

———. *Henry Demarest Lloyd and the Empire of Reform.* Philadelphia, 1963.

Deutscher, Isaac. *The Prophet Armed, Trotsky: 1879–1921.* New York, 1954.

Dombrowski, James. *The Early Days of Christian Socialism in America.* New York, 1936.

Draper, Theodore. *American Communism and Soviet Russia.* New York, 1960.

———. *The Roots of American Communism.* New York, 1966.

Dreiser, Theodore. *Dawn.* New York, 1931.

Dubofsky, Melvyn. "Success and Failure of Socialism in New York City, 1900–1918: A Case Study." *Labor History,* IX (Fall 1968), 361–75.

———. *We Shall Be All: A History of the IWW.* Chicago, 1969.

———. *When Workers Organize.* Amherst, Mass., 1968.

Dulles, Foster Rhea. *Labor in America.* Northbrook, Ill., 1966.

Dunn, Jacob Piatt. *Memorial and Genealogical Record of Representative Citizens of Indiana.* Indianapolis, 1912.

Dunning, N. A., ed. *The Farmers' Alliance History & Agricultural Digest.* Washington, D.C., 1891.

Duss, John S. *The Harmonists: A Personal History.* Harrisburg, Pa., 1943.

Eastman, Max. "The Chicago Conventions." *The Liberator,* Oct. 1919, 5–19.

———. *Heroes I Have Known.* New York, 1942.

———. *The Trial of Eugene Debs.* New York, n.d.

Eckler, A. Ross, and Jack Zlotnick. "Immigration and the Labor Force." *Annals of the American Academy of Political and Social Science,* CCLXII (1949), 92–101.

Ehrmann, Bertha. "Reminiscences of Max Ehrmann." *Indiana Magazine of History,* XLVI (Sept. 1950), 249–58.

———, ed. *The Journal of Max Ehrmann.* Boston, 1952.

Elliott, John L. "Eugene V. Debs, the Man." *The Standard* (Dec. 1926), 104–6.

Engdahl, John Louis. *Debs and O'Hare in Prison.* Chicago, n.d. [1919].

Esarey, Logan. *History of Indiana from Its Exploration to 1922. Also an Account of Vigo County from Its Organization,* edited by William F. Cronin. 3 vols. Dayton, Ohio, 1922.

Estes, George. *Railway Employees United: A Story of Railroad Brotherhoods.* Portland, Oreg., 1931.

Evans, David Owen. *Social Romanticism in France, 1830–1848.* London, 1951.

Faulkner, Harold U. *American Economic History.* New York, 1924.

Federation of Organized Trades and Labor Unions of the United States and Canada. *Report of the First Annual Session . . . held in Pittsburgh, Pennsylvania, on November 15, 16, 17 and 18, 1881.* Cincinnati, 1882.

———. *Report of the Third Annual Session of the Federation of Organized Trades and Labor Unions of the United States and Canada, Held in New York City, N.Y., August 21, 22, 23 and 24, 1883.* Cambridge, Mass., 1883.

Fenton, Edwin. *Immigrants and Unions, a Case Study: Italians and American Labor, 1870–1920.* New York, 1975.

Fetherling, Dale. *Mother Jones: The Miner's Angel, a Portrait.* Carbondale, Ill., 1974.

Finley, George W. "A Quaker Pioneer in Indiana: James Milton Finley." *Indiana Magazine of History,* XXVI (Mar. 1930), 34–42.

Finn, J. F. "AF of L Leaders and the Question of Politics in the Early 1890s." *Journal of American Studies,* VII (Dec. 1973), 243–65.

Flynn, Elizabeth Gurley. *Debs, Haywood, Ruthenberg.* New York, 1939.

———. *The Rebel Girl, an Autobiography: My First Life (1906–1926).* New York, 1973.

Foner, Philip S. *History of the Labor Movement in the United States.* 4 vols. New York, 1965.

Foreman, Grant. *A History of Oklahoma.* Norman, Okla., 1942.

Foster, William Z. *From Bryan to Stalin.* New York, 1937.

———. *History of the Communist Party of the United States.* New York, 1952.

Foulke, W. D. *A Review of the Indiana General Assembly, Regular and Special Sessions, 1884–5.* Indianapolis, 1886.

Fox, Dixon Ryan, ed. *Sources of Culture in the Middle West Background Versus Frontier.* New York, 1934.

Fredrickson, George. *The Inner Civil War: Northern Intellectuals and the Crisis of Union.* New York, 1968.

Freeman, Joseph. *An American Testament, a Narrative of Rebels and Romantics.* New York, 1936.

Fritsch, William A. *German Settlers and German Settlements in Indiana.* Evansville, Ind., 1915.

Frumerman, Harry. "The Railroad Strikes of 1885–86." *Marxist Quarterly,* I (Oct.–Nov. 1937), 394–405.

Gabriel, Ralph H. "Evangelical Religion and Popular Romanticism in Early Nineteenth Century America." *Church History,* XIX (Mar. 1950), 34–47.

Garraty, John A. *The New Commonwealth, 1877–1890.* New York, 1968.

Gaston, Herbert E. *The Nonpartisan League.* New York, 1920.

Gavett, Thomas W. *Development of the Labor Movement in Milwaukee.* Madison, 1965.

Gedicks, Al. "The Social Origins of Radicalism among Finnish Immigrants in Midwest Mining Communities." *Review of Radical Political Economics,* VIII (1976), 1–31.

Gephart, Ronald M. "Politicians, Soldiers and Strike: The Reorganization of the Nebraska Militia and the Omaha Strike of 1882." *Nebraska History,* 46 (Mar. 1965), 89–120.

Ghent, W. J. "Feudalism or Individualism." *The Independent,* 10 July 1902, 1647–50.

———. *To Skeptics and Doubters.* New York, 1911.

————. "Why Socialists Are Partisans." *The Independent*, 26 Oct. 1905, 967–71.

Gieske, Millard L. *Minnesota Farmer-Laborism: The Third-Party Alternative.* Minneapolis, 1979.

Gilbert, James. *Designing the Industrial State: The Intellectual Pursuit of Collectivism in America, 1880–1940.* Chicago, 1972.

Gillmore, Parker. *Prairie Farms and Prairie Folk.* 2 vols. London, 1872.

Gilman, Nicholas Paine. *Socialism and the American Spirit.* Boston, 1893.

Ginger, Ray. *The Bending Cross: A Biography of Eugene Victor Debs.* New Brunswick, N.J., 1949.

Glaser, William A. "Algie Martin Simons and Marxism in America." *Mississippi Valley Historical Review*, XLI (Dec. 1945), 419–34.

Glück, Elsie. *John Mitchell, Miner: Labor's Bargain with the Gilded Age.* New York, 1929.

Goldberg, Harvey, ed. *American Radicals.* New York, 1957.

Goldwater, Walter. *Radical Periodicals in America, 1890–1950.* New Haven, 1964.

Gompers, Samuel. *The American Labor Movement: Its Makeup, Achievements and Inspirations.* Washington, D.C., 1914.

————. *America's Fight for the Preservation of Democracy.* New York, 1917.

————. *Eight Hours: The Workers and the Eight-Hour Work Day and the Shorter Workday, Its Philosophy.* Washington, D.C., 1915.

————. *Real Farmers vs. Professional Farmers.* Washington, D.C., 1920.

————. *Seventy Years of Life and Labor.* 2 vols. New York, 1925.

————. *Socialist Methods versus Trade Union Methods.* Washington, D.C., 1912.

Goodwyn, Lawrence. *Democratic Promise: The Populist Movement in America.* New York, 1976.

Goren, Arthur. "A Portrait of Ethnic Politics: The Socialists and the 1908 and 1910 Congressional Elections on the East Side." In Joel H. Silbey and Samuel T. McSeveney, eds., *Voters, Parties and Elections.* Lexington, Mass., 1972.

Green, James R. *Grass-Roots Socialism: Radical Movements in the Southwest, 1895–1943.* Baton Rouge, 1978.

"Grocer's Progress: An Indiana Story." *Fortune*, 45 (Jan. 1952), 72–73, 120–24.

Gronlund, Laurence, G. C. Clemens, and G. A. Hoehn. *Three in One: A Trinity of Arguments in Favor of Social Democracy.* Chicago, 1898.

Gresham, Matilda. *Life of Walter Quintin Gresham, 1832–1895.* 2 vols. Chicago, 1919.

Gutman, Herbert G. "Protestantism and the American Labor Movement: The Christian Spirit in the Gilded Age." In his *Work, Culture and Society in Industrializing America.* New York, 1976.

————. "The Worker's Search for Power: Labor in the Gilded Age." In H. Wayne Morgan, ed., *The Gilded Age: A Reappraisal.* Syracuse, N.Y., 1963.

Haber, Samuel. *Efficiency and Uplift: Scientific Management in the Progressive Era, 1890–1920.* Chicago, 1964.

Haldeman-Julius, Emmanuel. *My Second 25 Years: Instead of a Footnote an Autobiography.* Girard, Kans., 1949.

————, and Marcet Haldeman-Julius. *Dust.* New York, 1921.

Haldeman-Julius, Marcet. "The Funeral of Eugene V. Debs." *Haldeman-Julius Monthly*, Dec. 1926, 3–16, 126.

Haller, John S., and Robin M. Haller. *The Physician and Sexuality in Victorian America.* Urbana, Ill., 1974.

Hanford, Ben. *Fight For Your Life!* New York, 1909.

Hassam, Loren. *An Historical Sketch of Terre Haute, Ind., Its Advantages for Manufacture and Attractions as a Home.* Terre Haute, 1873.

Hawthorne, Julian. *The Subterranean Brotherhood.* New York, 1914.

Haywood, William D. *Bill Haywood's Book: The Autobiography of William D. Haywood.* New York, 1958.

_____, and Frank Bohn. *Industrial Socialism.* Chicago, 1911.

Headley, John T. *Pen and Pencil Sketches of the Great Riots.* New York, 1877.

Hendrickson, Gordon O. "The Red Special in Colorado." *Colorado Magazine,* LI (Summer 1974), 216–27.

Hendrickson, Kenneth E., Jr. "Tribune of the People: George R. Lunn and the Rise and Fall of Christian Socialism in Schenectady." In Bruce M. Stave, ed. *Socialism and the Cities.* Port Washington, N.Y., 1975.

Herron, George D. *The Day of Judgement.* Chicago, 1904.

_____. *Social Meanings of Religious Experience,* edited by Timothy L. Smith, New York, 1969.

_____. *Why I Am a Socialist.* Chicago, 1900.

Hesseltine, William B. *Third-Party Movements in the United States.* Princeton, 1962.

Hibben, Rev. W. W. *Rev. James Havens, One of the Heroes of Indiana Methodism.* Indianapolis, 1872.

Hickey, T. A. *The Land?* Hallettsville, Tex., n.d.

Hicks, Granville. *John Reed: The Making of a Revolutionary.* New York, 1936.

Higham, John. *Send These to Me: Jews and Other Immigrants in Urban America.* New York, 1975.

_____. *Strangers in the Land: Patterns of American Nativism, 1860–1925.* New York, 1967.

Hillquit, Morris. *History of Socialism in the United States.* New York, 1910.

_____. *Loose Leaves from a Busy Life.* New York, 1934.

Hilton, George W., and John F. Due. *The Electric Interurban Railways in America.* Stanford, 1960.

Hinrichs, A. F. *The United Mine Workers of America and the Non-Union Coal Fields.* New York, 1923.

Holbrook, Stewart H. *James J. Hill, a Great Life in Brief.* New York, 1955.

Holliday, Rev. F. C. *Indiana Methodism: Introduction, Progress, and Present Position of Methodism in the State.* Cincinnati, 1873.

Holmes, John Haynes. "Debs—Lover of Men." *Unity,* 15 Nov. 1926, 165–68.

_____. *I Speak for Myself: The Autobiography of John Haynes Holmes.* New York, 1959.

Hook, Sidney. "A Gallant American Rebel." New York *Times Book Review,* 17 July 1949.

Houstoun, Mrs. M. C. F. *Hesperos: or Travels in the West.* 2 vols. London, 1850.

Howe, Henry. *Historical Collections of Ohio.* 2 vols. Cincinnati, 1902.

Howe, Irving. "An Answer to Critics of American Socialism, an Analysis of Their Method and Politics." *The New International,* XVIII (May-June 1952), 115–52.

_____. *World of Our Fathers.* New York, 1976.

_____, and Louis Coser. *The American Communist Party. A Critical History.* New York, 1962.

Hubbard, Kim, ed. *A Book of Indiana.* Indianapolis, 1929.

Hunter, Robert. *Scabs Are Scabs.* New Orleans, 1913.

Hurt, Walter. *Eugene V. Debs. An Introduction.* Williamsburg, Ohio, n.d.

Iglehart, John E. "The Life and Times of John Shrader, including the Introduction and Progress of Methodism in Southwestern Indiana." *Indiana Magazine of History,* XVII (May 1921), 3–49; XVII (June 1921), 118–49.

Industrial Brotherhood of the United States. *Constitution and Rules of Order.* Cleveland, 1874.

Industrial Workers of the World. *Proceedings. The Founding Convention of the IWW.* New York, 1905.

Ingalls & Company, comp. *The Advantages and Attractions of Terre Haute, Indiana, as a Business and Manufacturing Center, Its Educational Institutions, and Review of Its Growth and Progress, with Business Directory and Statistical Tables.* Terre Haute, 1872.

Jensen, Vernon H. *Heritage of Conflict: Labor Relations in the Nonferrous Metals Industry up to 1930.* Ithaca, N.Y., 1950.

Jobson, Rev. Frederick J. *America and American Methodism.* New York, 1857.

Johnson, Oakley C., ed. *An American Century: The Recollections of Bertha W. Howe, 1866–1966.* New York, 1966.

Jones, Howard Mumford, and Walter B. Rideout, eds. *Letters of Sherwood Anderson.* Boston, 1953.

Jones, Mary. *The Autobiography of Mother Jones.* Chicago, 1972.

Jordan, Philip D. *The National Road.* Gloucester, Mass., 1966.

Joseph, Samuel. *Jewish Immigration to the United States, from 1881 to 1910.* New York, 1914.

Karni, Michael G., Matti E. Kaups, and Douglas J. Ollila, eds. *The Finnish Experience in the Western Great Lakes Region: New Perspectives.* Turku, Finland, 1975.

Karsner, David F. *Debs Goes to Prison.* New York, 1919.

_____. *Debs, His Authorized Life and Letters.* New York, 1919.

_____. *Talks with Debs in Terre Haute.* New York, 1922.

Karson, Marc. *American Labor Unions and Politics, 1900–1918.* Carbondale, Ill., 1958.

Kaufman, Stuart Bruce. *Samuel Gompers and the Origins of the American Federation of Labor, 1848–1896.* Westport, Conn., 1973.

Kazin, Alfred. *On Native Grounds.* Garden City, N.Y., 1956.

Kelley, O. H. *Origin and Progress of the Order of the Patrons of Husbandry in the United States: A History from 1866 to 1873.* Philadelphia, 1875.

Kero, Reino. *Migration from Finland to North America in the Years between the United States Civil War and the First World War.* Turku, Finland, 1974.

Kerr, Charles. *A Socialist Publishing House.* Chicago, 1904.

_____. *What Socialism Is.* Chicago, n.d.

_____. *What to Read on Socialism.* Chicago, 1906.

Kerr, May Walden. *Socialism and the Home.* Chicago, 1901.

Kipnis, Ira. *The American Socialist Movement, 1897–1912.* New York, 1972.

Koenig, Louis W. *Bryan, a Political Biography of William Jennings Bryan.* New York, 1971.

Kolehmainen, John I., and George W. Hill. *Haven in the Woods: The Story of the Finns in Wisconsin.* Madison, 1965.

Kopelin, Louis. *The Life of Debs.* Girard, Kans., n.d. [1920].

Korman, Gerd. *Industrialization, Immigrants and Americanizers: The View from Milwaukee, 1866–1921.* Madison, 1967.

Kostiainen, Auvo. *The Forging of Finnish-American Communism, 1917–1924. A Study in Ethnic Radicalism.* Turku, Finland, 1978.

Kreuter, Kent, and Gretchen Kreuter. *An American Dissenter. The Life of Algie Martin Simons, 1870–1950.* Lexington, Ky., 1969.

Kuhns, Frederick. "A Sketch of Congregationalism in Indiana to 1858." *Indiana Magazine of History,* XLII (Dec. 1946), 343–52.

La Monte, Robert Rives, and Louis C. Fraina. *The Socialist Attitude on the War.* New York, 1917.

Lasch, Christopher. *The Agony of the American Left.* New York, 1969.

Laslett, John H. *Labor and the Left.* New York, 1970.

———, and Seymour Martin Lipset, eds. *Failure of a Dream? Essays in the History of American Socialism.* Garden City, N.Y., 1974.

Lee, Robert, and Martin E. Marty, eds. *Religion and Social Conflict.* New York, 1964.

Leibowitz, Irving. *My Indiana.* Englewood Cliffs, N.J., 1964.

Leinenweber, Charles. "The American Socialist Party and 'New' Immigrants." *Science & Society,* XXXII (Winter 1968), 1–25.

Lenin, N. *A Letter to American Workingmen.* Brooklyn, 1918.

Le Prade, Ruth, ed. *Debs and the Poets.* Pasadena, Calif., 1920.

Lewis, Lena Morrow. *The Socialist Party and Women Suffrage.* Chicago, n.d.

Liebman, Arthur. *Jews and the Left.* New York, 1979.

Lilenthal, Meta Stern. *Women of the Future.* New York, 1916.

Lindsey, Almont. *The Pullman Strike.* Chicago, 1967.

Lindstrom, David Edgar. *American Farmers and Rural Organizations,* edited by Herbert M. Hamlin. Champaign, Ill., 1948.

Lingenfelter, Richard E. *The Hard Rock Miners. A History of the Mining Labor Movement in the American West, 1863–1893.* Berkeley, 1974.

Lippincott, J. B., and Company. *A Complete Pronouncing Gazetteer or Geographical Dictionary of the World.* Philadelphia, 1893.

Lippmann, Walter. "On Municipal Socialism, 1913: An Analysis of Problems and Strategies." In Bruce M. Stave, ed., *Socialism and the Cities.* Port Washington, N.Y., 1975.

Litwack, Leon F. *North of Slavery.* Chicago, 1961.

Lizabeth. *The Key That Fits the Lock: Or Justice to the Toiler.* Girard, Kans., 1902.

Llano del Rio Colony. *Co-operation in Action.* Los Angeles, 1914.

Lloyd, Henry Demarest. *Men, the Workers.* New York, 1909.

———. *The Safety of the Future Lies in Organized Labor.* Chicago, 1893.

Lloyd, William Bross. *The Socialist Party and Its Purposes.* Chicago, 1918.

London, Jack. *The Dream of Debs.* Chicago, n.d. [1910].

Lowe, Caroline A. *The Wage-Earning Woman and the Ballot.* Chicago, n.d.

McCaleb, Walter F. *Brotherhood of Railroad Trainmen.* New York, 1936.

MacCartney, Frederic O. *The Old Slavery and the New.* Rockland, Mass., 1896.

McGuire, P[eter] J. "The American Federation of Labor—Its History and Aims." In William Trant, ed., *Trade Unions: Their Origin and Objects, Influence and Efficiency.* Washington, D.C., 1915.

McMurry, Donald L. *Coxey's Army: A Study of the Industrial Army Movement of 1894.* Seattle, 1969.

———. "Federation of the Railroad Brotherhoods, 1889–1894." *Industrial and Labor Relations Review,* VII (Oct. 1953), 73–92.

_____. *The Great Burlington Strike of 1888: A Case History in Labor Relations.* Cambridge, Mass., 1956.

McNaught, Kenneth. "American Progressives and the Great Society." *Journal of American History*, LIII (Dec. 1966), 504–20.

McNeill, George E. *The Philosophy of the Labor Movement.* Chicago, n.d. [1893].

McWhiney, Grady. "Louisiana Socialists in the Early Twentieth Century: A Study of Rustic Radicalism." *Journal of Southern History*, XX (Aug. 1954), 315–36.

McWilliams, Wilson Carey. *The Idea of Fraternity in America.* Berkeley, 1973.

Malkiel, Theresa S. *To the Union Man's Wife.* Chicago, n.d.

_____. *Why You Should Be a Socialist.* Chicago, n.d.

_____. *Woman and Freedom.* Milwaukee, n.d.

Marcy, Mary. *A Free Union.* Chicago, 1921.

Markham, Edwin. "Labor Hopeless and Hopeful." *The Independent*, 8 Feb. 1900, 353–55.

Markle, Augustus R. "Historical Fiction and Fictitious History." *Indiana Magazine of History*, XLV (June 1949), 173–74.

Martin, Edward Winslow. *The History of the Great Riots. Being a Full and Authentic Account of the Strikes and Riots on the Various Railroads of the United States and in the Mining Regions. . . . Together with a Full History of the Molly Maguires.* Philadelphia, 1877.

Marty, Martin E. *Righteous Empire. The Protestant Experience in America.* New York, 1970.

Matthews, John Michael. "The Georgia 'Race Strike' of 1909." *Journal of Southern History*, XL (Nov. 1974), 613–30.

Matthiessen, F. O. *Theodore Dreiser.* N.p., 1951.

Maurer, James Hudson. *It Can Be Done.* New York, 1938.

May, Henry F. *The End of American Innocence.* New York, 1959.

Mead, Sidney. *The Lively Experiment: The Shaping of Christianity in America.* New York, 1963.

Meek, W. H. *Sentimental Socialism.* Girard, Kans., 1902.

Middletown, P. Harvey. *Railways and Organized Labor.* Chicago, 1941.

Miller, Sally M. "Socialist Party Decline and World War I, Bibliography and Interpretation." *Science and Society*, XXXIV (Winter 1971), 398–411.

_____. *Victor Berger and the Promise of Constructive Socialism, 1910–1920.* Westport, Conn., 1973.

Montgomery, David. *Beyond Equality: Labor and the Radical Republicans, 1862–1872.* New York, 1967.

_____. *Workers' Control in America.* New York, 1979.

Moore, E. E. *Moore's Hoosier Cyclopedia.* Connersville, Ind., 1905.

Moore, R. Laurence. *European Socialists and the American Promised Land.* New York, 1970.

Morais, Herbert M., and William Cahn. *Gene Debs: The Story of a Fighting American.* New York, 1948.

Mordell, Albert. *Clarence Darrow, Eugene V. Debs and Haldeman-Julius: Incidents in the Career of an Author, Editor and Publisher.* Girard, Kans., 1950.

Morgan, H. Wayne. *Eugene V. Debs, Socialist for President.* Syracuse, N.Y., 1962.

Morris, James O. *Conflict within the AFL: A Study of Craft versus Industrial Unionism, 1901-1938.* Westport, Conn., 1974.

Morse, Rev. C. M. "The Church and the Working-Man." *The Forum*, Feb. 1889, 654-61.

National Resources Committee. *Farm Tenancy: Report of the President's Committee.* Washington, D.C., 1937.

Nearing, Scott. *The Debs Decision.* New York, 1919.

Nelson, Caroline. *Nature Talks on Economics.* Chicago, 1912.

Niebuhr, H. Richard. *The Kingdom of God in America.* New York, 1959.

_____. *The Social Sources of Denominationalism.* New York, 1929.

Niebuhr, Reinhold. "Biblical Faith and Socialism: A Critical Appraisal." In Walter Leibrecht, ed., *Religion and Culture, Essays in Honor of Paul Tillich.* New York, 1959.

Notarianni, Philip F., and Joseph Stipanovich. "Immigrants, Industry, and Labor Unions: The American West, 1890-1916." *Journal of Historical Studies*, 3 (Fall/Winter 1978), 1-15.

Nottingham, Elizabeth K. *Methodism and the Frontier: Indiana Proving Ground.* New York, 1941.

Oakey, C. C. *Greater Terre Haute and Vigo County.* 2 vols. Chicago, 1908.

"Oh, The Moonlight's Fair Tonight along the Wabash." *Fortune*, 19 (May 1939), 75-78, 132-36.

O'Hare, Kate Richards. "Home to Kate." *The National Rip-Saw*, Nov. 1921, 1-16.

_____. *Law and the White Slaver.* St. Louis, 1911.

_____. *"Nigger" Equality.* St. Louis, n.d.

_____. *Socialism and the World War.* St. Louis, 1919.

_____. *Wimmin Ain't Got No Kick.* Chicago, n.d.

[Oklahoma Socialist Party.] *Platform and Campaign Book, Oklahoma Socialist Party, 1916.* [Oklahoma City, 1916.]

Ollila, Douglas J. "From Socialism to Industrial Unionism (IWW): Social Factors in the Emergence of Left-Labor Radicalism among Finnish Workers on the Mesabi, 1911-19." In Michael G. Karni, Matti E. Kaups, and Douglas J. Ollila, eds., *The Finnish Experience in the Western Great Lakes Region: New Perspectives.* Turku, Finland, 1975.

Oneal, James. "Debs Turns Seventy." *The New Leader*, 7 Nov. 1925, 4.

_____. *Militant Socialism.* St. Louis, 1912.

_____. *Sabotage, or Socialism vs. Syndicalism.* St. Louis, 1913.

_____. "The Socialists in the War." *American Mercury*, Apr. 1927, 418-26.

_____, and Robert Minor. *Resolved: That the Terms of the Third International Are Unacceptable to the Revolutionary Socialists of the World.* New York, 1921.

_____, and G. A. Werner. *American Communism: A Critical Analysis of Its Origins, Development and Programs.* New York, 1947.

O'Neal, Judson. *Terre Haute's Shame: A Record of Graft and Swindle Unparalleled.* Terre Haute, 1915.

Painter, Leonard. *Through Fifty Years with the Brotherhood of Railway Carmen of America.* Kansas City, Mo., 1941.

Passi, Michael. "Fishermen on Strike: Finnish Workers and Community Power in Astoria, Oregon, 1880-1900." In Michael G. Karni, Matti E. Kaups, and Douglas J. Ollila, eds., *The Finnish Experience in the Western Great Lakes Region: New Perspectives*, Turku, Finland, 1975.

Paulson, Ross E. *Radicalism and Reform: The Vrooman Family and American Social Thought, 1837-1937.* Lexington, Ky., 1968.

Pepper, John. *Underground Radicalism: An Open Letter to EUGENE V. DEBS and to All Honest Workers within the Socialist Party.* New York, n.d. [1924].

Peterson, H. C., and Gilbert C. Fite. *Opponents of War, 1917-1918.* Seattle, 1971.

Phillips, Clifton J. *Indiana in Transition: The Emergence of an Industrial Commonwealth, 1880-1920.* Indianapolis, 1968.

Pinkerton, Allan. *Strikers, Communists, Tramps and Detectives.* New York, 1878.

Powderly, Terence V. *The Path I Trod,* edited by Harry J. Carman, Henry David, and Paul N. Guthrie. New York, 1940.

Pratt, William C. " 'Jimmie Higgins' and the Reading Socialist Community: An Exploration of the Socialist Rank and File." In Bruce M. Stave, ed., *Socialism and the Cities.* Port Washington, N.Y., 1975.

Preston, William, Jr. *Aliens and Dissenters: Federal Suppression of Radicals, 1903-1933.* New York, 1966.

Quandt, Jean B. "Religion and Social Thought: The Secularization of Postmillennialism." *American Quarterly,* XXV (Oct. 1973), 390-409.

Quint, Howard H. *The Forging of American Socialism.* Columbia, S.C., 1953.

――――――. "Julius A. Wayland, Pioneer Socialist Propagandist." *Mississippi Valley Historical Review,* XXXV (Mar. 1949), 585-606.

Reed, George Irving. *Encyclopedia of Biography of Indiana.* 2 vols. Chicago, 1895-99.

Reed, Louis S. *The Labor Philosophy of Samuel Gompers.* New York, 1930.

Remy, Charles F. "The Election of Beveridge to the Senate." *Indiana Magazine of History,* XXXVI (June 1940), 123-35.

Reynolds, Steven M. *The Revolution in Our Day.* Terre Haute, 1909.

Ricker, A. W. *Free Love and Socialism.* St. Louis, 1911.

Ridge, Martin. *Ignatius Donnelly, the Portrait of a Politician.* Chicago, 1962.

Robbins, Edwin Clyde. *Railway Conductors: A Study in Organized Labor.* New York, 1914.

Robins, Lucy. *War Shadows.* New York, 1922.

Robinson, Arthur. "The Great Dreamer—An Interview with Eugene V. Debs." *Collier's,* 20 Nov. 1926, 11, 39.

Roe, Wellington. *Juggernaut: American Labor in Action.* Philadelphia, 1948.

Rogers, Thomas Wesley. *The Occupational Experience of One Hundred Unemployed Persons in Bloomington, Indiana.* Bloomington, 1931.

Rogin, Michael Paul. *Fathers and Children: Andrew Jackson and the Subjugation of the American Indian.* New York, 1975.

Roll, Charles. *Colonel Dick Thompson, the Persistent Whig.* Indianapolis, 1948.

Roseboom, Eugene H., and Francis P. Weisenburger. *A History of Ohio.* New York, 1934.

Rosenberg, Leonard B. "The 'Failure' of the Socialist Party of America." *Review of Politics,* XXXI (July 1969), 329-52.

Rudolph, L. C. *Hoosier Zion: The Presbyterians in Early Indiana.* New Haven, 1963.

Russell, Charles Taze. *The Battle of Armageddon.* New York, 1925.

Salmons, C. H., ed. *The Burlington Strike.* Aurora, Ill., 1889.

Salvatore, Nick. "Railroad Workers and the Great Strike of 1877: The View from a Small Midwestern City." *Labor History,* 21 (1980), 522-45.

Sancton, Thomas A. "Looking Inward: Edward Bellamy's Spiritual Crisis." *American Quarterly*, XXV (Dec. 1973), 538-57.

Sanger, Margaret. *An Autobiography*. New York, 1938.

Sanial, Lucien. *Territorial Expansion*. New York, n.d.

Schlesinger, Arthur M., Jr. *History of American Presidential Elections, 1789-1968*. 4 vols. New York, 1971.

Schmidt, Louis Bernard. *Topical Studies and References on the Economic History of American Agriculture*. Philadelphia, 1923.

Schorer, Mark. *Sinclair Lewis, an American Life*. New York, 1961.

Seeds, Russel M., ed. *History of the Republican Party of Indiana*. Indianapolis, 1899.

Seretan, L. Glen. *Daniel DeLeon: The Odyssey of an American Marxist*. Cambridge, Mass., 1979.

Shannon, David A. "Eugene V. Debs: Conservative Labor Editor." *Indiana Magazine of History*, XLVII (1951), 357-64.

———. "Socialism and Labor." In C. Vann Woodward, ed., *A Comparative Approach to American History*. New York, 1968.

———. *The Socialist Party of America, a History*. Chicago, 1967.

[Sheahan, W. H.]. *Grand Lodge, Brotherhood of Railroad Trainmen. Report from Office of Grand Secretary and Treasurer*. Galesburg, Ill., 1891.

Sheean, Vincent. *Dorothy and Red*. New York, 1963.

Shepperson, Wilbur S. *Retreat to Nevada: A Socialist Colony of World War I*. Reno, 1966.

Shoaf, George H. "Debs and the 'Appeal to Reason,' a Personal Memoir." *American Socialist*, Nov. 1955, 10-19.

Shover, John L. "The Progressives and the Working Class Vote in California." In Joel H. Silbey and Samuel T. McSeveney, eds., *Voters, Parties and Elections*. Lexington, Mass., 1972.

Silvin, Edward, ed. *Index to Periodical Literature on Socialism*. Santa Barbara, 1909.

Simons, Algie M. *The Agricultural Revolution*. Chicago, 1912.

———. *The American Farmer*. Chicago, 1903.

———. *Class Struggles in America*. Chicago, 1906.

———. *The Man under the Machine*. Chicago, 1899.

———. *The Philosophy of Socialism*. Chicago, n.d.

———. *Socialism vs. Anarchy*. Chicago, 1901.

Simons, May Wood. *Socialism and the Organized Labor Movement*. Chicago, n.d.

———. *Woman and the Social Problem*. Chicago, 1899.

Slaner, Philip A. "The Railroad Strikes of 1877." *Marxist Quarterly*, I (Apr.-June 1937), 214-36.

Smith, Duane A. *Rocky Mountain Mining Camps, the Urban Frontier*. Bloomington, Ind., 1967.

Smith, Rev. John Lewis. *Indiana Methodism: A Series of Sketches and Incidents, Grave and Humorous Concerning Preachers and People of the West*. Valparaiso, Ind., 1892.

Smith, Timothy L. "Historic Waves of Religious Interest in America." *The Annals*, CCCXXXII (Nov. 1960), 9-19.

———. "Religion and Ethnicity in America." *American Historical Review*, LXXXIII (Dec. 1978), 1155-85.

_____. "Religious Denominations as Ethnic Communities: A Regional Case Study." *Church History*, XXXV (June 1966), 207–26.

Social Democracy of America. *Constitutions of Local Branches, State Unions, and the National Council of the Social Democracy of America.* Chicago, 1898.

The Social Democratic Party of America. N.p., n.d.

Socialist Labor Party. *Daniel DeLeon, the Man and His Work. A Symposium.* New York, 1926.

_____, and Socialist Party. *Proceedings of New Jersey Socialist Unity Convention.* New York, 1906.

Socialist Party of America. *National Convention of the Socialist Party Held at Chicago, Illinois, May 10 to 17, 1908.* Chicago, 1908.

_____. *National Convention of the Socialist Party Held at Indianapolis, Indiana, May 12 to 18, 1912.* Chicago, 1912.

_____. *National Convention of the Socialist Party Held in Masonic Temple Chicago, Illinois, May 15 to 21, 1910.* Chicago, 1910.

_____. *Report of the Socialist Party of the United States to the International Socialist and Trade Union Congress.* Amsterdam, Holland, 1904.

Socialist Society, USA. *Eugene Victor Debs (1855–1955): The Centennial Year.* New York, 1956.

Souvenir Volume, Golden Wedding Anniversary. Terre Haute, 1899.

Starr, George W. *Industrial Development of Indiana.* Bloomington, Ind., 1937.

Stave, Bruce M., ed. *Socialism and the Cities.* Port Washington, N.Y., 1975.

Stead, William T. *If Christ Came to Chicago!* Chicago, 1894.

Stern, Meta L. *To Wives of Toilers.* Chicago, n.d.

_____. *Votes for Working Women.* Chicago, n.d.

Stetler, Henry G. *The Socialist Movement in Reading, Pennsylvania, 1896–1936: A Study in Social Change.* Philadelphia, 1974.

Stewart, Ernest D. "The Populist Party in Indiana." *Indiana Magazine of History*, XIV (Dec. 1918), 332–67; XV (Mar. 1919), 53–74.

Stolberg, Benjamim. *Tailor's Progress: The Story of a Famous Union and the Men Who Made It.* New York, 1944.

Stone, Irving. *Adversary in the House.* New York, 1947.

Stott, William T. *Indiana Baptist History, 1798–1908.* Franklin, Ind., 1908.

Strong, Bryan. "Historians and American Socialism, 1900–1920." *Science and Society*, XXXIV (Winter 1971), 387–97.

Suggs, George G., Jr. *Colorado's War on Militant Unionism.* Detroit, 1972.

Swanberg, W. A. *Norman Thomas, the Last Idealist.* New York, 1976.

Sweet, William Warren. *American Culture and Religion: Six Essays.* Dallas, 1951.

_____. *Circuit-Rider Days in Indiana.* Indianapolis, 1916.

_____. *Makers of Christianity.* New York, 1937.

Swichkow, Louis J., and Lloyd P. Gartner. *The History of the Jews of Milwaukee.* Philadelphia, 1963.

Swinton, John. *1860–Lincoln; Debs–1895.* Terre Haute, 1895.

_____. *Address before the American Federation of Labor Convention.* Philadelphia, 1892.

_____. *Striking for Life.* New York, 1894.

Taft, Philip. *The A.F. of L. in the Time of Gompers.* New York, 1957.

Tams, W. P., Jr. *The Smokeless Coal Fields of West Virginia.* Morgantown, 1963.

Taylor, George Rogers, and Irene D. Neu. *The American Railroad Network, 1861–1890.* Cambridge, Mass., 1956.

Terkel, Studs. *American Dreams: Lost & Found.* New York, 1980.

Terre Haute City Directory, 1877. Terre Haute, 1876.

Terre Haute City Directory, 1879–1880. Terre Haute, 1879.

Terre Haute City Directory, 1882. Terre Haute, 1882.

Terre Haute City Directory, 1887. Terre Haute, 1887.

Terre Haute *Express. 77th Anniversary. Historical Industrial Record of the Prairie City.* Terre Haute, 1900.

Terre Haute Public Schools. *Twelfth Annual Report . . . for the School Year Ending August 31, 1875, with the Course of Study and General Rules and Regulations.* Terre Haute, 1875.

Thebaud, Rev. Augustus J., S.J. *Three-Quarters of a Century (1807 to 1882): A Retrospect Written from Documents and Memory in 1882 and the Following Years.* New York, 1904.

Thompson, Fred. *The I.W.W. Its First Fifty Years (1905–1955).* Chicago, 1955.

Thornbrough, Emma Lou. *Indiana in the Civil War Era, 1850–1880.* Indianapolis, 1965.

Trachtenberg, Alexander. *The Heritage of Gene Debs.* New York, 1930.

———, ed. *The American Socialists and the War.* New York, 1917.

Trissal, Francis M. *Public Men of Indiana: A Political History from 1860 to 1890.* Hammond, 1922.

Trotsky, Leon. *My Life.* New York, 1930.

Tussey, Jean Y., ed. *Eugene V. Debs Speaks.* New York, 1970.

Tuttle, William. *Race Riot: Chicago in the Red Summer of 1919.* New York, 1970.

Vail, Rev. Charles H. *The Mission of the Working Class.* Chicago, n.d.

Van Deusen, John G. "Did Republicans 'Colonize' Indiana in 1879?" *Indiana Magazine of History,* XXX (Dec. 1934), 335–46.

Vanzetti, Bartolomeo. *Background of the Plymouth Trial.* Chelsea, Mass., 1926.

———. *The Story of a Proletarian Life.* Boston, 1923.

Vincent, Henry A. *The Editor with a Punch: Wayland.* Massillon, Ohio, 1912.

———. *The Story of the Commonweal.* Chicago, 1894.

Visher, Stephen S. "Distribution of the Birthplaces of Indianaians in 1870." *Indiana Magazine of History,* XXVI (June 1930), 126–42.

Vorse, Mary Heaton. *A Footnote to Folly: Reminiscences.* New York, 1935.

Walden, May. *Socialism and the Home.* Chicago, n.d.

———. *Woman and Socialism.* Chicago, n.d.

Waldman, Louis. *Labor Lawyer.* New York, 1945.

Ware, Norman. *The Labor Movement in the United States, 1860–1895.* New York, 1929.

Warren, Fred D. "J. A. Wayland and the 'Appeal to Reason.' " *American Socialist,* Mar. 1957, 12–15.

———. *Warren's Defiance.* Chicago, n.d. [1912].

Watson, Thomas Edward. *Socialists and Socialism.* Thomson, Ga., 1910.

Wayland, J. A. *Leaves of Life: A Story of Twenty Years of Socialist Agitation.* Girard, Kans., 1912.

Webb, Walter Prescott. *The Great Plains.* New York, 1931.

Weinstein, Allen. *Prelude to Populism: Origins of the Silver Issue, 1867–1878.* New Haven, 1970.

Weinstein, James. *Ambiguous Legacy: The Left in American Politics.* New York, 1975.

————. *The Decline of Socialism in America, 1912-1925.* New York, 1967.

————, and David W. Eakins, eds. *For A New America: Essays in History and Politics from 'Studies on the Left,' 1959-1967.* New York, 1970.

Wells, H. G. *The Future in America. A Search after Realities.* New York, 1906.

Welter, Barbara. "The Cult of True Womanhood: 1820-1860." *American Quarterly*, XVIII (Summer 1966), 151-74.

Welter, Rush. *Popular Education and Democratic Thought in America.* New York, 1962.

Wentworth, Franklin H. *The Women's Portion.* New York, 1910.

Western Business Guide, 1882-83, Illustrated. Cincinnati, n.d.

Western Federation of Miners. *Official Proceedings of the Fourteenth Annual Convention . . . Held in Odd Fellows Hall at Denver, Colorado, on May 28th to June 13th, 1906.* Denver, 1906.

Whitfield, Stephen J. *Scott Nearing: Apostle of American Radicalism.* New York, 1974.

Wiebe, Robert. *The Search for Order.* New York, 1967.

Wiley, Rev. Allen. "Methodism in Southeastern Indiana." *Indiana Magazine of History*, XXIII (1927), 3-64, 130-216, 239-332, 393-466.

Williams, B. H. *Eleven Blind Leaders, or "Practical Socialism" and "Revolutionary Tactics."* New Castle, Pa., n.d.

Wittke, Carl. "Immigration Policy Prior to World War I." *Annals of the American Academy of Political and Social Science*, CCLXII (Mar. 1949), 5-14.

————. *Refugees from Revolution: The German Forty-Eighters in America.* Philadelphia, 1952.

Woodward, C. Vann. *The Origins of the New South.* Baton Rouge, 1966.

————. *Tom Watson, Agrarian Rebel.* New York, 1963.

Wright, Benjamin F. "Political Institutions and the Frontier." In Dixon Ryan Fox, ed., *Sources of Culture in the Middle West, Background versus Frontier*

Wyllie, Irvin G. *The Self-Made Man in America.* New York, 1954.

Yellen, Samuel. *American Labor Struggles, 1877-1934.* New York, 1974.

Young, Art. *On My Way.* New York, 1928.

Dissertations and Theses

Anderson, Paul H. "The Attitude of the American Leftist Leaders toward the Russian Revolution (1917-1923)." Ph.D. diss., Notre Dame University, 1942.

Barkey, Frederick A. "The Socialist Party in West Virginia from 1898 to 1920: A Study in Working Class Radicalism." Ph.D. diss., University of Pittsburgh, 1971.

Belissary, Constantine G. "The Rise of the Industrial Spirit in Tennessee, 1865-1885." Ph.D. diss., Vanderbilt University, 1949.

Burke, Maurice H. "Chauncey Rose: His Life and Contribution to Education." M.A. thesis, Indiana State Teachers College, 1937.

Bush, Charles C. "The Green Corn Rebellion." M.A. thesis, University of Oklahoma, 1932.

Drummond, Robert R. "Terre Haute, Indiana: A City of Non-Growth." Ph.D. diss., Northwestern University, 1953.

Grooms, Marvin Edward. "Eugene Victor Debs: The Kansas Years." M.A. thesis, Indiana State University, 1970.

Holzman, Hanni M. "The German Forty-Eighters and the Socialists in Milwaukee: A Social Psychological Study of Assimilation." M.A. thesis, University of Wisconsin, 1948.

Ridgley, Ronald H. "Terre Haute during the Civil War." M.A. thesis, Indiana State Teachers College, 1958.

Scharnau, Ralph W. "Thomas J. Morgan and the Chicago Socialist Movement, 1876–1901." Ph.D. diss., Northern Illinois University, 1970.

Stevenson, George James. "The Brotherhood of Locomotive Engineers and Its Leaders, 1863–1920." Ph.D. diss., Vanderbilt University, 1954.

Index

NICK SALVATORE is a Maurice and Hinda Neufeld Founders Professor of Industrial and Labor Relations and a professor of American Studies at Cornell University. He received the Bancroft Prize in American History and the John H. Dunning Prize in American History for *Eugene V. Debs: Citizen and Socialist.* He is also author of *Singing in a Strange Land: C. L. Franklin, the Black Church, and the Transformation of America* and *We All Got History: The Memory Books of Amos Webber.* Find him at www.nicksalvatore.com.

The Working Class in American History

The University of Illinois Press
is a founding member of the
Association of American University Presses.

Composed in 10/12 Times Roman
with Times Roman display
at the University of Illinois Press
Manufactured by Cushing-Malloy, Inc.

University of Illinois Press
1325 South Oak Street
Champaign, IL 61820-6903
www.press.uillinois.edu